Dictionary of
Victorian
Wood Engravers

Rodney K Engen

Chadwyck-Healey

First published 1985

Chadwyck-Healey Ltd
20 Newmarket Road
Cambridge CB5 8DT

Chadwyck-Healey Inc.
623 Martense Avenue
Teaneck, NJ 07666

Engen, Rodney K.
    Dictionary of Victorian wood engravers.
    1. Wood-engraving, British – 19th century
    – Dictionaries
    I. Title
    769.941'03'21   NE1143

ISBN 0-85964-139-2

Frontispiece: Dante Gabriel Rossetti's 'The Maids of
Elfen-Mere', from *The Music Master*, 1855, wood
engraved by the Dalziel Brothers. 'It is, I think, the
most beautiful drawing for an illustration I have
ever seen: the weird faces of the maids of Elfen-
Mere, the musical timed movement of their arms
together as they sing, the face of the man, above all,
are such as only a great artist could conceive'
(Burne-Jones). See pp. 224–25.

Printed in Great Britain by
Redwood Burn Limited, Trowbridge, Wiltshire.

Contents

Acknowledgements

I should like to record my appreciation of the numerous individuals, libraries, museums and their staffs who have helped in the compiling of this book over the last four years: the staff of the British Library, in particular Mr David Pasey, the Manuscript Department and Mr Arthur Searle; the British Museum Department of Prints and Drawings, in particular Mr Martin Tillerman for help with the Dalziel collection; the Boston Museum of Fine Arts Print Department; the Guildhall Library; Hampstead Public Library, Swiss Cottage; the Institute for Historical Research and Dr K. Manley; the Bodleian Library, Oxford, in particular the staff of the Constance Meade collection and Sheila Edward for providing copies of the collection catalogue; Sotheby's (Belgravia) and Mr Michael Heseltine of Sotheby's (Bloomfield Place); St Bride's Printing Library; University of California, Los Angeles, especially Mr Brooke Whiting and his staff for the Evans collection material provided and their assistance during my visit; University of Reading, especially Dr J. A. Edwards, Keeper of the Printing and Publishing Archives; the Victoria and Albert Museum Library and Print Department.

Of the numerous individuals who helped with my research may I mention in particular Mr Shaun Hammond for his tireless editorial assistance; Mr Ian Hodgkins; Mr Ruari McLean for his support and constant interest in the book; Mr John Porter for help with the Whittinghams and Byfields; Reverend J. S. Reynolds for invaluable assistance with his engraver relatives; Sarah Phelps Smith for her assessment of the Hartley Collection, Boston; and Mr Peregrine Stevenson for his help with translations.

Rodney Engen
London 1984

Preface

The technical skill and influence of the nineteenth-century British wood engraver and his draughtsmen assistants is now recognised by scholars, historians of printing history and book collectors to be a major factor in our visual record of the period. The draughtsman illustrator who prepared his drawing for the engraver, and the publisher who enjoyed commercial rewards from his engraved books and magazines, were dependent on the wood engraver. In turn, the reading public's knowledge of the world was regulated through the flood of engraved illustrations produced during the heyday of the wood engraver's art. When Thomas Bewick declared 'the use of the woodcuts will know no end', and set out to establish his unrivalled reputation for work on wood, the so-called 'British School' of wood engraving was born. Bewick's pupils spread their knowledge through their own engraving businesses in London; his opponents, engravers like Robert Branston, turned away from his white-line techniques in favour of the black-line imitations of metal engravings, which they called the 'London School'. By the 1830s a burgeoning continental marketplace lured numerous British engravers to France, Germany, Belgium and Sweden; later even to America, to teach the skills that made British wood engraving a much sought after commodity.

Engravers soon grew prosperous, with armies of apprentice assistants and various offices for printing and publishing as well as engraving. The rise of the engraver-businessman meant that men like Ebenezer Landells, Edmund Evans, and publishers like Charles Knight and Charles Whittingham could make a fortune from the boom in wood engraved magazines and books. By the 1850s and 60s the intricate, jewel-like surfaces of book illustrations drawn on wood by some of the period's more noted and talented draughtsmen were engraved by the hugely successful engraving firms like the Dalziel Brothers, the Swains or the Lintons. They trained assistants or took on 'outside' engravers who had trained under various trade school programmes; women wood engravers were especially popular as they could work at home and were generally reliable.

By the 1880s the boom was threatened by the growing use of the photoengraving technique, a process which eventually replaced the wood engraver's monopoly on reproductive techniques. Process, as it was called, was greeted with dismay by the less optimistic; others, like the Swains, adopted it into their own engraving business. Nevertheless, it was almost certain that the new technique would bring about the end of the prosperous wood engraving business, and many London wood engraving firms went bankrupt. However, by the 1890s wood engraving had turned in upon itself in search of its artistic roots, and the rise of the engraver-craftsman concerned with artistic integrity began to play an influential role in the Private Press movement, as we know it today. Figures such as William Morris and his disciples, engravers like Bernard Sleigh and Robert Gibbings produced articles and engravings to keep the art of the wood engraver alive and well to the present day.

We look to the nineteenth-century British wood engraver with a mixture of awe and respect, if only for the sheer amount of tedious work that was produced from wood blocks during the period. It was the so-called 'woodpecker', the facsimile engraver, who accepted long hours, the pressure of deadlines and tedious technical skills, to produce his translation of a pencil drawing upon a small boxwood block for mechanical printing. It was his ability to translate those same faint lines into intricate web-work patterns of black or white lines of an astonishing tonal range, which earned him the reputation and admiration of his continental colleagues. Much of his output was strictly for the trade – the shop bills and catalogue work on which many an apprentice was weaned. But when given the opportunity, as Bewick in his *British Birds*, or the Dalziels in their Rossetti engravings, he could produce masterworks on the woodblock. And, being printed in large numbers, the engravings were influential barometers of public and artistic taste, worthy of serious study today.

A survey of critical opinion among present day historians shows how attitudes toward the nineteenth-century wood engraver have changed from respectful interest to praise. The major writer in the field, Ruari McLean, wrote in 1967: 'The skill of the wood-engraver was often much greater than that of the artists whose work they were responsible for reproducing; their profession was at the very heart of the Victorian book and magazine world' (*Reminiscences of Edmund Evans*, 1967, p.viii). Percy Muir wrote in 1971, while discussing the Dalziel wood engravings of John Leech: 'This is yet one more reminder of the importance of the engraver throughout our period from William Harvey onwards, especially on wood but also on steel, and it is rewarding, where names are given or can be deciphered, to observe the deftness and ability of the best of them, the beauty of their craftmanship and their ingenuity in solving the intricate problems set them by artists' (*Victorian Illustrated Books*, 1971, pp.106–7). More recently Simon Houfe claimed 'At its worst such facsimile wood engraving was hackwork, at its best it expressed perfectly the growing strength of draughtsmanship within the British School' (*The Dalziel Family*, 1978, p.1). Finally, Ronald Russell concluded (in his *Guide to British Topographical Prints*, 1979, p.147): 'As an art form wood engraving still continues. But much research still needs to be done on the workshop craftsmen of the nineteenth century, whose products as they grow in age will surely come to be more highly valued.' Such remarks must serve as the basis for the present dictionary.

Introduction

It is an unfortunate fact that, despite the acknowledged importance of the British wood engraver and draughtsman of the nineteenth century, no full reference work exists in English to provide their names, biographies and lists of work engraved. There is no English equivalent to the French history, Pierre Gusman's *La Gravure sur bois en France au XIXe siecle*, 1929; while the Americans are served by Duyckinck and Stauffer. The nearest to a British history with reference section is William Chatto and John Jackson's *Treatise on Wood Engraving*, 1839, which Henry Bohn augmented with a partial list of contemporary engravers and draughtsmen in 1861. Other standard authorities, notably Forrest Reid and Gleeson White, only mention wood engravers in passing reference to the draughtsmen illustrators they discuss at length. More recently the pioneering work of Ruari McLean, Percy Muir, Keith Lindley, and most recently Eric de Maré's survey, have provided strong hints at the need for such a reference work; one which would incorporate the growing amount of research recently done and serve as a sourcebook for future research. The nearest to this, which lists draughtsmen illustrators almost exclusively, is Simon Houfe's *Dictionary of British Book Illustrators*; and even here little is made of a draughtsman's abilities on the woodblock itself.

This volume then, is intended as the companion volume to my *Dictionary of Victorian Engravers, Print Publishers and Their Works*, 1979. That work gave an account and list of British metal engravers, etchers and lithographers of the nineteenth century, with special reference to reproductions of the famous paintings engraved during the period. Indeed some of the engravers listed there also worked on wood and are listed in this, the second volume, *Dictionary of Victorian Wood Engravers*. Together the two volumes will, I hope, provide a sourcebook for future research by students and collectors, perhaps historians and curators, into the influence, both visual and technical, of the British engraver.

There are nearly 2,000 entries listed in this second volume. Each is either a wood engraver, a draughtsman who worked on wood, or an engraving firm. I have culled my information from the sources listed in the bibliography below. In addition I discovered that such major reference works as Nagler, LeBlanc, Bénézit, and Thieme-Becker failed to include those provincial wood engravers who exerted such an influence outside London. For these I consulted the provincial trade and post office directories which generally listed wood engravers and firms capable of providing engraved work, and give their addresses. They are included here to indicate the scope of the wood engraver's profession throughout the country. London trade and post office directories also provided names and addresses of numerous individual entries. But these are recorded with caution, since it is widely accepted that many entries were misprinted, mis-spelled, or easily confused. Consequently every effort has been made to include variant facts and check discrepancies in names and addresses, often against signatures on the engravings themselves. In some instances only a name and directory address is known; this is considered a valuable starting point and is listed, if only to indicate what an engraver considered important to include in his own directory entry.

I have also augmented this information with entries from diaries and published memoirs by engravers, publishers, and artist-draughtsmen, to help fill out an entrant's life and give special reference to his engraving activities. These sources are quoted, with reference given in the text, and in the reference section at the end of each entry. I have also searched the collections of major museums like the British Museum, the Victoria and Albert Museum, and the Bodleian Library to find the engraved work itself. Book illustrations were generally examined at the British Library, although its catalogue fails generally to list work by engravers or draughtsmen illustrators.

The period covered is 1800–1900. There are a few variations, notably late eighteenth-century wood engravers listed for their future influence on the art, or early twentieth-century figures (usually born by 1880), who continued the discipline of their Victorian masters. Most of the engravers covered are British; continental and American engravers are included only if their work was known by or published for the British public.

The terminology adopted is (1) wood engraver (2) wood cutter (3) draughtsman on wood (4) woodcut designer. The distinction is made between a wood engraving and a woodcut: strictly speaking a wood engraving is made by a burin or graver against the grain of a wood block, and a woodcut by a knife used to cut along or with the grain. This distinction was not always made, particularly in the nineteenth century, when the woodcut and wood engraving were spoken of synonomously, without technical distinctions. I have used, however, the period's term 'cut' for any wood engraved illustration (e.g. '34 cuts to . . .'), and 'plate' for full-page engravings.

The treatment of engraving firms includes not only those firms exclusively devoted to wood engraving, but also the more enterprising which branched out into colour printing, lithography, metal engraving, wood block and paper supply, and later process blocks. The first criterion, however, was whether a firm could produce wood engravings; other facilities are merely noted, with references to sources for further reading (i.e. colour printing surveys) which fall outside the scope of the present dictionary.

The draughtsmen generally worked in pencil on the wood block; later in ink on paper for photographic transfer of the drawing onto the block. They were usually aspiring young artists, painters, designers or architects, who found that by drawing on wood they could earn a steady income to support their greater ambitions as gallery artists. Many eventually gave up this work when they became established in the galleries. Their careers are outlined here to provide a basis with which to judge their importance as woodblock illustrators.

Format

The format chosen is similar to that used in the companion, Volume I.

(1) The name of the wood engraver, draughtsman or engraving firm, followed by dates of working life. Firm names often involved a partnership or sons taken in by their fathers: members of these partnerships are listed and cross-referenced when known.

(2) A statement of the artist's importance followed by biographical detail. Engravers are given particular emphasis as to which workshop or master engraver they trained under, and generally these individuals are cross referenced to help form a picture of the activity within a workshop. In addition firms' or engravers' addresses are often followed by those fellow-engravers whom I discovered shared the same address in the directories. Addresses are followed by reference to the directory and to the period listed (e.g. POD, 1846–57). The

directory abbreviations are explained in the bibliography section, 'General References Consulted'. Variant street numbers are given in brackets.

(3) A selection of engraved work arranged chronologically.

(4) A discussion of working methods used.

(5) A critical assessment or evaluation by period or current experts with references given for further research.

(6) A small section for the more accomplished artist, whose career included painting or exhibiting in the galleries, honours awarded there, followed by place and date of death.

(7) A select list of work in those collections examined.

(8) Engraver's signature. This is a complex subject and remains open to many variations. Engravers often signed their initials, occasionally their full surname; but more often they remained anonymous, their work stamped with the name of their master-employer. Some of these are listed in Nagler (*Monogrammisten*), or LeBlanc; others were compiled from studying the engravings themselves. Placement of signatures varied as well: the most common position was in the lower right hand corner; others appeared in the lower left hand corner (usually reserved for the draughtsman's initials, however, and too easily mistaken for the engraver), or in the centre. Some wrote in an elaborate script which they worked into the overall design to avoid spoiling the delicacy of the artist's design. Some can also be found with initials in reverse (the block was always engraved in reverse).

(9) A bibliography of sources consulted or useful for further information, generally listed by author's name only. The full reference is found in the Bibliographies. The reference 'Volume I' refers to the companion volume, *Dictionary of Victorian Engravers, Print Publishers and Their Works*, which also gives a full bibliography.

Distinctions abbreviated in the Dictionary

(see also Bibliography for abbreviated references given in the text)

A	Associate Member
FRGS	Fellow of Royal Geographical Society
FRS	Fellow of Royal Society
FSA	Fellow of Society of Antiquaries
H	Honorary Member
RA	Royal Academician
RCA	Royal Canadian Academician
RI	Member of Royal Institute of Painters in Watercolours
ROI	Member of Royal Institute of Painters in Oil-colours
RSA	Royal Scottish Academician

Bibliography

General Reference Works Consulted

[Note: The following three bibliographies include all books consulted and abbreviated in the dictionary.]

For specific information on print reference books see Howard C. Levis, *A Descriptive Bibliography of the Most Important Books in the English Language Relating to the Art and History of Engraving and Collecting of Prints*, 1912–13 (reprinted Dawsons 1974); also L. Mason, *Print Reference Sources, 18th to 20th Centuries*, Millwood, N.Y., 1975 and its supplement, *Fine Print References*, 1982. There is a selective but useful bibliography in M. Melot's *Prints*, 1981. A contemporary reference work of use for detail is E. C. Bigmore and C. W. H. Wyman, *A Bibliography of Printing*, 1880 (reprinted 1969).

Andresen – A. Andresen, *Handbuch für Kupferstichsammler*, Leipzig, 1870–73 (continuation of Heller below).

Art Journal – *Art Journal* 1849–1912 (originally *Art Union* 1839–48).

Baker – W. S. Baker, *American Engravers*, Philadelphia, 1875 (superseded by Stauffer below).

Bartsch – Adam Bartsch, *Le Peintre-Graveur*, 21 vols, Vienna, 1803–21, supplements, 1843, 1854 (reprinted Philadelphia, N.Y., 1980).

Bénézit – *Dictionnaire des Peintres, Sculpteurs, etc.*, 8 vols, 1910 (rev. ed. 1966).

Béraldi – Henri Béraldi, *Les Graveurs du XIXe siècle*, 12 vols, Paris, 1885–92.

British Library – British Library Catalogue of Printed Books.

British Museum – Catalogue of Prints and Drawings in the Department of Prints and Drawings, British Museum, London.

Bodleian Library – Constance Meade Collection, Bodleian Library, Oxford.

Bruillot – Franz Bruillot, *Dictionnaire des Monogrammes*, 3 vols, Munich, 1832–34.

Bryan – Michael Bryan, *Dictionary of Painters and Engravers*, 5 vols, 1903–05 (new edition, Port Washington, 1964).

Bushnell – George Herbert Bushnell, *Scottish Engravers*, 1949.

Callen – Anthea Callen, *Angel in the Studio*, 1979.

Chatto – *see* 'Wood Engraving' section.

Clayton – *English Female Artists*, 1876.

Clement and Hutton – C. E. Clement and L. Hutton, *Artists of the Nineteenth Century*, 1879.

DNB – *Dictionary of National Biography*, 1885–1937.

Dodd – Thomas Dodd, *Connoisseur's Repertory, or a Biographical History of Painters, Engravers, Sculptors and Architects, 1550–1800*, Volume A–B only, 1825 (original MS in BM, Add Mss 33, 401, unpublished).

Engen – R. K. Engen, *Dictionary of Victorian Engravers, Print Publishers and Their Works*, Cambridge, 1979 (referred to as 'Volume I').

Fielding – Mantel Fielding, *Dictionary of American Painters, Sculptors and Engravers*, rev. ed., 1974.

Fincham – H. N. Fincham, *Artists and Engravers of British and American Book Plates*, 1897.

Garrett – *see* 'Wood Engraving' section.

Glaser – Curt Glaser, *Die Graphik der Neuzeit vom Anfang des 19 Jahrhunderts bis zur Gegenwart*, Berlin, 1922.

Graves – Algernon Graves, *Royal Academy Exhibitors, 1769–1904*, 8 vols, 1905–06 (reprinted 1970).

Gusman – *see* 'Wood Engraving' section.

Hake – Henry M. Hake and F. O'Donoghue, *Catalogue of Engraved British Portraits Preserved in the Department of Prints and Drawings in the British Museum*, 6 vols, 1908–25.

Heller – J. Heller, *Praktisches Handbuch für Kupferstichsammler*, 2 vols, Bamberg, 1823–36 (*see also* Andresen).

Hind – Arthur M. Hind, *A History of Engraving and Etching*, 1923 (reprinted 1963) (*see also* 'Wood Engraving' section).

Hodgson – W. H. Hodgson, *Hodgson's Booksellers', Publishers' and Stationers' Directory for London and County*, 1855 (referred to as 'Hodgson's').

Houfe – Simon Houfe, *Dictionary of British Book Illustrators and Caricaturists 1800–1914*, Woodbridge, 1978.

Johnstone – *Johnstone's London Commercial Guide and Street Directory*, 1817.

Keppel – Frederick Keppel, *The Golden Age of Engraving*, N.Y., 1910 (with essays on English illustrators of *Punch*, C. Keene, G. DuMaurier).

Kelly – F. Kelly and Company. Series of London commercial street directories which took over the London Post Office directories (POD), from 1840 and included classified trade lists of engravers; also *Kelly's Post Office Directory of Stationers, Printers, Booksellers, Publishers and Paper Makers of England, Scotland, Wales and principal towns of Ireland*, 1872–1900 (referred to as 'Kelly's').

Labouchère – Norna Labouchère, *Ladies' Book-plates*, 1895.

LeBlanc – C. LeBlanc, *Manuel de l'amateur d'estampes*, 4 vols, Paris, 1854–89.

Linton – *see* 'Wood Engraving' section.

LSDS, LSDN – *see* POD.

McLean – *see* 'General Surveys' section.

Nagler – G. K. Nagler, *Allgemeines Kunstler-Lexicon*, 22 vols, Munich, 1835–52 (although W. J. Linton claimed this was not trustworthy on English wood engravers and illustrators); *Die Monogrammisten und die Jenigen Künstler aller Schuler*, 5 vols, Munich, 1858–79 (useful for engravers' signatures).

Ottley – W. Y. Ottley, *History of Engraving upon Copper and in Wood*, 1816; *Notices of Engravers*, 1831; *Dictionary of Recent and Living Painters and Engravers*, 1866.

Passavant – Johann D. Passavant, *Le Peintre-Graveur*, 6 vols, Leipzig, 1860–64.

Pigot – J. Pigot. Series of London trade directories published by J. Pigot and Company, 1823–40.

POD – Series of London Post Office directories, 1830–1900. Also of use were the London suburban directories North and South, 1860–. (These are referred to as POD, LSDS, LSDN; *see also* Pigot, Robson, Kelly, Hodgson directory entries.)

Redgrave – Samuel Redgrave, *Dictionary of Artists of the English School*, 1878 (reprinted 1970).

Reid – *see* 'General Surveys' section.

Robson – W. Robson. Series of classified London trade directories which ran concurrent with Pigot (q.v.), 1820–42.

Savage – William Savage, *Dictionary of the Art of Printing*, 1841.

Slater – J. H. Slater, *Engravings and Their Value*, rev. ed., 1929.

Spielmann – *see* 'General Surveys' section.

Stauffer – D. M. Stauffer, *American Engravers*, 2 vols, N.Y., 1907 (*see* Baker above).

Strickland – Walter George Strickland, *Dictionary of Irish Artists*, 2 vols, 1913, reprinted 1971.

TB – U. Thieme and F. Becker, *Allgemeines Lexikon der Bildender Kunstler*, 37 vols, Leipzig, 1927.

Todd – W. B. Todd, *A Directory of Printers*, 1800–40, 1972.

UCLA – University of California, Los Angeles (Edmund Evans papers).

VAM – Catalogue of Prints and Drawings in the Department of the Victoria and Albert Museum (originally South Kensington Museum), London.

Volume I – *see* Engen above.

Wakeman and Bridson – Geoffrey Wakeman and Gavin Bridson, *A Guide to Nineteenth Century Colour Printers*, Loughborough, 1975 (*see* 'General Surveys' section).

Waters – Grant M. Waters, *Dictionary of British Artists Working 1900–1950*, 2 vols, Eastbourne, 1975.

White – *see* 'General Surveys' section.

Who's Who – *Who Was Who*, 1897–1915, 1916–28.

Wood – Christopher Wood, *Dictionary of Victorian Painters*, Woodbridge, 1971.

General Surveys of Nineteenth Century British Illustration

A selective list of useful books, published in London unless stated otherwise.

Balston – T. Balston, 'English Book Illustration, 1880–1900' in J. Carter's *New Paths in Book Collecting*, 1934.

Bland – David Bland, *A History of Book Illustration*, 1958.

Blackburn – Henry Blackburn, *The Art of Illustration*, 1894.

Burch – R. M. Burch, *Colour Printing and Colour Printers*, 1910.

Crane – Walter Crane, *Of the Decorative Illustration of Books Old and New*, 1896 (reprinted 1972).

Cundall – Joseph Cundall, *History of British Watercolour Painting*, 1908.

Du Maurier – George Du Maurier, *Social Pictorial Satire*, 1898.

Everitt – Graham Everitt, *English Caricaturists and Graphic Humourists of the Nineteenth Century*, 1893.

Friedman – Joan M. Friedman, *Colour Printing in England*, New Haven, 1978.

Hall – John N. Hall, *Trollope and his Illustrators*, 1980.

Hamerton – P. G. Hamerton, *The Graphic Arts*, 1882.

Hardie – Martin Hardie, *English Coloured Books*, 1906 (reprinted 1973); *Watercolour Painting in Britain*, 1968.

Harvey – John R. Harvey, *Victorian Novelists and their Illustrators*, 1970.

Hinton – A. H. Hinton, *A Handbook of Illustration*, 1894.

Hodgson – Pat Hodgson, *The War Illustrators*, 1977.

Hodson – J. S. Hodson, *An Historical and Practical Guide to Art Illustration*, 1884.

Jackson – Holbrook Jackson, *The Eighteen-Nineties*, 1913 (reprinted 1976).

Jackson – Mason Jackson, *The Pictorial Press, Its Origins and Progress*, 1885.

James – Philip James, *English Book Illustration, 1800–1900*, 1947.

Johnson – Diana Johnson, *Fantastic Illustration and Design in Britain, 1850–1930*, Rhode Island Museum of Art, Providence, 1979.

Kitton – F. G. Kitton, *Dickens and his Illustrators*, 1899.

Layard – G. S. Layard, *Tennyson and his Pre-Raphaelite Illustrators*, 1894.

Lewis – C. T. Courtney Lewis, *The Story of Picture Printing in England during the Nineteenth Century*, 1928.

Maas – Jeremy Maas, *Victorian Painters*, 1969.

McLean – Ruari McLean, *Victorian Book Design and Colour Printing*, 1963 (rev. ed. 1972).

Maré – Eric de Maré, *The Victorian Woodblock Illustrators*, 1980; 'The Boxwood Illustrators' in *Penrose Annual*, 1970, pp.49–68.

Muir – Percy Muir, *Victorian Illustrated Books*, 1971.

Pennell – Joseph Pennell, *Pen Drawing and Pen Draughtsmen*, 1889; *Modern Illustration*, 1895; *The Illustration of Books*, 1896.

Peppin – Bridgit Peppin, *Fantasy Book Illustration*, 1975.

Price – R. G. G. Price, *A History of Punch*, 1957.

Quayle – Eric Quayle, *The Collector's Book of Books*, 1971; *The Collector's Book of Children's Books*, 1971 (rev. ed. 1984).

Ray – Gordon N. Ray, *The Illustrator and the Book in England, 1790–1914*, Pierpont Morgan Library, New York, 1976.

Reid – Forrest Reid, *Illustrators of the Sixties*, 1928 (reprinted 1975).

Reynolds – Graham Reynolds, *Victorian Painting*, 1966.

Russell – Ronald Russell, *Guide to British Topographical Prints*, Newton Abbot, 1979.

Sketchley – R. E. D. Sketchley, *English Book Illustration of Today*, 1903.

Sparrow – W. S. Sparrow, *Book Illustration of the Sixties*, 1939.

Spielmann – M. H. Spielmann, *The History of Punch*, 1895.

Slythe – R. Margaret Slythe, *The Art of Illustration, 1750–1900*, Library Association, 1970.

Studio – *The Studio* (London), 'Modern Pen Drawings', Winter 1900–01; 'Modern Book Illustrators and Their Work', Special No., 1914; 'British Book Illustrators Yesterday and Today', Special No., 1923.

Taylor – John Russell Taylor, *The Art Nouveau Book in Britain*, 1966 (reprinted 1980).

Thorpe – James Thorpe, *English Illustration of the Nineties*, 1935 (reprinted 1975).

Twyman – Michael Twyman, *Printing, 1770–1970*, 1970.

Wakeman – Geoffrey Wakeman, *XIX Century Illustration, Some Methods*, Loughborough, 1970; *Victorian Book Illustration – The Technical Revolution*, Newton Abbot, 1973.

Whalley – Joyce Whalley, *Cobwebs to Catchflies: Illustrated Books for the Nursery and Schoolroom, 1700–1900*, 1974.

White – Gleeson White, *English Illustration, 'The Sixties', 1857–70*, 1897 (reprinted 1970); 'Children's Book Illustrators' in *The Studio*, Special No., 1897–98.

Williamson – C. N. Williamson, 'Illustrated Journalism in England: Its Development' in *Magazine of Art*, 1890, pp.334ff.

Wood – Sir H. T. Wood, *Modern Methods of Illustrating Books*, 1887.

Bibliography of Nineteenth Century Wood Engraving

The following selected list of books, periodical references, practical manuals and reference books was culled from the catalogues of the British Museum, Victoria and Albert Museum libraries, from reference books cited in the 'General Reference Works' section and sources given under individual entries in the dictionary itself. It includes American and continental sources when applicable to nineteenth-century wood engraving and only omits references to individuals (e.g. Thomas Bewick) which are found under the entries for each artist-engraver in the main dictionary. Publication was generally in London unless otherwise stated.

Avermaete – Roger Avermaete, *La gravure sur bois moderne de l'occident*, Paris, 1928 (reprinted 1977).

Baldry – A. L. Baldry, 'The Future of Wood Engraving' in *The Studio* (London), 1898, pp.10–16.

Balston – Thomas Balston, *English Wood Engraving, 1900–1950*, 1951.

Beedham – R. John Beedham, *Wood Engraving*, 1921.

Binyon – Laurence Binyon, *The Artist Engraver*, 1894; *The Followers of William Blake*, 1925.

Bliss – Douglas Percy Bliss, *A History of Wood Engraving*, 1928 (reprinted 1964). The best survey with chapters on nineteenth-century master engravers.

Book Collector – *Book Collector*, Winter 1968 (article on Andrew Reid collection of blocks, Newcastle University).

Boston Museum of Fine Arts – A. V. S. Anthony (introduction), *Exhibition of American Engravings on Wood*, Boston, 1881; *Exhibition of the Society of American Wood-Engravers*, supplemented by an Exhibition of Old and Modern Woodcuts and Wood-Engravings, selected from the Gray Collection . . . and other sources, Boston, 1890; S. H. Phelps, 'The Hartley Collection of Victorian Illustration' in *Boston Museum Bulletin*, vol 71, 1973.

Bracquemond, – Félix Bracquemond, *Etude sur la gravure sur bois et lithographie*, Paris, 1897.

Brevière – *De la Xylographie*, 1833.

Brivois – Jules Brivois, *Bibliography of books engraved on Wood in the Nineteenth Century*, Paris, 1883.

Brown – William N. Brown, *Wood Engraving*: a practical and easy introduction to the study of the art, 1899.

Caxton – Caxton Celebration Catalogue of the Loan Collection Connected with the Art of Printing, 1877.

Chamberlain – Walter Chamberlain, *Wood Engraving*, 1978 (a practical guide with historical introduction).

Chambers – Chambers' Miscellany of Useful and Entertaining Tracts, No. 85, *Wood Engraving*, Edinburgh, c.1870?

Champfleury – *Histoire de l'Imagerie Populaire*, Paris, 1869.

Charnley – Emerson Charnley, *Specimens of Early Wood Engraving*, 1858 (a similar volume to one published by Joseph Crawhall, 1889).

Chatto – William Chatto, 'The History of Wood Engraving', serial in *Illustrated London News*, May–June 1844; *Gems of Wood Engraving from the Illustrated London News*, with history of the art, 1848 (rev. ed. 1849).

Chatto and Jackson – William Chatto and J. Jackson, *A Treatise on Wood Engraving*, 1839, enlarged by Henry Bohn, 1861 (reprinted Detroit, 1969) (the standard Victorian history and technical guide).

Cirker – B. Cirker, *1800 Woodcuts by Thomas Bewick and his School*, N.Y., 1962.

Collins – John Collins, *The Art of Engraving on Metal, Wood and Stone*, Burlington, New Jersey, 1858.

Colvin – S. Colvin, *Early Engraving and Engravers in England*, 1905.

Cundall – Joseph Cundall, *A Brief History of Wood-Engraving*, 1895 (reprinted Kennebunkport, Maryland, 1979) (*see also* 'General Survey' section).

Dalziel Brothers – *A Record of their Work, 1840–1890*, 1901 (reprinted 1980) (*see* Houfe below).

DeVinne – Théodore L. DeVinne, 'The growth of wood-cut printing' in *Scribner's Monthly* (N.Y.), April 1880, pp.860–74.

Dobson – Austin Dobson, *Thomas Bewick and his Pupils*, 1899.

Dodd – William Dodd, *Specimens of Early Wood Engraving*: being impressions of wood-cuts in the possession of the publisher (Dodd), Newcastle, 1862.

Dodgson – Campbell Dodgson, *Contemporary English Woodcuts*, 1922.

Duplessis – Georges Duplessis, *Les graveurs sur bois contemporains*, Paris, 1857 (originally in *L'Artiste*).

Duyckinck – E. A. Duyckinck, *Early American Wood-Engravers*, N.Y., 1877.

Emerson – William A. Emerson, *Practical Instruction in the Art of Wood Engraving*, for Persons wishing to learn the Art without an Instructor, East Douglas, Massachusetts, 1876; *A Handbook of Wood Engraving*, with Practical Instruction in the Art, N.Y., 1881 (reprinted 1884).

English Influences on Vincent Van Gogh, Arts Council catalogue, 1974–75 (charts the wood engraved illustrations Van Gogh collected).

Evans – *Reminiscences, see* McLean.

Exhibition of Wood Engravings at the Paris Ecole de Beaux Arts, May 1902.

Farleigh – John Farleigh, *Engraving on Wood*, Leicester, 1954 (handbook for the beginner).

Fildes – P. Fildes, 'Photo-transfer of Drawings in Woodblock Engraving' in *Journal of the Printing Historical Society*, 1969.

Firmin-Didot – A. Firmin-Didot, *Essai typographique et bibliographique sur l'histoire de la gravure sur bois*, Paris, 1863.

Fox – Celina Fox, 'Woodengravers and the City', in I. B. Nadel and F. S. Schwarzbach (eds.) *Victorian Artists and the City*, N.Y., 1980.

Friedländer – Max J. Friedländer, *Der Holschnitt*, Berlin, 1917 (revised by H. Mähle, Berlin, 1970).

Fuller – S. E. Fuller, *A Manual of Instruction in the Art of Wood Engraving*, Boston, 1867 (second edition 1879).

Furst – Herbert E. A. Furst, 'The Modern Woodcut' in *Print Collector's Quarterly*, July–October 1921, pp.151–70; *The Modern Woodcut*: A Study of the Evaluation of the Craft, 1924.

Garrett – Albert Garrett, *The History of British Wood Engraving*, Tunbridge Wells, 1978 (a well illustrated survey by a wood engraver with select biographies of engravers); *British Wood Engraving of the Twentieth Century*, 1980 (rather thin pictorial survey).

Gilks – Thomas Gilks, *The Art of Wood-Engraving*. A Practical Handbook, 1866 (second edition 1867); *A Sketch of the Origin and Progress of the Art of Wood Engraving*, with a Chapter Explaining a Box of Materials Used in the Process, 1868 (both probably the most popular and useful Victorian practical guides to engraving written by a wood engraver whose entry appears in the dictionary).

Graphic – *The Graphic Portfolio*, 1876 (a selection of 50 wood engravings from the most influential wood engraved illustrated publications of the 1870s).

Grolier Club – *Books and Prints Illustrating the Origin and Rise of Wood Engraving*, N.Y., 1890; *Modern Wood Engraving Works of the Society of American Wood Engravers*, N.Y., 1890.

Grupe – E. Y. Grupe, *Instruction in the Art of Photographing on Wood*, Leominster, Massachusetts, 1882.

Gusman – Pierre Gusman, *La Gravure sur bois et d'épargne sur métal*, Paris, 1916; *La Gravure sur bois en France aux XIXe siècle*, Paris, 1929; *L'Art de la gravure*, Paris, 1933.

Hamerton – Philip Gilbert Hamerton, *The Art of the American Wood-Engraver*, N.Y., 1894 (with extensive bibliography of wood engraving).

Hamilton – S. Hamilton, *Early American Book Illustrators and Wood Engravers, 1670–1870*, Princeton, N.J., 1958.

Hardie – Martin Hardie, *Catalogue of Modern Wood Engravings in the Victoria and Albert Museum*, 1906; *Catalogue of Prints, Wood Engravings after Sir John Everett Millais in the Victoria and Albert Museum*, 1908.

Hartley – Harold Hartley, 'The 1860s Illustrators' in *Print Collector's Quarterly*, vol 11, 1924 (*see also* S. K. Phelps in Boston Museum entry above).

Hayden – A. Hayden, *Chats on Old Prints*, 1908.

Heller – J. Heller, *Geschichte der Holzschneidekunst von der altesten bis auf die neusten zeiten*, Bamberg, 1823.

Hentschel – C. Hentschel, 'Process Engraving' in *Journal of the Society of Arts*, 20 April 1900, pp.469ff.

Herkomer – Herbert Herkomer, 'Drawing and Engraving on Wood' in *Art Journal*, 1882, pp.136ff.

Hind – Arthur M. Hind, *An Introduction to a History of the Woodcut*, 1935 (reprinted 2 vols 1963).

Hirth – G. Hirth and R. Muther, *Meister holzschnitte aus vier Jahrhunderten*, Munich, 1893.

Holme – Geoffrey Holme (ed.), *Modern Woodcuts and Lithographs by British and French Artists*, N.Y., 1919; *Representative Art of our Time*, 1903 (with essay by Charles Hiatt, 'The Modern Aspect of Wood Engraving').

Houfe – Simon Houfe, *The Dalziel Family*, 1978 (Sotheby sale catalogue).

Humphreys – Henry Noel Humphreys, *Masterpieces of the early Printers and Engravers*, 1870.

Jackson – Christine E. Jackson, *Wood Engravings of Birds*, 1978 (discusses Victorian engravers of birds and their work in general).

Jackson – John Jackson, *see* Chatto.

Jansen – H. Jansen, *Essai sur l'origine de la gravure en bois et en taille-douce*, 2 vols, Paris, 1808.

Johnson – Una Johnson, *American Woodcuts 1670–1950*: A Survey of Woodcuts and Wood Engravings in the United States, Brooklyn, N.Y., 1950.

Jourov – Alexandre Jourov and Eugénie Tretiakova, *La gravure sur bois*, Moscow, 1977.

Knight – Charles Knight, *Passages of a Working Life during Half a Century*, 3 vols, 1864–65 (autobiography by one of the pioneers of Victorian popular wood engravings used in the books and magazines he published; *see* his dictionary entry).

Kouwenhoven – John A. Kouwenhoven, *Adventures of America, 1857–1900:* A Pictorial Record from *Harper's Weekly*, N.Y., 1938 (selections of wood engravings from a major American publication of the period).

Kristeller – Paul Kristeller, *Kupferstich und Holzschnitt im vier Jahrhunderten*, Berlin, 1905 (reprinted 1922).

Laborde – Léon de Laborde, *Essai de gravure pour servir à une histoire de la gravure en bois*, Paris, 1833.

Laffan – W. M. Laffan (introduction), *Engravings on Wood by Members of the Society of American Wood Engravers*, N.Y., 1887.

Lindley – Kenneth Lindley, *The Woodblock Engravers*, Newton Abbot, 1970 (the most current technical survey of the Victorian wood engraver).

Linton – William J. Linton, 'The Engraver: His Function and Status' in *Scribner's Magazine* (N.Y.), June 1879, p.241; 'Art in Engraving on Wood' in *Atlantic Monthly*, June 1879, pp.706–13; *Some Practical Hints on Wood-Engraving for the Instruction of Reviewers and the Public*, Boston, 1879; *The History of Wood Engraving in America*, Boston, 1882 (reprinted N.Y., 1976); *Wood Engraving: A Manual of Instruction*, 1884; *The Masters of Wood Engraving*, 1889; *Memories*, 1895 (American edition, *Threescore and Ten Years, 1820–90, Recollections by W. J. Linton*, N.Y., 1894).

Lippman – F. Lippman, *Kupferstiche und Holzschnitte alter Meister in Nachbildungen*, 10 vols, Berlin, 1888–89.

Lüdemann – W. von Lüdemann, *Geschichte der Kupferstich-Kunst . . . Holzschneide- und Steindruck-Kunst*, Dresden, 1828.

Lützow – C. von Lützow, *Die vervielfältigende Kunst der Gegenwart*, Vol 1, 'Der Holzschnitt', Vienna, 1887–1903.

Mackley – George Mackley, *Wood Engraving*, 1948 (reprinted Old Woking, 1981) (recognized as the most competent manual for the beginner by one of the best British contemporary wood engravers, with a chapter 'Bewick and Some Modern Engravers' and bibliography).

McLean – Ruari McLean (ed.), *The Reminiscences of Edmund Evans*, 1967 (contains much about wood engraving in London 1840s–90, artists and publishers, referred to as 'Evans *Reminiscences*').

MacMurtrie – Douglas C. MacMurtrie, *The Book: the Story of Printing and Bookmaking*, third edition 1943.

MacNab – Iain MacNab, *Wood Engraving*, 1947 (manual by successful contemporary British wood engraver).

Maré – Eric de Maré, *The Victorian Woodblock Illustrators*, 1980 (chapters on draughtsmen and wood engravers).

Marx – G. W. Marx, *The Art of Drawing and Engraving on Wood*, 1881 (second edition with list of dealers and materials necessary).

Meister werke der Holzschneide Kunst, 1879.

Morris – William Morris, *Some German Woodcuts of the Fifteenth Century*, Kelmscott Press, 1897 (with an article by Morris and cuts from works in his library).

Mueller – Hans A. Mueller, *Woodcuts and Wood Engraving: How I Make Them*, N.Y., 1939.

Naumann – R. Naumann and R. Weigel, *Archiv für die zeichnenden Künste mit besonderer Beziehung auf Kupferstecher und Holzschneidekunst und ihre Geschichte*, 6 vols, Leipzig, 1855–62.

O'Connor – John O'Connor, *The Technique of Wood Engraving*, N.Y. and London, 1971.

Passavant – Johann David Passavant, *Le peintre-graveur*, 6 vols, 1860–64 (reprinted N.Y., 1966).

Pennell – Joseph Pennell, 'The True Condition of Wood-Engraving in England and America in *National Review*, vol 25, May 1895, pp.343–50.

Pichon – L. Pichon, 'The New Book Illustration in France' in *The Studio* (London), Special Winter No., 1924.

Pilinski – Adam Pilinski (ed.), *Monuments de la Xylographie, Reproduction Facsimile*, 8 vols, Paris, 1882–86.

Portland Art Museum – *Masterpieces in Wood*: The Woodcut Print from the Fifteenth to the Early Twentieth Century, Portland, Oregon, 1976.

Reiner – Imre Reiner, *Woodcut, Woodengraving*: A Contribution to the History of the Art, St. Gall, Switzerland, 1947.

Rumpel – Heinrich Rumpel, *Wood Engraving*, N.Y., 1974 (also as *La Gravure sur Bois/Der Holschnitt*, Geneva, 1972).

Ruskin Art Club – *Modern Wood Engraving*, Los Angeles, 1890.

Ruskin – John Ruskin, *Ariadne Florentina*: Six Lectures on Wood and Metal Engraving, delivered 1872, published 1876; *The Art of England*, 1883 (lectures as Slade Professor at Oxford including 'The Fireside' on the period's favourite illustrators and wood engravings).

Salaman – Malcolm C. Salaman, 'The Graphic Arts of Great Britain' in *The Studio* (London), Special No., 1917; 'The Woodcut of Today at Home and Abroad' in *The Studio*, Special No., 1927; *The New Woodcut*, N.Y., 1930.

Sander – David M. Sander, *Wood Engraving*: An Adventure in Printmaking, N.Y., 1978.

Schasler – Max A. Schasler, *Die Schule der Holzscheneidekunst*, Leipzig, 1866.

Schrader – J. L. Schrader and Diane Johnson, *The Woodcut Revival 1800–1925*, Lawrence, Kansas, 1968.

Sewter – A. C. Sewter, *Modern British Woodcuts and Wood-Engravings*, Whitworth Art Gallery, Manchester, 1962.

Sinclair – Hamilton Sinclair, *Early American Book Illustrators and Wood Engravers*, 1958 (supplement 1968).

Sleigh – Bernard Sleigh, *Wood Engraving since 1890*, 1932 (survey by one of the period's leading revivalist engravers with comments on Victorian predecessors).

Smillie – T.W. Smillie, 'Photographing on Wood for Engraving', Smithsonian Miscellaneous Collections, Washington D.C., vol 47, 1905.

Stevens – J. Stevens, 'Woodcuts dropped into the Text' in *Studies in Bibliography*, vol XX, 1967.

Typographica 10 (1964) (article on stock-blocks).

Vizetelly – Henry Vizetelly, *Glances Back Over Seventy Years*, 1893 (autobiography by wood engraver and publisher with recollections of many period artists and engravers).

Weigal – R. Weigal, *Holzschnitte berühmter meister*, Leipzig, 1851–54 (*see also* Naumann entry).

Wilkinson – W. T. Wilkinson, *Photoengraving and Photogravure*, 1890; *Photo-engraving and Photo-lithography in Line and Half-tone*, 1888.

Woodbury – George E. Woodbury, *A History of Wood Engraving*, London and N.Y., 1883 (reprinted Detroit 1969).

'Wood Engraving as an Employment for Women' in *Alexandra Magazine*, April 1865.

Alphabetical List of Engravers

ABATE and Clerville fl.1850s
London wood engraving firm, with an office at
24A Cardington Street, Hampstead Road, NW
(POD,1856). Their neighbour was the noted
engraver Mason Jackson (q.v.).

ABBOTT, Henry fl.1850s
London wood engraver, who worked at 89 Chancery
Lane, WC (POD,1859). He shared the premises with
F.Anderson (q.v.).

ABNER, John fl.1850s
Draughtsman illustrator, who drew on wood some of
the one hundred illustrations to Charles MacKay's
The Home Affections,1856. These were wood
engraved by the Dalziel Brothers (q.v.).
[White]

ABSOLON, John 1815-95
Draughtsman on wood, painter and illustrator,
listed by Chatto as 'an illustrator of popular story
books, most of which have been published or edited
by Mr Cundall'. Edmund Evans (q.v.) explains in his
Reminiscences (p.26) how Absolon was one of the
early artists who contributed designs on wood blocks
to his colour printed railway novel covers. Absolon
was born in Lambeth, May 1815, and studied under
the Italian, Ferrigi, and at the British Museum. He
started portrait painting in oils aged fifteen and was
assistant to Grieve, the theatrical scene-painter,
for about four years, before going to Paris about
1835. He became a watercolour painter and a member
of the New Water Colour Society in 1835 (resigned
1858, rejoined 1861, as treasurer). He is especially
noted for drawings of the battle fields of Crécy and
Agincourt which were published by Graves and
established a popular reputation. Many of his
paintings were engraved in black and white and
colours. He died on 26 June 1895. As a draughtsman
on wood Absolon is noted for his designs in the style
Houfe calls 'midway between the illustrators of the
old tradition like Mulready and the new generation of
the 1860s. He was most successful in figure drawing
and particularly so in his contemporary genre
subjects and his illustrations to children's books,
outlined and with very little shadow'. Of these the
British Library catalogue lists about forty-three
titles, while White claims among the best are his
designs for The Poetical Works of J.Beattie and
W.Collins,1846, wood engraved by Samuel Williams
(q.v.). He also made drawings for Peter Parley's
Annual in the late 1846s, printed by Reynolds and
Collins (q.v.); and drawings for sixty-two plates
printed in four to five colours from wood blocks for
Joseph Cundall's Songs, Madrigals and Sonnets
(1849), which earned him £36 for 'drawing and
designs'. His other work for Cundall included
Favourite Pleasure Books for Young People,1859;
Rhymes and Roundelayes,1858; The Poetical Works

of Oliver Goldsmith; Lockhart's Spanish
Ballads,1841, and Bohn's illustrated edition of
Longfellow's Poems,1856, which were wood engraved
by Thomas Bolton (q.v.). His drawings also
appeared engraved in periodicals like the
Churchman's Family Magazine,1864, and Art
Journal,1862. The British Museum owns his
designs engraved by the Dalziels (q.v.).
[For a list of illustrated work see British Library
catalogue and partial list in Houfe; also Bryan;
Chatto; White; McLean, Victorian Book Design;
Reminiscences of E.Evans,1969]

ADAM, John fl.1872-1900
Scottish wood engraver, who worked during the
second half of the nineteenth century in Edinburgh.
He had offices at 6 India Buildings, Edinburgh
(Kelly's,1872), 6 Forest Road (1876,1880) and
15 Meadow Place (1900).

ADAMS, Joseph Alexander 1803-80
Wood engraver, praised by W.J.Linton as among the
masters of the art in the Branston pattern, noted
for his quality engravings. He was born in New
Germantown, New Jersey in 1803 and was
apprenticed to a printer but self-taught as an
engraver. In 1831 he came to England, where he
studied with numerous British wood engravers,
the result of which can be seen in his frontispiece to
Treasury of Knowledge,1834, published in New York.
He re-engraved the English edition of Scripture
Illustrations and is best known for 1600 cuts 'nearly
all done by his pupils' to a Bible, published in New
York. He spent several years in Europe, then
returned to America to work with scientific
inventions, inventing a printing press named after
himself.
[Linton, Masters of Wood Engraving]

ADENEY, Thomas Samuel fl.1846-86
London wood engraver, who worked from 1846 in the
city. His offices changed numerous times over the
forty years he worked there. The directories list
42 Frederick Place, Hampstead Road (POD,1846),
19 Harpur Street, Red Lion Square (POD,1848) and
13 Millman Street, Bedford Row (POD,1851,
Hodgson's,1855). Two years later he moved again to
6 Regent Place, WC (POD,1857), which changed to
4 Regent Place (POD,1860). In 1862 he added an
office at 33 Essex Street, Strand which he retained
until 1881; then he moved to 23 Southampton
Buildings, WC and remained there until sometime in
1886, when this became the address of Danielsson
and Company (q.v.).

AITKEN
Little is known of this wood engraver.
Hake lists his wood engraved bust portrait
of the Victorian author, Douglas Jerrold,

after a photograph.

ALCOCK, John fl.1870s
London wood engraver, who worked at 3 Gunpowder
Alley, Shoe Lane, EC (POD,1873).

ALDRIDGE, John fl.1869-83
London wood engraver, who worked for over
fourteen years in the city, first at 8 Barnsbury
Terrace, Liverpool Road, N (POD,1869), then at
343 Liverpool Road (POD,1870). In 1875 he added an
office at 13 Paternoster Row, EC which had been
exchanged (by 1878) for 199 Strand, although this
second establishment only lasted for about a year,
disappearing from POD in 1879. After 1883 the firm
may have adopted the name Aldridge and Davis (q.v.).

ALDRIDGE and Davis fl.1883-?
London wood engraving firm, listed at 17 Gough
Square, EC (POD,1883). This address was later
taken by R.A.Cheffins (q.v.). Davis may be the
wood engraver Frederick William Davis (q.v.), who
set up on his own about 1887 at 75 Fleet Street, EC
(POD,1887).

ALLAN, Sir William 1782-1850
Occasional draughtsman on wood, prominent Scottish
painter of historical and oriental subjects and scenes
of Russian life. He was elected ARA,1825, RA,1835
and PRSA,1838. Allan is listed here for his drawings
on wood of oriental subjects to the Murray edition of
J.G.Lockhart's Ancient Spanish Ballads,1841, which
appeared alongside works by his draughtsmen
colleagues David Roberts, William Simson, Henry
Warren, C.E.Aubrey, Louis Haghe, William Harvey
and others (qq.v.). This book was impressive:
according to McLean, 'it must have been -- after
Baxter's Pictorial Album of 1837 -- the most
colourful and lavish book, produced for the gift book
market, that London had yet seen'.
[Wood; DNB; Redgrave; McLean]

ALLANSON, John ?-1859
English wood engraver, who worked in Leipzig,
Germany, after an apprenticeship with Thomas
Bewick (q.v.). He wood engraved most of Ludwig
Richter's 151 drawings to Musäus, Volkmarchen
der Deutschen, 1842, for which he was known
through the English selective edition, Legends
of Rubezahl and Other Tales. From the German
of Musäus, published by Joseph Cundall, 1845.
Allanson joined with William Nicholls (q.v.)
as Allanson and Nicholls and from their
Leipzig office they became known for their
expert English-style black-line wood engravings.
The inferior German engraving market turned to them
for help, but they jealously guarded their work and
once turned away an unsuitable trainee without
showing him their latest work in progress. Allanson

died in London in 1859.
[Muir, Victorian Illustrated Books,pp.215,
228]

ALLANSON and Nicholls
(see Allanson, John)

ALLARD, Henry
(see Allard, William and Henry)

ALLARD, William and Henry fl.1872-1900
Birmingham wood engravers, who worked during the
second half of the nineteenth century. Henry worked
with William at 8A New Edmund Street (Kelly's,1872)
but he fails to appear again. The firm is then listed
in William Allard's name alone, and operated from
4 Victoria Buildings, Temple Row (Kelly's,1876).
It remained there until 1900.

ALLDIS, Edward Thomas fl.1870s
London wood engraver, who worked at 33 Castle
Street, Holborn, EC (POD,1871). He shared the
premises that year with the wood engraving firm,
Minton and Stranders (q.v.).

ALLEN, Walter James fl.1859-91
Occasional draughtsman on wood, genre painter and
illustrator, listed by White and Houfe for his
contributions to the Churchman's Family Magazine,
1864, and the Illustrated London News,1888-91.
These were primarily drawings of comic animals,
humanised dogs and children. The British Library
lists his illustrations to F.Paladan-Müller, The
Fountain of Youth,1867. Allen exhibited at the Royal
Academy and other venues from 1859-61.
[Houfe; Bénézit; White]

ALLINGHAM, Mrs Helen
(see Paterson, Helen)

ALLON, Arthur fl.1850s
Draughtsman on wood of architectural subjects, notably
a three-quarter page drawing 'Bird's-Eye View of the
Crystal Palace and surrounding Country', engraved
in the Illustrated London News,14 June 1851. The
British Museum owns designs by 'A.Allom' (sic),
engraved by the Dalziels (q.v.) in 1852.

ALSOP, G.A. fl.1820s
London wood engraver, who worked during the early
part of the nineteenth century. Pigot listed his office
at 23 Moor Street, Edgware Road (Pigot,1822-23).
He may be related to the W.Allsop (sic) listed by
Johnstone in 1817 as 'Wood Letter Cutter'.

ANASTASI, Auguste Paul Charles 1820-89
French draughtsman of wood engravings and
landscape painter, who worked for Henry Vizetelly
(q.v.) in the early days of the Illustrated London

News. He was a pupil of Delacroix, Corot and Delaroche, and specialised in views of Normandy, Holland and Rome, but abandoned painting due to his blindness.
[Houfe; H.Vizetelly, Glances Back,1893]

ANDERSON, Alexander 1775-1870
American wood engraver, listed here for his importance in introducing the work of Bewick and Thompson to America. W.J.Linton calls him (Memories, pp.221-22) 'worthy of notice as the first engraver in wood in the USA'. Anderson was the son of a Scottish copper-plate printer. He studied Hogarth's work as a boy, and engraved on copper at the age of twelve, but soon became a doctor. Upon his retirement in 1798 (Bryan,1796) following a yellow fever epidemic that killed his family, he then returned to engraving first on copper, then on wood. His most notable work was 300 wood engravings for an American edition of Bewick's Quadrupeds,1802, which Linton praised as 'admirable copies, only reversed'. This led to the conclusion that Anderson's career, engraving primarily after English work, was influential, but not original. He engraved designs 'of equal fidelity, though he had no genius in design and even as an engraver was hardly to be called great'. After 1830 he devoted himself exclusively to wood engraving, and became an honorary member of the National Academy of Design, NY in 1843. He died in Jersey City on 17 January 1870, with his engraving tool in his hand. According to Fincham, Anderson signed his work 'A Anderson sculp (sc)'. This was found on seven bookplates done in 1800 and 1810.
[For a full account of Anderson's life and work, see Art Journal,1858, pp.271ff; also F.M.Burr, Life and Works of Alexander Anderson, NY., 1893; B.J.Lossing, A Memorial of Alexander Anderson, NY., 1870; A Collection of 150 engravings by Alexander Anderson, NY., 1873; A Brief Catalogue of Books illustrated by Alexander Anderson,1885]

ANDERSON, David John fl.1860-80
London wood engraver, who worked for over thirteen years in the city from a number of offices which he shared with engraver colleagues. He worked at 123 Chancery Lane, WC (POD,1866), which he shared with G.C.Freudemacher, E.T.Hartshorn, T.Powney and W.D.Willis (qq.v.). He moved to 75 Fleet Street, EC (POD,1868), then to 72 Ludgate Hill, EC (POD,1870), then to 130 Fleet Street, EC (POD,1873), then to 47 Fleet Street, EC (POD,1878), and finally to 98 Strand, WC (POD,1879). The British Library lists his book, Jewish Emancipation, published for him in 1857.

ANDERSON, Frederick fl.1857-88
London wood engraver, who worked for about thirty years in several offices shared with engraver colleagues. The first was at 13 Curistor Street,

Chancery Lane (POD,1857), which he shared with F.J.Kemplen (q.v.); the second at 44 Charrington Street, NW (POD,1858); the third at 89 Chancery Lane, WC (POD,1859), shared with Henry Abbott (q.v.); and the fourth at 8 Dane's Inn, Strand, WC (POD,1861), shared with C.M.Gorway, E.T.Hartshorn, J.H.Rimbault and J.Watkins (qq.v.). The London directory also lists Frederick Anderson and Company at 5 Newgate Street, EC (POD,1887), which engraved five full-page illustrations 'Daughters of George III', after drawings of Johann Heinrich Ramberg, to the English Illustrated Magazine,1886-87. These were in imitation of eighteenth-century chalk drawings.

ANDERSON, John 1778-?
Wood engraver of the 'Bewick School', Anderson was born in Edinburgh, son of Dr James Anderson, editor of The Bee and customer of Thomas Bewick (q.v.). He received a 'classical education' (Redgrave), then was apprenticed to Thomas Bewick from 10 September 1792 to ? September 1799. There he worked on the first part of Bewick's British Birds; engraved illustrations for Bloomfield's The Farmer's Boy,1800; Maurice's Grove Hill,1799; and an edition of The Letters of Junius. Bain explains that his style used thin horizontally biased foliage as in the nature vignettes of The Farmer's Boy. Redgrave concludes that Anderson, 'formed a style of his own, and showed much ability, but did not long follow his profession'. In fact he went abroad about 1804, 'on some speculation' (Redgrave), and was lost to wood engraving. He died sometime in the early nineteenth century. The British Museum owns his engravings to Grove-Hill's A Descriptive Poem, and after drawings of G.Samuel.
[Redgrave; Bénézit; TB; I.Bain, T.Bewick, Record, 1979]

ANDERSON, W.
Wood engraver of nature scenes. The British Museum owns a landscape with punter on a stream and a series of bird vignettes, attributed to Anderson. They are wood engraved in a competent yet uninspired black-line technique.

ANDERTON, William fl.1880s
Shrewsbury wood engraver, who worked from 41 High Street (Kelly's,1889).

ANDREW, Best and Leloir
(see Best, Adolphe)

ANDREW, J. (John) fl.1840s
London wood engraver, who engraved for the early numbers of the Illustrated London News in 1842 and Charles Knight's Penny Magazine, October 1841, after B.Sly (q.v.). His style is best seen in a costume scene at London's Guildhall engraved

after a third page drawing by John Gilbert for the
Illustrated London News,19 November 1842. Its
rather faint black line shows a limited understanding
of shade and over-emphasis on pattern. He taught
the engraver Theodore Carreras (q.v.). J.Andrew
worked from 302 Strand and 29 New Street, Dorset
Square (POD,1840) while a 'John Andrew' worked at
1A Grove Terrace, Bayswater (POD,1848).

ANDREW and Company fl.1880s
London firm of draughtsmen on wood, which
operated from 67 Strand, WC (Kelly's,1880).

ANDREW and Wagner fl.1840s
London wood engraving firm, which operated from
10 Crawley Street, Somerstown (POD,1846).

ANDREWS, George Henry 1816-98
Occasional draughtsman on wood of figure and
landscape subjects; also marine painter. He was
born in Lambeth in 1816 and trained first as an
engineer. By the 1850s he was working as
draughtsman for wood engraved illustrations of
naval subjects and became the principal naval
artist for the Illustrated London News,1856-60. He
also contributed to the Illustrated Times,1859 and
The Graphic,1870. Bohn in Chatto and Jackson lists
him among the prominent new draughtsmen for wood
engravings and lists his drawings for Ministering
Children,1856. His skills in combining landscape
drawing with a thorough knowledge of engineering
are best seen in his early works, such as 'Quarries
in the Holyhead Mountain', a half page drawing for
the Illustrated London News,3 September 1853.
Andrews also earned a reputation as a painter,
exhibiting at the Old Watercolour Society,1840-50,
at the Royal Academy from 1850-93 and at the
Royal Society of British Artists. He was elected
FRGS and member of the Royal Watercolour Society.
He died in Hammersmith on 31 December 1898. The
British Museum owns his drawings wood engraved by
the Dalziel Brothers (q.v.) in 1861.
[For an account of his work see M.H.Schilling,
George Henry Andrews, Weimer,1855; also Bénézit;
TB; Graves; Bryan; Redgrave; Chatto; Houfe]

ANDREWS, J. (James) fl.1830-61
Draughtsman on wood of botanical subjects, noted by
White for his wood engraved drawings to Household
Song,Kent,1861, done with Birket Foster and
Samuel Palmer (qq.v.). The British Library lists his
nine illustrated works from 1837-65, including
several also coloured by Andrews; such as his
'12 bouquets drawn and coloured from nature' to
L.A.Twamley's Flora's Gems, (1837); twenty-four
plates drawn and coloured to Robert Tyas's Flowers
and Heraldry,1851; and twelve colour illustrations to
Choice Garden Flowers,c1850.
[White; British Library catalogue; Bénézit]

ANDREWS, N. fl.1890s
Suburban London wood engraver, who worked at
32 Foulden Road, Stoke Newington, N (LSDN,1894).

ANDREWS, William fl.1878-1900
London wood engraver, who worked at 28 Essex
Street, Strand, WC (POD,1878-86) shared with
J.T.Morrell, later with G.Ferguson (qq.v.). His
office changed to the prominent engraving area in
the city, Falcon Court, 32 Fleet Street, EC
(POD,1897-99), which he shared with William
Frederick Jeffries (q.v.).

ANDREWS and Jewitt
(see Jewitt, Orlando)

ANELAY, Henry 1817-83
'Mr H.Anelay is well known to the public as a
draughtsman on wood, especially in the departments
of portrait and figure drawing', Bohn wrote in 1861
of this landscape painter and illustrator. Anelay was
born in Hull in 1817, lived in Sydenham from 1848
and began work as a portrait illustrator under the
tutelage of Stephen Sly (q.v.). Sly must have
secured work for him on the publications of Charles
Knight (q.v.), notably London,1840, and Penny
Magazine,1841-42. His drawings here were engraved
by A.Clarke, Murdon, I.Holloway, L.Jewitt,
James Field, and Sly himself (qq.v.). He provided
numerous plates for the new Illustrated London
News.1843-55, engraved by Frederick James Smyth
(q.v.); these included a large portrait of the
American novelist, Harriet Beecher Stowe,
15 January 1853. Houfe believes that in the same
year he may have been sent to Constantinople by
the paper. Henry Vizetelly explains, rather
brutally, that Anelay was 'certainly credited with
having produced in the earlier numbers some of the
worst figure subjects the paper ever published'
(Vizetelly, Glances Back). As a book illustrator,
Anelay called upon his experiences drawing 'the
good little boy and girl of the most commonplace
religious periodicals' (White), which included
British Workman,1855, and Band of Hope Review,
1861. Some of his best work may be seen in Bohn's
edition of Sandford and Merton, engraved by George
Measom (q.v.); figures in Merrie Days of England,
Kent, c1860-61; Favourite English Poems; and an edition
of Uncle Tom's Cabin,1852. He is also responsible
for eight drawings to Beeton's edition of Robinson
Crusoe,1862, engraved and printed by W.Dickes
(q.v.) and believed by McLean to be one of the first
colour printed Robinson Crusoes in England. The
British Library lists sixteen works illustrated by
him, including 130 illustrations to My Pet's
Picture-Book,1873, one of his last works. The
British Museum owns his designs engraved by the
Dalziels (q.v.). Anelay was also a landscape
painter who exhibited from 1845 in London, notably

at the Royal Academy, 1858-73.
[Houfe; Chatto; White; Bénézit; McLean; Bodleian]

ANGAS, George French 1822-86
Topographical draughtsman illustrator, born in 1822
in Durham, son of a founder of South Australia. He
studied anatomical drawing and lithography in
London, travelled to Malta and Sicily and published
his observations in 1842. He served as director of the
Sydney Australia Museum in 1851, having emigrated
there in 1843. Although primarily a lithographic
artist, the Dalziel Brothers (q.v.) wood engraved
several of his drawings in 1866 (a collection now in
the British Museum). He also exhibited at the Royal
Academy and the Royal Society of British Artists,
1843-74.
[For a list of lithographic illustrations see Houfe]

ANGERERS and Son, Fruworth and Company fl.1860s
London wood engraving firm, with two offices:
1 Palace Road, Upper Norwood, Crystal Palace
Station, and 146 Cheapside (POD,1866-67).

ANNESLAY, Lady Mabel 1881-?
Wood engraver, born at Anneslay Lodge, London in
1881. She studied art at the Frank Calderon School
of Animal Painting, 1895 and studied wood engraving
under Noel Rooke (q.v.) at the Central School,
1920-21. She became member of the Society of Wood
Engravers in 1924, then moved to County Down,
Ireland. She continued to engrave, despite the loss
of her right hand. She died in New Zealand.
[Garrett]

ANSDELL, Richard 1815-85
Occasional draughtsman on wood of animal subjects,
also prominent sporting and animal painter. He was
born in Liverpool in 1815, educated at the Blue Coat
School, Liverpool Academy and with the portrait
painter W.C.Smith in Chatham. He set up as an
artist first in Liverpool, then from 1847 in London.
He first exhibited at the Royal Academy from 1840,
then the British Institution from 1846, eventually
exhibiting a total of over 150 pictures. He was
elected RA in 1870, collaborated with T.Creswick
and W.P.Frith on large canvases, and achieved a
considerable reputation. As an illustrator on wood,
he contributed his prestigious name to various
'Sixties School' periodicals, notably the plate,
'Coming through the Fence' in Once a Week,1867;
he also drew for the Illustrated Times,1855-56, and
Rounds and Roundelayes,1858. Houfe described
these efforts as the work of 'a rare illustrator' of
'a few spirited designs to books'. Ansdell died in
Farnborough in 1885.
[For a full account of his painting see Wood (with
bibliography); also Houfe; White; Bénézit; Bryan;
Chatto]

APPLETON, Alfred John fl.1865-1910
London wood engraver, who worked from various
offices shared with his engraver colleagues. These
include 3 Bouverie Street, EC (POD,1865) shared
with the firm G.T.Izod and Company (q.v.),
32 Fetter Lane, EC (POD,1872) shared with
G.F.Sheern (q.v.) and 8 Palsgrave Place,
Strand (POD,1874) shared with C.Simpson and
O.Humphreys (qq.v.). He moved to 7 Bolt Court,
Fleet Street, EC (POD,1877) but remained there for
only a year, returning to Bouverie Street, where he
worked from No.4 until 1893. That year he moved
yet again to 11-12 Bell's Buildings, Salisbury Square,
EC (POD,1894-1901). By 1910 the firm is listed at
6 Dorset Street, Salisbury Square, EC.

APPLETON, Arthur Lawrence fl.1880s
London wood engraver, who worked from
168 Fleet Street, EC (POD,1886) which he
shared with the noted wood engravers
C.Branscombe, E.S.Gascoine, and
W.Purchese (qq.v.).

APPLETON, Frank fl.1877-95
London wood engraver, who worked from 180 Fleet
Street, EC (POD,1877), then 120 Salisbury Square,
EC (POD,1884), then 89 Farringdon Street, EC
(POD,1887), an address which he shared with the
wood engravers W.J.Potter, L.Knott, H.Prater,
C.Riches, H.Thornton and G.F.Horne (qq.v.).
From 1891 Appleton worked at 10 Red Lion Court,
Fleet Street, EC, where he remained until
about 1895, sharing the premises with Joseph
Williamson (q.v.).

APPLETON and Copping fl.1860s
London wood engraving firm, with an office at
Grecian Chambers, Devereux Court, Strand, WC
(POD,1864). (See also Copping, George James)

APPLETON and Sheern fl.1870s
London wood engraving firm, with an office at
81 Fleet Street, EC (POD,1870). (See also Sheern,
George Frederick)

ARCHER, James 1823-1904
Draughtsman on wood, prominent Scottish painter of
genre, portraits, landscapes and historical scenes.
He was born in Edinburgh in 1823, and was a pupil
at the Trustees' Academy under Sir William Allan.
He began chalk portraits and exhibited his first
historical painting at the Royal Scottish Academy in
1849. He moved to London in 1862, where he
exhibited at the Royal Academy, 1840-1904, the
British Institution and the Society of British Artists.
He was elected ARSA 1850 and RSA 1858. He died
in Haslemere on 3 September 1904. Chatto lists
Archer as a professional draughtsman on wood of
figure subjects. These included his illustrations to

Burns' Poems and 'two rather powerful blocks'
(White) called 'To Mary in Heaven' for Kent's
Household Song,1861, a major commission
shared with Birket Foster, Samuel Palmer,
G.H.Thomas, A.Solomon and others (qq.v.).
Such work was in keeping with Archer's reputation
as the first Victorian to do children's portraits in
period costume.
[Houfe; White; Chatto; TB; Art Journal,1871,
pp.97-99; for full biography see Wood]

ARCHER, John Wykeham 1808-64
Draughtsman on wood, watercolourist,
topographical illustrator, etcher, engraver. He
was born in Newcastle-upon-Tyne on 2 August 1808,
the son of a prosperous tradesman. He came to
London in 1820 and was apprenticed to the animal
engraver John Scott, of Copple Row, Clerkenwell.
He then worked as an engraver in Newcastle in
partnership with William Collard; then in Edinburgh,
and from 1831 in London, working with the noted
metal engravers W. and E.Finden. Much of his
work here was of topographical subjects engraved
on metal. He slowly abandoned engraving for
watercolour, was elected ARWS in 1842 and
exhibited at the New Watercolour Society, 1842-64.
He died in London on 25 May 1864. As a draughtsman
on wood, Archer was a prolific artist. Chatto noted
his 'antiquarian and architectural' subjects,
although most of these were etched and engraved on
metal from his original drawings. He began work
on wood for Charles Knight's publication, London,
1841. This led to numerous drawings for the
Illustrated London News,1847-51, engraved by
W.J.Linton and Mason Jackson (qq.v.). Most of
these were animal subjects or reproductions of
famous paintings. W.J.Linton notes that
Archer's drawing of Mulready's painting, 'Choosing
the Wedding Gown', was the first work for the
Illustrated London News which he engraved single-
handed. It was followed by 'Peacock at Home' and
'Dead Birds' after Lance, also engraved by Linton.
By 1851 Archer had completed a half page
reproduction, 'The Hay Cart' after Philips
Wouwerman, which was engraved by Jackson for
the Illustrated London News,14 June 1851. Fincham
explains Archer signed a crest design bookplate,
'Archer Eng^r' in 1850.
[Chatto; LeBlanc; Redgrave; Bryan; DNB; Houfe;
also Volume I (for metal engravings)]

ARCHIBALD and Stoole fl.1880s
Provincial wood engraving firm, with an office at
44 Whitefriargate, Hull (Kelly's,1880).

ARMITAGE, Edward 1817-96
Occasional draughtsman on wood, painter of
historical and religious subjects. He was born in
London in 1817, attended the Ecole des Beaux-Arts

in Paris in 1835, studied under Delaroche, won the
Houses of Parliament competition in 1847, visited
Russia during the Crimean War and returned home
to paint military pictures. He exhibited at the Royal
Academy, 1848-93, was elected ARA 1867 and RA
1872, serving as Academy painting lecturer in
1875. As a draughtsman on wood, Armitage is
noted by Chatto for his figure subjects, notably to
Lyra Germanica,1861; he also illustrated with
J.Leighton (q.v.) Pupils of St John the Divine,
1867-68, and the Dalziels' Bible Gallery,1880.
[For a study of his pictures see J.P.Richter,
Pictures and Drawings...of Edward Armitage,1898;
for biographical information see Wood; Houfe; DNB;
Bryan; Chatto; White; British Library catalogue]

ARMSTEAD, Henry Hugh 1828-1905
Draughtsman and engraver on wood, prominent
sculptor. Born in London on 18 June 1828, he
studied at the Royal Academy Schools and exhibited
from 1851, notably his famous sculptural groups
for the Albert Hall and the Albert Memorial. He
was elected ARA 1875 and RA 1879. He died on
4 December 1905. As a draughtsman, wood engraver
he worked primarily with the Dalziel Brothers
(q.v.) who interpreted the occasional drawings he
made for books and periodicals during the 1860s.
These include the Pre-Raphaelite composition, 'A
Song Which None but the Redeemed Ever Sing', in
Good Words,1861, praised by White as 'amongst
the most interesting of the comparatively few
illustrations by the RA'; 'Fourth Sunday in Lent'
for Churchman's Family Magazine's first number,
1863; and 'The Trysting Place', for Eliza Cook's
Poems,1865, which was engraved by the Dalziels
and which, according to White, 'deserves republication .
Drawings of note were those to Willmott's Sacred
Poetry,1862 and to Touches of Nature,1866. The
culmination of his work for the Dalziels was the
two designs he made for their celebrated Bible
Gallery,1880, which were republished as Art
Pictures from the Old Testament,1897. The
British Museum owns his designs engraved by
the Dalziels (q.v.), 1860-63.
[White; Houfe; TB; Bénézit; Who's Who,1906;
Art Journal,1874; Clement]

ARMSTRONG fl.1830s
London wood engraver, who worked at Duke Street
and Stamford Street (POD,1837).

ARMSTRONG, George fl.1860s
London wood engraver, who worked at 8 Dane's Inn,
Strand (POD,1862), an office which he shared with
C.M.Gorway, E.T.Hartshorn, J.H.Rimbault and
J.Watkins (qq.v.).

ARMSTRONG, John fl.1820s
Wood engraver of the 'Bewick School'. Armstrong
is described by Bewick (Bewick Memoir,p.200) as
his last apprentice 'who is now pursuing his business
in London' (c1827). The British Library lists a John
Armstrong 'of Newcastle-upon-Tyne', author of The
Young Woman's Guide to Virtue, Economy, and
Happiness, 6th edition (1825?) and 'Improved
edition', with twelve engravings, 1828, published
by Mackenzie and Dent. There is also a
'J.Armstrong', London wood engraver listed at
14 Thomas Street, Saddler's Wells, St John's
Street Road (Johnstone,1817).

ARMSTRONG, Thomas fl.1840s
London wood engraver, who worked from 132 Fleet
Street (POD,1845). He was one of the growing
number of wood engravers who worked for the
illustrated book market and was described by
Spielmann as one of Ebenezer Landells' 'outside
engravers' -- that is a freelance who undertook
commissions for the more established engraving
firms. Armstrong is especially noted for his work
after natural history subjects. The ten illustrations
which he 'cleverly engraved' (Chatto) for
S.C.Hall's Book of British Ballads,1842, after
drawings by F.W.Fairholt were in a clean, black-
line style which relied on fine outline reminiscent
of etched lines with the use of deep shadow detail to
designate spatial distances between individual
figures. The British Museum owns a series of
proofs, including the vignette 'Bewick's Tomb'. He
signed his engravings: 'THOS ARMSTRONG'.
[Chatto; Bénézit; Spielmann; TB; Nagler (Monogram)]

ARMSTRONG, William fl.1840-60s
London wood engraver, who worked at 12 Rodney
Street, Pentonville (POD,1851-2). Chatto
introduced him in a section marked 'Engravers on
Wood not before mentioned' and cites his work on
Don Quixote,1841, the Illustrated News and Clever
Boys,1860, but little is known of his life. The
British Museum owns several engravings after John
Gilbert (q.v.) signed 'W ARMSTRONG'.

ARMSTRONG, William fl.1890s
London wood engraver, who worked at 10 Red Lion
Court, Fleet Street, EC (POD,1896-7), an address
which he then shared with the noted wood engraver
W.E.Barker (q.v.)

ARROWSMITH, William fl.1887-1910
London wood engraver, who worked from 30 Holborn,
EC (POD,1887), which he shared with the engraving
firms Hay and Peach, and Mitchell and Pitt (from
1890). He then moved to 2 Charterhouse Street, EC
(POD,1892-1910). The Dalziel Brothers (q.v.)
claim in their Record that William Arrowsmith was
one of their pupils.

ARTHUR, Robert fl.1870-90
Scottish wood engraver, who worked from 60 Kyle
Street, Glasgow (Kelly's,1872), which later became
Robert Arthur and Sons (POD,1889).

ARTIST, Frederick fl.1880s
Provincial wood engraver, who worked in
Northampton at Parade and Alcombe Road
(Kelly's,1889).

ARTISTIC Engraving Association
London wood engraving firm, listed at 203 Gray's
Inn Road (POD,1869). (See also Taylor, Arthur)

ASKE, William Henry fl.1859-64
   Frederick fl.1864-67
London wood engravers. William worked at
9 Essex Street, Strand, WC (POD,1859), which he
shared with the wood engravers Dorrington and
Potter (q.v.). He moved to 188 Strand
(POD,1861-64) which he shared with R.H.Moore
and J.P.Wall (qq.v.). The directories then list
the wood engraver Frederick Aske at this address
(POD,1864-67), an office he then shared with
R.H.Moore, and J.P.Wall (qq.v.).

ATKINSON, John Henry fl.1880s
Provincial wood engraver who worked at 31 Bishop
Lane, Hull (Kelly's,1880).

ATKINSON, John Priestman fl.1864-94
Draughtsman on wood for Punch. He began in 1864,
as an official in the General Railway Manager's
office, Derby where he made drawings for the local
paper, the Derby Ram. He was introduced to the
editor of Punch where his first cut appeared -- an
initial T -- in volume 48. He continued, according to
Spielmann, on the 'outside staff', using the name
'Dumb Crambo Junior' and specialised in comic·
genre scenes throughout the 1860s and 70s. Later
he turned completely to art, studied in Paris, and
was a close friend of Harry Furniss (q.v.). His
style as draughtsman was much in the quick-sketch
vein, not unlike Furniss, Hine or Newman, which
made engraving his work difficult. He also drew on
wood for Punch Pocket-Books, from 1877, the
Illustrated London News,1881, 1884, the Cornhill,
1883, and other papers. Many of these were wood
engraved by Joseph Swain (q.v.).
[Houfe; Spielmann; British Library catalogue]

AUBREY, C.E. fl.1840s
Draughtsman on wood. Aubrey contributed
drawings to the important edition of Ancient
Spanish Ballads,1842, engraved by Henry Vizetelly
(q.v.), and published by Murray. The style he used
is that of the etching needle, that fine delicate line
most effective for his sylvan subjects.
[McLean, Victorian Book Design]

AUSTIN, J. fl.1817
London wood engraver, who worked at 14 Paul's
Alley, Barbican (Johnstone,1817). He was probably
related to Richard Austin (q.v.).

AUSTIN, Richard T. and Son fl.1800-20s
Wood engraver, listed by Redgrave as a pupil of
John Bewick (q.v.), who worked during the first
part of the nineteenth century. He was awarded a
silver medal and 10 guineas in 1802 by the Society
of Arts for his 'masterly cut', 'England, Ireland
and Scotland receiving the offerings of genius'. He
worked in London engraving for numerous booksellers as well as exhibiting landscapes at the
Royal Academy in 1803 and 1806. Later he is listed
in the directories as 'R.Austin and Son' at 14 Paul's
Alley, Barbican (Pigot,1822-27). Austin's engravings
were generally small vignettes. His earliest work
was for R.Dodsley's Economy of Human Life,1810,
after Craig's designs, engraved with Henry Hole
(q.v.), and cuts to Linnaeus' Travels in Lapland,
1811. These set the pace for such commissions as
the several hundred woodcuts of scriptural subjects
after Craig, Thurston and others published by
Ackermann of the Strand. They earned him a steady
but largely undistinguished reputation. 'He was a
clever artist, and much employed by the booksellers, but he did nothing to promote the art,
which in his day began to rise in estimation',
Redgrave claimed; while Bryan called him a wood
engraver 'of moderate ability'. Chatto dismissed
him: 'a wood engraver named Austin executed
several cuts, but did nothing to promote the art'.
The British Museum owns several of his biblical
engravings after Craig. He signed his work: 'Austen',
'Austin', 'R.Austin', or 'Austin sc' (taken from
five bookplates listed by Fincham,1810-25).
[Redgrave; Bryan; Bénézit; Dodd]

AYLING, Joseph J.
London wood engraver and block maker, who listed
an office in the directories at 4 Crane Court, Fleet
Street, EC (POD,1885-86). An advertisement
claimed he also produced photo-zinc blocks,
'specimens sent post free'. He may be related to
the London portrait painter J.Ayling, who exhibited
at the Royal Academy, 1823-42.
[TB; Bénézit]

BABBAGE, Frederick fl.1878-94
London wood engraver, who worked at 84 Fleet
Street, EC (POD,1878) which he shared with R.Boston
and A.Myerson, 1878-81, and F.Long, 1879 (qq.v.).
Later he moved to 8 Essex Street, Strand, WC
(POD,1885-94) where he worked with J.Dickinson,
1885-94 (q.v.). Among his engraving commissions
were the illustrations after drawings by F.Villiers
(q.v.) to 'The Banqueting House' by Austin Dobson,

engraved in a black-outline style but printed with a
greyness of overall tone, for the English Illustrated
Magazine,1883-84.

BACON, E. and Son fl.1878-79
London wood engraving firm, with offices at
23 Wormwood Street, EC, and 62 and 63 Chalk
Farm Road, NW (POD,1877). The following year
the firm appeared at Wilfrid Works, Chalk Farm
Road, NW.

BAGG, Thomas fl.1832-59 William fl.1856-59
London wood engravers. Thomas worked first at
8 Hart Street, Bloomsbury (Pigot,1832-36) then
moved to 63 Gower Street (POD,1848). From 1856
he shared this with William Bagg, an artist whom
Bénézit listed for the painted and engraved portraits
which he exhibited at the Royal Academy and the
British Institution from 1827-29. The British
Museum owns a series of nature vignettes of the
seasons by Thomas Bagg. He signed his work:
'T.Bagg'.

BAGOT, Richard fl.1870s
Provincial wood engraver, who worked at Wards
Buildings, Deansgate, Manchester (Kelly's,1876).

BAILEY, John 1750-1819
Wood and copper engraver, etcher and draughtsman.
Bailey was self-taught, and early in his career he
engraved for Hutchinson's Histories of
Northumberland and Durham,1781-84, and Culley's
Observations on Live Stock,1807. Redgrave
explains that 'His works, which were both on wood
and copper, are very creditable productions, but
better in engraving than design'. He later became
a friend of Thomas Bewick (q.v.) and as land-
surveyor, agent of Lord Tankerville at Chillingham,
showed Bewick the subject of his master work, the
Chillingham Bull; he also commissioned the drawing
and engraving of his ram for an agricultural report
which he wrote. In this context he was the author of
Agricultural Surveys of Northumberland,1794, and
Durham,1810, and also of an essay on the
'Construction of the Plough',1795.
[TB; Redgrave; Fincham; LeBlanc; Bewick,
Memoir; Bénézit]

BAIN, Alexander Stewart fl.1880s
Provincial draughtsman on wood, who worked at
33 Caroline Street, Jarrow, Durham (Kelly's,1889),
a city in which his draughtsmen colleagues George
Johnstone and Samuel Kelly (qq.v.) also worked.

BAKER, George Joseph fl.1870s
London wood engraver, who worked at 9 Essex
Street, Strand, WC (POD,1874-75), an address he
shared with several wood engraver colleagues,
such as J.Bye, J.Desbois, W.Murden,

P.Roberts and F.Watkins (qq.v.). Baker was a competent black-line engraver who used a finely etched line for his nature vignettes and anatomical diagrams. The British Museum owns a delicate hen's foot engraving by him. He signed his work: 'G J BAKER'.

BAKER, Russell fl.1888-89
London wood engraver, who worked at 5 Catherine Street, Strand, WC (POD,1888-89). He may be the engraver listed by LeBlanc and Bénézit for his plate, 'Mary, Queen of Scots, going forth to execution', after J.Stephanoff.

BAKER, William Henry fl.1889
Provincial wood engraver, who worked at 58 Victoria Street, Bristol (Kelly's,1889). Fincham lists two armorial crest bookplates engraved by 'W.M. (sic) Baker s^{ct} Southampton', both dated 1840, which may be the work of this engraver.

BALCOMB, John Thomas fl.1876-89
London draughtsman, specialist illustrator of scientific and biological subjects. He worked at 33 Essex Street, Strand, WC (Kelly's,1876-80), an address shared with the wood engravers and draughtsmen W.E.Hastie, R.H.Keene, and the prodigious W.J.Palmer (qq.v.). By 1889 Balcomb had moved to 23 Southampton Buildings, WC. Balcomb is noted for his scientific drawings in the Illustrated London News,1876-83, including full page drawings of 'Historical Treasures in the Loan Collection of Scientific Apparatus, S.Kensington', 16 September 1876, and a half-page drawing, 'Professor Graham Bell's Telephone', 15 December 1877.

BALE, Edwin R.J. fl.1870-80s
London landscape and genre painter, noted here as the director of art for Cassell and Company, publisher of some of the most important wood engraved illustrations of the period. He was born in London in 1842, studied at South Kensington and Florence Academy, and exhibited paintings at the Royal Academy, 1870-83.
[Bénézit; TB; Who's Who,1908; Graves]

BALE and Holman fl.1863-66
London wood engraving firm, also manufacturer of wood blocks, with an office at 87 Great Titchfield Street, W (POD,1863-66).

BALLINGALL, William fl.1872-80
Scottish wood engraver, who worked at 35 Cockburn Street, Edinburgh (Kelly's,1872), 12 Teviot Place (1876), and 25 North Bridge, Edinburgh (1880). Bénézit lists an 'A.Ballingall', Edinburgh painter, who worked during the second half of the nineteenth century and exhibited watercolours at the New

Watercolour Society, 1883.

BANBURY, Henry fl.1870s
Provincial wood engraver who worked at 24 Albion Hill, Leicester (Kelly's,1872).

BANFIELD and Barber fl.1870s
London wood engraving firm, whose office at 5 Racquet Court, Fleet Street (POD,1870-72), was adjacent to that of the prominent wood engraver Edmund Evans (q.v.).

BANKS, John Henry fl.1870s
London wood engraver, who worked at 55 Drury Lane (POD,1871).

BANKS and Company fl.1874-75
London wood engraving firm, with suburban office at 11 Lavender Road, Clapham Junction, SW (POD,1874). The following year they added 13 Lavender Road, as well as offices at 7, 8 Great Winchester Street Buildings, EC (POD,1875).

BANNISTER, Frederick fl.1880-1910
London draughtsman, engraver on wood. He began work as a draughtsman at 268 Strand, WC (Kelly's,1880). By 1885 he had moved to 44 Fleet Street, EC (POD,1885-89), then 10 Bolt Court, Fleet Street (POD,1890-1910) which he shared (1900-01) with the wood engraver G.Bolak (q.v.). Houfe lists an 'F.Bannister' as a figure artist noted for his contributions to the Strand Magazine,1892.

BARAGWANATH and Hiscocks fl.1890s
London wood engraving firm, with an office at 13 Hatton Garden, EC (POD,1896-97). This became Hiscocks and Company (q.v.) the following year.

BARBANT, Charles ?-1922
French wood engraver, who reproduced drawings by English draughtsmen. He was born in Paris, was a pupil of his father and worked first with Adolphe Best (q.v.). He engraved for various French magazines and books: Journal des Journaux,1845, Histoire de L'Empereur Napoleon, and Jour du Monde. He also engraved several blocks after drawings by Gustave Doré (q.v.), and even illustrated the work of Jules Verne (Les Indes Noires). He exhibited at the Salon,1869-82. According to Bénézit, 'Il présente dans ses oeuvres plus d'habileté que son pere'. He is known to have engraved the drawings of G.H.Thompson for 'The Industries of the English Lake District', a series for the English Illustrated Magazine,1883-84, which remains competent and clear, engraved with a good understanding of adequate light and dark to make the scene of a man splitting wood for basket weaving a convincing one, despite the fact that Barbant probably had never

seen the sight himself.
[Bénézit; Gusman; TB (full bibliography)]

BARBER, Alfred and Company fl.1873-84
London wood engraving firm, with various offices
recorded over an eleven year period: 18 Shoe Lane,
Fleet Street, EC (POD,1873), 36 Charles Street,
Hatton Garden, EC (POD,1874), 80 Cowcross
Street, EC (POD,1875-76) and 8 Red Lion Court,
Fleet Street, EC (POD,1877). By 1880 the firm had
become Alfred Barber and Company with two
offices: 33 Charles Street, Hatton Garden, EC and
30 Ludgate Hill, EC (POD,1880-84). Finally an
'Alfred Barber' is listed at 47 Swinton Street, WC
(POD,1910), who may in fact be the painter Alfred R.
Barber, listed by Bénézit as exhibiting 1879-93 at
the Society of British Artists.

BARFOOT, Thomas fl.1880s
Provincial wood engraver, who worked at 11 Union
Passage, Birmingham (Kelly's,1889).

BARFORD and Newitt fl.1880-1900
Provincial wood engraving firm, with an office at
26 Queen Street, Wolverhampton (Kelly's 1880-1900).

BARKER, Ellis fl.1898-1910
London wood engraver, who worked at 10 (3) Red Lion
Court, Fleet Street, EC (POD,1898-1901) and was
listed in the London directory as late as 1910 when
he was working at 33 Fetter Lane, EC.

BARKER, Henry fl.1884-85
London wood engraver, who worked at
19 Featherstone Buildings, Holborn, EC
(POD,1884-85).

BARKER, Walter and Son fl.1857-97
London wood engraver, established for over forty
years in the city. Walter Barker was one of the
primary 'Sixties School' engravers whose work
after M.J.Lawless (q.v.) appeared in such
magazines as the Churchman's Family Magazine,
1863 (notably the drawing, 'One Dead') and London
Society, Volume IV (a wood engraving after a
Lawless drawing, 'Honeydew'). Both show how he
managed to retain much of the lightness of touch of
Lawless' pencil. (For a reproduction of 'One Dead'
see Reid, p.54.) Walter Barker worked at 151 Strand,
WC (POD,1857), then moved to 49 Carey Street, WC
(POD,1864) where he remained until at least 1875.
However, by 1883 he had taken his son into the
business and moved to 325 Strand where they
remained for just one year, the premises given up
to H.R.Edwards (q.v.). They then moved to
172 Strand, WC (POD,1884-91), an address which
they shared with Collings and Company (q.v.),
where they were listed not only as wood engravers
but also as draughtsmen on wood. The firm moved

yet again to Monument Chambers, King William
Street, EC (POD,1891-97) but it is no longer
listed in the London directories after that date.
Walter Barker signed his engravings: 'W.BARKER Sc.'

BARLOW, Thomas C. fl.1872-89
Scottish wood engraver, who worked also as
printer and printers' wood-type cutter, first at
341 St Vincent Street, Glasgow (Kelly's,1872), then
103 Bath Street, Glasgow (1880-89).

BARNARD, Alfred George fl.1875-80
London wood engraver, who worked at 4 Bell's
Buildings, Salisbury Square, EC (POD,1875), then
as 'A.George Barnard' at 61 Fleet Street, EC
(POD,1879). By the following year Barnard had
moved to the suburbs at 21 Dumbleton Road,
Camberwell, SE (LSDS,1880). There may be some
relation between Alfred George Barnard and the
watercolourist George Barnard (fl.1832-90), an
artist draughtsman who contributed a drawing to
the Illustrated London News,1858.
[Wood; Houfe; Bénézit]

BARNARD, Frederick 1846-96
Draughtsman on wood, occasional wood engraver
and prominent illustrator of books and magazines.
He was born on 26 May 1846 in St Martin's-le-
Grand, London, studied at Heatherley's in 1863, and
in Paris under Bonnat. Although Barnard painted in
oils, he admitted to being most comfortable with pen
and ink, and established a reputation for his genre
and social realism themes. These appeared as
wood engravings in the Illustrated London News,
1863-96; Punch,1864, 1884; Broadway,1867-74;
London Society,1867-68; Cassell's Family Magazine,
1868; Once a Week,1869; Good Words,1869, 1891-92;
and others (see Houfe for full list). His best work is
the series of London sketches for George R.Sims'
How the Poor Live,1883, engraved for the Pictorial
Times. Barnard exhibited work at the Royal Academy,
1866-87, and at the Paris Exhibition, 1878. He died
of burns in Wimbledon on 28 September 1896.
Barnard established himself as a professional wood
engraver and draughtsman when he set up offices at
139 Fleet Street (POD,1877). He moved to 57 and
58 Chancery Lane, WC (POD,1883) which he shared
with the engravers J.Fenton and J.Sachs (qq.v.).
He moved to 130 Fleet Street, EC (POD,1885-90)
after which his name disappears from the directories.
As a draughtsman for wood engravings, Barnard was
well-served by his engravers. His work for the
Illustrated London News was interpreted by the
prominent engravers Joseph Swain and W.J.Palmer
(qq.v.) who retained much of the light, sketchy
touch of his drawings of actors and their stage
performances. The Dalziel Brothers (q.v.)
maintained a long friendship with him and he did
sixty-six of the 100 drawings for their edition of

<u>Pilgrim's Progress</u>. 'Our long connection with
Barnard was of close intimacy and friendship;
he was a delightful companion, amusing, and full
of bright repartee, and would often set the table in
a roar' (Dalziels' <u>Record</u>,p.338). Barnard's nine
drawings to their 'Household' edition of Dickens,
1871-79, earned him the Dalziels' admiration as
'one of the foremost illustrators of Dickens'.
[For a biography and list of works <u>see</u> Houfe;
Wood; DNB; Bénézit; TB; Bryan; Spielmann; White]

BARNARD, James fl.1880-1900
London draughtsman on wood, who worked at Viaduct
Chambers, 38 Holborn Viaduct (Kelly's,1880-1900).
He may be related to J.Langton Barnard, fl.1876-
1902, the London domestic genre painter.
[Wood; TB; Bénézit]

BARNARD, William fl.1870s
London wood engraver, who worked at 308 City Road,
EC (POD,1872-73).

BARNARD, William fl.1890-1902
Suburban London wood engraver, who worked at
3 Trinity Square, Brixton, SW (LSDS,1894-1902).

BARNARD, William S. 1774-1849
London occasional wood engraver, who more generally
engraved portraits in mezzotint. Although
predominately known for these metal engravings,
especially 'Summer' and 'Winter' after Morland,
printed in colours and 'much prized' (Redgrave) he
is also known to have wood engraved (according to
LeBlanc). He was for several years keeper of the
British Institution and died on 11 November 1849.
[LeBlanc; Nagler; TB; Redgrave]

BARNES, G.E. fl.1860s-70s
Draughtsman illustrator, known to have contributed
drawings to the <u>Broadway</u> c1867-74, he specialised
in architectural subjects. He also exhibited at the
Royal Society of British Artists, 1866. The British
Museum owns engravings after 'E Barnes' engraved
by the Dalziel Brothers (q.v.), 1866.
[Houfe; White]

BARNES, Robert 1840-95
Draughtsman illustrator on wood of rural figures. He
worked at Berkhamsted, later Ormonde House,
Cliveden Place, Brighton and established a
reputation for magazine and book illustrations of
'semi-bucolic serials' in <u>Good Words</u>,1869, 1891;
and the <u>Sunday Magazine</u>,1865-66, 1869. He also
illustrated a Charles Reade story in the <u>Cornhill</u>,
1864, and contributed to others in 1869-70, 1884. Reid
claims that he was an important 'Sixties School'
illustrator who contributed to most of the period's
major magazines, although his work lacked a real
sense of invention, borrowing too much from Walker

and Pinwell, whose rural subjects he imitated. He
continued such work throughout the 1890s; by then
the wood engraver had lost his patronage and his
drawings were process engraved. He was elected
ARWS in 1876 and exhibited at the Royal Academy,
1873-91. He continued to illustrate until within a
year of his death, for instance to <u>A Prisoner of War</u>,
1894. But he is perhaps best known for his
illustrations to Thomas Hardy's <u>The Mayor of
Casterbridge</u> for <u>The Graphic</u>,1886, where he
served as staff artist. As a draughtsman on wood,
Barnes had a firm grip on his pencil; his drawings
remain, according to Reid 'bold, strong, and very
much alive'. However they were generally of striking
similarity: 'a family of the well-to-do farming
class, healthy, sturdy, producing no disquieting
variations from the sound yeoman stock that has
reached back from generation to generation'. His
most important achievement here is in the eight
drawings engraved by J.D.Cooper (q.v.) for
<u>Pictures of English Life</u>,1865, as idyllic and
formalised as any of his later works. He was well
suited for such work, and well served by his
engravers, including Joseph Swain (q.v.). Reid
reproduces (p.258) Swain's engraved proof
copiously corrected by Barnes in the margins; his
pencil notes for tonal changes and intricate detail
corrections show how meticulously he worked with
his engravers.
[For a list of illustrated work <u>see</u> Houfe; Reid;
White; TB; <u>also</u> A.Jackson, <u>Illustrators of
T.Hardy</u>,1981]

BARNSBY, J. fl.1817-24
London wood engraver, who worked at Angel Court,
Strand (Johnstone, Pigot,1817-24).

BARR, John fl.1830s
Provincial wood engraver, who worked at
18 Bordesley Street, Birmingham (Pigot,1835).

BARR, Solomon fl.1835-42
Provincial wood engraver, who worked at Howe
Street, Birmingham (Pigot,1835), then as 'wood
engraver and printer' at 42 Cherry Street,
Birmingham (Pigot,1842).

BARRETT, Alexander fl.1856
London wood engraver, who worked at 7 Palsgrave
Place, Strand (POD,1856).

BARRETT, William fl.1883-1901
London wood engraver, who worked at 57 and 58
Chancery Lane, WC (POD,1883-91) which he
shared with J.Fenton, F.Barnard and J.Sachs
(qq.v.). He is last listed in the London directory
at 33 Fetter Lane, EC (POD,1901).

BARROW
Wood engraver, illustrator, listed by Houfe as
'working in a rather crude and old fashioned style'.
W.J.Linton and Charles Knight claim he was
Charles Dickens' uncle and proprietor of The Mirror
of Parliament,1828, who employed John and Charles
Dickens. He lived in Norwood where the young
Dickens visited at weekends, although the friendship
ended in 1834. Barrow, as an illustrator, left at
least two works: a drawing of Queen Victoria's visit
to the Midland counties to the Illustrated London
News,1843, and illustrations to Gulliver's Travels,
1864.

BARROW, M.T. fl.1890s
London wood engraver, who worked at 2 Whitefriars
Street, EC (POD,1897).

BARTLETT, Richard fl.1892-1900
London wood engraver, who worked at 148 Cheapside,
EC (POD,1892-1900). He took over from the firm
Bartlett and Norman (q.v.).

BARTLETT and Norman fl.1886-91
London wood engraving firm, with an office at
12 and 14 Catherine Street, Strand, WC (POD,1886),
then 148 Cheapside, EC (POD,1889-91). After that
date the firm became Richard Bartlett's alone (q.v.).

BARTON, H.S. fl.1858-63
Draughtsman on wood, who designed for the Dalziel
Brothers (q.v.). The British Museum owns
Dalziel engravings for a series of decorative
cabinet safe designs, 1858; a religious icon
engraved and dated 5 September 1859; and several
cuts dated 1862-62, notably illustrations to Wood's
Natural History,1863.

BARTON, John
Provincial wood engraver, who worked at Ann Street,
Birmingham (Pigot,1842).

BASTIN, J. (John) fl.1840s
Prominent London wood engraver. One of his
earliest works and his most successful was the
numerous engravings after Jacque and Fussel
engraved with G.Nicholls (q.v.) to L.Sterne's
A Sentimental Journey through France and Italy,
1840. This was followed by ten engravings after John
Tenniel's (q.v.) drawings to S.C.Hall's Book of British
Ballads,1842. McLean claims his engraved designs
after William Harvey (q.v.) to J.G.Lockhart's
Ancient Spanish Ballads,1841-42, contributed to
making the book the most lavish gift book yet to
appear in England. Bastin also engraved nautical
vignettes after J.W.McLea drawings to Charles
Gray's Lays and Lyrics,1842; and contributed
engravings to Charles Knight's publications, for
instance, the 'Land We Live In' series. The Bodleian

Library has his cuts to Charles Knight's Merry
Wives of Windsor in the 'Cabinet Shakespeare' series,
1843. He also engraved after Tenniel's drawings a
second time, for the illustrated German tale,
Undine,1845. Nagler explained that John Bastin was
a young artist of the 'engraved wood cut school'
whose work 'leistet aber vorzügliches in seinem
fache'. The British Museum owns his engravings
after J.Absolon, G.F.Sargent, F.Taylor,
J.Tenniel, J.Thorne and E.M.Ward. He signed
his engravings: 'J.BASTIN', 'JB' (superimposed).
[LeBlanc; Bénézit; Hake; Nagler; McLean,
Victorian Book Design,1972]

BATES, Dewey 1851-99
Draughtsman illustrator and painter, who was born
in Philadelphia in 1851 but had settled in England by
1880. There, he worked for galleries such as the
Royal Academy, the Royal Institute of Painters in
Watercolours and the Royal Society of British
Artists. He also contributed drawings to the English
Illustrated Magazine,1884-87, including those after
his own article, 'About Market Gardens', wood
engraved by W.Quick and O.Lacour (qq.v.); and those
to 'Walks in the Wheatfields' by Richard Jeffries
were engraved by R.Paterson, H.F.Davey and
O.Lacour (qq.v.). Bates died in Rye, Sussex in 1899.
[Houfe; Clement; TB; Bénézit]

BATTEN, John Dixon 1860-1932
Designer of wood cuts, painter and illustrator. He
was born in Plymouth on 8 October 1860, studied at
the Slade under Légros and exhibited pictures at
the Royal Academy, the New Gallery and the Grosvenor
Gallery. An influential figure, Batten's primary
skill was in book illustrations in a style derived
from German wood cuts and the Arts and Crafts
figures like William Morris and his followers who
adopted mythological themes and Celtic, Norse
and Indian legends. These were drawn in pen and
ink in a style reminiscent of the Birmingham School
of illustration. As a designer of wood cuts, Batten was
one of the prominent figures of the revival at the end of
the century, who rediscovered the hard-edged line and
flat shapes of Japanese prints. Hind explains that
one of his best was 'Eve and the Serpent',proof
1895, which was published in 1896, and cut by
Frank Morley Fletcher (q.v.) This was 'among the
earliest English prints in the Japanese method'.
[For a list of illustrated work see Houfe; also
Gusman; Hind]

BATTERSHELL, John Robert fl.1862-92
London wood engraver, who worked at 17 Tooks
Court, Chancery Lane, EC (POD,1862). He moved
to 154 Fleet Street, EC (POD,1870-92) which he
shared with fellow engravers A.Bradstock and
D.W.Williamson (qq.v.). He continued to engrave
here and to paint for the London galleries, where he

exhibited his work from 1872-75.
[Bénézit]

BAXTER, George 1804-67
Early wood engraver, prominent colour printer and occasional lithographer. He was born in Lewes, Sussex on 31 July 1804, son of John Baxter, a printer publisher for whom he first worked. He learned wood engraving well enough to help with his father's publications; by 1827 he is listed in Select Sketches in Brighton, published by John Baxter, as 'George Baxter, designer and engraver on wood at 37 High Street, Lewes'. After his marriage that same year, he moved to London, where he studied wood engraving with Samuel Williams (q.v.). His early engravings here were signed 11 Great Distaff Lane, Cheapside, probably the address of a local printer. By 1829 he had not only engraved two blocks for a Charles Knight publication, The Menageries, but had also achieved his earliest colour print from seven printings on wood blocks. He continued to augment his experimentation into colour printing by work as a wood engraver; by 1833, according to C.T.Lewis, Baxter 'had secured for himself the reputation of being one of the foremost of the wood engravers of his time'. His work for the Conchologist's Companion, a guide for shell collectors,1833, which involved much detailed engraving, was that year praised by the Athenaeum as 'a very beautiful specimen of wood engraving'. It is at this time that he appears in the London directories as a wood engraver, working from 29 King Square, Goswell Street (Pigot,1832-36). Among his other commissions were illustration engravings for Mary Russell Mitford's Our Village, 1835, which the authoress praised to her father, 'I never saw engravings on copper (sic) more beautifully finished'. There were also 'some excellent cuts' for Redding on Wines; Ellis's Missionary Annual and other books done about 1833. In 1834 Baxter devised a new method of polychromatic printing from wood blocks and was sufficiently confident to patent it and take it up commercially from new premises at 3 Charterhouse Square in 1835. By 1837 he had produced his famous 'Cabinet of Paintings', and he continued his printing work at the expense of wood engraving until the patent ran out in 1849. Baxter renewed his patent but was challenged by his apprentice George Leighton (q.v.) who claimed that he had only learned colour printing, not wood engraving, as Baxter's apprentice. Most of this colour printing activity which used a metal intaglio plate as printing base, the colours alone from wood blocks, falls outside the scope of this book. But it is important to mention a George Baxter who reappears in the London directory as a wood engraver at 11 Northampton Square (POD,1846), but only in that year. Even more relevant is the fact that Baxter

trained several prominent figures in the wood engraving, draughtsmanship field, notably Harrison Weir (q.v.), who worked at an early stage on wood blocks, Alfred Crewe, Alfred Reynolds, Thomas Dowlen, Thomas Thompson, Charles Gregory and George Cargill Leighton (qq.v.), the last two being the most distinguished of the group. The British Museum owns a series of intricate black-line engravings of printing presses by Baxter. He signed his early wood engravings: 'BAXTER SC' or 'BAXTER SC 29 King Square'. [For a complete biography and account of Baxter see C.T.Courtney Lewis, George Baxter,1908; also A.Ball and M.Martin, The Price Guide to Baxter Prints,1974; see also Volume I]

BAXTER, Robert William fl.1870s
London pupil of the prominent wood engraver William Dickes (q.v.). He began work for Dickes on 20 March 1874 at 109 Farringdon Road, EC, at a time when the firm 'employed a number of hands' (Docker), namely five artists and at least two wood engravers. Baxter excelled in his work and became an expert in chromolithography and the aquatint colour-block processes.
[A.Docker, The Colour Prints of W.Dickes,1924]

BAYES, Alfred Walter 1832-1909
Draughtsman and painter, noted as an informal pupil of the Dalziel Brothers (q.v.) He was born in La Férte-sous-Jouarre in 1832, and worked for most of his life in London. He first drew for various manufacturers' catalogues, then under the tutelage of the Dalziels, for fairy stories and children's books and various 'Sixties School' magazines, such as London Society,1865; Sunday Magazine,1866; Boy's Own Magazine; and Aunt Judy's Magazine. He later gave up such work for painting, and exhibited at the Royal Academy, 1858-1903, the British Institution, 1859-67 and the Royal Institute of Painters in Watercolours, 1890-1902, as well as the Society of British Artists, the New Watercolour Society. He was elected RE and RWS. The Dalziels remembered that the illustrator H.S.Marks first brought Bayes to them and since he had 'shown a wonderful capacity for design', they allowed him to frequent their studios. There, along with G.Kilburne and C.A.Ferrier (qq.v.), Bayes drew on wood for the Dalziels. 'Whatever progress he made in our studio was the result of the practice derived from the subjects given to him, and owing to the advantage of his seeing a great variety of drawings by the leading artists of the time. He was very industrious and rapid' (Dalziels' Record). Among his important works done with them were a large number of drawings for Hans Andersen's Tales, a set of drawings of biblical history and a set for the New Testament published by Routledge and Warne.

Houfe also lists illustrations to Taylor's Original Poems,1868, and Mrs Ewing's Old Fashioned Fairy Tales,c1880. The British Museum owns his designs engraved by the Dalziel Brothers (q.v.) in 1863,1865.
[Houfe; White; Bénézit; TB]

BAYLEY, Thomas Samuel fl.1883-94
London wood engraver, who worked during the lean later years of reproductive wood engraving, from his office at 5 Wine Office Court, EC (POD,1883-86). By 1894 he had in fact left the centre of London for 61 Crofton Road, Camberwell, SE (LSDS,1894). Among his works are engraved illustrations of topographical scenes for the English Illustrated Magazine,1883-86; notably to the series, 'Two Centuries of Bath', 1883 and a third-page illustration, 'The Castle, Heidelberg',1884 after a drawing by E.R.Butler. This was engraved rather poorly, sacrificing clarity for an indistinct atmosphere.

BAYNE, Herbert fl.1890-1900
London wood engraver, who worked with John Carpenter (q.v.) at 57 Bishopsgate Street Within, EC (POD,1890). Then with W.J.Metcalf (q.v.) he engraved at 11 and 12 Bow Lane, EC (POD,1892-1900).

BEAUCE, Jean-Adophe 1818-1875
French draughtsman and military painter. He was born in Paris on 2 August 1818, and went on numerous military expeditions to Algeria, Syria and Mexico. He is listed here for his sketches on wood for the Illustrated London News,1859-60, 1862, which included sketches of Garibaldi. He died in Boulogne on 13 July 1875.

BEAVAN, Henry fl.1860s
London wood engraver, who worked at 3 Falcon Court, Fleet Street, EC (POD,1861).

BECK
(see Inchbold and Beck)

BECKER, F.P. fl.1860s
Engraver of two subjects to Dickens' Christmas Books. Fincham lists him as collaborator on an armorial bookplate for Henry D'Esterre Hemsworth, wood engraved with Edward Churton, 26 Holles Street, London, and dated 1860.

BEDE, Cuthbert (Reverend Edward Bradley) 1827-89
Occasional wood engraver, illustrator and author. He was born in Kidderminster in 1827, educated at University College, Durham, was ordained in 1850 and became Vicar of first Denton, Peterborough, 1859-71, and then of Stretton, Oakham, 1871-73, and finally of Lenton with Harby, 1883-89. He died in Lavington in 1889. Bede learned wood engraving

techniques from George Cruikshank (q.v.) who also trained him in the skills needed to draw on the block. Bede's first drawing appeared in Punch, 1847, where he contributed until 1856. He also drew on wood for the Illustrated London News,1851,1856 (sketches to Mr Verdant Green, originally planned for Punch); the Illustrated London Magazine,1855; and Churchman's Family Magazine,1863. He illustrated his own books, The Adventures of Mr Verdent Green,1853-56, and Little Mr Bouncer, c1877, in what Houfe calls 'a jolly careless style'. The British Museum owns his designs engraved by the Dalziel Brothers (q.v.) in 1855,1858.
[Houfe; Spielmann]

BEDWELL, Frederick LeB. fl.1860s
Amateur draughtsman on wood who contributed sketches of South America to the Illustrated London News,1869. He was the Assistant Pay-Master on H.M.S.Actaeon during the China coast survey 1862, then on H.M.S.Nassau during the admiralty survey of South America.

BEEBY, John fl.1870s
London wood engraver, who worked at 20 East Clayton Street (Kelly's,1876). An advertisement claims that he was also a seal and gem engraver, die sinker, stamp cutter, designer and illuminating artist and stationer.

BEECH, Henry Auguste fl.1860s
London wood engraver, who worked at 227 Pentonville Road, N (POD,1868).

BEECH, J. fl.1850s
Draughtsman on wood, who helped to reproduce the popular paintings of the day for illustrated magazines. Graves lists his drawing on wood of Wilkie's 'Rabbit on the Wall', engraved by the noted wood engraver W.J.Linton (q.v.), which was exhibited at the Royal Academy, 1857.

BEEDHAM, Ralph John 1879-1975
Probably the last professional reproductive wood engraver, according to Garrett. He was born at Whitecross Street, Cripplegate, London in 1879 and apprenticed in 1893, aged thirteen and a half, to the old-established wood engraving firm, Hare and Company, Essex Street, Strand (q.v.). He remained there for six years, during which time wood engraving had been surpassed as a reproductive medium by photographic half-tone blocks etched on copper. He worked as engraving instructor at the LCC School of Photo-engraving and Lithography, taught such major figures as Joan Hassall, instructed Eric Gill in lettering and became his assistant in lettering for the remainder of Gill's life. His later work, on Robert Gibbings' blocks and other projects, during the mid-twentieth

century falls outside the scope of this book.
[Garrett]

BEEFORTH, John Peter fl.1876-89
London draughtsman, who worked at 40 Wellington
Street, Strand, WC (POD,1876-89).

BEESLEY, Arthur fl.1880-1900
Provincial wood engraver, who worked at York
Passage, High Street, Birmingham (Kelly's,1880).
By 1889 he had joined with another engraver,
Middleton, to become Beesley and Middleton, listed
at the same address until 1900.

BEILBY, Ralph 1743-1817
Master and later partner of Thomas Bewick (q.v.).
Coming from a talented family of skilled craftsmen
engravers and enamel painters, Beilby established an
engraving business in Newcastle. He apprenticed
Thomas Bewick at the age of fourteen (1 October
1757), to learn all aspects of metal engraving from
him, since he described himself as an 'Engraver-in-
general'. Later, after Bewick had served his
apprenticeship, he returned to Beilby as partner for
twenty years, 1777-97. More important, it is believed
that Beilby and Bewick were taught wood engraving by
Dr Charles Hutton (q.v.) so that they could engrave
his diagrams for the Treatise on Mensuration
published in parts from 1768, since 'there was not
then in that part (Newcastle) any artist who had ever
seen such engraving executed'. Hutton recalled
(Newcastle Magazine,June 1822) his role as
'instructing those persons [Bewick and Beilby] how to
cut out and square the blocks, and to cut or engrave
on the smooth surface of them the necessary lines
and letters in the diagrams, by which, in frequently
attending them for their instruction, we got the cuts
tolerably well executed'. But Beilby was not as
interested in the technique, as Bewick recalls
(Memoir,p.41): 'While we were going on in this way
we were occasionally applied to by printers, to
execute Wood cuts for them, in this branch my
master was very defective, what he did was wretched
& he did not like it--on which acc^t such jobs were
given to me'. Also Beilby was a difficult man and had
ignored his apprentice's poor health even when a
doctor 'cursed' him for keeping young Bewick
'doubled up at a low bench, which would eventually
destroy him and his passion'. Later Bewick found
him a difficult partner: there was a row over
authorship of the History of British Birds, over
which Beilby eventually gave in and returned to
watch-glass and clock engraving, leaving Bewick
with the business. He died on 4 January 1817, aged
seventy-four. Beilby signed his engravings:
'R.B.' or 'R.Beilby Sculp^t N castle'.
[See James Rush, The Ingenious Beilbys,1973; DNB;
A.Dobson, T.Bewick and His Pupils; also Bewick
bibliography under his entry below]

BELL, George Charles fl.1860s
London wood engraver, who worked at 37 Ludgate
Hill, EC (POD,1863), an office taken over from
T.Williams (q.v.).

BELL, J. fl.1874-94
Draughtsman, who worked as a special artist for
the Illustrated London News reporting events in the
Russo-Turkish War and Constantinople,1874-78,
and Mombassa,1890. He began work for the
Illustrated London News as a post office reporter.
His full and half-page drawings of the Central
Telegraph Establishment, its pneumatic tubes,
instrument gallery, and several views were complex
on the spot records engraved between 28 November
and 19 December 1874. His military reports were
engraved the following year by Henry Sargent
(q.v.) for the Illustrated London News.
[Houfe]

BELLENGER, Albert 1846-?
French wood engraver, born in Pont-Audemer on
18 June 1846. He was the brother and instructor of
the wood engraver Clement-Edouard (q.v.) and
brother of artist Georges Bellenger. He was the
pupil of the noted wood engraver A.F.Pannemaker
(q.v.) in Paris, where he exhibited at the Salon
from 1873, earning a medal in 1884. He engraved
for various French magazines, such as Le Monde
Illustré, L'Art, and L'Illustration; and in England
for the Magazine of Art, after works by Hubert
Herkomer (q.v.) and Alma-Tadema. He was engraver
to the London publisher Cassell, Petter and Galpin
(q.v.) who published some of the most successful
illustrated children's books. He also engraved
Gustave Doré's illustrations (q.v.) to London and
his History of the Crusades. He exhibited work in
England from 1875-81, notably a wood engraved
version of 'The Music Lesson', after the painting
by Frederic Leighton, exhibited at the Royal
Academy, 1881.
[Gusman; Beraldi; Bénézit; Graves]

BELLENGER, Clement-Edouard 1851-?
French wood engraver, brother of the wood engraver
Albert (q.v.), and the artist Georges, whose
drawings he engraved. He was born in Pont-Audemer
in 1851, was a pupil of Albert, and achieved a
reputation for illustrations after drawings by French
artists for French magazines; also for engraved
illustrations to Zola's novels and a Victor Hugo story.
Gusman described him as a very artistic engraver
of the 'new school' during the last quarter of the
nineteenth century, and notes his 135 plates after
Dunki, done as late as 1897. He also engraved a
half-length portrait of the English flower painter,
William Jabez Muckley (1835-1905) for L'Art,1882.
[Gusman; Hake]

BELLEW, Frank Henry Temple 1828-88
Draughtsman of humorous subjects on wood in
an outline style which he adopted for the mid-century
magazines. He was born in Cawnpore in 1828 and
emigrated to America where he contributed
drawings of local life to English Punch, 1857-62,
and also civil war themes to the Illustrated Times,
1861. He died in New York in 1888.
[Houfe; Bénézit; Spielmann]

BEMROSE, W.B. and Sons fl.1849-1900
Provincial wood engraving, lithographic and colour
printing firm. The firm began as letterpress
printers, founded in 1826 by William Bemrose
(1792-1880) at Market Place, Derby. Bemrose
formed a partnership with his two sons: (Sir) Henry
Howe Bemrose (1827-1911) and William Bemrose,
Junior (1831-1908) and listed the firm as W.Bemrose
and Son in 1849 and William Bemrose and Sons in
1854. By 1880 they appear as a wood engraving firm
in Kelly's Stationers' Directory with an office at
Irongate and a works at Midland Place, Derby
(Kelly's, 1880-1900). They were employing sixty-one
printers and about thirty-nine artists including wood
engravers, lithographers and showcard artists by
1880, and eventually branched out into publishing.
They had opened a London office by the mid 1860s:
21 Paternoster Row (POD, 1866-73); 10 Paternoster
Row (POD, 1874-80) and 23 Old Bailey
(POD, 1881-1901).
[For a discussion of colour printing work see
Wakeman and Bridson; British Lithographer, 1891-92,
pp.85-89; British Printer, July/August 1892, pp.5-13;
see also H.H.Bemrose, The House of Bemrose,
Derby, 1926]

BENEWORTH fl.1820-40
English wood engraver, who worked primarily after
French subjects. He engraved after Grandville; for
Le Vieux Vagabond, Les Prédictions de Nostradamus;
signed plates to the work of Molière, 1835-36, and
the History of Gil Blas, 1835; as well as engraved
illustrations to the Magasin Pittoresque. Gusman
claimed that Beneworth was one of the new group of
engravers who worked under the influence of Charles
Thompson (q.v.) from about 1820 onwards.
[Glaser; Gusman]

BENHAM, Jane E. (Mrs Hay) fl.1850-62
Draughtsman, illustrator and painter. She studied
under Kaulbach in Munich then travelled to Italy,
married and lived in Paris. She exhibited at the
Royal Academy, 1848-49, and other exhibitions
1859-62, but is primarily noted for her sympathetic
illustrations to Longfellow. Among these are
Evangeline, 1850, with Birket Foster and John
Gilbert (qq.v.); Longfellow's Golden Legend, 1854;
and Bogue's edition of Poems by Henry Wadsworth
Longfellow, 1854, illustrated with Birket Foster,

John Gilbert and E.Wehnert (qq.v.). White claims
that this was 'the earliest English illustrated
edition of any importance of a volume that has been
frequently illustrated since'. She also illustrated
Beattie and Collins' Poems, 1854.
[Houfe; White]

BENNETT, Charles Henry 1829-67
Draughtsman, illustrator of humorous subjects and
caricaturist, listed by Chatto among the most
significant professional draughtsmen on wood of the
1860s. He was probably self-taught and began
illustration on wood for Diogenes, August 1855, and
the Comic Times, 1855, graduating to work for Henry
Vizetelly (q.v.) on the Illustrated Times, 1856, where
he achieved wide popularity for his Darwinian series,
'Studies in Darwinesque Development' and the more
widely known 'Shadows' series. Vizetelly criticised
his portrait drawing in which he felt he 'usually
failed in his attempts at a characteristic portraiture'.
He drew for Punch, 1865-67, with over 230 drawings
which, despite the short two-year span, earned him
Spielmann's claim as 'one of the brightest and most
talented draughtsmen Punch has ever had'. Much
of Bennett's work was for engraved book illustration,
in collaboration with some of the period's major
engravers. Edmund Evans (q.v.) employed him to
draw for his railway novels series of colour printed
wood engravings. The Dalziels (q.v.) claimed that
they 'knew him well', and were always impressed
with the care Bennett showed in the engraving of his
work: 'A more earnest man concerning his work we
never met...time should never be allowed to enter
into the question; the task should be defined, but
never trammelled by "How long will it take?"'
(Dalziels' Record, p.330). Among his book works
are those which Chatto listed: Poets' Wit and Humour;
Quarles' Emblems, 1860; and Proverbs with Pictures,
1858-59. He also illustrated Aesop's Fables, 1857; his
famous Pilgrim's Progress, 1859, sponsored by
Charles Kingsley; Fairy Tales of Science, 1859;
Nine Lives of a Cat, 1860; Stories Little Breeches
Told, 1862; London People, c1864; Mr Wind and
Madame Rain, c1864; Lemon's Fairy Tales; and The
Sorrowful Ending of Noodledo, 1865. He also
appeared in other magazines apart from those
mentioned above, like the Illustrated London News,
1857, 1866; the Cornhill, 1861, where his series
'The Excursion Train' was inset with the text
rather than issued as separate plates, as was
usually the magazine's policy; The Welcome Guest,
1860; Good Words, 1861; London Society, 1862-65;
Every Boy's Magazine, 1864-65; and Beeton's
Annuals, 1866. The British Museum owns several
proof engravings by the Dalziel Brothers (q.v.).
[Houfe; White; Chatto; Spielmann; Evans,
Reminiscences; Vizetelly, Glances Back]

BENNETT, Henry Watson fl.1889-1901
London wood engraver, who worked at 3 Chandos
Street, Covent Garden, WC (POD,1889) and
10 and 11 Bedford Street, Strand, WC (POD,1890),
then Dacre House, Arundel Street, WC (POD,1892)
which he shared with J.J.Macnamara (q.v.). They
also worked together when the office changed to
5 Arundel Street (POD,1894), then 10 Norfolk Street,
Strand, WC (POD,1895). By 1901 Bennett had
returned to 3 Arundel Street.

BENNETT, W. fl.1855
London wood engraver, who worked at 16 Lavinia
Grove, Caledonian Road (Hodgson's,1855).

BENNITT, Colonel Ward fl.1870s
Amateur draughtsman on wood, who contributed
several initials and social cartoons to Punch,1875.
His post as lieutenant in the 6th Inniskilling
Dragoons forced him to draw only at night, but the
night work affected his eyesight and he gave it up.
[Houfe; Spielmann]

BENSON fl.1840s
Houfe lists this illustrator, who contributed a
drawing wood engraved in the Illustrated London
News,1844. He worked in Plymouth.

BENWELL, Joseph Austin fl.1860s
Draughtsman, illustrator and painter, who worked
in Kensington. He was noted for Eastern subjects
and travelled to India and China prior to 1856 and to
Egypt and Palestine, 1865-66. He contributed
drawings to the Cornhill,1860; the Illustrated London
News,1863-64; Welcome Guest,1860; and illustrated
Capper's Our Indian Army. He was also a
watercolourist and exhibited at the New Watercolour
Society from 1865, also at the Royal Academy and
the Royal Society of British Artists.
[Houfe]

BERARD, Evremond de fl.1852-63
French draughtsman and landscape painter, who
contributed drawings of Madagascar wood engraved
for the Illustrated London News,1863.

BERNSTROM, Viem Victor 1845-1907
Swedish wood engraver, who worked in London from
1860. He was born in Stockholm in 1845, attended
the Stockholm Academy, went to London and then
moved to New York in 1871, where he worked for
ten years for Harper and Company, publishers of
many of his illustrated works. He was awarded a
medal at Chicago, 1893, and at Buffalo, 1901. His
most impressive engraved work was 'The Mystery
of Life', after Carl Marr.
[TB; Gusman; Bénézit]

BERRY, Alfred fl.1870-1910
London wood engraver, who worked at
17 Devonshire Square, E (POD,1870-72). He
disappears from the directories until 1879, when
he was working from 53 Paternoster Row, EC
(POD,1879-1910), sharing the address from
1894-98 with C.A.Ferrier (q.v.), himself a
prolific wood engraver.

BERRY, R. fl.1822-24
London wood engraver, who worked at 6 St Dunstan's
Court, Fleet Street, EC (Pigot,1822-24).

BERRYMAN, J. (John) fl.1815-40
London engraver on wood and brass, who worked at
6 St Dunstan's Court, Fleet Street in 1815. There he
produced a large print of a fish, various
certificates, advertisements, an announcement for a
Society of Shipwrecked Mariners in Norfolk,
diagrams and initial letters of intricate design which
he engraved in a fine black-line style. This he
successfully adopted in a series of engraved
reproductions of classical statuary at Holkam Hall,
Norfolk. A group of the proofs for these are in the
British Museum. The London directories list a
John Berryman, wood engraver, at 11 Gough Square,
Fleet Street, EC (Johnstone,1817, Pigot,1822-39,
POD,1840). He may be related to the landscape
painter of that name who exhibited at the Royal
Academy, 1802-09. J.Berryman signed his early
engravings: 'J.B. sc' or 'Berryman'.

BERT, Hal fl.1880s
Provincial wood engraver, who worked at Octagon,
Plymouth (Kelly's,1889).

BERTRAM, John A. fl.1880s
Scottish wood engraver, who worked at 23 Jamaica
Street, Glasgow (POD,1880).

BERTRAND, Antoine (Alphonse) 1823-?
French wood engraver, whose work appeared in
English magazines. He was born in Paris in 1823
and was the pupil of Henry Brown (q.v.) at the
Royal School of Engraving, and of Henry Harrison
(q.v.), who taught him wood engraving. He worked
in Paris, exhibited at the Salon, 1864-79, and engraved
for French magazines such as Magasin Pittoresque,
after Gustave Doré and Tony Johannot (qq.v.). He
also engraved plates for l'Histoire de l'Empereur
Napoléon. Bénézit lists his 'Portrait of Princess
Clementine of Metternich', after Lawrence, and
remarked that Bertrand was 'perhaps known as
Alphonse'. Under that name appeared a signed wood
engraving of porcelain and bronze objects, engraved
in an ornate outline style after designs by La Hoche,
in the Illustrated London News,9 August 1851.
[Gusman; Bénézit; LeBlanc]

BEST, Adolphe 1808-60
French wood engraver, who encouraged a large
number of young engravers and worked for numerous
French and occasionally for English magazines. He
was born in Toul in 1808 and by 1833 had joined forces
with Hotelin, Leloir and Regnier (qq.v.). They
engraved for the early numbers of Magasin
Pittoresque, mostly after English subjects taken
from English magazines. He also engraved after
Adolph Menzel's drawings to his History of
Frederick the Great. He rarely worked alone,
but usually in collaboration as Best and Cie; Best
and Leloir; Best, Hotelin and Cie; or Best, Leloir,
Hotelin, Regnier. Yet his influence appeared in
their many collaborations: a history of the Old and
New Testaments, books on garden plants, the fine
arts, as well as in work for various English art
magazines. There are engravings signed Best,
Leloir, Hotelin, Regnier in the Illustrated London
News, notably a three-quarter page engraving,
'The French Chamber of Peers', after Eduard
Renard and K.Girardet, 1 February 1845, engraved
in a clear, very even black-line style. Gusman
explains how Best joined forces with the influential
J.Andrew about 1834, and together as Best and
Andrew they engraved for Roujoux's History of
England. They also included Leloir in work for the
Illustrated London News, most notably in the
engraved title which the magazine used from 1843
(originally engraved by S.Sly (q.v.) in 1842). This
was signed 'Andrew, Best et Leloir sc'. They also
engraved together on Magasin Pittoresque,1834-36;
L'Illustration; Musée des Familles; and after Tony
Johannot's (q.v.) drawings to Don Quixote,1836. They
established considerable reputations for reviving the
French interest in wood engraved illustration, which
borrowed from the recent revival in England.
Signatures on Best's work and collaborations varied:
'B H et ^{C}' (Best and Hotelin) or 'BHLR' (Best, Leloir,
Hotelin, Regnier) or 'ABL' (Andrew, Best and Leloir).
[For further discussions of their French engraving
see Gusman (1929,p.148); LeBlanc; Nagler;
Bénézit; and Glaser; see also Best, Regnier and
Company entry below]

BEST, Regnier and Company
Part-English wood engraving firm, comprised of
Adolphe Best (q.v.) and his partners Regnier and
later Hotelin and Leloir (qq.v.). They worked in
Paris and employed the Dresden born wood engraver
William Barnard (q.v.). They engraved drawings
for Curmer's edition of Paul et Virginie,1839 and
for Doré's edition of Balzac's Les Contes Drôlatiques,
1855, published in England in 1860. They engraved
for many other famous French illustrated books of
the romantic period.
[Muir, Victorian Illustrated Books,1971,p.215]

BEWICK, John 1760-95
Wood engraver and draughtsman, younger brother
of Thomas Bewick (q.v.). He is listed here for his
influence on his brother. He was born at
Cherryburn House, Eltringham, Northumberland in
March 1760 and apprenticed to his brother from
1777-82. Thomas Bewick recalled that when John
joined him, 'I was extremely happy--we lodged
together, he arose early in the Morning, lighted
our fire--...as well as any servant Girl could have
done' (Bewick's Memoir). His work with Thomas
possibly included illustrations to Gay's Fables,1779
(although Bewick fails to mention his brother's
apprentice work). After five years John Bewick was
given his freedom and left for London. He
established an office at Clerkenwell Green on
15 October 1787 and worked for most of his life in
the capital. His brother recalled that, 'He was as
industrious in London as he had been with us & had
plenty of work to do--he was almost entirely
employed by the Publishers & Booksellers in London,
in designing and cutting an endless variety of blocks
for them & as he was extremely quick at his work he
did it slightly & at a very low rate for them--'.
During his period in London John wrote many valuable
letters to his brother in which he discussed the
London printing and publishing trades, drew
animals from London Zoo for Thomas, criticised
his recent work, and expressed frequent concern at
his brother's reluctance to come south and promote
the sales of his books. He also purchased supplies
of boxwood for blockmaking and sent it back to
Newcastle for Thomas. (For selections from these
letters see I.Bain, The Watercolours of Thomas
Bewick,1981,Vol.I). John's first London work was
largely poorly paid blocks for children's books,
published by Newbury and Dr Trusler; he also
worked for the publisher William Bulmer. His work
included Children's Miscellany, Honours of the
Table, or Rules for Behaviour during Meals,
History of a School-Boy and New Robinson Crusoe,
dated 1788, with signed cuts. But it was in work of
the 1790s, especially for Poems by Goldsmith and
Parnell,1795, for which he watercoloured vignettes
(now in the British Museum), that John showed the
high degree of finish and control that matches his
brother's skill. The Bewick scholar Austin Dobson
concluded: 'Much of his work bears evident signs of
haste, as well as of an invention which was far in
advance of his powers of execution. He had
evidently a keen eye for character, and considerable
skill in catching strongly marked expression' (DNB).
Iain Bain concluded of John Bewick the engraver:
'His nature was more light-hearted than his
brother's and he had a good eye for the fashions
of the time. His work and his letters display much
of his gaiety of spirit. The manner of his engraving
particularly in the foliage of trees and the marking
of rocks displays a horizontal bias' (Thomas

Bewick, Record,1979,p.95). John Bewick contracted tuberculosis in 1793 and was forced to support himself by teaching drawing to boys at the Hornsey Academy, under Nathaniel Norton. He returned to Cherryburn, Ovingham in the summer of 1795 and died there on 5 December 1795, aged thirty-five. His last works were for William Bulwer: six drawings on wood for Le Grand's Fabliaux,1796, later engraved by Thomas; also drawings to Somerville's The Chase,1796, which Thomas finished and engraved after his brother's death. [For a list of John Bewick's work see J.G.Bell, Catalogue of Works...by Thomas and John Bewick, 1851; A.Dobson, Thomas Bewick and his Pupils, 1884; also Chatto and Jackson and DNB. A selection of his drawings is in the British Museum; some reproductions appear in I.Bain, Watercolours of Thomas Bewick,1981,Vol.I; D.Esselmont, John Bewick,1980; also I.Bain's Thomas Bewick, Record,1979; Thomas Bewick's bibliography below]

BEWICK, Robert Elliot 1788-1849
Wood engraver and draughtsman, especially of architectural and perspective subjects, the only son of Thomas Bewick (q.v.). He was born in Newcastle on 26 April 1788, and was the last apprentice of note in his father's workshop, serving a term from 26 May 1804 - 26 May 1811. He was made a partner on 1 January 1812, and was responsible for running the business during his father's illness. He supervised the normal jobbing work of copper etchings for bill heads and bookplates, he helped with his father's Aesop's Fables,1818 and drew and watercoloured at least seventy-six fish for the uncompleted History of British Fishes (see I.Bain, Watercolours of Thomas Bewick,1981). At least 150 of his drawings are in the British Museum. Robert Bewick was a skilful draughtsman who made up for his lack of originality with an impressive sense of accuracy. 'My Son is busy in drawing such fishes as we can meet with--& I am very happy to find he finishes them with inimitable accuracy--so it appears to me-- I also trust he is going to be a keen naturalist', Bewick wrote to Dovaston, 3 June 1824 (G.Williams, Bewick to Dovaston,1968,p.33). Unfortunately his father's domineering nature and his own indifferent health throughout his life prevented him from achieving a reputation of his own. He was especially interested in perspective and architectural drawing which he drew with etching needle fineness. He was only competent as a wood engraver, but as an etcher and engraver on copper he proved an impressive artist who 'deserves attention' (Bain). His father's influence over him continued to 1825, when Bewick secured new commissions for his son to engrave; but he was reconciled that Robert's reputation would never equal his own. And yet Bewick wrote in the prospectus to British Fishes, 'the exertions of my son, from the accuracy and beauty of his drawings

cannot be surpassed'. He clearly hoped Robert would come round and continue in his own wood engraver footsteps, as he concluded in his Memoir: 'I may be allowed to name my own Son & partner, whose time has been taken up with attending to all the branches of our business & who I trust will not let Wood Engraving go down, & tho' he has not shewn any partiality towards it--yet the talent is there, if he will & I hope call it forth...' (Bewick's Memoir,p.200). Robert probably suffered from either consumption or asthma, and died unmarried in Newcastle on 27 July 1849. His work is in the British Museum and Newcastle's Northumbrian Natural History Society. He signed his engravings: 'R.E.Bewick'.
[For a discussion of works see I.Bain, Watercolours of Thomas Bewick,Vol.I,pp.84-85; also I.Bain,Thomas Bewick, Record,1979; DNB; Bewick, Memoir; Linton, Masters of Wood Engraving]

BEWICK, Thomas 1753-1828
Wood engraver, draughtsman and watercolourist, said to be the father of the English wood engraving revival. He was the brother of John Bewick and father of Robert Elliot Bewick (qq.v.). He was born at Cherryburn House, Eltringham, Northumberland on 10 or 12 August 1753, the eldest son of a farmer, John Bewick (1715-85), and educated at Mickley, then at Ovingham Parsonage School under Reverend Christopher Gregson. While there he spent his spare moments drawing in chalk and studying the woodcut inn signs and crude prints of the locality which he drew with pen and ink and blackberry juice; he later used brush and colours on the hunting scenes and natural history subjects which he sold to his 'rustic neighbours'. He became in their eyes 'an eminent painter', and the walls of their houses were ornamented with an abundance of my rude productions, at a very cheap rate'; his work he recalled was 'in their opinion, as well as my own, faithfully delineated' (Memoir,pp.7-8). It was this taste for drawing that determined his training as a metal engraver, and he was apprenticed to the Newcastle engraver Ralph Beilby (q.v.) from 1 October 1767 - 1 October 1774. Bewick recalled how Beilby 'began with me upon a system of riged [sic] discipline, from which he never varied nor relaxed'. He was never taught how to draw, only to copy from such books as Copeland's New Book of Ornaments,1746. He was taught to prepare for the commercial work of the metal engraver, where all jobs 'coarse or fine' for letter heads, stationery, banknotes and labels, were gratefully accepted. He recalled the office 'filled with the coarsest kind of steel stamps--pipe Mould--Bottle moulds--Brass Clock faces--Door plates--Coffin plates-- Bookbinders Letters & stamps--Steel, Silver & gold Seals--Mourning Rings--Arms crests &

cyphers on silver & every kind of job, from the Silver Smiths--writing engraving of Bills, bank notes, Bills of parcels, shop bills & cards...'. Here Bewick worked 'till my hands became as hard & enlarged as those of a blacksmith'. Beilby did not like engraving on wood, nor was he good at it. When Dr Charles Hutton (q.v.) proposed publication of his Treatise on Mensuration,1768, which required fine linear charts, young Bewick was given the task of engraving these on wood, under Hutton's instructions. This was followed by further wood engraving commissions until Bewick had produced 151 wood blocks in just four years (to 1771). Bewick especially liked the job of drawing on the wood. Most of his wood engraved work during his apprenticeship was for children's books, chiefly for Thomas Saint, a Newcastle printer publisher. (For a discussion of these see DNB). Beilby sent impressions of some of these, notably those to a book of fables, to the Society for the Encouragement of Arts and Bewick received a premium of 7 guineas for them on 4 January 1776. His apprenticeship ended in October 1774. He remained at home in Cherryburn for two years, and walked to Scotland where he made numerous sketches, then he spent nine months in London from 1 October 1776, working primarily for Isaac Taylor, who provided 'plenty of work'. This was also the year Thomas Saint published his engravings in Select Fables,1776. He disliked London intensely and returned to Newcastle on 22 June 1777, joining in partnership with his old master Beilby from 1777-97. They took on Bewick's brother John Bewick (q.v.) as an apprentice engraver at this time, and Bewick continued his spare-time wood engraving. He engraved Fables of the Late Mr Gay, and Tommy Trip's History of Beasts and Birds, both 1779, for Thomas Saint, the latter 'supposed to have been a first draft of the more famous "Quadrupeds" and "Birds"' (DNB). In 1872 he released his brother from his five year apprenticeship and John eventually moved to London, where he provided a valuable link between the printing and publishing world there and his brother's publications. He proved a major influence: he drew for Thomas's various animal projects, criticised his publications, ordered boxwood blocks and tried in vain to lure Thomas back to London. Bewick's wood engravings were still done 'after hours', his bread-and-butter work remaining the metal engravings for which Beilby trained him. He began cutting blocks for his first major book A General History of Quadrupeds in 1785; it was published in 1790, with text by Beilby, and reached eight editions by 1824. He engraved the famous Chillingham Bull in 1789, which was declared 'Bewick's best and most ambitious work' to date (DNB). Other work of the period included copper engraved illustrations to Consett's A Tour through Sweden Swedish-Lapland, Finland and Denmark,1789. But the row that erupted with Beilby over the 'Quadrupeds'

publication resulted in Bewick contemplating dissolving his partnership in 1790, although it was to be seven years before the two actually went their separate ways. During five of those seven years, 1790-97, Bewick worked with John on illustrations for William Bulwer. They produced Poems of Goldsmith and Parnell,1795, and were at work on Somerville's The Chase and Le Grand's Fabliaux when John died, in December 1795. Thomas completed his brother's drawings and engraved them for eventual publication in 1796. The following year Bewick produced the first volume of his 'high water mark' as an artist engraver, the History of British Birds, Land Birds,1797. It marked the end of his partnership with Beilby, who continued as a watch-glass and clock engraver, while Bewick was forced to struggle for a living by metal engraving captions, bank notes and labels, which left little spare time for wood engraving. In fact it was not until 1804 that he produced his second volume of British Birds, Water Birds. By then he had taken on as apprentice his son Robert Elliot Bewick (q.v.) who having been made partner on 1 January 1812, remained with his father to run the business until his death. It was also in 1812 that Bewick began work on drawings for his Aesop's Fables, for which project he also employed his apprentices William Harvey and William Temple (qq.v.). Nevertheless Bewick remembered the strain of the work: 'The execution of the fine work of the Cuts, during the day light, was very trying to the Eyes, & the compiling or writing the Book by candle light in my Evenings at home, together injured the Optic nerve & that put the rest of the nerves out of tune...' (Memoir,p.132). In 1822 Bewick began writing his autobiography and continued to direct his son Robert's efforts to become a wood engraver equal to his own standard. They planned a History of British Fishes, on which Robert worked diligently, and for which he was praised by his father for his accurate drawings. But this was left uncompleted. The Quadrupeds, British Birds and Fables went through numerous editions which had to be supervised (see S.Roscoe, Thomas Bewick, a Bibliography Raisonné,1953, for a list). In 1827 he was visited by the American naturalist artist James Audubon, and completed 221 pages of his autobiography. The following year he returned briefly for a second visit to London. He died at 19 West Street, Gateshead on 8 November 1828, and was buried in Ovingham. The last work he engraved, done that year, was a large (14" x 17") print of a dying horse, 'Waiting for Death', issued posthumously by Robert in 1832. Thomas Bewick was not the inventor of a new method of engraving on wood. Rather, he perfected the use of the metal engraver's tools, and something of his own methods, on the boxwood block. This involved using the graver to cut across the grain of the wood block, in contrast to the then more commonly practised method of cutting with a knife or chisel along the grain of the wood to produce the crude black outlines of woodcut illustrations popular during the late eighteenth century. It is believed that he was introduced to this method, which had already been in use for some ten years in the south, by Dr Charles Hutton for his Treatise on Mensuration. Hutton, who apparently knew the techniques, had 'procured the necessary blocks of boxwood from London with the tools proper for cutting or carving on them, instructing those persons [Beilby and Bewick] how to cut out and square the blocks, and to cut or engrave on the smooth surface of them the necessary lines and letters in the diagrams, by which, in frequently attending them for their instruction, we got the cuts tolerably well executed...' (Hutton in The Newcastle Magazine, June 1822,pp.321-22). From this early technical training Bewick emerged the master of the medium. It was said that he was 'an artist of genius whose hand, eventually vastly skilled and trained in fine work on metal, was by this happy chance brought to a sympathetic medium, and that he later developed to full perfection a creative manner of engraving that could never be satisfactorily employed by a craftsman trained only in reproductive skills' (Bain in Bewick's Memoir,p.259). Bewick's artistic skill lay in his belief in the 'white-line' style of wood engraving. Rather than viewing the design on the block as a raised outline, which was inked and printed to imitate the original drawing, he saw the block on which the design was transferred as a solid black surface, from which the drawing emerged in white lines, every stroke of the graver a white modulation of form and dark colour. He rarely, if ever, used cross-hatching to shade, and the isolated black lines in some white areas were achieved with broad, freehand white-line cutting, rather than the meticulous cutting away from around the drawn lines done by the 'facsimile' engraver. To succeed with such a delicate approach to his work, Bewick supervised the printing of his engravings and devised various innovations on the presses. (For a discussion see Bain in Bewick's Memoir,pp.260-62.) He is said to have invented a two-line engraving tool to cut an even, single black line for diagrams and figure outlines, the tool cutting two white lines with a black line between them. This is still admired by present generations of engravers. In fact, so skilful were his efforts, that one of Bewick's wood blocks, engraved for a Newcastle paper, gave 900,000 prints without serious wear to the block surface. Bewick left a large number of pencil drawings and watercolours to help in the study of his working methods. Most of these are in the British Museum and Natural History Society of Northumbria. He does not mention how he prepared his blocks for engraving, but we know it was generally his custom first to prepare a minute

accurate pen and pencil drawing, sometimes in delicate watercolour finish (as seen in I.Bain's The Watercolours of Thomas Bewick,1981). These were heavily leaded on the back with a soft pencil, then placed over the block, folding the edges over the edge to steady the position. A fine hard point traced the outline of the drawing and the pressure transferred the line onto the surface of the block, itself covered in brick dust to pick up the pencil carbon more readily. The most impressive fact, however, is that Bewick did not draw in the details to a great extent but rather filled in the foregrounds, landscapes and foliage of trees with his graver directly on the block. Here is where his assurance and artistic abilities were brought into play. Bewick was an accomplished draughtsman and watercolourist, a dedicated perfectionist who drew exactly what he saw in nature. When asked to alter and beautify his drawings of local cattle for their admiring owners he refused: 'I would not put lumps of fat here & there to please them where I could not see it'. He believed that if he had become a painter he would not have copied Old Masters: 'I would have gone to nature for all my patterns, for she exhibits an endless variety--not possible to be surpassed & scarcely ever to be equalled' (Memoir,p.203). He drew his birds from museum specimens but much preferred the more naturalistic carcasses freshly killed and sent to him for immediate drawing. This led to his honest confession of why he enjoyed wood engraving: 'the sole stimulant with me was the pleasure I derived from imitating natural objects (& I had no other patterns to go by) & the opportunity it afforded me of making & drawing my designs on the Wood...' (Memoir,p.187). Once he concluded the ideal life for a wood engraver was to live in the country, 'surrounded by pleasing rural scenery & fresh air', and never to sit too long over a block, but vary the work load, with occasional visits to the city for discussions with fellow workers. Bewick grudgingly accepted the need for pupils, and despite the fact that he wondered if he could have done without them, he managed and trained a large number of influential engravers and draughtsmen. The awards and successes which many of them achieved gave him much pride, while others brought constant worry by their delinquent behaviour. The total number of Bewick apprentices was about eighteen, spread throughout his engraving career. They normally served a seven year term and were usually paid for their work during the final three years; but conditions differed depending upon the premium paid at the time of their being indentured. Several worked for a period before signing on, either on trial or because they had not reached the age of fourteen. Unfortunately Bewick rarely attributes an apprentice's work, which means the controversy over attributions continues today (see Chatto and Jackson, A Treatise on Wood Engraving,1839, of which the original MS is in the London Library; also I.Bain, Memoir,1975; Thomas Bewick, Vignettes,1978; Thomas Bewick, Record,1979; Watercolours of Thomas Bewick, 1981, with a chart of apprentices). Bewick listed sixteen apprentices of note in his Memoir: John Bewick, John Laws (silver engraver), John Johnson, Robert Johnson, Charlton Nesbit (noted for his first success in London), Henry Hole (a troubled reprobate), John Anderson, Edward Willis (his chief wood engraver who later helped compile the Bewick section of Chatto and Jackson), John Harrison (Bewick's nephew, noted for script engraving on metal), Henry White, Luke Clennell, Isaac Nicholson, William Harvey, William Temple, John Armstrong and Robert Bewick (qq.v.). He fails to mention John Jackson (q.v.). W.J.Linton in Masters of Wood Engraving,1889, lists these sixteen and notes that 'these are not all'. Bewick's reputation was fiercely guarded by his eldest daughter Jane Bewick (1787-1881). When her father was alive she censored his work, especially the 'offensive vignettes', about which Bewick considered that 'these notions of the ladies border upon the fastidious'. She refused later to be dragged into the controversy over Bewick's pupil Robert Johnson when Chatto prepared his Treatise. In 1862 she edited and published her father's A Memoir of Bewick, written by Himself, much of which Bewick had addressed to her. She declared with self-satisfaction that it made her 'now feel--my Father's fame unassailable' (see Jane Bewick entry in DNB). To add to his fame, a collection of Bewick's work appeared at the Fine Art Society, 1880, and Bewick's reputation among his colleagues and later Victorian disciples remained strong. W.J.Linton (q.v.) was perhaps his greatest disciple; his Practical Hints on Wood Engraving,1889, clearly sets out Bewick's white-line methods. Bewick's works were re-issued in numerous editions by the Victorians, who found his rural idylls in miniature an appealing escapist pastime. 'Bewick was truly a countryman... for though no person was capable of closer application to his art within doors, he loved to spend his hours of relaxation in the open air, studying the character of beasts and birds in their natural state; and diligently noting those little incidents and traits of country life which give so great an interest to many of his tailpieces', remarked Chatto and Jackson in 1839. Wordsworth wrote a ballad with the line, 'Oh that the genius of Bewick were mine'. Charlotte Brontë wrote a poem about Bewick and made Jane Eyre excited over Bewick's History of British Birds. John Ruskin and Carlyle took his work seriously, although Ruskin regretted his inability to record 'higher' elements in art, in favour of the lower classes and rustics. By the 1920s, Bewick's work had reached the collectors, and Slater, in Engravers

and Their Works,1928, pointed out: 'Collectors of single cuts by Thomas Bewick should look out for impressions having the representation of a thumb-mark, sometimes found in the upper margin. The presence of this mark shows that Bewick issued the print himself, his object being to put a stop to speculation on the part of his workmen, who were suspected of taking impressions out of the office and selling them'. For collections of Bewick's work see the British Museum, the Victoria and Albert Museum, and the Newcastle Museum, Natural History Society of Northumbria. Bewick signed his engravings: 'TB', 'TB sculpt', 'Bewick Sculpt' or later 'T.Bewick & Son Sculpt'.
[For a full bibliography see Iain Bain, Bewick Memoir,1975, which annotates the various publications available during and after Bewick's life; the same author's catalogue, Thomas Bewick, Record,1979; Thomas Bewick Vignettes,1978; and Watercolours of Thomas Bewick,1981 are the most helpful for layman and scholar]

BIDGOOD, William fl.1880s
Wood engraver of archaeological and topographical subjects. The British Museum owns a collection of delicate outline engravings of various artefacts and archaeological objects, engraved in a fine black-line style; a series of illuminated letters with insert engravings of various country houses; and a series of large engravings of churches, engraved in a dense tonal manner. Bidgood was truly a diverse and talented facsimile engraver. He signed his engravings: 'W BIDGOOD', 'WB sc'.

BIGG, Alfred L. fl.1860-63
London wood engraver, who worked at 11 (33) Little Russell Street, Covent Garden, WC (POD,1860-63).

BILLING, Edward fl.1826-38
London wood engraver, who worked at 187 Bermondsey Street (Pigot,1826-38).

BILLING, Martin, Son and Company fl.1889-1900
Provincial wood engraving firm, with an office at Livery Street, Birmingham (Kelly's,1889-1900).

BILLINGS, John fl.1880s
London wood engraver, who worked at Hare Place, 47 Fleet Street, EC (POD,1882).

BIRBECK, Robert fl.1880s
Provincial wood engraver, who worked at 313A Broad Street, Birmingham (Kelly's,1889).

BIRD, John Alexander H. 1846-?
Draughtsman illustrator, painter of animal subjects. He was born in Harington on 23 May 1846 and exhibited paintings, especially of horses, at the

Royal Academy, the Royal Institute of Painters in Watercolours, and the Canadian Academy. His illustrations to the magazine Dark Blue,1871-72, were dismissed by White as 'commonplace designs' when wood engraved by C.M.Jenkin (q.v.). [Bénézit; Houfe; White]

BISHOP, David fl.1886-87
London wood engraver, who worked at 10 Red Lion Court, Fleet Street, EC (POD,1886-87), a favourite district for wood engravers of the period.

BISSAGER, Frederick fl.1858-59
London wood engraver, who worked at 150 Paradise Row, Islington, N (POD,1858-59).

BLACKBURN, Mrs J. (née Wedderburn) 1823-1909
Draughtsman illustrator of birds, much influenced by the wood engravings of Thomas Bewick. She visited London from her Scottish home in 1840, and was told by Landseer that he could teach her nothing about drawing. She exhibited at the Royal Academy, 1863-75, and married a Glasgow University mathematics professor but continued to draw and paint until the 1890s. She died in Edinburgh in 1909. Her drawings appeared in Good Words,1861, as full-page wood engravings on tinted paper. Her series Scenes from Animal Life,1858, and Birds drawn from Nature,1862, were praised by the Bookseller: her 'delineations of animals are equal to Landseer'. She also illustrated The Instructive Picture Book, 1859, and W.J.M.Rankins' Songs and Fables,1874. The British Museum owns her designs engraved by the Dalziel Brothers (q.v.), 1855-63. [Houfe; White; Bénézit]

BLACKMAN, Richard fl.1886-1901
London wood engraver and draughtsman, who worked first at 5 Ludgate Circus Buildings, EC (POD,1886), then moved to 29 Ludgate Hill, EC (POD,1887-1901), sharing the office in 1888 with the noted wood engraver E.Whymper (q.v.).

BLACKSTAFFE and Pritchard fl.1876-89
Wood engraving firm, with offices at 106 Newhall Street, Birmingham (Kelly's,1876), 11 Dale End, Birmingham (Kelly's,1880), and 13 Carr's Lane, High Street, Birmingham (Kelly's,1889).

BLAIKLEY, Alexander 1816-1903
Draughtsman and portrait painter. He was born in Glasgow in 1816 and exhibited at the British Institution, the Royal Academy and the Royal Society of British Artists, 1842-67. He contributed a drawing which was wood engraved for the Illustrated London News,1856.

BLAKE, William 1757-1827
Occasional wood engraver, best known for metal engravings and paintings. He is included here for what one writer calls his 'triumphantly passionate, but virtually unknown wood engravings' (Smith, W.J.Linton,p.3). He was born in London at Golden Square on 28 November 1757, the son of a hosier, and was a pupil, aged ten, at William Pars' Drawing School, then apprenticed to the engraver James Basire. He began engraving drawings of London churches which prepared him for admission to the Royal Academy School as an engraving student in 1779, exhibiting there from 1780. From then onwards he worked as a commercial engraver in line, mostly on metal, for trade publications and after other artists' designs in such publications as The Wit's Magazine,1784, Harrison's Novelists Magazine, Wollstonecraft's Works,1791, and works by William Hayley, 1800-09. His visionary books, from Songs of Innocence,1789, to the incomplete illustrations to The Book of Job, 1825, were done throughout this period. As a wood engraver, Blake was a contemporary of Bewick, although he gained much from his own early metal engraving experiences and did not attempt wood engraving until about 1820. His relief printing from etched copper plates, and engraving on zinc and pewter in the 'wood cut manner' (of white line on a black background) influenced those wood engravings he did. And yet, unlike Bewick, he brought his own inventive directness and sense of rough, spontaneous freedom to the medium. In fact his cuts to Thornton's The Pastorals of Virgil,1821, were thought too crude by the publisher, who tried to get a so-called 'trade' wood engraver to re-cut them. But Blake's friends persuaded him to leave the blocks intact and insert a statement in the book explaining that the engraver was in fact an artist of 'some repute'. All these blocks were small, about 1.5" x 3", and mostly done in a white-line technique in groups of four on one block (two proofs of the completed seventeen blocks still exist). Oddly, W.J.Linton (q.v.), in Masters of Wood Engraving, disregards these engravings, although they were much admired by the Victorians. Linton later re-engraved them on metal for Gilchrist's Life of Blake, on the advice of Rossetti. Also seventeen designs were published in America in 1899, with Selwyn Image (q.v.) decorations. Blake also wood engraved for Phillips' Pastorals,1820-21. Both works achieved what Hind claimed was Blake's unsurmountable position in the history of wood engraving: he remains 'by far the greatest genius' and much of his wood engraving 'is so isolated and unique it falls into no survey of the general development of the art'. Technically, Blake had much in common with Bewick, for both used mostly a white line on a black background. Both also maintained the small scale of all their blocks, often using figures in

landscape settings, and both were technical innovators whose works influenced future generations, although Blake's influence took longer to develop and was less widespread. On the other hand, Blake's wood engravings are less carefully rendered, they lack the delicate greys and crisp cutting of Bewick, and altogether give a more suffused, mysterious effect, often with the background left in its original black and with only the fine incised line for tonal effects.
[For a discussion of Blake's wood engravings, see Chamberlain; also for Blake's book illustrations see Sir Geoffrey Keymes, A Bibliography of William Blake, 1921 and his subsequent studies; also DNB; Houfe; Slater; Hind]

BLANCHARD, Ph. fl.1853-60
Draughtsman illustrator, who made drawings for French papers and contributed French subjects wood engraved for the Illustrated London News, 1853.

BLANCHARD, William fl.1860s
London wood engraver, who worked at Tottenham Green Park, Tottenham, N (LSDN, 1860).

BLANPAIN, Peter fl.1890-95
London wood engraver, who worked at 7 Great Percy Street, WC (POD, 1890), and later at 40 Wharton Street, Lloyd Square, WC (POD, 1895).

BLATCHFORD, Montagu fl.1876-81
Draughtsman for Punch, although an amateur artist. As a Halifax carpet designer, he was skilful enough to adopt the popular Linley Sambourne-Charles Bennett comic style and have his work wood engraved by J.Swain (q.v.) in 1876. He was largely supplanted a few years later by Harry Furniss (q.v.), but continued to draw for Punch, sporadically after 1881. When the editor Tom Taylor died, he felt his drawing had been pushed aside for that of younger draughtsmen and returned to his business commitments in Halifax.
[Houfe; Spielmann]

BLUCK, Benjamin fl.1872-89
Provincial wood engraver, who worked at 27 Great Charles Street, Birmingham (Kelly's, 1872), 4 New North Street, Birmingham (Kelly's, 1876), 90 New Street, Birmingham (Kelly's, 1880) and finally at 2 Lincoln's Inn, Corporation Street, Birmingham (Kelly's, 1889). He may be related to J.Bluck, the early nineteenth century London aquatint engraver listed by LeBlanc.

BOLAK, George fl.1900-01
London wood engraver, who worked from 10 Bolt Court, Fleet Street, EC (POD, 1900-01), an office occupied by wood engravers since 1842. (See also Mason, Abraham John)

BOLTON, Thomas fl.1851-93
Prominent wood engraver, who appears in the London directories and worked in the city for over forty years. Chatto describes him as 'an artist of considerable repute' and Gusman places him in the school of wood engravers who continued the early influence of W.Harvey, C.Thompson and C.Gray (qq.v.) and shared in the reputations enjoyed by colleagues W.Folkard, Edmund Evans, and the Dalziel Brothers (qq.v.). Moreover he had foresight enough to engrave the first book of photographic wood engravings: C.Winkworth's Lyra Germanica, 1861. Bolton worked in London at 331 Strand (POD, 1851), 14 St Augustin Road, Camden Town (Hodgson's, 1855) and 3(7) Dane's Inn, WC (POD, 1857), where he wood engraved and remained listed in the directories until 1894. Among his engravings are illustrations after John Absolon (q.v.) to Bohn's edition of Longfellow's Poems and Poems and Songs of Robert Burns. He employed apprentices such as the noted engraver William Harcourt Hooper (q.v.) who helped with his work. One of the reasons why Bolton survived into the 1890s was his pioneering work with photographic transfer engraving. His first attempt was taken from a negative made by John Leighton (q.v.) of Flaxman's relief, 'Deliver Us from Evil' which was transferred onto a wood block and engraved without the need of a preliminary drawing. Chatto reproduces this work (p.577) but fails to explain how the process worked, only that 'Mr Bolton has just invented a process by which the powers of photography may be applied direct to the production of subjects from nature or art on wood, and from which the engraving can be made without the intervention of drawing'.
[Chatto; Wakeman; Gusman]

BONNER, George fl.1880s
Provincial wood engraver, who worked at Beatrice Street, Oswestry, Salop (Kelly's, 1889).

BONNER, George Frederick fl.1844-59
London wood engraver, who worked at 23 Warwick Square (POD, 1844), 1 Bennett's Hill, Doctor's Common (POD, 1855) and finally 2 Falcon Court, Fleet Street, EC (POD, 1859). He probably apprenticed the fourteen year old George Housman Thomas (q.v.) in 1838; this is contrary to the general belief that it was George Wilmot Bonner (q.v.), who had died two years previously

BONNER, George Wilmot (William) 1796-1836
Prominent early wood engraver, master of several important figures in the art, notably W.J.Linton, W.H.Powis and Henry Vizetelly (qq.v.). He was born in Devizes on 24 May 1796, was educated at Bath, and came to London where he was apprenticed to his uncle, the wood engraver Robert Branston, Senior (q.v.), and later to James Henry Vizetelly

(q.v.) at Vizetelly and Branston. He eventually set up his own wood engraving business and 'became a good draughtsman and skilled engraver, and was distinguished by his ability in producing gradations of tint by a combination of blocks' (Redgrave). He apprenticed W.J.Linton (q.v.) in 1828. Linton moved in with the Bonner family at 12 Canterbury Row, Kennington, and worked diligently for his master whom he described as 'a clever artist, and a good master'. Linton recalled how Bonner insisted that his apprentices learned all processes of wood engraving from the cutting of wood blocks to the finest graver work. He also demanded drawings of his apprentices, made from nature so that they did not become mere mechanical copyists. He sent Linton to draw the 'Red House', Battersea, bridges on the Thames, animals at the London Zoo, and to copy pictures in the Dulwich Picture Gallery. He also taught him how to saw a box block and, in opposition to wood engravings, to cut designs on its side for the trade placards that demanded large, bold letters and striking, if not crude, designs. Not all his apprentices appreciated this training however. The opinionated Henry Vizetelly, who came to Bonner about 1835, dismissed his master as a 'second-rate wood engraver, who itensified in his woodcuts the conventional mannerisms of the bold watercolour drawings which he was somewhat adept at producing'. By that time Bonner employed several assistants, with at least two living with his family. He listed his home-workshop in the London directory for four years, at 12 Canterbury Row, Kennington Road (Pigot,1832-36). Vizetelly claimed that his master died of 'brain fever' on 3 January 1836, when Vizetelly was still an apprentice. Bonner's achievement as a wood engraver was to adopt Bewick's white-line style in a competent but somewhat uninspired manner. W.J.Linton explained in his Masters of Wood Engraving: 'For this alone he stands nearly with the Masters: his work being always intelligently graver-drawn, cut at once, as by the Newcastle men, with little attention given to, or wanted for, any after-refinement'. Such work began as early as 1822, when Bonner engraved plates to William Savage's Practical Hints on Decorative Printing, including the plate 'Mercy'. This book was a pioneering work in the history of colour printing. Then followed fourteen engravings after William Harvey's designs to Northcote's Fables,1828, second series,1833; and engravings to the Tower Menagerie, 1829, in which he excelled in engraving animals. He engraved a series of guidebooks such as The Picturesque Pocket Companion to Margate, Ramsgate, Broadstairs,1831, and Kidd's New Guide to the 'Lions' of London,1832 (both guides printed by Charles Whittingham (q.v.) at the Chiswick Press); Doings in London, c1836, engraved after Robert Cruikshank (a copy of which is now in the Bodleian Library); Zoological Gardens,1835; and Picturesque

Excursions,1839. Bonner worked for William Pickering as well, and supplied wood engraved fish and vignettes to Pickering's edition of Walton and Cotton's Compleat Angler. He also worked with the noted woman wood engraver of the Chiswick Press, Mary Byfield (q.v.), on Francis Douce's The Dance of Death in Elegant Engravings on Wood,1833. Much of this work was well above the average standard for the period, and some of his blocks were re-used after his death. The British Museum owns a series of proof engravings by Bonner after W.Harvey, T.Landseer, D.Roberts and R.Cruikshank. Bonner signed his engravings in a sinewy handwriting, worked into the overall design: either as 'Bonner' or 'G.Bonner sc'.

[Muir; White; Redgrave; Russell; Linton, Masters of Wood Engraving; Vizetelly, Glances Back; McLean, Victorian Book Design; Bénézit; TB]

BONNEWELL, William Henry and Company
fl.1862-75
London wood engraving firm, with offices at 76 W.Smithfield, EC (POD,1862), and as Bonnewell and Company at 87 Holborn Hill, EC (POD,1864), which expanded into four offices, 85 and 86 Holborn Hill and 27 and 28 Field Lane, EC (POD,1865). The firm then moved to 16 Old Bailey, EC, and 169 Fleet Street, EC (POD,1870). By 1873 the Fleet Street address was dropped and by 1875 was replaced by Green Arbour Court, EC (POD,1875), the last year in which the firm appeared in the London directory.

BOOT, William Henry James 1848-1918
Draughtsman, illustrator and landscape painter. He was born in Nottingham in 1848, studied at the Derby School of Art and then moved to London where, working from Hampstead, he devoted his early career to illustration. He drew for the first numbers of The Graphic,1870-81, for which he is included here. His work was engraved by some of the period's finest reproductive wood engravers, among them E.Whymper (q.v.). He also contributed to the Illustrated London News,1884-86; Good Words, 1890; the Quiver,1890; Boy's Own Paper; Art Journal; and Magazine of Art, although most of these later works were process engravings. His book work included Edward Whymper's Scrambles amongst the Alps,1871. He became Art Editor of Strand Magazine,1895-1915 and a member of RBA, 1884 and Vice-President,1895-1915, exhibiting there, 1889-1913 and also at the Royal Academy, 1874-84. He died on 8 September 1918. His illustrations wood engraved by E.Whymper are in the British Museum.
[For a full list of illustrations see Houfe]

BORDERS, F. fl.1860-89
Wood engraver, noted for nine engravings after
William Quiller Orchardson's drawings for the first
volume of Good Words,1860. These included 'One
in Every Circle' reproduced by Reid (p.201).
Gleeson White said of these engravings, 'Admirable
in their own way, one cannot but feel that the
signature leads one to expect something much more
interesting; and, knowing the quality of
Mr Orchardson's later work, it is impossible to
avoid throwing the blame on the engraver'. Borders
also engraved a bookplate for A.Love, after a
'pictorial' drawing of S.J.Groves, dated 1880
(Fincham). The British Museum owns a large
landscape engraving, dated 1889, and a political
cartoon. He signed his engravings: 'F.BORDERS Sc',
'FRED BORDERS SCULP', 'FB' (superimposed).

BOSTON, Robert fl.1878-1901
London wood engraver, who worked at 84 Fleet
Street, EC (POD,1878-81) which he shared with
F.Long, F.Babbage, A.Myerson and C.Ridgway
(qq.v.). Boston later reappears in the directory at
81 Chancery Lane, WC (POD,1890-1901).

BOTHAMS, Walter fl.1882-1925
London draughtsman, illustrator and landscape
painter. He worked with the Dalziel Brothers (q.v.)
and provided drawings of rural life for the Illustrated
London News,1883-84, 1894. He worked in London,
Salisbury, 1885-1902, and Malvern, 1903-25. He
also exhibited at the Royal Academy, the Society of
British Artists and the New Watercolour Society,
1882-91.
[Houfe; Bénézit; Dalziels' Record]

BOUCHER, William H. ?-1906
Draughtsman illustrator, who worked for the
Dalziel Brothers (q.v.). He contributed cartoons to
their magazine Judy,1868-87, succeeding J.Proctor
(q.v.). He exhibited at the Royal Academy, 1888-91,
and died on 5 March 1906.
[Houfe; Dalziels' Record]

BOUGHTON, George Henry 1833-1905
Draughtsman, illustrator and painter. He was born
near Norwich on 4 December 1833, the son of a
farmer, and brought up in Albany, New York. He
returned to England in 1853, studied art in London,
returned to New York, where he stayed from 1854-
1859, went to France to study under Edouard Frère
and then settled in London in 1862, where he
illustrated for various magazines. His drawings of
historical costume scenes for the Illustrated London
News,1870-82, were greatly admired by Van Gogh.
He also contributed to Good Words,1878; Pall Mall
Magazine; and The Trial of Sir Jasper,1878, a
collaboration volume with John Gilbert, John Tenniel
and Birket Foster (qq.v.). His illustrations to Rip Van

Winkle,1893, were wood engraved by W.Spielmeyer
(q.v.). He was a regular exhibitor at the Royal
Academy, the British Institution and the Grosvenor
Gallery, and was elected ARA,1879, and RA,1896.
He died on 10 January 1905.
[Houfe; White]

BOURNE, Arthur fl.1888-92
London wood engraver, who worked at 26 Poppins
Court, Fleet Street, EC (POD,1888-92) shared
with Henry and Alfred Dix (q.v.).

BOUTALL
(see Walker and Boutall)

BOW, Charles fl.1850s
Draughtsman, who contributed a wood engraved
drawing to the Illustrated London News,1855.

BOWCHER, John fl.1871-85
London wood engraver, who worked at 70 Leighton
Road, Kentish Town, NW (POD,1871) and
28 Stonecutter Street, EC (POD,1876), following an
unsuccessful partnership as Hazard and Bowcher
(q.v.) in 1875. He reappears at 35 Woodsome Road,
Highgate, N (LSDN,1880), then returns to the city
at 140 Strand, WC (POD,1885), after which he
disappears from the directories.

BOWERS, Miss Georgina (Mrs Bowers-Edwards)
fl.1866-80
The second woman draughtsman on Punch, who
contributed initials, vignettes, and social subjects
from 1866-76. Many of these were engraved by
Joseph Swain (q.v.) who first helped her to draw on
wood. She lived at Holywell House, St Albans. She
was first encouraged to draw by the Punch artist,
John Leech (q.v.). She also illustrated for Once a
Week,1866; London Society,1867; and the books
Canters in Cramshire, c1880; and Mr Crop's
Harriers, c1880. She was an avid huntswoman;
many of her subjects were of that sport. She
exhibited in London,1878-80. The British Museum
owns several designs engraved by the Dalziel
Brothers (q.v.),1866.
[Spielmann; Houfe; TB; Clayton]

BOYLE, The Hon. Mrs Richard ('E.V.B.')
1825-1916
The only competent woman illustrator, draughtsman
to emerge before 1860. She was advised by Eastlake
and Boxall and admired by the Pre-Raphaelites,
whose work, especially that of Holman Hunt, Millais
and Arthur Hughes she in her turn admired and used.
She married in 1845, but continued to illustrate
fantasy books: A Children's Summer,1853;
Child's Play,1858; her most successful work The
May Queen,1861, Woodland Gossip,1864; and her
most well known, The Story Without an End,1868,

with coloured illustrations. She also contributed to
the Illustrated London News, Christmas number,
1863. She exhibited at the Dudley and the Grosvenor
Gallery,1878-81, and died on 30 July 1916.
[For a full list of illustrated work see Houfe]

BRACKETT, Oliver
Wood engraver and bookplate designer. According
to Gleeson White, 'Mr Oliver Brackett, in a
charming woodcut for Walter H.Brackett, and a few
other unpublished designs, shows admirable grasp
of decorative principles, so that it is a matter of
surprise not to find more examples of his designs'.
(Studio, Winter,1898-99,p.37).

BRADLEY, Basil 1842-1904
Draughtsman illustrator and painter of sporting
subjects. He studied at the Manchester School of Art,
frequently exhibited in London and provincial galleries
and became ARWS,1867 and RWS,1881. He is included
here for his wood engraved drawings to the major
magazines, Once a Week,1866; Cassell's Magazine,
1867; and as the chief equestrian artist to The Graphic
from its early days, 1869-76. His work here was
engraved by that paper's prominent wood engravers.
[Houfe; TB; Clement; Cundall; Graves]

BRADLEY, C.H. fl.1852-60
Draughtsman illustrator for Punch, who generally
drew initials and social subjects borrowed from
Tenniel's (q.v.) style. These appeared 1852-60 and
totalled thirty-five cuts, wood engraved by Joseph
Swain (q.v.).
[Spielmann; Houfe]

BRADLEY, Charles William fl.1885-86
London wood engraver, who worked at Gresham
Press Buildings, 2 Little Bridge Street, EC
(POD,1885). The following year he moved to
29 Chiswell Street, EC (POD,1886).

BRADLEY, Reverend Edward
(see Bede, Cuthbert)

BRADLEY, James Thomas fl.1880s
Provincial wood engraver, who worked at
162 Edmund Street, Birmingham (Kelly's,1889).

BRADLEY, William George fl.1882-96
London wood engraver, who worked at 303 Strand,
WC (POD,1882-86). He then joined in partnership
as Evans and Bradley. He reappears alone in
the directories as Bradley and Company at the same
address (POD,1889-96).

BRADSTOCK, Alfred
London wood engraver, who worked with David W.
Williamson (q.v.) first at 154 Fleet Street, EC
(POD,1884), then at 7 New Court, Carey Street,

WC (POD,1889-96). Bradstock is dropped from the
directory after that date, but Williamson remains.

BRAGER, Jean Baptiste Henri Durand 1841-1879
French draughtsman illustrator and marine painter.
He was born in Dole, France, on 21 May 1814,
studied with Eugene Isabey and travelled throughout
Europe and Africa for his subjects. He contributed
views of the Piedmont Campaign and of Palermo
wood engraved in Henry Vizetelly's (q.v.) Illustrated
Times,1859-60.

BRAHAM, Alfred and Ernest fl.1887-1910
London wood engravers and draughtsmen, who
worked at 181 Queen Victoria Street, EC
(POD,1887-1910).

BRAILSFORD, Joseph
(see Pawson and Brailsford)

BRAMWELL, John and Samuel fl.1880s
Provincial wood engravers, who worked in Chapel-
en-le-Frith, Stockport (Kelly's,1889).

BRANDARD, Robert 1805-1862
Occasional draughtsman and wood engraver,
primarily known for his metal engraved plates on
Turner's Picturesque Views in England and Wales,
after Stanfield and Callcott. He was born in
Birmingham in 1805, the brother of the engravers
Edward and William Brandard, came to London in
1824 to study with Edouard Goodall, and set up as
a professional engraver in Islington. He exhibited
work at the British Institution, 1835-58, Royal
Society of British Artists, 1831-47, the Royal
Academy and the Old Watercolour Society, and
died in Kensington on 7 January 1862. Hind
described Brandard as a wood engraver who had
the 'bad tendency' of trying to imitate metal line
engraving on the wood block. Such work involved
some illustrations to Charles Knight's London,
1841-42. It was believed that Brandard apprenticed
the young John Greenaway (q.v.), but this was
R.E.Branston (q.v.).
[LeBlanc; TB; Bryan; DNB; Houfe; Bénézit; Slater;
for a discussion of the Brandards as metal
engravers see Volume I (with bibliography)]

BRANDLING, Henry Charles fl.1847-61
Draughtsman on wood, watercolour painter,
lithographer. He was noted for his architectural
subjects and figures included in such works as The
Merchant of Venice,1860, illustrated with
G.H.Thomas, Birket Foster and W.H.Rogers
(qq.v.), which White calls 'a trifle belated in style'.
He also drew for Wilkie Collins' Rambles beyond
Railways,1851. He exhibited at the Old Watercolour
Society, 1853-57, and the Royal Academy, 1847-50.
[Houfe; Chatto]

BRANSCOMBE, Charles fl.1886-1910
London wood engraver, who worked at 168 Fleet
Street, EC (POD,1886) which he shared with
A.L.Appleton (q.v.). This changed to 108 Fleet
Street (POD,1889-90). By 1892 Branscombe had
joined with the Riches Brothers (q.v.) to become
Branscombe and Riches, but this apparently lasted
only one year. He was again on his own from 1893,
and shared his office with J.Hare (q.v.) from
1896-99. He continued to appear in the directories
until 1910.

BRANSTON, Charles fl.1856-78
London wood engraver, who worked at 21 Tavistock
Terrace, Upper Holloway (POD,1856), 4 Beaufort
Buildings, Strand, WC (POD,1863), and 6 Fetter
Lane, Fleet Street, EC (POD,1866) which he shared
with H.Crane and R.Pringle (qq.v.). He reappears
in the directories at 4 Salisbury Court, EC
(POD,1876-77), and he also worked in that year
from 13 Edith Road, Peckham, SE (LSDS,1876).
This then became the office of Branston and
Company (q.v.).

BRANSTON, Elizabeth fl.1832-34
London wood engraver, who worked at 13 Golden
Terrace, White Conduit Fields (Pigot,1832-34).

BRANSTON, Frederick William fl.1830-49
London wood engraver, comic draughtsman
illustrator and watercolourist. He was the brother
of the prominent wood engraver Robert Branston
(q.v.). He began his career as an artist in London
in the 1830s, where he exhibited at the Royal
Academy in 1833 and contributed to Hood's Comic
Annual,1830. By the mid 1830s he was working as
wood engraver for various French magazines and
books. These included Magasin Pittoresque; Léon
de Laborde's Essai de Gravure,1833; and
Dr Wordsworth's La Grèce Pittoresque, for which
he worked on the 300 total cuts with the most
prominent English reproductive wood engravers of
the period: E.Evans, John Orrin Smith, W.T.Green,
M.A.Williams, R.Hart, G.W.Bonner, C.Gray,
E.Landells, S.Sly, T.W.Williams, and J.Wheeler
(qq.v.). By 1838 he had engraved cuts to Vue de Rouen
and the medieval miniatures by Théophile Fragonard to
Les Evangiles,1838; followed by cuts to Vue de Harre,
1841. Gusman described this French work as
engraved 'avec une grande finesse et précision de
coupe'. In England Branston engraved four designs
of William Harvey's for Northcote's Fables,1828;
cuts after W.Prior to J.F.Murray's Environs of
London,1842; designs of J.Franklin, E.M.Ward,
H.J.Townsend and J.N.Paton to S.C.Hall's Book of
British Ballads,1842; and John Franklin's designs
to The Book of Nursery Tales,1845. He was soon
associated with many of the influential engraved books
of the English wood engraving revival. He worked in

London and appeared in the directories at
4 Crescent Place, New Bridge Street (POD,1848),
and 48 Paternoster Row (POD,1849). By 1861 Bohn
in Chatto and Jackson could praise his engraving
influence and describe him as 'one of our best
engravers', reproducing his work after a John
Martin biblical design. The British Museum owns
a series of proof engravings by Branston after
designs of William Harvey, Edwin Landseer,
Richard Redgrave, David Roberts and E.M.Ward.
He signed his work: 'F W BRANSTON', 'FRED
BRANSTON' or 'F BRANSTON SC'.
[McLean, Victorian Book Design; Gusman; Houfe]

BRANSTON, Robert (Allen Robert) 1778-1827
One of the leaders of the revival of British wood
engraving. He was born in Lynn, Norfolk, in 1778,
the son of a copper-plate engraver and heraldic
painter, to whom he was apprenticed. When nineteen
years old he settled in Bath and set up as painter
engraver. In 1799 (1802, Chatto) he came to London
where he engraved musical scores and taught
himself wood engraving, eventually establishing
himself as a major figure in that field. His first
engraving on wood was for lottery bills, then for
various book illustrations. This work included
some plates for Wallis and Scholey's History of
England,1804-10; Bloomfield's Wild Flowers,1806;
Ackermann's Religious Emblems,1808-10 after
J.Thurston designs, engraved with C.Nesbit and
Luke Clennell (qq.v.), which Bliss praised as such
charming engravings in 'one of the most notable books
of the century'; G.Marshall's Epistles in Verse,
1812. For a reprint of Puckle's The Club,1817, he
was joined by his apprentice John Thompson, Charlton
Nesbit, W.Hughes, H.White, and Mary Byfield (qq.v.).
He also engraved the title-page to Chorley's Metrical
Index,1818. His best work, however, was 'The
Cave of Despair' after John Thurston's design, in
Savage's Practical Hints on Decorative Printing,
1822, which shows his skill in white-line and
black-line styles and which many considered to be
the finest wood engraving ever done at the time.
He also planned a series of Fables with Thurston's
designs, intended to rival Bewick, his contemporary,
but abandoned the project after a few cuts; he also
tried a number after birds, again to rival Bewick,
'but though beautifully cut, they were essentially
inferior to Bewick's' (DNB). Branston's signature
is on ten engravings after W.Harvey to Northcote's
Fables,1828, although they were probably done by
his son Robert Edward Branston (q.v.) (proofs are
in the British Museum). Similarly an 'R.Branston',
wood engraver, is listed as working at Holloway
(Pigot,1822-23). Robert Branston, Senior, died in
Brompton, in 1827. As a wood engraver Branston
was the leader of the so-called 'London School' of
black-line engraving. He perfected the skills, then
passed them on to his apprentices, such as

G.W.Bonner, A.J.Mason, G.Watts, Charles and
John Thompson (qq.v.). His talent for cutting fine
lines made his wood engraving look like intricate copper
engraving. He was always in conscious rivalry with
Bewick, although he was some twenty-three years
Bewick's junior. Yet he failed to achieve such artistic
distinction, and especially failed with the trees
and natural scenery that Bewick had mastered. He
did excel in human figures and interiors of 'gradations
of light' (Redgrave). Branston senior signed his
work: 'R.Branston sc', 'RB' (superimposed).
[Nagler; C.T. Lewis; Linton, Masters of Wood
Engraving; Bénézit; Chatto; Heller; TB; Gusman;
DNB; Redgrave]

BRANSTON, Robert Edward fl.1840s-50s
London wood engraver and occasional draughtsman,
son of the noted wood engraver Robert Branston
(q.v.), brother of Frederick Branston (q.v.). Branston
formed a partnership with John Wright, as Branston and
Wright (q.v.), 1829-35 and apprenticed John Greenaway
(q.v.). Then with Charles Whiting, who had acquired Sir
William Congreve's process for security printing in
colours in 1830, he formed another partnership as
Whiting and Branston. They became noted for colour
printed lottery tickets, ornamental borders, cheques
and bank notes. When the firm broke up, before 1840,
Whiting remained at their office, Beaufort House,
Strand, and Branston joined James Henry Vizetelly,
Senior (q.v.) to form Branston and Vizetelly at
35 Fleet Street (later 76), with a sleeping partner,
Mr Whitehead. They trained W.H.Wills and
G.W.Bonner (qq.v.). Their first publication was the
Boy's Own Book. They employed Ebenezer Landells
(q.v.) as engraving supervisor, but the firm quickly
failed, by 1841, and some of the book projects were
given to Vizetelly's sons, James and Henry (qq.v.).
Branston then worked independently with his
apprentice William Dickes (q.v.) on such books as
the Abbotsford edition of Scott's Waverley Novels,
1842-47, the drawings for which Branston had done
on wood. They worked at 36 St Andrews' Hills
(POD,1840,1848-57). During this time Branston and
Dickes developed a method of printing in metallic
relief. They made a specimen for William Savage's
Dictionary of the Art of Printing,1841-, a pen and ink
drawing by A.W.Callcott, colour engraved from
seven blocks. Robert Branston was especially
competent in engraving the drawings of Sir W.Allan
and Clarkson Stanfield (qq.v.).
[C.T.Lewis; DNB; McLean; Wakeman; Bliss]

BRANSTON, W. fl.1817
London wood engraver, listed by Johnstone's
Directory (1817) at Upper Holloway. This may in
fact be a misprint for Robert Branston, Senior (q.v.).

BRANSTON and Company fl.1878-91
London wood engraving firm, with offices at
27 Stonecutter Street, EC (POD,1878),
119 Salisbury Square, EC (POD,1879), shared with
J.J.Marchant (q.v.) in 1880, and 75 Imperial
Buildings, New Bridge Street, EC (POD,1883-91).

BRANSTON and Vizetelly
(see Branston, Robert Edward)

BRANSTON and Wright fl.1829-38
London wood engraving firm, a partnership between
Robert Edward Branston (q.v.) and John Wright
(q.v.), with an office at 4 New London Street
(Pigot,1832-34). Their work was printed by Charles
Whittingham, Senior (q.v.) and they are best known for
their engravings after drawings of William Harvey (q.v.);
The Tower Menagerie, including a History of
Quadrupeds and Birds,1829 (54 cuts); The Gardens
and Menagerie of the Zoological Society; a vignette
to J.Britton's Picturesque Antiquities; after William
Harvey's drawings to Dr Percy's The Beggar's
Daughter of Bednall Green,1832; and the French
edition, Paul et Virginie,1838. The Bodleian Library
owns a series of pencil-marked proofs to the Menagerie
which shows the care the firm took in their work and
in their collaboration with their printer Whittingham.
They signed engravings: 'B&W', 'BW'.
[Nagler; Bodleian; Warren, Charles Whittingham,
1896; Linton, Masters of Wood Engraving]

BREND'AMOUR, Richard and Company fl.1880-88
German based wood engraving firm, founded by
Richard Brend'Amour, a wood engraver born in Aix
la Chapelle of French parentage on 16 October 1831.
He was the founder and senior member of a
Düsseldorf art printing firm, whose early output
is fully listed in TB and Glaser (p.222). The firm
also had offices at 31 Paternoster Square, EC
(POD,1880-83), and as Brend'Amour and Company
at 19 Ludgate Hill, EC (POD,1887-88). Their work
in England included a full page engraving, 'Clovelly
Pier at Half-Tide', after L.R.O'Brien's drawing in
The English Illustrated Magazine,1884-85. This is
a rather strong engraving, the black outline heavily
printed but tightly cut on the block.
[TB; Glaser; Bénézit]

BRETT, Edward (Edwin) John fl.1864-70
London wood engraving firm, with offices at
262 Strand, WC (POD,1864), 3 Thanet Place,
Strand (POD,1867), 3 Warwick Court, High Holborn
(POD,1868), and as 'Edwin [sic] Brett' at 173 Fleet
Street (POD,1870).

BREWER, Henry William ?-1903
Occasional draughtsman on wood, architectural
illustrator of panoramic views. He was born and
educated in Oxford, lived most of his life in North

Kensington and exhibited at the Royal Academy from 1858. He was one of the early illustrators of The Graphic,1870-1901, his work being engraved by the magazine's major wood engravers. He also contributed to The English Illustrated Magazine, 1887, and several 1890s process engraved papers.

BREWER, William Henry fl.1843-86
London wood engraver and draughtsman illustrator, who worked at 9 Red Lion Court, Fleet Street (POD,1843) where he remained for over forty years as engraver and draughtsman, although the office number changed to 13 (1845), 16 (1846) and 14 (1855). In about 1873 he added a second office at 3 Gough Square, Fleet Street, EC (POD,1873-86). By 1876 Brewer was listing himself in the London directory as a draughtsman only (Kelly's,1876-80). Houfe lists a W.H.Brewer, watercolourist of a drawing to Dickens' Master Humphrey's Clock, 1840, and another of fairies.

BREWTNALL, Edward Frederick 1846-1902
Draughtsman illustrator and landscape painter. He began as draughtsman for various Sixties magazines: Once a Week,1867 and Good Words for the Young, 1869; and provided various narrative drawings to early numbers of The Graphic,1870-74,1889; Punch,1870; the Illustrated London News,1873-74, 1892; Cassell's Family Magazine; the English Illustrated Magazine,1887; the Quiver,1890; Black and White,1891; Pall Mall Magazine,1892. More notably, Brewtnall worked as draughtsman for the Dalziel Brothers (q.v.): he contributed to the Bible Gallery,1880 and according to Dalziels' Record, he also drew ten illustrations to their Pilgrim's Progress. In addition Brewtnall exhibited at the Royal Society of British Artists from 1868, was a member 1882-86, exhibited at the Royal Watercolour Society from 1875, and was elected a member in 1883. He died in Bedford Park on 15 November 1902.
[Houfe; Bénézit; TB; Bryan; Dalziels', Record]

BRIDGES
(see Lockwood, Joseph and Bridges)

BRIDGES, Samuel fl.1880-94
London suburban wood engraver, who worked at 20 Brownlow Road, Dalston, E
(LSDN,1880-94).

BRIERLY, Sir Oswald Walters 1817-1894
Draughtsman, marine painter. He was born in Chester in 1817, studied at Sass's School, at Plymouth, and travelled round the world in 1841. During his travels he provided drawings to the Crimean War, and accompanied the Royal Family on various tours. His work was wood engraved in the Illustrated London News,1851,1854 (Crimea) and 1855 (Finland). He was elected ARWS in 1872 and RWS in

1890. He became Marine Painter to the Queen in 1874, and was knighted in 1885.
[Houfe; TB; Bénézit; Bryan]

BRINE, Thomas (J.G.) fl.1840s
Early draughtsman for Punch, who studied in Paris and London and worked closely with A.S.Henning (q.v.). He contributed a total of about twenty-four drawings of cartoons to Punch from 1841. 'He was a poor and often a 'fudgy' draughtsman, gifted with extremely little humour', as Spielmann dismisses him, and he was poorly paid: '...it is impossible to say, looking at these sketches, that his efforts were seriously underpaid'. On the other hand the young apprentice Edmund Evans (q.v.) admired Brine's work: 'he had a very refined style of drawing and was certainly a clever artist (Reminiscences,p.11). It is believed he taught Birket Foster (q.v.) figure drawing, and as J.G. (sic) Brine (Bénézit) contributed to Hall's Book of British Ballads,1842.
[Bénézit; TB; Houfe; Spielmann; Evans Reminiscences]

BRISTOL, Goldsmith's Alliance fl.1880s
Provincial wood engraving firm, also known as William Langford, Sons and Company with an office at 30 College Green, Bristol (Kelly's,1889).

BROMLEY, Charles James fl.1860-75
London wood engraver, who as Charles Bromley worked at 28 Chancery Lane, WC (POD,1860), then at 6 Grafton Road, Kentish Town, NW (POD,1863). Charles James Bromley appears at Grecian Chambers, Devereux Court, WC (POD,1872-75)..

BROMLEY, Clough W. fl.1880-1904
Engraver, illustrator, landscape and flower painter. He worked in Clapham, London, contributed works to numerous London galleries, including the Royal Academy and New Watercolour Society from 1872. He drew pastorals for the English Illustrated Magazine, 1885-87, 1896, notably drawings to 'London Commons' by Robert Hunter, wood engraved by R.Paterson, J.A.Quartley, O.Lacour and O.Jahyer (qq.v.).
[TB; Bénézit; Houfe]

BROMLEY, Valentine Walter 1848-1877
Draughtsman illustrator and painter, born on 14 February 1848 in London, where he was a pupil of his father, a watercolour painter. He began drawing on wood for The Graphic,1872-73; he was also frequently employed on the Illustrated London News, 1873-79, generally for complicated society scenes like the Tichborne trial, crowd scenes such as 'Tourists on the Tramp', 15 August 1874, engraved by H.Linton (q.v.) and several double-page drawings of the Pyramids, the war in Spain, and driving cattle in Nebraska, 21 August 1875, engraved by W.J.Palmer (q.v.), done after he had travelled to America

with Lord Dunraven. This resulted in his illustrations to Dunraven's The Great Divide. He also drew for Punch, 1876. He exhibited at the Royal Academy and the Royal Society of British Artists, 1867-74, and the New Watercolour Society, and died at Fallows Green, Harpenden, at the tragically young age of thirty. The Illustrated London News' obituary called him a 'clever and promising artist'. [For a full biography see DNB; Bryan; Redgrave; Clement; Bénézit; Houfe]

BROOKES, Warwick 1808-1882
Draughtsman illustrator. He was born in Salford in 1808 and was a pupil at the new Manchester School of Design. He organised a group of students intent on life study under the name of 'The United Society of Manchester Artists'. Brookes was head designer of the Rossendale Printing Company, 1840-66 and was encouraged by the Prince Consort, whom he frequently visited in London. He contributed briefly as an illustrator, with wood engraved headpieces for A Round of Days, 1866; and drawings to Marjorie Fleming, 1884; and WB's Pencil Pictures of Child Life, 1889.
[Houfe; Bénézit; TB; Bryan]

BROOKS, Herbert James
London draughtsman, who worked at 12 Paul Street, EC (Kelly's, 1900).

BROOKS, James Frederick fl.1870s
Provincial wood engraver, who worked at 121 Arundel Street, Sheffield (Kelly's, 1872).

BROWN
(see Walker and Brown)

BROWN, A.
Draughtsman listed by Houfe as contributing architectural subjects to the Illustrated London News, 1847.

BROWN, Ford Madox 1821-1893
Occasional draughtsman on wood, and prominent painter. He was born in Calais in 1821, studied art in Belgium and Rome, worked on the edge of the Pre-Raphaelite circle and took in Rossetti (q.v.) as a pupil. Reid claims that Brown made only nine drawings on wood blocks, but these are truly masterly and typical of the extreme care Brown took with detail. His first, 'The Prisoner of Chillon' to Willmott's Poets of the Nineteenth Century, 1857, involved a three day study of a decaying corpse in a mortuary to get the main figure right before drawing onto the 3.75" x 5" wood block for the Dalziels to engrave, with the 100 other cuts in the book. 'It is a beautiful but distinctly macabre design', Reid explains of the prison scene, 'the grim amusement on the face of the saturnine grave-digger being masterly, while nothing could be more realistic

than the dead body, which lies with its head dropping back into a pit and its stiffened limbs outstretched. Yet, though the face of the open-mouthed corpse conveys all the horror of death, and by no means recent death, it is wonderful how a delicate beauty shines through that visible corruption. Portions of the drawing suggest a certain mauling on the part of the engraver, but both in conception and execution it ranks among the masterpieces'. Then followed three designs to Lyra Germanica, 1868; a drawing to Once a Week, 1869; his best known drawing to Rossetti's 'Down Stream' for Dark Blue, 1871; and three drawings to the Dalziels' Bible Gallery, done in the 1860s but not published until 1880-81. These Brown called 'etchings' because of the pure line work necessary for the engraver. There are later appearances unacknowledged by Reid in the Builder, 1887; Brown Owl, 1891; and Mathilde Blind's Dramas in Miniature, 1897; but most were process engraved.
[For a full biography see F.M.Heuffer, Memoir of Ford Madox Brown, 1896; Wood; Bénézit; White; Reid; Houfe]

BROWN, Henry 1816-1870
Brother of the noted wood engraver William Brown (q.v.), who was born in England of English parents but, like his brother, spent his working life on the Continent. He served as engraver in Paris from 1840, became head of the Royal School of Engraving, La Haye, 1840, and numbered among his pupils Antoine Bertrand and Auguste Trichon (qq.v.).
[Bénézit]

BROWN, Isaac L. fl.1868
Draughtsman, who contributed wood engraved drawings to London Society, 1868, in company with some of the major draughtsmen illustrators of the day -- Walter Crane, John Gilbert, W.Small and F.Barnard (qq.v.).

BROWN, James fl.1887
Draughtsman illustrator, who contributed to the Dalziels' comic magazine Judy, 1887..

BROWN, John fl.1820-56
Draughtsman of architectural subjects, architect and County Surveyor of Norfolk. He drew a church scene for the Illustrated Times, Christmas 1856, and exhibited at the Royal Academy, 1820-44. He may be the J.Brown who contributed the half-page engraving 'Old and New Buildings in Threadneedle Street', after C.W.Sheeves, in the Illustrated London News, 10 February 1855.

BROWN, John Law fl.1876-89
Scottish wood engraver, who worked at 5 Keir Street, Edinburgh (Kelly's, 1876-89). Fincham mentions a landscape bookplate engraved by J.Brown of Lawn Market, Edinburgh, dated 1800

and signed 'JB'.

BROWN, J.O. or J.B. fl.1860s
Draughtsman, who contributed a drawing to Good
Words, 1860, a work which White dismisses as calling
'for no particular comment'; and also, as 'J.B.', a
series of full-page animal illustrations printed on tinted
paper from 1861, according to the magazine's
prospectus. Brown also exhibited at the Royal Society
of British Artists, 1862. The British Museum owns
designs by 'J.Browne' to Wood's Natural History,
1862, engraved by the Dalziel Brothers (q.v.).
[Houfe]

BROWN, J.R. fl.1874-90
Draughtsman illustrator, who worked for The Graphic,
1874-77, 1885-88, a regular contributor of both comic
and social realism subjects. He worked in Sefton
Park, Liverpool, and exhibited a work there in 1889.
[Houfe]

BROWN, Maynard fl.1878-99
Draughtsman illustrator, painter of historical
subjects. He lived in Nottingham and exhibited at
the Royal Academy, 1878-87, and other London
galleries. Houfe lists an M.Brown who contributed
landscapes for the Illustrated London News, 1888.
There is also a drawing by him in the Church
Monthly, 1899.
[Houfe; Bénézit; Graves]

BROWN, Thomas fl.1880s
Provincial wood engraver, who worked at Minor
and Scurr's Yard, 57 Briggate, Leeds (Kelly's, 1889).
He is not to be confused with Thomas Harry Brown
(q.v.). There is also, according to Houfe, a Thomas
Brown, fl.1842-56, illustrator of The Complete
Poetical Works of William Cowper, Gall and Inglis,
c1840.

BROWN, Thomas Harry 1881-?
Wood engraver, landscape painter in oil and
watercolour. He was born in Manchester on
17 December 1881, became an outstanding pupil of
the Manchester Academy and lived and worked in
the city. He exhibited at the Royal Cambrian Academy
and in Lancashire galleries.
[Waters]

BROWN, William fl.1870s
Provincial wood engraver who worked at 152 Church
Street, Preston, Lancashire (Kelly's, 1872). He was
an extremely versatile engraver: an advertisement of the period claims that he was a 'Designer,
draughtsman, die sinker, engraver, lithographer by
steam power, commercial and general lithographer'
doing 'copper plate printing of mechanical and
architectural drawings'.

BROWN, William ('W.B.') 1814-1877
Wood engraver, born in York in 1814, brother of the
noted engraver Henry Brown (q.v.). William worked
most of his life in Brussels, notably engraving after
Raphael, Rubens and other Old Masters. These
engravings appeared in the French Histoire des
Peintres de Toutes les Ecoles, 1849-75. Brown taught
at the Brussels Academy, Adolphe Pannemaker (q.v.)
being one of his pupils. He died in Belgium on
15 August 1877; his obituary notice was in the Art
Journal of that year (p.368). He may be the W.Brown
('W.B.') who began his career as a draughtsman
for Punch from 1844; his 'Statue of Jenkins' 'pleased
Punch readers greatly', according to Spielmann.
He also illustrated The Comic Album which was
'deservedly popular in its day'.
[Houfe; Spielmann; Gusman; Bénézit; TB]

BROWNE, Hablot Knight ('Phiz') 1815-1882
Occasional draughtsman on wood, prominent
humourist illustrator, watercolourist. He was born
in Kennington in 1815, educated in Suffolk and then
apprenticed to the metal engraver William Finden.
He opened his own engraving studio and attended the
St Martin's Lane School, then on the death of Robert
Seymour, succeeded him as Dickens' illustrator for
Pickwick Papers, 1836, and also illustrated Dickens'
Sunday under Three Heads the same year. He
continued in his Regency style caricature-like
illustrations until the 'Sixties School' supplanted him.
He was paralysed in 1867 and moved to Brighton in
1880, where he died in 1882. One of his sons was the
artist Walter Browne (q.v.). Browne was never
comfortable drawing on wood, his style being too
fine-lined and sketchy to be adequately engraved or
printed. His son Edgar recalled the problems in a
letter: 'Browne was an accomplished etcher, but he
was never at home with the technique of woodcutting.
He never seemed able to realise what changes an
engraver might make in the appearance of his
drawing. As a rule, the tendency was to increase
the amount of white shown, and thereby thin the line,
and also in free drawing to substitute something
more mechanical. He never cured himself of using
a mixed method of drawing and leaving the engraver
to find his way out of it, which he generally did by
cutting away anything that offered difficulty' (letter
quoted in Buchanan-Brown, Phiz, p.26).
Browne was intent on repeating the same dense
surfaces and delicate details which he had achieved
in his etchings, as seen in his earliest wood
engravings, namely to Sunday under Three Heads,
1836; and to E.Caswall's Morals for the Churchyard,
1838. There are also good examples of the
decorative vignette style of the period in his
Handbook of Swindling, 1839. His work was engraved
by some of the early period's most proficient wood
engravers E.Landells, C.Gray and T.Williams (qq.v.);
he is known to have drawn about 300 designs for

wood engravings from 1839-1850 (compared with 800 etchings), followed by 232 from 1851-60, and 227 from 1861-70. Some of the best are to Master Humphrey's Clock,1840-41, engraved by Landells; and twelve designs to the Routledge Shilling Toybook The Young Ragamuffin,1866, engraved by the Dalziels. He was, however, best suited to the smaller books, in the romantic tradition borrowed from France in the 1840s. Those of note are St. Patrick's Eve,1845; A Romance of a Mince-Pie, 1848; James Haunay's Hearts are Trumps,1848; G.P.R.James' The Fight of the Fiddlers,1849; Lever's Nuts and Nutcrackers; and Brough's Ulf the Minstrel,1859. By the 1860s his work was showing the weaknesses which his younger colleagues had mastered, yet he continued drawing on wood for Routledge's series of illustrated novels of Fielding and Smollet,1857; Ainsworth's Ovingdean Grange, 1860; and Sir Guy de Guy,1864, engraved by Edmund Evans (q.v.), who admired his work from his apprentice days. Evans points out that the early Browne drawings were not engraved by him but by another E.Evans (Edward Evans (q.v.)) (see Reminiscences,p.20). Browne also contributed to numerous magazines, such as Punch,1842-44, 1861-69; the Illustrated London News,1844-61; the Illuminated Magazine,1845; Illustrated London Magazine,1835-55; and the Illustrated Times, 1855-56. The British Museum owns several designs engraved by the Dalziel Brothers (q.v.). [For a complete account of his work see J.Buchanan-Brown, Phiz,1978; also Houfe; Chatto; Spielmann; Bénézit]

BROWNE, Hablot T. fl.1880s
The London directories list a Hablot T.Browne, wood engraver, working at 5 Arundel Street, Strand (POD,1883-84).

BROWNE, Walter fl.1870s-80s
Draughtsman engraver, son of Hablot K.Browne (q.v.). He began training with Bonnat as an illustrator engraver, until on 19 May 1870 Phiz wrote to the Dalziel Brothers (q.v.), recommending his son for work with them: 'I think you would find his style of work suited to some of the many publications you engrave for. What he has hitherto done for publishers has been satisfactory'. Walter was then taken up by Mark Lemon who accepted a few drawings for Punch which appeared until 20 November 1875. He was then lured away by what Spielmann calls 'a delusive offer of Tom Hood's of constant work on Fun, so that he closed the door in his face, and had henceforward to look to news drawing and book illustration for advancement'.

BROWNLOW, Charles Victor 1863-?
Occasional wood engraver, etcher and landscape painter. He was born on 28 May 1863, was the pupil of the wood engraver J.W.Whymper (q.v.) and

contributed wood engravings to the English Illustrated Magazine,1889-90, after Philip Norman's drawings to 'Eton College', and one after W.B.Gardner's 'From Moor to Sea', a competent landscape engraving. Brownlow worked in London, exhibited an etching at the Royal Academy,1892, and then emigrated to America, working in Germantown, Pennsylvania in 1909, then Philadelphia. [See Volume I for his work on metal and for a bibliography; also Fielding]

BRUER, Jeffrey fl.1870s
London wood engraver, who worked at 12 Sergeant's Inn, EC (POD,1878).

BRUNTON, William S. fl.1859-71
Draughtsman illustrator of Irish parentage, founding member of the Savage Club. He contributed numerous sketches of social life to the Dalziel Brothers (q.v.) as 'Billy Brunton' and was a draughtsman for Punch,1859, where his 'Annamite Ambassadors' series paved the way for Harry Furniss's successful 'Lika Joko' series. He also drew for the Illustrated Times,1861,1866; London Society,1863,1865,1868; the Dalziels' Fun,1865; Tinsley's Magazine,1867; Broadway, 1867-74; and Moonshine,1871. The British Museum owns several designs engraved by the Dalziel Brothers (q.v.), 1863,1865. [Houfe; Dalziels' Record]

BRUWIER, Charles fl.1860s
London wood engraver, who worked at 27 Fetter Lane, Holborn, EC (POD,1866) which he shared with E.Heaviside (q.v.).

BRYDEN, Robert 1865-1939
Scottish wood engraver and cutter, etcher and sculptor. He was born in Coylton, Ayrshire on 11 June 1865, educated at the local school, Ayr Academy and then came to London after some years as an architect's assistant. He also studied at the Royal Cambrian Academy and the Royal Academy Schools. He travelled to Belgium, France, Italy, Spain and Egypt, making etchings of the subjects he saw there. In 1899 he produced a folio series of thirty-three woodcut portraits, Men of Letters of the Nineteenth Century; as well as the woodcut border for William Strang's 'The Labourer', an unusually large work (2 x 2.40 metres) (both are now in the British Museum). When his woodcut of Burns appeared in The Dome, April 1900 (printed from two blocks) according to the editor, it 'awoke so much interest that another cut by him seems to be taken for granted': the promised work was 'The Little Philosopher', December 1900. Bryden was a prolific printmaker: between 1898-1910, he produced 450 etchings and woodcuts which secured his position among the new generation of

revivalist wood engravers alongside Bernard Sleigh, Louise Glazier and W.O.J.Nieuwenkamp (qq.v.). He was elected ARE,1891 and RE,1899, and died on 22 August 1939. He signed his work: 'B' (dated). [Gusman; Waters; Houfe; Hake; TB; Bénézit]

BUCHANAN, Mrs Lucinda (Lucy) fl.1870-86
London wood engraver, who worked at 180 Fleet Street, EC (POD,1870) with T.D.Collins (q.v.) and 183 Holloway Road, N (POD,1874). From 1876 she worked as Mrs Lucy C.Buchanan at 4 Red Lion Court, EC (POD,1876-86).

BUCKLEY, John fl.1876-80
London draughtsman, who worked at 45 Blackstock Road, N (Kelly's,1876-80). He may be related to J.E.Buckley, a painter of historical subjects who exhibited at the Society of British Artists, 1843-61.

BUCKMAN, Edwin 1841-1930
Draughtsman illustrator and watercolourist. He was born on 25 January 1841 and was educated at King Edward's School, Birmingham and Birmingham Art School. He was an influential original contributor to The Graphic,1869-71,1889 (about twenty-four drawings); then to the Illustrated London News, 1871-76 (about ten drawings). These Van Gogh admired, 'drawn especially broadly and boldly and in a whole-hearted manner' and were mainly of grim social scenes like 'A London Dustyard', or crowds like 'A Republican Procession in London', many wood engraved by his relation H.Buckman (q.v.). Edwin was later drawing master to Queen Alexandra. He exhibited at the Royal Academy until 1877, and at the Royal Watercolour Society and was elected ARWS,1877. He died on 15 October 1930. [Houfe; Bénézit; TB]

BUCKMAN, H. fl.1875-80
Wood engraver, who engraved for the Illustrated London News several full-page plates after Edwin Buckman (q.v.). These include 'Quiet Times: A Sketch on Hampstead Heath', 9 October 1875; and 'Homeless', 30 December 1876. He also engraved a mother and child with stippled faces and tight cross-hatched backgrounds to give the appropriate gloom; and a series of sketches, 'Whitsuntide Holiday Sketches' of rather crudely engraved figures against slight landscape backgrounds. Buckman signed his work: 'H BUCKMAN Sc'.

BUCKMAN, William Rice fl.1868-78
London wood engraver, illustrator who worked at East Temple Chambers, Whitefriars Street, EC (POD,1875), shared with H.Sargent (q.v.), and at 16 Clifford's Inn, EC (POD,1877-78). Houfe explains that a W.R.Buckman contributed illustrations to Good Words,1868, and Cassell's Magazine,1870.

BUCKNELL, A. fl.1883-84
Wood engraver, who engraved an illustration by F.Villiers (q.v.) to 'The Emperor and his Marshall', for the English Illustrated Magazine,1883-84. This was engraved in a rather crude manner and relied on dark gouges to fill in the stark, blank white areas.

BUDD, Nathaniel fl.1880-1900
Provincial wood engraver, who worked at 3 Queen Street, Wolverhampton (Kelly's,1880-89), then, as Nathaniel Budd and Son, 'draughtsmen', at 40 Litchfield Street (Kelly's,1900).

BULLETI, Anton L. fl.1876
Provincial wood engraver, who worked at 17 Eldon Square, Newcastle-upon-Tyne (POD,1876).

BUNCHER, A.J. and Company fl.1889-1900
Provincial wood engraving firm, with offices at 33 and 34 Whittall Street, Birmingham (Kelly's, 1889-1900).

BURBROOK, Charles Alfred fl.1890s
London wood engraver, who worked at 67 Imperial Buildings, EC (POD,1893).

BURGESS, A. fl.1866-67
London wood engraver, who worked at 7 Montpelier Road, and exhibited three wood engravings at the Royal Academy, 1866-67. These are 'Twelfth Night', Act II, scene 2; and 'All's Well that Ends Well', Act II, scene 2, both after H.C.Selous (q.v.) in 1866; and 'A Study', 1867. [Bénézit; Graves]

BURKITT and Saunderson fl.1880-1900
Provincial wood engraving firm, with an office at 25 Scale Lane, Hull (Kelly's,1880-1900).

BURLINSON, J.
The British Museum owns several of his designs, wood engraved by the Dalziel Brothers (q.v.), to Goldsmith's Works, and Ballad Stories,1863-67.

BURNE-JONES, Sir Edward Coley Bt. 1833-98
Occasional draughtsman on wood, painter, illustrator, and designer. He was born in Birmingham on 28 August 1833, educated at King Edward's School, Birmingham then at Oxford where he was influenced by the writings of John Ruskin and the paintings of Rossetti. He was a prolific painter and occasional illustrator: for Sixties magazines like Good Words, two works, 1862-63, engraved by the Dalziel Brothers (q.v.), and some books like Mrs Gatty's Parables from Nature, one work, 1865; and one work for the Dalziels' Bible Gallery, c1863, published 1880-81. Burne-Jones was in fact introduced to the Dalziels by Holman Hunt who wrote to them on 21 November 1861 (at the time when the

Dalziels were engraving all cuts for Good Words)
and asked if his friend might draw for them: 'He is
perhaps the most remarkable of all the younger men
of the profession for talent, and will undeniably, in
a few years fill the high position in general public
favour which at present he holds in the professional
world. He has yet, I think, made but few drawings
on wood, but he has had much practice in working
with the point both with pencil and pen-and-ink on
paper, and so would have no difficulty with the
material'. The Dalziels visited his studio and were
so impressed with Burne-Jones' work that they
commissioned the 'Bible Gallery' drawings and
bought his paintings. His early drawings for wood
engraving were strong, heavily outlined and almost
independent of the text itself, avoiding the common
fault of the period -- too much detail and fine line --
that, when engraved, turned into mere grey flatness.
Burne-Jones who planned to work with his fiancée
Georgiana (q.v.), was aware of the need for good
engraving and wrote in a letter to his sister-in-law,
Miss Macdonald, who liked wood engraving
'I see that for the engraving I want, the most perfect
design and beautiful drawing is needed, more than in
pictures even, for in them so many other qualities
come in and have their say...But in engraving
every faculty is needed,--simplicity, the hardest of
all things to learn--restraint in leaving out every
idea that is not wanted--perfect outline, as correct
as can be without effort, and still more essentially,
neat--and a due amount of quaintness,...As to
scribbly work...Nearly all book illustration is full
of it--drawings...that have wild work in all the
corners, stupid senseless rot that takes an artist
half a minute to sketch and an engraver half a week
to engrave...' (quoted in Harrison and Waters,
Burne Jones,pp.72-73). He returned to
illustration in 1865 with William Morris' The
Earthly Paradise and The Story of Cupid and Psyche,
both abandoned and unpublished. The last years of
Burne-Jones' life, 1892-98, were spent in
partnership with William Morris (q.v.) and the
Kelmscott Press, for which he designed and Morris
engraved illustrations. These range from various
frontispieces to A Dream of John Ball, a King's Lesson,
1892; to woodcut designs to The Golden Legend,1892;
and the most famous The Works of Geoffrey Chaucer,
1896. The style of these later designs was borrowed
from his study of Italian models, for instance, the
Hyponerotomachia, of which he owned a copy, and
from which he learned clear, simple shading
lessons. The originality of these woodcuts, with
expert typography, continued to influence private
presses well after the turn of the century.
Burne-Jones was elected ARA,1885 and ARWS,1886,
and created Baronet,1894. The British Museum owns
two designs engraved by the Dalziel Brothers,
1862-63.
[For a list of books illustrated see Houfe; for

biographies see Harrison and Waters, Burne-Jones,
1973; see also P.Fitzgerald, Burne-Jones,1976;
Burne-Jones, Arts Council,1975]

BURNE-JONES, Georgiana (née Macdonald)
fl.1850-80
Wife of the painter and illustrator Edward
Burne-Jones (q.v.) who had before her marriage
trained with Ford Madox Brown and also at the
local branch of the Birmingham Government School
of Design, when she lived in that city. Later she
collaborated with Rossetti's wife and made a book of
her husband's designs. She was expert enough at
wood engraving for the young George Du Maurier
(q.v.) to send his wife Emma to her for engraving
instruction. Ruskin wrote to her of this 'woman's
mission': 'I'm delighted to hear of the woodcutting.
It will not, I believe, interfere with any motherly
care or duty and is far more useful noble work than
any other of which feminine thought and nature are
capable. I can't imagine anything prettier or more
wifely than cutting one's husband's drawings on the
wood block--there is just the proper quality of echo
in it...' It is believed that among Georgiana's wood
engravings after her husband's designs are the works
for the abandoned The Earthly Paradise,1865-6, for
which she had earlier prepared herself with a cut,
'Ladies watching Knights Depart for Battle', c1858,
described in the Arts Council catalogue, 1975, as
'very clumsy'. During the 1860s period when
Burne-Jones worked with William Morris, Georgiana
apparently joined forced with Jane Morris and wrote
in her Memorials,1904,I,p.213, 'Oh, how happy we
were, Janey and I, busy in the morning with
needlework or wood-engraving...'.
[A.Callen, Angel in the Studio,pp.10,181]

BURNETT, William Hawtrey fl.1876-77
London wood engraver, who worked at 5 Wine Office
Court, EC (POD,1876-77). He may be related to
William H.Burnett, the landscape and architecture
painter who exhibited at the Royal Academy and the
British Institution, 1844-60.
[Bénézit; TB]

BURNHAM, Henry and Company fl.1874-92
London firm of wood engravers and draughtsmen,
with offices at 74 Fleet Street, EC (POD,1874),
35 Bouverie Street, EC (POD,1875), 80 Fleet
Street, EC (POD,1881) and 8 Sergeant's Inn, Fleet
Street, EC (POD,1892).

BURROWS, Henry fl.1850s
Wood engraver, who was originally from London
but who lived in Headington, near Oxford about
1851, where he probably worked for the noted
engraver Orlando Jewitt (q.v.).
[The Library,1964,p.326]

BURTON, E.J. fl.1847-49
Draughtsman, who contributed drawings to Punch,
1847-49 which Spielmann described as 'unimportant'.

BURTON, J.
(see Burton and Heeley)

BURTON, William Paton 1828-83
Draughtsman and landscape painter. He was born in
Madras in 1828, educated in Edinburgh, with the
architect David Bryce, but left for a travelling
career painting scenes on the Continent and in
Egypt. As a draughtsman he contributed to Willmott's
Sacred Poetry of the 16th, 17th, and 18th centuries,
1862, which White claimed was perhaps the most
important book of that year. He also drew for
A.A.Proctor's Legends and Lyrics,1865, 'all
engraved by Horace Harral (q.v.), who cannot be
congratulated upon his rendering of some blocks'
(White); and for the anthology Golden Thoughts from
Golden Fountains,1867. Here his drawings were
originally printed in sepia. Burton died near
Aberdeen on 31 December 1883. The British Museum
owns several designs engraved by the Dalziel
Brothers (q.v.), 1861-63, including cuts to
Goldsmith's Works, and Ballad Stories,1863-67.

BURTON, William Shakespeare 1830-1916
Occasional draughtsman illustrator, minor
Pre-Raphaelite painter. He studied at the Royal
Academy Schools, winning a gold medal there in
1851 and exhibited at the Royal Academy and the
Royal Institute of Painters in Watercolours, most
notably his famous painting, 'Wounded Cavalier'.
His one known illustration, 'Romance of the Rose',
was wood engraved for Once a Week,1865 (p.602).
[Houfe]

BURTON and Heeley fl.1820-89
Wood engraving and draughtsman firm, with an office
at Caxton Chambers, 14 Cranby Street, Leicester
(Kelly's,1889). The firm was probably started by
J.Burton, a wood engraver who engraved an armorial
woodcut book plate for the Town Museum Library,
Leicester, 1820, and signed it 'J Burton sc'.

BUSHNELL, A.
Draughtsman illustrator, who contributed a wood
engraved drawing to Good Words,1861.

BUSS, Robert William 1804-75
Draughtsman, illustrator and painter. He was born
in London in 1804, the son of R.W.Buss, an engraver
and enameller, and studied drawing with George Clint.
He began his carrer as a draughtsman on wood for
Charles Knight's publications, particularly the
Penny Magazine, from 1841, his drawings engraved
by I.Holloway and W.Quartley (qq.v.): also Knight's
Shakespeare, London, Old England, and a Chaucer.

Other work involved etchings on steel for the works
of Mrs Trollope, Harrison Ainsworth and Marryat.
He was also editor of the Fine Art Almanack,
wrote a book, The Principles of Caricature,1874,
and exhibited at the Royal Academy, the British
Institution and the Royal Society of British Artists,
1826-59. He died in Camden Town, 1875. The
British Museum owns his designs engraved by the
Dalziel Brothers (q.v.), 1839-47.
[For his engraved work on metal see Volume I
(with bibliography)]

BUSST, John fl.1889
Provincial wood engraver, who worked at Old
Square Chambers, Corporation Street, Birmingham
(Kelly's,1889).

BUTLER, Lady (Elizabeth) (née Thompson)
1846-1933
Illustrator, painter of battle scenes. She was born
in Lausanne in 1846, studied at South Kensington
with Kate Greenaway (q.v.), Florence and Rome,
and specialised in accurate military paintings and
equestrian subjects. She contributed drawings to
The Graphic,1873,1889 and illustrated poetry and
memoirs. She exhibited at the Fine Art Society,
1877, the Royal Academy from 1873 and various
other galleries. She died on 2 October 1933.
[E.Butler, An Autobiography,1923; Houfe; Wood]

BUTLER, James John fl.1886
London wood engraver, who worked at 73 Imperial
Buildings, Ludgate Circus, EC (POD,1886).

BUTLIN, George Louis fl.1862-84
London wood engraver of animal subjects, who
worked at 33 Essex Street, Strand, WC
(POD,1862-66), shared with W.J.Palmer and
R.H.Keene (qq.v.), and at 7 Chalcot Terrace,
Regent's Park, NW (POD,1868-71), then returned
to 33 Essex Street until 1875. He reappears at
Queen's Villas, Chingford (LSD,1880-84). The
British Museum owns a number of his animal
engravings, one after Joseph Wolf inscribed
'engraved for E.Whymper' (q.v.).

BUTTERWORTH (Charles) and Heath fl.1856-1910
London wood engraving firm, with an office at
356 Strand (POD,1856-83). The firm's name changed
to Charles Butterworth in 1884, and an office
continued at 115 Strand (POD,1889-1910).
Butterworth and Heath were a prominent engraving
firm known for competent wood engravings for the
Religious Tract Society publications such as The
Mirage of Life,1859, after John Tenniel (q.v.)
drawings; also for magazines like The Critic,1860;
Leisure Hour,1866, after Simeon Solomon (q.v.);
Sunday at Home,1869, after C.Staniland, E.Armitage
(qq.v.); a portrait of Queen Victoria, aged fifteen,

in Girl's Own Paper, after George Hayter;
portraits for Reformatory and Refuge Journal,
1874. Several of their engraved portraits and
reproductions of objects are in the British Museum.
Butterworth signed his work: 'BUTTERWORTH Sc'.
[see also White; Hake; Fincham]

BYE, John fl.1868-82
London wood engraver, who worked at 9 Essex
Street, Strand, WC (POD,1868-82), premises
shared with W.Murden, J.Desbois, H.C.Mason and
P.Roberts (qq.v.).

BYFIELD, Ann 1830-? Mary, Junior 1840-?
London wood engravers, known as the 'Misses
Byfield'. They were the daughters of the wood
engraver John Byfield (q.v.) and sisters of Edward
Byfield (q.v.), who carried on the family engraving
traditions after several members had died. They
were probably taught to engrave by their aunt Mary
Byfield (q.v.) and set up as 'artist engravers on
wood' at 47 Florence Street, Islington. Their work
included new illustrations engraved for the eighth
edition of Bradley and Goodwin's A Manual of
Illumination,1861, published for Winsor and Newton.
[The Private Library,Winter 1980]

BYFIELD, C.
Nagler lists this wood engraver, possibly related to
the Byfield family of engravers, and gives one work:
Tales of humour, gallantry and Romance,1824, after
sixteen drawings by George Cruikshank (q.v.).
These were signed: 'CB'.

BYFIELD, Ebenezer 1790-1817
London wood engraver, brother of the noted engravers
John and Mary Byfield, Senior (qq.v.). He trained in
the Byfield family wood engraving profession and
worked with his brother John and sister Mary on
Thomas Dibdin's Bibliographical Decameron,1817,
although he did not survive to see his work published
that year. He died early in 1817 at the age of twenty-
seven, leaving his engraver son, Louis (q.v.) to
continue his work. An 'E.Byfield' wood engraver
appears in the London directory once, working at
Eden Grove, Holloway (Johnstone,1817).
[Redgrave; LeBlanc; Bénézit; The Private Library,
Winter 1980]

BYFIELD, Edward 1838-60
London wood engraver, son of John Byfield (q.v.),
brother of Ann and Mary, Junior (qq.v.) and nephew
of Mary, Senior (q.v.). According to the 1851 census
he was a 'pupil to the wood engraving', although
little is known of his output. The Bodleian Library
has an engraved border for the Chiswick Press,
after a design by one of the Whittingham daughters
(q.v.). This is marked 'engraved by Mary and her
nephew Edward Byfield'. Edward also helped his aunt

by signing her business receipts, but died at the
tragically young age of twenty-two in 1860.
[The Private Library, Winter 1980; Bodleian]

BYFIELD, John 1788-1841
London wood engraver, brother of the noted
engravers Mary, Senior and Ebenezer Byfield (qq.v.),
with whom he worked. He began engraving with Mary
for Thomas Dibdin, who described him in
Reminiscences of a Literary Life, as 'an artist,
whose gratitude is equal to his ability, and whose
ability is strengthened by his care and integrity.
I owe chiefly to him and to his sister all the wood
embellishments of the Bibliotheca Spenciana, and
Tour; and the greater part of those in the
Decameron, and the whole of those in the present
work, are from the same quarter'. By the 1830s
John Byfield was engraving, again with Mary, Senior,
for Pickering-Whittingham publications, including
the ninety cuts to Pickering's Icones Veteris
Testamenti,1830 and The Dance of Death Exhibited
in Elegant Engravings...by F.Douce,1833,
engraved with W.Bonner (q.v.). He also engraved
four cuts with Mary to The London Stage,1824, in
the first two of four volumes. He worked for the
bibliographer John Martin, for whom he engraved
Martin's Bibliographical Catalogue,1834; and he
engraved a cut for an edition of Gray's Elegy,1835,
and several bookplates, listed by Fincham, in
1830 and 1840. He was known to charge as much as
£2-3 for vignette engravings, but still suffered
financial problems towards the end of his life,
probably the result of his large family of six
children. They included the noted engravers Ann,
Edward and Mary Byfield (qq.v.). John Byfield
remains a highly regarded wood engraver of the
post-Bewick period: Nagler calls him one of the
'superior still living English wood engravers'; the
DNB claims that he 'held a high position in his
profession', with works executed 'with great skill
and fidelity'. He worked first at Paradise Row,
Holloway (Johnstone,1817), then Cornwall Place,
Holloway (Pigot,1822-27), then 4 Brooksby Street,
Islington (Pigot,1832-34) and finally at 30 Upper
Park Street, Liverpool Road, Islington (Pigot,1836).
The British Museum owns his engravings after
R.Seymour (q.v.) and two intricate black-line
engraved ewers. He signed his engravings:'J.Byfield'.
[Redgrave: LeBlanc; Bénézit; Heller; DNB; Nagler;
G.Keynes, W.Pickering,1969; The Private Library,
Winter 1980]

BYFIELD, Louis 1816-86
London wood engraver, son of Ebenezer Byfield
(q.v.) but brought up by his uncle John (q.v.) and
wood engraver aunt Mary, Senior (q.v.), to become
his aunt's 'mainstay' in later life. He worked and
lived with his wife in the crowded Byfield family
home at 30 Upper Park Street, Islington, where he

engraved at least two known works: local architectural scenes for the ill-fated Islington Magazine,
July and August 1838, one of Canonbury House, and
one of St Mary's Church in 1750. After that date he
apparently set up as 'undertaker and engraver' and
perhaps engraved with his aunt Mary, contributing
to S. Lewis's History and Topography of the Parish of
St Mary's, Islington, 1842. He married twice but had
no children, and served as his aunt Mary's business
assistant during her later years, signing her
receipts. He signed his work: 'LOUIS BYFIELD SC'.
[The Private Library, Winter 1980]

BYFIELD, Mary, Senior 1795-1871
Prominent London wood engraver, best known for
her engravings for Pickering-Whittingham
publications. She was the sister of the wood
engravers Ebenezer and John (qq.v.) with whom she
worked. By the age of sixteen she was professionally
competent as a wood engraver, and appeared in the
London directories as such from 1822. Her early
work was for Thomas Dibdin's Bibliomania and
Typographical Antiquities and she engraved with her
brother John, Bibliotheca Spenciana, Tour, and
Bibliographica Decameron. She then began her
association with the younger Charles Whittingham
(q.v.), the printer-engraver who was the same age
and with whom she worked for over forty years.
She engraved almost all the Chiswick Press
ornaments for him, continuing to engrave after his
retirement in 1860. One of the most important early
commissions for him was blocks for Holbein's
'Dance of Death' included in Illustrations of the Old
Testament, 1830, engraved with John and printed
by Whittingham. Through Whittingham she began an
association with the publisher William Pickering for
whom she produced many fine books, including
Queen Elizabeth's Prayer Book of 1569, 1853. Here
every page has a Byfield engraving based on
sixteenth-century designs and work by Holbein,
Dürer and others. There was a total of over a
hundred blocks engraved for this book alone, and
since they were detachable they were reused later
in other Whittingham publications. McLean
declared it 'a triumph of printing as well as
illustration and topography'. Many of Mary Byfield's
engravings for Whittingham were done after designs
by his daughters, Charlotte and Elizabeth
Whittingham (qq.v.), whom she had trained to draw
on wood. Generally these were elaborate floral or
insect encrusted borders which she engraved in
fine stipple or intricate black-line. (There are a
number of these engravings and the preliminary
designs in the Constance Meade Collection,
Bodleian Library.) Mary Byfield worked from the
Islington area of London. The London directories
first list her at Cornwall Place, Holloway
(Pigot, 1822-27), then 4 Brooksby Street, Islington
(Pigot, 1832-34). By 1842 she had moved to a

converted fourteenth-century priory at Canonbury
Place, Islington. She is next listed in the
directories at 30 Upper Park Street, Islington
(POD, 1844) which was the crowded family home of
her brother John Byfield, his wife, their six
children and their orphaned nephew Louis Byfield
(q.v.), whom Mary trained and adopted. In fact the
other six children also helped their aunt to
engrave so that Mary remained with the
family until at least 1861, when she disappears
from the directories. In addition Mary Byfield
worked with the most proficient draughtsmen and
wood engravers of the 1840s period. She engraved
with Orlando Jewitt (q.v.) on his famous Memorials
of Cambridge, 1841. Through Whittingham she was
placed in contact with many fine artist-engravers,
including J.A. Montagu (q.v.) the strong medievalist
draughtsman, S. Williams and T.H. Shepherd (qq.v.).
The architectural draughtsman Henry Shaw (q.v.)
employed her to engrave an alphabet book of stunning,
intricate designs published as E. Jesse's A Summer's
Day at Windsor, and A Visit to Eton. The Bodleian
Library owns a highly uncharacteristic grotesque
which she engraved for a joke--a full page head of
'Anthanasius Gasker, Esq.' for the 'Library of
Useless Knowledge', a parody of Charles Knight's
'Library of Useful Knowledge' series of the period.
For all her work Mary Byfield achieved small but
enthusiastic critical support: the writer and wood
engraver G.W. Marx (q.v.) wrote of her in his
The Art of Drawing and Engraving on Wood, 1881,
that since wood engraving was now 'one of the
branches of art labour in which ladies may engage
and practise with every probability of success and
fair remuneration', the example of Mary Byfield
should be followed: 'This lady's productions were in
all respects, equal to those of her compeers,
J. Byfield and [Abraham ?] Mason'. Mary Byfield
signed her engravings: 'Mary Byfield Sc' or
'BYFIELD SC'. This makes identification especially
difficult since much of her early work was done
with John Byfield as 'BYFIELD Sc'.
[For a discussion of the Byfields see The Private
Library, Winter, 1980; also for relations with
Pickering see Sir G. Keynes, William Pickering,
1960; McLean, Victorian Book Design;
A. Warren, Charles Whittingham, 1896]

BYFIELD, Mary, Junior
(see Byfield, Ann)

BYRNE, Claude fl. 1880s
Draughtsman illustrator and painter, who worked at
Rathmines, Dublin. He exhibited at the Royal
Hibernian Academy, 1884 and contributed drawings
of Irish distress to the Illustrated London News, 1886.

BYRNE, E.R. fl.1870s
Draughtsman, who contributed wood engraved
drawings of marine subjects to The Graphic,1873.

CALDECOTT, Randolph 1846-86
Draughtsman illustrator, watercolourist and
sculptor. He was born in Chester on 22 March 1846,
educated at King's School, worked at a Manchester
bank, while he developed his sketching skill and
contributed to local periodicals Will o' the Wisp,
1867, and The Sphinx,1867. This was followed by a
trip to London and success at drawing for London
Society,1871-72, and Punch,1872,1883. His drawing
on wood was taught by the prominent wood engraver
Joseph Swain (q.v.): 'I sent one block to Swain, who
returned it as too sketchy and asked me to try again.
I did so; and he then sent me blocks for the other
scenes. After these had been in his hands a few days
I received a note from him to say that they were
accepted and if I liked to send any more drawings to
him he would shew them for approval' (quoted in
M.Hutchins, Yours Pictorially,1976,p.16). He drew
travel sketches for the Harz Mountains,1872, and
for The Graphic,1873-86, and collaborated with the
noted wood engraver James D.Cooper (q.v.) on the
first successful double venture, Old Christmas, and
Bracebridge Hall,1876-77. These were seen by the
wood engraver Edmund Evans (q.v.) who was
looking for a new artist to draw for his colour
printed toybooks series, and Caldecott began
work on the first of sixteen, The House that Jack
Built,1878. The series ended in 1885 with The Great
Panjandrum Himself. He also drew for Mrs Ewing,
who was less than pleased with the expensive and
dilatory Evans, and although some of his drawings
were process engraved, this proved unsuccessful
and Evans had to be re-instated. Caldecott also
sculpted relief plaques, painted oils and watercolours
and exhibited at the Royal Academy,1872-85. He died
on an American sketching tour, in St Augustine,
Florida, on 12 February 1886.
[For a complete account of his life and work, see
R.Engen, Randolph Caldecott,1976; also H.Blackburn,
Randolph Caldecott,1886]

CALLAWAY, Reverend William Frederick fl.1855-61
Amateur draughtsman for Punch, to which he
contributed about two sketches, 1855, although one
had been redrawn by Leech (q.v.) before publication.
He was also a Baptist minister of York and
Birmingham. He exhibited at the Royal Academy, the
British Institution and others, from 1855-61.
[Spielmann, Bénézit; TB]

CALLIE, William fl.1870s
Wood engraver, who worked in London at Aldine
Chambers, Paternoster Row (POD,1875).

CALVERT, Edward 1799-1883
Occasional wood engraver, noted for his series of
Arcadian visions which remain a major influence on
modern wood engraving; also a noted painter. He
was born on 20 September 1799 in Appledore, near
Bideford, Devon and joined the Navy at fifteen years
old, which he left in 1820 to become an artist. He
settled in Plymouth where he studied under
A.B.Johns, a friend of Turner and fellow landscape
painter, and came to London at the end of 1824
where he was admitted to the Royal Academy Schools.
He soon became one of the group of artists, 'the
little band of brothers', gathered round William
Blake (q.v.) including: Samuel Palmer (q.v.), George
Richmond, Francis Oliver Finch, Henry Walter and
Welby Sherman (q.v.). When Blake died on 12 August
1827 Calvert and George Richmond were at the funeral.
He exhibited at the Royal Academy from 1825-36,
and during his so-called 'Shoreham' period, 1827-31,
he produced his series of remarkable wood
engravings on Arcadian themes. From then on he
painted in oil and watercolour mainly to please
himself, mostly on the mythological subjects which
he found so fascinating after a visit to Greece. He
died in London on 14 July 1883. As a wood engraver
Calvert was one of the most talented of all artist-
engravers although his output was noticeably small:
he made just eleven prints, of which just seven
were from wood blocks, two being on copper and
two lithographs. He was very aware of the
difficulties of resolving the craftsman versus
artistic nature of the print, and although it seems
he was a self-taught engraver, he had the ability to
understand the capabilities of the medium.
His wood engraving style borrowed heavily
from his mentor William Blake, but he was
more confident and direct. 'With nothing
am I more impressed than with the
necessity in all great work, for suppressing the
workman and all the mean dexterity of practice',
he wrote of engraving. 'Wood engraving, of all
things, most ready for dexterity, reads us a good
lesson'. His method of engraving on wood began
with a drawing directly on the block, which he cut
with various tools, such as a tinter, a round
scorper, spitsticker and burin. He occasionally
used the black-line style, but in this he preferred
the less sharply contrasted use of flicks and dots,
rather than the more methodical parallel lines or
cross-hatching. All seven of his blocks were small
and square cut, and show no sign of the lowering
process used by Bewick (q.v.). His subject matter
was generally landscapes in a romantic mood, less
stylised or symbolic than Blake's, although Blake's
influence continued in the engravings until 1830.
Most of his wood engravings were nominally
published as soon as they were completed, the first,
'The Ploughman, dated 22 September 1827. This was
followed by 'The Cyder Feast', 10 October 1827;

'The Brook', 29 June 1829; 'The Lady with the Rooks', 1829; 'The Return Home', 1 March 1830; 'The Chamber Idyll', n.d. [1831] ; and the unpublished works, 'The Bacchante', probably engraved by Calvert, a second version being by Welby Sherman (q.v.). There is also an eighth work, a 'Landscape', designed by Calvert and said to be engraved by his son Samuel (q.v.). Calvert's wood engravings were known only to a small circle of friends until they appeared in some memorial exhibitions after his death and when his son Samuel had all his father's published line and wood engravings reprinted from the original plates and blocks for his Memoir, 1893. Although here much of the wood engraved delicacy was lost, nevertheless this book exposed Calvert, the printmaker, to a larger public and made his reputation, albeit posthumously. It was followed about twenty years later, in 1904, by a second reprint of just thirty copies by the Carfax Gallery. By then, Calvert the wood engraver had established a considerable reputation among the revivalists of the art, who readily admitted their debt to this forgotten master. Hind claimed that he held a position 'unique as a reflection of Blake's spirit among the wood engravings of Blake's own contemporaries'. Also from his most highly regarded 'The Chamber Idyll' and the second most popular 'The Cyder Feast', of which more reproductions are made than any other of his works, Calvert remains today one of the major influences on modern wood engraving.
[For a discussion of Calvert's engravings see A.J.Finberg in Print Collector's Quarterly, Vol.17, 1930; also DNB; S.Calvert, Memoir of Edward Calvert, 1893; L.Binyon, Followers of William Blake, 1925; Arts Council, S.Palmer and His Circle, 1957; and biography by Raymond Lister, Edward Calvert, 1962]

CALVERT, Frederick fl.1890s
Wood engraver, who worked in London at 58 Fleet Street, EC (Kelly's, 1893), which he shared with W.F.Jeffries (q.v.). Calvert may in fact be related to the watercolourist, engraver Frederick Calvert, listed by Bénézit and TB, who worked in London 1811-44, produced thirty-nine plates to Picturesque Views of Staffordshire and Shropshire, 1830, worked for the Archaeological Journal and exhibited from 1827-44 at the British Institution and the Society of British Artists.

CALVERT, John fl.1872-76
Provincial wood engraver, who worked at 21 St Nicholas Street, Leicester; by 1876 he had expanded his business to 21 and 23 St Nicholas Street (Kelly's, 1872-76).

CALVERT, Samuel
Son of the noted wood engraver Edward Calvert (q.v.), who first reprinted his father's work in his Memoir of Edward Calvert, 1893. It is believed that Samuel wood engraved the unpublished design, 'Landscape', after his father's drawing, of which the only known impression is in the British Museum. It depicts two sheep drinking, while in the distance there is a cottage and a flock of sheep grazing on a hillside.

CALVERT, William fl.1859-61
London wood engraver, who worked at 10 East Harding Street, EC (POD, 1859-61).

CAMERON, George fl.1860s
London wood engraver, who worked at 1 Shawfield Street, Chelsea, SW (POD, 1863). Fincham lists a bookplate in the Chippendale style signed 'G.Cameron sc'.

CAMERON, Hugh 1835-1918
Draughtsman, portrait and genre painter, who was born in Edinburgh in 1835, where he studied at the Trustees Academy. He worked in Edinburgh and at Largs, travelled on the Continent, was elected ARSA, 1859, RSA, 1869, and RWS, 1878, and also exhibited at the Grosvenor Gallery, the Royal Academy and the Royal Society of British Artists. He is listed here for his drawings to the wood engraved publications, Pen and Pencil Pictures from the Poets, 1866; two of the fifty total wood engravings to Idyllic Pictures, 1867; and to Good Words.
[Houfe; White]

CAMPBELL, Edward Voullaire fl.1847-90
London wood engraver, who worked at 15 Edward Street, Wenlock Road (POD, 1847), 1 Charles Street, City Road (POD, 1852-57) and 13 Bouverie Street, Fleet Street, EC (POD, 1862-71) which he shared with A.Gascoine (q.v.). By 1872 he had moved to the prominent wood engraver district, 6 Red Lion Court, EC (POD, 1872-90), which he shared during the years 1888-90 with E.Wright (q.v.).

CAMPBELL, J.G. and Company fl.1872-1900
Provincial wood engraving firm, with an office at Press Lane, 194 High Street West, Bishopwearmouth, Durham, Sunderland (Kelly's, 1872-1900).

CAMPFIELD, G.
Wood engraver, known to have engraved the Burne-Jones designed title-page to William Morris' The Earthly Paradise (original edition, 1868) when it was published in subsequent editions.

CANHAM, Arthur Charles fl.1879-1910
London wood engraver, who worked first in
partnership as Purchese and Canham (q.v.), then
from 1890 independently from an office at
168 Fleet Street, EC (POD,1890-1901); by 1910
this address was 152 Fleet Street, EC.

CANHO, Samuel fl.1890s
London wood engraver, who worked at
10 Featherstone Buildings, WC (POD,1896).

CARLILE, Lieutenant W.O. fl.1873
Draughtsman, known to have contributed a wood
engraved drawing to the Illustrated London News,
1873. He was elected RA.

CARMICHAEL, John Wilson 1800-68
Draughtsman illustrator and marine painter, born
in Newcastle-upon-Tyne in 1800. He went to sea at
an early age, and was apprenticed to a shipbuilder,
during which time he made drawings of his work.
He worked primarily in watercolour, but from 1825
tried oils, and became a regular exhibitor to the
London galleries, where he had moved in 1845.
He also worked as draughtsman for the Illustrated
London News which sent him to the Baltic during the
Crimean War, 1853-56. He left London in 1862 due
to illness and settled in Scarborough where he died
on 2 May 1868.
[Houfe]

CARPENTER, John fl.1890-91
London wood engraver who worked at 57 Bishopsgate
Street Within, EC (POD,1890-91), which he shared
with Herbert Baynes (q.v.).

CARPENTER, William 1818-99
Wood engraver, draughtsman, painter and etcher of
oriental subjects. He was born in London in 1818,
son of the portrait painter, Mrs M.S.Carpenter
and the radical writer William Carpenter. He was a
fellow pupil, with Henry Vizetelly (q.v.), of the
noted wood engraver Orrin Smith (q.v.), and in
addition to training as wood engraver he wrote plays.
He gave both up to join the army, and was posted to
India where he sketched the country's manners and
customs for some of the first colour reproductions
to appear in the Illustrated London News,1857-59.
These were done during the Indian Mutiny, a period
of intense British interest in that country. A number
of these works were later exhibited at South
Kensington in 1881. Vizetelly recalls how Carpenter
returned to England after pleading insanity.
[Houfe; Vizetelly, Glances Back]

CARPENTER, William John fl.1878-88
London wood engraver, perhaps related to William
Carpenter (q.v.) since POD lists him as 'William
John Carpenter junior'. He worked from

168 Rotherthithe New Road, SE and 148 Cheapside,
EC (POD,1878-81), the following year retaining only
the Rotherhithe address (POD,1882-88). Bénézit
and TB record a William John Carpenter,
architectural painter in oil and watercolour, who
worked in London and exhibited from 1885-95 at
the New Watercolour Society and the Society of
British Artists.

CARPUE, Daniel fl.1830s
London wood engraver, who worked at 3 Old
Montague Street, Whitechapel (Pigot,1836).

CARR, David 1847-1920
Draughtsman, figure and bird painter, born in
London in 1847, educated at King's College, London
and articled to an engineer. He left to become an
art student under Legros at the Slade, then worked
in Paris in 1881. He exhibited at the New
Watercolour Society, the Grosvenor Gallery, the
New Gallery, the Royal Academy from 1875 and the
Royal Institute of Painters in Watercolours, and
also designed several West Country houses. As a
draughtsman on wood he designed birds and landscapes
for the Pall Mall Gazette, and the English Illustrated
Magazine,1884-87, notably illustrations to W.Syme's
'Loch Fyne', engraved by O.Lacour (q.v.). He died
on 25 December 1920.
[Houfe; Bénézit; TB; Who's Who,1911; Graves]

CARR, Francis (Frank) Arthur fl.1878-96
London draughtsman and wood engraver, who worked
at 233 Strand (POD,1878-79), 10 Duke Street,
Adelphi, WC (POD,1880-81), 114 Farringdon Road,
WC (POD,1886-92), and 33 Wharton Street, WC
(POD,1895-96).

CARRALL, Michael William fl.1822-23
Provincial wood engraver, who worked at Walm-Gate,
York (Pigot,1822-23).

CARRERAS, Theobald 1829-95
English wood engraver, born in 1829 of Spanish
parents. He was the engraving pupil of J.Andrew
(q.v.) and established himself as a successful wood
engraver for over twenty years. The British
Museum owns a roundel after Sir Noel Paton and
a Gainsborough portrait engraving. TB claims that
Carreras' work was often mistaken for
J.D.Cooper's (q.v.). He signed his engravings:
'T Carreras sc'.
[see Percy Roberts MS in the British Museum]

CARRICK, J.Mulcaster fl.1854-78
Draughtsman illustrator and painter of landscapes
in the Pre-Raphaelite style. He exhibited these at
the British Institution,1854, the Royal Institute of
Painters in Watercolours, and the Royal Society of
British Artists, 1856. Some were oil painted versions

of illustrations. He drew four wood engraved illustrations to Charles MacKay's The Home Affections, 1858, and some to A.A.Procter's Legends and Lyrics, 1865. The British Museum owns his landscape designs wood engraved by the Dalziel Brothers (q.v.), 1857-58.
[Houfe; White]

CARTER, C.
Little is known of this wood engraver who worked after portrait paintings of noted eighteenth century English artists. The British Museum owns two such wood engravings: 'Hon. Mary Graham' after T.Gainsborough, and 'Margaret, Countess of Carlisle', after J.Reynolds.
[Hake]

CARTER, Harry (Henry) 1821-80
Prominent wood engraver, magazine proprietor, born in Ipswich in 1821, who set up as a London wood engraver, notably for the Illustrated London News in the 1840s. He established himself as 'Henry' [sic] Carter and Company' at 114 Upper Stamford Street (POD, 1846), which became 'Henry Carter' when it moved to 112 Fleet Street, EC (POD, 1848). During this period he became acquainted with the prominent wood engraver W.J.Linton (q.v.). He then moved to America about 1848, and under the pseudonym Frank Leslie, established Frank Leslie's Illustrated Newspaper (American version of the British Illustrated London News) for which he engaged Linton as his artistic director, thus helping to establish that engraver in America. Linton repaid the favour by mentioning Carter in his own autobiography and also in History of American Wood Engraving. Carter made a fortune from an empire of illustrated publications which he skilfully managed. He died on 10 January 1880 in New York.
[TB; Bénézit; Linton, Memories and History of American Wood Engraving]

CARTER, Samuel John 1835-92
Draughtsman illustrator and painter of animal subjects, who was born in Swaffham, Norfolk, in 1835, studied in Norwich and exhibited paintings at the British Institution, 1863-66, the Royal Academy, the Royal Society of British Artists, 1861-68, and the Grosvenor Gallery. He achieved a considerable reputation for his animal drawings and sketches of farm shows in the Illustrated London News, 1867-89, many of these engraved by the prominent engraver of animal subjects John Greenaway (q.v.). He also contributed to The Graphic, 1886.
[Houfe; Bénézit]

CARTER, Stephen Salter fl.1848-67
London wood engraver, who worked at 6 Bouverie Street, Fleet Street, EC (POD, 1848). By 1856 he

had joined forces to become Stephen Carter and Rowland, with an office at 4 Bradley Terrace, Wandsworth Road (POD, 1856-60). By 1863 Carter was working on his own at new premises, 48 Paternoster Row, EC (POD, 1863-67).

CARTER and Dalton fl.1871-74
Wood engraving firm, probably the partnership of Stephen Carter and James Dalton (qq.v.), with a London office at 21 Paternoster Row, EC (POD, 1871-74).

CARTWRIGHT and Rattray fl.1889-1900
Provincial wood engraving firm, with offices at Caxton Works, Hyde, and 28 Brown Street, Manchester (Kelly's, 1889-1900).

CASELLA, Miss Julia
Sculptor, who contributed a wood engraved illustration to The Graphic, 1880, and exhibited at the Grosvenor Gallery, 1885.

CASEY, James R. and Son fl.1880s
London draughtsman firm, with an office at 6 Godliman Street, EC and 4 Paul's Bakehouse Court, EC (Kelly's, 1889).

CASH, John fl.1880s
Provincial wood engraver, who worked at 8 Mosley Street, Newcastle-upon-Tyne (Kelly's, 1889).

CASSELL, Petter and Galpin
Prominent publisher of wood engraved illustrations, which commissioned some of the period's most skilful engravers, such as John Greenaway (q.v.). There is an indication that the firm also issued wood engravings under its own name, namely those for the periodical Once a Week, after Paul Gray, signed 'C P & G Sc' (from a copy in the Bodleian Library).

CASSON, William fl.1865-1910
London wood engraver, who worked at 3 Mary Avenue, EC (POD, 1865-68), 24 Bucklersbury, EC (POD, 1872-84), and 62 and 63 Basinghall Street, WC (POD, 1886-1910).

CATHCART, Frederick Henry fl.1881-94
London wood engraver, who worked at 152 Fleet Street, EC (POD, 1881-88), the office shared with H. Prater and A.Scott (qq.v.); and 11 Ludgate Hill. EC (POD, 1889-94), shared with H.Prater again from 1893.

CATTELL, Arthur Sylvans and Company fl.1881-84
London wood engraving firm, with offices at 17 and 18 Bear Alley, EC (POD, 1881-82), then 28 Farringdon Street, EC, and 16,17 and 18 Bear

Alley, EC (POD,1883-84). The firm also specialised in 'zinco typography'.

CATTERMOLE, George 1800-68
Draughtsman illustrator, watercolourist, born in Dickleburgh, Norfolk in 1800, brother of the topographical artist Reverend R.Cattermole and uncle of the illustrator Charles Cattermole. He worked first as an architectural draughtsman and contributed to Britton's English Cathedrals,1832-36, but by the 1830s was specialising in historic incidents, prompted by his own edition of Poetical Prose Works of Sir W.Scott, drawn in fine, intricate pen lines, sometimes re-drawing works in watercolour. He achieved considerable success as an illustrator of Charles Dickens, notably Barnaby Rudge and The Old Curiosity Shop in Dickens' Master Humphrey's Clock,1841, engraved by Charles Gray (q.v.). He also exhibited at the Old Watercolour Society and the Royal Academy, 1819, and the British Institution, 1827, refused a knighthood in 1839, and was patronised by the Queen, but failed in later life as an oil painter. He was elected AOWS,1822, and OWS,1833. He died in London in 1868.

CHABOT, Charles fl.1844-51
London wood engraver, who worked at 9A Skinner Street, Snowhill (POD,1844-51). Bénézit and TB list a Charles Chabot, London lithographer, 1815-82.
[Wakeman and Bridson]

CHADWICK, John William fl.1880-1900
Provincial wood engraver and draughtsman, born in England. He worked in Birmingham at 56 Ann Street (Kelly's,1880), 100 Colmore Row (Kelly's,1889) and Gothic Arcade, Snowhill (Kelly's,1900). His son was the landscape painter Ernest Albert Chadwick.

CHALK, Frederick fl.1860s
London wood engraver, who worked at 37 Castle Street, Holborn, EC (POD,1865), an office which he shared with E.S.Gascoine (q.v.).

CHALON, Alfred Edward 1780-1860
Draughtsman, portrait and history painter, who was born in Geneva in 1780 the younger brother of the artist John Chalon. He moved to Kensington where he and his brother worked for the rest of their lives. Chalon entered the Royal Academy Schools in 1797, and exhibited at the Royal Academy from 1810. He was primarily a watercolourist, noted for his fashionable portraits of famous contemporaries; he was Painter in Watercolour to Queen Victoria, founded the Sketching Society in 1808, exhibited at the British Institution, 1807-38 and the Royal Academy, 1810-60 and was elected ARA in 1812, and RA, 1816. As a draughtsman illustrator he was noted for brown

wash caricatures intended for private circulation only. He illustrated several books with his portrait paintings, and contributed a design for wood engraving to the Illustrated London News,1843. He died at Campden Hill, Kensington, 3 October 1860. [Houfe; Wood]

'CHAM' Comte Amedée Charles Henri de Noé 1819-79
French draughtsman on wood and lithographic caricaturist, who was born in Paris on 26 January 1819, tried study at the Ecole Polytechnique, but turned instead to a drawing career, working under the caricaturist Charlet and with Paul Delaroche. He rose to the height of the caricaturist profession, publishing his first series of lithographs in 1839. He worked in London during the autumn of 1843 and scandalised the British public with his drawings of the Queen and Albert. These were reprinted in England in the Pictorial Times (the paper, founded in 1843 by Henry Vizetelly (q.v.) and, ironically, printed by Spottiswoode, Printer to the Queen). Vizetelly recalls how 'Cham', as he signed his work, was an 'exceedingly rapid draughtsman.... [although it was] evident he did not care two straws about depicting either minute or broad shades of character'. He cites the time when Mark Lemon, then editor of Punch, sent a large bundle of boxwood blocks to Cham for filling and how Lemon was amazed when the entire bundle was returned the next morning, each block completely covered and with a note asking for 'more woods'. His work appeared in Punch, in 1859. Cham died in September 1879.
[Beraldi; Gusman; Vizetelly, Glances Back; Houfe]

CHANDLER Brothers fl.1888-90
London wood engraving firm, with an office at 328 High Holborn, WC (POD,1888-90).

CHAPMAN, Captain E.F.
Amateur draughtsman illustrator, who travelled to Asia in 1874 and returned sketches on wood of the Yakund Expedition for engraving in the Illustrated London News.

CHARLTON, George Edmund fl.1880s
London wood engraver, who worked at 112 Fleet Street, EC (POD,1886), which he shared with A.Gascoine (q.v.).

CHARLTON, John 1849-1917
Draughtsman illustrator, painter of animal and battle subjects, who was born in Bamburgh, Northumberland in 1849 and studied at the Newcastle School of Art under W.B.Scott (q.v.) and in London at South Kensington under J.D.Watson (q.v.). He became noted for society

and royal subjects, which he drew in London, his home from 1874. Two years later he began as artist for <u>The Graphic</u>, and provided illustrations for their wood engravers from 1876-95, notably sketches of the Egyptian Campaign of 1882 which led to his paintings of battle scenes and a reputation as a leading military painter. He exhibited these at the New Gallery, the Royal Academy, the Royal Scottish Academy and the Royal Society of British Artists from 1871, where he was elected RBA,1882, and ROI,1887. He died in London on 5 November 1917. [Houfe; Wood]

CHASEMORE, Archibald fl.1868-1901
Draughtsman illustrator, first associated with <u>Punch</u> which was then under the careful eye of its editor Mark Lemon, who proposed his first contribution: 'You may try your hand at a large drawing, but let it be broad fun. We don't want any more ladies and pretty children'. Chasemore's first work was altered by Charles Keene, but he contributed thirty-three drawings on wood to <u>Punch</u> from 1868-75 and one belatedly in 1879. Then he was taken up by the Dalziels for their rival comic paper, <u>Judy</u>, to which he contributed drawings from 1875-89, also to their later <u>Ally Sloper's Half Holiday</u>. He later drew for <u>Pick-Me-Up</u>,1901 and the <u>Boy's Own Paper</u>. Some of his work appeared in the London galleries from 1874-78, but his style, generally in pen and ink, was rather stiff although his political subjects were more competent and, according to Houfe, 'amusing and collectible'.
[Bénézit; TB; Spielmann; Houfe]

CHATTO, William Andrew 1799-1864
Although neither a wood engraver nor draughtsman on wood, Chatto's name as an early chronicler of wood engraving is important to include here. With John Jackson (q.v.) he produced the pioneering <u>Treatise on Wood Engraving</u>,1839, with a revised second edition with added material by Henry Bohn, 1861. This had a major influence on the revival of wood engraving, and was followed by Chatto's <u>Gems of Wood Engraving from the Illustrated London News</u>, 1848. But, as W.J.Linton points out in his <u>Masters of Wood Engraving</u>,1889, Chatto 'was only a most conscientious and excellent bibliographer, not by any means qualified, even with such help as he had from Jackson, to criticise and judge the works which he chronicled and described'. Indeed Chatto's real connection with wood engraving was the fact he was a Newcastle man like his collaborator John Jackson, both inhabitants early on of the city which had, through Bewick, played the primary role in reviving wood engraving. But Chatto soon moved to London where he worked in the wine trade and used his spare time to write topographical essays under the pseudonyms Stephen Oliver,Junior and Joseph Fume. He tried to be thorough and the real value of his

<u>Treatise</u> was his reliance on information given during interviews with Bewick's apprentices such as Edward Willis and William Harvey, also E.Landells and C.Nesbit (qq.v.). But in the end his appreciation of Bewick in the <u>Treatise</u> shows little knowledge of the facts.

CHEFDEVILLE, L. fl.1889-90
Wood engraver, known to have engraved for the <u>English Illustrated Magazine</u>,1889-90, 'Hoorn and Enkhuizen' after a drawing by Reginald Blomfield, and 'Potters in Rhineland' after Harry Furniss.

CHEFFINS, Richard Albert (Alfred) fl.1868-91
London wood engraver, who worked at 15 Essex Street, Strand, WC (POD,1868), shared with R.S.Marriott (q.v.), 46 Fleet Street, EC (POD,1870-72), 24 Curistor Street, EC (POD,1873-74), 268 Strand, WC (POD,1875-77) and 42 Essex Street, Strand, WC (POD,1878-79), where he remained until 1886, the number changing first to 9 (1880), then 8 (1885). He then moved to 2 Johnson's Court, Fleet Street, EC (POD,1887-88), 169 Fleet Street, EC (POD,1889) and 4 then 17 Gough Square, EC (POD,1890-91). He may be related to the London lithographers Charles F. and Charles Richard Cheffins.
[Wakeman and Bridson]

CHELTNAM, Charles S. fl.1850s
Prominent wood engraver, who began his career as an assistant to Smith and Linton (q.v.) during the early days of the <u>Illustrated London News</u>, for which they engraved after prominent watercolourists. He joined forces in partnership as Smith and Cheltnam (q.v.), working in London from 85 Hatton Garden (POD,1851). He engraved Richard Doyle's illustrations to Ruskin's <u>King of the Golden River</u>, 1850-51 and various half and full page illustrations to the <u>Illustrated London News</u>,1852-54, after paintings by J.P.Knight, C.Beyas and W.Hensley. His style is clear, though the figures are rather poorly engraved. Cheltnam had set up on his own by 1856, and worked at 1 Barnard's Inn, Holborn (POD,1856).
[W.J.Linton, <u>Masters of Wood Engraving</u>]

CHESHIRE, George fl.1890s
London wood engraver, who worked at 1 Norfolk Street, Strand, WC (POD,1895), which he shared with G.Meek and R.Cousins (qq.v.).

CHESHIRE, William and James Reynolds fl.1862-1901
London wood engravers and draughtsmen. William Cheshire began in partnership as Cheshire and Dickenson, 48 Paternoster Row, EC (POD,1862), then 2 Ivy Lane, Newgate Street, EC (POD,1863) and the following year worked at the same address on his own. He moved to 42 Paternoster Row, EC

(POD, 1867-78), during which time he joined with James Reynolds Cheshire, with whom he worked until at least 1896. By 1879 they had opened a new office at 23 Holborn Viaduct, EC (POD, 1879-1901). The firm engraved full page illustrations to the Illustrated London News, 1877, the Art Annual, 1885 (a whole length portrait of the painter Sir John Millais), and English Illustrated Magazine, 1883-84, also notable animal illustrations of Charles Whymper and those of J.W.North (qq.v.) to Richard Jeffries' 'Summer in Somerset', 1887-88. The British Museum owns an engraving of humming birds after Charles Whymper. They signed their work: 'W.J.R.Cheshire sc', 'W. & J.R.Cheshire'.

CHILDS, C.K. fl.1850s
Wood engraver and draughtsman, who produced a series of drawings which he engraved for the Art Journal, 1850. These included portraits of William Westall, James Ward, David Octavius Hill, William Linton and William Muller. The British Museum owns the Muller work, a drawing after a sculpted bust and also an engraving of the stairs to the Palace of Xerxes. He signed his engravings: 'C K CHILDS D. ET SC'.
[Hake]

CHILDS, George
Nineteenth century black-line wood engraver. The British Museum owns a series of intricate patterned engravings of Indian temples attributed to him. He signed his work: 'G CHILDS'.

CHINN, Joseph fl.1880s
Provincial wood engraver, who worked at Lyceum Chambers, 97 Hanover Street, Liverpool (Kelly's, 1889).

CHIPMAN, J.G.
Nineteenth century wood engraver. The British Museum owns a wharf scene engraved in black-line style with a stark white sky for contrast.

CITY Wood Engraving Company fl.1889-1900
Provincial engraving firm, with an office at Arcade Chambers, St Mary's Gate, Manchester (Kelly's, 1889-1900). There was also a London office from 1893, managed by Richard Goodhind (q.v.) at 138 Fleet Street, EC (POD, 1893-96).

CLARK, James
Wood engraver, who was apprenticed to the Dalziel Brothers (q.v.). He remained with them after his training and worked as a Dalziel assistant for over forty years.
[Dalziels' Record]

CLARKE, Miss A. fl.1840s
Wood engraver associated with the publications of Charles Knight (q.v.). She engraved for Knight's Penny Magazine, September 1841, cuts after Anelay (q.v.); also cuts to Knight's edition of William Lane's The Arabian Nights' Entertainments, 1839. Copies of these are in the Constance Meade Collection, Oxford. Miss A.Clarke may be related to Harriet Ludlow Clarke (q.v.).

CLARKE, Edward Francis C. fl.1867-87
Draughtsman illustrator, painter and architect. He practised in London, where he exhibited from 1872-87 at the New Watercolour Society, the Royal Society of British Artists, 1882-84, the Royal Institute of Painters in Watercolours and the Royal Scottish Academy. He is listed here for his illustrations wood engraved in the Churchman's Shilling Magazine, 1867, also Dark Blue, 1871-73.
[Houfe; White]

CLARKE, Harriet Ludlow fl.1840s
Wood engraver of landscape and topographical subjects. She engraved 'The Avenue, Hampton Court' for Charles Knight's 'The Land We Live In' series, 1847-, and a series of dogs after drawings by Edwin Landseer. Both are in the British Museum. She signed her engravings: 'H L CLARKE' and 'H CLARKE SCULP'.

CLARKE, Joseph and Son fl.1889-1900
Provincial wood engraving firm, with offices at Edgar Street, Princess Street, and 28 Kennedy Street, Manchester (Kelly's, 1889-1900).

CLARKE, Joseph Clayton 'Kyd' fl.1883-94
Draughtsman illustrator and caricaturist, who drew wood engraved illustrations for an edition of Dickens in 1883, and a caricature of Beardsley in 1894.
[Houfe; Bénézit]

CLARKE, Miss Maude V. fl.1887-90
Draughtsman illustrator, who contributed to the English Illustrated Magazine, 1887, the Illustrated London News, 1889, and the Sporting and Dramatic News, 1890.

CLAXTON, Adelaide (Mrs George Turner) fl.1858-c1905
Draughtsman and watercolourist for wood engraving, the daughter of the artist Marshall Claxton and sister of Florence (qq.v.). She and her sister were taken in their teens around the world at which time they developed their skills at drawing satirically 'the social follies of both hemispheres', as Henry Vizetelly explained. He secured their drawings for his Illustrated Times, and both were set on their careers of watercolouring and drawing for wood engraved books and magazines. These included

A Shillingsworth of Sugar Plums,1867; Brainy Odds & Ends,1900; and contributions to magazines like the Illustrated London News,1858; the Illustrated Times,1859-66; London Society,1862-65,1870; Judy,1871-79; Bow Bells; Echoes; and Sidelights on English Society,1881. She also exhibited pictures at the Royal Academy, the Royal Society of British Artists, 1865-76, the Society of Women Artists, 1880-89, and the Society of British Artists. She established a London office as draughtsman at 319 Strand, WC (Kelly's,1889), then 62 Strand, WC (Kelly's,1900), under her maiden name, although she married George Gordon Turner about 1874. The British Museum owns her designs engraved by the Dalziel Brothers (q.v.) in 1862-63.
[Houfe; Bénézit; TB; Graves; Clayton]

CLAXTON, Florence A. (Mrs Farrington) fl.1855-79
Draughtsman illustrator, daughter of the artist Marshall Claxton and sister of the artist Adelaide (qq.v.), with whom she often worked, although her work is better executed. She specialised in historical and romantic illustrations, her first being the wood engraved plate, 'Miserable Sinners', to Henry Vizetelly's Illustrated Times,1855, to which she continued to contribute until 1867. She also drew for the Illustrated London News,1860, her drawings engraved by the prominent wood engraver Thomas Gilks (q.v.); also for Churchman's Family Magazine,1863; Good Words,1864; and 100 drawings to The Adventures of a Woman in Search of her Rights, 1871. Her oil and watercolour paintings appeared at the Royal Academy, 1859-67, the Royal Society of British Artists, 1865-73, and the Society of Women Artists, 1896. The British Museum owns her designs wood engraved by the Dalziel Brothers (q.v.), 1862-65.
[Houfe; TB; Bénézit; Clayton; Graves]

CLAXTON, Marshall C. 1811-1881
Draughtsman illustrator and painter of historical subjects, born in Bolton in 1811, the pupil of John Jackson, RA and a student at the Royal Academy Schools. He travelled with his two daughters Adelaide and Florence (qq.v.) to Australia in the 1850s where he was the first man to exhibit his pictures. He returned through Ceylon and India and sketched the life and scenery there, providing drawings for the wood engravers of the Illustrated London News,1852-58; the Illustrated Times,1859; and Churchman's Family Magazine,1863. He also exhibited work at the British Institution, 1833-67, the Royal Academy and the Royal Society of British Artists, 1832-75.
[Houfe; White]

CLAYTON, Benjamin
Draughtsman illustrator of military subjects, who contributed drawings for wood engravings to Vizetelly's Illustrated Times,1856-60.
[Houfe]

CLAYTON, Eleanor (Ellen) Creathorne c1846-?
Irish novelist and illustrator, born in Dublin. She was a student at the British Museum after which she drew humorous works for the magazines, and designed calendars and valentines throughout the 1870s. She is known to have illustrated Miss Milly Moss,1862.
[Houfe]

CLAYTON, John R. fl.1850s-60s
Wood engraver and draughtsman on wood, who specialised in figure subjects, and is largely associated with the Dalziel Brothers (q.v.), his friends for over fifty years, according to their Record. They had met as fellow students at the Clipstone Life School, Clayton having first trained as a sculptor with Sir Charles Barry, who taught him to appreciate the decorative arts: 'During this period, however, his wonderful facility for design found easy outlet in drawing on wood', recalled the Dalziels, who commissioned Clayton to draw on wood for the Illustrated London News ('for which he did much beautiful work'). Rossetti consulted him during the traumatic genesis of his designs on wood to Moxon's editions of Tennyson's Poems in 1854 and Clayton gave the right though misleading response: 'Clayton was of opinion that it was much more the thing for the purpose than the drawings made by [Arthur] Hughes, which, however, turns out a complete mistake, as Hughes's drawings, also cut by Dalziel, have come, with one exception, quite remarkably well'. But then Rossetti was always a difficult draughtsman for engravers to work with. The Dalziels thought enough of Clayton's draughtsmanship to believe that he should have been elected RA, and he executed a number of designs for classic 'Sixties School' publications: George Herbert's Poetical Works, 1856; Pilgrim's Progress, 1856; Course of Time,1857; Poets of the Nineteenth Century,1857; Dramatic Scenes and Other Poems, 1857; Lays of the Holy Land,1858; The Home Affections,1858; Krummacher's Parables,1858; Barry Cornwall's Poems, and Longfellow's Tales of a Wayside Inn,1867, illustrated with B.Foster, Tenniel and Thomas Dalziel (qq.v.). Gradually Clayton gave up illustration in favour of stained glass work. The British Museum owns his designs wood engraved by the Dalziel Brothers.
[Chatto; Bénézit; Houfe; Fincham; Dalziels' Record]

CLEGHORN, John fl.1840-80
Wood engraver, wood carver, sculptor and painter,
who exhibited at the Royal Academy, the British
Institution and the Society of British Artists,
notably landscapes. He began as illustrator to
Winkle's Illustrations to the Cathedral Churches,
1836-37, and for Charles Knight's London, 1842,
and between 1840-60 engraved on wood several bookplates with armorial or seal designs: Fincham lists
ten. He had a London wood engraving office at
4 Charlton Place, Islington (Hodgson's, 1855). He
signed his work: John Cleghorn des', 'Cleghorn',
or 'J.Cleghorn'.
[TB; Bénézit; Graves; Fincham]

CLEMENT, Charles J.
Little is known of this reproductive wood engraver
listed by Gusman. He was born in Neuf-Brisach,
Haut Rhine, and collaborated on numerous works
for bibliophiles.

CLEMENT, Joshua fl.1868
London wood engraver who worked at St Paul's
Chambers, 15 Paternoster Row, EC (POD, 1868),
an address he shared then with the wood engraver
C.W.Sheeres (q.v.).

CLEMENTS, William fl.1830s
Liverpool wood engraver, who moved to London and
opened a business as a printseller and free-lance
reporter on the arts. He was an intimate and agent
for the Liverpool collector Joseph Mayer and early
friend of the Dadd family, encouraging young
Richard Dadd (q.v.)

CLENNELL, Luke 1781-1840
Prominent early wood engraver, draughtsman,
illustrator and watercolourist of the Bewick School.
He was born in Ulgham, near Morpeth,
Northumberland on 8 April 1781, the son of a
farmer, worked with his uncle Thomas Clennell, a
Morpeth grocer and tanner, and developed his
drawing skills enough for a local nobleman to
recommend him for apprenticeship to Thomas
Bewick (q.v.). He served his apprenticeship to the
Newcastle engraver from 8 April 1797 to 7 April
1804, and became one of Bewick's most skilful
assistants, as engraver as well as watercolourist
and draughtsman. He contributed many tailpieces to
the second volume of British Birds and a greater
part of the engravings to Hodgson's The Hive, 1806
and cuts for the Wallis-Scholey History of England.
As the result of Bewick's business practice of taking
three of the five guineas paid for each of the Scholey
cuts, Clennell sent a proof to the publisher claiming
he was the engraver and subsequently moved to
London under the publisher's tutelage, arriving in the
autumn of 1804. There he worked on engraving
John Thurston's (q.v.) drawings, which he first

heightened, and then improved in clarity by slightly
altering the outline of the animals. Thurston
gradually relented to this interpretative treatment
after seeing how much his work was improved.
In May 1806 Clennell received the gold palette
from the Society of Arts for 'an engraving on wood
of a Battle', followed by another gold medal in
1809, this time for his largest cut, a heading for
the diploma of the Highland Society, after Benjamin
West's design. The encircled figures were copied
on wood by Thurston, who was paid £15; Clennell
was paid 150 guineas. Linton called this work 'the
greatest accomplishment of wood engraving daring,
on so large a scale, to compete with engraving on
copper'. This was perceptive since it is known that
after two months work, Clennell had to re-do the
block after the first one, several pieces of box
veneered upon beech, had suddenly split beyond
repair. Chatto claimed that it was a typical Clennell
piece: 'This cut is characteristic of Clennell's style
of engraving--the lines are in some places coarse,
and in others the execution is careless; the more
important parts are, however, engraved with great
spirit; and the cut, as a whole, is bold and effective.
Cross-hatchings are freely introduced, not so much,
perhaps, because they were necessary, as to show
that the engraver could execute such kind of work,--
the vulgar error that cross-hatchings could not be
executed on wood having been at that time extremely
prevalent among persons who had little knowledge of
the art, and who yet vented their absurd notions on
the subjects as if they were undeniable truths'.
Clennell's other work included engravings after
Thurston for Beattie's Minstrel, 1807 and his famous
vignette of a ship in a gale for Falconer's Shipwreck,
1808, of which Chatto claims: 'Perhaps no engraving
of the same kind, either on copper or wood, conveys
the idea of a storm at sea with greater fidelity. The
drawing was made on the block by Thurston; but the
spirit and effect,--the lights and shadows, the
apparent seething of the waves, and the troubled
appearance of the sky,--were introduced by
Clennell'. He also engraved seven of Thurston's
twenty-one designs for Ackermann's Religious
Emblems, 1809, with his engraver colleagues C.Nesbit,
R.Branston and H.Hole (qq.v.) (with whom he shared his
apprenticeship at Bewick's). His last work of note
was the series of cuts in the 'black-line' manner
after pen and ink drawings on blocks by Thomas
Stothard to illustrate Samuel Rogers' Pleasures of
Memory, and Other Poems, 1810, a volume which
remains a favourite for collectors of Stothard
('pure Stothard', Linton called it), and which TB
claims was Clennell's best work. Clennell was a
stylist who represented a major break-through
for wood engraving. His skills as a draughtsman and
watercolourist allowed him not only to copy skilfully
but to create on the block. He was 'our consummate
workman' to Linton, one who had the eye and the

hand to develop a freer, more spirited style on the block than even Bewick had managed. Much of this, according to Bain, was the result of his escape from his master and independence in London. The section on technique in Chatto's Treatise cites Clennell's accomplishments as an example for budding wood engravers to follow in order to learn the elusive skill of recording reflected light and engraved tonal contrasts: 'Of all modern engravers on wood, none understood the advantages of their art in this respect better than Bewick and Clennell; the cuts of their engraving are generally the most effective that have ever been executed'. The encouragement which Clennell received for his watercolours led to his abandoning wood engraving about 1810, in favour of painting in oil and watercolour. He achieved some success in the galleries, was elected AOWS in 1812, was an exhibitor at the Royal Academy in 1812 (his work engraved twice) and was awarded 150 guineas by the British Institution for a competition picture of the Life Guards at Waterloo, which was engraved and published in 1821. He excelled at fishing and marine scenes as well as romantic landscapes which served as book illustrations, notably in Border Antiquities of England and Scotland, 1814-17. But it was the Waterloo picture which proved his downfall: 'So much fatigue, vexation, and disappointment was experienced by the artist in assembling the materials for this picture that he became insane, and, with brief lucid intervals, continued so until his death', wrote Austin Dobson in the DNB. Indeed Clennell's wife also 'gave way' and she died leaving their three children and the insane father to fend for themselves, assisted partly by sales of an engraved version (ironically) of the Waterloo picture, and by an Artist's Fund. Although Clennell managed to paint and compose 'half-articulate verses', he never entirely regained his reason and died on 9 February 1840 in Newcastle Lunatic Asylum. The British Museum owns a collection of proofs after J.Thurston, Stothard, and the Highland Society Diploma. [For an account of his later years see Chatto and Jackson, pp.521-27, also Chatto's article in the Illustrated London News, 18 May 1844; biographical detail may be found in the entry for the DNB, and in Austin Dobson's Thomas Bewick and his Pupils, 1884; see also Linton's Master of Wood Engraving; and I.Bain, Watercolours of Bewick, 1981]

CLERVILLE
(see Abate and Clerville)

CLIFT, Leslie E. and Company fl.1893-1900
London wood engraving firm, with offices at 1 Holborn Place and Red Lion Yard, High Holborn, WC (POD, 1893-98) and 7 Bride Court and 22 Bride Lane, EC (POD, 1899). By 1900 the firm had become proprietors of Hare and Company (q.v.).

CLINT, Elizabeth c1815-?
Wood engraver, daughter of Luke Clint and Elizabeth Byfield (q.v.), niece of the engravers John and Ebenezer Byfield and Mary Byfield (qq.v.). After her mother's death she joined with her Uncle John and Aunt Mary Byfield to help with the family wood engraving business. She engraved cuts for Felix Summerley's A Hand-Book for Hampton Court, 1841; various animal seals in a coat of arms published in T.Moule's Heraldry of Fish, Van Voorst, 1842; and at least two other works by her are known. She was thirty-six when she appeared in the 1851 census as 'engraver on wood' by then following in her Aunt Mary's footsteps as an independent businesswoman engraver.
[McLean, Victorian Book Design; The Private Library, Winter 1980]

COATS, Andrew Craig fl.1883-90
London wood engraver, who worked at 3 Bouverie Street, EC (POD, 1888), which he shared with the engraver E.C.Dalton (q.v.); later he moved to 62 Strand, WC (POD, 1890). He engraved several illustrations to the English Illustrated Magazine, 1883-90, including the drawings of A.Morrow (q.v.); 'Parcel Sorting Room, General Post Office', after Harry Furniss; and a fine copy of a Zoffany painting which he engraved on wood in rich, painterly tones, 1887-88. He was most successful, however, in engraving architectural subjects such as Nottingham Castle, or London Bridge Steps.

COBB, Thomas fl.1863-78
London wood engraver, who worked at 177 Camberwell N.Road, Camberwell Street (LSDS, 1863), then 4 Meadow Place, Kennington Oval S (POD, 1864-66), and finally moved into the city at 27 Southampton Buildings, WC (POD, 1867-78).

COCKING, John James fl.1883-88
London wood engraver, who worked at 70 Imperial Buildings, Ludgate Circus, EC (POD, 1884-86), then at 181 Queen Victoria Street, EC (POD, 1887-88). Like A.C.Coats (q.v.) he engraved for the English Illustrated Magazine after A.Morrow; also after a painting by Watteau, 1883-84; a vignette by Alfred Parsons to 'Shakespeare Country', 1884-85; and one of Heywood Sumner's illustrations to 'Undine', 1886-87.

COCKSHAW, Alfred Charles fl.1880s
Provincial wood engraver, who worked at 15 Pocklington's Walk, Leicester (Kelly's, 1889).

COGHLAN, Cornelius fl.1870s
London draughtsman on wood, who worked at 47 Aldermanbury, EC (Kelly's, 1876).

COLDWELL, William Henry fl.1874-77
London wood engraver, who worked at 180 Fleet
Street, EC (POD,1874), which he shared with
T.D.Collins (q.v.); and 123 Chancery Lane, EC
(POD,1877), shared with W.J.Potter (q.v.).

COLE, C.W. fl.1884-1905
Illustrator of comic subject for wood engravings
in The Graphic,1884-85 and in collaboration with
C.J.Staniland (q.v.) of Japanese views for the same
magazine,1887
[Houfe]

COLE, Timothy 1852-1931
Major reproductive wood engraver, noted for his
masterful engravings of 'Old Master' paintings.
He was born in London on 6 April 1852, but moved
to America where he studied with Bond and Chandler.
He set up an engraving business first in Chicago,
then New York and was employed for many years
engraving on wood for the Century Magazine and
Scribner's Magazine. He achieved a reputation and
much critical acclaim for his wood engravings of
'Old Master' paintings by Dutch, Italian, Spanish
and English painters, reproduced in a tonal manner
to simulate their brush work and painted surfaces.
For these he was awarded a gold medal in Paris and
St Louis, 1904, and honourable mention again in
Paris, 1910. Cole's working methods were unique.
He worked from a photograph of the painting to be
copied, translating it first into line, then working it
over in stipple to simulate the rich surfaces of painted
canvas for which he was justly famous. However he
apparently did not have the painting photographed on
the block, as one might have expected. Even when he
used half-tone blocks for engravings after Tissot's
paintings of the 'Life of Christ' (for The Century) he
achieved a unique effect. He 'shows you how the
graver was used lavishly to heighten the lights on
a half-tone block; a trick which soon became
unnecessary' (Sleigh). Cole's engravings were
generally recognised by engraver colleagues as high
points in the history of wood engraving. The 1890s
revivalist engravers looked to his work for
inspiration; Bernard Sleigh (q.v.) wrote of his 'The
Honourable Mrs Graham' and 'Mother and Child'
engraved for The Century,1895, that 'my positive
opinion [is] that they represent the high-water mark
of human skill with the graver upon wood' (Wood
Engraving since 1890). The Liverpool Art Gallery
purchased about twenty Cole engravings at this time,
while Joseph Cundall in his Brief History of Wood
Engraving,1895, described Cole as the saviour of
wood engraving; 'for the brilliant band of wood
engravers which has formed in America still
continues to give us excellent examples of their
skill, and especially we may mention the inimitable
copies of paintings by the old masters by Timothy
Coles [sic]'. Cole was often linked with fellow

engravers Henry Marsh and W.J.Linton (qq.v.).
Linton himself praised Cole and discussed his work
in his History of Wood Engraving in America,1882.
Present day critics continue to admire Cole's work.
Chamberlain used it in his historical survey as
'possibly the ultimate examples of facsimile
engraving'. Hind was more cautious and described
his total dependence on tone without outline as
carrying 'the tonal responsibilities of mixed black
and white-line work to its extreme limits'.
[For a list of work see W.J.Stillman, Old Italian
Masters Engraved by Timothy Cole,1888; John C.
Van Dycke, Old Dutch and Flemish Masters
Engraved by Timothy Cole,1893; Old English
Masters Engraved by Timothy Cole,1896; and
C.H.Chaffin, Old Spanish Masters Engraved by
Timothy Cole,1901; see also Alphaeus Cole,
Margaret Ward, Timothy Cole, Woodengraver,
N.Y. (Pioneer Press) 1935; Fielding]

COLEMAN, William ?-1807
Early wood engraver, who achieved distinction by
several awards from the Society of Arts, 1775-77.
He died at Duke's Court, Bow Street, December
1807.
[Redgrave; TB; Bénézit]

COLEMAN, William Stephen 1829-1904
Draughtsman on wood, illustrator, figure and
landscape painter and etcher. He was born in
Horsham, Sussex in 1829, the son of a physician.
He was a keen naturalist, which fact inspired his
drawing when he came to London and called on the
Dalziel Brothers (q.v.). They employed him as a
draughtsman and he quickly achieved success, most
notably in the series of natural history books by
Reverend J.G.Wood, who praised his accuracy and
meticulous skill at getting good specimens for his
illustrations: to The Common Objects of the Country,
1858, and Natural History Picture Book,1861. He
also wrote A Book on British Butterflies,1860; and
British Bird's Eggs, originally commissioned by
the Dalziels, but colour printed by Edmund Evans
(q.v.) in 1896, after having colour printed several
early nature books. This latter led to his revision
of the colour work in the 'Butterfly' book. He
worked in collaboration with Harrison Weir and Wolf
(qq.v.) and contributed many zoological drawings
on wood to magazines like the Illustrated Times,
1856 and the Illustrated London News,1857; also
to such books as S.C.Hall's The Book of the Thames,
1859, engraved by the Dalziels, Butterworth and
Heath (qq.v.); and The Book of South Wales,1861; as
well as Mary Howitt's Tales. As a painter he
exhibited from 1866-79 and the Dalziels bought
'hundreds' of his oils and watercolours which
ranged from butterfly paintings for Christmas
cards to a life-size nude. He was later associated
with the Minton Pottery Studio as a designer and was

also on the Dudley Gallery committee until 1881. He died on 22 March 1904 at St John's Wood. The British Museum owns a collection of his designs wood engraved by the Dalziel Brothers.
[Chatto; Houfe; Bénézit; TB; Dalziels' Record; for etchings see Volume I]

COLLIDGE, Henry fl.1860s
London wood engraver, who worked at 37 Castle Street, Holborn, EC (POD,1866), which he shared with the noted engraver E.S.Gascoine (q.v.).

COLLIER, The Hon. John 1850-1934
Illustrator, prominent figure and portrait painter, born in London on 27 January 1850, son of the 1st Baron Monkswell. He was educated at Eton and the Slade under Poynter, and under J.P.Laurens in Paris. He did illustrations only rarely and was rather a weak pen and ink draughtsman, but Thomas Hardy secured him for the serialised The Trumpet Major, Good Words,1880, Hardy sending him sketched details to ensure accurate drawing. This was not successful and Collier's work led the magazine's editor to worry about subsequent 'nasty block-cutting'. Later Collier tried again, for Thackeray's Ballads,1894, and contributed to the English Illustrated Magazine,1890-91. He also exhibited his portraits at the Grosvenor Gallery, the Royal Academy, and the Royal Society of British Artists, and wrote a manual of oil painting. He died on 11 April 1934.
[A.Jackson, Illustrators of T.Hardy,1981; Wood]

COLLINGS, Thomas Penson fl.1866-89
London wood engraver, draughtsman on wood and illustrator, who specialised in detailed engravings of ornaments and works of art. He worked at 38 Surry (sic) Street, Strand, WC (POD,1866-73) and 172 Strand, WC (POD,1874-81). This latter then became Collings and Company (q.v.) which existed at least until 1896 at the same London address. Among Collings' engraved work was a series of intricate medical cuts of the human voice box, 'The Singing Voice', in the English Illustrated Magazine,1885-86. He also contributed to The Graphic,1875-89.

COLLINGS and Company fl.1882-96
London wood engraving firm, originated by Thomas Penson Collings (q.v.) at 172 Strand, WC (POD,1880-96), then 163 Strand, WC (POD,1900).

COLLINS, Henry fl.1883-84
London wood engraver, who worked at 4 Newgate Street, EC (POD,1883-84). Fincham lists an H.Collins, engraver of five bookplates from Chippendale and armorial designs. He worked in London at 113 Piccadilly (1810) and 164 Strand (1840,1850). He signed his work: 'H.Collins sc'.

COLLINS, Robert fl.1864-69
London wood engraver, who worked at 123 Chancery Lane (POD,1864-69), an address shared with G.C.Freudemacher, E.T.Hartshorn, T.Powney, W.D.Willis, and R.Cooper (qq.v.). Robert Collins may be the Robert C.Collins listed by Bénézit as born in Edenderry, Ireland and who worked in America at one time.

COLLINS, Thomas Dawson fl.1867-1910
London wood engraver, who worked at 14 Queen Street, Soho, W (POD,1867), 33 Newman Street, W, and 180 Fleet Street, EC (POD,1868-74), an address shared with Mrs C.Buchanan and W.H.Coldwell (qq.v.). He moved to 97 Fleet Street, EC (POD,1875-1900) which was shared with M.Laurie (q.v.). He remained there until 1901, then moved to 4 Ludgate Circus, EC (POD,1900-1910).

COLLINS, Thomas Hogarth fl.1870-73
London wood engraver, who worked at 13 Stamford Street, EC (POD,1870-73).

COLLINS, William B. fl.1843-63
Wood engraver and colour printer. He was apprenticed to George Baxter (q.v.) and about 1843 formed a partnership with Charles Gregory (q.v.), another Baxter apprentice, as Gregory and Collins. Then about 1844, with Alfred Reynolds (q.v.), the firm appeared as Gregory, Collins and Reynolds (see Charles Gregory entry). When Gregory left, Collins and Reynolds continued as colour printers from wood blocks, appearing in the directory at 3 Charterhouse Square (POD,1848). There they engraved for Peter Parley's Annual,1849, after J.Absolon's (q.v.) drawings. By late 1849 they had been bought up by George Cargill Leighton (q.v.). William Collins disappears from directories until 1859, then at 107 Dorset Street, Fleet Street, EC (POD,1859-63) he worked as wood engraver and oil colour printer, printing the title-page of Peter Parley's Annual,1852, wood engraved by W.G.Mason (q.v.). By 1861 the firm had become Collins and Company.
[For a discussion of colour work see Wakeman and Bridson; also McLean, Victorian Book Design; Lewis]

COLLINS and Company
(see Collins, William B.)

COLLINS and Reynolds
(see Gregory, C. and Collins, William B.)

COLLINS and Wall fl.1884-85
London wood engraving firm, probably composed of Henry Collins (q.v.) in partnership with James Charles Wall (q.v.), who took over the office and worked there alone from 1891.

COLLIS, John and Company fl.1883-98
London wood engraving firm, with offices at
138 Fleet Street, EC and 72 Denmark Hill, EC
(POD,1883-87), later 52 Fleet Street, EC
(POD,1888-93), then 166 Fleet Street, EC
(POD,1894-98).

COLOMB, Wellington fl.1865-70
Draughtsman illustrator and landscape painter, who
contributed a drawing on wood to Good Words,1864.
He also exhibited paintings at the Royal Academy and
the Royal Society of British Artists, 1865-70.

COMAN, Thomas fl.1875-87
London wood engraver, who worked at 10 Bolt Court,
Fleet Street, EC (POD,1875-87), an address shared
with A.Fairhall, R.G.F.Sweeting, A.J.Wilson and
E.Scrivens (qq.v.).

COMMERCIAL and Artistic Engraving and
Publishing Company fl.1889-1900
London firm of wood engravers and draughtsmen,
with an office at 174 Fleet Street, EC (POD,1889),
then 160 Fleet Street, EC (POD,1895-1900).

CONCANEN, Alfred 1835-86
Draughtsman, illustrator and marine painter, the
son of the painter Nicholas Condy. He taught art in
descent, and began to draw music cover designs in
1859, soon to become a prolific and skilful interpreter
of music. His designs include those for H.S.Leigh's
Carols of Cockayne,1874, J.Greenwood's Low Life
Deeps,1874, and The Wilds of London,1876, and
illustrations to Wilkie Collins' The Queen of Hearts,
1875. He also contributed to the Illustrated Sporting
and Dramatic News.
[Houfe]

CONDY, Nicholas Matthew 1818-51
Draughtsman, illustrator and marine painter, the
son of the painter Nicholas Condy. He taught art in
Plymouth, and contributed naval illustrations on wood
to the Illustrated London News,1845-50.
[Houfe]

COODE, Miss Helen Hoppner fl.1859-82
Draughtsman illustrator and watercolourist, the first
woman cartoonist on Punch, to which she contributed
nineteen drawings from November 1859 to January
1861. She also contributed small drawings to Once a
Week,1859. She worked from Notting Hill, London
and Guildford, Surrey, and specialised in figure
subjects although her drawing was often brittle and
the figures rather insignificant. She exhibited at the
British Institution, 1859-66, and the Royal Academy
and the Royal Society of British Artists, 1876-81.

COOK, Mary Ann fl.1830s-40s
Wood engraver, who engraved cuts to Charles
Knight's (q.v.) publication, William Lane's
Arabian Knights' Entertainments,1839.
[Bodleian Library]

COOKE, Edward William 1811-80
Draughtsman illustrator, wood engraver, marine
watercolourist and topographer, born at Pentonville
on 27 March 1811, the son of the engraver George
Cooke. He began his career at the age of nine with
wood engravings of plants which appeared in
J.C.Loudan's Encyclopedia of Plants,1829, and
Loddidge's Botanical Cabinet,1817-33. After his
meeting with the marine painter Clarkson Stanfield
in 1825, he turned to drawing boats and to the study
of shipping, which led to extensive travels in Europe.
His paintings and engravings relate to the illustrations
he made for Coast Sketches, British Coast,1826-30,
and Fifty Plates of Shipping and Craft,1829. He also
drew on wood for Good Words,1863, and etched
several works on metal plates. He exhibited work at
the British Institution, 1835-67, the Royal Academy
and the Royal Society of British Artists, 1835-38,
1876 and was elected ARA in 1851, RA in 1864. He
died at Groombridge, Kent, on 4 January 1880. The
British Museum owns a collection of proof designs
engraved by the Dalziel Brothers (q.v.), 1861,1864.
[Houfe; for metal engravings see Volume I (with
bibliography)]

COOKE, Edwin and Company fl.1900
London firm of draughtsmen, with an office at
152 Upper Thames Street, EC (Kelly's,1900).

COOMBE, A.E. fl.1886-89
Wood engraver, who worked for the English
Illustrated Magazine. He engraved with R.B.Lodge
(q.v.) the illustrations of W.B.Gardner (q.v.) to the
series, 'Surrey Mill Wheels', 1886, and 'Surrey Farm
Houses', 1888. These were large, very competent
works showing a good understanding of tone and
contrast.

COOPER, Alfred W. fl.1850-1901
Draughtsman on wood, and one of the best of the
secondary 'Sixties School' illustrators. He lived and
worked in London, 1853-54, and had moved to
Twickenham by 1866 where he apparently worked for
the rest of his life. He began drawing on wood for
periodicals, borrowing his style from J.E.Millais (q.v.).
His drawings first appeared in Good Words,1861;
London Society,1862-68; and the Churchman's Family
Magazine,1863. The drawings for the latter are
strongly influenced by Frederick Walker (q.v.). Other
works appeared in Tinsley's Magazine,1868; Dark
Blue,1871; The Graphic, 1870; British Workman;
and Aunt Judy's Magazine. He was also employed by
the wood engraver Edmund Evans (q.v.) to design

covers to his famous railway series of 'yellowbacks'.
He exhibited work in London from 1850-1901, notably
at the British Institution, 1853-66, the Royal Society
of British Artists, 1852-80, the Royal Institute of
Painters in Watercolours and the Royal Institute of
Painters in Oil-Colours. The British Museum owns
his designs engraved by the Dalziel Brothers (q.v.),
1862, 1863, 1866.
[Houfe; Evans Reminiscences; TB; Bénézit]

COOPER, George William fl.1880s
Provincial wood engraver, who worked at
13 Adelaide Street, Birmingham (Kelly's,1880).

COOPER, James Charles fl.1873-75
London wood engraver, who worked at 111 Long
Acre, WC (POD,1873-75).

COOPER, James Davis 1823-1904
Prominent London wood engraver and draughtsman
on wood, who engraved after the major artists of
his day. He was born in 1823, and first appears in
the London directories at 10 Ely Place, Holborn
(POD,1849) but by 1855 he had moved to 26 Gt. James
Street, Bedford Row (POD,Hodgson's,1855-60). By
the following year he had established a workshop at
188 Strand, which he shared at various times with
W.H. and F.Aske, E.S.Gascoine, R.H.Moore,
C.Roberts, and J.P.Wall (qq.v.); he remained there
for the remainder of his working life, and is listed
as late as 1900 in the directories. Cooper worked in
association with the colour printer Richard Clay
during the 1850s and 60s. He also took out Patent
710 in 1857, for making engraved blocks from which
electrotypes could be made for relief printing. As a
wood engraver he features prominently in Bohn's
supplement to Chatto (pp.550-51) which lists his
early engravings: eighty engravings after Percival
Skelton to Murray's Childe Harold,1859; engravings
after Birket Foster and Harrison Weir (qq.v.) to
Select Poems and Songs of Robert Burns,1858;
several engravings to Rhymes and Roundelayes, for
which 'Mr Cooper is favourably known to the artistic
world'; Poetry and Pictures from Thomas Moore,
1858; The Merrie Days of England,1859; Favourite
English Poems,1858; and after B.Foster to
Bloomfield's Farmer's Boy,1858. By the 1860s he had
distinguished himself enough to take on work for various
publishers: he engraved a full-page plate, 'St Barbara
to Henry Shaw's influential A Handbook of the Art of
Illumination,1866, this and his border design being
printed in brown ink by Charles Whittingham (q.v.);
twelve cuts after John Franklin to St George and the
Dragon,1868; sixteen unusually large cuts after
Robert Barnes, E.M.Wimperis (qq.v.) and others
to Pictures of English Life,1865; and he also engraved
with W.J.Linton (q.v.) after T.Morten's illustrations
to Gulliver's Travels,1865. In addition he was a
prominent engraver for magazines, beginning

with landscapes for the Illustrated London News in
1851, although these were rather crude, as in his
block of 'The Moorland Stream', 22 February 1851,
after H.Jutsum, which shows its seams and in which
the sky is rather crudely ruled. He improved enough
to contribute a double-page engraving, 'The Drover's
Halt', after R.Ansdell, 25 October 1873, and
continued to contribute to the Illustrated London
News throughout the 1870s. This work led to his
most prestigious commissions during the 1880s,
namely for the Art Journal, and for the English
Illustrated Magazine,1883-88, after such noted
artists as Alfred Parsons, Hugh Thomson, Randolph
Caldecott, Rossetti and Du Maurier (qq.v.). Cooper
is perhaps best known for his collaboration with
Randolph Caldecott. They worked together on
Caldecott's first book success, Old Christmas,1875,
and this was followed by Bracebridge Hall,1876, and
the Aesop's Fables,1883, all evidence that Caldecott
owed much to Cooper's skills as a wood engraver of
fine, clear line and a faithful engraver-copyist after
Caldecott's original drawings which Cooper
interpreted on the block. He even secured the
admiration of that arch critic of the wood block,
John Ruskin, who had Cooper engrave some Kate
Greenaway drawings and his own sketches of clouds
(see Art Journal,1884,pp.105-8). He also engraved
after photographs of the Queen and Albert. He died
on 27 February 1904. Some of Cooper's work was
actually done by Theobald Carreras (q.v.). The
British Museum owns Cooper's engravings after
various artists: R.Barnes, H.K.Browne, Birket
Foster, Henry O'Neil, F.W.Moody, D.G.Rossetti,
and R.Caldecott; also engraved architectural subjects;
and cuts to the Illustrated London Almanack,1851.
He signed his work: 'J COOPER SC', 'J Cooper'.
[Chatto; Hake; White; TB]

COOPER, Richard fl.1860s
London wood engraver, who worked at 123 Chancery
Lane, WC (POD,1867), an office which he shared
with E.T.Hartshorn, T.Powney, and W.D.Willis
(qq.v.).

COPAS, John Robert fl.1860s
London wood engraver, who worked at 46 Alfred
Street, Barnsbury, N (POD,1868).

COPAS and Company fl.1890s
London wood engraving firm, with an office at
41 Gray's Inn Road, WC (POD,1892-1901).

COPE, Charles West 1811-90
Occasional draughtsman on wood, prominent painter
of historical subjects. He was born in Leeds on
28 July 1811, educated at Leeds Grammar School,
and went to London in 1826 where he studied at
Sass's in 1827 and the Royal Academy Schools in
1828. He travelled to Paris, 1831 and Italy, 1833-35,

becoming an expert on Renaissance fresco techniques. He was also an etcher and illustrator and a founding member of the Etching Club, to whose publications he contributed numerous illustrations (see Volume 1). He exhibited at the British Institution and the Royal Academy, 1833-82 and was elected ARA in 1843, RA in 1848. Cope is listed here for his early drawings on wood, which according to Bohn were primarily figural subjects for Book of Favourite Modern Ballads, Adams' Allegories, Excelsior Ballads, Burns' Poems, and Poetry of Thomas Moore. He also drew illustrations (unsigned) for Nursery Rhymes, Tales and Jingles, 1844. The British Museum owns his designs wood engraved by the Dalziel Brothers (q.v.), 1855, 1863.
[Wood; Chatto; McLean; Bénézit; TB; C.H.Cope, Reminiscences, 1891]

COPLESTON, Josiah fl.1865-72
London wood engraver, who worked at 1 Pickett Place, WC (POD, 1865), then 6 Newcastle Street, Farringdon Street, EC (POD, 1870-72).

COPPING, George James fl.1860s
London wood engraver, who worked at 137 Barnsbury Road, N (POD, 1867). He may be the Copping of Appleton and Copping (q.v.).

COPSEY, D. fl.1870s
Wood engraver, who engraved the full-page illustration, 'Russian Stage-Coach Pillaged by Steppe Robbers near the Sea of Aral', in the Illustrated London News, 17 October 1874. The engraving is especially good for its atmospheric use of uniform parallel lines to describe the barren landscape.

CORBOULD, Alfred Chantrey ?-1920
Draughtsman illustrator, primarily for Punch. He was introduced to the paper by his uncle Charles Keene (q.v.), who also advised him on drawing for wood engraving: '...the execution would render the drawing rather difficult to engrave, and you want a little more study and practice in "the human face divine" to please the newspaper people. I never give advice on these matters, but I can tell you from my own experience I don't think drawing on wood is a good road to stand on as an artist; but if you don't agree with me and wish to go in for this particular branch, it seems to me that you should article or apprentice with some engraver of large business for a certain time on certain terms. This is how I began, and have been sorry for it ever since!' Corbould persisted and contributed to Punch, 1871-90, working under three editors, to whom he first sent slight sketches for approval. He specialised in sporting subjects that Spielmann claimed 'raised their author to very near the front rank of popularity'. He also contributed drawings for Edmund Evans' (q.v.) series of wood engraved railway novel covers. This work led to

further drawing on wood for The Graphic, 1873-89; the Illustrated London News, 1876, as a 'Special Artist' in Servia; the Cornhill, 1883; Daily Graphic; Black and White, 1891, and others. He also exhibited at the Royal Academy, the Royal Hibernian Academy, the Royal Institute of Painters in Watercolours, the Royal Institute of Painters in Oil-Colours and the Royal Society of British Artists where he was elected RBA, 1893.
[Spielmann; Evans Reminiscences; Houfe; TB; Bénézit]

CORBOULD, Edward Henry 1815-1905
Painter who occasionally drew on wood, also etcher and sculptor. He was born in London on 5 December 1815 and became a pupil of his father Henry Corbould, another prolific illustrator. He studied at Sass's and the Royal Academy Schools and began illustrating for books and magazines. He was appointed drawing master to the Queen's children in 1851, a post which he retained until 1872. He specialised in figure and architectural subjects, his illustrations including those for Lalla Rookh, 1839, the major work for S.C.Hall's Book of British Ballads, 1842, engraved with T.Wakefield and J.Bastin (qq.v.); some of the nearly 100 wood engravings to an edition of Bunyan's Pilgrim's Progress, 1849; Tupper's Proverbial Philosophy, 1854; Willmott's Poets of the Nineteenth Century, 1857; Merrie Days of England, 1858-59; also Favourite Modern Ballads; Burns' Poems; Poetry of Thomas Moore; Barry Cornwall's Poems; and Thornbury's Legendary Ballads, 1876. He also contributed illustrations to periodicals like The Sporting Review, 1842-46; the Illustrated London News, 1856, 1866; London Society, 1863; Churchman's Family Magazine, 1863 and Cassell's Magazine, 1870. He also drew designs for the engraver Edmund Evans (q.v.). He exhibited work at the British Institution, 1846, the Grosvenor Gallery, the New Watercolour Society, the Royal Academy and the Royal Society of British Artists, 1835-42. The British Museum owns his designs wood engraved by the Dalziel Brothers (q.v.).
[Chatto; Houfe; Evans Reminiscences; Bénézit; TB; Nagler (as 'Edwin'); Linton, Masters of Wood Engraving]

CORNER, James Mackenzie fl.1872-1900
Scottish wood engraver, who worked in Edinburgh at 8 Brighton Street (Kelly's, 1872), 1 Park Street (Kelly's, 1876-80), and 25 Scotland Street (Kelly's, 1900).

CORNILLIET, Jules 1830-86
French draughtsman illustrator and history painter, who was born in Versailles in 1830, studied with Ary Scheffer and H.Vernet, and exhibited at the Salon in 1857. He is included here for his wood engraved drawings of the Franco-Italian campaign for the Illustrated London News, 1859.

CORPE
(see Rees and Corpe)

COTMAN, Frederick George 1850-1920
Landscape and genre watercolourist and oil
painter, nephew of J.S.Cotman. He was born in
Ipswich, attended the Royal Academy Schools in
1868 and travelled with the Duke of Westminster
to the Mediterranean as his watercolourist recorder.
He occasionally illustrated: his work is known
engraved on wood for the Illustrated London News,
1876, 1880. But he largely painted for the galleries,
being elected RI in 1882, ROI,1883, and died at
Felixstowe on 16 July 1920.
[Houfe]

COULDEREY, Thomas W. fl.1877-98
Draughtsman illustrator and domestic painter,
who set up as draughtsman on wood in London at
10 Sergeant's Inn, Fleet Street, EC (Kelly's,1880).
He drew for Charles Reade's A Woman Hater,1877;
and contributed to the Illustrated London News,1888,
1894; Cassell's Family Magazine; and English
Illustrated Magazine,1891-94. He also exhibited
at the Royal Academy,1883-93, the Royal Society
of British Artists and the Royal Institute of Painters
in Watercolours, worked at 12 New Court, Lincoln's
Inn from 1883-86, then moved to Pulborough and
Chichester, Sussex, 1890-93 and to Brighton, 1897.
[Houfe;Bénézit]

COULLIE, Falcon fl.1870s
London wood engraver, who worked in the
engraving district, 15 Wine Office Court, EC
(POD,1874).

COUSENS, William James fl.1890s
London wood engraver, who worked at 2 and 3
Stonecutter Street, EC (POD,1897).

COUSINS, Robert fl.1894-95
London wood engraver, who worked at 1 Norfolk
Street, Strand (POD,1894-95), which he shared
with G.Cheshire and J.C.Saunders (qq.v.).

COWAN, William fl.1872-80
Scottish wood engraver, who worked at 15 St James
Square, Edinburgh (Kelly's,1872-80).

COWERN, Robert George fl.1889-1900
Provincial wood engraver, who worked at
Princess Street, Wolverhampton (Kelly's,1889),
then 60 Queen Street, Wolverhampton
(Kelly's,1900).

COWING, George Wetton fl.1880s
Provincial wood engraver, who worked at High
Street, Barnet, Hertfordshire, and Sun Street
Waltham Abbey, Essex (Kelly's,1880)

COWLAND, John fl.1850s
Little is known of this wood engraver listed by
LeBlanc as 'contemporary'.

COX, Everard Morant fl.1878-91
Draughtsman illustrator, who worked in London for
such comic magazines as Punch,1883, and provided
illustrations on genre and sporting subjects for the
Illustrated London News,1883-84,1888,1891. He
also exhibited at the Royal Academy, 1884-85.
[TB; Bénézit; Spielmann]

COX, William James fl.1880s
London wood engraver, who worked at 3 Falcon
Court, 142 Fleet Street, EC (POD,1886), which he
shared with H.Freeman (q.v.).

CRAFT, Percy Robert 1856-1934
Landscape and coastal painter, occasional
draughtsman on wood, who studied at Heatherley's
and the Slade under Legros and Poynter. He worked
in London until 1910 and briefly in Penzance,
Cornwall in 1890, a place which had inspired his
drawing for the Illustrated London News,1883. He
exhibited at the Royal Academy, the New Gallery,
the Royal Society of British Artists, the Royal
Society of Painter-Etchers and Engravers, the
Royal Institute of Painters in Oil-Colours and the
Royal Scottish Academy, and was elected RBA in
1898. He died in London on 26 November 1934.
[Houfe]

CRAIG, Edward Gordon 1872-1966
Wood engraver, etcher, writer, actor and theatrical
designer, producer, who was largely responsible for
keeping wood engraving alive at the end of the
nineteenth century. He was born in Stevenage,
Hertfordshire, on 16 January 1872, son of
E.W.Godwin and Ellen Terry. He was educated at
Heidelberg and Bradfield, but on his move to
Uxbridge in 1893 he came under the influence of
William Nicholson and James Pryde (qq.v.) nearby
at Denham. Nicholson taught him wood engraving for
which Craig published woodcuts in his own periodical
The Page,1898-1901 produced at The Sign of the
Rose, Hackbridge. Craig studied Renaissance wood
engravings and architecture at this time, and from
1893-98 produced a number of energetic and bold
yet chunky woodcuts, most notable being those of
character studies of Henry Irving and Ellen Terry,
with whom he joined as theatre manager of the
Imperial Theatre, Westminster, 1903. His approach
to wood engraving brought a new dimension to its
previous reproductive qualities, 'an aesthetic form,
centred upon formal values and the expression of
aesthetic emotion', according to Albert Garrett. His
early engraved work showed the strong influence of art
nouveau, which went into the little books he produced,
also his understanding of black and white-line which

he later adopted in this theatrical designs. He
was also his own editor, illustrator and publisher
for The Mask,1908-29 and The Marionette,
and contributed to the influential The Dome,1898-99.
He was a founder member of the Society of Wood
Engravers in 1919 although he never fully adopted
their 'white-line' style. He later headed the splinter
group, the English Wood Engraving Society in 1926,
in opposition to the original group. He continued to
design for the stage and to write extensively until his
death in 1966. Sixty of Craig's best wood engravings
are seen in his own compilation, Woodcuts and Some
Words,1924, in which he claimed to have produced
about 517 woodblocks by that time, 'and the prize I
received for my work was a medal. As it is a curious
medal which only the engraver can get, those of us
who have it are a bit proud of it. It is worn on the
hand, and yet it is not of gold nor a ring. It is a
bump--nothing handsome. It is fixed on the palm of
the right hand in a straight line below the third
finger. Diamonds and pearls are not so rare'. The
British Museum owns a collection of signed proofs
by him. Craig signed his woodcuts: 'C'.
[For list of works see Ifan Kyrle Fletcher,
Bibliography of Edward Gordon Craig; Victoria and
Albert Museum catalogue,1967; also Houfe; Garrett;
Maré; Bénézit; Studio,xxiii,pp.246-57]

CRAIG, Francis fl.1820-50s
Wood engraver, who worked during the early
nineteenth century, associated with the school of
reproductive engravers like Luke Clennell and
R.Branston (qq.v.). He used a heavy thick black-line
style. Nagler lists his engravings to The Provincial
and Picturesque Scenery of Scotland,1819, and after
the drawings of the painter William Marshall Craig
(q.v.) in A Course of Lectures on Drawing, Painting
and Engraving,1821. The British Museum has a series
of agricultural subjects; also cuts to Travels in Lower
Hungary. He signed his work 'FC', 'F Craig sc'.
[LeBlanc; Nagler; Bénézit; TB; Bruillot]

CRAIG, William Marshall c1765-1834
Occasional draughtsman on wood, illustrator,
miniature and portrait painter. He is best known as
drawing master to Princess Charlotte in 1812,
miniature painter to the Duke and Duchess of York
in 1820 and as a painter in watercolours to the Queen.
He worked from Manchester in 1788, the year he
exhibited at the Royal Academy; by 1791 he had moved
to London. From about 1821 he worked as draughtsman
on wood and shared with John Thurston (q.v.) 'the
honour of being one of the principal designers on
wood' (DNB). He had proposed a Scripture Illustrated,
1806, which was engraved by the period's most
competent engravers, e.g. Thomas Bewick, Luke
Clennell, Charlton Nesbit, R.Branston, R.Austin,
H.Hole, and J.Lee (qq.v.). Later his Lectures on
Drawing, Painting and Engraving,1821 was engraved by

Francis Craig (q.v.). He also drew for various
publications of Charles Whittingham (q.v.). He
worked either directly on wood or from ideas
provided by a book's author, which he worked up
into drawings on the block.
[For a list of works illustrated see Houfe; also
Redgrave; Bénézit; TB; DNB; Bodleian Library;
Fincham; LeBlanc]

CRANE, Henry James fl.1856-87
London wood engraver and draughtsman on wood,
who worked at 255 Strand (POD,1856-57), 170 Fleet
Street, EC (POD,1858-59), 38 West Square, S
(POD,1861-64) then adding a second office at
6 Fetter Lane, EC (POD,1864-67) which he shared
with R.S.Marriott, C.Branston, F.Mellish,
R.Pringle (qq.v.). By 1868 this second office had
changed to 4 Bouverie Street, EC (POD,1868-73)
when it became the sole office (POD,1874-87),
shared briefly with A.J.Appleton (q.v.). Crane's
work included half and full-page illustrations to the
Illustrated London News,1875-76, generally of
horses after drawings by Sturgess, or various
special artist sketches.

CRANE, Walter 1845-1915
Draughtsman on wood, prominent illustrator,
painter, decorator and writer who was born in
Liverpool on 15 August 1845, and largely self-taught
as an artist illustrator. When he showed his designs
for eighteen pages of Tennyson's Lady of Shalott to
the wood engraver W.J.Linton (q.v.) he was so
impressed he took Crane on as apprentice without
the necessary premium. Crane began work at
thirteen years old in January 1859, and worked for
three years from the third floor of 33 Essex Street
with a row of about six engravers and six fellow
apprentices then employed by Linton. He was taught
by Linton's partner Harvey Orrin Smith (q.v.) who
showed him how to transfer a drawing onto the block,
but Crane was especially taken with his master's
skill at cutting such work: Linton's freedom of touch
upon the block was to him, 'astonishing'. Crane
became adept at animal drawing, was sent to London
Zoo to make sketches, and given half-drawn
illustrations of animals to sharpen up; he also drew
catalogue drawings of bedsteads and various highly
detailed domestic items, fashion plates, and medical
drawings. He quickly achieved a reputation for his
own skilful drawing and Linton sent him out as
special reporter for The Illustrated News of the
World to record aspects of London life. In January
1862 Crane was given his indenture of apprenticeship
with a note from Orrin Smith confirming his success:
'Returned with thanks and full expression of
satisfaction at Walter Crane's thorough good
conduct, his readiness, his industry and his ability'.
Crane later recalled his valuable apprenticeship and
how Linton had 'implanted a sense of necessary

relationship between designing, material, and method of production--of art and craft, in fact--which...has had its effect in many ways'. Crane is best known for his colour printed Picture Book series engraved by Edmund Evans (q.v.) and published by Routledge, but he also had work engraved by the Dalziels and Joseph Swain (qq.v.). He was also a noted figure in the art education field, taught design at various institutions, and lectured and wrote about the importance of design theory. His influence survived the turn of the century and even now there is a recent revival of interest in his work. The British Museum owns his designs wood engraved by the Dalziel Brothers (q.v.),1862-63.
[For a complete account of his career and work, I.Spencer, Walter Crane,1975; also R.Engen, Walter Crane as Book Illustrator,1975; W.Crane, Artist's Reminiscences,1907]

CRANSTON, William Alfred fl.1863-79
London wood engraver, who worked at 156 Strand, WC (POD,1863-64), which he shared with E.Skill and S.V. and A.Slader (qq.v.). He then moved to 266 Strand, WC (POD,1865) which was then also the office of the prominent engravers J.Swain and E.Whymper (qq.v.). By 1871 Cranston had moved to 174 Fleet Street, EC (POD,1871-79).

CRAWHALL, Joseph 1821-96
Illustrator, engraver of chap-books and ballad writer, best known for his highly original productions of handcoloured woodcuts to illustrate his earthy ballads, which he printed at 'Ye Leadenhall Press, Newcastle'. He was born at West House, Newcastle, in 1821, and ran the family rope business while pursuing his father's interest in antiquarian books. On his own retirement he began his series of chap-books with The Compleatest Angling Book That Ever Was Writ,1859, and a new edition in 1881 with his own woodcuts which he then called 'sculptures'. These books were printed in small editions (the first was forty copies) and were his attempt to restore the personality of books at a time when rapid printing processes were making the book-as-object an obsolete concept. He produced, illustrated and engraved his own books throughout the 1880s (the British Library catalogue lists at least thirteen) and with W.Nicholson (q.v.) was an influence in private book production. He was also a friend of the Punch illustrator Charles Keene, for whom Crawhall supplied the jokes that appeared as illustrations in Punch. He was secretary of the Newcastle Arts Club and compiled Specimens of Early Wood Engraving, 1889. His designs without text appeared as Impresses Quaint,1889. He died in 1896.
[For a complete list of his work, see Adrian Bury, Joseph Crawhall,1959; Charles S.Felver, Joseph Crawhall,1972; Bénézit; Houfe; British Library catalogue; Garrett]

CREALOCK, Lieutenant-General Henry Hope 1831-91
Amateur illustrator artist, educated at Rugby, who joined the army in 1848 and served during the Crimean War, during the Indian Mutiny, in New Brunswick, 1865, and in Zululand, 1879. He is listed here for illustrations to The Illustrated Times,1855, secured by Henry Vizetelly (q.v.), and various illustrations to books such as Wolf-Hunting and Wild Sport in Lower Brittany,1875, G.J.Melville's Katerfelto,1875, and W.D.Davenport's Sport,1885. [Houfe]

CREBER, Theophilus fl.1880-89
Provincial wood engraver who worked at 60 and 61 Union Street, Plymouth (Kelly's,1880-89).

CRESWICK, Thomas 1811-69
Occasional draughtsman on wood, landscape painter and etcher, who was born in Sheffield, Yorkshire on 5 February 1811. He was educated at Hazelwood, near Birmingham and rapidly developed a talent for drawing. He used this to devise his famous landscape scenes which appeared in various books and magazines, done in collaboration with the animal painters Ansdell and Goodall, and figure painters Phillip and Frith. Bohn explained in Chatto and Jackson that 'Mr Creswick, RA, the distinguished painter, has occasionally drawn on wood, but more as a favour than part of his metier', and cites Ruskin's mixed reactions to Creswick's drawings to 'The Nut Brown Maid' in Book of British Ballads; engraved by J.Williams (q.v.). Creswick also drew vignettes for Moxon's edition of Tennyson's Poems, 1857 and contributed to Bohn's illustrated Walton's Angler, engraved by Mason Jackson (q.v.); Early English Poems,1863; and the Churchman's Family Magazine,1863. In addition Creswick was an early member of the Etching Club and produced various etched illustrations. He was elected ARA in 1842, RA,1851, where he exhibited from 1828 and also exhibited at the British Institution in 1829-30. He died in Bayswater, London on 28 December 1869. [Chatto; Houfe; LeBlanc; DNB; Clement; Bénézit; Barlow, Catalogue of Works of Thomas Creswick, 1873; also Volume I for discussion of his etchings]

CREWE, Alfred fl.1835-50
Wood engraver, apprenticed to the noted George Baxter (q.v.) on 20 July 1835 for seven years, after which he remained as wood engraver with Baxter until about 1840. He then worked with Ebenezer Landells (q.v.), where he met Birket Foster and Edmund Evans (qq.v.), and worked for Landells on part of the panoramic view of London for the Illustrated London News. Later Crewe quit Landells for Henry Vizetelly (q.v.), with whom he had worked for six years by 1849. It was through Crewe that B.Foster was in fact introduced to Vizetelly,

initiating that successful artist-patron collaboration. Nothing is known of Crewe in later years.
[C.T.Lewis, Picture Printing,p.66]

CROOK, John fl.1870s
Provincial wood engraver, who worked at 35 Cannon Street, Birmingham (Kelly's,1876).

CROOK, John, Junior fl.1870s
Provincial draughtsman on wood, who worked at 29 Temple Row, Birmingham (Kelly's,1876) and was probably related to John Crook (q.v.).

CROOK and Bradley fl.1880s
Provincial wood engraving firm, with an office at 162 Edmund Street, Birmingham (Kelly's,1880).

CROPSEY, Jaspar Francis 1823-1900
Occasional draughtsman on wood, and painter, who was born in Rossville, New York, 1823, worked in New York 1845-62, travelled to Turkey but settled in London in 1857. He drew on wood for The Poetical Works of E.A.Poe,1857 and The Poetry of Thomas Moore. He also exhibited at the Royal Academy, 1845-62, and died in Hastings-on-Hudson, 1900.
[Chatto; TB; Art Journal,1860,pp.198-9]

CROSSFIELD
(see Iago and Crossfield)

CROWE, Eyre 1824-1910
Illustrator and painter, born in London on 3 October 1824, the son of an historian. He studied with W.Darley and at the Paris Atelier of Delaroche; also the Royal Academy Schools in 1844. He drew for the Illustrated London News,1856-61, following his move to America, was elected ARA in 1875 and exhibited at the British Institute, 1850,1861, the Royal Academy and the Royal Society of British Artists,1854,1856. He was Thackeray's cousin and secretary, and he accompanied him to America and wrote and illustrated With Thackeray in America,1893, and Haunts and Homes of W.M.Thackeray.
[Houfe]

CROWE, J.A. fl.1840s-50s
Wood engraver and illustrator, who worked for the Illustrated London News as special correspondent in the Crimea, 1855-56. He also engraved for Charles Knight's The Penny Magazine,1841, after F.Fairholt's drawing series, 'A Day in a Tobacco Factory' and 'A Day at the Coach Factory'.
[Houfe; Bodleian Library]

CROWLEY, Nicholas J. 1813-57
Draughtsman illustrator and portrait painter, born in 1813, probably in Ireland, who worked in Dublin. He briefly visited England in 1838, exhibited at the British Institution, 1839-57, the Royal Academy from 1835 and at the Royal Society of British Artists, 1836. He was also elected RHA,1838. He contributed wood engraved drawings to the Illustrated London News,1853-54.
[Houfe]

CROWQUILL, Alfred (pseudonym Alfred Henry Forrester) c1804-72
Comic draughtsman and writer, born in London c1804 (Redgrave 1805). He was contributing caricatures to the comic papers by the age of eighteen, and was gradually associated with The Hive, The Mirror, and the early numbers of Punch. He left Punch in 1844, where 'his place was easily and advantageously filled' (Spielmann) and built up a successful career as children's book illustrator. His drawings were done in a fine, fantasy style at times reminiscent of Richard Doyle or G.Cruikshank (qq.v.). Henry Vizetelly (q.v.) secured some for his Illustrated Times,1859, and Crowquill was also a frequent contributor to the Illustrated London News,1844-70. Bohn cites his illustrations to the Pictorial Grammar, 1850; eight drawings to S.C.Hall's Book of British Ballads; and The Adventures of Gooroo Simple. He also wrote extensively and was more generally known as a literary man for The New Monthly and Bentley's magazines. He exhibited briefly at the Royal Academy, 1845-46. He died in May 1872. The British Museum owns his designs wood engraved by the Dalziel Brothers (q.v.), 1839-47.
[For a list of illustrated works see Houfe; also Chatto; Redgrave; Spielmann; Evans Reminiscences]

CRUIKSHANK, George,Senior 1792-1878
Draughtsman on wood, caricaturist, etcher, painter and temperance spokesman. He was born at Duke Street, London on 27 September 1792, second son of the caricaturist Isaac Cruikshank. He worked for several years for his father engraving lottery tickets and chap-books, his first design being published in 1806. He quickly established himself as a Regency caricaturist and contributed to numerous journals and books, which became vehicles for his sprightly drawings, many of which were done for wood engravers. Although from 1823-35 these were mostly head and tailpiece vignettes to be dropped into the text, they were the result of over twenty years of experience drawing for wood engraving and etched plates. His style borrowed much from his early political cartoons; those swift pencil sketches which he made for William Hone's pamphlets, and the crude chap-book woodcut effect which he eventually abandoned once he had been commissioned by the more important periodicals. He used a large number of wood engravers to interpret his drawings, notably John Thompson (q.v.) for Mirth and Morality,1835 and Talpa,1852; or S. and T.Williams (qq.v.) whom he had recommended to the publisher John Murray.

Later he discovered the expert skill of Horace Harral (q.v.) who introduced the burgeoning 'sixties' style of firm black outline into Cruikshank's drawings for Mrs Ewing's The Brownies,1870. He was competent enough in his understanding of the wood engraver's skills to have taught the illustrator Cuthbert Bede (q.v.) the art of drawing on wood for Punch, although he himself steadfastly refused to draw for the magazine. He did contribute drawings to Bentley's Miscellany,1837-43; Ainsworth's Magazine,1842; Vizetelly's Illustrated Times; and its rival, the Illustrated London News,1877. Cruikshank turned to the temperance cause during the last thirty years of his life, and painted, drew and wrote under its influence. He exhibited at the British Institution, 1833-60, and at the Royal Academy. He died in Mornington Crescent on 1 February 1878. The British Museum owns designs wood engraved by the Dalziel Brothers (q.v.), 1839-47,1863,1866.
[For a list of his illustrated work see Houfe; William Feaver, George Cruikshank, Arts Council, 1974; J.Buchanan Brown, George Cruikshank,1980]

CRUIKSHANK, George,Junior fl.1886-94
Draughtsman illustrator, son of George Cruikshank (q.v.), in whose style he worked, albeit rather weakly. He contributed drawings to magazines throughout the 1870s and 1880s, notably to Beeton's Annuals,1866; London Society,1866,1874; Aunt Judy's Magazine,1866-71; the Illustrated London News,1882; and the Sphere,1894.
[Houfe; White]

CRUIKSHANK, (Isaac) Robert 1786-1856
Draughtsman caricaturist, illustrator and miniature painter, the eldest son of the caricaturist Isaac Cruikshank and brother of George Cruikshank (q.v.). He first served in the navy before setting up as a miniature painter in London, then changed to etching and caricatures in 1816,' no doubt under the influence of his successful brother George, although he himself achieved a considerable reputation from 1816-25. After the 1820s he dropped out of favour, a victim of the newer forms of caricature adopted by HB (John Doyle (q.v.)) and others. He did collaborate on at least one book with George: illustrations to the Universal Songster,1828, engraved on wood by J.R.Marshall (q.v.), using 'rather a coarse hand' (Bohn in Chatto and Jackson). Other drawings were wood engraved by Thomas Mosses and M.U.S. (qq.v.). The British Museum owns several engraved by the Dalziel Brothers (q.v.).
[For a list of illustrated work see Houfe; G.Everitt, English Caricaturists,1893; Chatto; and W.Bates, George Cruikshank...with some account of his brother Robert,1878]

CULLETON, Thomas fl.1840-70s
London wood engraver, who worked from 1840 at 2 Long Acre, then 25 Cranbourn Street, WC (POD,1860-76). He is listed by Fincham as an 'Heraldic stationer', noted for some thirty bookplates designed and engraved from 1840-70.
[TB; Fincham]

CUNNINGHAM, John fl.1840s-60s
London wood engraver, who worked at 6 Richard Street, Liverpool Road (POD,1848-51), then formed a partnership as Cunningham and Fry, at 108 Dorset Street, Fleet Street, EC (POD,1853). By 1855 the partnership had broken up and Cunningham was working alone in Dorset Street (POD,1853-64). His early engraving was for Charles Knight's publications, such as the Penny Magazine,1841, after drawings of Wells, F.Fairholt and Stanesby (qq.v.).
[Bodleian Library]

CUNNINGHAM and Fry
(see Cunningham, John)

CURREN, J.
Draughtsman on wood, who contributed two wood engraved sketches to Punch,1875-76.
[Spielmann]

CURREY, Miss Esme c1883-1973
Wood engraver, etcher, and tempera painter. She specialiséd in wood engravings of architectural subjects and portraits. She was born in Kensington, studied at the Slade, in Melbourne, and Goldsmith's College. She exhibited at the Royal Academy, the Royal Society of British Artists and the Royal Society of Painter-Etchers and Engravers. She was elected ARE in 1937. She was a competent etcher, worked in London and died on 29 March 1973.
[Waters]

CUTTS, Henry Whitmore and Company fl.1877-84
London wood engraving firm, with offices at 210 Strand, WC (POD,1876-80), then 7 Bell Yard, Temple Bar, WC (POD,1883-84). Cutts' engraved work included a half-page engraving 'The Poor Seamstress on Christmas Morning', after 'E.F.' for the Illustrated London News,22 December 1877, engraved in a clear, heavy 'sixties' black-line style.

CUTTS and Harrison fl.1873-75
London wood engraving firm, a partnership between H.Cutts and Henry Harrison (qq.v.), with an office at 4 Bouverie Street, Fleet Street, EC (POD,1873-75), which was shared with Henry Crane (q.v.). By 1876 Harrison had split up from Cutts and both were working independently.

DADD, Frank 1851-1929
Draughtsman illustrator and figure artist, born in
London on 28 March 1851. He trained at South
Kensington and the Royal Academy Schools, then
became a professional illustrator, drawing for
various popular magazines. He drew for wood
engravings in the Cornhill,1870-79, and The Graphic,
1876-1910, where he joined the staff in 1884 and
produced his characteristic paintings for boy's
adventure stories. He also worked for the Illustrated
London News,1878-84, for which he produced full
and double-page drawings wood engraved by
W.I.Mosses (q.v.) and others. His most impressive
work here was a large fold-out engraving, 'The New
Cabinet', 15 May 1880. Yet his technique of using
heavy brushwork and grey washes even at this early
period made such works difficult to wood engrave
accurately. In this instance Dadd benefited by the
advent of photo-engraving for his later engravings
for the Quiver,1882; Boys' Own Paper; and the
Windsor Magazine; and illustrations to such books as
J.H.Newman's Lead Kindly Light,1887; and
G.M.Fenn's Dick O' the Fens, 1888. Dadd was also
employed to produce portraits of William Pickering
and Charles Whittingham (q.v.). He also exhibited at
the Royal Academy, 1901, and was elected RI,1884,
ROI,1888. He was related by marriage to Kate
Greenaway (q.v.). He died in Teignmouth, Devon
on 7 March 1929.
[see also Houfe; A.Warren, Charles Whittingham,1896]

DADD, Richard 1817-86
Occasional draughtsman on wood, primarily painter
of fairies and intricate painted fantasies. He was
born in Chatham in 1817 and educated there and
at William Dadson's Academy. He moved to London
in 1834, where he made friends with such noted
artists as David Roberts and Clarkson Stanfield, who
recommended him for admission to the Royal
Academy Schools. He exhibited at the British
Institution, 1839, the Royal Academy and the Royal
Society of British Artists, 1837. He won the life
drawing medal at the Royal Academy in 1840, toured
the Continent and Near East in 1842, and returned
unstable. He brutally murdered his father and was
committed to first Bethlem Hospital, then Broadmoor,
where he spend the remainder of his life. Dadd's
only known drawings on wood are four designs for
'Robin Goodfellow' in S.C.Hall's Book of British
Ballads,1842, which Hall prefaced by the claim,
'examples of the genius of a large proportion of the
more accomplished artists of Great Britain--as
exhibited in drawing upon wood'. The drawings were
commissioned by Hall, who had secured the young
Tenniel, Kenny Meadows and John Gilbert (qq.v.)
as well. He assembled his artists at his house to
read out the ballads before handing over the wood
blocks on which the appropriate artist was to make
his design. Dadd had never drawn on wood before but

provided four highly imaginative designs in which he
incorporated to a greater extent than any other of the
artists the texts of his allotted ballads. 'Though he
had never drawn on wood before, Dadd's concern
with dramatic lighting at this period translates well
into the light and dark contrast of wood engraving,
and he shows an understanding of the medium's
potential which was not shared by all his friends who
worked on the volume. He enjoyed the work, and
only a few days before killing his father had written
to Hall offering to illustrate another ballad for the
second volume' (P.Allderidge, Richard Dadd,
pp.65-66).
[see Houfe; P.Allderidge, Richard Dadd,1974]

DADD, Stephen T. fl.1879-1914
Draughtsman illustrator and figure painter, who was
trained first as a wood engraver by John Greenaway
(q.v.), to whom he was related. He contributed
illustrations of domestic and animal subjects to
The Graphic,1882-91,1901; the Illustrated London
News,1889; Daily Graphic,1890; the Quiver,1890;
Sporting and Dramatic News,1890; Black and White,
1891; The Rambler,1897; Chums; and Cassell's
Family Magazine. He also exhibited at the New
Watercolour Society,1879-92, the Royal Society of
British Artists and the Royal Institute of Painters in
Watercolours. He worked at Brockley, South London.
[Houfe; R.Engen, Kate Greenaway,1981]

DALE, Henry Sheppard 1852-1921
Draughtsman illustrator for wood engravings, etcher,
engraver, landscape and architecture watercolourist.
He was born on 13 November 1852 and studied at
Cary's Art School, the Slade from 1871, and in Italy
from 1874-77. On his return he was taken up as a
draughtsman illustrator for wood engraved plates in
The Graphic,1879-81, and illustrated several books.
He also exhibited in the London galleries from 1878,
notably at the Royal Academy, the Royal Institute of
Painters in Watercolours and the Royal Society of
Painter-Etchers and Engravers, where he was
elected ARE in 1909. He died on 24 November 1921.
[Waters; for a list of metal engravings and etchings
see Volume 1]

DALTON, Ernest Charles fl.1884-1901
London wood engraver, who was a pupil of
W.J.Palmer (q.v.). He then set up at 3 Bouverie
Street, EC (POD,1884-89), sharing the premises
with H.F.Davey and A.C.Coats (qq.v.). He moved
later to 67 Great Ormond Street (POD,1890-1901).
The British Museum owns a landscape with small
boys after 'W S', engraved in strong tints.

DALTON, James fl.1866-93
London wood engraver, who worked at 9 Crimscot
Street, Bermondsey, SE (POD,1866), 48 Paternoster
Row (POD,1867), shared with S.S.Carter (q.v.) and

21 Paternoster Row (POD,1868-71). Dalton joined with Carter as Carter and Dalton (q.v.), then as Dalton and Carter, with an office at 21 Paternoster Row (POD,1875-83). He had broken with his partner by 1885 and moved to 60 Old Bailey, EC (POD,1885-92), then 7 Red Lion Court, Fleet Street, EC (POD,1893).

DALTON and Carter
(see Dalton, James)

DALZIEL, Alexander Aitcheson fl.1870s
Wood engraver and illustrator, son of Robert Dalziel and nephew of the Dalziel brothers (q.v.) with whom he trained as a wood engraver. His elder brother was the wood engraver John Saunderson Dalziel (q.v.). Alexander Dalziel illustrated The Colliers' Strike in S.Wales,1872, but shortly after his apprenticeship he married and moved to South Africa, 'where for a time he coupled scholastic work with his engraving' (Dalziels' Record,p.348). He later gave up engraving for teaching.

DALZIEL, Alexander John 1814-36
Wood engraver and illustrator, born in Wooler on 12 March 1814, the son of the artist Alexander Dalziel (1781-1832), and brother of the famous Dalziel brothers George, Edward, Thomas and John (qq.v.). He first served as a pupil of Isaac Nicholson (q.v.) in Newcastle for seven years where he worked with fellow pupil Charles Gray (q.v.). According to the Dalziels' Record, he 'proved himself a very skilful draughtsman and engraver'. He was a promising black and white illustrator but died of consumption in Newcastle on 23 December 1836.

DALZIEL Brothers fl.1840-1905
The most influential and successful firm of wood engravers, draughtsmen, printers and publishers of the period. Their work spanned over fifty years and encompassed almost every major illustrated book published in Britain from 1840-90. The firm began when George Dalziel (q.v.) came to London in 1835 and set up as a wood engraver. He was joined by his brother Edward in 1840 and together they signed work as 'G. & E.Dalziel' and operated from an office at 48 Albert Street, Mornington Crescent (POD,1848-52). This work included commissions from Ebenezer Landells (q.v.) for early issues of the Illustrated London News and Punch. They were the first to engrave John Leech's drawings for Punch, having also engraved its prospectus and first covers. Through their Newcastle connections they were taken up by the prolific draughtsman William Harvey (q.v.) and engraved many of his drawings from 1839-66, notably for the Abbotsford edition of Walter Scott,1842-43. Harvey introduced them to his employer, Charles Knight (q.v.), the publisher of numerous illustrated popular books and magazines, and Knight commissioned their engravings to his 'Shakespeare' and 'The Land We Live In' series,1854-56. About 1850 they entered into relations with the publisher George Routledge, which lasted over forty years, and it was through this connection that they were able to engrave and print the long series of illustrated books for which they became famous. 'For these "fine art" books, often issued in the name of other firms, the Dalziels made all the arrangements and undertook the financial risk, commissioning artists on their own responsibility to design the woodcuts, contributing part of the designs themselves, and engraving the blocks by their own hands or those of their pupils' (DNB). George and Edward were joined by their engraver sister Margaret Dalziel (q.v.) in 1851, and their brother John Dalziel (q.v.) in 1852. They appear in the London directories as the Dalziel Brothers, 4 Camden Street, N, Camden Town (POD,1856-58). Their plans for fine art books meant that they needed their own printing press, so they also established The Camden Press at 53 (later 110) High Street, Camden Town, in 1857. They remained there until the firm closed down in 1905, at first with John Dalziel living on the premises, and his brothers nearby in Camden Town, Primrose Hill and Hampstead. In 1860 they were joined by another brother, Thomas Bolton Gilchrist Dalziel (q.v.), who joined as a draughtsman partner from 1857-86. They continued to exert influence upon illustrated books and magazines throughout the 1870s and 1880s, but in 1893, the Official Receiver was called in to examine their substantial losses. The firm survived from 1893-1905 in the hands of Edward Dalziel's sons, Harvey Robert (1855-?), and Charles Davison Dalziel (1857-?), then under the name Dalziel and Company Limited. By the 1860s they had established what one critic thought 'more like a school of engraving than a business'. Their fine art publications demanded talented draughtsmen and apprentice engravers, who were largely taught by Thomas Dalziel. They included the draughtsmen trainees G.G.Kilburne, C.A.Ferrier, A.W.Bayes, Fred Walker, J.W.North, and George Pinwell (qq.v.). The engraver trainees included Francis Fricker, Harry Fenn and Charles Kingdon; the Dalziel nephews Alexander Aitcheson Dalziel and John Sanderson Dalziel; Phil Ebbutt, Hal Ludlow, George Gatcombe, Harry Leighton, E.J.Wallis, Walter Williams, William Arrowsmith, James Clark, and someone signed 'WY' (qq.v.). The Dalziel training was strenuous and demanding for not only did they insist on a nine hour stint at the engraver's bench, but afterwards every pupil was to work on drawing. Most of the Dalziels knew how to draw as well as engrave and they felt, understandably, that this was an essential skill for any novice wood engraver. The Dalziels were, in fact, keen collectors of paintings and often commissioned artists' works, such as watercolours from Burne-Jones, Watson, and Birket Foster (whom they offered £3,000 for thirty

watercolours, but were refused). (For an indication of the scope of their collections see S.Houfe, The Dalziel Family, 1978.) They themselves exhibited twenty-one wood engravings at the Royal Academy, 1861-70. A complete list of the Dalziel works has never been attempted, not even by Gleeson White. The Dalziels provided a list at the end of their Record, 1901, but this is unreliable. The British Library catalogue lists some seventy-four books; the British Museum Print Room has over fifty folio volumes of dated proofs, compiled at the time they were engraved, for their various books, magazines and trade publications (catalogues, fashion plates, scientific charts and graphs). These start from 1839. The Camden Press also printed colour plates for various books (although the Dalziels hardly mention colour printing in their autobiography). Their most successful colour work was for Routledge's children's books, although McLean points out that they 'never seriously rivalled Evans either in volume or quality, although their output was quite large' (McLean, Victorian Book Design, 1972, p.180). However, they were best known for their expertly wood engraved black and white illustrations which helped many a 'Sixties School' illustrator on his way to prominence. Their early designs were after George Cruikshank, John Leech, Richard Doyle, Kenny Meadows, F.R.Pickersgill, and John Gilbert (qq.v.). They formed links with the Pre-Raphaelites when asked by Millais (q.v.) in 1855 to engrave his drawings to the Moxon edition of Tennyson's Poems, 1857 (for which they eventually engraved fifteen cuts). They had also engraved after Millais, Rossetti and Arthur Hughes (qq.v.) for The Music Master and Day and Night Songs, 1855. Most of the illustrations by Rossetti and Holman Hunt were cut by them; Ford Madox Brown and Burne-Jones (qq.v.) contributed to their Bible Gallery, 1880. They were perhaps most successful in engraving after Millais, however, especially his Trollope illustrations -- Orley Farm, 1861 and Framley Parsonage, 1862. They initiated a Fine Art Gift Book from him, his famous Parables of Our Lord, 1864. They also helped interpret the drawings of G.Du Maurier, J.Tenniel, Birket Foster and Harrison Weir (qq.v.). Their most famous engravings were to Edward Lear's Book of Nonsense, 1862, and after Tenniel's drawings to Lewis Carroll's classics, Alice in Wonderland, 1866, and Through the Looking-Glass, 1872. Their influence on the 'Sixties School' of engraved illustration came largely through work for the illustrated periodicals. They were solely responsible for the engravings in the Cornhill, from its foundation in 1859, followed by a similar position on Good Words from 1862. Here they commissioned new draughtsmen like Fred Walker, G.J.Pinwell, A.B.Houghton, M.J.Lawless, J.D.Watson, Frederick Barnard, and J.W.North (qq.v.). 'Their aim was to preserve each line intact when the drawings were made, as Gilbert and Tenniel made them, by a pure

line method, but they often had the more difficult task of reproducing in facsimile a mixture of line and brush work, touched on the block with Chinese white, a practise habitual with later illustrators...' (DNB). When they found the task too difficult, or they wished to preserve the artists' drawings, they used photographic transfer onto the wood block (for instance Millais' work in the Bible Gallery. Book commissions during this period included: Staunton's Shakespeare, 1858-61, after John Gilbert's drawings; Lalla Rookh, 1861, after Tenniel; Pictures of English Landscape, 1862, after Birket Foster; Pilgrim's Progress, 1863, after J.D.Watson; The Arabian Nights' Entertainments, 1864, after A.B.Houghton and Thomas Dalziel; Home Thoughts and Home Scenes, 1865; Goldsmith's Works, 1865, after Pinwell; and their own A Round of Days, 1866; Wayside Poesies, 1867; and Bible Gallery, 1880. (For a list of work see Dalziels' Record, pp.353ff although dates are not to be trusted.) By the 1870s the Dalziels had turned to publishing and printing comic papers. They bought the paper Fun, started in 1865 as a penny rival to Punch. From 1870 to 1893 it was owned by George and Edward Dalziel, who commissioned illustrations from G.Pinwell, F.Barnard, J.Mahoney, Henry Doyle, and Hubert Herkomer (qq.v.), and articles by Austin Dobson, G.A.Sala and George Sims. In 1871 they bought Hood's Comic Annual, where George's articles often appeared. In 1872 they bought Judy, which they sold to their nephew Gilbert Dalziel (q.v.) in 1888. They were placed in charge of the illustrations and engravings to the Household edition of Dickens, 1871-79, and selected new illustrators such as James Mahoney, E.G.Dalziel, Charles Green, F.A.Fraser, A.B.Frost and Gordon Thomson (qq.v.). But it was the Dalziels' Bible Gallery, 1880-81, planned in the 1860s (when parts appeared at the Royal Academy) with its famous illustrators Millais, F.Leighton, S.Solomon, Holman Hunt and others, which marked the official end to their book engraving activities. The advent of photo-engraving meant many commissions were lost to that medium by the 1880s; and by 1893 the Dalziels' debts (£39,146) could not be ignored. The receiver was called in and told of 'the extinction of their wood engraving business owing to the introduction of automatic processes; to loss by colour printing owing to foreign competition; and to loss through competition generally'. The receiver commented that since the Dalziels were then over seventy years old, they 'could not keep up with the times' -- a crushing blow for so influential a firm. On the other hand, some of their critics would have welcomed their demise, for example W.J.Linton (q.v.) who saw them as responsible for the 'muddy darks and rotten fine work' of all European wood engraving of the period, when engravers merely 'followed the fashion of the Dalziel mania in England' and used the graver to outline and imitate the line

engraving, without considering the sense of tone.
White points out why this was so popular: 'Their
effort was to translate the draughtsman's line, not
to paraphrase it by tint-cutting'. Nevertheless their
influence in France was considerable. They engraved
for the Magasin Pittoresque which secured a large
public for their work, which was praised by Gusman
(p.216). Nagler claimed that the Dalziels were the
'most fruitful English engravers of our time', and
cited their 100 engravings to Willmott's Poets of the
Nineteenth Century, 1857. Bohn, in Chatto and
Jackson, claimed that 'Messrs. Dalziel are among
the most extensive of our wood-engravers, and have
taken part in all the illustrated works of importance
which have been produced during the last twenty years',
and devoted five pages to illustrations. The Dalziels'
reputation was firmly cemented into place when
George and Edward published their reminiscences,
The Brothers Dalziel, a Record of Fifty Years'
Work...1840-90, appropriately published at the end
of an era, in 1901. It is a fascinating account of their
working relationship with the period's most prominent
illustrators, publishers and authors, but regrettably
omits much about their competitors or their reception
as artistic supervisors to the period's most influential
publications. When it appeared, their rival Edmund
Evans (q.v.) lamented the fact he had been omitted
from its pages, and added of their printing from
original blocks, 'I doubt if the general public will care
for it, I believe they are more interested in process
now...' (letter dated 1901, University of California
Library). Today opinions still place the Dalziels at
the top of their field, although W.J.Linton probably
made better wood blocks for the presses. Their
Record has been republished (Batsford, 1980) and
their engravings appear on cards, posters and in
scholarly studies of the period. Their most recent
critic, Eric De Maré, dislikes their 'lack of overall
unity and simplicity in book design', and adds the
final note: 'Too often their engravings show
insufficient regard for the subjects they purport to
illustrate. They churned the books out, with thick,
rich, indented, and gilded covers, and sometimes
they would botch, using the same block in different
books in irrelevent contexts, often to the annoyance
of the designers (E.De Maré, The Woodblock
Illustrators, 1980, pp.57-58). The largest collections
of proofs are in the British Museum, the Victoria and
Albert Museum and the Boston Museum (Hartley
Collection). The Dalziel signatures varied:
'DALZIEL SC', 'G.DALZIEL'.
[For biographical information see individual entries
below; also Dalziels' Record, 1901; DNB;
S.Houfe, The Dalziel Family, 1978 (Sotheby Sale
catalogue). For colour printing see Wakeman and
Bridson]

DALZIEL, Davison
Wood engraver, youngest of the Dalziel brothers
(q.v.), who married Helen Galter, sister of the
Punch engraver William Galter (q.v.)

DALZIEL, Edward 1817-1905
Prominent draughtsman and wood engraver,
occasional watercolourist and oil painter. He was
one of the talented Dalziel family, born in Wooler,
Northumberland on 5 December 1817, the fifth son
of the artist Alexander Dalziel (1781-1832) and
brother of George, John, and Thomas Dalziel (qq.v.).
He was educated first in Newcastle, where he
trained as a businessman until his brother George
lured him to London about 1839. There they worked
together from 1840, engraving for Ebenezer Landells
(q.v.) as 'outside engravers' on various popular
illustrated books and magazines, including early
editions of Punch and the Illustrated London News.
He was particularly good at engraving Richard
Doyle's drawings. He was the leading light in the
firm of wood engravers, printers and publishers
known as the Dalziel Brothers (q.v.) and remained
there as engraver, draughtsman, later publisher
and printer until 1893. His brother Thomas recalled
Edward's invaluable keen sense of artistic judgement
and his success in finding new draughtsmen: 'The
extension and development of our transactions and
the carrying out of many of the fine art works which
we published, is unquestionably due to my brother
Edward Dalziel, and to this I am at all times ready
to bear unhesitating testimony' (quoted in White,
p.178). Edward was the brother who took the role of
the draughtsman illustrator most seriously. His
early days in London had been spent studying drawing
at the Clipstone Academy, where his fellow pupils
were Charles Keene and John Tenniel (qq.v.), and
he continued to paint throughout the 1890s (see
S.Houfe, The Dalziel Family, 1978, Items 3-7). He
successfully exhibited oil and watercolour paintings
at the British Institution in 1841; and two studies of
a head at the Royal Academy, 1865-66. Although as
an illustrator he was less gifted than his brother
Thomas, he contributed a considerable number of
drawings on wood for his firm to engrave. These
appeared in: Poetical Works of Bryant, 1857; Dramatic
Scenes, 1857; Poets of the Nineteenth Century, 1857;
Mackay's Home Affections, 1858; six drawings to the
Dalziels' Arabian Nights' Entertainments, 1865;
A Round of Days, 1866; The Spirit of Praise, 1866;
Ballad Stories of the Affections, 1866; Golden Thoughts
from the Golden Fountains, 1867; three to Ingelow's
Poems, 1867; North Coast, 1868; National Nursery
Rhymes, 1870; Dickens' The Uncommercial Traveller
(Household edition, supervised by the Dalziels, 1871);
The Graphic, 1873-74; and one drawing to the Dalziels'
Bible Gallery, 1880-81. His thirty drawings to Parnell's
The Hermit, drawn in 1855, were engraved and
privately printed by the Dalziels' Camden Press,

1904. Forrest Reid assessed Edward's talents as a
draughtsman on wood blocks: 'He made a few if any
designs for periodicals, and, though he contributed
to a fair number of books, his contributions were as
a rule limited to a drawing or two, and not all of
these signed. He was by no means a great
draughtsman, yet some of his drawings, especially
his drawings of children, have a charm which the
more conventional figure work of his brother
[Thomas] lacks. Rarely is anything he does, I dare
say, quite so accomplished as Thomas's best work
in landscape, but both had the great advantage of
knowing exactly what the craft of the engraver could
and could not reproduce'. Reid concluded, 'With
more practice Edward would, I think, have been the
best of the three Dalziels. Even as it is, he is the
most interesting (Reid,p.252). Edward worked
mainly from the Dalziel premises at 53 High Street,
Camden Town, but he registered as an engraver in
the London directories once, at 6 Bernard Street,
Regent's Park Road (POD,1856). During the mid
1860s he lived at 10 St George's Square (Graves,
Royal Academy Exhibitors). He married Jane Gurden
in 1847, and had five sons and four daughters. The
eldest son, Edward Gurden Dalziel (q.v.), and his
second son Gilbert Dalziel (q.v.), were both artists.
The third and fourth sons, Harvey Robert (b.13 March
1855) and Charles Davison Dalziel (b.16 January
1857) carried on the family business from 1893-1905,
then under the name Dalziel and Company Limited
until it closed down. Edward helped his brother
Gilbert to write their memoirs, The Brothers
Dalziel,1901. He died on 25 March 1905 at Fellows
Road, South Hampstead. The British Museum owns
a number of his engravings. He signed his work:
'ED' (superimposed), 'E.DALZIEL SC'.
[For biographical detail see S.Houfe, The Dalziel
Family,1978; Dalziels' Record; DNB;
for accounts of his work see Reid; White. His
paintings are listed in Catalogue of Choice
Collection of Watercolour Drawings...of Edward
Dalziel, Christies,19 June 1886; also reproduced in
Houfe]

DALZIEL, Edward Gurden 1849-89
Draughtsman illustrator, the eldest son of Edward
Dalziel (q.v.). He was born in London on 7 February
1849. He began work as a draughtsman on wood during
the 1860s, and contributed to Good Words, Good
Words for the Young, Sunday Magazine, People's
Magazine, The Day of Rest, and The Graphic. But
it was his numerous drawings for his father's
magazines Fun,1878-80 and Judy, with subjects of
country life and manners, the figures borrowed from
Pinwell and Walker, that were admired by his
contemporaries. He also illustrated various books:
Novello's National Nursery Rhymes, and Christmas
Carols and did five drawings with F.Barnard (q.v.) to
Strahan's Pilgrim's Progress. He illustrated for

his uncles their Household Dickens series, The
Uncommercial Traveller, Christmas Stories, and
Reprinted Pieces,1871-79, and one drawing to the
Dalziels' Bible Gallery,1880-81. These Millais
declared 'admirable'; John Gilbert wrote to his
father, 'Your son's drawings show an amazing care
and truth'. But Forrest Reid dismissed Edward's
contribution to the late sixties style which, he
thought, indicated 'confusion between the ornate and
the decorative...But even more than F.A.Fraser
and Wilfrid Lawson he represents the decadence,
and his solitary design in Dalziels' Bible Gallery,
'The Five Kings Hiding in the Cave', shows how
completely out of touch he was with the whole spirit
of the sixties' (Reid,p.266). Edward Dalziel was
also a painter. His uncles described him in their
Record as 'a young artist full of promise and great
ability. Had he given continued attention to his oil
painting he must undoubtedly have taken a very high
position. He exhibited many pictures at the Royal
Academy, the Grosvenor and other galleries, but
the allurement of black and white became too much
for him, and he laid aside his brush for the pencil'.
His landscape and genre work was exhibited at the
Royal Academy,1869-82; also at the Paris
Exhibition,1878. The British Museum owns a
number of his drawings for wood engravings.
[For biographical detail see Dalziels' Record;
DNB; TB]

DALZIEL, George 1815-1902
Draughtsman, wood engraver, occasional author of
poems and stories, the senior member of the
artistic family of Dalziels. He was born in Wooler,
Northumberland on 1 December 1815, the son of the
artist Alexander Dalziel (1781-1832), brother of
Edward, John and Thomas (qq.v.), or as they
became known, the Dalziel Brothers (q.v.). George
was educated in Newcastle, then at nineteen came to
London in 1835, where he worked for four years with
the wood engraver Charles Gray (q.v.). He then set
up on his own, but had joined with his brother
Edward by 1840, and together they formed what
would eventually become the Dalziel Brothers, wood
engravers, draughtsmen, printers and publishers.
George's early engravings were 'outside' work
commissioned by Ebenezer Landells (q.v.) for
Punch and the Illustrated London News. His own
earliest engraving of note was for S.C.Hall's Book
of British Ballads,1842, in which he collaborated
with the period's major engravers: W.Linton, Orrin
Smith, F.Branston, the Williams family,
H.Vizetelly, E.Landells, E.Evans and E.Whymper
(qq.v.). He became particularly proficient at
engraving after William Harvey's and Richard Doyle's
(qq.v.) drawings. He also produced some original
drawings, himself. He worked from 48 Albert Street,
Mornington Crescent (POD,1854-58), which he
shared with Edward; by 1857 they had taken on the

printing office at 53 High Street, Camden Town, where they established the Camden Press that continued in operation until 1905. George was the literary member of the family, who produced several volumes of poems and stories. He also wrote for the Dalziels' own comic publications Fun and Hood's Comic Annual. His works include: Mattie Grey and Other Poems,1873; Pictures in the Fire,1887; Dick Boulin's Four-in-Hand,1887; Who Lived There?,1887; In Memoriam (poems),1888; A Soldier's Sweetheart and Other Stories,1892; and Unconsidered Trifles (poems),1898. He and his brother Edward wrote their autobiography, The Dalziel Brothers,1901. George married in 1846 but had no children. When his wife died he moved in with Edward in Hampstead, and died at 107 Fellows Road, South Hampstead on 4 August 1902. The British Museum owns a number of his wood engravings. He signed his work: 'G.DALZIEL', 'G.D.', but later only as 'DALZIEL SC'.
[See Dalziels' Record; S.Houfe, The Dalziel Family,1978; DNB]

DALZIEL, Gilbert 1853-1930
Wood engraver, draughtsman illustrator and watercolourist. He was born in London on 25 June 1853, the second son of the wood engraver Edward Dalziel (q.v.) and brother of Edward Gurden Dalziel (q.v.). He was a pupil of the Dalziel Brothers (q.v.), where he learned wood engraving, then studied at South Kensington and the Slade, under its new head, Sir Edward Poynter. He exhibited genre watercolours at the Dudley Gallery and Crystal Palace from the age of thirteen, 1866-82, but like his brother Edward Gurden, he turned from painting to black and white illustration. He drew for many books and magazines including The Pictorial World, Quips, and Larks. He became editor of the Dalziel-owned Fun and started Ally Sloper's Half Holiday in 1884. In 1888 he took over the editorship of the Dalziels' Judy, and established its 'golden age', procuring illustrations from leading process illustrators, Bernard Partridge, Raven-Hill and Greiffenhagen. Gilbert Dalziel was the most talented member of the younger generation of Dalziels, but his sternest critics came from his father's generation, which he knew well. He was in fact named after John Gilbert (q.v.) who refused to become his godfather. He modelled for Frederick Walker's illustrations to Thackeray's 'Phillip', in the Cornhill. But when he became associated with the blatantly commercial comic paper, Ally Sloper, he brought shame on his father and uncles. According to Edmund Evans: 'I cannot but feel sorry for one of such a hardworking family as either George or Edward having any connection with such useless rubbish as Ally Sloper, whatever money was ever made out of it' (letter in University of California Library). Gilbert continued his artistic career and was ultimately responsible

for preserving his father and uncles' reputations by presenting collections of their engravings to various museums. He also helped Forrest Reid to compile his Illustrators of the 1860s,1928. He was a member of the Hampstead Society of Artists, and died on 13 May 1930.
[S.Houfe, The Dalziel Family,1978; TB; Who's Who, 1913; Waters; Dalziels' Record]

DALZIEL, John 1822-69
Wood engraver and talented draughtsman on wood, one of the Dalziel Brothers (q.v.). He was born in Wooler, Northumberland on 1 January 1822, the sixth son of the artist Alexander Dalziel (1781-1832), and brother of George, Edward and Thomas Dalziel (qq.v.). He trained as an engraver when he joined his brothers in London in 1852, as part of the Dalziel firm. He appears in the London directories at 3 Camden Street, N (POD,1851-54). His brothers described him as 'a skilful and highly accomplished engraver; but his health, unfortunately, gave way, and in early 1868 he had to give up all art work' (Record,pp.4,11). He contributed many designs for engraving during that period, but in 1868 retired to Cumberland, for the sake of his health and the scenery. He lived in Drigg until 21 May 1869, when he died, cutting short a promising career. He married twice: Harriet Carter in 1846; Elizabeth Wells in 1863, and had a son and two daughters. The British Museum owns engravings by him.
[For biographical detail see DNB; also Dalziels' Record]

DALZIEL, John Sanderson fl.1863-1900
Wood engraver, nephew of the Dalziel Brothers (q.v.). He was the son of the painter Robert Dalziel and brother of the wood engraver Alexander Aitcheson Dalziel (q.v.). He trained as a wood engraver with his uncles, then set up on his own in London, first at 9 Essex Street, Strand (POD,1863, listed as 'John Dalziel,Junior'), then at 3 Bouverie Street (POD,1869). The British Museum owns a collection of his work, including engravings of machines, printing presses and portraits after photographs. He subsequently emigrated to Canada and set up as 'Artist and Engraver on Wood, 85 St Urbain Street, Montreal'. His first engraving commission was of a cooking stove, for which he received $50. By 1876 he was working in Philadelphia, where he engraved 'a large number of elaborate, highly-finished works, chiefly of a scientific character, much of which has been reproduced in this country' (Dalziels' Record,p.348). The British Museum collection includes numerous engravings of natural history subjects, shells, insects, buds, for Century Magazine,1886 and the Century Dictionary,1884-88. A page of shells for the Smithsonian Institute, Washington, earned him

$800 and the praise of Professor Woolcot: 'most perfect'. There is also a large winter scene for Outing Magazine, c1880, which John inscribed '4 days= 32 hours work'. John had apparently moved to Colorado by 1900, where he grew fruit and engraved. 'English Robin' a large, delicate work, was done in his old age and inscribed 'photographed on wood by John Dalziel at the age of 86 years'. [S.Houfe, The Dalziel Family,1978; Dalziels' Record]

DALZIEL, Margaret 1819-94
Wood engraver, sister of the Dalziel Brothers (q.v.). She was born in Wooler, Northumberland on 3 November 1819, daughter of the artist Alexander Dalziel (1781-1832). In 1851 she lived in London where she engraved for over forty years for her brothers George, Edward, Thomas and John Dalziel (qq.v.). They remembered her as a willing and capable worker: 'we were fortunate enough to have the loyal and skilful help of our sister Margaret, who warmly entered into all our plans and worked very constantly upon the most highly finished engravings we produced' (Record,pp.19-20). She was a stout, mannish woman, but, as Edward recalled, 'the essence of kindness and generosity, a sister-mother to us all, and "Aunt Meg" to everybody'. Gleeson White praised her abilities as a wood engraver of works 'distinguished for their elaboration and fine feeling' (White,p.179). She engraved for the Dalziel Brothers until they retired in 1893, and died unmarried on 12 July 1894. Her engravings were signed under the general inscription of the workshop: 'DALZIEL SC'. [S.Houfe, The Dalziel Family,1978; Dalziels' Record]

DALZIEL, Thomas Bolton Gilchrist Septimus 1823-1906
Landscape and figure draughtsman, illustrator, painter, and occasional lithographer; one of the Dalziel Brothers (q.v.). He was born in Wooler, Northumberland on 9 May 1823, the seventh son of the artist Alexander Dalziel (1781-1832), and youngest brother of George, Edward, and John Dalziel (qq.v.). He was educated in Newcastle and unlike his brothers trained as a copperplate engraver, but did not continue this work after his apprenticeship. He came to London in 1843 and worked as an independent illustrator, drawing not only for his brothers George and Edward, but for other engravers as well. 'He did not take part in the engraving of blocks, but devoted himself to drawing on wood. He also undertook the important improvements to be carried out before a finished proof was submitted to the artist' (DNB). During the days before he joined his brothers in 1857 he moved to Dover to work as a landscape painter and draughtsman. In 1857 he joined in partnership with George, Edward

and John Dalziel as the Dalziel Brothers, and remained there as a draughtsman and supervisor until 1886. At first his work was borrowed from William Harvey (q.v.), but it became more individual by the 1860s, then came especially under the influence of A.B.Houghton (q.v.) while drawing for the Dalziels' Arabian Nights' Entertainments,1864. This proved 'a considerable tour de force for both men but showing that Dalziel's talent could stand up with that of a greater artist' (Houfe, The Dalziel Family, 1978). He also borrowed the rural style and subjects of Frederick Walker (q.v.) during the period. In fact Thomas was the only one of the Dalziel Brothers to reach full recognition as a draughtsman (although all could draw). He was a greater figure artist than Edward, and was allowed to express his talent in a large number of books that were either added to or initiated and financed by the firm. He was especially adept at landscape drawing, as Reid pointed out: 'To the uninitiated it would seem as if many of Thomas Dalziel's landscapes would be almost impossible to cut yet that the difficulties were always those which either his own hand or that of another could surmount, the prints themselves are there to prove' (Reid, p.252). By the 1860s, when the Dalziel firm had become an engraving factory, he and his brother Edward supervised the apprentices and searched for new draughtsmen. He preferred careful book illustration to the rapid deadlines and poor printing of magazines. His work first appeared in Willmott's Poets of the Nineteenth Century,1857; Dramatic Scenes,1857; Bryant's Poems,1857; Gertrude of Wyoming,1857; Mackay's The Home Affections, 1858; and Lays of the Holy Land,1858. He provided a hundred illustrations to Pilgrim's Progress,1865. This followed his most successful and powerful drawings researched and drawn with A.B.Houghton for the Dalziels' Arabian Nights' Entertainments,1865 (a later edition, of solely his own drawings,1877). He contributed to A Round of Days,1866; Ballad Stories of the Affections,1866; The Spirit of Praise,1866; Jean Ingelow's Poems,1867; Golden Thoughts from Golden Fountains,1867; North Coast,1868; National Nursery Rhymes,1870; Christmas Carols,1871; and the Dalziels' Bible Gallery,1881. Thomas Dalziel was a friend of A.B.Houghton as well as of his colleagues Pinwell and Walker. He nurtured a painter's ideals, however, and his watercolour and chalk landscapes and marine pictures were exhibited from 1846-74, notably at the British Institution, 1858; the Royal Academy, 1856-62; and the Royal Society of British Artists,1846,1866. When his brothers retired in 1893, he was living in Herne Bay, Kent, where he died on 17 March 1906. He married Louisa Gurden in 1856 and his two elder sons, Herbert (1853-1941) and Owen (1861-1942) were also successful painters. Thomas recalled of his work and influence as one of the Dalziel Brothers: 'We were constant and untiring workers with our hands, untiring because it was truly a labour of love' (White,p.178). The British Museum owns a collection of engraved and lithographed designs. [For a discussion of his work see White; Reid; DNB; TB; Dalziels' Record; S.Houfe, The Dalziel Family,1978 (reproductions of several paintings and drawings)]

DANIELSSON and Company fl.1886-97
London draughtsman and wood engraving firm, with offices at 23 Southampton Buildings, WC (POD,1886-87), 52 Beaumont Street, Portland Place, W (POD,1888-97) and by 1897 a second office at 19 Farringdon Avenue, EC. They also printed colour lithographs for books and magazines.
[For colour work see Wakeman and Bridson]

DANSE, A.
Draughtsman illustrator, who contributed illustrations to Rose G.Kingsley's 'The Belfry of Bruges' wood engraved by J.D.Cooper (q.v.). They appeared in the English Illustrated Magazine,1883. Beraldi lists the Brussels-born engraver Auguste Danse, who trained under Calamatta and worked after Leys and Bastien-Lepage.

DARLEY, Felix O.C. 1822-88
Prominent American wood engraver, one of the most noted exponents of mid-nineteenth century wood engraving. He was born in Philadelphia on 23 June 1822 where he became noted for his wood engravings to a local paper. His engravings to Washington Irving's History of New York,1850, set an exceptionally high standard of facsimile wood engraving, which he used for works of Dickens and Hawthorne as well. He was also a painter of historical subjects, portraits, and genre subjects which he exhibited at various galleries. He died in Claymore on 27 March 1888. The British Museum owns three proof engravings after his designs, engraved by the Dalziel Brothers (q.v.),1863.
[Stauffer; TB; Bénézit; Clement; Heller; Art Journal, 1888,p.256; Fielding]

DARLEY, J.Felix ?-1932
Draughtsman on wood, landscape and figure painter. He was noted for his drawings on wood to The Poetical Works of Edgar Allan Poe,1857; Poets of the West; and a drawing to London Society,1863 (according to Bohn in Chatto and Jackson). He worked in London from 1886, and in Addlestone, Surrey from 1898, and exhibited at the Royal Institute of Painters in Oil-Colours and the Royal Society of British Artists, where he was elected RBA in 1901. He died in Woking on 17 October 1932.
[Chatto; Houfe; White]

DARRE, G. fl.1883-89
French draughtsman illustrator, who worked exclusively for Parisian satirical publications. He came to London in 1883 and worked for various magazines. Five years later Joseph Swain (q.v.), who had engraved his work, persuaded him to submit work to Punch. There Darré found work from 1888-89, although his pen and ink drawings 'lacked true artistic quality and Punch's essential spirit' (Spielmann,p.560). He also worked for the Dalziels' Judy,1889, then abandoned illustration for commercial show-card work.

DAVEY, Harry Fitzner fl.1883-1900
London wood engraver, who worked at 3 Bouverie Street, EC (POD,1884). He disappears from the London directories until 1899 (his office becomes that of E.C.Dalton (q.v.)) then reappears at 172 Strand, WC (POD,1899), and 12 Burleigh Street, Strand, WC (POD,1900). Davey was a competent facsimile wood engraver who worked for the English Illustrated Magazine,1883-90, after landscape drawings by H.Ryland, A.D.McCormack, Clough Bromley, Walter Crane and W.Biscombe Gardner. He was equally competent at detailed work on flowers and plants, narrative sketches like 'Baking Brie' and 'Gathering Cider Apples' by W.J.Hennessy, and architectural details, as well as animals like 'Cats and Kittens' after drawings by Louis Wain. Davey also engraved portrait cuts for the Magazine of Art,1888, and after photographs for the Illustrated London News,1892. Houfe explained that there was also an H.F.Davey, topographer, who worked in Newcastle and contributed drawings to the Illustrated London News,1887.
[Hake; Houfe]

DAVEY, R. fl.1880s
Wood engraver, who worked for the English Illustrated Magazine,1883-84. He engraved vignettes of buildings after drawings of T.Sandys and H.Thomson to Austin Dobson's 'The Tour of Covent Garden'.

DAVIDSON, Thomas fl.1880-1908
Occasional illustrator, history and genre painter, who worked in Hampstead from 1880. He contributed figure subjects to Good Words,1880. He also exhibited at the Royal Academy, the Royal Society of British Artists, the Royal Hibernian Academy, and the Royal Institute of Painters in Oil-Colours.
[Houfe]

DAVIEL, Leon fl.1889-1930
French wood engraver, portrait painter and illustrator, born in Paris, where he was the pupil of Carolus-Duran. He specialised in figure subjects for the British magazines, 1889-1907. He began with topographical engravings for the English

Illustrated Magazine,1889-90, notably 'Eton College' after Philip Norman; then Good Words,1897; Black and White,1900; Pearson's Magazine; the Temple Magazine; and the Illustrated London News,1907. He also exhibited at the New Gallery, the Royal Academy and the Royal Institute of Painters in Oil-Colours, and worked in Chelsea, 1914-25.
[Bénézit; Houfe]

DAVIES, Charles fl.1880s
Wood engraver, who worked in London at 42 Essex Street, Strand, WC (POD,1883), which was earlier the office of Robert Davies (q.v.), and which Charles shared with G.F.Frasher (q.v.).

DAVIES, Frederick Peter fl.1851-57
London wood engraver, who worked with W.H.Joyce (q.v.) at 11 Bolt Court, Fleet Street, EC (POD,1851-54), then on his own at 162 Fleet Street, EC (POD,1855), and 23 Bouverie Street, Fleet Street, EC (POD,1857).

DAVIES, James fl.1872-77
London wood engraver, who worked at 9 Fountain Court, Strand, WC (POD,1872-77). He may be related to James Henry Davies, a landscape painter born in Manchester in 1848, who exhibited from 1872 at the Royal Academy, the Society of British Artists and other galleries.
[TB; Bénézit]

DAVIES, Robert fl.1880s
London wood engraver, who worked at 42 Essex Street, Strand, WC (POD,1880), where he shared the office with R.A.Cheffins and G.F.Frasher (qq.v.). By 1883 the address was occupied by Charles Davies (q.v.).

DAVIS Brothers fl.1890s
Provincial firm of draughtsmen on wood, who worked at 56 Livery Street and 126 Lionel Street, Birmingham (Kelly's,1900).

DAVIS, Frederick William fl.1887-88
Wood engraver, who worked in London at 75 Fleet Street, EC (POD,1887-88), an address he shared with R.Long (q.v.). He may be related to Frederick Davis, genre painter of Birmingham, who trained with his father, at the Antwerp Academy and Paris Ecole and exhibited at the Royal Institute of Painters in Watercolours, the Society of British Artists and the New Watercolour Society from 1891, and in Paris, 1900.
[See the Davis Brothers entry above; TB; Bénézit]

DAVIS, Lucien 1860-?
Draughtsman illustrator, born in Liverpool in 1860, the son of William Davis the artist. He was educated at the Royal Academy Schools, 1877, where he won

several prizes. He began as an illustrator for wood engravings to Cassell publications in 1878, followed by his most important work, drawings for wood engravings in The Graphic,1880-81. As a result of these he joined the staff of the Illustrated London News,1885, and contributed drawings until 1905. He also worked for the English Illustrated Magazine,1885, his series, 'The Pilgrimage of the Thames' being engraved by J.Cocking, J.C.Griffiths, J.D.Cooper, Waterlow and Company, T.W.Lascelles, R.Paterson, and O.Jahyer (qq.v.). He also drew for the Dalziels' Fun,1886-87; The Quiver,1890; and Cassell's Family Magazine. He was an exhibitor in London from 1878, notably at the Royal Academy, and was elected RI,1893. He also exhibited in Paris, 1900.
[Bénézit; Houfe]

DAVIS, M. 1710-84
One of the earliest London wood engravers, whose work for various printers helped to establish the groundwork for the revival of the art by the turn of the century. He specialised in scenes of London life, and worked at Salisbury Court, Fleet Street, for over fifty years, the address even then being a centre for engraving. He died on 28 January 1784, aged seventy-four.
[Redgrave; Bénézit]

DAVISON, William Arthur fl.1885-92
London wood engraver, who worked at 25 Bouverie Street, EC (POD,1885), then disappeared from the directories until 1892, when he worked at 38 King William Street, EC (POD,1892).

DAWSON, Alfred fl.1860-92
Wood engraver, etcher and landscape painter. He worked in Chertsey, etched after his father Henry Dawson's drawings, wood engraved and etched illustrations to C.E.Robinson's A Royal Warren of Picturesque Rambles in the Isle of Purbeck, Dorset, 1882, and to The Portfolio,1884-92. He exhibited in London from 1860, at the Royal Academy, the Society of British Artists, the British Institution, the Royal Society of Painter-Etchers and Engravers and the Royal Society of British Artists. Geoffrey Wakeman gives an Alfred Dawson as the first process blockmaking firm in England, working by 1871, which perfected the Typo-etching process of picture reproduction by 1884.
[Wakeman, Victorian Book Illustration; TB; Bénézit; see Volume I for etchings]

DAWSON and Wilmer, Dawson and Clift fl.1890-92
London wood engraving firm, with an office at 35 Essex Street, Strand, WC (POD,1890). This changed to Dawson and Clift (possibly Leslie E.Clift (q.v.)) (POD,1891-92).

DAY, John B. fl.1869-79
London wood engraver, lithographer, colour printer,
the son of the lithographer William Day (b.1823), of
Day and Haghe. John Day appears in the directories
as John B.Day (Day and Son) Savoy Steam Press,
3 Savoy Street, Strand (POD,1869-79) where he was
a wood engraver and colour printer, lithographer
(chromolithography, photolithography, according to
an 1869 advertisement).
[For his colour work see Wakeman and Bridson]

DAY, William H. fl.1889
Provincial wood engraver, who worked at Chatham
Buildings, 25 South John Street, Liverpool
(Kelly's,1889).

DAY and Collins Limited fl.1878-1910
London wood engraving firm, with an office at 10 and
11 Bridgwater Gardens, EC (POD,1878), then 29, 50,
52 Fann Street, EC (POD,1879-1910).

DEAN, Thomas William fl.1848-49
London wood engraver, who worked at 3 and 4 Poppin's
Court, Fleet Street, EC (POD,1848-49).

DEANE, William Wood 1825-73
Draughtsman on wood and watercolourist, born in
Liverpool Road, Islington on 22 March 1825, the
son of the animal draughtsman J.W.Wood (q.v.).
He abandoned an architectural career for painting,
attended the Royal Academy Schools in 1844 , and
travelled to Italy, 1850-52, and to Spain, visiting
the latter with his friend F.W.Topham (q.v.) who
also trained to draw on wood. Deane contributed
drawings of Naples on wood for Henry Vizetelly's
Illustrated Times,1856. He was a successful painter
and exhibited views of France, Spain and Venice at
the British Institution,1859-64, the Old Watercolour
the New Watercolour Society, the Royal Academy
and the Royal Society of British Artists,1857-66. He
died in Hampstead on 18 January 1873.
[Houfe]

DEAR, Mary E. fl.1848-67
Draughtsman on wood, portrait and genre painter.
She illustrated Hawthorne's The Scarlet Letter,1859
and contributed drawings on wood to The Illustrated
Times, Christmas, 1855 and the Art Journal,c1865.
She also exhibited at Colnaghi exhibitions in London,
at the Royal Academy and the Royal Society of
British Artists,1848-67, by then working in
Rottingdean, Sussex.

DEARLE, William fl.1874
London wood engraver, who worked at 14 Medburn
Street, Camden Town, NW (POD,1874).

DEE, George Horatio fl.1840s
Provincial wood engraver and general engraver,
who worked at St Augustine's Back, Bristol
(Pigot,1842). Fincham lists an armorial bookplate
for Daniel and David Burges signed 'Dee sc',
dated 1840.

DEEBLE, Edward Walter fl.1880-90
London wood engraver, who worked at 38 Liverpool
Road, N (POD,1880-90).

DEEBLE and Stanley fl.1870s
London wood engraving firm, with an office at
30 Liverpool Road, N (POD,1876), probably a
partnership between Edward Deeble and L.Stanley
(qq.v.).

DE GREY, First Earl (Thomas Philip Robinson)
The British Museum owns a small woodcut of the
Prince of Wales' crest, 'Ich Dien', dated November
1814, by this artist. It is signed: 'g'.

DE KATOW, Paul de 1834-97
Draughtsman illustrator and battle painter. He was
born in Strasbourg on 17 October 1834, trained with
Delacroix, and exhibited regularly at the Salon,
1839-82. He was a war correspondent who drew
illustrations of the Siege of Paris for the Illustrated
London News,1870, and also contributed to The
Graphic,1872. He also exhibited at the Royal Society
of British Artists,1872-73.
[Houfe]

DELAMOTTE, Mrs C. fl.1864-65
London wood engraver, who worked at 14 and 15
Beaufort Buildings, WC (POD,1864-65), shared
with Freeman G.Delamotte (q.v.).

DELAMOTTE, Freeman G. fl.1845-68
London wood engraver, who worked at 127 Chancery
Lane (POD,1845-46), 7 Orange Street, Bloomsbury
(Hodgson's,1855), 6 Hobury Street, King's Road,
Chelsea (POD,1856), and 14 and 15 Beaufort Buildings,
WC (POD,1857-68) where he worked with
Mrs C.Delamotte (q.v.). Houfe lists 'E.Delamotte',
a draughtsman who contributed decorative initials
to the Illustrated London Magazine,1855. Freeman
may be related to Philip Henry Delamotte (1821-89),
colour printer (see Wakeman and Bridson).

DELAMOTTE, William Alfred 1775-1863
Draughtsman on wood, and watercolourist. He was
born in Weymouth on 2 August 1775, worked under
Benjamin West in 1794, at the Royal Academy Schools
life class, and eventually settled in Oxford as a
drawing master and topographer. He made most of
the drawings on wood for Jean Ingram's Memorials
of Oxford,1837, in three volumes. These were
engraved by Orlando Jewitt (q.v.) and became his

most famous early engraved work. Delamotte was a
competent recorder of Oxford and the Thames valley.
His drawings were etched and lithographed for books.
He also exhibited his paintings at the British
Institution,1808-46, the Old Watercolour Society,
1806-8, the Royal Academy and the Royal Society of
British Artists,1829-31. He died at St Giles's Field,
Oxford, 13 February 1863. He is probably related to
the anastatic printer and photographer Philip Henry
Delamotte (1821-89) of Broad Street, Oxford (1849)
(see Wakeman and Bridson).
[Bénézit; TB; Nagler; Redgrave; Graves; H.Carter,
Orlando Jewitt,1962]

DELL, John H. 1830-88
Draughtsman illustrator and painter of rustic and
animal subjects. He worked in London and the
surrounding area: Hammersmith, Chertsey, New
Malden, and was best known for his thirty illustrations
to Nature Pictures,c1878, engraved by R.Paterson
(q.v.) which White described as the result of 'years
of patient painstaking labour on the part of artist and
engraver'; the book was 'not unworthy to a place
among the best' of the 'Sixties School' volumes. Dell
also exhibited at the British Institution,1851-67,
and the Royal Society of British Artists,1851-86.
[Houfe; White]

DEL ORME, Eugénie fl.1880s
Wood engraver who worked in Paris, where he
achieved an honourable mention. He also engraved
work for the English Illustrated Magazine signed
'E.H.Del Orme & Butler'. This included 'Duck Huts
on the Marais', 1886-87, after David Murray,
engraved in a rather rough style, the foreground
foliage being scratched and unsympathetic to the
horizontal lines of the sky; also 'Potato Planting'
after A.D.McCormick and 'St Sennen Cove, Cornwall',
after C.Napier Hemy, 1887-88.
[Bénézit]

DEROY, Isidore Laurent 1797-1886
Architectural illustrator, painter and lithographer
well known in France. He exhibited at the Salon and
drew churches and castles for various British
publications including the Illustrated London News,
according to Vizetelly.
[Vizetelly, Glances Back]

DESBOIS, Joseph fl.1871-90
Wood engraver, who worked in London at 9 Essex
Street, Strand, WC (POD,1871-90) with numerous
engraver colleagues. These included J.J.Woolley,
J.Bye, H.C.Mason, G.Puttock, G.J.Baker,
R.A.Cheffins, and W.Limming (qq.v.).

DESCHAMPS, Emile
French wood engraver, who worked for a number of
French publications. He was the pupil of Brevière

and is listed in Gusman for his wood engravings.
He is listed here for his portrait engraving of
Gladstone, half-length, owned by the British
Museum.
[Bénézit; Beraldi; Hake; Gusman]

DEVER fl.1859-76
Draughtsman for wood engravings, genre and flower
painter. He contributed eight caricatures on wood
for Punch about 1864, which Spielmann thought 'none
can see without being reminded of some of the
grotesque types which later on were adopted by
Mr E.T.Reed in his earlier work'. He also
exhibited his paintings at the Royal Academy from
1859-76.
[Bénézit; TB; Spielmann]

DE WILDE
Wood engraver, who contributed ten ornamental
engravings after John Leighton (q.v.) to Richard
Pigot's Moral Emblems,1860. These were intricate,
baroque borders with Leighton's tailpiece drawings
set within circles. This may be the Belgian genre
and portrait painter August de Wilde (1819-86).
[Bénézit; British Library catalogue]

DICKENSON
(see Cheshire, William)

DICKES, William 1815-92
Wood engraver, draughtsman on wood, pioneering
colour printer. He was born in Beechencliff, near
Bath, on 7 May 1815, and apprenticed to the wood
engraver Robert Branston,Junior (q.v.) about 1831.
He attended the Royal Academy Schools in 1835,
where he gained several medals for his drawing.
He was commissioned by W.H.Lizars to illustrate
The Naturalist's Library, c1840, and also drew on
wood for Charles Knight's London,1841, and Captain
Marryat's Masterman Ready,1841, and drew a full
page illustration, 'The Throne-Room and Palace of
Holyrood', engraved by S.Sly (q.v.) for the
Illustrated London News, 3 September 1842. It was in
this year that he was commissioned by Robert Cadell
to draw illustrations and supervise the engraving
(mostly on wood) for the Abbotsford edition of Scott's
Waverley Novels,1842-47. This proved a useful
contact since he was to supervise the drawing and
engraving of some of the period's most promising
illustrators and engravers, such as Birket Foster,
Edmund Evans, and even his master, Robert
Branston (qq.v.). It was this Waverley commission
that established Dickes as a wood engraver. From
among a series of intricate border engravings, dies,
a needle book pattern and a fine engraved cheque, all
now in the British Museum, there is a four page
advertisement (probably dated 1847): 'William Dickes,
Designer and Engraver on Wood and in Glyphography.
Illustrator of the Abbotsford Edition of the Waverley

Novels'. Dickes then listed his current achievements: Professor Bell's British Quadrupeds, and Book of British Reptiles; Yarrell's British Fishes; Blaine's Encyclopedia of Sporting; Martingale's Sketches of Sporting; Sir William Jardine's Naturalist's Library ('Marsupiata' volume). He singled out his zoological engravings to Voyage of Her Majesty's Ship Beagle; Portfolio of the Earl of Derby; engravings for the Zoological Society of London; and finally the Abbotsford edition of the Waverley Novels. The advertisement concluded: 'From his character as an Artist, and his Experience in conducting researches for pictorial purposes, at most of the London and Parisian Libraries, and other Institutions, W.Dickes feels confident that he can be of essential service to Publishers and Authors having works to illustrate and who yet may be unable from want of time, to seek the necessary Authorities for themselves'. By 1846 Dickes had set up on his own as an 'Artist and Engraver on Wood & Copper' at 48 Salisbury Square, Fleet Street, EC (POD,1846-48), later moving to 4 Crescent Place, Bridge Street, Blackfriars (POD,1849-51), where he also began lithography and colour printing in oil colour from wood blocks. During this period he achieved a reputation for his competent wood engravings, 'representative for all the many long forgotten wood engravers who worked to a high standard of craftsmanship in order to produce relatively cheap books which instructed and entertained in a popular manner' (C.Jackson,p.14). His wood engravings included H.Warren's cover design to Simm's & McIntyre's Parlour Library, 1847-62; five colour engravings to Amalie Winter's Michael and the Twins,1850; and thirteen (of thirty) border designs by H.Noel Humphreys to The Poets' Pleasuance,1847; he re-engraved cuts from Cundall's Babes in the Wood of 1849, drew and engraved for H.Noel Humphreys' Sentiments and Similes of William Shakespeare,1851 (for which Dickes received 64s 6d); and a frontispiece of his own design for Charles Kingsley's Glaucus, or Wonders of the Shore, 1855. Dickes continued to develop his colour printing techniques. When he moved to 5 Old Fish Street, Doctor's Common about 1852, he became an 'Engraver and oil colour printer', having obtained a Baxter licence about 1850, and exhibited specimens of oil colour printing from raised surfaces (probably from wood blocks) at the Great Exhibition of 1851. He also exhibited in Paris, 1855, the year he took out an advertisement in Hodgson's directory which listed eleven works available from 'William Dickes, Designer, Engraver on wood, and Printer of book illustrations in oil colours'. Another advertisement, c1854, quoted by C.T.Lewis, Colour Printing,p.182, shows a prolific Dickes, capable of numerous jobs: 'artist and engraver on wood, lithographer and colour printer, undertakes, at moderate charges, drawing and engraving on wood, steel engraving, lithography, chromolithography, letterpress colour printing, and

copper-plate engraving'. Dickes married Sarah Bloomfield in 1841 and raised a family of nine children, six sons and three daughters, some of whom he brought into his business. The firm had become William Dickes and Company by 1864, when he took two sons: Walter Dickes (?-1913) and William Frederick Dickes (1843-1920) in with him. By then he had larger premises at 109 Farringdon Road, EC, five storeys of printing and engraving works where he trained five artists and two engravers (including young Joseph Swain (q.v.) before he went to Orlando Jewitt). By 1867 this had become his sole office: it remained listed in the directories until 1875. During that time the firm won prizes for colour printing at the London International Exhibition,1862, in Dublin,1865, and Paris, 1867. Dickes became the principal colour printer for the Society for the Promotion of Christian Knowledge, People's Magazine, Gentleman's Journal, The Queen and the Religious Tract Society, producing work for the middle and lower middle-class reading public. By the early 1870s his business had begun to slacken off, and he retired in 1873. He died of acute nephritis on 26 February 1892, aged seventy-six, at 75 Loughborough Park, Brixton. He signed his engravings: 'W.DICKES Sc'.
[For a complete account of Dickes' life and career as a colour printer see A.Docker, The Colour Prints of William Dickes,1924; also Lewis; Burch; Wakeman and Bridson. See also British Library catalogue; McLean; Chatto; Spielman; Houfe; C.Jackson]

DICKES, William Frederick
Wood engraver of birds. The British Museum owns a faint black-line engraving of a vulture for The Life of the Zoological Gardens.

DICKINSON, John fl.1885-94
London wood engraver, who worked at 8 Essex Street, Strand, WC (POD,1885-94), an address he shared with R.A.Cheffins and F.Babbage (qq.v.). Bénézit lists the London genre painter J.Reed Dickinson, fl.1870-81, who may be related.

DIETRICH, Charles (Carl)
Wood engraver, whom Gusman lists as working for the French magazines, such as Magasin Pittoresque, Arts et Métiers au 19c, and who is known to have engraved a half-length portrait, on wood, of the Victorian painter, Sir John Millais, after a photograph. This was published in the Art Annual, 1885.
[Hake; TB]

DINKEL, Joseph fl.1833-61
Prominent botanical and architectural draughtsman on wood, who was born in Munich but who lived and worked in London from 1840, the year he exhibited at the Royal Academy. He travelled throughout

Europe for the Linnaean Society and the Royal
Geological and Palaeontological Societies, and
worked from 1828 onwards illustrating Louis Agassiz's
Poissons Fossiles,1833-43. He also produced clear,
highly-shaded drawings of shells and bones, engraved
by James Lee (q.v.), for Dr Mantell's geological
books, such as Medals of Creation and Petrifications
and their Teachings. By 1861 Dinkel was often being
employed by Professor Owen and Thomas Bell,
President of the Linnaean Society. Bohn in Chatto and
Jackson concludes that Dinkel was 'a very accurate
draughtsman of subjects of Natural History,
especially Fossil remains; but though he has most
practice in this department, he also undertakes
Architectural and Engineering drawings'.
[Chatto; Bénézit; TB; Houfe]

DIX, Henry and Alfred fl.1880-98
London wood engravers, who worked at 21 Castle
Street, Holborn, EC (POD,1880-82), an address
shared with J.Fenton and J.Ford (qq.v.). This
changed to 26 Poppins Court, EC (POD,1883-92),
which Henry and Alfred shared for five years with
Henry and A.Bourne (qq.v.). By 1897 they were
working at 25 Farringdon Avenue, EC (POD,1897-98).

DIXIE, George William fl.1885-87
London wood engraver, who worked in partnership
as Reade and Dixie (q.v.) then independently at
295 Strand, WC (POD,1886-87).

DIXON, E.
Wood engraver, whom Gusman lists as having worked
on various illustrated novels. He engraved on Paul
et Virginie; and signed one work, 'Salles de Bal à
l'Hotel de Ville', in 1846.

DIXON, Henry and Annie fl.1842-68
Henry Dixon was a London wood engraver, who
worked at 36 Halliford Street, Lower Road, Islington
(POD,1856-57). He engraved small architectural
cuts for the Illustrated London News, like the rather
crude 'Thurgarton Church', 30 July 1842. By 1858 he
had been joined by Annie Dixon, who engraved as
Mrs Annie Dixon from 36 Halliford Street
(POD,1858-68). She had been born in Horncastle,
Lincolnshire and by 1858 had established herself as
a miniature painter who was favoured by the aristocracy
(including the Queen). She died in February 1901.
[TB; Bénézit]

DIXON, John Jeffrey fl.1893-1910
London wood engraver, who worked at 89 Farringdon
Street, EC (POD,1893-1910), an address he shared
with the engravers W.J.Potter, L.Knott, F.Thorpe,
and W.Ginn (qq.v.).

DOBELL, Clarence M. fl.1857-66
Draughtsman illustrator and figure painter. He drew
on wood for Good Words,1860 and Once a Week,1865
and he illustrated One Year,1862 for Macmillan,
which White dismisses as being 'in the sterile crop
of the year 1862'. He worked in London, 1857-65,
then Cheltenham, and exhibited at the British
Institution, 1858-66, the Royal Academy and the
Royal Society of British Artists, 1857-66.
[Houfe; White]

DOBSON
(see McKelvie and Dobson)

DOBSON, James fl.1860s
London wood engraver, who worked at 3 Bouverie
Street (POD,1868), an address he shared with
W.H.Tilby (q.v.).

DOBSON, William Thomas Charles 1817-98
Draughtsman illustrator and biblical painter. He was
born in Hamburg in 1817, entered the Royal Academy
Schools in 1836, and taught at the Government School
of Design in 1843. He abandoned his work in 1845 to
travel abroad, returning to exhibit works at the Old
Watercolour Society, the Royal Society of British
Artists and the Royal Academy, where he was
elected ARA,1860, RA,1871, and RWS,1875. He
illustrated some of the nineteen works for the
important volume, A.A.Procter's Legends and
Lyrics,1865, engraved by Horace Harral (q.v.),
'who cannot be congratulated upon his rendering of
some blocks' (White,p.128).
[Houfe; White]

DODD, D. fl.1822-28
London wood engraver, who worked at Branch-Row,
Hoxton (Pigot,1822-23). He engraved three cuts to
Northcote's Fables,1828: 'Paper Kite'; 'Lion and
Snake'; and 'Snow-drop and Primrose'. These are
in the British Museum. He signed his work:
'Dodd sc'.

DODD, Daniel George fl.1854-65
London wood engraver, brother of John Dodd (q.v.),
who worked at 53 Skinner Street, Snowhill
(POD,1854-60), then moved to Richmond, where he
worked at 5 Clarence Villas, St Mary's Grove,
Richmond, SW (POD, LSDS,1863-65).

DODD, I. fl.1820-30
Anglo-American wood engraver, who worked on
portraits and ornament. He signed a full page portrait
of George IV on the cover of The Mirror,1830, for
which he provided several other wood engraved
illustrations. He also engraved two armorial bookplates for the Annand family, 1820,1830, signed
'I Dodd sculpt'. The British Museum owns a
competent engraving of Chatsworth signed 'I.DODD'.

[Fincham; Bénézit; TB]

DODD, John Robert fl.1820s-30s
London wood engraver, brother of Daniel Dodd (q.v.), who worked at 22 Charles Street, City Road (Pigot,1826-27). He is probably the J.Dodd who engraved two cuts to Northcote's Fables,1828: a tailpiece for Gay's 'Fable of Dog and Fox' and 'Angler'.

DODGSON, Charles Lutwidge (Lewis Carroll) 1832-98
Creator of the 'Alice' books, and occasional draughtsman on wood and illustrator of his own work. He was born in Daresbury, Cheshire on 17 January 1832 and was educated at Rugby and Christchurch, Oxford, where he spent the remainder of his life as a don. Dodgson made his first drawing on wood in mid July 1863 at the suggestion of Mr Coombe, printer to the Clarendon Press, who introduced him to the sculptor Thomas Woolner, to advise Dodgson on anatomical drawing. Three weeks later he delivered his drawing on the block to Orlando Jewitt (q.v.), wood engraver of Camden Town, London, who discouraged Dodgson's drawing ambitions. Dodgson then decided to employ a professional illustrator, eventually securing John Tenniel (q.v.) in February 1864. Dodgson remained a severe critic of illustration throughout his life.
[See Anne Clark, Lewis Carroll,1979,pp.129-30]

DODGSON, George Haydock 1811-80
Landscape draughtsman on wood, painter and topographer. He was born in Liverpool on 16 August 1811, and apprenticed to George Stephenson, the railway engineer, 1827-35. He began to paint and moved to London in 1836 where he drew its architecture. He specialised in landscape illustration throughout the 1850s, drawing extensively on the Thames, Whitby and Wales. He used these drawings to illustrate various periodicals, for example seven plates to the Cambridge Almanack,1840-77 and numerous drawings on wood of landscapes, drawn with E.Duncan (q.v.) for the Illustrated London News, 1853-56, which were admirably engraved by W.J.Linton (q.v.). Linton in fact praised Dodgson's work in his Masters of Wood Engraving. Dodgson illustrated the important 'Sixties School' volumes, Lays of the Holy Land,1858, and C.Mackay's The Home Affections,1858. Dodgson also exhibited at the British Institution, the Old Watercolour Society, the Royal Academy and the Royal Society of British Artists,1835-39, and was elected ARWS,1842-47, then OWS,1848. He died at 28 Clifton Hill, St John's Wood, on 4 June 1880. The British Museum owns the designs engraved by the Dalziel Brothers (q.v.): a landscape vignette,1856; a view of Jerusalem,1857. [Bénézit; TB; Bryan; DNB; Chatto; Linton, Masters of Wood Engraving; Art Journal,1880,p.300]

DODSHON, George Monteith fl.1884-91
London wood engraver, who worked at 27 Chancery Lane, WC (POD,1884-86), then 39 Hunter Street, WC (POD,1887-91).

DOLAMARE
Wood engraver, who engraved after William Small (q.v.). He engraved a battle scene after Schonberg, which is in the British Museum collections.

DOLBY, Edwin Thomas fl.1849-70
Draughtsman illustrator of architectural and landscape subjects, who specialised in views of churches. He contributed drawings for wood engraving to Recollections of the Great Exhibition, 1851; views of Denmark for the Illustrated London News,1854; views of the Crimea for the Illustrated Times,1855 and for The Graphic,1870. He also exhibited at the New Watercolour Society as a candidate,1850-64, and at the Royal Academy, 1849-65.
[For books illustrated see Houfe]

DOLLING
(see McDougle and Dolling)

DORE, Paul Gustave Louis Christophe 1832-83
Draughtsman illustrator on wood, painter and sculptor. He was born in Strasbourg on 6 January 1832, took up lithography at the age of eleven, then moved to Paris, and contributed a weekly page to Philipon's Journal Pour Rire, from 1848. That year he also exhibited pen and ink drawings at the Salon, and made his reputation as an illustrator with his Rabelais,1854, followed by a series of English and French classics. He came to the attention of the British public with drawings for wood engraved illustrations in the Illustrated London News, from 1853 onwards, including Crimean sketches from 1855-56, 1858. These attracted the attention of Henry Vizetelly who commissioned drawings for his Illustrated Times,1855-60, and recalled, 'His rapidity with his pencil was extraordinary, and though he eventually became overburdened with work he under no circumstances refused it'. Doré charged just £6 for a newspaper sized drawing at that time, despite the amount of work involved in his crowded sketches, in which every figure was carefully delineated in the final engraving. His most successful works included The History of Don Quixote,1863; Coleridge's The Ancient Mariner,1865; The Adventures of Baron Munchausen,1866; Fables of La Fontaine,1867; Tennyson's Idylls of the King,1867-68; Dante's Inferno,1866; and his own illustrated version of the Bible,1867. He visited and drew views of London in the late 1860s, which appeared as London-A Pilgrimage,1872, his large, atmospheric drawings wood engraved by P.Jonnard and Pannemaker (qq.v.). Doré illustrated over 119 books, and such work

brought him a substantial British reputation. He opened his own gallery in London to exhibit and sell his work, particularly his large paintings which were unsuccessful and taxed his later years. Doré was prolific enough to keep a dozen or more wood engravers in constant employment, the most notable being the Pannemakers, also H.Pisan, P.Jonnard, Charles Barbant, Adolphe Gusman, and Hildibrand (qq.v.). His British engravers were J.Findlay for the Tennyson work and W.J.Linton (qq.v.). Doré's style grew more involved and he became dependent on his engravers to understand the complexities of his designs. E.J.Sullivan in the Art of Illustration cites the time when Doré was overworked and exhausted drawing a vast building with numerous windows for a Balzac story. He gave up and scribbled 'Etc' over the remaining windows to be finished by the engraver. The engraver, however, engraved the block just as it arrived, with an 'Etc' reversed over the space intended for more windows. His later works did not in fact have the ink detail carefully worked out for the engravers to follow, rather he relied more on wash to suggest tone, which the engraver was to interpret in lines as he saw fit. Ironically his reputation in France waned when he tried to steer away from such demanding illustrations in favour of painting. He grew bitter about the adverse criticism and once told Vizetelly, 'If I had to begin my life again I wouldn't make a single drawing. If it were not for my drawings more justice would be rendered to my paintings' (Vizetelly, Glances Back,I,p.391). [For a complete bibliography of Doré's illustrated work see Blanchard Jerrold, Gustave Doré,1891; also M.Rose, Gustave Doré,1947; also Gusman; Slater; Bliss; Nagler; Hind; TB (with book list); Beraldi; Glaser (on Doré's engravers); Linton, Masters of Wood Engraving]

DORRINGTON, Alfred Robert fl.1862-1910
London wood engraver, who worked at 9 Wine Office Court, EC (POD,1862) which he shared with George Dorrington (q.v.). He moved to 22 Chancery Lane, WC (POD,1864-72) and then again to 68 Fleet Street, EC (POD,1873-82). By then he was advertising as a firm of 'draughtsmen and engravers in every class of speciality; illustrating manufacturers' catalogues, specimen books issued yearly'. He also made and produced wood blocks for engraving. By 1883 Alfred Dorrington and Company had moved to 8 Stanhope Street, Strand, WC (POD,1883-1901), and added photography on wood to their list of skills ('special deep photo process blocks'). The firm was still in the London directory at 33 Furnival Street, EC (POD,1910) at the turn of the century.

DORRINGTON, George fl.1838-1901
London wood engraver, particularly noted for his early engravings after the caricaturist Robert Seymour (q.v.) and vignettes to Goldsmith's Vicar

of Wakefield,1841. Edmund Evans (q.v.) recalled how as a young man he saw an advertisement for an apprentice wood engraver to Dorrington in a local London coffee house, offering a premium of thirty pounds, but he was warned off by his printer employer, who had never heard of Dorrington. George Dorrington worked in London at 2 Union Place, City Road (Pigot,1838-40), then 143 Blackfriars Road (POD,1846), 1 Burleigh Street, Strand (POD,1849-50), 4 Ampton Street, Gray's Inn Road (POD,1851-59), McLean's Buildings, New Street Square and Fetter Lane, EC (POD,1860). By 1861 he was working at 9 Wine Office Court, EC (POD,1861-64) which he shared with Alfred Dorrington (q.v.), 9 Hand Court, Holborn, WC (POD,1865-85) then 33 Packington Street, N (POD,1886-1901).
[LeBlanc; Bénézit; TB; British Museum; Evans, Reminiscences]

DORRINGTON, William fl.1817-34
London wood engraver and wood letter cutter who worked at 6 City Garden Row, City Road (Johnstone's,1817), 52 Charles Street, City Road (Pigot,1823-24) and 35 Charles Street (Pigot,1832-34). The British Museum owns four engravings after G.Cruikshank (q.v.) by 'W & G Dorrington, Engravers on Wood, 52 Charles Street, City Road'.

DORRINGTON and Potter fl.1860-61
London wood engraving firm, who worked at 9 Essex Street, Strand (POD,1860-61), which they shared with W.H.Aske (q.v.). Potter is possibly William John Potter (q.v.).

DOUCE, A.
Wood engraver of landscape vignettes after Harry Fenn (q.v.). These are in the British Museum.

DOWER, J. fl.1855-77
Pentonville map engraver, who worked at St Pauls, 28 Ludgate Street, Pentonville. He contributed various maps to the Illustrated London News, 1855-77, including ones of Sebastapol, Savoy and Nice, India, and the Ottoman Empire.

DOWERS, Henry and Company fl.1880s
London wood engraver, who worked at 7 Bolt Court, EC (POD,1880).

DOWLEN, Thomas fl.1840s
Wood engraver, apprenticed to George Baxter (q.v.), who probably worked for J.Kronheim (q.v.) about 1849, at the instigation of Charles Gregory (q.v.).
[C.T.Lewis, Picture Printing,1928]

DOWNARD, Ebenezer Newman fl.1849-92
Draughtsman illustrator, painter of historical subjects who specialised in genre subjects. He drew

full-page illustrations to the Illustrated London News, 1871-79, notably 'To the Squire's Hall', December 1871, engraved by F.Wentworth (q.v.); Landseer's 'Pet Dog "Tiney" and Pet Cat', 19 September 1874, engraved by J.Greenaway (q.v.); and a series of four scenes, 'Canal Life', 10 October 1874. He also exhibited at the British Institute,1861-66, the Royal Academy, the Royal Society of British Artists, the Royal Hibernian Academy and the Royal Institute of Painters in Oil-Colours.
[Houfe; Bénézit]

DOWNES
(see Smith, T.J., Son and Downes)

DOWNES, E. fl.1850s
London wood engraver, who worked at 2 Walnut-Tree-Walk, Lambeth (Hodgson's,1855).

DOYLE, Charles Altamont 1832-93
Draughtsman illustrator of humorous subjects, born in London in 1832, the son of the caricaturist John Doyle and brother of Richard and Henry (qq.v.). He was largely an amateur artist, employed as a civil servant most of his life, but managed to develop a sprightly, fairy-like style for the works he drew for wood engraving. These included the sixty drawings to 'Alice'-inspired fantasy, Jean Jambon's Our Trip to Blunderland,1877, and drawings for various periodicals: the Illustrated Times,1859-60; Good Words,1860; London Society,1863-64; and The Graphic, 1877. He also exhibited at the Royal Scottish Academy, and lived in Scotland where he raised a family, which included Sir Arthur Conan Doyle. He fell prey to alcoholism, and was eventually confined to an asylum. He died in Dumfries in 1893. The British Museum owns proof wood engravings of his designs, by the Dalziel Brothers (q.v.), 1863.
[M.Baker, Doyle Diary,1978; R.Engen, Richard Doyle]

DOYLE, Henry Edward 1827-92
Wood engraver, caricaturist, portrait painter and painter of religious subjects. He was born in Dublin in 1827, the son of the caricaturist John Doyle and brother of Charles and Richard Doyle (qq.v.). He trained in Dublin but worked in London as a wood engraver and draughtsman for satirical journals, making several small cuts for Punch, from 1844, including 'The Great Gun' series, 1845, then was cartoonist of Fun,1867-69 as 'Hen' or 'Fusbos'. He wished to be known as a religious painter and in 1869 became Director of the National Gallery of Ireland. He exhibited enough to become ARHA,1872, RHA,1874, and was awarded CB in 1880. He died in Dublin on 17 February 1892. The British Museum owns proof wood engravings of his designs, engraved by the Dalziel Brothers (q.v.), 1863, 1866.
[Spielmann; R.Engen, Richard Doyle,1984]

DOYLE, James William Edmund 1822-92
Heraldic artist and illustrator, the eldest son of John Doyle and brother of Charles, Henry and Richard Doyle (qq.v.). He was born in London in 1822, studied with his caricaturist father, and made drawings from youth onwards to please his father. He described himself as 'the manipulator' of drawings on blocks. His primary work was illustrations to his own history book, A Chronicle of England, drawn in 1842, and colour printed in a masterly fashion from over ten wood blocks by Edmund Evans (q.v.), in 1864, after Doyle's own coloured proofs. He also compiled the Historical Baronage of England,1886. He died in London in 1892. The British Museum owns historical subjects engraved by the Dalziel Brothers (q.v.).
[McLean; C.T.Lewis; R.Engen, Richard Doyle,1984]

DOYLE, Richard (Dick Kitcat) 1824-83
Draughtsman illustrator and painter of fairies. He was born in London in September 1824, the second son of the caricaturist John Doyle and brother of Henry, Charles and James Doyle (qq.v.). From an early age Doyle trained himself as an illustrator: his first book, privately printed for his family, was Home for the Holiday,1836 (published 1887). His masterly Journal,1840, was a record of his early life and ambitions with his artistic family (published 1887). His first published book was The Eglington Tournament,1840, followed by etched work with John Leech (q.v.) on W.H.Maxwell's Hector O'Halloran. He quickly established himself as an illustrator on wood and steel, signing his work 'Dick Kitcat' and could have been a major figure in the field , had it not been for an early inadequate training and his tragic experience on Punch, where he served as its youngest illustrator from 1843-50. He resigned over the paper's anti-papist policies, Doyle being a staunch Roman Catholic, and after much disillusionment tried to make his living as book illustrator, then as a painter of fairies and landscapes. His most important book was drawings to In Fairyland,1870, a remarkable folio of sixteen colour plates printed in eight to twelve colours from wood blocks by Edmund Evans (q.v.). Doyle learned to draw on wood blocks from Joseph Swain (q.v.) who supervised the first, 'a bad, smudgy thing', for Punch. This was gradually improved so that his fine, intricate borders and initial letters with chivalric scenes and wide-eyed ladies became his hallmark. His cover design for Punch was used until 1954. Unfortunately Doyle had not been trained in figure drawing, and this made his drawing essentially amateurish throughout his life, despite his attempt to compensate by the proliferation of figures of great detail. Nevertheless his work was praised by Holman Hunt. He illustrated Ruskin's King of the Golden River,1851, and he was included by Bohn in Chatto and Jackson. He continued to contribute to numerous

books and magazines throughout the 1850s-1870s. Doyle also exhibited paintings at the Royal Academy, 1868-83. He died in London at his club on 11 December 1883. The British Museum owns a collection of his designs engraved by the Dalziel Brothers (q.v.) during the 1860s.
[Houfe; D.Hambourg, Richard Doyle,1948; Chatto; Spielmann; Evans Reminiscences; C.Wheeler (ed), Richard Doyle's Journal,1981; R.Engen, Richard Doyle]

DRUMMOND, James 1816-77
Draughtsman of ornithological subjects, painter of historical subjects. He was born in Edinburgh in 1816, entered the Trustees Academy, studying there under Sir William Allen, and exhibited at the Royal Scottish Academy, 1835 onwards. He was elected ARSA in 1846, RSA,1852. He also exhibited at the Royal Institute of Painters in Watercolours. He drew on wood for Good Words,1860; and illustrated J.Andersen's Ancient Spanish Weapons,1881.
[Houfe; White; Wood]

DUDLEY, Henry
Wood engraver, listed by J.S.Hodson's Guide to Art Illustration,1884, as having engraved 'An Old Seal', 'said to be one of the finest specimens of wood engraving ever done', which was exhibited at the Caxton celebrations, South Kensington Museum,1877.

DUDLEY, Howard 1820-64
Wood engraver, who was born in London in 1820, the only son of George Dudley of Tipperary, and Sarah, daughter of a Salisbury Square, London, coal merchant. Howard Dudley lost his father at an early age and moved with his mother to Easebourne, near Midhurst, Sussex, where he developed a lifelong interest in the neighbourhood. At fourteen he was determined to illustrate works of local history and antiquities, so he set up a small printing-press and produced a small volume, Juvenile Researches or a Description of Some of the Principal Towns in the Western Part of Sussex and the Borders of Hants... illustrated by numerous wood engravings executed by the author,1835. Dudley also set the type and as a self-taught engraver, drew and engraved from his own wood blocks, printing each page as he finished it. 'These, though very rough, show great taste, and are very remarkable for an artist of so tender an age' (DNB). It was so successful that Dudley reprinted it in a larger format. The following year he published a similar volume, The History and Antiquities of Horsham,1836, illustrated with thirty woodcuts of his own and four lithographs. He also planned 150 wood engravings to The History and Antiquities of Midhurst, but had to abandon the project since he had become a professional wood engraver with greater demands on his time. He practiced his wood engraving first in Edinburgh, from 1845-52 where he married Jane Ellen, then in London where he appears as a

wood engraver in the directories at 28 Holford Square, Pentonville (POD,1856-67). He died there on 4 July 1864, aged forty-four.
[Bénézit; DNB; Gentleman's Magazine,1865; British Library catalogue]

DUDLEY, Robert fl.1858-93
Draughtsman illustrator, lithographer and painter of landscapes. He drew Birmingham scenes for the Illustrated London News,1858, and continued to draw for their wood engravings until 1873; also for the Illustrated Times,1861; The Boys' Own Magazine, 1863; London Society,1864-71; and The Graphic, 1869. He also exhibited at the Royal Academy, 1865-91 and the Royal Institute of Painters in Watercolours, working in Kensington, 1865-75 and in Notting Hill from 1875, where he died about 1893. The British Museum owns a design wood engraved by the Dalziel Brothers (q.v.), 1865.
[TB; Bénézit; Houfe]

DUGARD, Henry fl.1876-1900
Provincial wood engraver, who worked in Birmingham at 8A Coleshill (Kelly's,1876), 45 Bull Street (Kelly's,1880), Bond Street (Kelly's,1889), and 22 Charlotte Street (Kelly's,1900).

DUKE, Louis fl.1870s
Provincial wood engraver, who worked at 106 Newhall Street, Birmingham (Kelly's,1872).

DUKES, John Palmer fl.1878-96
London wood engraver, who worked at 42 Essex Street, Strand, WC (POD,1878), shared with R.A.Cheffins and J.Bowcher (qq.v.). By 1896 he had reappeared in the directories at 48 Broad Street, Bloomsbury (POD,1896).

DU MAURIER, George Louis Palmella Busson 1834-96
Draughtsman illustrator on wood, and novelist. He was born in Paris where he returned as an art student, 1856-57, after a brief period as a chemistry student in London. He studied in Antwerp, but then lost an eye which hindered his plans to become a painter. So he returned to London to draw on wood sporadically as a black and white illustrator, first for second-rate magazines, then the major ones such as Punch, from 1860-96, where he served as a regular social cartoonist, succeeding John Leech in 1864. He also contributed to the Illustrated London News,1860; Once a Week,1860-68; the Illustrated Times,1862; London Society,1862-68; and the Cornhill,1864, 1870, 1875-80; as well as major 'Sixties School' volumes such as English Sacred Poetry,1864; Legends and Lyrics,1866; and Touches of Nature,1867. Du Maurier drew for wood blocks, first making numerous pen sketches on paper, but by 1864 these were directly drawn on the

block in pencil ('...I think that in boldness of
execution & character they are better'). He planned
to use his fiancée Emma to wood engrave these
drawings, but soon gave the idea up, as Du Maurier
wrote to his mother in 1861: 'We saw a she engraver
at Islington, and I saw several engravings; it is
impractical and I thought she had better give it up;
I shall want her eyes for something else, and to make
her so good an engraver that she should engrave my
things in preference to Swain or Dalziel would require
some 6 or 7 years, at it all day' (D.Du Maurier,
The Young Du Maurier,1951,p.96). Most of
Du Maurier's work was wood engraved by Joseph
Swain (q.v.) although the Dalziels occasionally sent
him early commissions. By 1880 he had used
photography for wood engraving, as he explained
to Thomas Hardy, who commissioned
illustrations to A Laodicean; Hardy wrote to the
American Harper and Brothers '...he should much
prefer to send you his original drawings on the paper,
& let you photograph & engrave them. He
[Du Maurier] adds that your engravers work so much
more carefully than ours that he could finish the
drawings in better style if he knew they were to be
cut in America, & thinks it would be a pity to lose
the advantage'. Du Maurier was one of the first
draughtsman illustrators to appreciate the value of
his original drawings, and kept a collection in a
safe for his children's future. He also exhibited
work at the Royal Academy,1870-90; the Old
Watercolour Society,1870-93, and the Fine Art
Society and organised several one man showings of
drawings,1884,1887,1895,1897. The British Museum
owns his designs wood engraved by the Dalziel
Brothers (q.v.).
[For biographical details see L.Ormond, George
Du Maurier,1969; for book list see Houfe;
see also Spielmann; Bryan; Graves]

DUNCAN, A. fl.1853-62
Draughtsman figure painter, who worked in London.
He drew on wood for Coleridge's Ancient Mariner,
1856 which he illustrated with Birket Foster and
E.H.Wehnert (qq.v.). He also exhibited at the
British Institution,1855-62, and the Royal Society of
British Artists, 1853-62.
[Houfe; White]

DUNCAN, D.M. fl.1880-82
Draughtsman, figure painter, who contributed a
wood engraved drawing to Good Words,1880, and
exhibited in Glasgow,1880-82.

DUNCAN, Edward 1803-82
Draughtsman on wood, etcher, aquatinter, marine
and coastal painter. He was born in London on
20 October 1803 and was apprenticed to the aquatint
engraver Robert Havell and his son. He then worked
for Fores, the printsellers, before giving up all

engraving for watercolour. He developed as a
draughtsman on wood, and worked with W.J.Linton
(q.v.) who engraved his work for the Illustrated
London News,1847-58,1868. Linton described
Duncan as 'the most accurate of draughtsmen,
whose true realism stood him in the place of
imagination'. He explained how Duncan would
present him with a coloured drawing on the block
which Linton translated into black and white
engraved line, such as 'Old Mill, Landscape',
drawn by Duncan and G.Dodgson (q.v.) and
engraved by Linton. Other outstanding drawings
were 'Sketches in Hainault Forest', a two and a
half page drawing engraved by Orrin Smith (q.v.)
in a tight, compact style for the Illustrated London
News,22 November,1851; and a large fold-out drawing
of 'The British Fleet at Spithead', 6 August 1853.
Duncan also contributed drawings to Poems and
Pictures,1846; Willmott's Poets of the Nineteenth
Century,1857; C.Mackay's The Home Affections,
1858; Lays of the Holy Land,1858; Favourite English
Poems,1859; Book of Favourite Modern Ballads,
1860; Montgomery's Poems,1860; Once a Week,1866;
Book of Rhymes and Roundelayes; Moore's Poems;
and The Soldier's Dream, many of which were
praised by Bohn in Chatto and Jackson. He fully
illustrated Bohn's edition of Southey's Life of Nelson,
engraved by H.Harral (q.v.). As a painter Duncan
exhibited at the British Institution, 1833-57, the New
Watercolour Society, the Royal Academy and the
Royal Society of British Artists, 1830-82, and was
elected member of the Royal Watercolour Society.
He died in London on 11 April 1882. The British
Museum owns a design by him engraved by the
Dalziel Brothers (q.v.) in 1857.
[For a discussion of his etchings see Volume I; also
see Chatto; Slater; Walker's Quarterly,October 1923;
TB; Bénézit; Graves; Linton, Masters of Wood
Engraving]

DUNN, Edith (Mrs T.O.Hume) fl.1862-1906
Occasional illustrator, painter of domestic scenes,
who worked in Worcester, 1863, and in London,
1864, where she exhibited at various galleries, such
as the Royal Society of British Artists, 1862-67, and
the British Institution,1864-67. She contributed a
drawing to The Quiver,1866. The British Museum
owns three designs engraved by the Dalziel Brothers
(q.v.), 1865-66.
[Houfe; White]

DURAND, Godefroy 1832-?
Special artist illustrator, born in Düsseldorf of
French extraction, in 1832. He joined the permanent
staff of The Graphic in 1870 and supplied military
and equestrian subjects for many years until 1890.
He also exhibited at the Royal Academy and the
Royal Society of British Artists, 1873.

DURHAM, C.J. ?-1889
Draughtsman illustrator and figure painter. He
taught at the Slade and contributed industrial
drawings to the Illustrated London News regularly
from 1861-74. He also exhibited at the Royal Academy,
1859, and the Royal Society of British Artists,
1872-80.
[Houfe]

DUTERTRE, Victor 1850-?
French wood engraver, born in Thilouze, Indre-et
Loire, 10 February 1850. He was a pupil of the
engraver J.A.Quartley (q.v.), exhibited at the Salon,
where he received an honourable mention, 1896,
third class 1899, and he specialised in reproductions
and vignette illustrations. He worked in London at
30 and 31 New Bridge Street, Blackfriars, EC
(POD,1877-78).
[Bénézit; Gusman]

DUTTON, Edward C. and Company fl.1900s
Provincial wood engraver, who worked at County
Chambers, B.Martineau Street, Birmingham
(Kelly's,1900).

DUTTON, Thomas G. fl.1858-79
Draughtsman and marine watercolourist. He worked
in London and contributed drawings of shipping for
wood engravings to the Illustrated London News,1877.
He also exhibited at the Royal Society of British
Artists, 1858-79.

DUVERGIER, Ernest (Elphage Alfred) fl.1857-94
London wood engraver, who worked at 8 Gough
Square, EC (POD,1857-58), 9 Wine Office Court,
(POD,1859), 16 Essex Street, Strand, WC
(POD,1862-63), 6 Thanet Place, Strand, WC
(POD,1875-82), 61 Fleet Street, EC (POD,1883-90)
shared with W.Roberts (q.v.) and then at the same
address as 'Elphage Alfred Duvergier' (POD,1891-94).

DYAS, Edward
Wood engraver, who trained himself and worked near
Madeley, Shropshire. He was best known for woodcuts
to Alexander's Expedition, a poem by Dr Beddoes,
printed in 1792, but not published. Redgrave described
Dyas as a 'clever self-taught artist' and Chatto
mentions his work.

DYCE, William 1806-64
Occasional draughtsman illustrator on wood,
prominent Scottish painter and decorator. He trained
as a painter under the Nazarene and Renaissance
influence. He painted portraits and frescoes, and
sympathised with the Pre-Raphaelites. He is listed
here for an unsigned illustration to Nursery Rhymes,
Tales & Jingles,1844 and an illustration on wood for
the Dalziels' Bible Gallery (see Dalziel Brothers).
[For biographical detail see Wood; also TB; Bénézit;

McLean, Victorian Book Design,p.57]

EADE, Charles fl.1868-94
London draughtsman and wood engraver, who
worked at 4 Goldsmiths' Street, Gough Square, EC
(POD,1868-71), 8 Featherstone Buildings, WC
(POD,1872-76), 71 Fleet Street, EC (POD,1879-85),
171 Queen Victoria Street, EC (POD,1886), then
4 Ludgate Circus (POD,1894-95).

EADES, Charles fl.1880-1900
Provincial wood engraver, who worked in Birmingham
at 1 Upper Mill Lane (Kelly's,1880-89), and later at
2 Upper Mill Lane (Kelly's,1900).

EARL, Benjamin fl.1880-1900
London wood engraver, who worked at 7 and 8 Dyers'
Buildings, EC (POD,1880-86), and 84 Fetter Lane,
EC (POD,1895-1900).

EARL, William fl.1857-67
London wood engraver, who worked at 10 Red Lion
Court, Fleet Street, EC (POD,1857-67).

EARL(E), William Elden fl.1839-68
Wood engraver, who worked at Surrey Street,
Norwich (Pigot,1839), then in London from 1856 as
W.E.Earle at 7 Regent Street, Lambeth Walk
(Hodgson's,1855, POD,1856-59), then 146 Regent
Street (POD,1860-68). The British Museum owns
several small engravings, crudely cut, of figures,
attributed to W.E.Earle. He signed his work:
'W.E. EARL'.

EATON, Edwin fl.1870s
Provincial wood engraver, who worked at
31 Cemetery Road, Rotherham, and 28 Change
Alley, Sheffield (Kelly's,1872). Fincham lists the
engraver 'Eaton', of 69 Park Street, London, who
designed and engraved an armorial bookplate for
Francis Thornhill Baring, dated 1851.

EBBUTT, Phil fl.1880-1903
Draughtsman, illustrator of figure and humorous
subjects, who began as a pupil of the Dalziel
Brothers (q.v.), being recommended to them by
George D.Sims. The Dalziels recall young Ebbutt's
'natural taste for drawing, and [being] quick
at design'. They employed him on political cartoons
and historical romances, on Jack and Jill and social
character sketches for Fun,1886-87, finding him an
'industrious, willing worker', but his progress was
hindered by an affliction of the eyes, which now and
again demanded complete rest'. He was also one of
the original artists for the Daily Graphic,1890,
worked for The Quiver,1892, the Lady's Pictorial,
1895, and The Graphic,1901-03. He opened a London
office as a draughtsman on wood at 319 Strand, WC

(Kelly's,1889).
[Dalziels' Record]

EDISON Engraving Company fl.1896-1901
London wood engraving firm, with an office at
167 Strand, WC (POD,1896-1901).

EDMONSTON, Samuel 1825-?
Draughtsman on wood of figure subjects, landscape
and marine painter. He was born in Edinburgh in
1825, was the pupil of Sir William Allan and the
Royal Scottish Academy Schools, and worked in
Edinburgh, as watercolourist and pastel artist. He
illustrated Pen and Pencil Pictures from the Poets,
1866; Burns' Poems; and exhibited work at the Royal
Academy, 1856-57, and the Royal Scottish Academy.
[Chatto; Bénézit; TB; Clement; Graves]

EDMUND, William fl.1880s
Provincial draughtsman, who worked at 8 Loadman
Street, Newcastle-upon-Tyne (Kelly's,1889).

EDMUNDSON, Christopher fl.1880s
London suburban wood engraver, who worked at
16 Mount Pleasant Road, Finsbury Road, Finsbury
Park, N (LSDN,1880).

EDWARDS, D. fl.1850-57
Draughtsman illustrator, who contributed two
drawings to the hundred in Reverend Robert
Willmott's The Poets of the Nineteenth Century,
1857, engraved by the Dalziel Brothers (q.v.).

EDWARDS, Henry Russell fl.1880s
London wood engraver, who worked at 325 Strand,
WC (POD,1884).

EDWARDS, Kate fl.1865-79
Competent 'Sixties School' illustrator, who drew for
wood engravings in London Society,1865-66; and
Once a Week,1867, and who exhibited work at the
Royal Society of British Artists, 1879.
[Houfe; White]

EDWARDS, Louis
Draughtsman illustrator of military subjects, which
he contributed for wood engravings to the Illustrated
London News,1889.

EDWARDS, Mary Ellen (Mrs Freer, 1866-69,
Mrs Staples, 1872-) 1839-c1910
Prolific 'Sixties School' draughtsman illustrator and
figure artist. She was born in Kingston-upon-Thames
on 6 November 1839 and established a reputation for
competent drawings for wood engraving. She drew
for Puck on Pegasus,1862 and Parables from Nature,
1861,1867; then Churchman's Family Magazine,
1863-64; London Society,1864-69; Family Fairy
Tales,1864; The Quiver,1864; Once a Week,1865-68;

Legends and Lyrics,1865; The Sunday Magazine,
1865; Good Words,1866; Aunt Judy's Magazine,1867;
Cassell's Magazine,1867-70; Churchman's Shilling
Magazine,1867; Broadway,1867-70; Idyllic
Pictures,1867; Illustrated Book of Sacred Poems,
1867; Argosy,1868; Dark Blue,1871-73; The Graphic,
1869-80; the Illustrated London News,1880 onward;
Quiver,1890; and Girl's Own Paper. Her best work
was engraved by Joseph Swain (q.v.) for the Cornhill,
in which appeared her thirty-two illustrations to
Trollope's The Claverings,1866-67. After this she
tended to repeat herself and present a weak style.
She contributed to most illustrated periodicals for
adults from The Quiver to The Graphic, and her
work in these was much admired by Van Gogh, who
associated her with Du Maurier and P.Marquoid
(qq.v.). The British Museum owns five proof
engravings by the Dalziel Brothers (q.v.),1865-66.
[For a list of works see Houfe; also discussions in
White; Reid]

EGAN, P.
Draughtsman on wood, who contributed the drawing,
'Waterloo Picture Coursing Meeting', wood
engraved by J.Andrew (q.v.) to the Illustrated
London News, 3 December 1842.

ELLIS, Edwin John 1841-95
Draughtsman illustrator, landscape and marine
painter. He was born in Nottingham in 1841, studied
art with Henry Dawson and settled in London, after
art studies in France. He presented initial letter
and quarter-page drawings to Mark Lemon, editor
of Punch, which appeared from 12 December 1867.
As Ellis recalled: 'They were all more or less
pinched and painful things, and Mr Lemon did not
conceal from me that "he was not knocked over by
them". But they were drawn on the block--not on
paper--and from the strangeness and discomfort of
it came the tight-elbowed style of the work. Of what
I did altogether, only about a third were printed;
half were paid for; but what they paid for they did
not print, and what they printed they did not pay for'
(Spielmann,p.537). Ellis also contributed to London
Society,1868-69; and Cassell's Magazine,1870. He
wrote and illustrated Fate in Arcadia,1868-69, and
because of his interest in and championing of
William Blake's poetry, he published The Real Blake,
1907. He was also a popular landscape painter and
exhibited at the Royal Academy and the Royal Society
of British Artists,1868-91.
[Spielmann; Bénézit; Houfe]

ELLIS, Tristram James 1844-1922
Illustrator, landscape painter, watercolourist and
etcher, born in Great Malvern in 1844. He travelled
extensively to the Continent and Near East and
exhibited works at the Grosvenor Gallery, the New
Gallery, the Royal Academy and the Royal Society of

British Artists, and was elected ARE,1887. By the
1880s he had illustrated magazines and books like
A.C.Stephen's Fairy Tales of a Parrot,1873; and
done 'How a Bone is Built', a medical illustration
engraved by J.D.Cooper (q.v.) for the English
Illustrated Magazine,1883-84. He also etched
illustrations to On a Raft through the Desert,1881.
He died on 25 July 1922.
[TB; Houfe; Who's Who,1914]

ELMORE, Alfred 1815-81
Occasional illustrator, history and genre painter. He
was born in Clonakilty, County Cork, on 18 June
1815, moved to London to study art at the British
Museum and the Royal Academy Schools, travelled
extensively and exhibited at the Royal Academy,
1834 onwards, being elected ARA,1846, RA,1857,
and RHA,1878. He contributed a frontispiece
illustration for wood engraving to Charles Mackay's
The Home Affections,1858, and to Mrs S.C.Hall's
Midsummer Eve,1842. He died in Kensington on
24 January 1881. The British Museum owns proof
engravings of his designs, engraved by the Dalziel
Brothers (q.v.), 1839-47.
[Houfe; Wood (bibliography)]

ELTZE, Fritz ?-1870
Draughtsman illustrator, who was introduced to
Punch in May 1864, after Joseph Swain's (q.v.)
inquiry and accepted as social illustrator following
John Leech's death that year. He specialised in
scenes from Scotland Yard and his boyhood home in
Ramsgate, where he had suffered from progressive
consumption. His comic views led to half-page
'socials' and a sympathetic treatment of childhood,
which he contributed until September 1870 (later
works from stock, 1872,1875). Spielmann concludes,
'Eltze, one of Punch's tall men, by the way, was a
pleasing draughtsman whose work, in its curious
absence of lining, had a striking appearance of
originality in its practically broad outline'. Eltze
also contributed to Good Words,1864; Sunday
Magazine,1865; Once a Week,1866-67; Mark Lemon's
A New Table Book,1866; and Legendary Ballads,1876.
[Spielmann; Houfe; H.C.Ewart, Toilers in Art,1891]

ELWES, Alfred Thomas fl.1872-84
Draughtsman illustrator of animals and birds, which
he contributed to the Illustrated London News,1872-77.
He also illustrated The Pleasant History of Reynard
the Fox,1872; and drew for The Graphic,1875; and
the Cornhill,1883-84.

EMERSON, William A.
Wood engraver, author, who wrote and illustrated
the popular Practical Instruction in the Art of Wood
Engraving for Persons to Learn the Art without an
Instructor,1876, new edition,1881.
[Levis]

EMERY, Charles fl.1880s
London draughtsman, who worked at 83 Forest Road,
Dalston, E (Kelly's,1880).

EMMOTT and Company fl.1880s
Provincial wood engraving firm, with an office at
New Bridge Street, Strangeways, Manchester
(Kelly's,1889).

EMSLIE, Alfred Edward 1848-1918
Draughtsman illustrator, watercolourist and genre
painter. He exhibited in London from 1867 and
developed his draughtsmanship skills drawing for
the Illustrated London News from the 1870s and
regularly in the 1880s, also then for The Graphic,
1880-85. These were works of social realism, such
as 'At Work in a Woollen Factory', Illustrated
London News,1883, much praised by Van Gogh who
collected his work. Emslie was elected ARWS,1888,
exhibited at the Grosvenor Gallery, the Royal
Academy, the Royal Society of British Artists, the
Royal Watercolour Society and the Fine Art Society,
1896, and won a medal at the Paris Exhibition,1887.
[Houfe; English Influences on Van Gogh]

ENGBERG, Jones 1833-?
Swedish wood engraver, who studied in London,
Paris, then returned to his own studio in Sweden
and later went to New York. According to Gusman,
he contributed engravings to various nineteenth
century publications.

ERSKINE
(see McFarlane and Erskine)

ETHERINGTON, Alfred and Edward fl.1849-80
English wood engravers, who worked in Paris
during the 1860s. They engraved architectural
subjects for French magazines such as Magasin
Pittoresque, and also for Histoire des Peintres
de Toutes les Ecoles,1849-75. Later Alfred worked
in London at 3 Bouverie Street (POD,1880). Edward
was a friend and engraver of Gustave Doré (q.v.).
The British Museum owns a series which he engraved
in a dull grey manner after Karl Girardet. They
signed their work: 'A E[superimposed]THERINGTON',
'E.ETHERINGTON'.
[Bénézit; TB; Gusman (for list of French work)]

EVANS, Alfred fl.1876-1900
Provincial wood engraver, who worked at
55 Whitechapel, Liverpool (Kelly's,1876), then with
Thomas Evans at Central Chambers, S.Castle
Street, Liverpool (Kelly's,1880-1900).

EVANS, Edmund 1826-1905
Prominent wood engraver, colour printer,
occasional etcher and watercolourist. He earned a
reputation as 'the last of the great commercial wood

engravers'. He was born in Southwark on 23 February 1826, and was educated at a school in Jamaica Row kept by Bart Robson, an old sailor, until November 1839, when he became a thirteen year old 'reading boy' at Samuel Bentley's printing works, Bangor House, Shoe Lane. There he remained from November, 1839 - May 1840, but his speech impediment prevented him from reading in the composing room, and he became a workroom sweeper and errand boy. He became fascinated by the wood engravings printed there, especially those for the London publisher Van Voorst, and after drawing his own design after one of these on slate, he upset the office when he tried to print it on the presses. He was sent to Mr Fley, the firm's overseer, who instead of reprimanding him introduced him to Ebenezer Landells (q.v.) a wood engraver and personal friend. Landells agreed to take young Evans (then fourteen) as an apprentice wood engraver at a £30 premium, for a period of seven years, and he started in 1840. Evans worked at Landells' succession of workshops: 76 Fleet Street, then his private home in Thornhill Road, Barnsbury, and when work for the Illustrated London News demanded a larger staff, Landells moved with them to St Bride's Court, and finally Holford Street, Pentonville. According to his autobiography, Evans apparently enjoyed each of these moves and his apprenticeship; and Landells gradually came to admire his skills. There Evans befriended fellow-apprentice Birket Foster (q.v.) and the two often went off on sketching trips together in search of new engraving material. There is a fascinating sketch-book of sixty-six watercolours, drawings in ink and pencil, dated 1840-47, now in University of California Library, which Evans kept during these escapades and which shows the influence of Foster's draughtsmanship. They were both to enjoy painting and engraving all their lives. Evans often worked in collaboration with Birket Foster on those nature vignettes which he engraved for the early issues of Punch or the Illustrated London News (which Landells helped to start). He recalled that this strenuous work was always done under the shadow of a weekly deadline: 'I worked considerably at overtime, for the I.L.N. generally required night work, so I was totally unfit for work for a day or two after the drives of getting the blocks in to time. I often had to get to Landells by from four or five in the morning to take up the block' (Reminiscences, p.14). He was also sent round to deliver and collect proofs and drawings at Punch or Illustrated London News' offices, or from Landells' outside engravers, the Dalziels (q.v.). Once he took Dickens a drawing for his approval. He engraved 'a lot' for Punch, especially 'those little things they did early on, silhouettes-'. The office was often filled with visiting artists and writers, and Evans recalled the number of drawings that they merely stuffed into drawers: 'Outside artists used to send drawings hoping they would be accepted: one man, I remember, brought several drawings on wood, packed in a fancy flower-basket with cabbage leaved between them--I suppose he was afraid of being seen carrying a basket except of fruit!' Such an atmosphere of enterprise and activity greatly impressed young Evans and his fellow apprentice John Greenaway (q.v.), and inspired their own ambitions to set up as engravers. Evans completed his apprenticeship in May 1847 and despite Landells' pleas to continue as one of his staff engravers, he insisted that he must set up on his own. He struggled at first, engraving sporadically for the Illustrated London News from 1847. His first cuts here were landscapes: a view of Wordsworth's house, Rydal Mount; a view of Funchal, Madeira; and one of Lannercost Priory. But even his apprenticeship failed to train him well enough to succeed without practice: 'To my sorrow Nathaniel Cooke told me that he was willing to give me work for the I.L.N. but I could not engrave quite well enough. The fact was that I engraved the blocks too fine, fitted for book-work printing, not newspaper printing...' (Reminiscences,p.20). Undeterred, Evans planned new landscape engravings after Birket Foster's drawings, and together they initiated various series such as the 'Seasons' and the 'Watering Places of England'. Evans engraved these in as fine a manner as possible, and admitted the influence of Thomas Bewick (q.v.). He also became quite adept at engraving the atmospheric designs of sea and landscape of Samuel Read (q.v.), a skill he shared with his fellow apprentice John Greenaway (q.v.). By 1850 he had set up an office at Wine Office Court, near the Cheshire Cheese, and took on his younger brother Frederick Evans (q.v.) as pupil, and W.L.Palmer (q.v.) as assistant. The noise of his press annoyed the lawyer below them and forced them to abandon these premises. Frederick found others, 4 Racquet Court, Fleet Street, where his engraving firm remained for over fifty years. Evans was also fortunate in his early book commissions. Ingram, Cooke and Company commissioned Birket Foster's illustrations to Ida Pfeiffer's Travels in the Holy Land,1852, and Evans engraved them for three printings: a brown outline key block, a buff and a blue tint block. This was probably Evans' first colour work and led to further work: Fern Leaves from Fanny's Portfolio,1853, again engraved from brown key block, but only a second lighter brown tint block. The cover to Mayhew's Letters Left at the Pastrycook's,1853, he engraved and printed in blue and red on yellow tinted paper, and this inititated the so-called 'yellow-backs'. These were railway novels with colour printed covers, printed in red and blue (occasionally green) upon yellow tinted enamel paper. They were so successful, designed by the major artists for wood engraving, that Evans built

up a substantial number of orders from not only
Ingram, Cooke and Company, but also George
Routledge and Warne, Smith, Elder and Company
and others, and eventually American publishers as
well. The Constance Meade Collection, Bodleian
Library, has some 350 proofs of these 'yellow backs'.
Although Evans soon became known for his colour
work, he did produce some effective black and white
wood engravings during the 1850s. He considered
that his 'best works' were cuts to an edition of Sir
Walter Scott's Poetical Works, 1853-56; George
Herbert's Poetical Works; and Cowper's Task,
1855-56. His interest in the countryside and in the
growing market for natural history guidebooks
resulted in what some regard as his masterpiece of
black and white engraving: the colour and uncoloured
drawings (largely of W.S.Coleman) to Reverend
J.G.Wood's Common Objects series, 1857-, published
by Routledge. McLean declared that Evans' intricate
uncoloured engravings in Common Objects of the
Microscope, 1861 were 'miraculously fine: even
Bewick never surpassed these'. But it was Evans'
colour printing which secured his success and
brought in the necessary commissions to keep his
staff of engravers which had grown to about thirty by
the 1860s and 70s. Of his earliest successes, he
recalled, 'those were red letter days in my life!'
He used the process of printing in oil colour from a
series of wood blocks which descended from the
chiaroscuro engravers, and was most akin to his
immediate predecessor, George Baxter (q.v.),
although Evans did not use Baxter's steel or copper
key plate. His first successful colour work was for
Poems of Oliver Goldsmith, 1858. This was produced
from Birket Foster's drawings on wood, which
Evans first engraved in outline, then produced a
proof of for Foster to watercolour as he wanted the
tints. 'This was followed most carefully by Evans,
who bought the actual colours used by the artist,
ground them by hand, and did the printing on a hand
press' (DNB). Evans recalled 'It was a great labour
to engrave the colour blocks as they were done'
(letter in University of California Library). The
success of this book (it sold out; a second edition with
additional illustrations was done in 1859), led to
Foster's and Evans' collaboration on Thomas
Miller's Common Wayside Flowers, 1860, again
published by Routledge. Most of these early (1858-60)
colour engravings were done in from six to eight
colours. They led the way to the commission which
Evans declared to be 'the most carefully executed
book I have ever printed', James Doyle's A Chronicle
of England, 1864. Its eighty-one illustrations from
nine or ten colour blocks were 'printed on a hand
press for the last time' (DNB). The even more
remarkable work which followed was for Doyle's
brother, Richard Doyle's In Fairyland, 1870. Its
sixteen large colour plates from eight to twelve
blocks was probably the largest single book Evans

ever printed and surely the most remarkable. From
1865-69 Evans engraved numerous six-penny Toy
Books for George Routledge and Ward and Lock. In
1877 he decided to initiate his own series of children's
books, which were to be distributed by George
Routledge. He secured the young illustrator Walter
Crane (q.v.) for the first of these, The Baby's
Opera, 1877, and Crane eventually found himself
linked with Evans' other children's illustrators,
Randolph Caldecott and Kate Greenaway (qq.v.).
Together they produced some of the most influential
colour engraved children's books ever printed.
Evans built up a masterful relationship with his
artists and they in turn learned to produce the
appropriate drawings with simple outlines and flat
washes reproduced almost in facsimile. Evans
described the process, which started with Crane:
'They were originally drawn on wood by Crane, the
black only: the treatment of each subject was quite
original, masses of black being freely used, so that
when the proofs were painted as a guide for the
colour printer, the intention was clearly seen from
the beginning: a flesh tint, a red with a fraction of
brown in it, a dark blue with brown added, a yellow
with raw sienna, were the only printings required to
obtain a very good artistic effect. Of course the
most was made of this limited scale of colouring by
engraving and crossing the colours, either solid
or in gradations of engraving' (Reminiscences,
p.34). By the 1880s, Evans had apparently tried to
adapt Caldecott's and Kate Greenaway's drawings
to the new process method of photo-engraving for
their planned venture, Mavor's English Spelling-
Book, 1885. This would allow the original drawings
to be saved, and retain some of the original
intentions of the artists. He provided Caldecott with
a choice; 'I shewed him some drawings by Kate
Greenaway which I had photographed on wood and
engraved in the usual way, also some similar
drawings which I had reproduced by this process.
but R.C., Kate Greenaway and myself liked the
engraved ones best'. It does indicate that Evans was
willing to adapt to changes in his profession by the
1880s, but in fact all his work with Crane, Caldecott
and Greenaway was wood engraved in the standard
way. Evans was always a capable if somewhat
over-trusting businessman, who found that his firm
had grown to such proportions that he was overshadowed as engraver by his staff of assistants.
He enlarged his firm by taking over 116 Fleet
Street which led into Racquet Court, later also
119 Fleet Street where he 'put up a steamengine and
boiler with many extra machines'. His only regret
was the darkness which forced the use of gas light,
'a very expensive as well as an unsuitable light
for printing in colours'. With this growth came new
demands on his time. He could no longer merely
engrave: 'I engraved a considerable number of
drawings by various artists who had not made their

name, and they got me to engrave their drawings
and were very disappointed, and even disgusted,
because their drawings, when engraved, did not
come up equal to those drawn by Birket Foster, and
they evidently thought I, as engraver, was alone to
blame! I could not help thinking, "You cannot make
a silk purse out of a sow's ear"' (Reminiscences,
p.32). Nevertheless, Evans managed to instil in his
artists and engravers a devotion to his business and
his abilities as an engraver, which proved his
greatest asset. Caldecott recalled, during a turbulent
collaboration with Mrs Ewing, that Evans had trained
a staff of assistants to engrave so that he was able to
'superintend their work and to give advice and make
suggestions thereon at such moments as he could
spare from his growing occupations of waiting in
publishers' lobbies, or corresponding with authors,
of seeking out suitable materials to his trade, of
discovering draughtsmen who might be trusted to
return to him a block of wood with a fair design
pencilled thereon instead of selling it for a few
immediate pence, and of interviewing such artists
as called upon him either to solicit employment, to
request instant and inordinate reward for work done,
or to point out that his engraving of their drawings
was "sickening" (I quote the word usually used).'
Caldecott concluded, 'Therefore E.E[vans], [J.D.]
Cooper and others wear tall silk hats, have extensive
establishments, and seldom, if ever touch a block
themselves' (quoted in M.Hutchins, Yours Pictorially,
1976,pp.104-05). Evans described his duties as
totally exhausting: 'My work at Racquet Court kept
me fully employed in mind and body: I had to direct
the engravers even to the direction of the lines in the
colour blocks, and the printers in the tones of the
inks for printing, often mixing the inks, so when my
day's work was done I did not feel inclined to go to
any of the places of amusement' (Reminiscences,
p.48). He chose instead to move in 1864, to a large
house in the country, at Witley, Surrey. There his
neighbours included George Eliot, Tennyson, the
Allinghams, Birket Foster and a host of his artist
protégés who came for visits. Evans retired from
his demanding business in 1892, and turned it over
to his two sons, Edmund.Wilfred (b.1869) and
Herbert (b.1871). He suffered a stroke and paralysis,
and was forced to move to Ventnor, Isle of Wight.
But despite paralysis in his right hand he managed to
continue to engrave as late as 1898, when on holiday
in Ramsgate he recalled: 'I engraved on wood 4 or 5
hours each day in the 8 weeks I was at Ramsgate.
Colour works for my sons at Racquet Court' (letter
in University of California Library.) He also
watercoloured and sold a few pictures, mainly
landscapes painted while on holidays. 'Last year I
did 6 little art pictures from nature and sold them',
he wrote on 25 October 1897. He also tried his hand
at etching landscapes; three were successful enough
to be accepted at the Royal Academy,1873-80. Evans

retained a close interest in his son's business
during his retirement. It was perhaps significant
that he was supervising the colour printing of plates
to his protégée's biography, Kate Greenaway,1905,
when he died in Ventnor, on 21 August 1905. His
sons continued the business, which by 1904 was
moved to Swan Street, Borough, SE, and specialised
in the three-colour process. Even Evans admitted
towards the end of his life that this was an
improvement from hand engraving on wood blocks:
'I must say I like those 3 colour works (without the
aid of the poor Engraver)...I only wish it had come
my way--in my time' (letter in University of
California Library). (For a discussion of the work of
the Racquet Court Colour Press see the British and
Colonial Printer and Stationer, 31 March 1904,p.3.)
The business continued to thrive into the 1960s, having
amalgamated with W.P.Griffith Limited in 1953.
The largest collections of Evans' work are in the
Constance Meade Collection, Bodleian Library
(colour printed work, books, proofs); the British
Museum (a collection of small vignette proofs); and
UCLA Library (manuscripts and drawings and
sketches). Evans signed his black and white
engravings: 'EDMUND EVANS SC, 'E EVANS SC'.
[For an account of Evans' life and his autobiography
see R.McLean, Reminiscences of Edmund Evans,
1967 (with bibliography of engraved work); also
DNB; TB. For a discussion of his engraving business
see British and Colonial Printer,31 March 1904,
7 September 1905; also Hardie; Burch; McLean,
Victorian Book Design; for colour printing see
Wakeman and Bridson]

EVANS, Edward fl.1838-48
London wood engraver, not to be confused with
Edmund Evans (q.v.) who knew this engraver's work
after Phiz (q.v.) drawings and was often confused
with him. Edward Evans worked in London at
53 Wynyatt Street, Goswell Road (Pigot,1838),
14 President Street, W (POD,1840), and
91 Bartholomew Close (POD,1846-48). Evans' work
included a cover engraving after Phiz to Harry
Lorrequer's Charles O'Malley,1839; a vignette
after William Harvey (q.v.) to Ancient Spanish
Ballads,1841-42 (signed 'EVANS Sc'); illustrations
after J.Franklin and H.Warren (qq.v.) to S.C.Hall's
Book of British Ballads,1842; a frontispiece in two
colours to Sir Uredale Price on the Picturesque,
1842; and illustrations after William Harvey to
Charles Knight's Penny Magazine,October 1845.
He signed his work: 'E.EVANS Sc' or 'EVANS Sc'.
[Evans Reminiscences; Bodleian Library]

EVANS, Frederick fl.1850s
Wood engraver assistant to his elder brother,
Edmund Evans (q.v.). He was taken on as a pupil
when Evans set up in London at Wine Office Court,

c1850, where he worked under the assistant, W.L.Palmer (q.v.). When Evans was forced to move in 1851, Frederick found the new premises, 4 Racquet Court, Fleet Street, which remained under Evans' control for the next fifty years. Engravings of plants and animals and a page of insects and moths done by Frederick are in the British Museum. He signed his work: 'F EVANS'. [McLean; Evans Reminiscences]

EVANS, George Joseph fl.1853-1901
London wood engraver, who worked at 42 Acton Street, Gray's Inn Road (POD,1853-68), 17 Great Ormond Street, WC (POD,1869), 25 New Ormond Street, WC (POD,1870-77), 10 Ampton Place and Ampton Street, WC (POD,1878-81). The following year the firm became Evans and Company (POD,1882-88), but reverted to George J.Evans and Son at 1 Ampton Street, Gray's Inn Road, WC (POD,1889-94), then to George J.Evans, at 57 Rochester Road, NW (POD,1895-1901).

EVANS, Henry fl.1880-95
London wood engraver, who worked at 8 Red Lion Court, Fleet Street, EC (POD,1880-95). The directories also listed another Henry Evans, wood engraver, who worked at 303 Strand, WC (POD,1880-86), which became Evans and Bradley (POD,1887-88). (See also Bradley, William George)

EVANS, Thomas Joseph
(see Evans, Alfred)

EVANS, William H. fl.1880s
Provincial wood engraver, who worked at 9 South Castle Street, Liverpool (Kelly's,1889). (See also Evans, Alfred)

EYRE, Colonel Vincent
Amateur draughtsman, colonel in the Bengal Artillery. He contributed drawings of India to the Illustrated London News, wood engraved in 1857.

FAHEY, Edward Henry 1844-1907
Occasional draughtsman, oil and watercolour painter of architectural subjects. He was born in London in 1844, studied at South Kensington, the Royal Academy Schools, and in Italy, and achieved a reputation for paintings hung at the New Gallery, the Grosvenor Gallery, the New Watercolour Society, the Royal Academy, the Royal Society of British Artists, the Royal Hibernian Academy, and the Royal Institute of Painters in Watercolours. He was elected ARI,1870, RI,1876, and ROI,1883. Fahey is listed here for his architectural drawings wood engraved in The Graphic,1870, 1877. He died in Notting Hill, 13 March 1907.

FAIRFIELD, A.R. fl.1861-87
Draughtsman illustrator, born into an artistic family. He spent just three months at South Kensington in 1857, then began drawing on wood for Fun,1861, which prepared him for drawings to The Leisure Hour. Its editor Dr James Macaulay sent Fairfield to Joseph Swain (q.v.), the Punch engraver, for wood blocks and Swain soon saw his talent for block drawing and introduced the young artist to the Punch editor, Mark Lemon. Fairfield began his work for Punch with drawings in the special Shakespeare Jubilee number, followed by twenty-four cuts,1864-65 and a final one in 1887. He also contributed to Thornbury's Legendary Ballads,1876. He was in addition a talented portrait caricaturist.
[Spielmann; Houfe]

FAIRHALL, Alfred fl.1872-76
London draughtsman, who worked at 8 Bouverie Street, Fleet Street, EC (Kelly's,1872) and 10 Bolt Court, Fleet Street, EC (Kelly's,1876), an office shared with Thomas Coman (q.v.).

FAIRHILL and Miller fl.1870s
London wood engraving firm, with an office at 84 Fleet Street, EC (POD,1875), possibly a partnership between Alfred Fairhall (sic) and John Fenwick Miller (qq.v.).

FAIRHOLT, Frederick William c1814-66
Wood engraver, draughtsman on wood and antiquarian. He was born in London c1814 (1818, Bryan, Bénézit), the son of German immigrant parents. He won the Society of Arts medal at an early age and took up scenery painting in the theatre. In 1835 he became an assistant to the wood engraver Stephen Sly (q.v.) at whose premises he met and befriended the engraver and antiquarian Llewellyn Jewitt (q.v.). It was probably through Sly, who then worked prolifically for Charles Knight's publications, that Fairholt also began to draw and engrave for Knight: he drew on wood for Knight's London,1841, and for Knight's Penny Magazine, 1841. Most notable of these is his series 'A Day in a Tobacco Factory', Penny Magazine,November 1841, engraved by M.Sears, Leonard, J.Cunningham, E.Crowe, S.Slader and T.Wragg (qq.v.). This was followed by the illustrations to 'A Day at the Coach Factory', December 1841. Fairholt developed a keen interest in medieval heraldry and design and established a reputation (according to Bohn in Chatto and Jackson) 'for his knowledge of costume and medieval art, which he has exemplified in a considerable number of shaded outlines, mostly drawn and engraved by himself'. He became the chief illustrator and engraver for the British Archaeological Association's journal, The Archaeological Album. He edited and illustrated Costume in England,1856; and Labarte's

Arts of the Middle Ages; and wrote articles on antiquarian subjects for early numbers of the Art Union (later Art Journal), where he served as an assistant editor under S.C.Hall. He also drew and engraved Pilgrimages to English Shrines, 1850; a series on pottery manufacture, 1855; illustrated a catalogue of the Earl of Londesborough's collection, Miscellanea Graphica, 1854, and accompanied the Earl in 1856 on a tour of Italy and Egypt. He died in Brompton, London on 3 April 1866. The British Museum owns a series of proof engravings after his designs engraved by the Dalziel Brothers (q.v.), 1839-47. He signed his engravings: 'F.W.F.'.
[TB; Redgrave; Bryan; DNB; Chatto; Nagler; Bodleian; S.C.Hall, Retrospect of a Long Life, 1883, Vol.I, p.362; for a list of illustrated works see Houfe; also account of later career in S.C.Hall, Retrospect of a Long Life, 1883]

FAKLANDER, Ida D.M. 1842-?
Swedish wood engraver, born in 1842. She was a pupil of Edward Skill (q.v.), and came to London in 1850, where she worked engraving for The Graphic. Later she returned to Sweden and became the head of her own studio.
[Gusman]

FALKNER, George and Sons fl.1860-1900
Provincial wood engraving firm, with an office at Imperial Buildings, 170 Deansgate, Manchester (Kelly's, 1889-1900). Fincham lists four bookplates designed and engraved (one lithographed) by the firm, dated 1860, 1870 and two in 1883. Their work was signed: 'Falkner Eng. Manchester', 'G.F.S.Fec' (Falkner & Sons).

FARRELL, James fl.1880s
Provincial wood engraver, who worked at 65 Hanover Street, Manchester (Kelly's, 1889).

FARRELL and Jenson fl.1880s
Provincial wood engraving firm, with an office at 56 Arcade Chambers, Manchester (Kelly's, 1889).

FARRELL and Jepson fl.1890-93
London wood engraving firm, with an office at 62 Fleet Street, EC (POD, 1890-91), then 138 Fleet Street, EC (POD, 1893) before becoming the City Wood Engraving Company (q.v.).

FATIO, Morel fl.1843-59
Italian draughtsman illustrator, who contributed wood engraved topographical drawings of France to the Illustrated London News, 1843; and of Italy to the Illustrated Times, 1859.

FAULKNER, Lucy fl.1861-78
Occasional wood engraver, embroiderer, designer, china painter and writer. She was the sister of

Charles and Kate Faulkner and became associated with William Morris (q.v.) from 1861, working for his firm Morris, Faulkner and Company. About 1861 Lucy married the wood engraver Harvey Orrin Smith (q.v.) and learned the techniques well enough to engrave a wood block, 'Cupid Leaving Psyche', 1868, to William Morris's uncompleted The Earthly Paradise. She later published The Drawing Room, its Decoration and Furniture, 1878.
[Callen, Angel in the Studio]

FAWCETT, Benjamin 1808-93
Wood engraver and prominent colour printer from wood blocks, said to be one of three most notable letterpress colour printers (with J.Kronheim and William Dickes (qq.v.)). He was born in Bridlington, Yorkshire in 1808, the son of a sailor, who died early. He was apprenticed to the local stationer, printer and bookseller, Forth, in about 1823, and by 1831 had moved to Middle Street, Driffield to open his own stationer and printing business. Sometime during this early period he had met and perhaps studied briefly with Thomas Bewick (q.v.) and had been inspired by the master's wood engravings, which he tried during the next few years to emulate. From his Middle Street office, where he remained for nineteen years, Fawcett produced his own wood engraved editions of cheap children's books, drawing books, primers and copy books, one an exact reproduction of Bewick's 'Tiger' in British Quadrupeds. Another, of bird stories, is also Bewick-inspired. The only exception was the engravings he made after drawings of John Gilbert to a Kings and Queens booklet. For this work he employed a small number of excellent engravers including John Stabler and W.D.Ridley (qq.v.). His workroom was supervised by a relative of his wife, Miss Augusta Woodmansey, who oversaw the number of colourists he employed to tint his engravings. In fact when his first wife died about 1841 Fawcett married one of these colourists, Martha Porter, and she and their four daughters continued to do much of her husband's colouring. By 1844 Fawcett had begun his famous collaboration with Reverend Francis Orpen Morris, whose naturalist books Fawcett engraved and printed. These ranged from A Bible of Natural History, with 160 wood engravings, to the daunting seven year project, A History of British Birds, 1851-57, in six volumes, with 357 wood engravings all by Fawcett and specimen plates coloured by his wife. Such intricate and accurate work allowed Fawcett to develop his own engraving style, goaded on by the severe criticisms of Morris who took extreme care with his own work. The engraving style utilised a simple foreground technique with no backgrounds, the occasional tree or bramble being engraved for two tones, one black, one uniformly grey. He avoided cross-hatching, in favour of a minute, fine-lined tonal quality reminiscent (and

presumably borrowed from) Bewick. Then followed the Morris series of monthly publications, Nests and Eggs of British Birds,1852-56 with a total of 223 wood engravings by Fawcett; A History of British Butterflies,1852-?; A History of British Game Birds and Wildfowl,1855, with sixty Fawcett engravings, some also drawn by him ('B.Fawcett del'). By 1856 Fawcett had experimented enough to produce striking colour printed plates for watercolour reproductions. These appeared in Shirley Hibberd's Rustic Adornments for Homes of Taste,1856, his earliest full colour work, with eight plates in gold and colours. He adopted a unique colour printing process, engraving on Turkish boxwood (matured for three years before use) for key and colour blocks in extremely fine line, only using hand presses, then touching up by hand. It is believed that some of the tonal effects, apart from stipple, line and ink shadings, came from the grain of the wood block itself (he never used electrotypes). He also used some fifty-one tints of coloured inks. The process was unique for the use of wood blocks to print watercolours (as opposed to Baxter's metal oil colour prints). Its success led to a larger printing works at East Lodge, from 1850-95, with outbuildings for printing, engraving, colouring and binding, and eventually using a staff of between fifty and sixty. These included the apprentice, later a noted draughtsman engraver, A.F.Lydon, and his brother Frederick (qq.v.). Numerous colour plate books were turned out by such authors as Hon. Mrs Ward, Telescope Teachings,1859; E.J.Lowe's, Beautiful Leaved Plants 1861 ('an ambitious task and a triumph of wood engraving and colour printing'); a series of smaller books for naturalists, also the largest colour plate book, British Freshwater Fishes, 1879, and The Ruined Abbeys of Britain,1882. However by the 1870s the colour printing business had begun to suffer, then Fawcett lost his eyesight and in 1883 A.F.Lydon left so that fewer books were produced. Fawcett died early in 1893 and his business continued under his son, but did not flourish, being sold at an auction in January 1895. He was awarded medals at the International Exhibitions, 1866-67 and 1881-82. The British Museum owns a collection of colour nature engravings. He signed his engravings: 'B Fawcett'.
[For a complete account of his colour work see Reverend M.C.F.Morris, Benjamin Fawcett,1925, which lists eighty-eight works; also Ray Resmond, 'Benjamin Fawcett' in Festschrift für Claus Nissen, Weisbaden, Pressler,1973,pp.91-135; Wakeman and Bridson; Lewis; C.Jackson]

FAWCETT, George fl.1880s
Provincial wood engraver, who worked at Beverley Road, Great Driffield, Yorkshire (Kelly's,1880).

FAWKES, Lionel Grimston 1849-1931
Draughtsman illustrator of Irish extraction essentially an amateur and member of the Royal Artillery. He contributed a drawing for wood engraving to Punch,1875, and forty full-page drawings to Trollope's The Way We Live Now, 1874-75, long believed to have been done by Luke Fildes. He also illustrated his aunt's The Washburn and Other Poems,1879.
[Spielmann; Houfe; N.John Hall, Trollope and his Illustrators,1980]

FAY, Henry fl.1880s
London draughtsman, who worked at Hare Place, 47 Fleet Street, EC (Kelly's,1880).

FAZAKERLEY, William fl.1880s
Provincial wood engraver, who worked at 58 Duke Street, Liverpool (Kelly's,1889).

FELLER, F. 1848-1908
Illustrator and painter, born in Bumpliz, Switzerland on 28 October 1848. He studied in Geneva, Munich and Paris and settled in London, where he specialised in comic genre subjects and mountaineering drawings for the Illustrated London News,1880-84; Black and White,1891; St Pauls,1894; Good Cheer,1894; and Chums. He also exhibited at the Royal Academy and the Royal Society of British Artists,1878-95, and died in London on 6 March 1908.
[Houfe]

FENN, Harry 1845-1911
Prominent draughtsman on wood, painter, water-colourist and etcher. He was born in Richmond, Surrey on 9 September 1845, and was one of the Dalziel Brothers' (q.v.) earliest pupils whom they trained to draw and engrave on wood. Later his landscapes were wood engraved by A.Douce (q.v.). He moved to New York, aged nineteen, and established a prominent reputation as 'the most popular landscape draughtsman in America' (Dalziels' Record) noted especially for Picturesque America,1870, 'one of the most brilliantly successful illustrated books ever published, according to the Dalziels. He travelled to Europe and the Near East for a future series. He died in Montclair, New Jersey, 21 April 1911.
[Bénézit; TB (with bibliography); White; Dalziels' Record; Fielding]

FENNELL, John G. 1807-85
Draughtsman, landscape, watercolourist, who studied with Henry Sass in London and became a friend of Hablot Browne, Phiz (q.v.), Dickens and Thackeray. He drew on wood for Charles Knight's Penny Magazine,October 1841, engraved by Jackson.
[Bodleian Library; Houfe]

FENTON, John fl.1880-85
London wood engraver, who worked at 21 Castle
Street, Holborn, EC (POD,1880-82) shared with
H.Dix, and J.Ford (qq.v.), then at 57 and 58
Chancery Lane, WC (POD,1883-85), shared with
F.Barnard, W.Barrett and J.Sachs (qq.v.).

FERGUSON, George fl.1885-1910
London wood engraver, who worked at 28 Essex
Street, Strand, WC (POD,1885-86), shared with
W.Andrews (q.v.). He reappears as G.Fergusson (sic)
at 19 Primrose Hill, SE (POD,1898-1900),
5 Whitefriars Street, EC (POD,1901) and 72 Fleet
Street, EC (POD,1910).

FERGUSON, James fl.1817-66
Illustrator and landscape painter. He worked in
London, Edinburgh, Darlington and Keswick, and
made vignette illustrations to Scott's Gertrude of
Wyoming. He was probably also illustrator for Army
Equipment,1865-66. He exhibited at the British
Institution, 1821-57, the Royal Academy and the
Royal Society of British Artists, 1827,1849,1856.
[Houfe]

FERRIER, Charles Anderson fl.1858-98
Wood engraver, born in Arbroath, Scotland, where
he tried wood engraving on his own, then moved to
London. There he was taken up as a young Scot 'of
varied abilities' by the Dalziel Brothers (q.v.) who
had met Ferrier through William Harvey. 'He was a
youth of considerable promise and full of enthusiasm
for his art', the Dalziels recalled, although his first
studies were crude, despite his friends' claims for
his 'genius'. He was apprenticed with W.G.Kilburne
and A.W.Bayes (qq.v.), but his enthusiasm led to
various achievements. He became the London
correspondent of his home newspaper after two
months in London, working in his lunch hour. He was
also a scientist, later a member of the Royal Societies,
and as a staunch teetotaller, a personal friend of
George Cruikshank, with whom he shared temperance
work. The Dalziels concluded that Ferrier left their
establishment, 'one of the most remarkable men who
had their beginning in our studio'. Ferrier then set
up on his own, working in London's printing district
as wood engraver at 8 Wine Office Court, Fleet Street,
EC (POD,1858), 23 Bouverie Street, Fleet Street,
EC (POD,1859-64), 11 Gough Square, EC
(POD,1865-67), 9 Red Lion Court, Fleet Street, EC
(POD,1868-76) and 73 Fleet Street, EC (POD,1877-79).
At 64 Fleet Street (POD,1880-87) he shared his office
with noted engravers D.H.Luxmore, I.Holdaway,
J.F.Miller, E.A.D.Minns and G.F.Sheern (qq.v.).
Ferrier continued to work as a wood engraver into the
late 1890s, from 53 Paternoster Row, EC (POD,1894-
98), shared during the first year with A.Berry
(q.v.). His engraved work included engravings after
paintings for the Illustrated London News, notably

'The Abdication of Mary, Queen of Scots', after
A.Johnson's painting, 26 May 1855, and 'The
Missing Partner', after Frederick Barnard,
February 1871. Fincham lists two book plates
engraved by Ferrier, one for Princess Alice, dated
1850, and two sizes for Queen Victoria's Windsor
Library,1860. Ferrier signed his work:
'C.A.Ferrier Sc'.
[Dalziels' Record; Houfe]

FIELD, James
The British Museum owns a wood engraving of a
prisoner after H.Anelay (q.v.) by James Field.

FIELD, Walter and Company fl.1891-96
London wood engraving firm, with an office at
9 Furnival Street, EC (POD,1891) shared with
C.Peinligh (q.v.), then at 2 The Facade, Cloak Lane,
EC (POD,1896).

FIELD and Thompson fl.1887-90
London wood engraving firm, with an office at 10 and
11 Cursitor Street, EC (POD,1887-90).

FILDES, Sir Samuel Luke 1844-1927
Draughtsman illustrator on wood, prominent genre
painter of English and Venetian subjects. He was born
in Liverpool on 18 October 1843, and studied at the
Liverpool Mechanics Institute, Warrington School of
Art, South Kensington and Royal Academy Schools.
Intent on becoming a book illustrator, he began his
career as a draughtsman on wood for illustrated
periodicals after he obtained an introduction to one
of the period's leading wood engravers, William
Luson Thomas (q.v.). Thomas approved of his
drawings on wood blocks and offered him a job
redrawing parts of other artists' drawings to make
them ready for engraving. Then followed two
drawings to Foxe's Book of Martyrs, a monthly
serial, May, July, 1866, and an introduction to the
noted engraver Joseph Swain (q.v.) who commissioned
drawings for Once a Week,1866-69; Good Words,
1867-68; Sunday Magazine,1868; Illustrated Readings,
1867-68; Cassell's Magazine,1868-70; Quiver,
1868-69; Sunday at Home,1868 and Gentleman's
Magazine,1869-70. Thomas engaged Fildes for his
new publication The Graphic,1869-74,1880, for
which Fildes produced some of his most notable
drawings which he eventually turned into paintings.
Many were admired by Van Gogh. Other work
appeared in the Cornhill,1870-73; Leisure Hour,
1870; Pictures from English Literature,1870; and
the Illustrated London News,1880. Fildes also drew
for books and made the acquaintance of Charles
Dickens in 1869, illustrating his Edwin Drood,1870,
engraved by C.Roberts (q.v.). He also illustrated
Charles Reade's Peg Woffington,1868, and Griffith
Grant; Wilkie Collins' The Law and the Lady and
Miss or Mrs,1885; and Thackeray's

Catherine,1894. He gave up drawing on wood about 1872, in favour of oil painting, exhibiting at the Royal Academy,1872-1927. But in 1873 he took up a pencil to draw for The Graphic an unusual portrait of Emperor Napoleon II on his deathbed, from a photograph, an achievement which the Times called 'a remarkable instance of speedy production joined to a high degree of artistic merit'. Thomas had persuaded Fildes to make the drawing on the wood block, to save time (rather than on paper for photographic transfer onto the block), and Fildes received the portrait photograph on Monday evening at 7 o'clock. He worked all night and finished the drawing at 10 o'clock on Tuesday morning. The block was then broken into thirty pieces and distributed to thirty separate engravers who completed the cutting by 10 o'clock on Wednesday morning. By 10 o'clock on Thursday morning the pieces had been reassembled, the joints smoothed out, and four copper electrotypes were made for the printers from his block. Fildes was able to earn a considerable amount for his drawings, especially when publishers used photographic transfer techniques and preserved his original drawings which they sold for as much as £50 each. He took advantage of this fact to amass a considerable fortune. He was more noted later as a popular Edwardian portrait painter, his subjects including state portraits of royalty. He was elected ARA,1879, RA,1887, knighted in 1906 and died 27 February 1927.
[For biographical detail see L.V.Fildes, L.Fildes, 1968; Houfe (full book list); TB (full bibliography)]

FINDLEY, J. fl.1825-68
Wood engraver, etcher and aquatint engraver. He is known for a wood engraving after Gustave Doré (q.v.) to Moxon's edition of Tennyson's Enid, illustrating the death of Earl Doorm at the hand of Geraint. This was published by Moxon, 1 November 1868, and declared to the Printsellers' Association. J.Findlay (sic) worked in London from 1825-57.

FISHER, Albert Edward fl.1894-95
London wood engraver, who worked at 1 Norfolk Street, Strand, WC (POD,1894-95) which he shared with G.Meek, R.Cousins and J.C.Saunders (qq.v.).

FISHER, Eden and Company fl.1880-1900
London wood engraving firm, with offices at 50 Lombard Street, EC and 97 Fenchurch Street, EC (Kelly's,1880-89), then 6,7,8 Clement's Lane, Lombard Street, and 95-97 Fenchurch Street (Kelly's,1900).

FITCH, Oswald fl.1890s
London wood engraver, who worked at 57 Moor Lane, EC (POD,1891). He may be related to the colour printers John N.Fitch (1840-1927) and Robert Fitch,

who are listed in Wakeman and Bridson.

FITZCOCK, Henry 1824-?
Draughtsman illustrator and painter of historical subjects. He was born in Pentonville in 1824 and studied at the Royal Academy Schools and with Benjamin Haydon. He began his career exhibiting at the British Institution,1853-64, the Royal Society of British Artists,1853-72, and the Royal Academy, primarily literary subjects from Longfellow and Cowper. This prepared him for drawing for wood engravings in various magazines, such as the Illustrated London News,1856-60 (a record of a Swedish trip); and Churchmen's Family Magazine, 1864. He also illustrated books like John Bunyan's The Holy War,1864; and All About Shakespeare.

FITZGERALD, John Anster 1832-1906
Occasional illustrator, prominent painter of fairies, who was born on 25 November 1832, and painted for the London galleries, the Royal Academy, the Royal Society of British Artists, the Royal Institute of Painters in Watercolours, and the Royal Society of Painters in Oil-Colours, living 1845-1903 in Newington. He contributed wood engraved fairy subjects to the Christmas numbers of the Illustrated London News,1863,1876-77.
[Houfe; Wood]

FITZGERALD, Michael fl.1871-91
Illustrator of social subjects such as Irish peasants and middle class life, which he contributed for wood engravings to such magazines as the Illustrated London News,1872-86,1891 and Pictorial World, 1874-75, engraved in a dark, rather crude wood-cut manner. These were greatly admired by Van Gogh, who considered the sympathetic representations of Irish poor and Welsh miners striking, and that one of an English prison was 'as beautiful as a Regamey' (q.v.). Fitzgerald also contributed to Dark Blue,1871-73, and later the Cornhill,1885. Some of his work was exhibited at the Royal Academy, the Royal Society of British Artists and the Royal Hibernian Academy, 1875-85.
[Houfe; English Influences on Van Gogh]

FITZPATRICK, Edmond fl.1848-72
Draughtsman illustrator of Irish social subjects, and of figures, contributor to the Illustrated London News,1848,1853-59. He also made drawings for wood engraving in the London Society,1872. Some were exhibited at the British Institution,1867, and the Royal Society of British Artists, 1856-70. He was elected ARHA,1856. The British Museum owns several proof engravings from his designs engraved by the Dalziel Brothers (q.v.), 1860, 1862.

FLEMING, Benjamin fl.1874-78
London wood engraver, who worked at 119 Salisbury
Square, EC (POD,1874-78). His engravings included
various half-page plates after drawings from special
artists for the Illustrated London News,1875-76,
notably a series of drawings of the New Zealand gold
fields, 10 April, 8 May 1875, and a Buddhist temple,
after 'RW', 11 December 1875.

FLEMING, William Vaughan fl.1880s
Provincial wood engraver, who worked at 19 Chapel
Walks, Manchester (Kelly's,1889).

FLETCHER, Frank Morley 1866-1949
Woodcut artist and portrait painter. He was born in
Whiston, Lancashire in 1866, studied in Paris at the
Atelier Cormon, and exhibited at major London
galleries from 1888, and in Paris and America. As
a woodcut artist he helped to influence the revival of
interest in wood as a print medium. He worked with
J.D.Batten (q.v.), cutting his designs for the
Japanese-inspired colour woodcuts which gained
them both a considerable reputation. Their
collaboration on 'Eve and the Serpent',1895 (proof)
1896 (published) was heralded as the first colour
woodcut in the 'Japanese style'. Fletcher's work led
to his own influential book, Wood-block Printing,
1916; the edition of 2,000 included individual prints
in each volume. He served as a member of the
council of International Society of Sculptors, Painters
and Gravers,1903-09 and was head of the Art
Department, Reading University,1898-1906, but moved
to America in 1923, where he died on 2 November
1949. His pupils included Professor A.Seaby (q.v.).
[Waters; Hind]

FLORIAN, Frederic and Ernest fl.1890s
Swiss-Italian process wood engravers. Frederic
went to France where he worked with his brother
Ernest engraving French and foreign bank notes,
and they became noted for their understanding of
photo-engraving. Gusman describes Frederic as a
'good draughtsman as well as an impeccable engraver'
who utilised a 'soft touch' technique upon the wood
block. He devised a theory centred upon the light and
darks of the photo-engraving, and believed the
engraving and typography surrounding it should be
considered as a tonal unit, and the block printed to
standards set by the overall impression of the full
page (see Gusman, Volume I,p.259). The brothers
engraved after various artists such as Luc-Olivier,
and Merson and worked for various periodicals such
as Revue Illustré, and Harpers, in collaboration
with the editor Edouard Pelletan. They are listed
here for their engravings after William Hatherell's
designs to Thomas Hardy's Hearts Insurgent,
published in Harper's New Monthly,1895.
They signed their work: 'FLORIAN'.
[Gusman; A.Jackson, Illustrators of T.Hardy,1981]

FOLKARD, William A. fl.1830-50
London wood engraver and draughtsman on wood,
who provided wood engravings to various books.
These included comic illustrations to Tom Hood's
Comic Annual,1834; Jenning's Landscape Annual,
1835-36; and engravings after Théophile Fragonard
to Les Evangiles,1838, engraved with John Wright
M.Sears, Charles Laing, Powis and Robert Hart.
His most successful engravings were among the
nearly 400 after John Gilbert, J.H.Townsend and
others to S.C.Hall's Book of English Ballads,
1842. This book Bohn described as 'the first
work of any consequence that presented a
combination of the best artists of the time'. Some
cuts he engraved with Thomas Gilks (q.v.).
Folkard also designed and engraved bookplates:
Fincham lists eight (including one for Frederick
Folkard) done from Folkard's early office at
260 Regent Street; they were dated 1830, 1840, 1850.
By 1840 he had joined forces with J.Wright as Wright
and Folkard (q.v.); then he worked on his own from
4 New London Street (POD,1842). The British
Museum owns engravings after J.Gilbert and
D.Roberts. He signed his work: 'Folkard sc', or
'W.A. FOLKARD Sc'.
[Chatto; Gusman]

FOOTHORAPE, John fl.1876-80
Provincial wood engraver, who worked in Birmingham
at 54A Bread Street (Kelly's,1876), then 56 Great
Charles Street (Kelly's,1880).

FORCROY
Wood engraver, listed by LeBlanc as a pupil of
Adam, who worked during the early part of the
nineteenth century.
[Nagler; Bénézit; LeBlanc]

FORD, George Harry fl.1886-1910
London wood engraver, who worked in partnership
with J.C.Wall (q.v.) as Ford and Wall,
31 Paternoster Square, EC (POD,1886-90), then on
his own at 29 Paternoster Square, EC
(POD,1892-1910). He is not to be confused with the
London lithographer George H.Ford (1809-76).
[Wakeman and Bridson]

FORD, James fl.1881-82
London wood engraver, who worked at 21 Castle
Street, Holborn (POD,1881-82), shared with H.Dix
and J.Fenton (qq.v.).

FORRESTER, Alfred Henry
(see Crowquill, Alfred)

FORRESTIER, Amedée 1854-1930
'Special' draughtsman, illustrator, probably born in
Belgium. He came to England to work for the
Illustrated London News,1882, and drew for wood

engravings as 'special artist', regularly until 1899. His subjects were mostly royal occasions and ceremonial events. He also illustrated for most major magazines like the Strand Magazine,1891; English Illustrated Magazine,1895-96, as well as books such as Wilkie Collins' Blind Love, 1890; Bret Harte's Barker's Luck,1896. He exhibited briefly at the Royal Society of British Artists,1882-83. He died on 14 November 1930. [For a complete list of works see Houfe]

FOSTER, Francis W. fl.1880s
London wood engraver, who worked at 3 and 4 Red Lion Passage, EC (POD,1886).

FOSTER, Myles Birket 1825-99
Draughtsman illustrator and painter of pastoral landscape scenes, who the Dalziels called 'one of England's most popular landscape draughtsmen'. He was born in North Shields, Northumberland on 4 February 1825 and moved to London in 1830 where, after schooling he was apprenticed to the wood engraver Ebenezer Landells (q.v.), Bewick's pupil, and from 1841-46, worked with fellow apprentice Edmund Evans (q.v.). He first trained to engrave on wood but proved talented as a draughtsman and changed to drawing on wood, drawing first for Punch, 5 September 1841 then for the Illustrated London News,1847-57, and its annual almanacks. Many of these drawings were engraved by Edmund Evans. McLean (in Victorian Illustrated Books, p.179) claimed that Landells' decision to restrict Foster to drawing on wood was a mistake: 'For this he had perhaps a fatal facility: he might have been a greater artist than Bewick, if his art had undergone the discipline and concentration of wood engraving'. The Dalziels remembered how Foster broke his arm during his apprenticeship, and on his own initiative made up the lost time when he recovered, working diligently in a little top room in Birch Court, making small drawings of pots and pans, teapots, grid-irons and other useful items for an ironmonger's catalogue. His cheerful comment was typical: 'It is right that I should return here and do this work; it is good practice, and will enable me to draw all these sorts of things with some practical knowledge'. Following his apprenticeship he was introduced to Henry Vizetelly (q.v.), who was immediately impressed with his drawings and shunned a rival draughtsman, Edward Duncan (q.v.), to employ Foster in 1846. 'One day a young fellow called upon me with a large round of boxwood, which he had covered with cleverly pencilled sketches of rural subjects, as a specimen of his abilities', Vizetelly recalled (Glances Back, Vol.I,p.309). Their collaborations included The Country Year Book,1847; and his famous Longfellow's Evangeline,1847, engraved by Vizetelly, which Bohn in Chatto and Jackson calls his 'first important illustrations'. By 1851 he had begun his noted relationship

with the Dalziel Brothers (q.v.) with eight drawings to Kirk White's Poetical Works, after which he illustrated several small books, such as Wordsworth's Poems, and Odes and Sonnets,1859. The Dalziels paid him well. He received £300 for some fifty drawings, and a pound each for vignettes. He was also one of the first artists to be colour engraved in the Illustrated London News,1857. In 1859 Foster gave up drawing on wood in favour of watercolour paintings of pastoral landscapes, for which he is best known today. He returned once to draw for wood engravings in 1862, again for the Dalziels. This was his famous Pictures of English Landscape: 'the last works of wood engraving likely to be produced by the artist', claimed the preface, and the thirty full-page engravings are masterpieces of the Dalziels' engraving skill. Foster also drew on wood for various poetry books, including those praised by Bohn: Adam's Allegories,1856; Book of Favourite Modern Ballads; Poets of the Nineteenth Century,1857; Christmas with the Poets, Favourite English Poems,1859; Home Affections,1858; Merrie Days of England; Barry Cornwall's Dramatic Scenes and Poems; Southey's Life of Nelson; and Gosse's Rivers of the Bible. Foster was elected ARWS,1860 and RWS in 1862. He died in Weybridge on 27 March 1899. The British Museum owns a number of proof engravings of his designs for the Dalziel Brothers. [For a complete list of illustrated work see Houfe; for biography Wood (with bibliography); DNB; Slater; Lewis; Evans Reminiscences; McLean, Victorian Book Design; Dalziels' Record]

FOUNTAIN Brothers fl.1870s
Provincial wood engraving firm, with an office at 3 Skinner Lane, Leeds (Kelly's,1872)

FOWLER, Thomas fl.1853-55
London wood engraver, who worked at 51 Exmouth Street, Clerkenwell (POD,1853-55).

FOX, Walter E. fl.1880s
Provincial wood engraver, who worked at 75 Godwin Street, Bradford, Yorkshire (Kelly's,1889).

FRAMPTON, Frederick Walter fl.1898-1901
London wood engraver, who worked at 71 Shoe Lane, EC (POD,1898), then 6 Gray's Inn Road, WC (POD,1899-1901).

FRANKLIN, John fl.1828-68
Draughtsman illustrator on wood, landscape, historical and architectural painter. He was born in Ireland and studied in Dublin before he settled in London in 1828. He had sent works to the Royal Hibernian Academy in 1826 and continued to exhibit there and at the British Institution, the Royal Academy and the Royal Society of British Artists. But he is listed here for his drawings on wood of

small border and figure subjects. These included small drawings to W.H.Ainsworth's Tableau from Crichton,1837; S.C.Hall's Ireland,1841; Midsummer Eve,1842; and The Book of Nursery Tales,1845, engraved by Frederick Branston (q.v.). W.J.Linton (q.v.) wood engraved his initials and border designs to The Psalms of David,1862, which were praised and printed by Edmund Evans (q.v.). Franklin also designed the cover to Peter Parley's Annuals, engraved by A.Reynolds, C.Gregory and W.B.Collins (qq.v.); and illustrations to St George and the Dragon, 1868, wood engraved by the master engraver J.D.Cooper (q.v.). The British Museum owns seven proof engravings by the Dalziel Brothers (q.v.) done in 1865.
[For a list of illustrations see Houfe; also Chatto; Bénézit; Nagler; McLean; TB; UCLA]

FRANKLIN, William H. fl.1880-1910
London draughtsman and wood engraver, who worked at 10 Bolt Court, Fleet Street, EC (Kelly's,1880), which he shared with Edward Scrivens, R.G.F.Sweeting, and A.J.Wilson (qq.v.). He then disappears from the London directories until 1894. He reappears at 33 Fetter Lane (POD,1894), then 6 Wine Office Court (POD,1896-1910), which he shared with C.Murray (q.v.).

FRASER, Miss
Draughtsman illustrator for Punch. She was the daughter of Colonel Fraser of the City Police and successfully contributed seven sketches to Punch, 1876, engraved by Joseph Swain (q.v.)
[Spielmann]

FRASER, Francis Arthur fl.1865-98
Draughtsman illustrator and figure painter, a prolific 'Sixties School' artist. He drew for wood engravings in numerous magazines: Sunday Magazine,1865-69; Once a Week,1867; Cassell's Magazine,1867-70; St Pauls,1870-71, namely eighteen plates for Ralph the Heir; a major contribution of seventy-five cuts to Good Words, 1869-72; London Society,1870; and the Illustrated London News,1874. From 1878 he was employed by Fun, and became its cartoonist in 1898. Among his book illustrations were those to Household editions of Dickens' Great Expectations,1871; eight frontis-pieces to Trollope's Chronicles of Barsetshire,1878; and Mark Twain's The Innocents at Home,1897. He also exhibited work at the Royal Academy and the Royal Society of British Artists.
[Houfe; N.John Hall, Trollope and his Illustrators, 1980]

FRASER, John fl.1880s
Scottish wood engraver, who worked at 21 Elder Street, Edinburgh (Kelly's,1880). Fincham lists a pictorial bookplate engraved by Fraser and Clark

of Edinburgh.

FRASHER, George Frederick fl.1880-1910
London wood engraver, who worked at 42 Essex Street, Strand, WC (POD,1880-1901), and added a second office at 61 Gracechurch Street, EC (POD,1883-90), which he shared with W.S.Norman (q.v.).

FREEMAN, Henry fl.1840-90
Draughtsman wood engraver, who worked at 3 Falcons Court, 142 Fleet Street, EC (POD,1886-89), which he shared with W.J.Cox and Mathew Griffith (qq.v.). A 'Freeman' illustrated the series, 'The Cartoons of Raphael', for Charles Knight's Penny Magazine, October 1841, engraved by Stephen Sly (q.v.).
[Bodleian Library]

FREEMAN and Freeman fl.1897-1910
London wood engraving firm, with an office at 23 Farringdon Avenue, EC (POD,1897-1910).

FREER, Mary Ellen
(see Edwards, Mary Ellen)

FRENCH, Cecil 1879-1953
Woodcut artist, who worked in a sylvan style reminiscent of Edward Calvert (q.v.). The British Museum owns a series of colour woodcuts. He signed his work: 'C F' (superimposed).

FRENCH, Henry fl.1868-75
Draughtsman illustrator, described by the Dalziels (q.v.) as 'a clever and popular artist'. He was the son of an accomplished wood engraver of the 'Bewick School', and presumably learned to draw for various magazines under his influence. He contributed drawings for wood engravings by the Dalziels in London Society,1868; Sunday Magazine,1869; Good Words,1869; and twenty illustrations to the House-hold edition of Dickens' Hard Times.
[Dalziels' Record; Houfe]

FREUDEMACHER, George C. fl.1861-76
London draughtsman and wood engraver, who worked at 123 Chancery Lane (POD,1861-66). He shared this office with T.Powney, E.T.Hartshorn, D.J.Anderson, and W.D.Willis (qq.v.). He worked here until at least 1876 (Kelly's,1876), although then listed as a draughtsman on wood only.

FRICKER, Francis (Frank) fl.1844-93
Wood engraver, assistant to the Dalziel Brothers (q.v.) for whom he worked for forty years. He was apprenticed early in 1844 as the first Dalziel pupil, and shared the office with fellow apprentice James Clark (q.v.). The Dalziels remembered him as 'a steady, industrious fellow, who was always punctual

and reliable. He became a good engraver, and remained with us, without intermission--with the exception of two or three weeks holiday in each year (which we had a practice of giving to all our pupils)--until we broke up our establishment in 1893' (Dalziel's Record). He became their master proof printer according to a letter from Gilbert Dalziel to Harold Hartley, c1928 (Boston Museum), 'Frank Fricker took most of the Dalziel proofs and did them awfully well, too'.
[Dalziels' Record; Boston Museum]

FRIEDLÄNDER, C. fl.1887-88
Wood engraver, for the English Illustrated Magazine, 1887-88, notably illustrations to the article 'Glimpses of Old English Homes'. Bénézit and TB list a Camilla Friedländer, nature painter born in Vienna, 10 December 1856, who made a debut in 1864.

FRISTON, David Henry fl.1853-78
Draughtsman illustrator, who worked in Regent's Park, 1854, and Kensington, 1863, the year he contributed to Churchman's Family Magazine. He drew on wood for Edmund Evans' (q.v.), early books for Tinsely's Magazine, 1867; contributed numerous theatrical sketches of London performances, notably pantomimes, for the Illustrated London News, 1869-78, and Dark Blue, 1871-73. He also exhibited at the British Institution, 1854-67, the Royal Academy and the Royal Society of British Artists, 1863.
[Houfe; Evans Reminiscences; Bénézit; TB]

FRITH, William Powell 1819-1909
Prominent Victorian genre painter, occasional draughtsman on wood. He was born on 9 January 1819 and studied under Sass and at the Royal Academy Schools, where he exhibited from 1840. He became the master of narrative painting, with works like 'Derby Day', 1853, and 'The Railway Station', 1862. He is listed here for one known drawing on wood, listed by Bohn in Chatto and Jackson: figure subjects to S.C.Hall's Book of British Ballads, 1842. He was elected ARA, 1845, RA, 1853 and created CVO, 1908. He died in St John's Wood, 2 November 1909.
[Chatto; Wood]

FRÖHLICH, Lorens 1820-1908
Draughtsman illustrator, painter and engraver. He was born in Copenhagen on 25 October 1820, studied in Denmark, Munich, Dresden and Rome, and contributed illustrations to various British publications. These included Mrs Gatty's Parables from Nature, 1861; A.A.Procter's Legends and Lyrics, 1865, poorly engraved by Horace Harral (q.v.). He also did a drawing for wood engraving in the Illustrated London News, 1872 and contributed to various British children's stories, illustrating What Makes Me Grow, 1875. He was appointed professor of the Academy of Fine Art, Copenhagen

in 1877, where he died on 25 October 1908.
[Houfe; White]

FROMENT, Emile Alphonse fl.1880s
French wood engraver, who was born in Paris, a member of the Froment engraving family, who engraved during the nineteenth century. He was the son of Eugène Froment (q.v.) whose works his resembled. He received an honourable mention at the Salon, 1892, and engraved editions of Pelletan.
[TB; Bénézit]

FROMENT, Eugène 1844-1900
French wood engraver, born in Sens (Yonne) 2 December 1844, a member of the Froment wood engraving family. He was pupil of Tauxier, at the Ecole des Arts Décoratifs and went to London to work engraving for various magazines such as The Graphic, with W.L.Thomas and C.Roberts (qq.v.). Among his best work here was after Hubert Herkomer (q.v.), 1877, also after W.Small and C.Green. He engraved for the Illustrated London News, several large full-page and double-page drawings, notably 'Sketches in Albania' after R.Caton Woodville, 10 April 1880, engraved in dark outline against a white background; also 'A Flower Show' after Emslie, 3 July 1880, a double-page engraved in stark outline and stipple technique. Froment also engraved for various French publications for instance L'Art and L'Illustration, and exhibited at the Salon from 1866, where he achieved a third class medal, 1875, a second class, 1884 and a gold medal, 1900. Gusman described Froment as 'one of the most perfect engravers of the second half of the nineteenth century' and claimed that 'His burin always kept this steadiness and sobriety in execution which he gained from English engraving...'. Even towards the end of his life, working after Ribot and Benjamin Constant, 'faithful to the old wood engraving school, to the profound colouring deeply engraved and free in style, during the last years of his life he executed engraving with extreme delicacy, without giving the impression of affectation. His confident use of the burin sympathetically followed the work of the illustrator which he used to interpret. Not one of his engravings is banal in its interpretation. They can even surpass the most highly regarded examples of his contemporaries...' (Gusman, pp.187-88).
[For a biography and list of works see Gusman]

FROMENT, Ferdinand Florentin fl.1880s
French wood engraver, member of the Froment wood engraver family. He was a pupil of W.J.Linton (q.v.) and exhibited at the Sociétaire des Artistes Français, from 1887. He was awarded an honourable mention in 1889.
[Bénézit]

FROST, Arthur Burdett 1851-1928
Draughtsman illustrator and painter. Born in
Philadelphia on 17 January 1851, he came to
England in 1877, but returned home in 1878,
where he was associated with Harper's magazine
from an early period, training his draughtsman's
skills for wood engraving. Pennell considered him
the finest comic artist in America. He drew for
the Household Edition of Dickens' American Notes,
1871, engraved by the Dalziel Brothers (q.v.) and
for Lewis Carroll's Phantasmagoria, 1911; and
contributed a drawing to the English magazine,
the Quiver, 1882.
[Muir, Victorian Illustrated Books (with book
list); Houfe]

FRY
(see Cunningham, John)

FURNISS, Harry 1854-1925
Prolific draughtsman, caricaturist and author. He
was born in Wexford, Ireland in 1854, and began to
draw first for his own Irish version of Punch, then
for Punch itself, after he had moved to London in
1873. His first work was the result of innocence
rather than talent, for by 1869 he had steered
himself toward drawing and engraving periodical
work. 'He imagined every artist had to engrave his
own work, and so set to and taught himself engraving,
and for some years engraved his own work on wood.
That method had this advantage, that if he were pushed
for time, he could easily cut out one or two, or a
half dozen figures, and put in a few scribbles by
reversing the tool, and so get through the work
within the specified time. As he only engraved his
own work, he did not apply these tricks to the
drawing of any other artist' (Journal of Society of
Arts, 20 April 1900, p.472). Most of this early work
was for the Illustrated London News, 1876-86, where
he was an over-worked 'special' artist: 'I sat up all
night and drew a page on wood, ready for engraving,
and sent it off by the first train in the morning. It
was in the press before my rival's rough notes left
Liverpool. One would hardly think, to see candles
stuck in my boots, that the hotel was the Old Adelphi.
I trust the "special" of the future will find the electric
light, or a better supply of bedroom candlesticks. All
day again sketching, and all night hard at work,
burning the midnight oil (I was nearly writing books)
...And after another day of this kind of thing, I
reached home without having had an hour's sleep.
Oh! a "special's" life is not a happy one' (H.Furniss,
Confessions of a Caricaturist, Vol.I, 1901, p.68). His
early drawings here included a full-page, 'Mr Gladstone
in Birmingham', 9 June 1877. Furniss developed a
skill for caricature and could draw directly on the
block, after stalking his subjects to make rapid
pencil sketches, sometimes on a piece of card, or
even the inside pocket of his overcoat. He then

reworked in ink to produce anything from a thumbnail sketch to a full-page drawing, portraits and all,
in an hour or so. Most of his Punch work was
engraved by Joseph Swain (q.v.), the chief Punch
engraver. This appeared from October 1880 to
21 February 1894. He then left after an argument,
having never been a salaried staff member. He also
contributed drawings to Vanity Fair, 1881; the
Cornhill, 1883-85; the English Illustrated Magazine,
1883-86, 1889-90, wood engraved by O.Lacour,
L.Chefdeville, and W.H.Hooper (qq.v.); and The
Graphic, 1889. He also did illustrations to Lewis
Carroll's Sylvie and Bruno, 1889. Many other works
appeared well after the turn of the century. Furniss
exhibited at the Royal Academy, the Royal Hibernian
Academy, and the Fine Art Society, 1894, 1898. He
died in Hastings on 14 January 1925.
[For biographical detail see his own autobiography,
Confessions of a Caricaturist, 1901; also Spielmann;
TB (bibliography); Houfe (book list)]

FUSSELL, Alexander c1814-1909
Draughtsman on wood, primarily of ornithological
subjects in the Bewick tradition. He was born in
Birmingham, son of an artist, and exhibited in
London at the British Institution from 1838, and
elsewhere until 1881. He is best known for his series
of bird drawings to William Yarrell's History of
British Birds, 1837-, which he drew on wood from
1836-56, and which included 579 small cuts in
volume one alone, engraved by John Thompson
(q.v.). He also drew for an edition of Sterne's
Sentimental Journey, 1840, engraved by J.Bastin
and J.Nicholls (qq.v.). The British Museum owns
his designs engraved by the Dalziel Brothers (q.v.),
1839-47.
[Jackson; Bénézit; TB; Graves; Nagler]

FUSSELL, Joseph fl.1821-45
Draughtsman on wood, landscape painter. Houfe
believes that he was probably the brother of
Alexander Fussell (q.v.) and painted from Sadlers
Wells, and Bloomsbury, 1821-45. He is listed here
for drawings for wood engravings to Charles
Knight's London, 1841. He also exhibited at the
British Institution, 1822-45, and the Royal Society
of British Artists, 1821-45.

FYFE, William Baxter Collier 1836-82
Draughtsman illustrator and figure painter. He was
born in Dundee in 1836 and studied art at the Royal
Scottish Academy in Edinburgh, specialising in
Scottish genre subjects. He is listed here for his
one drawing wood engraved in Good Words, 1861,
which White claimed helped to make the magazine's
second volume a marked improvement on the first.
This appeared with drawings by J.Wolf, A.W.Cooper
and C.H.Bennett (qq.v.). Fyfe worked in London
from 1863, and exhibited at the Royal Academy, the

Royal Institute of Painters in Watercolours and the Royal Society of British Artists. The British Museum owns a proof engraving of his design, by the Dalziel Brothers (q.v.), 1861.
[Houfe; White]

GABER, August 1823-91
German reproductive wood engraver, born in Koppernig on 14 November 1823. He is listed here for his influence among the Victorian engravers, particularly after John Ruskin praised his engraved reproductions of A.Ludwig Richter's (q.v.) drawings and paintings (see Ruskin's Elements of Drawing,1857). He also taught the engraver M.Klinkicht (q.v.). Gaber was associated with Hugo Bürkner's atelier, and established himself in Dresden, then Berlin. He married Richter's daughter in 1852, and died in Berlin in September 1891.He signed his work: 'GABER', 'GA' (superimposed).
[For a discussion of his work see Glaser; Bénézit; Nagler; TB]

GAILDRAU, Jules 1816-98
French draughtsman illustrator, born in Paris on 18 September 1816. He worked as draughtsman for wood engravings to the numerous French papers such as L'Illustration, and according to Vizetelly drew on wood for the Illustrated London News during its early issues. He also exhibited at the Salon,1848-57. He died in Paris, January 1898.
[Houfe; Vizetelly, Glances Back]

GALBRAITH, James Scott fl.1877-82
London wood engraver and draughtsman, who worked at 4 Crane Court, Fleet Street, EC (POD,1877). He joined with Alfred Henry Gibson (q.v.) as Galbraith and Gibson, retained his old office and appeared in the directories as a draughtsmen firm (POD,1878-81). Later Galbraith broke away and again worked alone (POD,1882).

GALBRAITH and Gibson
(see Galbraith, James Scott)

GALLY, Arthur fl.1894-1901
London wood engraver, who worked at 7 Dane's Inn, Strand, WC (POD,1894-1901).

GALTER, William fl.1830s-40s
London wood engraver, who was employed by Ebenezer Landells (q.v.) at his engraving premises, 22 Bidborough Street, St Pancras. He worked with various more notable engraving pupils such as Edmund Evans and John Greenaway (qq.v.), and engraved for Punch, but according to Spielmann he left 'to take Orders', presumably religious training. His sister Helen Galter married Davison Dalziel (q.v.); his uncle by marriage was the engraver

Ebenezer Landells (q.v.).

GARDNER, Thomas fl.1870s
Provincial draughtsman on wood, who worked at Wharfage, Ironbridge, Salop (Kelly's,1876). By 1880 there was a Thomas Gardner, wood engraver, working at 1 Garden Street, Withy Grove, Manchester (Kelly's,1880).

GARDNER, Thomas and Company fl.1880s
Provincial wood engraving firm, with an office at Beechan Cliff, Dudley Road, Birmingham (Kelly's,1889).

GARDNER, W.Biscombe c1849-1919
Prominent and prolific wood engraver, landscape painter and etcher. He was born about 1849, and by 1872 had established himself as a valuable and proficient draughtsman on wood for magazines, especially The Graphic. He worked from his London office at East Temple Chambers, 3 Whitefriars Street, EC (Kelly's,1872), then developed his wood engraving skill to set up as a wood engraver at 108 Fleet Street, EC (POD,1883-86). He specialised in reproducing paintings by popular artists like Alma-Tadema, Leighton, G.F.Watts, Burne-Jones and Hubert Herkomer; these were exhibited at the Royal Academy from 1878-1900. His skills proved best used on portrait engravings. These included the portraits, now in the British Museum: of the engraver W.J.Linton (q.v.) (exhibited at the Royal Academy, 1891); of Professor Ruskin, after Herkomer's painting (published in Magazine of Art, 1891 and exhibited at the Royal Academy, 1891); of the Duke of Albany, taken from a photograph and published in a supplement to the Pictorial World, 2 April 1884; and of Gladstone, in the Illustrated London News,March 1894. The publisher John Lane issued Gardner's wood engraved portrait of George Meredith, after a painting by G.F.Watts. This was listed in Lane's 1896 catalogue issued as signed proofs on Japanese vellum edition for 1 guinea each. Gardner's importance lies in his impressive, large full and double-page engravings to The Graphic, the Illustrated London News,1872-80, and English Illustrated Magazine,1887-88,1891-92. He used a firm outline style then filled in with various tonal techniques: stipple surfaces (e.g. 'Mrs Reynolds' after Reynolds), or the erratic, deep gouging of his graver to reproduce the thick paintwork of C.J.Staniland's 'Love at First Sight' (a double-page in the Illustrated London News,15 May 1873) or Rubens' 'The Descent from the Cross' (the Illustrated London News,18 August 1877). He also engraved copies of Landseer's famous canine painting, 'Be It Ever So Humble', and Gerome's painting, 'The Gladiators'. Each tested his abilities to adopt the graver for various painterly effects. He also drew on wood for others to engrave.

These drawings included those in the English Illustrated Magazine,1886-90, engraved by the noted wood engravers A.E.Coombe, R.B.Lodge, H.F.Davey, O.Lacour, C.V.Brownlow, R.Paterson, A.C.Coats, W.Spielmeyer, and J.D.Cooper (qq.v.). Gardner's influence continued even after the emergence of the process block, which had threatened the livelihoods of many less proficient and adaptable engravers. The wood engraver Bernard Sleigh (q.v.) notes in his Wood Engraving since 1890 that Gardner's process engraving of a Burne-Jones pencil drawing was an object lesson: 'only by the aid of a lens will you be in the least able to appreciate such skill. The process block had by now reached a stage of perfection, and a corresponding cheapness of production, which were bound to supersede this laborious hand engraving, and the last breath of facsimile work may be seen in this curious attempt to combine the human hand and the machine'. Gardner also painted in watercolours and in oil, etched landscapes which he exhibited at the New Gallery, the Royal Academy, the Royal Institute of Painters in Watercolours, the Royal Institute of Painters in Oil-Colours and the Royal Scottish Watercolour Society, and won a silver medal at the Paris Exposition, 1900. He worked in London, Tower Hill, Dorking and Haslemere, Surrey, also in Tunbridge Wells, from 1906. Like so many of his engraver colleagues, he eventually succumbed to alcoholism. Edmund Evans wrote of him (14 December 1903, Evans MS, UCLA) 'Biscombe Gardner seems to have dried up, not a good expression--I heard he had taken to drinking & don't respect this...'. The British Museum owns several landscape engravings by him. He signed his work: 'W Biscombe Gardner'. [Bénézit; TB; Graves; Hake; Hayden, Chats on Old Prints,1909,p.125]

GARLAND, Charles Trevor fl.1874-1907
Draughtsman illustrator, painter of landscapes, portraits and children. He worked in London for The Graphic,1874, contributing regularly to such galleries as the Royal Academy, the Royal Society of British Artists, the Royal Institute of Painters in Watercolours and the Royal Institute of Painters in Oil-Colours. He contributed drawings for Christmas issues of the Illustrated London News, 1881-86,1892-93.
[Houfe]

GARLAND, George fl.1874-81
London wood engraver, who worked at 1 Howard Street, Strand, WC (POD,1874-81).

GARLAND, Henry fl.1854-92
Occasional draughtsman illustrator, landscape and painter of genre and animal subjects. He was born in Winchester and worked in North London from 1854, then Leatherhead, Surrey, from 1887. He started his career with a drawing for the Illustrated London News,1868, but later exhibited paintings regularly at the Royal Academy, the Royal Society of British Artists and the Royal Institute of Painters in Oil-Colours.
[Houfe]

GASCOINE, Alexander fl.1870-94
London wood engraver, who worked at 13 Bouverie Street, EC (POD,1870), shared with E.V.Campbell (q.v.), 12 Bell Yard, Temple Bar, WC (POD,1871-77) and 112 Fleet Street, EC (POD,1881-87), shared with G.E.Charlton (q.v.). By 1889 he had become Alexander Gascoine and Company at 30 Fleet Street, EC (POD,1889-93), then last appeared at 116 Chancery Lane (POD,1894).

GASCOINE, Edward Stanley fl.1865-94
London draughtsman and wood engraver, who worked at 37 Castle Street, Holborn, EC (POD,1865-66) shared with H.Collidge (q.v.); 188 Strand, WC (POD,1867); Beaufort Chambers, 16 Beaufort Buildings (POD,1868-70); 268 Strand, WC (POD,1873-76) shared with W.Purchase (q.v.); and 168 Fleet Street, EC (POD,1884-94), during which time he became E.S.Gascoine and Company, London draughtsmen firm (Kelly's,1889). He engraved for various magazines, in a grey-tint technique, including the English Illustrated Magazine, 1883-84, after Hugh Thomson and C.Napier Hemy and 'A Young Cricketer', after Gainsborough. The 1886-87 issue included his full-page engraving after Dewey Bates, 'By the Riverside', a girl picking apples, which was unfortunately rather poorly engraved, in that flecks of white and indistinct dark grey foliage did nothing to achieve the clarity such a work demanded. However, Gascoine continued to work into the mid 1890s for publications such as the Church Monthly,1895, after Fred W.Burton's drawing. The British Museum owns his engravings after Alfred Parsons and G.L.Seymour. He signed his work: 'E Gascoine' (script).

GASCOINE, John
Draughtsman illustrator, whom White mentions as contributor to the magazine London Society,1865.

GASKIN, Arthur Joseph 1862-1928
Designer and illustrator for wood engravings, portrait painter. He was born in Birmingham in 1862, educated in Wolverhampton, and studied art at the Birmingham School of Art, where he eventually taught. He is listed here for his bold designs for the new revival of wood engraving, done under the influence of William Morris (q.v.) and his Kelmscott Press, for which Gaskin designed Spencer's The Shepheardes Calender,1896. He also drew illustrations to various 1890s magazines, including the Yellow Book,1896, and Quarto,1897. He

exhibited at the New Gallery, the Royal Academy, the Royal Society of British Artists and the Royal Society of Painter-Etchers and Engravers, and died on 4 June 1928.
[Waters; Houfe]

GATCOMBE, George fl.1887-97
Draughtsman illustrator who specialised in theatrical subjects. He began work as a pupil of the Dalziel Brothers (q.v.), being introduced through Phil Ebbutt (q.v.). The Dalziels found that Gatcombe had an early 'taste for drawing' rather than engraving, and he was a rapid workman who developed his 'elegant social' themes to appear in the Dalziel publications, Fun, 1887-92, and Ally Sloper's Half Holiday, 1890; as well as The Rambler, 1897. He also drew for numerous book commissions, for instance Tom Hood's Comic Annual, and political cartoons and historical designs, all of which made him 'a good all-round black and white artist'.
[Dalziels' Record]

GATELEY, John fl.1880s
Provincial wood engraver, who worked at 21 Weaman Street, Birmingham (Kelly's, 1889).

GAUGNIET
French draughtsman, who contributed a design for wood engraving to the Illustrated London News, 1848.

GAUNT, Percival Charles fl.1890s
London wood engraver, who worked at 24 Bouverie Street, EC (POD, 1892).

GAVARNI, H.G.S. Chevalier (called Paul) 1804-66
Prominent draughtsman illustrator on wood, caricaturist, engraver and lithographer. He was born in Paris on 13 January 1804, studied machinery design at the Conservatoire des Arts et Métiers, and worked as an architectural etcher. He became Chevalier Gavarni, designer of theatrical and fashion plates in 1829, and developed an interest in Parisian life which he turned into entertaining caricatures for French magazines. He joined the staff of Charivari (French version of Punch). He left for England on 21 November 1847 and remained there for four years. He met prominent artists and was commissioned to draw on wood for the Illustrated London News, 1848-55. He also produced his series of tinted wood engraved drawings, Gavarni in London, 1849-50. On his return to Paris he produced Les Anglais Peints par Eux-Mêmes, 1851. Some believe he profited artistically by his English visit and developed a wetter, broader watercolour technique. Gavarni was a prolific draughtsman on wood, lithographic stone and metal plate: he produced over 2,000 known drawings of which 320 were on wood. One of the finest 'Prisoners in the Vaults of the Hotel de Ville, Paris, June 1848' was wood engraved by Henry Linton (q.v.)

and exhibited at the Royal Academy in 1855. Gavarni had lost his popularity by the late 1850s and died of consumption in Paris on 24 November 1866.
[For a list of drawings see Oeuvres Choisies de Gavarni, 1846-48; also E. and Jules de Goncourt, Gavarni, Paris, 1924; also Spielmann; Graves; Bénézit; TB; Beraldi; Print Collector's Quarterly, 1916]

GEAR, J.W. fl.1821-52
Occasional draughtsman, engraver and portrait painter, who contributed a drawing for wood engraving to the Illustrated London News, 1848. He specialised in watercolour family groups, theatrical personalities, and porcelain painting, and exhibited at the Royal Academy and the Royal Society of British Artists, 1821-52.
[Houfe]

GEDAN, H. fl.1889-90
Wood engraver, who worked for the English Illustrated Magazine, 1889-90. He contributed topographical scenes, of Ceylon, 'Lace-making in Ireland', Osterley Park, and Thames views from photographs.

GELDARD, Charles fl.1862-68
London wood engraver, who worked at 7 New Inn, Strand, WC (POD, 1862-68).

GELDERD, Ralph fl.1880s
Provincial wood engraver, who worked at 2 Bridge Street, Shrewsbury (Kelly's, 1889).

GEORGE, L. and Company fl.1886-89
London wood engraving and draughtsman firm, with an office at 11 Queen Victoria Street, EC (POD, 1886-87, Kelly's, 1889).

GERARD, Alphonse (Louis-Alphonse) 1820-?
French wood engraver who was born in Paris in 1820, was the student of H.D. Porret in 1836, and began wood engraving with 'Scènes Populaires' after H. Monnier, 1838. From about 1840 he began engraving after numerous French draughtsmen such as Delaroche and Gavarni (q.v.) and worked with J. Barre on several illustrated magazines, including L'Artiste; L'Illustration; and Magasin Pittoresque. Some of his engravings were for English magazines like the Illustrated London News, 1860, after French draughtsmen. Gerard exhibited at the Salon, 1853-69. He signed his engravings: 'G sc', 'G' (script).
[Nagler; Beraldi; TB]

GERBEAUX, Franc fl.1895-99
Wood engraver, who worked in London at 90 Chancery Lane, WC (POD, 1895-99).

GERE, Charles March 1869-1957
Wood engraver, draughtsman, illustrator, designer
of stained glass and portrait painter. He was born in
Gloucester in 1869, educated in Birmingham and
Italy, and with A.J.Gaskin (q.v.) was associated
with the so-called Birmingham School of illustration.
He designed for wood engravings in the Kelmscott
Press works: frontispiece to William Morris' News
from Nowhere,1893; also for various 1890s
magazines: the Quest,1894-96; and Yellow Book,
1896. He drew for the Ashendene Press's Morte
d'Arthur and Dante, engraved by W.H.Hooper and
J.B.Swain (qq.v.). Walter Crane (q.v.) noted in his
Of the Decorative Illustration of Books Old and New,
1896, that Gere was an outstanding wood engraver:
'Mr Gere has engraved on wood some of his own
designs, and he thoroughly realises the ornamental
value of bold and open line drawing in association
with lettering, and is a careful and conscientious
draughtsman and painter besides.' Gere exhibited at
the New English Art Club, 1910-24, the New Gallery,
at the Royal Academy from 1890-1956, and the
Royal Hibernian Academy and the Royal Watercolour
Society. He was elected ARWS in 1921, RWS in 1927,
ARA in 1933 and RA in 1939.
[Houfe; Waters]

GIBBINGS, Robert John 1889-1958
Wood and copper engraver. He was born on 23 March
1889 in Cork, Ireland and educated at the local
University, then in London at the Slade. He studied
engraving under Noel Rooke (q.v.) at the Central
School, 1912, and produced his first white-line wood
engravings in 1913. He formed the Society of Wood
Engravers in 1920 and published his first book,
Twelve Wood Engravers, 1921. He was director of
the Golden Cockerell Press, 1924-33 and lived in
Reading where he taught under Professor A.Seaby
(q.v.). He died on 19 January 1958. The British
Museum owns a number of small proofs.
[Garrett; Waters]

GIBBS, George fl.1850s
London wood engraver, who worked at 58 Fleet
Street, EC (POD,1854),.which became the office of
the prominent wood engraver Joseph Swain (q.v.).

GIBBS, William fl.1857-82
London wood engraver, who worked at 4 Thanet
Place, Strand, WC (POD,1857-60), 75 Fleet Street,
EC (POD,1875-81), shared with J.F.Nash (q.v.),
and then Hare Place, 46 Fleet Street, EC (POD,1882).

GIBBS and Company fl.1880s
Provincial wood engraver, who worked at 14 Hale
Street, Dale Street, Liverpool (Kelly's,1889).

GIBSON, Alfred Henry and Company fl.1882-95
London draughtsmen and wood engraving firm,
according to an 1885 directory advertisement,
creators of 'high class wood engravings for books,
journals, catalogues, &c in one or more colours,
exact reproductions of prints, chalk, or ink drawings,
steel or copper plates, by transfer and photo zinc
process'. Their office was at 4 Crane Court, Fleet
Street, EC (POD,1882-95).

GIFFORD, Francis (Frank) fl.1867-84
London wood engraver, who worked at 15 Essex
Street, Strand, WC (POD,1867), shared with
H.Lovejoy and R.S.Marriott (qq.v.), then as 'Frank
Gifford' at 1 Norfolk Street, Strand, EC
(POD,1882-84).

GILBERT, Achille-Isidore 1828-99
French occasional wood engraver, draughtsman,
etcher, lithographer and painter. He was born in
Paris on 6 April 1828, studied with Couture and
Bellocs, and entered the Ecole des Beaux Arts,
1843. He worked primarily as an engraver and
lithographer, and contributed numerous illustrations
to French magazines, notably L'Illustration, which
included 100 wood engraved portraits as well as
numerous lithographs, and also the Gazette des
Beaux Arts. He exhibited engravings at the Salon,
1851-80, and the London Royal Academy,1877-84,
many etched after prominent Victorian paintings.
[For metal engraving list see Volume I; Bénézit;
TB; Beraldi; Graves]

GILBERT, Frederick fl.1862-77
Draughtsman illustrator and watercolourist, the
brother of the noted illustrator Sir John Gilbert
(q.v.), with whom he lived in Blackheath. He drew
on wood for Cassell's Magazine,1866; Aunt Judy's
Magazine,1866; and London Society,1870. His style,
dismissed by White, as a 'facile understudy of
Sir John...differing as far as it well could', was
applied to genre and historical subjects, especially
to Tennyson's works. He exhibited at the Royal
Society of British Artists.
[Houfe; White]

GILBERT, Sir John 1817-97
Prolific draughtsman on wood and painter of
historical subjects, said to be the most influential
figure, with William Harvey (q.v.), in the revival of
nineteenth-century British wood engraving and
originator of the so-called 'Sixties School' style of
draughtsmanship on wood. He was born in
Blackheath in 1817, apprenticed to an estate agent,
then studied with the still-life painter George Lance,
teaching himself to draw on the wood block, engrave,
etch and model as well. He began drawing on wood
for Punch,1842. His frontispiece was used for the
second volume and wrapper for several years, and

he sporadically contributed drawings to Punch until 1882. But his first major contribution came in collaboration with Henry Vizetelly (q.v.) on the newly established Illustrated London News, in which his first drawings appeared early in 1842. He had done various transfer drawings on wood for Vizetelly, after Clarkson Stanfield designs to Poor Jack, and had come under Vizetelly's shrewd influence. He also provided large numbers of wood engraved drawings to the Illustrated London News, 1842-79, which one source (Dalziels' Record) listed as totalling at least 30,000, another 40,000 (Bryan) although both seem rather exaggerated. Vizetelly recalled those early days: 'In 1842 it would have been well-nigh impossible to have kept an illustrated paper, containing from twenty to thirty engravings weekly, going had not Mr John Gilbert's facile and imaginative pencil been available for the purpose.' And when Vizetelly started the rival paper, the Pictorial Times, which foundered in 1847 (replaced by the Illustrated Times, 1855) John Gilbert provided most of the wood engraved illustrations for this as well. The demands placed upon him by deadlines for these weekly magazines taught him to work quickly and directly upon the block itself, generally without models. During those early days he would receive the blocks from Vizetelly's messenger, who was told to go away for about an hour, then return for the finished drawings on the block. He established a reputation for elaborate allegories and for Christmas themes, for special editions. By the 1870s he had progressed enough to draw skilfully for numerous double-page engravings in the Illustrated London News, either from his own sketches ('The Balaclava Charge', 30 October 1875), or even from his by then famous historical watercolours ('Hark! Our Steeds at Present Service Neigh', 11 December 1875). For these he was paid enormous sums and taken up by such prominent engravers as the Dalziel Brothers (q.v.) who remembered his shrewd, if eccentric business manner: 'He took a small foot rule out of his pocket, measured the size of the two wood blocks, and said, "The price will be 35 shillings each, but I could not possibly give them to you tomorrow; but the next morning you may rely on having them."' The drawings were promptly sent as promised and thereafter Gilbert asked and received a guinea for each drawing. Gilbert worked at great speed as a 'special artist' for the magazines, recording current events as they happened directly upon the wood block. He could do as many as twelve blocks an hour, and yet the Dalziels were convinced that he still retained absolute control: 'There is no sign of haste, though many are sketchy; still, there is nothing which suggests that greater excellence would have attended greater elaboration.' Even the continental artists looked to Gilbert with awe and respect; one critic told Spielmann that though Gilbert shared Doré's 'fecundity' of output, his skill and accuracy were

superior to the Frenchman's. By 1872 he had earned the accolade, published in the Illustrated London News (16 March 1872): 'he developed an eminently daring, suggestive, picturesque, and playful style of wood engraving, quite novel in the history of the Art, which commends itself by its admirable appropriateness to the nature of the material and the method of printing'. Much of Gilbert's technique was further developed in drawing for numerous book illustrations. The first and most influential were the cuts engraved by W.A.Folkard (q.v.) which he contributed to the 400 engravings by numerous prominent artists to S.C.Hall's Book of English Ballads, 1842, described by Bohn in Chatto and Jackson as 'the first work of any consequence that presented a combination of the best artists of the time'. Gilbert went on to produce drawings for some of his most famous work: Staunton's Shakespeare's Works, issued in parts, 1856-58, the 832 illustrations drawn on wood over a four year period and the tailpieces and vignettes left until the end so that he would know how much space was available. The whole project was engraved by the Dalziel Brothers, who had two proof sets made, such was their admiration of Gilbert's work (one proof set is now in the British Museum). A further Shakespearean work was Gilbert's elaborate Shakespeare's Songs and Sonnets, 1860-62, in which his watercolours appeared as ten chromolithographs by Vincent Brooks, with thirty-two wood engravings and two colour engravings by Edmund Evans (q.v.). Evans recalled later how the illustrations were 'engraved on wood, printed with a tint with lights taken out or directed by Gilbert with white paint on the proof'. He concluded that although he 'had little dealings together' with him, 'I am glad I knew John Gilbert' (Evans MS, UCLA). Gilbert's drawings were wood engraved by the period's most skilful engravers: Henry Linton, the Dalziel Brothers, W.A.Folkard, Kirchner and Greenaway and Wright (qq.v.). He also taught the engraver Edward Morin (q.v.) and used Alfred S.Williams (q.v.) as an assistant. Gilbert's painting career was equally successful. He exhibited at the Royal Society of British Artists and the Royal Academy, where he was elected ARA in 1872, and RA in 1876. He exhibited at the Royal Watercolour Society where he served as PRWS in 1871. He lived with his artist brother Frederick Gilbert (q.v.) in Blackheath and died on 5 October 1897. The British Museum owns several proof engravings after his designs engraved by the Dalziel Brothers.
[For a complete list of illustrated work see Houfe; and TB; also Chatto; Spielmann; Bryan; Dalziels' Record; Vizetelly, Glances Back]

GILBERT, Sir William Schwenck ('BAB') 1836-1911
Amateur draughtsman illustrator, journalist and playwright. He was born in Southampton Street, Strand on 18 November 1836, educated in and pursued a

legal career as well as entering into an operatic collaboration with Sir Arthur Sullivan from 1869-96. He began his career in illustration, as 'Bab', to accompany humorous verses for Fun,1861, having first published them in Juvenile Verse Picture Book,1848. His work appeared briefly in Punch,1865 engraved by Joseph Swain (q.v.) but its editor Mark Lemon refused to take him on as staff member, and so Gilbert was dropped. He continued his comic sketches for Magic Mirror,1867-68; London Society, 1868; Good Words for the Young,1869; and The Graphic,1876, all wood engraved by Joseph Swain and other engravers. His style alternated between the savage creatures of his 'Bab Ballads' and fairy-like drawings of young girls. Gilbert's work was praised by Max Beerbohm, and he was knighted in 1907. He died in Harrow Weald, 29 May 1911. The British Museum owns several proof engravings by the Dalziel Brothers (q.v.), 1864,1866.
[Spielmann; Houfe]

GILES, Godfrey Douglas 1857-1923
Draughtsman illustrator and painter of horses and military scenes. He was born in India in 1857 and served as a professional soldier there, then in Afghanistan and Egypt. He studied art in Paris and regularly exhibited in London 1882-1904, at the Grosvenor Gallery, the Royal Academy, the Royal Society of British Artists, the Royal Institute of Painters in Oil-Colours and the Royal Scottish Academy. He is listed here for his drawings wood engraved by Edward J.Whymper (q.v.). They appeared in The Graphic,1885 (horses); he also contributed to Black and White,1891; and Vanity Fair, 1899-1900, 1903. The British Museum owns his drawings wood engraved by Edward Whymper.

GILES, Richard fl.1888-92
London wood engraver, who worked at 2 Tudor Street, Blackfriars, EC (POD,1888-92).

GILES, William 1872-?
Wood engraver, lithographer, etcher and painter of landscapes and birds. He was born in Reading on 19 November 1872, studied at a local art school and South Kensington, and worked in Chelsea. He travelled to Paris and worked in Germany, where he engraved his first colour wood engraving in 1903, in the Japanese style borrowed from F.Morley Fletcher (q.v.). His wood engravings of birds and landscapes are listed by Thieme-Becker. He exhibited at the Royal Academy, 1916-17, and the Society of Gravers-Printers in Colour, 1910-14, 1920.
[Hake; TB; Bénézit; Gusman; see Volume I for etchings]

GILKS, Edward fl.1848-51
London draughtsman on wood, who worked with Thomas Gilks (q.v.) at 4 Fenchurch Building

(POD,1848-49). He drew on wood for the Illustrated London News, generally small vignettes of topographical and architectural subjects,1850-51, engraved by Thomas Gilks. With Thomas he illustrated for Louisa S.Costello's The Falls, Lakes and Mountains of North Wales,1845.

GILKS, Thomas fl.1840-70s
London wood engraver, draughtsman, illustrator and writer on engraving. He worked at 1 Crown Court, Threadneedle Street (POD,1841-42), then joined the draughtsman Edward Gilks (q.v.) at 4 Fenchurch Building (POD,1848-49). He reappears in the directories on his own at 170 Fleet Street, EC (POD,1851-56), and advertised in Hodgson's,1855 as 'Mr Gilks, draughtsman, engraver on wood... begs respectfully to announce that he continues to execute all orders that he may be favoured with, in the best style, with promptness, and a due regard to moderation in charges'. By 1857 he was working at 21 Essex Street, Strand (POD,1857-65), then 9 Bedford Row, WC (POD,1866-71) and 11 King's Road, Bedford Row, WC (POD,1872-77). Gilks engraved numerous book and magazine illustrations, including John Leech's The Comic English Grammar, 1840; S.C. Hall's Book of British Ballads,1842, engraved with W.A.Folkard (q.v.); Man--from Cradle to Grave, a series of illustrations by John Gilbert (q.v.) (now in the British Museum); W.Sawyer's History of Westmoreland,1847; and H.Fitzcock's All about Shakespeare,1864, after illustrations drawn by Fitzcock. He also engraved large plates for the Illustrated London News,1850-60. These were mostly after the drawings of Edward Gilks and the paintings of Florence Caxton, as well as a series of Australian subjects engraved in the 1858 issue. Other magazines for which he engraved include London Society,1870, the year he exhibited at the Royal Academy. Gilks also wrote on engraving, his influential The Art of Wood Engraving, A Practical Handbook,1866, for Winsor and Newton, beginning with this claim for wood engraving: 'The Art has had for many years so great an attraction for the painter and amateur, that the author has been often requested to give private lessons in Wood Engraving and Lectures on its History and Practice.' This was followed by A Sketch of the Origin and Progress of the Art of Wood-Engraving,1868, which was sold with a box of wood engraving tools. He also wrote A Suggestive Hand-book to Art Criticism,1876. The British Museum owns his engravings after J.Gilbert, J.Leech, D.H.McKewan and H.Warren. Gilks signed his work: 'T G' (superimposed), 'T Gilks sc'.
[Bénézit; TB; British Library catalogue; Wakeman and Bridson (for colour printing); Hake; Houfe]

GILL, Arthur Eric Rowton 1882-1940
Wood engraver, draughtsman, painter and stone sculptor. He was born in Brighton on 22 February

1882, studied at the Chichester Art School, 1898, and the following year joined the lettering class of Edward Johnston at the Central School. He was apprenticed to an architect 1900-03, and taught gilding and lettering in London. He became a figure sculptor, exhibiting at the Chenil Gallery, 1911, and the following year visited the wood engraver Gwen Raverat (q.v.) at Royston. He was a founding member of the Society of Wood Engravers, 1920 and worked from Ditchling, then Capel-y-ffin, Abergavenny, and finally High Wycombe, Buckinghamshire. He died in Uxbridge on 17 November 1940. He is listed here as one of the primary influences on wood engraving at the turn of the century.
[Garrett; Houfe; Chichester Eric Gill Catalogue, 1967; M.Yorke, Eric Gill, 1981; Waters]

GINN, William fl.1901-10
London wood engraver, who worked at 89 Farringdon Street, EC (POD,1901-10). He shared the premises with the noted wood engravers William Williams, L.Knott, W.J.Potter and J.Dixon (qq.v.).

GIRONIMO, Henry fl.1870s
London wood engraver, who worked at 8 Dane's Inn, Strand (POD,1874). He shared the premises with the noted wood engraver T.Robinson (q.v.).

GLAZIER, Louise M. fl.1900-12
Wood engraver of the revivalist period and book-plate designer. She worked in Mitcham, 1902 and in Bruges in 1906. Her wood engravings were bold, yet with a sense of mystery. They appeared in various new periodicals which sought to revive wood engraving: The Dome, 1900, 'The Steps', 'The Garden'; also for Laurence Housman's (q.v.) magazine, The Venture, 1903, 'The Death of Pan'. These helped her to achieve a position of influence among budding new wood engravers. George Mackley praises her contribution in his classic manual, Wood Engraving, 1948, in which he links her work with that of Bernard Sleigh, Robert Bryden and W.O.J.Nieuwenkamp (qq.v.). She exhibited work with fellow female engraver Clemence Housman (q.v.) at the London gallery of John Baillie, 1 July 1903. She signed her work:'L M C' (superimposed).
[Houfe; Mackley]

GLIDDON, Charles fl.1865-70
Occasional wood engraver, illustrator. He drew for an edition of Walter Scott's Red Gauntlet and The Fortunes of Nigel, and wood engraved a portrait of James Henry Leigh Hunt, after Mrs Gliddon (probably Anne Gliddon, fl. c1840), owned by the British Museum.
[Hake]

GOATER, Alfred fl.1872-89
Provincial wood engraver and printer who worked at Mount Street Works, 30 Mount Street, Nottingham

(Kelly's,1872-76) with second premises at 27 Little Park Street, Coventry, Warwickshire (Kelly's, 1872-89). These premises continued into the 1900s as A.Goater Limited, printer of colour plates for magazines like Boy's Own Paper and Queen.
[Wakeman and Bridson]

GODARD, Pierre François 1768-1838
French wood engraver, the engraver of more then 8,000 designs, including English cuts to the second edition of Renouard's Buffon, 1812. Gusman explained how he was a soldier taken prisoner in Nantes during the Vendée war in 1792, but freed by the villagers to continue his wood engraving, having kept his tools in his war kit. He worked at Alençon, for the Fables of Fontaine and Aesop's Fables, and many of his works were in the local museum. His son, Pierre François Godard, 1797-1864, was also a wood engraver and much influenced by the English wood engravers such as C.Thompson (q.v.) with whom he engraved first for Brigand Espanol, 1824; then after a Thompson drawing of an antique vase, 'Temple de Gnide'. Gusman claimed that Godard junior was 'le plus redoubtable adversaire de Thompson et des Anglais'.
[For a list of French works engraved see Gusman]

GODART Brothers fl.1887-88
London wood engraving firm, with an office at 47 Imperial Buildings, New Bridge Street, EC (POD,1887-88). (See following two entries)

GODART, Frank fl.1881-88
London wood engraver, who worked at 45 then 52 Imperial Buildings, New Bridge Street, EC (POD,1881-83), shared with W.B.Pain (q.v.), then at 319 Strand, WC (POD,1884-88).

GODART and Hay fl.1889-91
London wood engraving firm, with an office at 39,40,41 Imperial Buildings, New Bridge Street, EC (POD,1889-91).

GODDARD, George Bouverie 1832-86
Draughtsman illustrator, painter of animal subjects. He was born in Salisbury, Wiltshire on Christmas Day 1832 and recognised as an infant prodigy. He travelled to London in 1849, studied animals at the London Zoo for two years, returned home briefly, then went back to London in 1857, where he had exhibited at the Royal Academy in 1856. There he drew animals on wood for Punch, 1865, and the Illustrated London News, 1865-84, graduating to large fold-out plates of animals: 'Royal Game', 4 March 1876, engraved by John Greenaway (q.v.); and the double page 'Driving Grouse on the Moors', 9 September 1876, engraved by W.Hollidge (q.v.). He also drew for Once a Week, 1866; London Society, 1868; and The Graphic, 1880-84. Spielmann recorded how Goddard shared a studio with Charles Keene

(q.v.) but eventually left Punch, after doing fourteen animal drawings, 'of which some were adjudged to contain the best horses seen in its pages since the death of Leech'. He then gave up drawing on wood to paint for the galleries, exhibiting at the Royal Academy and the Royal Society of British Artists, 1864-72. He died in Brook Green, London on 6 March 1886.
[TB; Bénézit; DNB; Bryan; Spielmann; Art Journal, 1886,p.158]

GODDART and Son fl.1880-1900
Provincial wood engraving firm, with an office at Silver Street, Hull (Kelly's,1880-1900).

GODTSCHALK, Charles fl.1888-89
London wood engraver, who worked at 180 Fleet Street, EC (POD,1888-89).

GODWIN, James ?-1876
Draughtsman illustrator, and genre painter. He studied at the Royal Academy Schools and worked in Kensington from 1846, where he drew on wood for various prominent 'Sixties School' publications: The Poetical Works of Edgar Allan Poe, 1853, seven drawings to Willmott's Poets of the Nineteenth Century, 1857, engraved by the Dalziels; Mackay's The Home Affections, 1858; and to the magazine London Society, 1863. He also provided drawings regularly to the Illustrated London News, 1853-67, generally of Christmas themes and decorative fillers in an exact, delicate style. He also exhibited at the British Institution, 1846, 1850, the Royal Academy and the Royal Society of British Artists, 1846-51. He died in London in 1876. The British Museum owns his designs engraved by the Dalziel Brothers (q.v.), 1860-66.
[Houfe; White]

GOODALL, Charles fl.1872-76
Provincial wood engraver, who worked at 2 Park Lane and 62 Boar Lane, Leeds (Kelly's,1872-76), then Cookeridge Street and Park Lane, Leeds Kelly's,1876). There was also a Charles Goodall, London lithographer and colour printer.
[Wakeman and Bridson]

GOODALL, Edward Angelo 1819-1908
Occasional draughtsman on wood, illustrator and landscape painter. He was born on 8 June 1819, the son of the metal engraver Edward Goodall (see Volume I) and brother of the draughtsman Walter Goodall (q.v.). After education at University College School, London, he became a travel artist, first in British Guiana and South America, and then as artistic correspondent for the Illustrated London News, 1855, in the Crimea. He drew landscapes for wood engravings in Willmott's Poets of the Nineteenth

Century, 1857, engraved by the Dalziels; and Rhymes and Roundelayes with his brother, Walter. He was elected ARWS, 1858 and RWS, 1864. He died on 16 April 1908. The British Museum owns his designs engraved by the Dalziel Brothers (q.v.).
[Chatto; Redgrave; Bryan; DNB (list of paintings); TB; Bénézit; Art Journal, 1870]

GOODALL, Walter 1830-89
Draughtsman on wood of figure subjects, painter and watercolourist. He was born in London on 6 November 1830, son of the engraver Edward Goodall (see Volume I) and studied at the Clipstone St Academy, the Government School of Design and the Royal Academy Schools in 1852. He worked primarily as a watercolourist, exhibited at the Royal Academy, 1853-87, and was elected RWS in 1853. As a draughtsman, he did drawings for the Vernon Gallery, published in the Art Journal, and also wood block drawings to illustrations for Rhymes and Roundelayes and Ministering Children, both mentioned by Bohn in Chatto and Jackson. He was paralysed in 1875 and died in Clapham, near Bedford on 14 May 1889.
[Chatto; Bryan; TB; Bénézit; DNB; Graves]

GOODHILL, Mr fl.1830s-40s
According to the diary of Llewelyn Jewitt (q.v.) when his engraver brother Orlando Jewitt (q.v.) moved to Oxford in 1838 and sought employees for his engraving business. 'He has engaged one--a Mr Goodhill, a draughtsman, but has met with no engravers' (The Library, 1964,p.326).

GOODHIND, George fl.1880-1900
Provincial draughtsman and wood engraver, who worked at Gascoigne Street, Boar Lane, Leeds (Kelly's,1880), then 1 Ann Street, Leeds (Kelly's, 1900).

GOODHIND, Richard and Company fl.1893-1910
London wood engraver, manager for the City Wood Engraving Company (q.v.) from 1893-96, but then worked on his own as Richard Goodhind and Company, 138 Fleet Street, EC (POD,1897-1910).

GOODING, Joseph fl.1855-90
London wood engraver, who worked at 8 Elizabeth Terrace, Liverpool Road (Hodgson's,1855) then 10 Red Lion Court, Fleet Street, EC (POD,1857-90), which he shared with William Earl and Albert Green (qq.v.).

GOODMAN, Arthur fl.1890-1913
London wood engraver, who worked at 6 Dowgate Hill, EC (POD,1894). He may in fact be Arthur Jule Goodman (fl.1890-1913), the American-born illustrator and 'special artist', who worked for Harper's from 1889 then came to London and worked as 'special artist' for the Pall Mall Gazette. He achieved a

reputation for his military subjects and contributed to such magazines as the Girl's Own Paper, 1890-1900; Pall Mall Budget,1893; the Illustrated London News,1893; St Pauls,1894; Good Words, 1894; and the English Illustrated Magazine,1895-97. [For Arthur Jule Goodman bibliography see The Idler, vol.9,pp.803-16]

GOODMAN, Walter 1838-?
Draughtsman illustrator, portrait painter. He was born in London on 11 May 1838, studied at Leigh's and travelled in Europe, and in Cuba, 1864-69, which inspired the text and wood engraved illustrations to The Pearl of The Antilles, or an Artist in Cuba. He also drew for wood engravings in the Illustrated London News, notably various full-page sketches of Russian peasantry, 28 April and 17 November 1877. He also exhibited regularly at the British Institution, 1859-61, the Royal Academy, 1872-88, the Royal Society of British Artists, 1859-90 and the Royal Scottish Academy. He worked in Brighton in 1889, then Henfield, Sussex in 1906.
[Bénézit; TB; Graves; Houfe]

GORMAN, William and Company fl.1889-1900
Scottish draughtsmen firm, with an office at 153 W. Nile Street, Glasgow (Kelly's,1889-1900).

GORWAY, Charles Milton fl.1830-64
London wood engraver, who began as one of Ebenezer Landells' 'outside' engravers c1840, which meant that while he was not apprenticed to Landells he was commissioned to do free-lance engravings, a position he shared with the young Dalziels and T.Armstrong (qq.v.). By early 1845 he had joined forces with his employer as 'Landells, Gorway and Provart' to wood engrave for the Illustrated London News, notably 'British Association, Cambridge', a full-page crowd scene, and 'Fireworks Temple, Vauxhall', a half-page, rather heavily-engraved plate, both 21 June 1845. There were also various smaller cuts of topographical interest but these engravings relied upon heavy background ruling at the expense of the rather mediocre figure engraving. They culminate in Gorway's own three pages of vignettes, 'The Eastern Counties Railway', 2 August 1845, which are small yet distinct engravings with a good sense of contrast. Other early commissions included engravings after Thomas Landseer to W.Kidd's edition of Robert Burns' Address to the Devil,1830, and some engravings to Appleyard's edition of Dickens' Nicholas Nickleby,1847, engraved with John Greenaway (q.v.). Since this last commission ended in Appleyard's bankruptcy, it is tempting to believe that Gorway suffered the same fate as his fellow engraver John Greenaway, and went unpaid for his engraving. He appears ten years later in the London directories as a professional wood engraver, with offices at 3 Dane's Lane

(POD,1857), 8 Dane's Inn, WC (POD,1858), and then 33 Devonshire Street, Islington, N (POD,1862-64). By 1866 Bohn in Chatto and Jackson could claim that Gorway 'has successfully engraved many of John Gilbert's designs', and include him in his list of engravers deserving 'honourable mention'. [Chatto; Spielmann; TB; Bénézit; Kitton]

GORWAY, Walter fl.1850-99
London wood engraver, who worked at 74 Swinton Street, Gray's Inn Road (POD,1860-67) and then 32 Rochester Square, NW (POD,1870-99). By 1900 the office was taken over by George Richard Gorway (q.v.). According to TB, Gorway worked on a number of serialised novels after John Gilbert drawings, for the London Journal. He also engraved for the Illustrated London News, notably a three-quarter page, 'The Outrage upon Sir John Coventry', after T.H.Maguire's painting, 14 July 1860. He signed his work: 'W Gorway Sc' (script).
[TB; Bénézit]

GORWAY, George Richard fl.1900-01
London wood engraver, who took over the office of the noted engraver Walter Gorway (q.v.). He appears in the London directories at 32 Rochester Square, NW (POD,1900-01).

GOSSE, Philip Henry 1810-88
Draughtsman and zoologist, who farmed in the United States and Canada before returning to England to take up the study of insects in 1839. He wrote and illustrated his own books, including: The Canadian Naturalist,1840; Introduction to Zoology,1843; Birds of Jamaica,1847; Rambles on the Devonshire Coast, 1853; The Aquarium,1854; Manual of Marine Zoology, 1855-56; Actinologia Britannica,1858-60; and Romance of Natural History,1860. Gosse was elected FRS in 1856, and was the father of Sir Edmund Gosse. The British Museum owns four proof engravings after his designs, engraved on wood by the Dalziel Brothers (q.v.), 1863-64.
[For biographical detail see E.Gosse, Father and Son,1907; A.Thwaite, Edmund Gosse,1984]

GOULD, Mrs M. fl.1853
London wood engraver, who worked at 18 Millbank Row, Westminster (POD,1853).

GOULD and Reeves fl.1884-1901
London wood engraving firm, with offices at 73 Wenlock Street, New North Road, N, and 15 Abbey Street, Bethnal Green, E (POD,1884-93), then at Wenlock Street and 27 Stonecutter Street, EC (POD,1894) and finally just at Wenlock Street (POD,1895-1901).

GOWARD, W.P. fl.1850s
Ipswich wood engraver, who moved to Headington
near Oxford about 1851 and possibly was employed by
the noted engraver Orlando Jewitt (q.v.).
[The Library,1964,p.326]

GOWER, S.J. fl.1860s
Little is known of this draughtsman, who drew for a
wood engraving in the Illustrated London News,1860.

GOWLAND, James fl.1839-55
English wood engraver of numerous vignettes to
illustrated novels. His importance is noted by Gusman
as a wood engraver for various French publications
such as the Magasin Pittoresque and L'Image; and
for various books: Ct de Laborde's Versailles,
1839, engraved with Godard, Charles Thompson,
J.Orrin Smith, W.T.Green, J.A.Wheeler, M.Sears,
Jackson and Best (qq.v.); La Fontaine Contes et
Nouvelles,1839, after T.Johannot and Fragonard,
engraved with C.Thompson, Sears and Best; De
L'Ardeche Laurent's Histoire de L'Empereur Napoleon,
1839, the total of 500 wood engravings by Gowland,
Sears, Thompson, Williams, Quartley, J.Orrin Smith,
Whithead and Sheeres (qq.v.); Abbé Prevost's Histoire
de Manon Lescaut,1839, the ninety engravings by
Gowland, Sears, Thompson, Williams, Mary A.
Williams, J.Orrin Smith, Gray and Timms (qq.v.);
Mme de Stael's Corinne ou L'Italie,1841-42, engraved
with Quartley and J.Orrin Smith; and Jules Janin's
L'Ane Mort,1842, from the 1829 original, engraved
with Thompson, Harrison, Gray, Quartley, Thomas
Williams and J.Orrin Smith. He worked in London
where the directories list an office at 2 Derby Street,
King's Cross (POD,1854-55). He signed his work:
'J.GOWLAND'.
[For list of works see Gusman; Glaser]

GRAHAM, Peter 1836-1921
Occasional draughtsman and landscape painter. He
was born in Edinburgh in 1836, and studied under
R.S.Lauder at the Trustees Academy, and with John
Ballantyne. He moved to London in 1866, where he
exhibited at the Royal Academy, and was elected
ARA,1877 and RA,1881. He contributed a drawing
for wood engraving in London Society,1878, but was
best known for his paintings of Scottish scenery which
he exhibited at the Royal Scottish Academy. He was
elected ARSA in 1860. He died in St Andrews on
19 October 1921.
[Houfe; White]

GRAHAM, Thomas Alexander Ferguson 1840-1906
Draughtsman illustrator and portrait painter. He was
born in Kirkwall in 1840 and studied at the Trustees
Academy, 1855 with fellow pupils Orchardson, Pettie,
P.Graham, and MacWhirter (qq.v.), then moved to
London where he exhibited from 1863. He contributed
nine drawings on wood to Good Words,1861-63, engraved

by the Dalziel Brothers (q.v.) and praised by White as
work 'of the power of an artist who has yet to be
"discovered" so far as illustrations are concerned'.
He exhibited portraits at the Grosvenor Gallery,
the New Gallery, the Royal Academy, the Royal
Society of British Artists, the Royal Institute of
Painters in Watercolours, the Royal Institute of
Painters in Oil-Colours and the Royal Scottish
Academy. He was elected HRSA in 1883. He died in
Hampstead on 24 December 1906. The British
Museum owns several proof engravings by the
Dalziel Brothers (q.v.), 1861-63.

GRANT, Charles Jameson fl.1831-46
Draughtsman wood engraver and caricaturist. He
drew for the penny radical papers during the
Chartist agitation. Houfe calls his work 'spirited if
rather coarse'. He signed his work: 'CJG'.
[For examples of his work, see M.D.George,
English Political Caricature,II,1959]

GRANT, George fl.1890s
London wood engraver, who worked at 89 Farringdon
Street, EC (POD,1891), which he shared with
W.J.Potter, L.Knott, H.Prater, and G.F.Horne
(qq.v.).

GRANT, William James 1829-66
Occasional draughtsman on wood, illustrator and
painter of historical subjects. He was born in
Hackney in 1829 and attended the Royal Academy
Schools in 1845, where he exhibited 1847-66. He
also exhibited at the British Institution,1849-63.
He was best known for historical and religious
paintings, his themes being taken from contemporary
poetry. This inspired his drawings on wood to
Favourite Modern Ballads, and Bloomfield's
Farmer's Boy, both works noted by Bohn in Chatto
and Jackson. He died in Hackney on 2 June 1866.
[Chatto; Redgrave; Houfe; Bénézit; TB; Bryan;
Graves; Art Journal,1866]

GRANT and Company fl.1876-89
London draughtsmen firm, with an office at 72 and
78 Turnmill Street, EC (Kelly's,1876), and second
premises at 30 Queen Victoria Street (Kelly's,1889).

GRAY
(see Payne and Gray)

GRAY, Charles ?-1847
English wood and metal engraver. He was born in
Newcastle, where he served as pupil to Isaac
Nicholson (q.v.), the Newcastle engraver and
Bewick disciple. He shared the work with
Alexander Dalziel (q.v.). He then moved to London
and worked under his fellow pupil Ebenezer
Landells (q.v.), after which he trained the young
George Dalziel (q.v.) for four years. He appears

in the London directories at 58 Seymour Street, Euston Square (Pigot,1838), and 19 Clarendon Square (POD,1842). There he engraved with Ebenezer Landells as 'LANDELLS & GRAY' various cuts after George Cattermole and Hablot Browne (qq.v.) for Dickens' Master Humphrey's Clock,1840-41; for Charles Knight's The Penny Magazine,October 1841; and most notably for Knight's edition of William Lane's Arabian Nights' Entertainments,1839. Gusman lists several cuts in French publications by E. (sic) Gray, probably a misprint for Charles: Les Evangiles,1838, after Fragonard, engraved with C.Thomas, T.Williams, J.Orrin Smith, F.W.Branston, Powis, Robert Hart, Sears, Charles Laing, John Wright and Folkard (qq.v.); Abbé Prevost's Histoire de Manon Lescaut, 1839, the ninety cuts engraved with M.Sears, T.Williams, Mary Williams, J.Orrin Smith, Gowland and Timms (qq.v.); Dr C.Wordsworth's La Grèce Pittoresque et Historique,1841, some of the 300 total cuts; and Jules Janin's L'Ane Mort,1842, engraved with Thompson, Timms, J.Orrin Smith, Rose, Harrison, Gowland and Quartley (qq.v.). The British Museum owns several small vignettes by Gray; also nature engravings signed 'LANDELLS & GRAY'. He signed his engravings: C. GRAY SC'.
[Houfe; Bénézit; TB; Dalziels' Record; Nagler; Kitton; Gusman; Bodleian Library; British Library catalogue]

GRAY, Miss Ethel 1879-1957
Woodcut artist, etcher, oil and watercolour painter. She was born in Newcastle on 14 May 1879, studied in York, Leeds and at South Kensington, under Leonardo Garrido and Stanhope Forbes. She exhibited at the Royal Academy, and lived in York and later in Scarborough. She died on 22 January 1957.
[Waters]

GRAY, Joseph William fl.1889-1900
Provincial wood engraver, who worked at 96 later 134 Deansgate, Manchester (Kelly's,1889-1900).

GRAY, Paul Mary 1842-66
Irish draughtsman illustrator. He was born in Dublin on 17 May 1842, attended a convent school and then taught drawing at the Tullabeg School. He then worked with the Dublin printseller, Dillon, and exhibited at the Royal Hibernian Academy, 1861-63. He moved to London in 1863, where to support his mother he 'was obliged by the necessities of his position to become a draughtsman on wood' (Strickland) and was taken up by Tom Hood who introduced Gray to various magazine publishers. His small initials for Punch,1863-65, and twelve drawings on wood to C.Kingsley's 'Hereward' for Good Words,1865, made him known, and thereafter he found work for many 'Sixties School' publications. His drawings were engraved by Joseph Swain, the Dalziels, W.J.Linton, and Charles Thompson (qq.v.). They appeared in Once a Week; London Society;

Shilling Magazine; Argosy; Quiver; Broadway; and such books as A Round of Days,1866; Idyllic Pictures,1867; Ghosts Wives,1867; The Spirit of Praise,1867; and The Savage Club Papers,1867. Gray also collaborated with the Dalziel Brothers on various of their 'Fine Art' publications; when they took over the magazine Fun, he joined the staff for twelve months. But consumption cut short Gray's promising career, and he died in London on 14 November 1866, aged twenty-four, after a trip to Brighton. The British Museum owns proof engravings by the Dalziel Brothers,1863-67; the Bodleian Library proofs to Once a Week and Good Words. [Strickland; Spielmann; Redgrave; Houfe; Reid; Bryan; TB; Bénézit; Art Journal,1867]

GRAY, Tom fl.1860-72
Draughtsman and subject painter, who worked at Howland Street, London in 1866. He drew on wood for London Society,1860, 1868 and a rural scene on wood for The Graphic. He also exhibited at the British Institution, 1866.
[Houfe; White]

GREATBACH, W. fl.1850s
London wood engraver, who worked at 2 Crescent Place, Morning Crescent (Hodgson's,1855). He may be the noted metal engraver William Greatbach (1827-65) (see Volume I).

GREATWOOD
(see Wright, Greatwood and Meek)

GRECO, J.
Wood engraver, who also drew illustrations to Sir Richard Burton's The Book of the Sword,1884.

GREEN, Albert fl.1870s
London wood engraver, who worked at 10 Red Lion Court, Fleet Street, EC (POD,1870).

GREEN, Alfred fl.1880s
Provincial wood engraver, who worked at Bond Street, Dewsbury, Yorkshire (Kelly's,1880).

GREEN, Charles 1840-98
Prominent draughtsman illustrator and painter. He was born in 1840, and studied at Heatherley's and with the noted draughtsman W.J.Whymper (q.v.). He achieved a substantial reputation for drawing on the block, many of his most successful figure and genre subjects being engraved by the Dalziel Brothers and Joseph Swain (qq.v.). He contributed to most of the major 'Sixties School' publications such as Once a Week,1860-65; Churchman's Family Magazine, 1863-64; the Illustrated London News,1866; Cassell's Magazine,1867; London Society; Sunday Magazine; Good Words for the Young; Sunday at Home; and English Sacred Poetry of the Olden Times,1864.

Notable illustrations were to <u>The Old Curiosity Shop</u>, for the Household edition of Dickens, 1871-79, engraved by the Dalziels, who praised his work: 'every picture is carefully studied both as to character, scene and subject' (the proofs of these are now in the Bodleian Library). His engraved scenes of London or Manchester poor and factory workers were much admired by Van Gogh when they appeared in <u>The Graphic</u>, from its earliest numbers, 1869-86. He also exhibited oil paintings at the Royal Academy, 1862-83 and other works at the Royal Institute of Painters in Watercolours and the Royal Society of Painters in Oil-Colours. He died in Hampstead on 4 May 1898.
[For a list of illustrated works <u>see</u> Houfe; Hardie; Bryan; Dalziels' <u>Record</u>; <u>English Influences on Van Gogh</u>]

GREEN, Henry Townley 1836-99
Draughtsman on wood for various 'Sixties School' publications. He was the brother of Charles Green (q.v.) and abandoned a banking career about 1867 to pursue his brother's artistic interests. He drew numerous illustrations, wood engraved by Joseph Swain and the Dalziels (qq.v.), of social subjects for <u>Once a Week</u>, 1867; <u>Sunday Magazine</u>, 1869; <u>Cassell's</u>, 1870; and <u>Good Words</u>, 1870. Van Gogh much admired his drawing, 'A City Church Congregation' in the <u>Illustrated London News</u>, 5 October 1872. By the 1880s he had turned to watercolours for the galleries and was elected ARI in 1875, RI in 1879 and ROI in 1883. He also exhibited at the Royal Academy and the Royal Society of British Artists.
[Houfe; <u>English Influences on Van Gogh</u>]

GREEN, John fl.1850s
Wood engraver, listed by Gleeson White as engraving illustrations to Robert Pollock's <u>The Course of Time</u>, 1857, after Birket Foster, John Tenniel and J.R.Clayton. He shared the engraving with Edmund Evans, the Dalziel Brothers and H.N.Woods (qq.v.).

GREEN, Julian fl.1880s
Provincial wood engraver, who worked at 19 Albion Street and Whitehall Road, Leeds (Kelly's, 1889).

GREEN, Richard fl.1872-75
London wood engraver, who worked at 46 Fleet Street, EC (POD, 1872-75), which he shared with W.H.Tilby (q.v.).

GREEN, W.
Wood engraver of the early nineteenth century. The British Museum attributes engravings by W.Green to an edition of <u>Pilgrim's Progress</u>, 1816, published in Derby. Green engraved in the crude, heavy black-line of the trade engraver of the period. He signed his engravings: 'W Green'.

GREEN, W.T. fl.1837-72
English wood engraver, best known for his engravings after Maclise, Stanfield, Richard Doyle, John Gilbert and John Martin. Green's early engravings were for <u>The Solace of Song: Short Poems</u>, 1837. According to Gusman, Green engraved for French editions of Ct. de Laborde's <u>Versailles</u>, 1839, engraved with Gowland, Thompson, J.Orrin Smith, and Sears (qq.v.), and for some of the 300 cuts to Dr C.Wordsworth's <u>La Grèce Pittoresque et Historique</u>, 1841. By this time he was an established engraver for Charles Knight's (q.v.) publications such as the <u>Penny Magazine</u>, December 1841, after T.H.Shepherd (q.v.); for Knight's <u>Pictorial Shakespeare</u> series, 'Hamlet', engraved with the Dalziel Brothers, J.W.Whymper and E.Landells (qq.v.); and for Knight's edition of Lane's <u>Arabian Nights' Entertainments</u>, 1839. He also engraved for the <u>Poetical Works of Goldsmith</u>, 1845; the illustrations of Richard Dadd (q.v.) to S.C.Hall's <u>Book of British Ballads</u>, 1842; and portrait engravings for the <u>Art Journal</u>, 1849-50. By 1850 he was engraving on wood for the <u>Illustrated London News</u>, 1850-51, notably after various landscape paintings, many rather poorly combining a fine-lined and stipple style or faint-ruled backgrounds to enhance rather weak figure drawing. By 1860 Green was included in the revised edition of Chatto and Jackson, where Bohn listed and praised his current work: Bible prints after John Martin; engravings to <u>Merrie Days of England</u>; <u>Favourite English Poems</u>; and several cuts after Daniel Maclise to Tennyson's <u>Princess</u>, 1860. Gleeson White claimed that Green's engravings after Samuel Palmer to Adams' <u>Sacred Allegories</u>, 1856, were his best work: 'had W.T.Green engraved no other blocks, he might be ranked as a great craftsman on the evidence of these alone'. Green engraved Marcus Stone's (q.v.) illustrations to Dickens' <u>Our Mutual Friend</u>, 1864; the small drawings of Richard Doyle (q.v.) to <u>Frederick Locker</u>, 1865 (Moxon's Miniature Poets series); and Kenny Meadows' illustrations to J.T.Trueba y Cosio's <u>Romance of the History of Spain</u>, 1872. The British Museum owns a large collection of Green's engravings after R.Ansdell, H.K.Browne, T.Creswick, R.Doyle, J.Gilbert, F.Goodall, W.Harvey, F.W.Hulme, R.Huskisson, D.Maclise, C.Stanfield, and E.M.Ward. He signed his engravings: 'W.T.GREEN Sc'.
[Gusman; Bodleian Library; Hake; White; TB; Bénézit; Chatto; Spielmann]

GREENAWAY, Alfred John (Johnnie) 1852-1938
Wood engraver, born in Islington, London, on 12 July 1852, the youngest of four. He was the pupil of his father, John Greenaway (q.v.) with whom he trained as a young man. However, he soon became discouraged and gave up the business of engraving to become a noted writer on chemistry and professional instructor at the Royal College of

Chemistry. He was the brother of Kate Greenaway (q.v.) who introduced him to John Ruskin and the two men collaborated on scientific projects, including photographs for Ruskin's Oxford lectures. He was one of the sole comforts of his sister's later life and after her death in 1901 devoted his time toward maintaining her posthumous reputation. [see R.Engen, K.Greenaway: A Biography,1981]

GREENAWAY, Catherine (Kate) 1846-1901
Prominent illustrator and watercolourist. She was born in Hoxton, London on 17 March 1846, the daughter of a proficient wood engraver, John Greenaway (q.v.). She quickly learned to draw from her father, who at that time worked for Punch and the Illustrated London News and spent his evenings engraving on the block while young Kate supervised. She soon tried her hand at drawing for wood engraving, aided by art school lessons at the local Government School, then the South Kensington branch, also evening classes in figure drawing at Heatherley's and the Slade. She perfected her drawing skills enough to begin work on wood blocks for various minor magazines and books. Some of her drawings were engraved by her father and published by his employer Cassell Petter Galpin. She established her reputation as a book illustrator with Under the Window, 1878-79, engraved on wood and printed in colours by the master engraver-printer Edmund Evans (q.v.), with whom she worked for the remainder of her life. She first sold her drawings for transfer onto the wood block, but later demanded payment for their use only, and had them returned to her by Evans. Her drawing was never as strong as the finished engraving; it is right to say she (and her colleagues Walter Crane and Randolph Caldecott (qq.v.)) were such successes as book illustrators because of the interpretative skill of their engraver Edmund Evans. He strengthened the outline and modulated the pastel tones of their original designs. She worked almost exclusively for wood engraving, with only brief experiments early on with colour lithography, when she was a greeting card artist for Marcus Ward. She also painted watercolours of children, and later rather poor attempts at oil portraits, which she exhibited at the Fine Art Society, 1894, 1898, 1902, the Royal Academy, the Royal Society of British Artists and the Royal Institute of Painters in Watercolours, where she was elected RI in 1889. She died in Hampstead on 6 November 1901.
[For biographical and full bibliographical material see R.Engen, K.Greenaway: A Biography,1981]

GREENAWAY, John 1816-90
Prolific wood engraver, especially noted for animal engravings after Harrison Weir (q.v.); also topographical draughtsman for the Illustrated London News. He was born in Mint Street, Southwark, London on 20 September 1816, the son of a cabinet

maker. He was first apprenticed to Robert Edward Branston (q.v.), the London wood engraver, for seven years from 1 February 1831. Afterwards he joined the enterprising Ebenezer Landells (q.v.) to engrave the early numbers of Punch and the Illustrated London News. There he worked alongside fellow engravers Edmund Evans, Birket Foster and William Galter (qq.v.). Greenaway set up on his own, and first appears in London directories in partnership with W.Wright (q.v.) as Greenaway and Wright (q.v.) at 48 Salisbury Square (POD,1846-48). There he worked after animal drawings of Harrison Weir, for children's books, and for a new illustrated series of Dickens. This was commissioned by the publisher Appleyard, to be engraved after John Gilbert (q.v.) illustrations and started well enough with Pickwick Papers completed and early numbers of Nicholas Nickleby on sale. But Appleyard went bankrupt and left his engravers unpaid. Wright then parted from John Greenaway, who left his office and became a freelance engraver, working in his Hoxton home. He worked primarily for the Illustrated London News as draughtsman engraver, and eventually set up again at 4 Wine Office Court (POD,1854-86). This was a small third floor office which from 1875 he shared with W.H.Tilby (q.v.). It was here that his young daughter Catherine (Kate) Greenaway came to visit and learn to draw on wood blocks. John Greenaway trained her in the evenings, when the family had gone to bed, and much of her success as an illustrator is due to his influence. Throughout the 1850s and 60s Greenaway developed a reputation for competent engravings and a reliable business manner. He was given the distinction of three pages in Bohn's chapter to Chatto and Jackson, 'Artists and Engravers of the Present Day', 1861. Bohn listed his engravings for The Poetry of the Year; Poems and Songs of Robert Burns; Poetry and Pictures from Thomas Moore; Favourite English Poems; Barry Cornwall's Dramatic Scenes and Poems; Bloomfield's Farmer's Boy,1858; Fable Book for Children; Favourite English Ballads,1859; James Montgomery's Poems,1860; Wood's Natural History; Cundall's Book of Nature,1860; and Campbell's Pleasures of Hope, 1861. He later engraved Harrison Weir's drawings to G.F.Townsend's Aesop's Fables,1867. He was a dedicated engraver and occasionally also worked as a 'special' reporter-draughtsman for the Illustrated London News. He was sent to draw scenes during the Rugeley murder trial, Staffordshire, and also drew the local scenery. He was sent to record the Opening of Parliament by the Queen. By the 1870s he had engraved a large number of works for the Illustrated London News, notably landscape works after Samuel Read and animals after Samuel Carter. Especially good was his large 'Prize Cats at the Crystal Palace Cat Show', after Harrison Weir, 22 July 1871, which culminated in further double-page and fold-out supplements by 1876. By then he was also working

for the children's publisher Cassell Petter Galpin
from whom he secured draughtsman work for
his daughter, which he then engraved. He had also
agreed to train various relatives to assist him,
including his niece, Miss Thorne (q.v.), a distant
relation, Stephen Dadd (q.v.) and later his own son
Alfred John (Johnnie) (q.v.). By 1887 he had only
brief commissions, and was largely supported by his
famous daughter. But he moved his office to the more
prestigious 143 Strand (POD,1887-91), which he
shared with W.J.Palmer and Thomas Symmons (qq.v.).
When he died in Hampstead on 26 August 1890, he had
retained his respected reputation, although his
engraving business had gradually dried up. The
Illustrated London News wrote a glowing obituary
and years later his old friend Edmund Evans
remembered him as 'a friend of mine since I was
14 years of age--a very good wood engraver'
(Evans MS, UCLA). John Greenaway's engraving
technique was competent if uninspired. He could
interpret the fine pencil lines of a Harrison Weir
animal drawing with as much confidence as he could
the stark, brooding seascapes of Samuel Read,
although the quality of dark tone occasionally became
obsessive and he needed to rely upon the effective
technique of flecked whites (e.g. seagulls, sea spray)
to restore overall tonal balance. His ability to retain
a sharp, clear outline was especially prized for the
children's books he engraved, including the early
works of Kate Greenaway, whose success depended
upon such controlled outlines for her formalised
children.
[For biographical detail see R.Engen, Kate
Greenaway: A Biography,1981; also TB; Chatto;
British Library]

GREENAWAY, Mary 1818-98 Rebecca 1803-89
Wood engraver sisters of John Greenaway (q.v.) and
aunts to Kate Greenaway (q.v.). They lived together
in Peabody Square, in London's East End, both
spinsters who worked for and were supported by their
brother. Mary was a book engraver and folder;
Rebecca a book binder.

GREENAWAY and Wright fl.1846-51
London firm of wood engravers, comprised of John
Greenaway and W.Wright (qq.v.). They were
commissioned by the publisher Appleyard to engrave
John Gilbert's illustrations to Dickens, issued
serially from 1847, and they had completed Pickwick
Papers and started on Nicholas Nickleby before
Appleyard went bankrupt. They worked at 48 Salisbury
Square (POD,1846-48), then 4A Wine Office Court
(POD,1851), after which time Wright broke the
partnership, leaving Greenaway with the debts.

GREENWOOD, John Frederic 1885-1954
Wood engraver, etcher and watercolourist. He was
born in Rochdale on 13 June 1885, and studied at
Shipley and Bradford Art Schools, 1904-08, then the
Royal College 1908-11. He taught at the Batley
School of Art, 1911-12, Battersea Polytechnic,
1912-27, Bradford School of Art, 1927-37, and at
Leeds College of Art. He was elected ARE in 1922,
RE in 1939 and RBA in 1940. He lived in Ilkley,
Yorkshire and died on 28 April 1954.
[Waters]

GREENWOOD, W.
Wood engraver and draughtsman of the mid nineteenth
century, who worked in a heavy black-line style.
The British Museum owns a series of landscape
vignettes and the larger engraving: 'Thornton Abbey,
Lincolnshire'. He signed his work: W GREENWOOD
DEL SC'.

GREGORY, Charles fl.1836-57
Wood engraver and colour printer from wood blocks,
described by C.T.Courtney Lewis as probably one of
the two, with George Cargill Leighton (q.v.), most
distinguished pupils of the wood engraver and colour
printer George Baxter (q.v.). He was apprenticed to
Baxter for seven years in April 1836 and remained
with him for four months after his release in 1843.
He then joined William Collins (q.v.), a fellow
Baxter pupil, in partnership as Gregory and Collins
and set up an office at 3 Charterhouse Square
(POD,1846). They produced a fancy red, blue, green
and gold title-page for Bishop Heber's Palestine,
1843, which Lewis believed was their earliest work.
Alfred Reynolds (q.v.) joined Collins and Gregory
and the firm changed to Gregory, Collins and
Reynolds, 'Engravers on wood & printers in colour,
gold & bronze', with an office in 1843 at 10 St James's
Street, Clerkenwell; in 1844 at 108 Hatton Garden;
and by 1846 at Baxter's old address of 3 Charterhouse
Square. They established a high reputation for
engraved colour work printed from wood blocks
(unlike their master George Baxter's method which
used intaglio metal plates) and usually in up to ten
colours. They engraved the drawings and watercolours
of Harrison Weir, T.Absolon and J.Franklin (qq.v.)
and produced reproductions which some regard as
equal to anything produced by Edmund Evans or the
Dalziel Brothers (qq.v.) in the 1860s. Among their
commissions were colour covers to Peter Parley's
Annuals,1846-49; for Felix Summerley's 'Home
Treasury' series (praised by the Art Union) and
numerous publications of Darton and Company,
Longmans and H.G.Clarke. By June 1849 Charles
Gregory had left the firm for work with Kronheim
(q.v.), and the business became known as Collins
and Reynolds (q.v.). Gregory worked for Kronheim
(earning 2 and a half guineas a week) alongside his
fellow Baxter apprentices Thomas Thompson and Thomas
Dowlen (qq.v.) and at his suggestion Kronheim took
up the Baxter licence. By 1857, however, the German
firm of Frauenkneit had taken over Kronheim and Gregory

became a partner.
[For colour work see Wakeman and Bridson;
C.T.Lewis; McLean, Victorian Book Design]

GREGORY, Charles 1849-1920
Illustrator, historical and genre painter. He was
born in Milford, Surrey and worked in London, 1880,
Godalming, 1894, and Marlow, Buckinghamshire. He
contributed three drawings for wood engraving to the
Illustrated London News,1876,1877,1879, but was
primarily known for his paintings. He exhibited at
the Royal Academy, the Royal Society of British
Artists and the Royal Watercolour Society where he
was elected ARWS in 1882 and RWS in 1884. He died
in Marlow on 21 October 1920.

GREGORY, Collins and Reynolds
(see Gregory, Charles)

GREGORY, Edward John 1850-1909
Draughtsman illustrator and painter. He was born in
Southampton on 19 April 1850 and educated locally
in the P. and O. Company's drawing office, 1865,
and with the noted illustrator Hubert Herkomer (q.v.),
who advised Gregory to study in London. He was a
pupil at the South Kensington and Royal Academy
Schools, 1871-75, worked as a decorative artist for
the new Victoria and Albert Museum, and began his
association with The Graphic, via its illustrators
Herkomer, Robert Walker Macbeth (qq.v.),
drawing on wood for various social and
theatrical events. Afterwards he freely transcribed
Franco-Prussian War sketches sent home from the
French army at the front by Mr Sydney P.Hall (q.v.).
These he signed with Hall. Later he specialised in
ship board scenes. These provided an opportunity to
develop his draughtsmanship skills during the
thirteen years he contributed to The Graphic, until
1883. Van Gogh admired these drawings and the DNB
concluded of Gregory's work, 'Probably his watercolours and some of his drawings on wood will have
more enduring fame than his oils'. Gregory exhibited
at the Royal Institute of Painters in Watercolours,
where he was elected RI,1876 and PRI,1898; also at the
Royal Academy, where he was elected ARA,1879 and
RA,1898; also at the Royal Institute of Painters in
Oil-Colours and the Royal Scottish Academy. He
settled in Great Marlow, Buckinghamshire and died
there on 22 June 1909.
[DNB; Houfe; TB; Graves]

GRENIER, P. fl.1873-77
London wood engraver, who worked at 172 Strand
(POD,1876-77). He contributed wood engravings to
the Illustrated London News,1873-75, notably full
and double-page plates of various landscapes and
topographical and architectural subjects. He used a
fine-line with stipple to describe the elaborate interior
of 'The London School Board's New Offices', a double-

page engraving, 10 April 1875; a tight, rough-
textured effect to 'Mural Decorations', after Arthur
Stocks, full page, 1 April 1876. He signed his work:
'P Grenier' (script).

GRESLEY, J.
The British Museum owns four proof wood engravings
by the Dalziel Brothers (q.v.) after designs by this
artist, engraved 1861, 1863.

GREW, Mrs Susannah fl.1880s
London draughtsman, who worked at 46 Libra Road
Park, Plaistow, E (Kelly's,1889).

GRIBBLE, Miss Vivien (Mrs Jones) ?-1932
Wood engraver and book illustrator. She studied art
at Munich, the Slade, and Central School. Her
illustrated books include Hardy's Tess of the
d'Urbervilles and Songs from the Princess. She lived
at Higham, near Colchester and died on 6 February
1932.
[Waters]

GRIFFIN and Duvergier fl.1840s
London wood engraving firm, with an office at
5 Whitefriars Street (POD,1848).

GRIFFITH, Mathew fl.1880s
London wood engraver, who worked at 3 Falcon
Court, 142 Fleet Street, EC (POD,1886), shared
with Henry Freeman (q.v.).

GRIFFITHS and Watson fl.1870s
London wood engraving firm, with an office at 4 Maria
Terrace, Albion Grove, Barnsbury, N (POD,1872).
By the following year Griffith had set up on his own
(see following entry).

GRIFFITHS, John Charles and Company fl.1872-95
London wood engraving and draughtsmen firm,
earlier Griffiths and Watson (q.v.). They advertised
in Kelly's, 1872, as 'Draughtsmen and engravers on
wood, 29 Paternoster Row, London EC', with
'numerous permanent staff of skilled artists and
engravers in every branch of Art'. The firm
specialised in figures, ornamental portraits,
landscapes, animals, flowers and heraldry. Their
offices were at 29 Paternoster Row, EC and 4 Maria
Terrace, Albion Grove, Barnsbury, N (POD,1873-74);
later 100 Fleet Street, EC (POD,1875-88), 41 Wych
Street, WC (POD,1889-93) and 7 Quality Court, WC
(POD,1894-95). Among the engravings done by
Griffiths were two half-page cuts after W.J.Hennessy
for the English Illustrated Magazine,1884-85. These
were rather dark, heavy-handed combinations of
gouges and stipple shading.

GRIFFITHS, Tom fl.1880-1904
Draughtsman illustrator and landscape painter. He is
listed here for his military drawings for wood
engravings in The Graphic,1880-87. Houfe explains
that he may have served as a 'special artist' in Africa,
1881, 'but it is more likely that he was an understudy to T.W.Wilson (q.v.) and worked up his
sketches at home'. He exhibited paintings at the
Royal Academy, the Royal Society of British Artists,
the Royal Hibernian Academy and the Royal Institute
of Painters in Watercolours, and lived in Amberley
from 1893 and Bideford from 1901.
[Houfe]

GRISET, Ernest Henry 1844-1907
Comic draughtsman of animals, who was born in
Boulogne-sur-Mer in 1844, and studied with Louis
Gallait, probably in Brussels. He came to England in
the mid-1860s and with his strange grotesques in the
spirit of Grandville, he attracted the attention of the
Dalziel Brothers (q.v.) who commissioned drawings
for their comic magazine Fun. Mark Lemon, editor
of Punch, offered him regular employment there,
and he provided sixty-three drawings in the wake of
the recently deceased Charles Bennett, 1867. But
after the first year he fell out of Lemon's favour when
his comic inventions did not prove popular enough.
He also drew for Once a Week,1867; Broadway,1867;
Good Words for the Young,1870-71; The Graphic,
1870-71; and Hood's Comic Annual,1878. His edition
of Aesop's Fables for Cassell was perhaps his most
inspired work, while his prolific output appeared in
his own Griset's Grotesques,1867. He also exhibited
animal drawings at the Royal Society of British
Artists, 1871-72. He died in England on 22 March
1907. The British Museum owns several proof
engravings by the Dalziel Brothers,1866.
[For biographical and bibliographical detail see
L.Lambourne, Ernest Griset,1980; Houfe; TB;
Spielmann]

GROVE, William fl.1880s
Provincial wood engraver, who worked at Clarence
Street, Kingston, Surrey (Kelly's,1880).

GROVES, S.J. fl.1845-80
Draughtsmen and wood engraver, who engraved
three subjects to Dickens' Christmas Books,1845-46;
contributed illustrations to Pen and Pencil Pictures
from the Poets,1866; and according to Fincham
designed a pictorial bookplate for A.Love,1880,
engraved by F.Borders (q.v.).

**GURNEY, Frederick K., Son and Company
fl.1876-89**
London draughtsmen firm, with offices at
16 Woodstock Street, W (Kelly's,1876) and a second
office at 21 later 45 Kirby Street, EC
(Kelly's,1880-89).

GUSMAN, Adolphe fl.1840-70
French wood engraver, best known for his wood
engravings after Gustave Doré (q.v.). He signed his
work in a variety of ways: as 'Gusmand' to 1841,
'Gusman' in 1850, 'Gusmand' to 1868, then 'Gusman'
after 1868.
[For full account see Gusman]

GUTHRIE, James Joshua 1874-1952
Wood engraver, illustrator, bookplate designer,
printer and author. He was born in Glasgow on
11 April 1874, was self-taught and learned printing
from Reginald Hallward. He established his own
press, the Pear Tree Press at South Harting,
Hampshire, in 1905, after founding and illustrating
his magazine Elf,1895. He was an accomplished
wood engraver in the romantic style of Blake,
Calvert and Palmer and yet he illustrated in a
rather eccentric technique on granulated cardboard
and plaster. He also wrote on Clemence Housman
(q.v.) who, with R.B.Lodge (q.v.), engraved
Guthrie's work.
[For a list of works see Houfe]

GUY, George fl.1880s
London wood engraver, who worked at 8 Dyer's
Buildings, Holborn (POD,1881).

GUYS, Constantin Ernest Adolphe Hyacinthe 1802-92
French draughtsman, influential figure artist in pen
and watercolour. He was born in Flushing, Holland
of French parents in 1802, and by the 1840s was in
England acting as tutor. There he gained employment
from the newly established Illustrated London News
in 1843 and contributed drawings on wood until 1860,
covering the Crimean War in 1854-56. He was later
special correspondent to Spain, Italy, Germany,
Turkey and Egypt. This work associated him with
the English press and even his French colleagues
praised his skill at dexterous pen and wash drawing,
although his contemporary popularity was limited.
He died in Paris in poverty in 1892.
[For bibliography see Houfe]

GYDE, Frederick fl.1854-60
London wood engraver, who worked at 7A Red Lion
Court, Fleet Street, EC (POD,1854-57), and then
17 Albion Grove, Barnsbury, N (POD,1859-60). He
was the uncle of the writer on nature, Richard
Jeffries, to whom he taught drawing. Jeffries
immortalised him in the character of Alere Flamma,
'a gifted engraver on wood and a delicate artist with
pencil' in his novel, Amaryllis at the Fair,1887. The
portrait was of an 'artist, engraver, bookbinder
connoisseur, traveller, printer, republican,
conspirator, sot, smoker, dreamer, poet, kind-
hearted, good-natured, prodigal, shiftless, man of
Fleet-Street, carpet-bag man, gentleman shaken to
pieces. He worked in his shirt sleeves and drank

stout, but nothing vulgar has ever been recorded against Alere Flamma--He frequented strong company--very strong meat--but no vile word ever left his lips'.
[S.J.Looker, R.Jeffries,1964,p.15]

HADDLETON, Walter John fl.1880s
Provincial wood engraver, who worked at 41 Frederick Street, Birmingham (Kelly's,1889).

HADFIELD, G.S. fl.1880s
Provincial wood engraver, who worked at 21 and 24 St James's Street, Derby (Kelly's,1889).

HALCROW, Reginald James fl.1883-87
London wood engraver, who worked at 5 Wine Office Court, EC (POD,1883-85) which he shared with T.S.Bayley (q.v.), then at 64 Fleet Street, EC (POD,1886-87), shared with J.T.Richardson and C.A.Ferrier (qq.v.).

HALL, Basil fl.1886-88
Illustrator, who contributed story illustrations for wood engravings in The Graphic,1886-87, also illustrations of social events in 1888. He specialised in military subjects.

HALL, Charles fl.1840s
Wood engraver assistant and skilled block cutter to George Baxter (q.v.). By 1851 he was helping the firm of Bradshaw and Blacklock.
[C.T.Lewis]

HALL, E. fl.1850s
Draughtsman illustrator, who contributed drawings on wood of genre and social subjects to the Illustrated Times,1856-59.

HALL, Harry fl.1838-86
Draughtsman illustrator and painter of equestrian subjects. He first painted horses at Tattersall's in London, then moved to Newmarket, and met the editor of Punch, Mark Lemon, who secured one drawing for his magazine, 1853. He also contributed to Sporting Review,1842-46; drawings on wood to the Illustrated London News,1857-58, 1866-67; and became chief artist on The Field. He also exhibited at the British Institution, 1847-66, the Royal Academy, 1838-86, and the Royal Society of British Artists, 1839-75. He was the father of the noted draughtsman Sydney Hall (q.v.).
[Houfe]

HALL, Henry Brayn fl.1850-99
Wood engraver, born in Camden Town, London, probably the son of the engraver Henry Bryan Hall, with whom he travelled to New York in 1850. By 1858 he had returned to London and spent a year with

the publisher Charles Knight (q.v.) who influenced his career. He set up business as Henry Hall, London wood engraver, at 89 Farringdon Street (POD,1890), which he shared with the engravers W.J.Potter, L.Knott, H.Prater, F.Thorpe and F.Appleton (qq.v.), then moved to 180 Fleet Street, EC (POD,1891). He subsequently returned to America and worked in New York as a metal engraver until about 1899. Among his more famous plates were 'The Death of Lincoln', and various officer portraits from the American Civil War.
[TB; Bénézit; Fielding]

HALL, Sydney Prior 1842-1922
Prominent draughtsman on wood, 'special' illustrator-reporter and painter. He was born in Newmarket on 18 October 1842, the son and pupil of Harry Hall (q.v.). He also studied with the illustrator Arthur Hughes (q.v.), and at the Royal Academy Schools. He began as draughtsman on wood to the Quiver, 1869, worked with his teacher Arthur Hughes on Tom Brown's School Days,1869; then drew for Dark Blue,1871-73; and for The Sketch. By 1870 he had established himself as a prominent draughtsman for wood engravings in The Graphic. He became their 'special artist' reporter and contributed drawings for thirty-six years (to 1906) including sketches of the Franco-Prussian War, which were touched up and prepared for engraving by E.J.Gregory (q.v.). He also accompanied the Prince of Wales to India for sketches on the spot such as 'The Pleasures of the Chase', 22 February 1876. He was a favourite painter to the Royal Family and exhibited at the New Gallery, the Royal Hibernian Academy, the Royal Institute of Painters in Watercolours and the Royal Academy, 1874-1920.
[Bénézit; TB; Houfe]

HALL and English fl.1880-1900
Provincial wood engraving firm, with offices at 71 High Street and 36 Union Street, Birmingham (Kelly's,1880-1900).

HALLAM, George Charles fl.1876-1901
London draughtsman and wood engraver, who worked as draughtsman at 9 Fountain Court, Strand, WC (Kelly's,1876), and 8 Danes Inn, WC (Kelly's,1880) which he shared with T.Robinson (q.v.). Then he disappears from directories until 1897 when he reappears as a wood engraver at 2 New Street Square, EC (POD,1897-98); then as George Hallam and Company at 154 Fleet Street, EC (POD,1899-1901).

HALLIDAY, B.C. fl.1850s
Draughtsman, who contributed drawings for wood engraving to Punch,1855, as 'Our Artist in the Crimea'.
[Spielmann]

HALSWELLE, Keeley 1832-91
Draughtsman illustrator and landscape painter. He
was born in Richmond, Surrey of Scottish parents on
23 April 1832, studied at the British Museum in
Edinburgh and started a career as draughtsman on
wood for various books and magazines. He drew
for the Illustrated London News, 1860; and for Good
Words, 1860 (six drawings which White claimed were
'badly drawn or spoilt by the engraver'); illustrated
The Princess Florella, 1860; Six Years in a House-
Boat; and Scott's Poems, c1866; and contributed
some forty drawings to Pen and Pencil Pictures
from the Poets, 1866. He also painted in Italy and
Paris, exhibited at the Royal Academy, 1862-91,
and the Royal Society of British Artists, 1875-79,
and was elected ARSA, 1865 and RI, 1882. The British
Museum owns several proof engravings by the Dalziel
Brothers (q.v.), 1861-62.
[Houfe; Art Journal, 1879, p.49]

HAMERTON, Robert Jacob fl.1830-91
Draughtsman and lithographer, occasional painter.
He was born in Ireland and taught drawing in County
Longford at the age of fourteen, then came to London
to study lithography under Charles Hullmandel, the
'father of lithography in England'. He began drawing
on wood for Punch, 1843-44, then sporadically until
1848, as 'one of the few Irishmen who have worked
on the paper' (Spielmann). His subjects for ten
cartoons in 1844 were Irish: 'striking for their
handling, if not at first for their finish', but as
Spielmann recalled 'he deserted the precincts of
Whitefriars, and soon after renounced wood-drawing
in favour of his more lucrative employment'. He
also drew on wood for G.à'Beckett's Comic
Blackstone; and 'his masterpiece in wood-draughts-
manship', the illustrations to John Forster's Life of
Goldsmith. He returned to the lithographer's stone
until 1891, and also painted in oil and watercolour
with brief appearances at the British Institution,
1831-47, the Royal Academy and the Royal Society
of British Artists, 1831-58, being elected member
in 1843. He was a close friend of the illustrator
H.G.Hine (q.v.).
[Spielmann; Bénézit; TB; Strickland]

HAMILTON, James fl.1880s
Provincial draughtsman, who worked at 211 Granville
Street Park, Sheffield (Kelly's, 1889). He is not to be
confused with the illustrator, James Hamilton
(1819-78) who was born in Ireland and went to
America at an early age.

HAMMOND, Bending and Company fl.1880s
Provincial wood engraving firm, with an office at
10 Butts Court, Leeds (Kelly's, 1889).

HAMMOND, J. fl.1860s
Wood engraver, added by Bohn to Chatto and
Jackson in 1861, as one of the 'engravers on wood
not before mentioned'. He engraved illustrations to
Poems and Songs of Robert Burns.

HAMMOND, J.G. and Company fl.1889-1900
Provincial wood engraving firm, with offices at
12-16 Scotland Passage and Moor Street,
Birmingham (Kelly's, 1889-1900).

HAMPSHIRE, William Joseph fl.1888-1901
London wood engraver and draughtsman, with an
office at 112 Fleet Street (POD, 1888), shared with
A.Gascoine (q.v.); then 30 Fleet Street, EC
(POD, 1889-91); and Falcon Court, 32 Fleet Street,
EC (POD, 1893-1901), shared with T.Hobbs,
W.Spielmeyer, W.Andrews and A.Martin (qq.v.).

HAMPTON, Margaret fl.1840s
Wood engraver, who engraved for Charles Knight's
the Penny Magazine, after Ratcliffe, October 1841;
and for W.F.Tiffin's series, 'Old Kitchen, Stoke
Manor House', November 1841.
[Bodleian Library]

HANCOCK, Charles fl.1856-65
London wood engraver, who worked at 29 Great
Percy Street, Pentonville (POD, 1856-62), then
moved to St Germain Villas, Lewisham, SE
(LSDS, 1863-65). He may be related in some way to
the C.Hancock mentioned by Chatto who patented a
method for metallic relief (Chatto and Jackson,
p.635). He may also have some connection with the
sporting artist Charles Hancock, fl.1819-68 (see
Houfe).
[TB; Bénézit; Chatto]

HANCOCK, Francis Albert fl.1872
London wood engraver, listed in the directory as
'Copperplate, steel and wood engraver', at 37 and
38 Wood Street, EC (LSDN, 1872).

HARCOURT, Thomas fl.1880s
Provincial wood engraver, who worked at 33 St Paul's
Square and 2 Caroline Street, Birmingham
(Kelly's, 1880).

HARDING, James Duffield 1798-1863
Draughtsman, watercolourist, topographer,
lithographer and teacher. He was born in Deptford
in 1798 and studied with Samuel Prout and Charles
Pye, the engraver. He worked as a landscape artist,
exhibiting at the Royal Academy from 1810. He was
also an excellent lithographer after Bonington,
Roberts and Stanfield. He is listed here for his
designs engraved on wood by the Dalziel Brothers
(q.v.), 1855-56. The proofs of these are now in the

British Museum.
[For a discussion of his prints see Volume I; also Houfe]

HARDWICK, John Jessop 1831-1917
Apprentice wood engraver, draughtsman on wood, landscape and flower painter. He was born in Bow, Middlesex on 22 September 1831, and at fifteen years old was apprenticed to the noted wood engraver and publisher Henry Vizetelly (q.v.). He learned to engrave well enough there to be taken up as a draughtsman on wood for the Illustrated London News. His landscape paintings were highly praised and he was encouraged by Ruskin and Rossetti, exhibiting work at the Royal Academy from 1861. He was elected ARWS in 1882.
[Waters]

HARDY, Evelyn
Draughtsman illustrator, who contributed a military drawing for wood engraving in the Illustrated London News, 1889; also illustrations to the Church Monthly, 1899.

HARDY, Heywood 1842-1933
Prominent painter of animal subjects, occasional illustrator, etcher and decorator. He originated in Bristol, but moved to London about 1870, where he made a reputation for landscape and animal paintings. He contributed a Christmas drawing for wood engraving in the Illustrated London News, 1876, and The Graphic, 1880 (printed in colour). He exhibited often and was elected RE, 1880, ROI, 1883, and ARWS 1885.
[For a discussion of his etchings see Volume I]

HARDY, Paul fl.1886-99
Illustrator and history painter. He worked in Bexley Heath, Kent and was a prolific illustrator of the boys adventure stories written by G.A.Henty and Bret Harte. He also illustrated for wood engravings in the English Illustrated Magazine, 1886, 'A Glimpse of Bristol and Clifton', engraved on wood by R.Paterson, O.Lacour and R.Lueders (qq.v.).
[For a list of illustrated work see Houfe]

HARDY, William fl.1874-80
London wood engraver, who worked at 222 Great College Street, Camden Town (POD, 1874-80).

HARE, Jabez fl.1845-51
London wood engraver, printer, who worked at 10 Nelson Square, Blackfriars Road (POD, 1845-46), 108 Fleet Street (POD, 1848-49), and 3 Arundel Street, Strand (POD, 1851). The Bodleian Library (John Johnson Collection) owns the letterbook of Hare's business, 12 December 1846 to 30 August 1847, with receipts and correspondence to his numerous clients, including those to the noted wood draughtsman, Samuel Read (q.v.).

HARE, Thomas Matthews and Company fl.1842-1910
London firm of wood engravers and draughtsmen, established in 1842. Thomas Matthews Hare contributed scientific illustrations on wood to the Illustrated London News, 1847-49, and appeared with his own engraving business in the London directories at 31 Essex Street, Strand (POD, 1854-87). The following year he added a second office at 7 Bride Court, Fleet Street, EC (POD, 1888-95), by then listed merely as Hare and Company. The firm turned to photo-mechanical block making and colour lithography and was working from three premises by 1899: 7 Bride Court, 22 Bridge Lane, 1 Holborn Place, WC, and Red Lion Yard, High Holborn, then under the proprietorship of Leslie Clift and Company (q.v.). They remained in the directories until well after 1910.
[For a discussion of colour printing see Wakeman and Bridson; also British Printer, Volume 5, 1892, pp.48-49; Volume 8, 1895, pp.269-72]

HARKER, E.
Draughtsman, who contributed a drawing for wood engraving in the Illustrated London News, 1860.

HARKNESS, John fl.1870s
Provincial wood engraver, who worked at 121 Church Street, Preston, Lancashire (Kelly's 1872).

HARLEY, Walter fl.1880s
London wood engraver, who worked at 90 Barnsbury Road, N (POD, 1881).

HARLING, O. fl.1860s
Draughtsman, who contributed two sketches to Punch, 1866, engraved by Joseph Swain (q.v.).
[Spielmann]

HARPER, Henry Andrew 1835-1900
Author, painter and occasional illustrator. He was born in Blunham, Bedfordshire in 1835 and specialised in landscapes of the Holy Land. He contributed a Christmas drawing for wood engraving to the Illustrated London News, 1872. He also went with the Earl of Dudley to the Near East. He exhibited at the Royal Academy, the Royal Society of British Artists and the Royal Institute of Painters in Watercolours, but failed to be elected to the New Watercolour Society. He died in Westerham in 1900.
[Houfe]

HARRADEN, Frederick fl.1872-76
London draughtsman, who worked at 180 Fleet Street, EC (Kelly's, 1872), shared with T.D.Collins (q.v.), then 4 Wine Office Court (Kelly's, 1876), the office shared with John Greenaway and W.H.Tilby (qq.v.). He may be related to the engraving family Richard Harraden (1756-1838), and his son Richard Bankes Harraden (1778-1862).

HARRADEN, William fl.1864-71
London wood engraver, who worked at 8 Gough
Square, Fleet Street, EC (POD,1864-71).

HARRAL, Alfred fl.1840-70
Wood engraver, brother of the prominent wood
engraver Horace Harral (q.v.), with whom he worked.
W.J.Linton in Masters of Wood Engraving, described
Alfred as the best of J.Orrin Smith's (q.v.) pupils
who established his reputation as a competent
engraver of Kenny Meadows' and John Gilbert's (qq.v.)
drawings on wood. He and his brother Horace served
as assistants to Smith and Linton (q.v.) for whom
they engraved numerous cuts to the Illustrated
London News. Alfred continued to work for
W.J.Linton (q.v.) after his move to America, notably
on his pet project, American Enterprise,c1870.
Gusman claimed that Alfred and Horace also
engraved for the French Magasin Pittoresque.
[LeBlanc; Gusman; Linton, Masters of Wood
Engraving]

HARRAL, Horace fl.1844-91
Prominent London wood engraver and etcher, brother
of Alfred Harral (q.v.) with whom he worked as
pupil to J.Orrin Smith (q.v.), then with Harvey Orrin
Smith and William Linton (qq.v.). They engraved
numerous cuts to the recently established Illustrated
London News, from their London office at 85 Hatton
Garden which by 1849 Linton had abandoned and
Horace Harral occupied in partnership with Smith as
Smith and Harral (POD,1849). By 1854 Horace Harral
had his own London office at 17 Essex Street, Strand
(POD,1854-55), then 11 Serjeant's Inn, Fleet Street,
EC (POD,1856-59). Both offices were shared with
W.L.Thomas (q.v.). He then moved to his best
known address, 4 Palgrave Place, Strand, WC
(POD,1861-81). By 1882 he appears in the directories
as Horace Harral Downey, Temple Chambers, Falcon
Court (POD,1883-91). Harral was a friend of Henry
Vizetelly (q.v.) for whom he engraved portraits of
artists for his Illustrated Times,1858; he also
continued to engrave for the Illustrated London News,
1850-71, notably after various paintings, or portraits
of artists and pastoral landscapes by G.B.Goddard.
He also engraved for London Society, after Charles
Keene,1868, Helen Paterson, 1870, and T.Morten;
although Reid claimed that his engraving for this 'is
rarely so satisfactory as that of Dalziel and Swain'.
He also engraved after Charles Green's 'Thinking
and Wishing' in Churchman's Family Magazine,
1864, and after M.E.Edwards to Trollope's The
Claverings, the Cornhill,1866-67. He became
associated with the new magazine, The Graphic
from 1870, and engraved after various artists
including Helen Paterson, whom he had promoted as
its first woman staff member. His book engravings
included cuts after Edward Duncan, praised by Bohn
in Chatto and Jackson; to Bohn's illustrated edition

of Southey's Life of Nelson; after George Thomas to
an illustrated edition of Longfellow's Poems; and after
Edward H.Wehnert (q.v.), to Coleridge's Ancient
Mariner,1857. He engraved cuts to Burns' Poems;
Campbell's Pleasures of Hope; and, after Charles
Keene, Favourite English Poems,1870, which Reid
criticised for 'its hardness and tightness'. Harral
was also a competent etcher and exhibited plates at
the Royal Academy, 1862-70. The British Museum
owns his engravings after Charles Keene; and a
proof series of mountain views. He signed his
engravings: 'H.HARRAL Sc', 'HORACE HARRAL'.
[Bénézit; Reid; Graves; TB; Hake; McLean,
Victorian Book Design; H.Vizetelly, Glances
Back; Chatto; Print Collector's Quarterly,1930;
for a list of his etchings see Volume I]

HARRIS
(see Skidmore and Harris)

HARRIS, Thomas fl.1888-90
London wood engraver, who worked at 10 Bolt Court,
Fleet Street, EC (POD,1888-90).

HARRISON, George fl.1890-93
London wood engraver, who worked at 22 Chancery
Lane, WC (POD,1890-91), which had previously
been the office of Henry Harrison (q.v.). By 1893
he had moved to 3 Tudor Street, EC (POD,1893).

HARRISON, Henry fl.1842-88
English wood engraver, who worked in Paris about
1842, engraving with George Housman Thomas
(q.v.) for various French books and magazines.
Gusman lists several including: Jules Janin, L'Ane
Mort,1842, engraved with Thompson, Gray,
Quartley, Gowland, Thomas Williams and J.Orrin
Smith (qq.v.); some of the 150 vignettes to La Normandie,
1843, engraved with Quartley; cuts to Dr Lemaout,
Le Jardin des Plantes,1842-43, engraved with
Godard, Landells and Thompson (qq.v.). Harrison also
taught wood engraving to the noted French engraver
Antoine Bertrand (q.v.). He moved back to England
and established an engraving office at 255 Strand
(POD,1848), later forming a partnership as Cutts
and Harrison (q.v.), then continuing on his own at
4 Bouverie Street, Fleet Street, EC (POD,1876-81).
By 1884 he had moved to 22 Chancery Lane, WC
(POD,1884-88), the firm eventually being replaced
by George Harrison (q.v.).
[see Gusman; also White]

HARRISON, John Joseph and Company fl.1888-1910
London firm of draughtsmen and wood engravers, who
worked at 43 New Oxford Street, WC (POD,1888-89).
Then the name and number changed to Harrison
Brothers, 83 New Oxford Street, WC (POD,1896-1901).
They were still engraving after the turn of the century,
at 7 Great Queen Street, WC (POD,1910).

HARRISON, Joseph William R. fl.1883-84
London wood engraver, who worked at 4 Crane
Court, Fleet Street, EC (POD,1883-84).

HARRISON, Margaret
Wood engraver and illustrator, featured by A.L.Baldry
in his article, 'The Future of Wood Engraving',
Studio,1898. Baldry reproduced her engraving of a
design for E.E.M.Creak (p.13), alongside work by
Bernard Sleigh (q.v.). She signed her work:
'M E H'.

HARRISON, Samuel fl.1880s
Provincial wood engraver, who worked at 46 Bull
Street, Birmingham (Kelly's,1889).

HARRISON, William Charles fl.1856-71
London wood engraver, who worked at 32 De Beauvoir
Square (POD,1856), 268 Strand (POD,1866-70),
shared with W.F.Measom and R.H.Moore (qq.v.),
and 30 Tavistock Street, WC (POD,1871).

HARRISON and Company fl.1880s
London wood engraving firm, with an office at
174 Fleet Street, EC (POD,1882). Fincham lists a
bookplate engraved by them for George Trueman.

HARRISON and Gray fl.1876-80
Provincial firm of draughtsmen and wood engravers,
with offices at 8A Lord Street and 10 St George's
Crescent, Liverpool (Kelly's,1876-80).

HART, Mark M. fl.1836-39
London wood engraver, who worked at 19 Maidenhead
Court, Wood Street (Pigot,1836), 25 Edmund Place,
Aldersgate Street (Pigot,1838), and 20 Gower Street,
Bedford Square (Pigot,1839).

HART, Robert fl.1833-69
London wood engraver, who worked at 20 Leigh
Street, Red Lion Square (Robson,1833), 44 Devonshire Street, Queen Square (Pigot,1836),
13 Gloucester Street, Queen Square (Pigot,1838-39),
then changed to 15 Gloucester Street (Pigot,1851-62),
33A Red Lion Square, WC (POD,1863-68), and
17 Great Ormond Street, WC (POD,1869), which he
shared with George Evans (q.v.). Hart began his
career as did Henry Harrison (q.v.), engraving for
various French publications. Gusman lists his cuts
after Théophile Fragonard to Les Evangiles,1838;
some of the 300 cuts to Dr Wordsworth's La Grèce
Pittoresque et Historique,1841; and numerous cuts
to the French magazine L'Image,1847, where his
work appeared alongside fellow English engravers
Gowland and Sears (qq.v.)

HARTSHORN, Edward Townsend fl.1861-90
London wood engraver, who worked at the workshop
8 Dane's Inn, Strand, WC (POD,1861-62), with fellow
engravers F.Anderson, G.Armstrong, C.M.Gorway,
J.H.Rimbault and J.Watkins (qq.v.). He moved to
another workshop address, 123 Chancery Lane
(POD,1864-82), shared with D.J.Anderson,
W.H.Coldwell, R.Collins, R.Cooper and T.Powney
(qq.v.). By 1884 he had appeared at 21 St Bride
Street, EC (POD,1884-85), then at 142 Fleet Street,
EC (POD,1890). His engravings included a portrait,
Robert Vernon, after Henry Pickersgill to the
People's Journal. This is now in the British Museum.
[Hake]

HARVEY, William 1796-1866
Wood engraver and prolific draughtsman illustrator.
He was born in Newcastle on 13 July 1796, the son
of the baths keeper at the Westgate. At fourteen he
was apprenticed to the wood engraver Thomas Bewick
(q.v.) serving from 27 November 1809 to 9 September
1817. He learned to engrave with fellow pupils
W.W.Temple, John Armstrong and Isaac Nicholson
(qq.v.), but since he excelled in drawing as well as
engraving, Bewick gave him Robert Johnson's (q.v.)
drawings to transfer onto wood blocks. Chatto and
Jackson claimed that one of his best cuts during this
period was a vignette engraving for the title-page of
Cheviot: A Poetical Fragment,1817, engraved after
his own drawing. Bewick was very pleased with his
apprentice, describing him as 'one of the first in
excellence...who both as an engraver & designer,
stands pre-eminent at this day'. He gave him a
copy of his History of British Birds on 1 January
1815, with a letter which sought to direct Harvey's
future: 'Don't trouble yourself about thanking me for
them; but, instead of doing so, let those books put
you in mind of the duties you have to perform through
life.' However, at the end of Harvey's apprenticeship
he left for London, where from September 1817 he
studied drawing with B.R.Haydon and anatomy under
Charles Bell, with fellow pupils Lance, Eastlake
and Landseer. He maintained contact with his old
engraving master throughout his life, however, and
by 1818 was to transfer many of Robert Johnson's
designs on wood, and to work with W.Temple on
Bewick's Aesop's Fables. As Bewick wrote
(5 February 1818) 'I hope to derive some assistance
in the cutting [of] the Fables from a young man who
left me last September. As he expressed a wish to
continue to work at them for me, I gave him a number
of designs with him to London, which I had, on his
acct. on the wood with a finish and accuracy of fine
miniature paintings, and flattered myself that I cou'd
put a finishing hand to them when he returned them;
...' (Memoir,p.244). During his training with
Haydon he drew and engraved in imitation of copper
engraving the much praised 'Assassination of
Dentatus', published in 1821. This was printed
from a large block (15" x 11.5", now in the British
Museum) formed by joining together seven separate
pieces of wood. It took three years to complete and,

due to poor printing, only a few impressions were taken. Haydon touched up the proofs with Indian ink to mask the obvious block joins. This engraving was regarded by Chatto and Jackson as 'unquestionably one of the most elaborately engraved wood-cuts that has ever appeared. It scarcely, however, can be considered a successful specimen of the art; for though the execution in many parts be superior to anything of the kind, either of earlier or more recent times, the cut, as a whole, is rather an attempt to rival copper-plate engraving than a perfect specimen of engraving on wood, displaying the peculiar advantages and excellences of art within its own legitimate bounds. More has been attempted than can be efficiently represented by means of wood engraving.' The wood engraver John Jackson (q.v.) praises Harvey's engraved reflected light, and points out that areas of the print, the right leg for example, 'is perhaps the most beautiful specimen of cross-hatching that ever was executed on wood; and in my opinion it is the best engraved part of the whole subject'. The work was to set a new style in elaborate engravings and influenced a new generation of wood engravers. It was given a substantial amount of praise in treatises and manuals of the wood engraver's art: W.J.Linton in his Masters of Wood Engraving, 1889, called it 'the most daringly ambitious wood engraving ever done'. Ironically the 'Dentatus' engraving also heralded the end of Harvey's engraving career. He turned instead to designing first for copper-plate then for wood engravers. On the death of John Thurston (q.v.) in 1822, he became his successor as chief designer for the wood engraving trade. He produced 3,000 illustrations to numerous books in the decade of 1828-38 alone, and his drawings on wood were engraved by the major wood engravers of the day, allowing for the first time the element of speed and impersonality in engraved illustration that was to sweep the Victorian print world. The eventual toll on such a prolific career was a total lack of humour in his subjects, a dogged insistence on revived rather than modern subjects, and a mannered elegance that soon slipped out of fashion. His first success as designer was his intricate drawings on wood to Henderson's History of Ancient and Modern Wines, 1824, which Harvey also engraved in a delicate black-line manner from finished drawings which he made directly on the block. Then followed the first and second series of Northcote's Fables, 1828, 1833, which Harvey drew onto wood from the composite pasted-down illustrations first collected and arranged by Northcote, only inventing the tailpieces and initials. His work was engraved by a collection of the 'most eminent engravers in England', among them John Jackson (q.v.) who engraved 148 cuts. Then came The Tower Menagerie, 1828; Zoological Gardens, 1830-31; Children in the Wood, 1831; Blind Beggar of Bethnal Green, 1832, engraved by Charlton

Nesbit (q.v.); Story without an End; Pictorial Prayer Book; and Lane's Thousand and One Nights, 1840, drawn with Lane's advice about costumes and oriental accessories. By 1840 Harvey had become the major draughtsman illustrator on wood for engravers. He worked in London, appearing in the directories at 24 Norfolk Street (Pigot, 1822-23), where he built up a workshop which included the young John Orrin Smith (q.v.). His drawings influenced a new generation of engravers, such as Edmund Evans (q.v.) who remembered buying Harvey's Northcote's Fables with his first earnings. Indeed the Art Union for 1839 claimed that 'The history of wood engraving for some years past, is almost a record of the works of his pencil'. He had a profound influence on John Gilbert and George Cruikshank (qq.v.) and a negative influence (notably for his lack of humour) on Kenny Meadows (q.v.) ('Beauty was Harvey's evil genius, and grace was his damnation'). He reached a greater audience when employed by the enterprising publisher Charles Knight (q.v.), who commissioned drawings for his various and prolific popular books and magazines: the Penny Magazine, 1842-45; Knight's London, 1841; Knight's Farmer's Library, 1847; and the 'Land we Live In' series. These were generally wood engraved by Knight's standard engravers, T.Williams, M.A.Williams, Wright and Folkard, S.Williams, J.Orrin Smith, or John Jackson (qq.v.). Harvey also drew for Punch, 1841-42, although his third version of the cover was rejected as too serious and his initial letters considered too graceful. He provided various decorative and political drawings for the Illustrated London News, 1843-59. Henry Vizetelly (q.v.) recalled how Harvey was given 'carte blanche to draw from life all subjects from London's zoos to the Tower'. The Dalziel brothers remembered how Harvey supplied them with a constant flow of drawings from 1839 to his death. Harvey remained an influential figure for over twenty years, with the only major competition during the period coming from the French. Chatto and Jackson concluded that 'As a designer on wood, he is decidedly superior to the majority of artists of the present day; and to his excellence in this respect, wood engraving is chiefly indebted for the very great encouragement which it has of late received in this country'. He represented a pinnacle of the fine engraved style of the 'Bewick School' which was by the 1840s being supplanted by the more dominant black-line engravers with commercial rather than fine art pretensions. His adherence to copper-lined accuracy in his engravings restricted his tonal range to greys, unlike the more varied range of his master Bewick. For this reason W.J.Linton, in Masters of Wood Engraving, called Harvey 'our one draughtsman', with secondary abilities as an engraver. He urged his readers not to 'underrate him as an engraver, however much I object to his influence as designer upon the engraver's art'.

Harvey lived in Richmond most of his later life, and died at Prospect Lodge on 13 January 1866, 'an amiable, unpretending man, and the last survivor of Bewick's pupils (DNB). The British Museum owns a large collection of Harvey's designs including Dalziel engravings, 1839-47; and proofs of the 'Dentatus' engraving; the Bodleian Library owns several to Charles Knight's series.
[For a full list of illustrated work see Houfe; British Library catalogue; see also Muir; Chatto; Slater; Hake; Redgrave; Bliss; McLean, Victorian Book Design; Evans Reminiscences; Vizetelly, Glances Back; TB; DNB; Nagler; A.Dobson, T.Bewick and his Pupils,1884; I.Bain, T.Bewick Memoir; Hind; Linton, Masters of Wood Engraving; Dalziels' Record]

HASLEHURST, George fl.1840s
Provincial wood engraver, who worked at Castle Street, Sheffield (Pigot,1841).

HASTIE, William Edward fl.1876-92
London wood engraver, who worked at 33 Essex Street, Strand, WC (POD,1878-80), once the office of W.J.Linton (q.v.), but which Hastie shared with R.H.Keene and W.J.Palmer (qq.v.). He moved to 33 Fetter Lane, EC (POD,1881-92), where R.H.Keene joined him again briefly in 1885. Hastie engraved for the Illustrated London News, after various 'special' reporters' sketches, such as a Malayan landscape, 1 January 1876; 'Royal Visit to India'; and 'Craft on the Hooghly', 22 January 1876.

HASWELL
Little is known of this draughtsman on wood, landscape artist and designer of initial letters of great detail, in the style of Richard Doyle (q.v.). He contributed wood engraved designs in the Illustrated London Magazine,1853-54.

HATCH, Charles fl.1880s
London draughtsman, who worked at 33 Great Queen Street, WC (Kelly's,1880). Fincham lists a 'Hatch, London' engraver of an armorial bookplate for Abbot, dated 1820 and signed 'Hatch 11 Lisle St'.

HATTON, Helen Howard (Mrs W.H.Margetson) 1860-?
Draughtsman illustrator, watercolourist and pastellist. She was born in Bristol, studied at the Royal Academy Schools and at Colarossi's in Paris, and worked mainly in Berkshire. She drew wood engraved illustrations for the English Illustrated Magazine,1885-86; to J.Hatton's 'Adventures on the Equator', engraved by J.D.Cooper (q.v.); and J.Hatton's 'Yarmouth and the Broads', engraved by O.Jahyer, Waterlow and Sons, H.F.Davey, and O.Lacour (qq.v.). She also exhibited watercolours at the Royal Academy, the Royal Institute of Painters in Watercolours, the Royal Institute of Painters in

Oil-Colours and the New Watercolour Society.
[Bénézit; Houfe; TB]

HAUCK, Oscar fl.1893-98
London wood engraver, who worked at 90 Chancery Lane, WC (POD,1893-98).

HAY, E. fl.1852-53
The British Museum owns proof wood engravings by the Dalziel Brothers (q.v.) after small scientific drawings by this artist. They were engraved 1852-53.

HAY, George 1831-1913
Draughtsman illustrator, historical and subject painter. He was born in Edinburgh in 1831, studied at the Royal Scottish Academy School and the Trustees Gallery, and worked as an architect before turning to painting pictures of Scottish life and history. He drew some of the forty total wood engravings in Pen and Pencil Pictures from the Poets,1866; contributed to Poems and Songs by Robert Burns,1875; and later illustrated part of Scott's Red Gauntlet,1894. He was elected ARSA,1869 and RSA,1876, and was secretary 1881-1907. He died on 31 August 1913.
[Houfe]

HAY and Peach fl.1885-89
London wood engraving firm, with an office at 30 Holborn, EC (POD,1885-89), also the office of W.Arrowsmith (q.v.). By 1890 Hay had left and joined with Godart as Godart and Hay (q.v.).

HAYDON, G.H. fl.1860-92
Occasional draughtsman, barrister and traveller. He went to Australia early in his career (his sketches appeared in Australian Illustrated about 1876) but had returned to England by 1860, where he was a member of the Langham Sketch Club, and a friend of Charles Keene and John Leech (qq.v.). He contributed twenty-two sketches and initials to Punch,1860-62, up until Leech's death, and served as a model for future angling cartoons there. He also served as steward of Bridewell and Bethlem Hospitals.
[Spielmann; Houfe]

HAYES, James fl.1860s
London wood engraver, who worked at 30 Stangate, Lambeth, S (POD,1860). He may be a relation of the Hayes family of painters.

HAYWOOD, William fl.1899-1910
London wood engraver, who worked at 36 Furnival Street, EC (POD,1899-1901), then 10 Bolt Court, Fleet Street, EC (POD,1910).

HAZARD and Bowcher fl.1870s
London wood engraving firm, with an office at 28 Stonecutter Street, EC. By 1876 John Bowcher (q.v.) had broken from his partner and was working

independently from the same address.

HEADINGTON, James John fl.1875-1900
London wood engraver, who worked at 40 Wellington
Street, Strand, WC (POD,1875-93) then at 236 High
Holborn, WC (POD,1894).

HEARD, Isaac fl.1880s
Provincial wood engraver, who worked at 38 S.Castle
Street, Liverpool (Kelly's,1889).

HEATH
(see Butterworth and Heath)

HEATH, Henry fl.1824-50
Draughtsman, lithographer and etcher of political
caricatures. He worked from 1824-30 in a loose,
coarse style, then imitated John Doyle 'HB' (q.v.),
etched in the style of Cruikshank (q.v.), and
lithographed in the style of Seymour. He is listed
here for a single cartoon drawing on wood for Punch,
1842. He emigrated to Australia to be replaced on
Punch by R.J.Hamerton (q.v.), who signed his
cartoons 'BH' to be as near as possible to 'the old
favourite' Henry Heath's 'HH'.
[Spielmann]

HEAVISIDE, Edwin fl.1866-77
London wood engraver, who worked at 27 Fetter
Lane, Holborn, EC (POD,1866), shared with
C.Bruwier (q.v.), then disappeared from directories
until 1876, when he was working at 5 Wine Office
Court, EC (POD,1876-77), shared with William H.
Burnett (q.v.). He is probably the brother of the
noted engravers John and Thomas Heaviside (qq.v.).

HEAVISIDE, John Smith 1812-64
Wood and metal engraver. He was born in Stockton-
on-Tees in 1812, the son of a builder, and did not
begin engraving until the age of twenty-six. He
worked in Oxford, primarily for publishers of
antiquarian works, spending much of his time on the
archaeological books of John Henry Parker, then set
up an engraving office in London at 6 Bellevue
Cottage, Camden Street, Camden Town (POD,1856),
then 5 Sutherland Terrace, Caledonian Road
(POD,1857). He died in Kentish Town on 3 October
1864, aged fifty-two. He was the brother of fellow
engravers Edwin and Thomas Heaviside (qq.v.).
Redgrave spells his surname 'Heavyside'.
[TB; Bryan; Redgrave; Houfe]

HEAVISIDE, Thomas fl.1849-51
Wood engraver, brother of Edwin and John Heaviside
(qq.v.). He engraved portraits of Thomas Bewick
after William Nicholson (originally published 1816);
Robert Owen after a photograph; and also various
small cuts to the Illustrated London News,1849-51,
including a crude use of the graver on figures set

against a flat grey background in 'Scandal', after the
painting by Abraham Solomon, a half-page engraving,
15 February 1851.
[Houfe; Hake]

HEBBLETHWAITE, Esmond fl.1871-75
London wood engraver, who worked at 2 King's Road,
Bedford Row (POD,1871-75), an address which he
shared with the noted engraver Thomas Gilks (q.v.).

HEBBLETHWAITE, Henry fl.1880s
London draughtsman, who worked from 1 Murray
Street, Camden Square, NW (Kelly's,1880). He may
be related to the illustrator H.Sydney Hebblethwaite,
noted by Thorpe for his promise and invention,
notably in his drawings to Pick-Me-Up,1899.

HEDLEY, Ralph c1851-1913
Wood engraver, genre, portrait and landscape
painter. He was born in Richmond, Yorkshire in
1851 (TB), 1848 (Waters) and was an evening pupil
at the Newcastle Art and Life School (later the Bewick
Club). He set up as a wood engraver at 11 Nesham's
Buildings, Newbridge Street, Newcastle (Kelly's,
1872-80). He also exhibited paintings at the Royal
Academy from 1879-1902, was a member of the
Royal Society of British Artists, and president of
the Bewick Club and Vice-President of the South
Shields Art Club. He lived at 22 New Bridge Street,
Newcastle, and died on 12 June 1913.
[TB; Waters; Graves; Who's Who,1914)

HEELEY
(see Burton and Heeley)

HEFFER, Edward A., of Liverpool fl.1860-85
Draughtsman, decorative designer and architect,
who contributed designs for wood engravings to the
Illustrated London News,1860-61.

HEMMONS, William C. fl.1880s
Provincial wood engraver, who worked at 23 Stephen's
Avenue, Bristol (Kelly's,1889).

HEMY, Charles Napier 1841-1917
Marine, landscape and still life illustrator and
painter. He was born in Newcastle-upon-Tyne on
24 May 1841 and studied with William Bell Scott (q.v.).
He sailed round the world, 1850-52 and entered the
Dominican order, studying at Newcastle and Lyons. He
then gave up the religious life for art, studying in
Antwerp under Henri Leys, and settled in London in 1870,
then in Falmouth. Hemy achieved a reputation for his
nautical paintings and drawings, which he contributed
to the English Illustrated Magazine,1883-87. These
included illustrations to 'An Unsentimental Journey
through Cornwall', 1883-84, engraved on wood by
O.Lacour, R.Paterson, W.M.R.Quick, E.Gascoigne,
J.D.Cooper, E.Schladitz, Balecz Istvan, O.Jahyer,

C.Barbant, and H.F.Davey (qq.v.). Hemy also exhibited paintings at the New Gallery, the Royal Institute of Painters in Watercolours and the Royal Scottish Academy; and was elected RWS,1897, ARA,1898, and RA,1910. He died on 30 September 1917.
[Wood; TB; Bénézit; Houfe]

HENDERSON, Frederick fl.1870s
London wood engraver, who worked at 32 Fleet Street, EC (POD,1878).

HENDERSON, George Lewis fl.1880s
London wood engraver, who worked at 32 King Street, Cheapside, EC (POD,1888).

HENLEY, Lionel Charles 1843-c1893
Draughtsman illustrator and genre painter. He was born in London in 1843, and studied art in Düsseldorf, but returned to England where he drew on wood for various magazines. These include London Society, 1865; Fun,1865 (engraved by the Dalziels (q.v.)); Foxe's Book of Martyrs,1867; and The Graphic,1870. He also exhibited regularly from 1862 at the Royal Academy, the Royal Society of British Artists, to which he was elected member in 1879, and the Royal Institute of Painters in Oil-Colours. The British Museum owns proof engravings by the Dalziel Brothers,1865-66.
[Houfe; White]

HENNEQUIN, A.Hauger fl.1870s
Wood engraver of French subjects for the Illustrated London News. He engraved the double-page, 'A Fight on the Railway', after De Neuville, drawn on wood by G.Massias, 15 August 1874.

HENNESSY, William John 1839-1917
Draughtsman illustrator, landscape and genre painter. He was born in Thomastown, Ireland in 1839, and after an abortive uprising fled to America with his family in 1848, remaining there until 1870. He studied at the National Academy in New York, 1856 and became a member in 1863 (1861, Fielding). His early works were engraved by his friend there, W.J.Linton (q.v.). Linton admired his 'romantic antecedents, a flamboyant manner, and a highly finished artistic technique'. Hennessy provided the friendship and artistic inspiration which Linton had once received from the illustrators, Scott, Duncan and Wehnert. Linton engraved after Hennessy's drawings to J.G.Holand's Katrina,1869; Edwin Booth in Twelve Dramatic Characters,1870; Elizabeth Browning's Lady Geraldine's Courtship,1869-70; and numerous drawings to Linton's magazine, American Enterprise, from 1870. It was in that year that Hennessy settled in Sussex and Normandy but he continued to send drawings for Linton to engrave in America. Later his son married Linton's daughter.

He also earned his living drawing on wood for magazines, such as the Illustrated London News; Dark Blue,1871-72; The Graphic,1872-76,1880; Punch,1873,1875 ('they were by no means of the excellence to which the artist afterwards attained', Spielmann); and Good Words,1880 ('among his best', Houfe); also English Illustrated Magazine,1884-92, notably illustrations to 'Calvados' by Mary Mather, engraved on wood by O.Jahyer, H.F.Davey, E.J.Ohme, and W.B.Gardner (qq.v.). Hennessy also exhibited at the Royal Academy, the Dudley Gallery, the Grosvenor Gallery, the Royal Hibernian Academy, and the Royal Institute of Painters in Oil-Colours, to which he was elected member in 1902.
[F.B.Smith, W.J.Linton,1973,pp.176-7; TB; Houfe]

HENNING, Archibald Samuel ?-1864
Draughtsman and comic illustrator. He was born in Edinburgh, the son of the sculptor John Henning, and assisted his father on various projects in London. He began as the first Punch cartoonist and contributed drawings and a wrapper design from 1841, the first, 17 July 1841 'roughly done but not ill-cut' by Landells (q.v.). He lasted out the following year, although his lethargy and loose slap-dash style soon forced him to leave Punch. Nevertheless he continued to draw on wood for various early magazines, the Squib, Great Gun, Joe Miller the Younger, Man in the Moon, the Comic Times, and the Illustrated London Magazine, 1854. Such work earned him the admiration of the wood engraver W.J.Linton (q.v.), who described Henning as 'a fair and prolific draughtsman on wood' (Memoirs,p.72). Houfe suggests that he may have turned to medical and natural history drawings by the 1850s.
[TB; Bénézit; Houfe; Evans Reminiscences; Spielmann]

HERBERT, Robert fl.1860s
London wood engraver, who worked at 7 Dane's Inn, Strand (POD,1861), which he shared with W.A.Shepherd and C.Stevens (qq.v.).
[LeBlanc]

HERDMAN, Robert 1829-88
Occasional draughtsman and painter of portraits and historical subjects. He was born in Rattray on 17 September 1829 and was a pupil of R.S.Lauder at the Edinburgh Trustees Academy. He travelled to Italy,1855-56, establishing himself as a portrait painter from 1861, the year of his ARSA election. He also exhibited at the Royal Academy and drew illustrations with Birket Foster for wood engravings in Poems and Songs of Robert Burns,1875. He died in Edinburgh on 10 January 1888.
[Houfe; White]

HERKOMER, Sir Hubert von 1849-1914
Draughtsman illustrator, painter and etcher, best
known for his drawings of social realistic subjects
for The Graphic. He was born in Waal, Bavaria on
26 May 1849, and settled in England in 1857,
studying art at South Kensington from 1866. He first
began drawing on wood blocks which he sent to the
Dalziel Brothers (q.v.) who remembered them as
'not very remarkable'. They accepted one ('Lonely
Jane') which appeared in Good Words for the Young,
1870, and on the strength of this, and drawings in
the Quiver,1868, and Sunday Magazine,1870, he
became cartoon draughtsman for the new comic
paper, the Censor, at £2 a week, but the paper
soon folded. Finally he was introduced to W.L.Thomas
(q.v.), the editor of The Graphic, who
was intent on commissioning illustrated subjects
from the artists themselves (not, as previously
done, from the engravers, who commissioned the
drawings themselves). When Herkomer showed him
his wood block drawing 'Gypsies on Wimbledon
Common', Thomas accepted it and any further
drawings for £8 a block, and from then on, Herkomer
recalled, he 'never lacked work'. His work appeared
in The Graphic,1870-79, where his drawings were
wood engraved by C.Roberts, M.Uhlrich and
Froment (qq.v.), and were very popular. Van Gogh
considered Herkomer to be the best of The Graphic
artists and collected his engravings. Herkomer
produced only seven double-page engravings during
the entire period in which he worked for The Graphic.
His most successful were: 'Christmas in a Workhouse',
Christmas 1876, engraved by C.Robert, and his
'Heads of the People' series, 1879, engraved by
M.Uhlrich. He was asked by Thomas Hardy to
illustrate Tess of the d'Urbervilles for The Graphic,
1891, but of the twenty-five wood engravings,
Herkomer drew only six, farming out the remainder
to his students. During his period on The Graphic he
also drew for wood engravings in the Illustrated
London News,1871-73; London Society,1872; the
Cornhill,1872; the Dalziels' Fun; and a title-page
for Black and White. He also etched but admitted his
wood block drawing had hindered this. He was later
noted for his large paintings of the poor and down-
trodden which he produced and exhibited at the
Grosvenor Gallery, the New Gallery, the Royal
Society of British Artists, the Royal Society of
Painter-Etchers and Engravers, the Royal Hibernian
Academy, the Royal Institute of Painters in Oil-
Colours, the Royal Scottish Academy, the Royal
Watercolour Society and the Royal Academy. He was
elected ARA,1879 and RA,1890. He was knighted in
1907 and died in Budleigh Salterton, 31 March 1914.
[For a description of his etchings and bibliography
see Volume I; also Houfe; DNB; A.Jackson,
Illustrators of Thomas Hardy,1981; Dalziels' Record;
TB (substantial entry and bibliography)]

HEROND, L.J.
French draughtsman illustrator, who contributed
scenes of Paris to Cassell's Illustrated Family
Paper,1857.

HERRING, Benjamin ?-1871
Draughtsman, sporting artist, son of the painter of
equestrian subjects, J.F.Herring (q.v.). He drew
for wood engravings in the Illustrated London News,
1850-60,1864. He also exhibited sporting pictures
at the British Institution and the Royal Society of
British Artists,1861-63.

HERRING, John Frederick 1795-1865
Draughtsman illustrator and painter of sporting
subjects. He was born in Surrey in 1795 and worked
as a coach painter, and later as a horse portraitist.
He contributed drawings for wood engraving in The
Sporting Review,1842-46; the Illustrated London
News,1844-45,1864; the Illustrated Times,1859;
and Bell's Life in London. He exhibited paintings at
the British Institution, the Royal Academy and the
Royal Society of British Artists. He died in 1865.
His son was the illustrator Benjamin Herring (q.v.).
[Houfe]

HETHERINGTON, William fl.1870s
Provincial wood engraver, who worked at 67 Villa
Street, Hockley, Birmingham (Kelly's,1876).

HEWITT, Charles fl.1880s
Provincial wood engraver, who worked at 14 Broad
Street Corner, Birmingham (Kelly's,1889).

HEWITT, George fl.1868-96
London draughtsman and wood engraver, who worked
at 66 (28) Ludgate Hill, EC (POD,1868-96), shared
with A.H.Lindsell (q.v.).

HEWITT, Henry fl.1894-1910
London wood engraver, who worked at 61 Fleet
Street, EC (POD,1894-1901), originally the office
of E.Duvergier (q.v.).

HEYWOOD, John fl.1872-1900
Provincial wood engraver, who worked at 141 and
143 Deansgate and 1, 3, 5, Brasenose Street,
Manchester (Kelly's,1872-76), then Cornbrook
Works, Manchester (Kelly's,1900).

HICKS, George Elger 1824-1914
Occasional draughtsman on wood, genre and portrait
painter. He was born in Lymington in Hampshire in
1824, abandoned a doctor's career for painting and
trained at the Bloomsbury and Royal Academy
Schools in 1844. He began as a draughtsman
illustrator on metal for Campbell's Gertrude of
Wyoming,1846 engraved by William Hole for the
Art Union (not to be confused with the Routledge-

Dalziel version,1857); then on wood blocks for
Adams' Sacred Allegories,1856, engraved by
W.T.Green (q.v.) ('had W.T.Green engraved no
other blocks, he might be ranked as a great crafts-
man on the evidence of these alone', White); also for
Bloomfield's The Farmer's Boy,1857; and Favourite
Modern Ballads,1859 (mentioned by Bohn in Chatto
and Jackson). Hicks was also a noted painter of
Victorian life, and exhibited at the Grosvenor
Gallery, the Royal Academy,1848-1905, the Royal
Scottish Academy. He was elected member of the
Royal Society of British Artists in 1889. He died in
London in 1914.
[Chatto; Clement; Bénézit (as Edgar); TB (as Elgar);
White]

HICKSON, Charles fl.1800s
Engraving apprentice to Thomas Bewick and Beilby
(qq.v.), at Newcastle from 18 April 1795 until
February 1800, when he 'absconded'. Bewick
probably recalls the turbulent period of Hickson's
training in the veiled description (Bewick Memoir,
p.237) of an unnamed apprentice, 'one of the most
impudent--malignant & worst apprentices we ever
had'. Fincham lists an armorial bookplate for
George C.Harvey engraved by 'Hickson', dated 1820.

HIDES and Spiers fl.1890s
Provincial firm of draughtsmen, with an office at
63 Norfolk Street, Sheffield (Kelly's,1900).

HILDIBRAND 1824-97
French wood engraver, born in Paris in 1824, the
engraving pupil of Leloir and Best (q.v.). He made
his Salon début in 1866 with two engravings after
Doré (q.v.) for his Dante, and became known for his
interpretative wood engravings of that artist. Some,
like plates to Doré's London: A Pilgrimage,1872
were published in London. He also engraved after
Giradet and Grandville, and worked for the Paris
publisher Hachette. He died in 1897.
[McLean, Victorian Book Design; Gusman]

HILL, Edmund (Hill and Company) fl.1875-1910
London wood engraver, with an office at 48 later 45
Essex Street, Strand, WC (POD,1875-1901), which
became Hill and Company by 1890 and moved later
to 41-42 Shoe Lane, EC (POD,1910). Hill engraved
portraits of George Augustus Selwyn, Bishop of
Lichfield, after a photograph (for a newspaper) and
a bust portrait of the Victorian painter Hubert
Herkomer, for the Queen. Both are in the British
Museum.
[Hake]

HILL, William fl.1880s
Provincial wood engraver, who worked at
43 Armoury Square, Bristol (Kelly's,1889).

HIND, R. fl.1853-55
London wood engraver, who worked at 12 later 13
Brewer Street, Goswell Road (POD,Hodgson's,
1853-55).

HIND, Robert Neal 1817-79
London draughtsman on wood, who worked at 11 Bolt
Court, Fleet Street, EC (Kelly's,1872-76), which he
shared with William Joyce (q.v.). The British
Museum owns a lithograph of his design. TB claims
'he drew for books and magazines on the wood block'.
[Bénézit; TB]

HINDE, Alfred fl.1880s
Provincial wood engraver, who worked at 44 Dudley
Street, Wolverhampton (Kelly's,1880).

HINE, Harry 1845-1941
Draughtsman on wood and watercolourist. He was
born in London on 27 February 1845, the son of the
artist H.G.Hine (q.v.). He is listed here for his
drawings on wood commissioned by the engraver
Edmund Evans (q.v.) for the 'Professor Pepper'
series, published by George Routledge. Hine was
also a painter who exhibited at the Royal Academy,
the Royal Society of British Artists and the Royal
Institute of Painters in Oil-Colours, and was
elected member of the Royal Institute of Painters
in Watercolours in 1877. He died on 20 October
1941.
[Evans Reminiscences]

HINE, Henry George 1811-95
Prominent early draughtsman on wood, and
watercolourist of coastal scenes. He was born in
Brighton on 15 August 1811, the son of a coachman,
and taught himself to draw and paint from nature by
painting the local Sussex scenery. He went to London
and was apprenticed to the stipple engraver Henry
Meyer (see Volume I). Then he worked for two years
in Rouen, France, before working for Ebenezer
Landells (q.v.) as a draughtsman on wood. Landells
started the paper Cosmorama and sent Hine out to
draw the London Docks on a wood block for
reproduction in the paper. Hine had first received
instructions for drawing on the block from Mr Wood
(q.v.), 'a master-engraver of the time' (Spielmann).
He began by drawing a comic dustman and his dog in
the block margin. Landells admired this and steered
Hine from landscapes to drawing comic figures for
Punch, for which he supplied drawings or 'blackies'
as he called the comic sketches with punning titles,
from 1841-44. He drew directly on the block,
sometimes from Landells' suggestions, and became
the chief stock-artist, and occasional artist of eight
Punch social cartoons, sharing the position
with John Leech (q.v.), as well as first illustrator
of Punch's Almanac. Gradually he was edged out of
Punch and took his pencil elsewhere. He drew

Christmas work for The Great Gun; drawings to Puck; Joe Miller the Younger; Mephystopheles; The Man in the Moon; The Illuminated Magazine,1843-45; the Illustrated London News,1847-55, holiday scenes, engraved by J.Walmsley (q.v.); Illustrated London Magazine,1853-54; and The Welcome Guest,1860. But it was his success as a Punch draughtsman which inspired his many engraver and draughtsman colleagues. Edmund Evans (q.v.) recalled how Hine worked with him at Landells' office in Bidborough Street: 'he had a very free hand and drew figures capitally. (It is a proof of the quantity of drawing on wood Hine made at this time that as a joke we used to open the drawers in which drawings were kept and say "Oh, here is one of Hine's drawings", or "Look here, here is a drawing by Hine", or "Why, see here is a lovely drawing by Hine", and so on for an unlimited time. He made dozens of little silhouette drawings for which I know he was paid 18/- a dozen, for I remember making many drawings in competition for this set of drawings)' (Evans Reminiscences,p.11). Hine also illustrated a serial by Wilkie Collins, 1843-44, and Horace Mayhew's Change for a Shilling, 1848. He gradually tired of drawing on wood and returned to watercolours of landscapes, London life, and of his favourite South Downs, in the style of his mentor Copley Fielding. He exhibited these at the Royal Academy, the Royal Society of British Artists and the Royal Institute of Painters in Watercolours, being elected member there in 1864 and Vice-President 1888-95. He died in London on 16 March 1895, leaving an illustrator son, Harry Hine (q.v.). Edmund Evans eulogised his friend Hine thus: 'he was a very jovial hard working man all his life, every body liked him, and he seem'd to like every body in return' (UCLA). The British Museum owns a series of Hine engravings including Dalziel proofs engraved 1839-47.
[Spielmann; Houfe; Bryan; Bénézit; TB; DNB (with bibliography)]

HIPSLEY, John Henry fl.1872-89
London draughtsman, who worked at 13 Bouverie Street, Fleet Street, EC (Kelly's,1872-80), then 3 Bolt Court, Fleet Street (Kelly's,1889). Houfe lists a John Henry Hipsley, fl.1882-1910, flower painter who worked in Liverpool, 1882, Hemel Hempstead, 1891, and Birmingham, 1899. He contributed to the Strand Magazine,1891.

HIRST, Mrs Dorothy, née Stephenson 1888-?
Wood engraver and oil painter. She was born in Harrogate, Yorkshire on 17 April 1888 but lived and worked in Holyport, Berkshire. She exhibited at the Royal Academy, the International Society of Sculptors, Painters and Gravers, and the Paris Salon.
[Waters]

HISCOCKS, C.W. and Company fl.1898-1901
London firm of wood engravers, known earlier as Baragwanath and Hiscocks (q.v.). They worked from 13 Hatton Garden, EC (POD,1898-1901).

HOBBS, Thomas fl.1865-95
London wood engraver, who worked at 8 Thanet Place, Strand, WC (POD,1865-68); 227 Strand, WC (POD,1875-81), shared with E.Rooker and F.Watkins (qq.v.); Temple Chambers, Falcon Court; and 32 Fleet Street, EC (POD,1886-95), shared with W.J.Hampshire (q.v.).

HODDER, James fl.1870s
London wood engraver, who worked at 100 Strand, WC (POD,1870).

HODDLE, George fl.1872-80
Scottish wood engraver, who worked at 26 Rintoul Place, Leith, N B (Kelly's,1872-80).

HODGE, Edward
(see London Ruling Company)

HODGSON, John Evan 1831-95
Occasional illustrator, painter of landscapes and historical subjects. He was born in London on 1 March 1831, studied at the Royal Academy Schools, and specialised in military and oriental scenes. He contributed a drawing for wood engraving in The Graphic,1876. He was a frequent exhibitor of paintings at the Royal Academy, elected ARA,1873, RA,1880, RE and ROI.

HODGSON, Thomas fl.1776-?
London wood engraver, printer and publisher. He was apprenticed to the Newcastle printer John Wood, and by 1776 was working in London as printer, engraver and publisher at George's Court, Clerkenwell. He was one of three awarded a bounty for wood engraving by the Society for the Promotion of Arts, for his cuts to Sir John Hawkins' History of Music,1776. When Thomas Bewick (q.v.) came to London briefly, Hodgson became his patron and provided engraving work and friendship for the disillusioned Bewick. In his Memoir Bewick recalled his friend thus: 'Having taken a liking to wood ingraving [sic], he employed most of his time in embellishing the endless number printed at the office of the old Ballads & Histories, with rude devises as head-pieces to them--He was a most assiduous, careful & recluse Man--...I understood he employed some Germans as well as myself, to cut blocks for him, he also employed me to make designs, for many of these cuts--when he died he left me a legacy of five pounds--& this was the first money I ever rec[d] that I had not wrought for' (Bewick Memoir,p.70). Hodgson was determined to persuade Bewick to draw and engrave for him, and when Bewick

declared his wish to return to Newcastle Hodgson proposed that 'he would begin by giving me as much as would keep me employed for 2 years' to be engraved there and sent back to London. Bewick's last word on his friend was rather less flattering: he pronounced Hodgson 'pregnant with religion, & pretended goodness, yet is ready to snatch at all advantages'. The British Museum owns a medieval-styled heraldic engraving to a Treatise on Music by Hodgson. [Redgrave; TB; Bénézit]

HOFFLER
Houfe lists this draughtsman on wood, who contributed drawings of Cuba for a wood engraving in the Illustrated London News, 1869. He may be the German, Adolph Hoeffler of Frankfurt, who was in North America, 1848.

HOGGAN, Thomas fl.1890s
London wood engraver, who worked at 12 Ludgate Square, EC (POD, 1894), which had earlier been the office of Pearson, Simmons and Knott (q.v.).

HOLE, Henry Fulke Plantagenet Woolicombe
c1781-c1820
Wood engraver of the Bewick School. He was born about 1781, the son of a Lancashire militia captain, and apprenticed to the wood engraver Thomas Bewick (q.v.) from 24 March to 3 October 1801. He was a fellow pupil with Luke Clennell (q.v.) and during his training he engraved some of Bewick's water birds to his History of British Birds. W.J.Linton dismissed these as 'poor'. He also engraved a bookplate in 1798. Bewick recalled how he had to bail Hole out of jail and how he suffered problems with an illegitimate child. Following his apprenticeship, Hole first remained in Newcastle for a period before moving to Liverpool. There he was patronised by Messrs Roscoe, Capel, Loff, MacCreery and other prominent local figures, occasionally appealing to his old master Bewick for help on the larger engravings. This work included: eight cuts after John Thurston (q.v.) to MacCreery's The Press, 1803, which is regarded as his best work; cuts to an edition of Mrs Hemans' Poems, 1808; some thirty-two designs by Thurston to Ackermann's Religious Emblems, 1809, engraved with R.Austin (q.v.); cuts after W.M.Craig to R.Dodsley's Economy of Human Life, 1810; and Six Views in the Neighbourhood of Liverpool, published in Gregson's Portfolio, 1817. Hole became a member of the Liverpool Academy and contributed to its exhibition, 'An Attempt to restore the Old Method of Crosslining on Wood', 1814. However he eventually inherited his uncle's estate at Ebberley Hall, Devonshire, and succumbing to a life of drinking and leisure, gave up engraving altogether. The date of his death is unclear: most sources list 1820, although most recently Iain Bain gives 1851. [Iain Bain, Watercolours of Thomas Bewick, 1981; Redgrave; Bryan; Bénézit; TB; DNB; Chatto; Fincham;

Linton, Masters of Wood Engraving; Dobson]

HOLIDAY, Henry James 1839-1927
Illustrator, stained glass artist, painter and sculptor. He was born in London on 17 June 1839, went to Leigh's Academy, the Royal Academy Schools, 1854, and influenced by the Pre-Raphaelites, became friends with Holman Hunt and Burne-Jones. He also formed his own sketching club while at the Royal Academy, joining with Albert Morre, Marcus Stone and Simeon Solomon. He established himself as an illustrator for wood engraving, with drawings for Lewis Carroll's The Hunting of the Snark, 1876, which were skilfully engraved, for all their intricate fantastic detail, by Joseph Swain (q.v.). He also illustrated The Mermaid by Hans Andersen, n.d. Holiday is best known for his stained glass designs, having set up his own glass factory in 1890, and as a decorative mural and mosaic artist. He also wrote extensively on artistic technique and exhibited work at the Grosvenor Gallery and the Royal Academy. He died on 15 April 1927.

HOLL, Francis Montague (Frank) 1845-88
Draughtsman, illustrator of social realist subjects, and portrait painter in oils. He was born in London on 4 July 1845, the son of the metal engraver Francis Holl (see Volume I). He studied at the Royal Academy Schools, 1861, won a travelling scholarship which he only partially completed, and began work as a black and white illustrator for wood engraving in the early 1870s. His illustrations on the wood block were of three types. First there were those drawn especially for The Graphic (some he later painted), which appeared January 1872, then regularly until 1876; then two in 1879, one in 1882, and one in 1883, totalling some twenty drawings altogether. These were mostly double-page social themes, such as 'Shoemaking at the Philanthropic Society's Farm School, Redhill' (18 May 1872) or 'Sketches in London - A Flowergirl' (22 June 1872). Secondly, there were those drawings done after his own paintings first exhibited from 1864 at the Royal Academy, the Grosvenor Gallery, the Royal Society of Painter-Etchers and Engravers, the Royal Hibernian Academy, the Royal Institute of Painters in Watercolours, and the Royal Scottish Academy; he was elected ARA, 1878, RA, 1883 (for portrait work). Thirdly, there were those twenty-six drawings illustrating Trollope's Phineas Redux, in The Graphic, July-December 1873. He also contributed two very expert military drawings to the Illustrated London News, 1881, 1884, which were much admired by Van Gogh. Holl died from heart disease on 31 July 1888.
[Houfe; DNB; Bénézit; TB; A.L.Baldry, Francis Holl; A.M.Reynolds, Life and Work of Francis Holl, 1912; English Influences on Van Gogh; N.John Hall, Trollope and his Illustrators, 1980]

HOLLAND, Henry fl.1876-1906
London draughtsman, who worked at 247 Strand, WC
(Kelly's,1876), which he shared with T.Hobbs,
E.Rooker and F.Watkins (qq.v.). Houfe lists a
Henry T.Holland, fl.1879-1906, illustrator and
figure painter, who contributed humorous subjects
for wood engravings in the Dalziels' comic paper
Judy,1879-87; later to Punch,1906. He worked from
Bloomsbury and exhibited at the Royal Institute of
Painters in Watercolours, 1887-90. The British
Museum owns proof engravings after designs of
'P.Holland' (sic), engraved by the Dalziel Brothers
(q.v.), 1853.

HOLLANDS, S.D. fl.1880s
Draughtsman illustrator, painter of still-life and
fruit. He contributed drawings for wood engraved
cuts and tailpieces in the English Illustrated
Magazine,1888.

HOLLIDGE, Thomas
(see Hollidge, William)

HOLLIDGE, William fl.1869-95
Prominent London draughtsman and wood engraver,
who worked at 5 Fetter Lane, EC (POD,1870-95).
The following year the directory's entry was for a
Thomas Hollidge, 5 Fetter Lane (POD,1896-98).
Among Hollidge's numerous commissions were cuts
to Cassell's Magazine,1869-70, and numerous full-
page engravings, generally after paintings, for the
Illustrated London News,1871-76. These included
reproductions from such noted artists as Henry Wallis,
William Hunt, Heywood Hardy, Helen Paterson, and
Henry Stacy Marks, as well as after drawings of
Alfred Johnson (qq.v.)

HOLLOWAY, Isaac Horatio fl.1841-82
London wood engraver, who worked at 18 Bouverie
Street, EC (POD,1878-80), shared with G.F.Sheern
(q.v.), then 64 Fleet Street, EC (POD,1881-82),
where Sheern also accompanied him. The directories
occasionally mis-spell his name as 'Holdaway'.
Among his early works are cuts for Charles Knight's
Penny Magazine,September-December 1841, after
drawings of R.W.Buss, H.Anelay and F.W.Fairholt
(qq.v.).
[Bodleian Library]

HOLMAN, Alfred R. fl.1877-78
London wood engraver, who worked at 65 Castle
Road, Kentish Town, NW (POD,1877-78).

HOLME, Robert Mountain fl.1866-70
London wood engraver, who worked at 81 Fleet
Street, EC (POD,1866-70).

HOLMES, Charles Herbert fl.1880s
Provincial wood engraver, who worked at 34 Bank
Street, Sheffield (Kelly's,1880).

HOLMES, George Augustus ?-1911
Occasional illustrator, genre painter, who worked
in Chelsea and contributed a drawing for a wood
engraving in the Illustrated London News,1882. He
also exhibited at the British Institution, the Royal
Academy, and the Royal Society of British Artists,
to which he was elected member in 1869.

HOLN
According to Nagler, LeBlanc and Heller this was an
early nineteenth century wood engraver, who signed
a religious cut in 1808. He also engraved the drawings
of John Thurston (q.v.).

HOLT, W.G. fl.1870s
Little is known of this comic draughtsman, figure
artist, who contributed three drawings; 'ambitious
cuts', wood engraved for Punch,1878.
[Spielmann]

HOOD, Thomas,Senior 1799-1845
Humorous draughtsman and poet. He was born in
London on 23 May 1799, the son of a bookseller.
While an adolescent living in Dundee he drew sketches
for the local paper, then returned to London to serve an
apprenticeship, first under Harris (probably John Harris,
Senior, see Volume I), then his uncle Robert Sands,
and finally the Le Keux brothers. While he developed
his literary skills he drew comic illustrations for
such publications as Whims and Oddities,1826-27
and The Comic Annual,1830,1834,1837-38, which
the young apprentice engraver W.J.Linton (q.v.)
recalled having engraved on wood for his employer
G.W.Bonner (q.v.). Hood borrowed heavily from
the satiric wit of the eighteenth century and
illustrated some of his own works, Hood's Own,
1838; Up the Rhine,1839; Hood's Magazine,1844,
he also commissioned John Leech (q.v.) to draw
for a collection of his literary pieces, Whimsicalities,
1844. Hood died on 3 May 1845, leaving a talented
illustrator and engraver son, Thomas Hood,Junior
(q.v.).
[DNB; TB (with full bibliography); Houfe;
Dalziels' Record; Redgrave]

HOOD, Thomas,Junior 1835-74
Draughtsman, wood engraver and humorist, born in
Wanstead, Essex on 19 January 1835, the only
surviving son of the noted draughtsman and poet,
Thomas Hood (q.v.). He attended various schools,
then Pembroke College, Oxford, and worked as
journalist, then amateur cartoonist during a clerk-
ship in the War Office,1860. By 1861 he had met
the Dalziel Brothers (q.v.) whom he had long
admired and wished to work with. He became the

editor and illustrator-engraver of their comic paper, Fun,1865-71. He also wrote for various magazines and published comic collections such as Tom Hood's Annual, from 1867, for which the cuts were engraved by the Dalziels, and to which a few 'Sixties School' illustrators contributed. He also wrote and illustrated various children's books with his sister, Frances Freeling Broderip (d.1873). He died in Peckham Rye, Surrey, 20 November 1874. The British Museum owns proof engravings of early designs engraved by the Dalziel Brothers (q.v.), 1861.

HOOPER, E. fl.1850s
London wood engraver, who worked at 13 Henrietta Street, Covent Garden (POD,1853). This may be the wood engraver of the title page to the serial novel Mary Price,n.d., published by John Dicks. It was signed 'E.Hopper' (sic), and is now in the Constance Meade Collection, Bodleian Library.

HOOPER, William Harcourt 1835-1912
Prominent London draughtsman and wood engraver. He was born in London on 22 February 1834, apprenticed to the noted wood engraver Thomas Bolton (q.v.) and began engraving after John Gilbert's (q.v.) drawings on blocks. 'When a boy he would be sent to Sir John Gilbert's house at Blackheath with a clean block and then go and watch the golfers on the green whilst Sir John drew the required illustration' (B.Sleigh, Wood Engraving since 1900,p.9). These appeared engraved in London Journal and later from 1850 in the Illustrated London News. Hooper later served as manager of Joseph Swain's (q.v.) engraving firm and under Swain's name engraved the work of many of the important 'Sixties School' illustrators such as Fred Walker for Wilkie Collins' Woman in White, C.Green, C.Keene, J.Leech, R.W.Macbeth, John Millais, F.A.Sandys, J.M.Smith, John Tenniel, and R.Caton Woodville (qq.v.). He was admired for his skill, especially by the influential critic John Ruskin, who visited Hooper's London office in 1885. Hooper set up on his own as a London draughtsman and wood engraver from 1872 at 28 Fleet Street, EC (Kelly's, POD, 1872-81). Hooper was a skilful outline engraver who eventually adopted the style of medieval woodcuts for various commissions. He engraved bookplates with Walter Crane (see Fincham). The British Museum owns a collection of his bold woodcut trade marks, cards, charts and maps; also a series of wood engravings after Selwyn Image (q.v.) for the Century Guild's Hobby Horse,1883-91. There are also a number of original Japanese-inspired woodcuts of silhouette flower arrangements and tonal woodcuts meticulously done to imitate Japanese brushwork; also a series of stained glass designs. Among Hooper's students of this outline engraving technique was the young Charles Ricketts (q.v.). The influence of William Morris (q.v.) began in 1891, when Hooper was employed as engraver for the Kelmscott Press.

He engraved the Golden Legend of Master William Caxton,1892, and the famous Kelmscott Chaucer, 1896, after Burne-Jones' designs; and also after Catterson Smith's ink renderings. By the 1900s he was employed by the Ashendene Press and engraved Charles Gere's designs to Morte d'Arthur, and Dante, 1909. He died in Hammersmith on 24 February 1912. The British Museum owns a large collection of his facsimile engravings, especially after J.Tenniel, H.Herkomer, Fred Walker, R.Caton Woodville, T.Mahoney, and proofs for the Kelmscott Chaucer. [TB; Fincham; Houfe; Sleigh; Hind; Bénézit]

HOPKINS, Alexander fl.1850s
London wood engraver, who worked at 4 Surrey Street, Strand, WC (POD,1859).

HOPKINS, Arthur 1848-1930
Draughtsman illustrator and watercolourist. He was born in London in 1848, brother of the poet Gerard Manley Hopkins, and illustrator Everard Hopkins (q.v.). He attended Lancing College, worked in the City, then entered the Royal Academy Schools, 1872, and began exhibiting pictures in the galleries that year. He also drew illustrations for the Illustrated London News,1872-98, engraved by Joseph Swain; then for the Cornhill,1875,1884; and The Graphic, 1874-86. He then became a valued staff illustrator to Belgravia, working for its editor Mary Elizabeth Braddon. He drew the twelve drawings to Thomas Hardy's The Return of the Native, serialised 1878. These were also engraved by Swain (q.v.); and Hardy considered them 'capital work', although Hopkins was dissatisfied with Swain's engraving. In fact the failures stemmed from Hopkins' own deficiencies with perspective and human anatomy. Hopkins also collaborated with Swain on Good Words,1873-74 (the proofs are in the Bodleian Library). His style borrowed much from Du Maurier and Frederick Walker, although his stiffer line kept Hopkins in the second rank of draughtsmen on wood. Nevertheless, his drawings for the Illustrated London News and The Graphic were much admired by Van Gogh. In later years he relied on watercolour paintings, and he exhibited at the Royal Academy, the Royal Institute of Painters in Oil-Colours, the Royal Watercolour Society, and the Fine Art Society. He dismissed his illustrations for the Quiver,1890 and Punch,1893-1902, as 'fearful...artistic hack work'. He died in Hampstead on 16 September 1930.
[TB; Bénézit; Houfe; English Influences on Van Gogh]

HOPKINS, Everard 1860-1928
Illustrator, watercolourist, born in London in 1860, the brother of Arthur Hopkins (q.v.) and the poet Gerard Manley Hopkins. He worked generally for magazines, after a Slade training, then became editor of the Pilot, and drew for wood engravings in

The Graphic,1883-85; the Illustrated London News, 1887-92; and continued through the 1890s in the Quiver,1890; Punch,1891-94; Black and White,1891; and Cassell's Family Magazine. He also exhibited at the Royal Academy, the Royal Watercolour Society, and the Royal Institute of Painters in Watercolours. He died on 17 October 1928. [Spielmann; Sketchley; TB; Bénézit]

HOPTON, Iliff fl.1893-94
London wood engraver, who worked at 3 Tudor Street, EC (POD,1893-94), shared with the noted wood engraver George Harrison (q.v.).

HORDER(S), Arthur fl.1871-72
London wood engraver, who worked at 100 Strand, WC (POD,1871-72). The directory spelling varied from 'Horder' to 'Hordes'.

HORNE, George Francis fl.1886-1900
London wood engraver, who worked at 30 Fleet Street, EC (POD,1886-87), shared with F.Thorpe (q.v.). He then moved to 89 Farringdon Street, EC (POD,1889-92), which he shared with Thorpe, W.J.Potter, L.Knott and H.Prater (qq.v.), and finally to 21 St John's Square, EC (POD,1893-1900).

HORNE, Thomas fl.1830-69
London wood engraver, who worked at 3 Thanet Place, Strand, WC (POD,1851-69). His work included twelve bookplates listed by Fincham, from armorial designs, signed 'T.Horne 233 Strand' (1830) and 'Horne Temple Bar' (1840,60).

HORNER, Jabez fl.1876-80
Provincial wood engraver and draughtsman, who worked at 54 Albion Street, Leeds (Kelly's,1876-80).

HORNUNG, Charles fl.1894-95
London wood engraver, who worked at 77 Gray's Inn Road, WC (POD,1894-95).

HORSLEY, John Callcott 1817-1903
Occasional draughtsman on wood, painter and etcher. He was born on 29 January 1817, studied at the Royal Academy Schools, then concentrated on book illustration, generally of historical or Shakespearean subjects. He is included in Bohn's appendix to Chatto and Jackson as a valuable draughtsman on wood, noted for figure designs to the Poetry of Thomas Moore, Burns' Poems, Tennyson's Poems, Favourite English Poems, Favourite Modern Ballads; and Milton's L'Allegro,1849, engraved on wood by W.J.Linton (q.v.). McLean also lists illustrations to Nursery Rhymes, Tales and Jingles,1844, and the Book of Common Prayer,1845, drawn on wood with H.Warren and G.Scharf (qq.v.), 'charming woodcut illustrations--...surprisingly of contemporary [i.e. modern] church scenes'. Horsley also etched

illustrations for publications by the Etching Club and for the Art Union. His paintings appeared at the British Institution and the Royal Academy, where he was elected member, 1864 and Treasurer, 1882 and served as professor of drawing. He died in Cranbrook 19 October 1903. The British Museum owns proof engravings from his designs on wood, engraved by the Dalziel Brothers (q.v.), 1839-47.
[For a list of illustrated works see Houfe; DNB; Chatto; McLean, Victorian Book Design; TB; Bénézit; Wood]

HORSLEY, Walter Charles 1867-1934
Draughtsman, figure and landscape painter. He was born in 1867, son of the noted painter J.C.Horsley (q.v.). He worked in London and contributed a drawing for wood engraving to The Graphic,1880. He also exhibited at the Royal Academy, the Royal Society of British Artists, the Royal Institute of Painters in Watercolours, and the Royal Institute of Painters in Oil-Colours.

HOTELIN
French wood engraver, who engraved with Adolphe Best (q.v.) as Best, Hotelin and Leloir.
[Gusman]

HOUGHTON, Arthur Boyd 1836-75
Prominent draughtsman illustrator on wood and painter. He was born in Kotagiri, Madras in 1836, studied at Leigh's, and the Royal Academy Schools and trained to draw on wood with the noted engraver J.W.Whymper (q.v.). He proved skilful enough for the Dalziel Brothers (q.v.) to commission four drawings on wood to Wilkie Collins' After Dark, 1862. He also did nine drawings to the short-lived magazine Entertaining Things,1 January 1862; contributed to London Society, 1862, 1866-68; and his most successful work, for Good Words,1862-68, engraved by the Dalziels. He soon gave up his painter's ambitions to draw full-time on wood blocks for numerous sixties magazines and books, his most important being ninety-three drawings for the Dalziels' Arabian Nights' Entertainments,1864, which the DNB praised as 'full of life and fancy; of gravity and passion; often wild and fantastic; but always in sympathy with the subject and never wanting in human character...His designs were often striking in their effects of black and white, but they were wanting in tone and gradation, a defect partly due perhaps to the loss of one eye'. He provided numerous drawings for small volumes of contemporary poetry, biblical stories, boy's adventures, and finally to the ill-fated Dalziels' Bible Gallery (posthumously,1881). For a complete list see P.Hogarth, A.B.Houghton, Victoria and Albert Museum catalogue,1975. Houghton should have achieved a considerable reputation for his drawings during his lifetime since his output and understanding of the tonal limitations of wood engraving were considerable,

and rivalled only Doré (q.v.) according to Paul Hogarth, despite having only one eye and migraine attacks. But he spent his lifetime pressurised by deadlines. He had a daunting variety of subjects to be contained upon a small block surface (generally 8" x 6" or 20 cm x 15.2 cm), many of which were done first with verses or text written around the finished engraving. Houghton's working method was to begin with a rough sketch, then a more defined drawing was traced or drawn on the whitened surface of the block. He then picked out details in 'H' degree pencil and highlighted in Chinese white before turning the block over to the engraver to follow. Once he told Rossetti how the entire process from rough sketch to finished block drawing took only two or three hours. This, and his photographic memory qualified Houghton to become one of the most skilful of 'special' reporter illustrators. When he was employed by the newly established weekly, The Graphic, to record aspects of America on a tour October 1869-April 1870, his observations caused considerable controversy, a sure sign of their success as engravings: later the western subjects in particular were enthusiastically reprinted in America. Houghton also served as special reporter in France during the Franco-Prussian War. He provided a total of 104 illustrations to The Graphic (his greatest number to any single periodical) from 1869-73, 1875. Houghton also exhibited his paintings sporadically at the British Institution, the Old Watercolour Society, and the Royal Academy, and was elected ARWS, 1871, and RBA. He died of progressive alchoholism in Hampstead on 25 November 1875. The Dalziels eulogised Houghton, 'The young Genius', as 'perhaps one of the most versatile of black and white draughtsmen of our time'. The British Museum owns proof engravings by the Dalziel Brothers (q.v.), 1862-65.
[DNB; Redgrave; TB; Bryan; Dalziels' Record; Hind; L.Housman, A.B.Houghton, 1896; P.Hogarth, A.B.Houghton, VAM catalogue, 1975]

HOUSMAN, Clemence Annie 1861-1955
Wood engraver, author and political activist. She was born in 1861 in Worcestershire, but moved to London with her brother Laurence (q.v.) late in 1883. There she studied art and wood engraving under the engraver Charles Roberts (q.v.), first at the Lambeth School of Art, later as free-lance engraver for Roberts on cuts for the Illustrated London News and The Graphic (until the paper abandoned wood engraving for process reproductions). Throughout the 1890s she was involved in the Private Press movement, engraving after Philip Connard in The Dome, October 1899, and for James Guthrie's (q.v.) Pear Tree Press. She is best known for her meticulous engravings after her brother's pen drawings for his fairy tale books. These include: The House of Joy, 1895 (re-touched process

engravings); his illustrations to her own tale The Were-Wolf, 1896 (cover, title and six designs); The Field of Clover, 1898; Of the Imitation of Christ, 1898; The Little Land, with Songs from its Four Rivers, 1899; The Blue Moon, 1904; and Prunella, 1907 -- all after Laurence Housman's designs. She also engraved her brother's frontispiece to Tennyson's Maud, 1905 (engraved with Reginald Savage (q.v.)), and several of his bookplate designs. Her work for James Guthrie included a large, intricate plate, 'The Evening Star' which she complained was too detailed to reproduce well; an edition of Rossetti's The Blessed Damozel (engraved with Reginald Lodge (q.v.)); and an edition of Milton's Hymn on the Morning of Christ's Nativity (engraved with Reginald Lodge). Other engraved work included illustrations of Paul Woodroffe (q.v.); an edition of Confessions of St Augustine, 1900; and ten Woodroffe drawings (only four used) to a newly translated edition (by Laurence Housman) of Aucassin and Nicolette, 1902. She also engraved architectural subjects like 'Camden' after William Strang (q.v.); a set of twenty-four plates after pen drawings by F.L.Griggs which included views of Chipping Campden. Clemence was also the author of a popular horror story, The Were-Wolf, 1896; a passionate tale The Unknown Sea, 1898; and a psychological reconstruction of the 'Morte d'Arthur', The Life of Aglovale de Galis, 1905. She was an avid suffragette, served a short period in Holloway gaol, and wrote such tracts as 'Women and Tax Resistance' and 'Conditions of Release'. Her later years were spent with her brother, Laurence, in Street, Somerset, where she abandoned writing and engraving for gardening and the encouragement of her brother. As a wood engraver, her style uses the traditions of Blake through the Pre-Raphaelites, Burne-Jones, Ricketts and Beardsley, yet 'falls naturally within the old category of line engraving...In technical range no engraver has carried the art further, except perhaps in the evaporation of lineal form in tones, which is aside from this and still awaiting a modern exponent, unless we except Mr Timothy Cole, the American engraver', wrote James Guthrie (Print Collector's Quarterly, II, 1924). Because she engraved few books and those mostly by her brother 'her self-effacement is complete', and yet 'her blocks are not only a marvel of faith, but a marvel of sympathy'. Unfortunately her own prints are rare since she did only a small number of burnished proofs (taken from the block without a press). She signed her engravings: 'C H Sc'.
[For a discussion and list of her engravings see R.Engen, Laurence Housman, 1984; also R.P.Graves, A.E.Housman, 1979]

HOUSMAN, Laurence 1865-1959
Draughtsman illustrator, painter and author. He was born on 18 July 1865 and with his sister Clemence

Housman (q.v.) went to London in 1883 to study art. His exhibited drawings and paintings showed the influence of Rossetti, Ricketts, Morris and the much admired sixties illustrator A.B.Houghton (qq.v.) whose works he edited and published in 1896. He was described as the last of the artists for facsimile wood engravers, and he made conscious attempts to emulate the Victorians not only in his drawings but also in his writing of poetry and for the stage. His own designs were most successfully engraved by his sister Clemence. His illustrations first appeared as forty-four drawings to George Meredith's Jump to Glory Jane, 1890, while his best known are to Rossetti's Goblin Market, 1893; J.Barlow's The End of Elfintown; and Shelley's The Sensitive Plant, as well as his famous drawings to stories by George Macdonald. He also contributed to various magazines including: the English Illustrated Magazine, 1893-94; Pall Mall Magazine, 1893 Yellow Book, 1894, 1896; Pageant, 1896; Parade, 1897; Dome, 1897-99; and Quarto, 1898. Housman retired with his sister to Street, Somerset and died there in 1959.
[For bibliographical list see I.Hodgkins, Housman catalogue, National Book League, 1975; also R.Engen, Laurence Housman, 1984]

HOWARD, George Ninth Earl of Carlisle 1843-1911
Amateur draughtsman for wood engraving, water-colourist. He was born on 12 August 1843, studied at South Kensington, was a patron to William Morris, Burne-Jones and J.D.Batten (q.v.), and served as MP for East Cumberland, 1879-80, 1881-85. He gathered around him a circle of artists and radicals at Naworth Castle, Cumberland and contributed drawings of it to the English Illustrated Magazine, 1884-85, engraved on wood by J.D.Cooper (q.v.) in a strong, dark tonal style. Howard also exhibited at the Royal Academy, the New Gallery, the Royal Hibernian Academy and the Royal Watercolour Society. He died on 16 April 1911.
[DNB; TB; Houfe]

HOWARD, Captain Henry R. ?-1895
Draughtsman, illustrator for wood engravings. He was born in Watford, began drawing from childhood, and trained in Hanover. He submitted drawings for wood engravings to Punch, which its editor Mark Lemon accepted although he sent Howard to John Tenniel and John Leech (qq.v.) to learn to draw on the wood block. His work appeared in Punch from 1851-67, although he lost money (£30) for his first efforts, after buying blocks from Joseph Swain (q.v.). He supplied various humanised beast and bird drawings as initial letters which totalled sixty-six cuts in 1853 and 122 by 1867 and earned him £100 a year. He hoped to succeed Leech as chief cartoonist but failed, and retired from Punch in 1867. He died on 31 August 1895. His 'work, though clever and ingenious, was weak' (Spielmann).

[Spielmann; Houfe]

HUARD, Louis ?-1874
Draughtsman illustrator. He was born in Aix-en-Provence and studied art in Antwerp but worked in London for over twenty years on various wood engraved illustrations to magazines. He began as the most frequent contributor to the British Workman, 1855, then graduated to the London Journal, 1859, succeeding Sir John Gilbert (q.v.). He provided several cuts to the Illustrated London News, 1861-63, 1875-76, 1881, and worked for James Hogg's London Society, 1863; Churchman's Family Magazine, 1863; Cassell's Magazine, 1865; and the Band of Hope Review, ('a perfect instance of a popular venture unconcerned, one would think, with art', White). Such harsh criticism of his abilities to draw for wood engravings, which he learned from rather inferior penny journals more concerned with circulation than quality, clouded Huard's reputation. He exhibited at the British Institution, 1857-72. The British Museum owns proof engravings after Huard, engraved by the Dalziel Brothers (q.v.), 1863-64.
[White; Houfe]

HUBBARD, George A. fl.1880s
Provincial draughtsman on wood, noted for map engravings. He worked in Bexley Heath, Kent (Kelly's, 1889) and was probably related to the draughtsman on wood, William Hubbard (q.v.).

HUBBARD, William and Son fl.1880s
Provincial firm of wood draughtsmen, noted for map work, with an office in Bexley Heath, Kent (Kelly's, 1880). (See also Hubbard, George)

HUGGINS, Edwin fl.1880-1900
Provincial draughtsman and wood engraver, who worked at William IV Yard, Briggate, Leeds (Kelly's, 1880), then at 60 Basinghall Street, Leeds (Kelly's, 1889-1900). The business was established in 1838 by William Huggins. According to an advertisement Edwin was specialising by the 1880s in 'wood letter and printing materials, blocks, lines and odd letters cut out', and selling 'wood type and poster blocks'.

HUGHES, Arthur 1832-1915
Prominent draughtsman illustrator and painter. He was born in London on 27 January 1832, educated at fourteen years old at the Government School of Design, Somerset House, under Alfred Stevens, entered the Royal Academy Schools, 1847, and exhibited there in 1851, 1854 and 1856. He became associated with the Pre-Raphaelites, and posed for Millais' 'The Proscribed Royalist', 1853. Their friendship inspired work on his most significant illustrations, to William Allingham's The Music Master, 1855, and his illustrations and paintings

were much admired by John Ruskin. Forrest Reid devoted six pages to Hughes and remarked: 'He never, indeed, became a first-rate draughtsman, still less such a master as Sandys, Millais, Houghton, or Keene. But he had what is rarer than clever draughtsmanship, a spark of genius, and a personal charm so persuasive that it goes far to make up for a somewhat wobbly technique.' Reid claims his most significant drawings for magazines were the 231 for Good Words, 1864-71: 'Here, in these pictures for children, he at last enters his own world--a world very close to that of Blake's Songs of Innocence.' His style derived as much from Pre-Raphaelite detail and composition (as in his Tennyson's Enoch Arden, 1866) as the fairy world of Richard Doyle, which reached fruition in George Macdonald's Dealings with Fairies, 1867, and At the Back of the North Wind, 1871. He continued to illustrate for books and magazines until the turn of the century and at one time taught the noted illustrator Sydney P. Hall (q.v.). He exhibited his paintings at the Grosvenor Gallery, the New Gallery, the Royal Academy, the Royal Institute of Painters in Water-colours and the Royal Institute of Painters in Oil-Colours, and lived a withdrawn existence at Kew Green, where he died on 22 December 1915. The British Museum owns proof engravings after Hughes, engraved by the Dalziel Brothers (q.v.), 1865, 1866. [For a list of works see Houfe; also Reid; Bénézit; TB; McLean, Victorian Book Design]

HUGHES, Arthur Ford 1856-1914
Draughtsman illustrator and landscape painter. He studied at Heatherley's, the Slade and the Royal Academy Schools, and worked in Wallington, Surrey, 1880, and London in 1890. He contributed headpiece designs for wood engraving to the English Illustrated Magazine, 1886-87. He also exhibited at the Royal Academy, the Royal Society of British Artists, the Royal Institute of Painters in Watercolours and the Royal Institute of Painters in Oil-Colours.

HUGHES, Edward 1832-1908
Draughtsman illustrator, portrait and genre painter. He illustrated for Once a Week, 1864-66; Shilling Magazine, 1865-66; Argosy, 1866; Sunday Magazine, 1866, 1869; Cassell's Magazine, 1870; for Hurst and Blackett's Standard Library; the Illustrated London News, 1870-75; and The Graphic, 1871. He worked with George Du Maurier (q.v.) on illustrations to Wilkie Collins' Poor Miss Finch, 1872. He specialised in historical subjects and worked in London from Chelsea and Notting Hill.

HUGHES, Hugh (Henry) 1790?-1863
Welsh wood engraver, draughtsman and lithographer. He was born in Pwllygwichiad, near Llandudno, son of Thomas Hughes, and was registered in the parish on 20 February 1790. He lost his parents while very

young and was educated by his grandfather and then apprenticed to a Liverpool engraver. He moved to London and learned oil painting. He painted a portrait dated 1812, and is perhaps the wood engraver listed by Johnstone as 'H. Hughes' who worked at 21 Wilderness-Row, St John's Street (Johnstone, 1817), where he was neighbour to the wood engraver J. Armstrong (q.v.). He then moved to his grandfather's farm, Meddiant Farm, Llansantffraid Glan Conway, Denbighshire, where he spent 1819-22 drawing and engraving his best known work, 'The Beauties of Cambria', 1823. This consisted of sixty landscapes ('cut with much ability', Redgrave) of North and South Wales, of which fifty-eight were drawn and all wood engraved by him. Chatto calls them 'singularly beautiful wood engravings' and reproduces four (pp. 539-40), while Nagler praises them for their delicate engraving. The DNB claimed: 'In his knowledge of natural form and masterly handling of the graver, Hughes has been compared with Bewick. His treatment of natural objects was realistic, and laborious, and his foliage is always truthful and graceful.' The book was published by subscription at one guinea or two guineas on India paper, and printed by John Johnson, printer to William Hughes (q.v.). Hughes also drew caricatures, lithographed Welsh scenery and became involved in religious politics. He published various tracts as well as works on Welsh antiquities, and edited his father-in-law's sermons. He married after 1823, but his three children died early. He died in Great Malvern on 11 March 1863. He signed his work: 'HH', 'H. Hughes'. [DNB; TB; Chatto; Linton, Masters of Wood Engraving; Redgrave; LeBlanc; Nagler; Bryan]

HUGHES, Jane fl. 1826-27
London wood engraver, who worked early in the century at 17 Hatfield Street, Blackfriars Road (Pigot, 1826-27). This was previously the office of William Hughes (q.v.).

HUGHES, John B. fl. 1880s
Welsh wood engraver, who worked at 9 New Street, Pwllheli, Carnarvonshire (Kelly's, 1880).

HUGHES, William 1793-1825
English wood engraver, born in Liverpool in 1793. He was an engraving pupil of Henry Hole (q.v.), the competent wood engraver who had come to Liverpool after a turbulent training under Thomas Bewick (q.v.). Hughes excelled in architectural subjects. Chatto claimed that some of his work was 'of considerable merit', while Linton (in Masters of Wood Engraving) noted the influence of Thurston, and the occasional use of the white-line technique. He concluded, 'All I find by him is good'. His engravings appeared first as illustrations to Gregson's Fragments towards a History of

Lancashire,1817, Dibdin's Decameron,1817 and Puckle's The Club,1817 (three headpieces and five tailpieces). He was working in London 1819-22 in partnership with the noted printer Charles Whittingham, the elder (q.v.), as Whittingham and Hughes, 12 Staining Lane. There they produced the Chiswick edition of British Poets (1822) in a hundred volumes. His later work included a collaboration with young John Jackson (q.v.) on Rutler's Delineations of Fonthill,1823 (ten vignettes); Johnson's Typographia,1824; and Ottley's History of Engraving and Mornings in Bow Street,1824, engraved after Cruikshank. For Charles Whittingham (q.v.) he engraved vignettes after Cruikshank to Washington Irving's Knickerbocker's History of New York,1824; and Butler's Remains,1827 (posthumously published). He also engraved portraits of William Caxton and J.Johnson. Hughes died in Lambeth on 11 February 1825, aged thirty-two. The British Museum owns his engravings after W.H.Brooke, G.Cruikshank and G.Cuitt. He signed his work: 'W HUGHES sc'.
[TB; LeBlanc; Redgrave; DNB; Bryan; W.J.Linton, Masters of Wood Engraving; Nagler; Heller; Bruillot; Chatto]

HUGHES, William fl.1822-14
London wood engraver, who worked early in the century at 17 Hatfield Street, Blackfriars Road (Pigot,1822-24). By 1826 this had become the office of wood engraver Jane Hughes (q.v.).

HUGHES, Wyndham Hope fl.1880s
Provincial draughtsman, who worked at All Saints Cottage, Holywell Hill, St Albans, Hertfordshire (Kelly's,1880).

HULL, Edward fl.1827-77
Draughtsman illustrator of figure subjects and genre painter. He worked in London where he contributed wood engravings to the Illustrated Times,1859-61, for the paper's originator, Henry Vizetelly (q.v.).

HULME, Frederick William 1816-84
Draughtsman on wood, illustrator and landscape painter. He was born in Swinton on 22 October 1816, and studied with a Yorkshire artist before coming to London in 1844. There, he worked as a draughtsman of landscapes in the manner of Creswick for various book and magazine engravings, notably the Illustrated London Magazine,1853; the Poetical Works of E.A.Poe,1853; S.C.Hall's Book of South Wales,1861; and Rhymes and Roundelayes; and the Art Journal. He published A Graduated Series of Drawing Copies in Landscape,1850. He also exhibited landscape paintings at the British Institution, the Royal Academy, the Royal Society of British Artists and the Royal Institute of Painters in Oil-Colours. He died in London on 14 November 1884.

The British Museum owns his designs engraved by the Dalziel Brothers (q.v.).
[Chatto; DNB; Bryan; Bénézit; TB]

HULME, Robert C. fl.1862-76
Draughtsman illustrator and still-life painter. He drew for wood engravings of various ceremonial subjects for the Illustrated London News,1864-69, 1873. He also exhibited paintings at the Royal Academy and the Royal Society of British Artists.

HUMPHREYS, Henry Noel 1810-79
Draughtsman on wood, ornamental illustrator, numismatist and naturalist. He was born in Birmingham on 4 January 1810, attended King Edward's School, worked in Italy and then returned to England in 1843 where he set up as a draughtsman on wood and designer of intricate yet knowledgeable detailed cuts for numerous books. These designs appeared first in W.B.Cooke's Illustrations of the Scenery of Rome, then in The Illuminated Calendar, 1845; as rich woodcut initials in his own account of The Coins of England,1846, and as thirty expert flower borders to The Poet's Pleasaunce, 1847, engraved on wood by H.Vizetelly and W.Dickes (qq.v.). From about 1851 he devoted himself entirely to writing (History of the Art of Writing, 1851, Printing,1855), and to drawing on wood for various elaborate gift books; he also produced the best chromolithographed plates to them, inspired by Italian and Flemish manuscript illumination of the Middle Ages. Such books included Tupper's Proverbial Philosophy,1854, engraved by H.Vizetelly, with whom he often worked (e.g. a decorative design to Vizetelly's Illustrated Times,1855); Rhymes and Roundelayes in Praise of Country Life,1857; W.Falconer's The Shipwreck,1858, engraved by H.N.Woods (q.v.); Thomson's Seasons,1859, engraved by the Dalziel Brothers (q.v.); Poems of Goldsmith,1859, with illustrations by Birket Foster, engraved and colour printed by Edmund Evans (q.v.); and Wordsworth's White Doe of Rylstone, 1859, engraved by H.N.Woods (q.v.). He also designed at least one of Routledge's 'New Toy Books': A Little Girl's Visit to a Flower Garden, colour printed by Edmund Evans. As a naturalist himself, he provided wood engravings printed in two colours and hand coloured for the Samson Low series of naturalist guides. This series included River Gardens,1857, Ocean Gardens,1857 and The Butterfly Vivarium,1858. McLean notes in conclusion that Humphreys was just that degree better as a draughtsman designer for wood engraving: 'There is an integrity and originality in Noel Humphreys' work as a designer which makes the similar work of his contemporaries, like T.Macquoid, T.Sulman and Harry Rogers look feeble. The width of his learning, in the fields of natural history, arms and armour, coins and

jewellery, was obviously great. But his ability and industry did not bring him affluence'. In fact Humphreys died intestate in London on 10 June 1879, leaving less than £800. The British Museum owns his designs engraved by the Dalziel Brothers (q.v.), 1863.
[For a list of works see DNB; Houfe; see also McLean, Victorian Book Design; Chatto; Bénézit; TB; Art Journal,1879,p.184]

HUMPHREYS, Owen fl.1870s
London wood engraver, who worked at 8 Palsgrave Place, Strand (POD,1874), an office which he shared with A.J.Appleton and C.Simpson (qq.v.).

HUMPHRIES, Edward John (Joseph) and Company fl.1880-96
London firm of wood engravers, who worked at 53 Hyde Road, N (POD,1880-83), then as Edward Humphries and Company at 84 Fleet Street, EC (POD,1893-96), shared with A. and H. Quartley (q.v.).

HUNT, Alfred fl.1860-84
Draughtsman illustrator and painter. He was a student of the Royal Academy Schools, worked as a painter in Yorkshire and then returned to London about 1860. There he joined the illustration staff of the Illustrated London News, and by 1865 was a regular contributor of large comic subjects, first in Christmas numbers, but by 1871 of full-page drawings of battle and rural scenes. He worked on various special artist sketches during the Ashanti War,1874; drew a double-page supplement 'The Royal Marriage at St Petersburg', 7 February 1874; a full-page 'The Prince of Wales Tiger Shooting', 25 March 1876; and a special foldout supplement, 'Chinese Immigration to America', 29 April,1876, engraved on wood by 'L.R.' (q.v.). Of this work Houfe remarks: 'His double pages present crowds of figures, usually rather wooden but interesting for period details'. He also drew illustrations with C.Green and P.Skelton (qq.v.) to Dr Cumming's Life and Lessons of Our Lord,1864.

HUNT, William Holman 1827-1910
Occasional draughtsman on wood, prominent Pre-Raphaelite painter. He was born in Wood Street, Cheapside, London on 2 April 1827 and worked as a clerk while receiving painting lessons from H.Rogers, portrait painter. He studied at the British Museum, the National Gallery, and the Royal Academy Schools after 1844, where he exhibited from 1846. He joined Rossetti and Millais (qq.v.) in 1848-49 to form the Pre-Raphaelite Brotherhood, and began a series of painting visits abroad. His subjects became more eastern and mystical after visits to Egypt, Syria, the Holy Land and Palestine. As a draughtsman illustrator, Bohn lists him for his

occasional figure subjects drawn on wood to Moxon's Tennyson's Poems,1857 (his famous 'Lady of Shalot' engraved by the Dalziels), and to Mrs Gatty's Parables from Nature,1861. He also drew for Once a Week,1860, engraved by Joseph Swain (q.v.); Willmott's Sacred Poetry,1862; Good Words,1862; Watt's Divine and Moral Songs,1865; and for Macmillan's 'Golden Treasury' series and Hurst and Blackett's Standard Library series, Studies from Life. Holman Hunt's influence on 'Sixties School' wood engraving was apparent from his early Tennyson drawing. Later in Once a Week, his 'At Night', 1860, was clear and compelling as was his understanding of highlight and spatial description within the confines of a small wood block. They remain major works, expertly engraved by Swain and the Dalziel Brothers (qq.v.). He was primarily a painter and exhibited at all the major London galleries, including the Grosvenor Gallery, the New Gallery, the Royal Society of British Artists, the Royal Hibernian Academy, the Royal Scottish Academy and the Royal Watercolour Society. He was awarded OM in 1905, and died on 7 September 1910. The British Museum owns proof engravings by the Dalziel Brothers (q.v.), 1857.
[Chatto; TB; Bénézit; Houfe; Wood (bibliography)]

HUSTLER, James fl.1866-68
London wood engraver, who worked at Joseph Swain's (q.v.) office, 266 Strand, WC (POD,1866-68).

HUTHSFERNER, R. fl.1880s
Wood engraver, who engraved a bust portrait of John Bright, M.P. after a photograph, in the February 1888 supplement of the Illustrated London News. This is now in the British Museum.
[Hake]

HUTTON, Dr Charles
Wood engraving instructor of Thomas Bewick and his employer Ralph Beilby (qq.v.). Hutton had learned to engrave on wood and to appreciate the qualities of boxwood blocks and tools while in London and approached Beilby to see if he could wood engrave the diagrams in his own Treatise on Mensuration. But it was Bewick who persisted and learned to engrave on wood the fine, even lines needed for the charts in Hutton's work, which was published in parts from 1768.
[For an account see Hutton's own article, Newcastle Magazine,1822; also I.Bain in Bewick Memoir,1975]

HUTTULA, Charles R. fl.1861-67
London wood engraver, who worked at 2 Great New Street, Fetter Lane, EC (POD,1861-67). He may be related to the genre painter Richard C.Huttula, fl.1866-88, who also illustrated the Broadway,

c1867-74, and W.H.G.Kingstone's Hurricane Harry, 1874.
[TB; Bénézit]

HYATT, Frederick fl.1879-90
London wood engraver, who worked at 140 Strand, WC (POD,1879-80), then 41 Wych Street, WC (POD,1890).

HYDE, Edgar
Draughtsman artist, who worked in Limerick, Ireland. He drew for wood engravings in Henry Vizetelly's the Illustrated Times,1859.

HYDE, Henry fl.1883-87
London wood engraver, who worked at 34 Richard Street, Liverpool Road, N (POD,1883-87). There may be a connection with Henry James Hyde, London genre painter, who exhibited at the Royal Society of British Artists, 1883-92.
[TB; Bénézit]

HYLAND, James B. fl.1880s
Scottish wood engraver, who worked at 6 Hanover Street, Edinburgh (Kelly's,1889).

IAGO, Charles Thomas fl.1879-97
London wood engraver, who worked at 267 Strand, WC (POD,1879-81), then disappears from the directories until 1890, when he was working at 12 New Court, Carey Street, WC (POD,1890-92). Iago then joins with Crossfield as Iago and Crossfield, and worked at the 12 New Court address (POD,1893-97).

IAGO and Crossfield
(see Iago, Charles Thomas)

ILLINGWORTH, S.E. fl.1860s
Draughtsman illustrator, who contributed a drawing for wood engraving to James Hogg's influential magazine, London Society,1868, which appeared with work by Charles Keene, John Gilbert and F.Barnard.

IMAGE, Selwyn 1849-1930
Pen and ink draughtsman for wood engravings, watercolourist and poet. He was born in Bodiam, Sussex in 1849, educated at Marlborough and New College, Oxford, and studied art at the Slade School, Oxford under John Ruskin. Although he took Holy Orders in 1872, and served as curate of various London churches, 1875-80, he also worked on drawings, in a firm, medieval style borrowed from William Morris and Walter Crane (qq.v.). Crane claimed that Image was one of the key figures in the modern revival of decorative book design and printing: 'Mr Selwyn Image did much to keep alive true taste in printing and book decoration, when they were but little understood' (Of the Decorative Illustration of

Books Old and New,1896). Image is perhaps best known for his designs for the Century Guild's Hobby Horse,1883-91, wood engraved by W.H.Hooper (q.v.). The British Museum owns a series of his ink drawings in preparation for these. The decorative vignettes, head and tailpieces were later reprinted in an edition of William Blake's XVII Designs to Thornton's Virgil, Portland, Maine, 1899. Other illustrations appeared as title-page and cover designs to L.Binyon's Lyric Poems,1894; Ernest Rhys' A London Rose,1894; E.R.Chapman's A Little Child's Wreath,1895-96; Michael Field's Stephania, 1895-96; and Vincent O'Sullivan's Poems,1895-96. He also designed stained glass and was elected member of the Art Worker's Guild, 1900, and Professor of Fine Art, Oxford, 1910-16. He died on 21 August 1930.
[Houfe; J.R.Taylor; Art Nouveau Book in Britain]

INCHBOLD and Beck fl.1880s
Provincial firm of wood engravers, with an office at 31 John William Street, Huddersfield (Kelly's,1880).

INGRAM, Master H. ?-1860
Amateur draughtsman on wood for his father Herbert Ingram's paper, the Illustrated London News. He contributed drawings on wood for 1859,1860, but then went with his father to America where he died in a steamer accident on Lake Michigan in 1860.

IRONS, Charles fl.1873-88
London wood engraver, who worked at 28 Essex Street, Strand, WC (POD,1873), shared with J.Rhodes and J.T.Morrell (qq.v.), 25 Upper Ground Street, Blackfriars Road, SE (POD,1874-76), and Old Bargehouse Wharf, Upper Ground Street, SE (POD,1877-84), then moved to the suburbs at 59 Cressingham Road, Lewisham, SE (LSDS,1888).

IRONS, Clarke and Company fl.1879-92
London wood engraver, who worked at 4 (23) (27) Bouverie Street, EC (POD,1879-90), then 74 Fleet Street, EC (POD,1891-92).

IRONSIDE, Edmund B. fl.1880s
Provincial wood engraver, who worked at 16 St John Street, Liverpool (Kelly's,1889).

ISTVAN, Balecz
Wood engraver, who engraved illustrations for the English Illustrated Magazine,1883-84, notably after C.Napier Hemy's (q.v.) drawings to 'An Unsentimental Journey through Cornwall', and after landscape paintings of L.R.O'Brien and E.J.Gregory. He was particularly skilful at engraving light in nature.

IZOD, George Thomas, and Company fl.1855-74
London wood engraver, brother of James Henry Izod (q.v.). He worked at 12A Gough Square (POD,1855-65),

Tudor Street, Blackfriars, EC (POD,1857-60), and
3 Bouverie Street, EC (POD,1863-67), shared with
A.J.Appleton (q.v.). George Izod then joins his
brother James as Izod Brothers, 41 Castle Street,
Holborn, EC (POD,1871-74). George then disappears
from the London directories, while his brother
continues to appear until 1910.

IZOD, James Henry fl.1869-1910
London wood engraver, who worked at 6 Wine Office
Court, EC (POD,1869-70), then joined with his brother
George Thomas Izod (q.v.) as Izod Brothers,
41 Castle Street, Holborn, EC (POD,1871-74). James
reappears on his own, working from 6 Wine Office
Court (POD,1875-80), which he shared with C.Murray
(q.v.). By 1893 he had moved yet again to
15 Clerkenwell Close, EC (POD,1893), then
27A Farringdon Street, EC (POD,1894-1901). He
continued to work as wood engraver from 15 Newbury
Street, Cloth Fair, EC (POD,1910).

JACKSON, J. fl.1875-77
Draughtsman on wood, who worked at 49 Cardington
Street, Hampstead Road, NW (POD,1875-77) and
specialised in drawings from 'special' reporters for
the Illustrated London News,1875-76. These were
half or full-page from such foreign parts as Burma
Spain, Paris, and Kostajnica, Yugoslavia.

JACKSON, James fl.1872-80
Provincial wood engraver, who worked with his
brother Robert Jackson (q.v.) at 7 and 8 Millgate,
Wigan, Lancashire (Kelly's,1872-80).

JACKSON, John
Wood engraver of the late eighteenth and early
nineteenth centuries. He was noted for engraved
illustrations to children's books, and worked for
many years in Smithfield, London. He is probably
the J.Jackson, wood engraver, of 5 Long Lane,
West Smithfield, (Johnstone,1817). Redgrave
concluded his short entry: 'He was a man of eccentric
habits, of whom little can now be learnt'.
[Bénézit; Bryan; Redgrave]

JACKSON, John 1801-48
Major wood engraver, born of 'humble parentage'
(DNB) in Ovingham, Northumberland on 19 April
1801. He drew from an early age and was placed
with the Newcastle firm of Armstrong and Walker,
engravers and printers, until it went bankrupt. Then
he transferred to Thomas Bewick (q.v.), also a
native of Ovingham, and served out a year's
apprenticeship at the age of twenty-three, from
19 June 1823 - 12 June 1824, but was not admired by
Bewick. He then went to London and worked for James
Northcote, RA and the noted Bewick pupil William
Harvey (q.v.), whose drawings to Northcote's

Fables,1828, Jackson expertly engraved with John Orrin
Smith (q.v.). He also engraved with William Hughes
(q.v.) a drawing of Mr Weare's murder for the
Observer: 'Henceforth Jackson was one of the first
engravers of illustrations on wood for popular
literature or journalism' (DNB). This distinction
was largely due to Jackson's collaborations with
Charles Knight (q.v.), for whom he engraved
numerous cuts to Knight's Penny Magazine, from 1832
onward, and was put in charge of all engravings by
others; also for Knight's Musical Library,1836;
Knight's Shakespeare; and, most notably, Knight's
publication of Lane's Arabian Nights' Entertainments,1839. He continued such collaborations with
Knight throughout all of his working life and Knight
published his and W.A.Chatto's influential Treatise
on Wood Engraving,1839, with about 300 cuts
engraved by Jackson (which are praised by Chatto
several times). Jackson also employed many
assistants from his London offices at 62 (76) Upper
Seymour Street, Euston Square (Pigot,1832-36),
then 12 Cardington Street, Hampstead Road (Pigot,
POD,1838-48). He certainly needed help for his
work for Knight could be daunting: Knight's Farmer's
Library and Cyclopedia of Rural Affairs, from 1847
onwards, was a monthly publication which alone
promised 'thousands of wood engravings' after
William Harvey and other draughtsman, all to be
either engraved by Jackson or farmed out to his
assistants. Other work included drawings to New
Sporting Magazine; and a cut in the Illustrated
London News, 31 December 1842. He wrote articles
to Hone's Every-day Book, and provided numerous
engravings for the publications of the Society for the
Diffusion of Useful Knowledge, and cuts for Martin
and Westall's Pictorial Illustrations of the Bible,
1833, engraved with W.Powis and W.J.Linton (qq.v.).
Gusman even lists several landscape engravings to
the French magazine, Magasin Pittoresque (founded
in 1833). All this led W.J.Linton to claim (in Masters
of Wood Engraving) that Jackson's role as engraver-
supervisor made study of his work difficult, 'so vast
an amount of work was under his direction that it is
not easy to identify his own actual performance'.
Jackson was also concerned for the history of his
profession, and collected material continually for
his Treatise on Wood Engraving. He joined with
William Andrew Chatto, who wrote most of the text,
while Jackson selected the subjects, contributed some
historical material, bore the cost of production and
engraved most illustrations (some of his best work
is found in the first edition, 1839). On the other hand,
Chatto edited and shaped the whole volume, which
ended in a dispute between the two authors over who
had produced the greater share of the book. Nevertheless it remains a good example of an historian-
engraver practising the love of his art, and is still
mostly linked with Jackson's name, despite numerous
discrepancies. A second edition was published with

145 new engravings and a new chapter on artists 'of
the present day' by Henry G.Bohn, 1861. The MS
of Chatto and Jackson is in the London Library.
Jackson continued to work up to his death, of chronic
bronchitis, in London on 27 March 1848. His brother,
Mason Jackson (q.v.) was trained by and worked with
him at his Cardington Street office from about 1846.
The young Ebenezer Landells (q.v.) worked for him
from 1829. His greatest disciple and engraver was
Joan Hassall, who carried his intense interest for
teaching and practising wood engraving into the
present. The British Museum owns a series of proofs
labelled to show 'the process of layering'; also
engravings after J.W.Archer, W.Harvey, T.Landseer,
W.H.Prior and H.C.Selous; the Bodleian Library owns
his work for C.Knight. He signed his work:
'JJ fecit', 'JJ' (superimposed).
[Redgrave; Hake; LeBlanc; Nagler; Heller; DNB; TB;
C.T.Lewis; Gusman; Linton, Masters of Wood
Engraving; I.Bain, Thomas Bewick, 1979]

JACKSON, John Baptist(e) 1701-80?
Chiaroscuro and colour wood engraver. Although not
of the nineteenth century, Jackson's influence as
engraver and colour artist on wood was recognised
after his death by engravers such as Thomas Bewick,
John Jackson and W.J.Linton (qq.v.). C.T.Courtney
Lewis claimed that he was the first known Englishman
to print from wood blocks in full colours. Jackson was
born in 1701 and apprenticed to the engraver Elisha
Kirkall (1685-1742), said to be the first exponent of
'white-line' engraving method, with whom he probably
engraved on anonymous cuts to Croxall's edition of
Aesop's Fables. He also engraved Dryden's Poems,
1717. By 1726 he was working in Paris on book
vignettes, under the major wood engraver Papillon,
until he left in 1731, for Venice. There he engraved
and studied for his plan to revive the disused art of
engraving in colours or chiaroscuro by superimposing
a number of different blocks over one another. His
first colour engraving was 'The Descent from the Cross',
1738, after Rembrandt's painting; by 1745 he had
published seventeen (twenty-four, Slater) similar
colour engravings after various Venetian painters.
After twenty years abroad, he returned to England
and started a business in Battersea, the first in
England, manufacturing paper printed in chiaroscuro
for wallhangings. He published his technical findings
as 'An Essay on the Invention & Printing in Chiaroscuro
...& The Application of It to the Making (of) Paper-
hangings, 1754, which was illustrated with the first in
'natural and proper colours from wood and typepress'
in England. This was the process which Thomas
Bewick found worth trying to revive by the 1820s,
'several impressions from duplicate, or triplicate
blocks, done and printed in this way, of a very large
size, were also given to me, as well as a drawing of
the press from which they were printed, many years
ago, by an old Man of the name of Jackson' (Bewick,

Memoir, p.194). Bewick went on to describe Jackson's
last years spent in his own town of Newcastle:
'Jackson left Newcastle quite enfeebled with Age, and
it was said ended his days, in an asylum, under the
charitable & protecting care of Sir Gilbert Elliot
Bart, at some place on the border near the Teviot
or on Tweedside'. The British Museum owns a large
number of his engravings. Jackson signed his
engravings: 'JBJ sculp'.
[For a complete account of Jackson's work see DNB;
TB (with bibliography); Jacob Kainen, J.B.Jackson,
Washington, DC, 1962; also Redgrave; Nagler;
LeBlanc; Heller; Bryan; C.T.Lewis; Hind; Chatto]

JACKSON, John George fl.1880s
Provincial wood engraver, who worked at 39 Newhall
Street, Birmingham (Kelly's, 1889). An advertisement
in the directory claimed that he did 'every description
of copper-plate and engraving on wood for catalogues,
price lists, pattern and general trade work...general
printer, die sinker, relief stamper'.

JACKSON, Mason 1819-1903
Wood engraver, born in Ovingham, Northumberland
on 25 May 1819. He was the younger brother and
trainee of the wood engraver John Jackson (q.v.).
His early work included engravings after Robert
Seymour for the green wrapper of Dickens' Pickwick
Papers, 1836, followed by engravings after H.Warren
to S.C.Hall's Book of British Ballads, 1842. By 1846
Jackson was established in London as a wood engraver,
and appeared in the directories at 12 Cardington
Street, Hampstead Road (POD, 1846-63), an office
shared with his brother John for two years. Later he
worked from 12 Pembroke Gardens, W (POD, 1866).
During the 1850s and 1860s Jackson established a
reputation as a competent and prolific engraver for
numerous popular magazines and books. He trained
the wood engraver E.M.Wimperis (q.v.) and became
the principal wood engraver for the Art Union of
London (later Art Journal), 1850-60. He also worked
for the innovative publisher Charles Knight (q.v.)
and engraved Knight's Shakespeare; Knight's
'Land We Live In' series, with H.Orrin Smith, Bastin,
and the Dalziels (qq.v.); and most notably Knight's
edition of Lane's Arabian Night's Entertainments, 1839.
Other work included engravings for Cassell's
Illustrated Family Paper, 1857 and cuts to the
Illustrated London Almanack, 1850-51. Of particular
importance is the fact that he was engraver to the
Illustrated London News, 1850-78 (art editor from
1860), a post he held for thirty years. Here he
engraved numerous full and double-page drawings
and paintings of prominent period artists, like
Frederick Goodall and the draughtsman John Gilbert
(q.v.). He was also a competent portrait engraver
of artistic and literary personalities: Tennyson (after
a photograph), John Leech, Daniel Maclise, Thomas
Creswick, Thomas Carlyle, David Roberts, and

Princess Alexandra of Denmark (after a photograph). Jackson was praised by Chatto in his article on wood engraving in the Illustrated London News, 1844 and was singled out by Bohn, in Chatto and Jackson, for his skilful engravings to Bohn's edition of Walton's Compleat Angler, after Thomas Creswick's drawings and his cuts to Ministering Children. He also established a reputation as an historian of his profession- the first historian of illustrated journalism in England. His The Pictorial Press: Its Origins and Progress, 1885, traced the rise of illustrated journalism from its early beginnings to late Victorian times. He also exhibited landscape paintings from 1856-79 at the Royal Academy, the Dudley Gallery and the Portland Gallery. He died in West London on 28 December 1903 and was buried at Brompton Cemetery. The British Museum owns his engravings after E.Armitage, J.Gilbert and W.Harvey, and various landscapes; the Bodleian Library owns his engravings for C.Knight. He signed his engravings: 'M JACKSON SC'.
[Chatto; Houfe; Bénézit; TB; DNB; Hake; LeBlanc]

JACKSON, Robert fl.1870s-90s
Provincial wood engraver, who worked with James Jackson (q.v.) at 7 and 8 Millgate, Wigan, Lancashire (Kelly's, 1872). He probably engraved a portrait of Harriet, Marchioness of Duffeerin and Ava, for the Illustrated London News, 1891, which is now owned by the British Museum.
[Hake]

JACKSON and Smith fl.1820s-30s
Joint collaboration between the wood engravers John Jackson and John Orrin Smith, about 1828. Their major work was for Whittingham's Sandford and Merton, engraved with Willis (q.v.) and a tailpiece, 'The Alderman's Funeral' to Northcote's Fables, 1828.

JACQUE, G.H.
French draughtsman, who contributed drawings for wood engraving in the Illustrated London News, 1851.

JAHYER, Octave Edouard Jean 1826-?
French wood engraver, who contributed to various English magazines. He was born in Paris on 26 November 1826, was a pupil at the Ecole des Beaux Arts, and exhibited from 1848 at the Salon, generally wood engravings after Baron, Doré, and Charles Jacques. He worked for numerous French magazines, Monde Illustré, and Magasin Pittoresque, and became an interpreter of Gustave Doré (q.v.) for Complainte du Juif Errant, 1856 and Contes Drolatiques, 1855. He also engraved on wood for the English Illustrated Magazine, 1883-87, after T.Napier Hemy, etchings of Constable, and drawings of Hugh Thomson to 'Days with Sir Roger de Coverley'; also after David Murray, Heywood Sumner's 'Undine' series, and Robert Jobling and Noel Paton's (qq.v.)

illustrations. He signed his work: 'O.Jahyer'.
[LeBlanc lists him as 'Jahyer, frères', suggesting he worked with a brother; see also Gusman; Bénézit; TB]

JAMES and Company
London draughtsmen firm, with an office at 79 Queen Street, EC (Kelly's, 1900).

JANET, Gustave 1829-?
Draughtsman on wood, lithographer. He was born in Paris in 1829, the brother of Janet-Lange (q.v.). He drew on wood for most of the leading French magazines, e.g. Monde Illustré and Revue de la Mode. He also drew for the English Cassell's Family Paper, 1853. Henry Vizetelly commissioned work from him, first for his Illustrated Times, 1855-56, then when Vizetelly moved to Paris as correspondent to the Illustrated London News, Janet drew for that paper, 1867-71. Vizetelly recalled that Janet was 'excellent in depicting such scenes as a ball or a reception at the Tuilleries, his women always being very gracefully drawn although they were remarkably alike in face... he was deficient in the knack of imparting the appearance of action or motion to his figures' (Vizetelly, Glances Back, II, p.337).
[Houfe; Bénézit; Beraldi]

JANET-LANGE, Ange-Louis 1815-72
Draughtsman, lithographer and painter. He was born in Paris in 1815, the elder brother of Gustave Janet (q.v.). He was commissioned by Henry Vizetelly (q.v.) to draw for his Illustrated Times, 1860, then for the Illustrated London News, because as Vizetelly recalled he drew on wood in a far more vigorous style than his brother. Janet-Lange achieved a reputation for his military episodes and drawings of Court pageants. He also drew, like his brother, for the English magazine Cassell's Family Paper, 1855.
[Gusman; Vizetelly, Glances Back]

JARVIS, Thomas fl.1841-48
London wood engraver and draughtsman. He worked in London at 30 Nicholas Lane, Lombard Street (POD, 1848) and drew on wood for Charles Knight's Penny Magazine, September 1841, engraved by Quartley and Sears (q.v.).
[Bodleian Library]

JEFFRIES, William Frederick fl.1890-1900
London draughtsman and wood engraver, who worked at 58 Fleet Street, EC (POD, 1890-93), Falcon Court, 32 Fleet Street, EC (POD, 1894-98), and then at 153 Chadwick Road, Peckham, SE (LSDS, 1898-1900).

JENKIN, C.M. fl.1871-76
Wood engraver, who worked for Dark Blue, 1871-73, engraving 'commonplace designs' of E.F.Clarke, W.J.Hennessey, M.Fitzgerald, D.H.Friston,

S.P.Hall, and J.A.H.Bird. He also engraved full, double and foldout page engravings to the Illustrated London News,1871-76. These, after Hennessey and Robert Barnes (q.v.), were engraved in a rather crude, heavy line, the faces over cut and printed too dark, and only when Jenkin stippled over the surface did a lighter grey clarity emerge. He signed his work: 'JENKIN Sc' (script. [White]

JENKIN, Thomas Williams fl.1897-1901
London wood engraver, who worked at 7 New Court, Carey Street, WC (POD,1897-1901) and shared the premises with D.W.Williamson (q.v.).

JENKINS, P.F.L. fl.1853-55
London wood engraver, who worked at 17 Eaton Street, Grosvenor Square (POD, Hodgson's,1853-55).

JENKINSON, Charles
London wood engraver, who worked at 109 Fleet Street, EC (POD,1900-01).

JENNINGS, Charles fl.1830s-40s
Wood engraver, who engraved cuts for Charles Knight, especially for his edition of Lane's Arabian Nights' Entertainments,1839. He signed his work: 'JENNINGS'.
[Bodleian Library]

JENNINGS, Edward fl.1865-88
Occasional illustrator and landscape painter. He drew on wood for Good Words,1880. He also exhibited at the New Watercolour Society, the Royal Academy, the Royal Society of British Artists and the Royal Institute of Painters in Watercolours.

JEWELL, Frederick William fl.1884-86
London wood engraver, who worked at Hare Place, 47 Fleet Street, EC (POD,1884-85), then 93 Fleet Street, EC (POD,1886).

JEWITT, Edwin fl.1848-64
Wood engraver, one of the four younger brothers and pupils of the wood engraver Orlando Jewitt (q.v.). He moved to Headington, near Oxford with the Jewitt family about 1838, but appears in London ten years later. There he worked as a wood engraver at 15 Hardwick Place, Commercial Road, E (POD,1848-55), then 1 Pickett Place, Strand (POD,1856-64). His engravings appeared in his brother Llewellynn Jewitt's (q.v.) Manual of Illuminated Missal Painting,c1860, with lithographs by Orlando; he engraved the title-page to Town Talk,1858. He signed his engravings: 'E.Jewitt'.

JEWITT, Henry ?-1875
Wood engraver, elder brother of Orlando Jewitt (q.v.) with whom he worked. When given the blocks,

with Orlando's drawings from objects on them, he developed a reputation for 'being able to cut the finest line of anyone in the trade'. A comparison of Orlando's preliminary drawings with the engraved blocks shows that Henry was more than the 'nameless drudge' some believed him to be (see H.Carter, Orlando Jewitt,1962). Although Henry 'added a somewhat rigorous and unsympathetic quality to the subjects' in many cases, according to Carter, the sheer intricacy of Orlando's architectural drawings, with their demands for fine lines, meant that Henry was at least a competent engraver. His engravings also appeared in his brother Llewellyn Jewitt's (q.v.) London Interiors,1841. He worked from Orlando's office, 20 Clifton Villas, as Jewitt, Keates and Reynolds from 1869 until his death in 1875. He signed his work: 'H.Jewitt'.
[See H.Carter, Orlando Jewitt,1962; also J.Horden in The Library,1964,p.326; J.H.Parker, ABC of Gothic Architecture,1881]

JEWITT, Llewellyn Frederick William 1816-86
Wood engraver, illustrator and antiquarian. He was born in Kimberworth, near Rotherham, Yorkshire on 24 November 1816, the youngest of the seventeen children of the topographer Arthur Jewitt. His brothers were the wood engravers Orlando (q.v.), with whom he worked and trained, Henry (q.v.), and Edwin (q.v.). In about 1818 he moved to Duffield, Derbyshire, where his father taught him drawing and Orlando taught him wood engraving ('before he was twenty-one', DNB). He met the draughtsman, wood engraver and antiquarian F.W.Fairholt (q.v.) in 1835, with whom he went to London three years later. Together they drew and engraved under Stephen Sly (q.v.) for the publications of Charles Knight (q.v.). These included Penny Magazine, Pictorial History of England, Pictorial Bible, Illustrated Shakespeare, Penny Cyclopedia, London, Palestine, and Old England. He also drew and engraved extensively for the Pictorial Times, the Illustrated London News, Literary World, Mirror, and Saturday Magazine. According to his biographer, like Fairholt, 'he issued so vast an amount of unsigned work that his labours can never be estimated' (W.H.Goss, Llewellyn Jewitt,1889,p.10). This included almost all of the drawings to London Interiors,1841, with engravings by his brother Henry; and an immense amount of tedious labour on a forty foot long architectural drawing of London from Hyde Park to Aldgate Pump, drawn to scale. Jewitt moved to Headington, near Oxford about 1846, to work with his brother Orlando on engraving illustrations to Parker's Glossary of Architecture, and Orlando's Domestic Architecture. After a few years he returned to London where he supervised the engraved illustration to Punch, during the period of Kenny Meadows, Thackeray and Leech (qq.v.). Poor health forced him to abandon this work and he moved to a succession

of jobs in various towns, first as librarian in
Plymouth, then in 1853 to Derby, where he started
the Derby Telegraph, serving as its editor until
1868. In 1860 he established the antiquarian magazine,
Reliquary, and continued as its editor until his death.
The latter part of his life was occupied in antiquarian
and archaeological pursuits, and he wrote extensively
on a variety of topics from ceramics to coins. (For
a list see Goss, also DNB.) His articles for
the Art Journal alone run through more than twenty
volumes. He died in Hollies, Duffield on 5 June 1886.
The British Museum owns some of his work.
[DNB; W.H.Goss, Life of Jewitt,1889; Bénézit;
H.Carter, Orlando Jewitt,1962; British Library
catalogue]

JEWITT, Thomas Orlando Sheldon 1799-1869
Prominent and prolific wood engraver, architectural
draughtsman. He was born in Chesterfield, in 1799,
the son of the topographer Arthur Jewitt and brother
of the wood engravers, Edwin, Henry and Llewellynn
(qq.v.). He was entirely self-taught as an engraver,
brought up in Buxton and Kimberworth, near Rotherham,
Yorkshire, where he produced his first published work,
wood engravings to his elder brother Reverend Arthur
George Jewitt's Wanderings of Memory,1815. Two
years later he contributed drawings of a Derbyshire
walking tour, which he wood engraved and etched, to
his father's Morning Star, or Yorkshire Magazine,
1817-18. He contributed numerous illustrations to a
local publisher's children's books, and nineteen of a
series of fifty juvenile tracts for Houlston of London.
When the family moved to Duffield, near Derby in
1818, Orlando was busy with numerous illustrations
for a new style of guide book initiated by his father
e.g. Peak Guide and Matlock Companion; and he
illustrated several: Stranger's Guide through
Cheltenham; Otley's Guide to the English Lakes;
Slater's Blenheim Guide. Orlando combined copper
and wood engravings in some of these: A Sketch
Historical and Descriptive of the Minster...of
Lincoln,1822; Simpson's History and Antiquities of
Derby,1826; his father's own Lincoln and Lincolnshire
Cabinet and Annual Intelligencer; and S.Glover's
History of the County of Derby,1829. It was the
intention of Arthur Jewitt at this point 'to establish
the engraving business for my sons', and Orlando had
business cards printed: 'O.Jewitt, engraver on wood,
Duffield, near Derby' (in the Constance Meade
Collection, Bodleian Library). The turning point in
Orlando's career came with the architectural wood
engravings from small blocks which he did for Matthew
Bloxam's Principles of Gothic Architecture,1829,
followed by Bloxam's Glimpse at the Monumental
Architecture and Sculpture of Great Britain,1834.
These set the pace and established his work routine,
travelling to the various architectural monuments to
make on the spot drawings of interiors and exteriors.
The result were the engravings for which he is best

remembered: the series of books he did for the
Oxford publisher, bookseller, printer J.H.Parker,
including J.Ingram's Memorials of Oxford,1837,
after drawings of W.A.Delamotte (q.v.), with steel
engravings by J.Le Keux. The Parker collaboration
brought Orlando and his family to Headington to be
near Oxford in 1838. There Orlando collected around
him his assistants, including his brothers Llewellyn,
Henry and Edwin, and his father Arthur. And yet he
appears in the London directories as 'Engraver on
wood, Oxford' (Pigot,1842) which suggests his
attempt to establish a link with the city at an early
stage. The 1840s saw Jewitt at the height of his
career as architectural draughtsman and engraver.
He would make intricate drawings from the object,
then turn over the blocks to his brother Henry, or
another assistant to engrave as the work increased.
From 1840-50 he became increasingly meticulous,
concerned to reproduce the smallest detail, despite
some obvious faulty overall draughtsmanship. In this
he depended to a large degree upon his assistants to
adapt the drawing into fine engraved line. His work
during this period included his associations with the
architectural designer Augustus Welby Pugin,
engraving Pugin's designs in True Principles of
Painted Christian Architecture,1841, although he was
probably restricted in these engravings. These were
followed by Glossary of Ecclesiastical Ornament,
1846. The difficulty here, according to Harry Clark,
Jewitt's biographer, was Jewitt's didacticism: 'his
architecture is easily comprehensible, but his
capacity for suggesting recession by atmosphere or
concentrating attention here or there by wit or
artifice is much less'. Jewitt relied upon flat planes,
and like a toy theatre his engravings lack the essential
sense of space; 'he was not a white-line engraver, and
his capacity to draw what met the eye rather than the
inquiring mind and to draw quickly and incisively is
limited accordingly'. Jewitt was offered the post of
Punch engraver, to succeed E.Landells (q.v.) about 1843,
but refused and suggested Joseph Swain (q.v.).
Nevertheless he was commissioned for drawings and
engravings descriptive of the vogue for gothic
architecture and between 1840-49 many of his earlier
works were republished, after he had re-engraved blocks
or added new cuts. He also spent seven years, from
1844-51, travelling for the work he produced in
T.Hudson Turner's Some Account of Domestic
Architecture in England,1851-59, three volumes,
published by Parker. He was also a keen amateur
archaeologist and wrote articles, lectures and guides
to various sites in and around Oxford. During the
mid-1850s he continued his ecclesiastical drawings
and added natural history commissions. He moved
to London sometime around 1857 (according to POD)
and set up his workshop with 'almost a monopoly of
the special class of wood engraving in which he
excelled' (DNB). He chose Camden Town in north
west London, where at 20 Clifton Villas he worked

until his death (POD,1857-69). The following year his brother Henry continued the firm as Jewitt, Keates and Reynolds. During this last period, Orlando 'did not refuse the dullest jobs', from hack-work advertisements of church furniture and clerical attire, to a chemistry textbook. He had also supplied three blocks to the Official Catalogue of the Great Exhibition of 1851. Among his London clients was the Oxford don, Charles Lutwidge Dodgson (q.v.) (the author Lewis Carroll) for whom he engraved a series of diagrams for £7 in 1859. Dodgson returned to Jewitt in August 1863, with a drawing for his first 'Alice' book drawn on wood. Jewitt apparently gave him some advice, possibly to turn the illustrations over to a professional. He did however agree to engrave the block and improve the drawing, and charged Dodgson £1.17s 6d for engraving 'head of a girl' and for a set of engraving tools, two pencils and nine boxwood blocks. Jewitt's workshop in Headington consisted of William Reynolds, a Baxter pupil; Henry Jewitt; Llewellyn Jewitt; Edward Keates, Orlando's future son-in-law; a Mr Goodhill, draughtsman; Henry Burrows, from London; W.P.Goward, from Ipswich; and William C.Watmough (qq.v.), a son or step-son of Orlando's sister Marianne. When Orlando moved to London most of these accompanied him and after his death, they formed a variety of successive partnerships: Jewitt, Keates and Reynolds (POD,1870-86), then Jewitt and Keates (POD,1887-1901). His last pupil to carry on the influence of the master died as late as 1949. (For an account of each engraver see separate entries.) Orlando Jewitt died at his Clifton Villas, Camden Square home on 30 May 1869. His influence remained in the hands of such writers as Chatto and Jackson, who praised his 'pre-eminent' gothic architectural and ornamental engravings in their Treatise: 'he is one of the very few who continue to combine designing and drawing with engraving'. J.H.Parker in ABC of Gothic Architecture,1881, claimed that he 'was a thorough artist and enthusiastic lover of the subject of Gothic Architecture'. Among his contemporaries Thomas Bewick, writing to Thomas Dovatson (23 November 1827), noted: 'I know nothing of Mr Jewett [sic], except seeing the name O Jewett, put upon some wood cuts--chiefly (I think) views of churches--in the Gentleman's Magazine--on which there was no scope to shew genius--all I can say of them is, that they are as well done as such things need be'. There are a number of watercolours and pencil sketches in the Constance Meade Collection, Bodleian Library, which suggests that Jewitt made preliminary studies and did not always draw directly upon the wood block. A selection of proofs are also in the British Museum. Jewitt signed his engravings: 'O.Jewitt' although many under this signature were probably done by assistants.
[For biographical and bibliographical detail see H.Clark, Orlando Jewitt,1962; also The Library,

1964,p.326; DNB; Redgrave; also W.Goss, Llewellynn Jewitt,1889]

JEWSBURY, Thomas Smith fl.1872-80
Provincial draughtsman and wood engraver, who worked at Arcade Chambers, 96 Deansgate, Manchester (Kelly's,1872-80).

JOBLING, Robert 1841-1923
Illustrator of panoramic views and river painter. He was born in Newcastle in 1841, trained there as a glass-maker, attended evening art classes at the Newcastle School of Art, and began to illustrate for various magazines. He drew for the Illustrated London Magazine,1885 and provided illustrations to R.J.Charlton's article, 'Newcastle on Tyne', in the English Illustrated Magazine,1885-86, wood engraved by E.Ohme, E.Schladitz, O.Jahyer, R.Lueders, and E.Gascoine (qq.v.). He also drew for The Graphic,1889, and did illustrations to Wilson's Tales of the Borders. He became a full-time artist in 1899, although he exhibited from 1878 at the Royal Academy and the Royal Society of British Artists. He died in Whitley Bay in 1923.
[Bénézit; TB; Houfe]

JOHANNOT, Tony 1803-52
French draughtsman on wood, etcher, lithographer and painter. He was born in Offenbach on 9 November 1803, the brother of the copper engraver Charles Johannot and the painter engraver Alfred Johannot with whom Tony worked. He established a reputation as the foremost French illustrator of the 1840s with his vignettes in the romantic tradition especially for those wood engraved in editions of Balzac, George Sand and Victor Hugo. He was known to the English public through translated editions of his works: 800 vignette drawings to Don Quixote,1836-37, English ed.1842, engraved by Lavoignat; Works of Molière,1835-36; Sterne's Sentimental Journey,1851; and Guinot's Summer at Baden Baden,1853. He also drew on wood for the Illustrated London News,1851. The following year he died, in Paris, on 4 August 1852.
[LeBlanc; Nagler; Muir; Beraldi; Houfe; Glaser]

JOHNSON, Alfred J. fl.1874-94
Illustrator and painter of figures and domestic subjects. He worked from North London, for various magazines. He did drawings for wood engravings in the Illustrated London News,1874-93, where he drew small one-page sketches, and worked on 'special' reporter sketches like 'The Famine in India', 13 June 1874, engraved by William Hollidge (q.v.), and on full-page and foldout drawings after various paintings, engraved by W.B.Gardner and Henry Linton (qq.v.). He also drew for the Quiver,1890, Strand Magazine,1894 and Wide World Magazine, and provided book illustrations to E.S.Turner's Seven Little Australians,1894. He also exhibited

paintings from 1875-87 at the Royal Academy, the Royal Society of British Artists and the Royal Institute of Painters in Watercolours.
[TB; Bénézit; Houfe]

JOHNSON, C.K.
Houfe lists this draughtsman illustrator, who drew comic genre subjects which were wood engraved for The Graphic,1887.

JOHNSON, Edward Killingworth 1825-96
Draughtsman on wood and rustic artist. He was born in Stratford-le-Bow in 1825 and trained himself to paint, attending life classes at the Langham Life School, but preferred working from nature, thus moving to the Essex countryside in 1871. While in London he served as assistant to the wood engravers Smith and Linton (q.v.) who were commissioned to provide engravings to the newly established Illustrated London News. He engraved after prominent water-colourists, the work no doubt inspiring his own later nature drawings. These he contributed to The Graphic, 1874-89, as 'Our Country Artist'. He was also well trained to draw on the wood block: in 1855 he was commissioned to draw on wood for Cundall's edition of Goldsmith's The Deserted Village. He also drew on wood for The Welcome Guest,1860; London Society, 1863; and Churchman's Family Magazine. As a painter, he exhibited at the Old Watercolour Society, the Royal Academy and the Royal Society of British Artists, and was elected AOWS,1866 and OWS in 1876. He died in his beloved Essex in Halstead on 7 April 1896. The British Museum owns proof engravings of his designs done for the Dalziel Brothers (q.v.), 1848-51.
[TB; Bénézit; Clement; Houfe; Linton, Masters of Wood Engraving]

JOHNSON, Herbert 1848-1906
Draughtsman illustrator, figure and landscape painter, etcher. He worked as a draughtsman for various magazines, specialising in military and ceremonial subjects, which he began to do during the early years of The Graphic,1870-89. The paper sent him to India as 'special' reporter of the Royal Tour in 1875, and to Egypt in 1882. He also drew for the English Illustrated Magazine,1888; Daily Graphic,1890; Girls' Own Paper; and Windsor Magazine. He worked in London, mostly in Clapham, and exhibited work at the Royal Academy, the Royal Society of British Artists and the Royal Institute of Painters in Oil-Colours.
[TB; Graves; Houfe]

JOHNSON, John ?-1797
Wood engraver, born in Stanhope in Weardale, the cousin of the wood engraver Robert Johnson (q.v.). He was apprenticed to Ralph Beilby and Thomas Bewick (qq.v.) in Newcastle, from Christmas 1782,

and managed to engrave a few tailpieces to Bewick's British Birds. He also drew 'The Hermit' to Bulwer's edition of Parnell's Poems. Bewick recalled that Johnson was an adaptable pupil, 'for whom we had a great regard....& who we put to do engraving on Wood, as well as other kinds of work--I think he would have shone out in the former branch--but he died of a fever, about the age of 22 when only beginning to give great promise of his future excellence'. He died in Newcastle in 1797.
[DNB; Bénézit; Heller; LeBlanc; Nagler; Bryan; Redgrave; Bewick Memoir]

JOHNSON, John fl.1826-28
London wood engraver, printer of wood engravings. He established himself as engraver and printer at the Apollo Press, 10 Brook Street, Holborn (Pigot,1826-27), where he printed the engravings after William Harvey's drawings to James Northcote's Fables,1828. The book's preface claimed that Johnson's 'skill in the difficult task of printing engravings on wood, has been long well-known and firmly established'.

JOHNSON, John fl.1870s
London wood engraver, who worked at 46 Fleet Street, EC (POD,1872), shared with the wood engraver R.Green (q.v.)

JOHNSON, Neville fl.1830s
London wood engraver, who worked at 14 Little New Street, Shoe Lane (Robson's,1832).

JOHNSON, Richard fl.1880s
Provincial wood engraver, who worked at 18 Scale Lane, Hull (Kelly's,1880).

JOHNSON, Robert 1770-96
Draughtsman and proficient early watercolourist for engravings of Thomas Bewick (q.v.). He was born in Shotley, near Ovingham, Northumberland, in 1770, the son of a joiner, cabinet maker and a Bewick family servant and cousin of the engraver John Johnson (q.v.). His mother secured his apprentice-ship to the Newcastle engraving business, Beilby and Bewick, which apprenticeship Robert served from 23 August 1787-23 August 1794, although he was a year too young and suffered poor health until Bewick nursed him. In fact Bewick quickly saw where Johnson's value lay, not as an engraver, but as a draughtsman and watercolourist of preliminary sketches and drawings to be used in transferring onto the block itself. Bewick kept Johnson away from the confined atmosphere of his workshop (partly because of his poor health) and sent him into the countryside to draw from nature. Bewick recalled in his Memoir (omitted from the first 1862 edition), how much he admired Johnson's skills: '...the next thing I put him to was that of colouring chiefly my

own designs...the practical knowledge I had attained in colouring was imparted to him...he soon coloured them in a stile superior to my own hasty productions ...in this way he became super excellent...' However, Johnson's actual contribution to Bewick's wood engravings (for which he is included here) is still shrouded in uncertainty: Chatto claimed he was 'almost wholly employed in copper plate engraving' at first, then made many designs for tailpieces of Bewick's British Birds, and possibly some drawings to Bewick's Fables,1818. But, as Bain points out in Bewick, Memoir,n.p.244) and Bewick Watercolours, I,pp.70-71, this 'seems highly unlikely'. According to DNB he worked on various designs for engraving: drawings to Bulmer's editions of Goldsmith's and Parnell's Poems,1795 and a drawing of St Nicholas' Churchyard, engraved on wood by Charlton Nesbit (q.v.), and engraved on copper by himself for the publisher Joseph Whitfield of Newcastle. He afterwards quarrelled with Whitfield and made him the subject of three engraved caricatures. After his apprenticeship he turned exclusively to painting. It was in fact painting which had been the basis of a court case with Bewick and Beilby in which he won back money received for drawings sold to the Earl of Bute, which he had done as an apprentice: he had claimed that such watercolour painting was not part of his apprenticeship training. He was then commissioned by Morrison, the Perth booksellers, to copy the portraits by Jameson at Taymouth Castle, for reproduction in Pinkerton's Iconographia Scotica, (published 1799), and had completed fifteen out of the nineteen promised when he caught a chill, and died painfully at Kenmore, Perthshire, on 26 October 1796, aged twenty-six. The DNB points out that two drawings by Johnson were also engraved on wood by C.Warren (q.v.) as illustrations to Gay's Fables and Ossian's Poems.
[DNB; Redgrave; Chatto; LeBlanc; Nagler; I.Bain, Thomas Bewick,1979]

JOHNSON, Thomas fl.1880s
Wood engraver, etcher and watercolourist. He was born in London and trained with the wood engraver F.Williams (q.v.), then moved to Brooklyn, USA, where he worked engraving numerous portraits for the Century Magazine and Harper's. His subjects included Longfellow,1883; Queen Victoria, after an oil painting by T.Sully for Century Magazine,1883; Browning; Tennyson; F.Holl; Franz Liszt; Andrew Lang, after a painting by W.B.Richmond; and John Bright, MP. (Many of these are in the British Museum.) He also engraved after photographs and Old Masters, particularly Rembrandt. His work appeared in England in the English Illustrated Magazine,1885-86, a full-page engraving of Lady Sarah Bunbury, after a painting by Reynolds, engraved on wood but in a poor imitation of steel engraving, the contrasts weak, the whole a flat featureless plate. Johnson exhibited

work in Berlin,1891, Vienna,1895, Paris,1900 and San Francisco,1915. He signed his work: 'T.Johnson'.
[Bénézit; TB; Hake; Fielding]

JOHNSTON, James fl.1851-63
London wood engraver, who worked at 36 Old Broad Street, City (POD,1851-58), then 35 Moorgate Street, EC (POD,1859-60), and 26 New Broad Street, EC (POD,1861-63). The British Museum owns engravings attributed to J.Johnston after W.Phillips, and an advertisement for the Penny Monthly, inscribed engraved 'for Edmund Evans'. He signed his work: 'J JOHNSON Sc', 'J J Sc'.

JOHNSTON, John Alfred fl.1887-99
London wood engraver, draughtsman, who worked at 108 Fleet Street (POD,1887-91) and shared premises with C.Branscombe (q.v.) and W.J.Riches, then at 29 Bouverie Street, EC (POD,1892-93), then 181 Queen Victoria Street, EC (POD,1894-99).

JOHNSTONE, Alexander 1815-91
Occasional illustrator, genre and history painter. He was born in Scotland in 1815 and studied at the Edinburgh Academy and Royal Academy Schools. He drew some of the 100 illustrations wood engraved by the Dalziel Brothers (q.v.) to Charles Mackay's The Home Affections (portrayed) by the Poets,1858. His work appeared there alongside that of such noted draughtsmen as Birket Foster, John Gilbert, T.B.Dalziel, S.Read, and John Tenniel (qq.v.). He also exhibited paintings at the British Institution, the Royal Academy, and the Royal Society of British Artists. He is not to be confused with the map engraver, Alexander Keith Johnston (1804-71). The British Museum owns a proof engraving after his design, engraved by the Dalziel Brothers, 1857.
[Houfe]

JOHNSTONE, George fl.1880s
Provincial draughtsman on wood, who worked at 31 Caroline Street, Jarrow, Durham (Kelly's,1889). His neighbour was the noted draughtsman A.S.Bain (q.v.).

JOHNSTONE, J.M. fl.1876-91
Wood engraver of artists' portraits, primarily for for Magazine of Art. His subjects included Ford Maddox Brown, painter, a sepia-toned self-portrait c1876; Sir Joseph Edgar Boehm, sculptor, after a photograph for Magazine of Art; William Powell Frith, painter, a self-portrait for Magazine of Art,1889; a portrait of Gladstone, aged seventy-nine, after H.J.Thaddeus for the Magazine of Art,1889; and Thomas Woolner, sculptor, after a photograph for the Magazine of Art, 1891. Most of these are in the British Museum.
[Hake]

JONES
Houfe explains that various wood engravings to the
Illustrated London News,1843, are signed 'Jones
del', that is drawn by Jones. (See also Jones, Charles,
Jones, James, Jones, V. and Jones, William)

JONES, Charles fl.1844-57
London wood engraver, who worked at 17 Houghton
Street, Clare Market (POD,1844), then afterwards
disappearing from the directories he reappears, at
126 Chancery Lane (POD,1855) and 4 Pemberton
Row, Gough Square (POD,1856-57).

JONES, Ferdinand Edmund and Son fl.1870s
London wood engraving firm, with an office at
11 Gough Square, EC (POD,1871).

JONES, George Alfred fl.1880s
Provincial wood engraver, who worked at Cullen's
Yard, Upper Parliament Street, Nottingham
(Kelly's,1889).

JONES, Henry fl.1880s
Provincial wood engraver, who worked at 4 Montague
Street, Liverpool (Kelly's,1889).

JONES, James and Company fl.1841-42
London wood engraving firm, with an office at 1 New
Gloucester Place, Hoxton (POD,1841-42).

JONES, N.
Wood engraver, known to have done an engraving of
Olympus for The Big Story Book. According to
William Allingham's diary (1 August 1866),
'[William] M[orris] and friends intended to engrave
the wood-blocks themselves--and M will publish the
book at his warehouse'.

JONES, Owen Carter 1809-74
Prominent ornamental draughtsman on wood,
architect and topographer. He was born in Thames
Street, London on 15 February 1809 and was a pupil
for six years of the architect Lewis Vulliamy, at the
same time studying at the Royal Academy Schools.
He travelled abroad in 1830 and visited the East in
1833, and Granada in 1834, where he began drawings
of the Alhambra for a book which took nine years to
complete. It was a monumental two volume work of
101 drawings lithographed after his own sketches,
with woodcuts by Henry Vizetelly (q.v.) as well as
steel and copper engravings. He next drew ornamental
decorations on wood for Lockhart's Ancient Spanish
Ballads,1842, which were drawn with C.E.Aubrey
and William Harvey, and wood engraved by Henry
Vizetelly, E.Evans and J.Bastin (qq.v.).
Unfortunately the wood engravings were done in an
earlier style than the accompanying lithographic
border designs, also by Jones. Throughout the 1840s
Jones played a major role in creating ornate Moorish

designed gift books which he devised from meticulous
study of historical ornamentation. Such work reached
a culmination in his classic lithographic work, The
Grammar of Ornament,1856. He also designed
various industrial objects and was appointed
superintendent of works at the Great Exhibition,
1851, and director of decoration of the Crystal
Palace,1852, where he designed the Egyptian,
Greek, Roman and Alhambra Courts, publishing his
designs afterwards. He also exhibited at the Royal
Academy from 1831-61, and died in London on
19 April 1874.
[For colour work see Wakeman and Bridson; also
McLean; Chatto; Redgrave; Houfe; DNB; TB]

JONES, V.
Houfe lists this contributor to the Illustrated London
News,1858, although uncertain whether he was an
engraver or draughtsman on wood.

JONES, William
London wood engraver, who worked at 24 Walcot
Square, Lambeth (POD,1848). Fincham lists a
W.Jones, designer of a 'Reward of Merit' bookplate,
engraved with W.Alexander of 1 York Street, Covent
Garden, dated 1820. The British Museum owns
several proof engravings by the Dalziel Brothers
(q.v.), 1866, after 'W.Jones'.

JONNARD, Paul Pacel ?-1902
Prominent French wood engraver, known for his
work after Gustave Doré (q.v.). He was born in
Paris, of Belgian parents and studied with François
Trichon (q.v.) exhibiting work at the Salon from
1863-66. He established a considerable reputation
for his large, skilfully engraved blocks, undaunted
by the demands of Gustave Doré's intricate tonal
ranges. He engraved Doré's Bible,1867, his Dante's
Paradise,1866, and his masterly illustrations to
Blanchard Jerrold's London,1872, an achievement
Chamberlain called 'graphically one of the most
effective of all nineteenth-century illustrated books'.
Jonnard also engraved for various English magazines,
most notably, according to TB, his reproduction of
Millet's 'Strickerin' for Cassell's Magazine of Art,
1889; also a series of sculpted artist portraits,
now in the British Museum, such as G.F.Watts
after A.Gilbert, for the Magazine of Art,1889;
a self-portrait of William Holman Hunt; Robert
Browning after Alphonse Legros; John Ruskin
after a sculpted bust by J.E.Boehm, for the
Magazine of Art,1891; and Ford Maddox Brown
after C.Dressler. Jonnard also engraved for
numerous French magazines and books. He died
in 1902. He signed his work: 'Jonnard' (script).
[Bénézit; TB; Gusman; Hake; Hayden, Chats on
Old Prints,1908]

JOSEPHS, Michael fl.1875-83
London wood engraver, who worked at 11 Buckingham
Street, Strand, WC (POD,1875-83).

JOYCE, Thomas and Son fl.1845-98
London wood engraving firm, listed first as Thomas
Joyce, 6 Well Street, Cripplegate (POD,1845-66),
66 Bartholomew Close, EC (POD,1867) and 7 Old
Bailey, EC (POD,1869-71). The following year the
firm changed to Thomas Joyce and Son, 58 Dorset
Street, EC (POD,1872-90). By 1893 a Thomas
Stewart Joyce ran the firm from 5 Whitefriars Street,
EC (POD,1893-98).

JOYCE, William Henry fl.1836-1901
London wood engraver, who worked first at
9 Martlett Court, Bow Street (Pigot,1836) then
25 Duke Street, Lincoln's Inn Fields and 11 Princes
Street, Drury Lane (Robson's,1837, Pigot,1838),
then moved into his main office, 11 Bolt Court,
Fleet Street, EC (Pigot,1839, POD,1840-95). In that
year 1896, there appeared a William Henry Joyce,
wood engraver of 6 Wine Office Court, EC
(POD,1896-1901), an office which he shared then
with C.Murray and W.H.Franklin (qq.v.).

JUSTYNE, Percy William 1812-83
Draughtsman illustrator and landscape painter, who
worked primarily for various magazines. He was
born in Rochester, Kent in 1812, lived in the Near
East and Spain, 1841-48, and specialised in drawings
of those areas' architecture and monuments, such as
illustrations to Smith's History of Greece; Ferguson's
Biblical Dictionary; and C.Kingsley's Handbook of
Architecture. He also drew illustrations for wood
engravings in Cassell's Illustrated Family Paper,
1857; Churchman's Family Magazine,1863; The
Graphic,1873: the Illustrated London News; and
Floral World. He also exhibited at the Royal Academy
and the Royal Society of British Artists. The British
Museum owns several proof engravings by the Dalziel
Brothers (q.v.), after his designs, 1860-64.

KEATES, Charles (Edward) fl.1870-1901
Wood engraver, who worked in London. He was the
son-in-law of the noted engraver Orlando Jewitt
(q.v.). He worked with Jewitt's brother Henry
Jewitt and William Reynolds (qq.v.) as Jewitt,
Keates and Reynolds, 20 Clifton Villas, Camden
Square, NW (POD,1870-86) and then when Reynolds
left he continued to engrave as Jewitt and Keates, at
the same address (POD,1887-1901). A family article
in The Library gives his name as Edward Keates and
describes him as the 'future son-in-law of Orlando
Jewitt'.
[The Library, 1964,p.326]

KEATS, Charles fl.1890s
Wood engraver, who worked with T.Sturge Moore
(q.v.) cutting ornamental borders for the Vale Press
books of Charles Ricketts (q.v.).
[J.R.Taylor, Art Nouveau Book in Britain,p.71]

KEELING, William Knight 1807-86
Occasional illustrator, portrait painter and watercolourist. He was born in Manchester in 1807,
where he was apprenticed to a wood engraver. He
then moved to London to study under the portrait
painter, W.Bradley, but later returned to Manchester
in 1835 and helped to found the Manchester Academy
of Fine Arts. He contributed an illustration to The
Chaplet,1840, but was primarily a painter. He was
an exhibitor at the British Institution and the Royal
Academy, and was elected NWS,1841. He died in
Manchester on 21 February 1886.
[Houfe]

KEENE, Charles Samuel 1823-91
Prolific draughtsman illustrator on wood, and etcher.
He was born in Hornsea, London, on 10 August 1823,
the son of a solicitor. From an early age he was
devoted to drawing, encouraged by his mother, but
after a private school and a period at Ipswich
Grammar School, he entered his father's solicitor's
office. While there he drew and watercoloured
historical and nautical subjects which his mother
helped to sell and these were the basis for Keene's
five years' apprenticeship to the noted wood engraver
Josiah Whymper and his brothers (q.v.). He combined
training for wood engraving with drawing at the
Clipstone Street Artists' Society, being a member from
1848-50. After leaving Whymper in 1852, he set up
as a draughtsman illustrator in the Strand (although
he does not appear in the London directories) and
worked for various magazines, especially the nearby
Illustrated London News,1850-56; then Punch,
1851-91. His drawings here secured his reputation
as the foremost interpreter of London's urban life,
and one source claimed that while those to 1865 were
issued anonymously, the total number of Punch
drawings was about 3,000. Such work soon taught
Keene the trials of drawing for the wood engraver
and he disliked the destruction of his originality by
the engraver. As he wrote to the budding Punch
artist A.Chantrey Corbould (q.v.), 'I never give
advice on these matters, but I can tell you from my
own experience I don't think drawing on wood is a
good road to stand on as an artist; but if you don't
agree with me, and wish to go in for this particular
branch, it seems to me that you should article or
apprentice yourself by legal agreement with some
engraver of large business for a certain time on
certain terms. This is how I began, and have been
sorry for it ever since!' (Spielmann,p.544).
Nevertheless, Keene became a frequent and prolific
contributor to magazines and books: he drew about

140 illustrations for the first issues of Once a Week, 1859-65,1867; Good Words, 1862 engraved by the Dalziel Brothers (q.v.); the Cornhill, 1864; and London Society, 1866-70. Much of his early sixties work was engraved on wood by Edmund Evans (q.v.) and the Dalziels, who tried in vain to tie him down to a single commission. When they wanted illustrations to a Don Quixote, Keene refused: 'He felt that his best efforts were due to Punch, but even with the proprietors of that journal he objected to be put on any fixed agreement--"No, I prefer to send in my drawings as I finish them, whatever they may be, and be paid for the work I have done"' (Dalziels' Record, p.178). This attitude, and his unusual working method – he always carried steel pens, ink and sketchbook in his pocket – made him a difficult draughtsman for the wood engraver to interpret. Joseph Pennell pointed out while discussing Keene's drawings (quoted in Print Collector's Quarterly, Volume 17,1930): 'They are drawn in black, blue, brown, and red lines, put down with pens, brushes, sticks, and his fingers; the various colours and methods are found in the same design, with very delightful results for everybody except the poor engraver. His paper alone was a serious drawback to excellence of reproduction. He liked to work on dirty brown scraps, upon the backs of old envelopes, or any odd pieces, in which the texture, the very imperfection would add a quality that was amusing. And on these grey or brown bits he drew with grey watery ink, with purple ink; he mixed up pencil and wash, pen and Chinese white, with which he gave modelling and relief to forms, afterwards to be photographed on to the wood, and engraved, as well as they could be engraved by Swain [q.v.] into pure block outline blocks, and printed upon pure white paper.' He even experimented with small pieces of wood tied to his pen holders for delicate softened expressions which 'were the despair of the most finished wood engravers'. Keene continued to draw on wood, despite the trials with his engravers, and only after December 1872 did he consent to work on paper, the design then being photographed on wood. His style changed as well, from tight intricate pencil line to a broader approach. Houfe gives three distinct phases: a Georgian burlesque and caricature, seen in Barrett's Book of Beauty, 1846; a hard Germanic line borrowed from Menzel by the 1850s; and a softer more delicate line in the 1860s. Keene was also an etcher of great skill. He was a dedicated artist and continued to work until his death in London on 4 January 1891. The British Museum owns proofs engraved by the Dalziel Brothers, 1856, 1861-62; over 100 proofs of Keene's Punch cartoons are in the Hartley Collection, Boston Museum.
[See also TB; Houfe (for book lists); G.S.Layard, Life and Letters of Charles Keene, 1892; and Work of Charles Keene, 1897; D.Hudson, Charles Keene, 1947; Reid in Print Collector's Quarterly,

1930; Chatto; Spielmann; DNB; Dalziels' Record; Bénézit; for a description of his etchings see Volume I]

KEENE, Robert Henry fl.1860-87
London wood engraver, who worked at 9 Wine Office Court, Fleet Street, EC (POD,1860-62), an office shared with fellow engravers G.Dorrington and E.Duvergier (qq.v.) then moved to W.J.Linton's (q.v.) old engraving office at 33 Essex Street, Strand, WC (POD,1863-85). Here he shared the premises with G.Butlin, J.Sachs, W.J.Palmer, and W.E.Hastie (qq.v.). By 1886 Keene had moved to 33 Fetter Lane (POD,1886-87).

KEFFORD, (John Warwick) and Pearson; Kefford and Company fl.1877-86
London wood engraving firm, a partnership between John Warwick Kefford and George William Pearson (q.v.). Their office as Kefford and Pearson was at 35 Bouverie Street, EC (POD,1877-80) and then 80 Fleet Street, EC (POD,1881-82). The following year Pearson left to set up on his own, and Kefford continued as John Warwick Kefford and Company, 74 Fleet Street, EC (POD,1886).

KELBIN, James fl.1897-1900
London wood engraver, who worked at 5 Fetter Lane, EC (POD,1897-1900). He shared the premises at first with W.Hollidge (q.v.).

KELLENBACH, Charles de fl.1883-86
Wood engraver, who worked for the English Illustrated Magazine, 1883-86. He engraved 'The Royal Collection of Miniatures at Windsor Castle', 1883-84; a taut, steel-like rendering of 'Crossing the Brook' after Reynolds, 1883-84; and illustrations of T.Macquoid to the 'In Umbria' series, 1885-86.

KELLY, Miss Lucinda C. fl.1848-56
London wood engraver, who worked at 9 Red Lion Court, Fleet Street, EC (POD,1848-51), then 153 Fleet Street, EC (POD,1852) and 15 (90) Nicholas Square, Hackney Road (POD, Hodgson's,1854-56).

KELLY, Samuel fl.1880s
Provincial draughtsman, who worked at 88 Albert Road, Jarrow, Durham (Kelly's,1889). There he specialised in marine subjects and worked in competition with fellow draughtsmen on wood, A.Bain and George Johnstone (qq.v.).

KELLY, Thomas fl.1802-35
Irish wood and copper engraver. He was a student of the Dublin Society's School, where he received prizes for his wood engravings in 1802 and 1803 and he remained in Dublin until 1827. He worked for the Dublin Society and for a Boston publisher in 1823, then travelled to America. He worked in Philadelphia

1831-33 and New York 1834-35, and was also associated with Joseph Andrews in Boston. He specialised in wood engraved portraits of famous people, such as Washington, Jefferson, Napoleon, and Byron. He died in New York about 1841.
[Strickland; Stauffer; TB; Bénézit; Fielding]

KELLY, William fl.1860s
London wood engraver, who worked at 9 Essex Street, Strand (POD,1864). He shared the premises with the noted engravers J.H.Pasco(e), C.Robinson, T.Robinson, and F.Watkins (qq.v.).

KEMP, George fl.1880s
Provincial draughtsman on wood, who worked in Clay Cross, Chesterfield (Kelly's,1889).

KEMP, Harrison and Company fl.1880s
London wood engraving firm, with premises at 23 Charterhouse Street, EC (POD,1881).

KEMP, William fl.1880s
London wood engraver, who worked at 146 Fleet Street, EC (POD,1880). He engraved cuts to the Illustrated London News, October, November, 1880. These were after 'special artist' sketches of Balmoral, engraved as delicate etched line against stark white backgrounds; and a confident full page engraving of salmon spearers. He signed his work: 'W Kemp Sc'.

KEMPLEN, Frederick fl.1857-58
London wood engraver, who worked at 13 Cursitor Street, EC (POD,1857-58). He shared the premises with F.Anderson (q.v.).

KEMPLEN, John fl.1871-72
London wood engraver, who worked at 172 Strand, WC (POD,1871), then at 4 Dyer's Buildings, Holborn, EC (POD,1872).

KENNARD, Edward
Draughtsman, who contributed sporting subjects for wood engravings in The Graphic,1888.

KEULEMANS, John Gerrard 1849-1912
Draughtsman, lithographer and painter. He is noted here for his designs for wood engravings (two signed, more unattributed) to a new edition of Yarrell's History of British Birds,1871-85. He worked in association with E.Neale and C.Whymper (qq.v.), and his drawings were engraved by R.C.West, George Pearson, and the Dalziel Brothers (qq.v.).
[C.Jackson, British Birds]

KEYL, Friederick William 1823-71
Prominent painter of animals and occasional illustrator for wood engravings. He was born in Frankfurt am Main, 17 September 1823, studied with Verboekhoven, and then came to London in May 1845,

specifically to study with the Victorian animal painter Edwin Landseer as his only pupil. He drew and painted animals, was a frequent exhibitor at the Royal Academy and the British Institution, 1847-72, and was patronised by the Queen. He is listed here as one of the earliest draughtsman illustrators for the Warne and Routledge 'Toy Book' series about 1865. His drawings were engraved on wood and colour printed by Edmund Evans (q.v.). He also drew on wood for the Illustrated London News, 1864-69; Churchman's Family Magazine,1864; Beaton's Annual,1866; and Gatty's Parables from Nature,1867. He died on 5 December 1871. The British Museum owns a proof engraving of his design by the Dalziel Brothers (q.v.), 1862.
[McLean, Victorian Book Design; Houfe; Bénézit; TB]

KILBURNE, George Goodwin 1839-1924
Wood engraver, draughtsman, watercolourist and painter. He was born in Norfolk on 24 July 1839 and was apprenticed for five years to the wood engravers, the Dalziel Brothers (q.v.), with whom he remained for one year after his training period expired. He also married the elder daughter of Robert Dalziel, niece of the Dalziel Brothers. They recalled Kilburne as one of the 'most industrious and constant workers', who was also obedient and skilful: 'He was one of the most satisfactory pupils we ever had. He took up engraving with great aptitude, and from the day he came to us his work was always good' (Dalziels'' Record). Kilburne was also a very skilful draughtsman whose apprentice drawing was 'so perfect, that it was published with the set to which it belonged'. His drawings appeared in the Illustrated London News, 1873; The Graphic,1873-77 (generally domestic or theatrical scenes); and the Cornhill,1884. He later gave up wood engraving, and drawing on wood for the watercolour paintings which were exhibited at the Royal Academy, the Royal Society of British Artists, and the Royal Institute of Painters in Watercolours, to which he was elected member in 1868. He also exhibited at the Royal Institute of Painters in Oil-Colours, to which he was elected member,1883. He died in September 1924.
[Houfe; TB; Bénézit; Dalziels' Record]

KING, Edward R. fl.1883-1924
Illustrator and genre painter of whom little is known. He drew for wood engravings in the Illustrated London News,1883-87 and the chilling realism of his rural and urban scenes was much admired by Van Gogh. He used a bold contrast to suggest the grimness of urban life, which the engraver caught in minute cross-hatching and a sculpted sense of form (see 'Workman's Train', Illustrated London News, 14 April 1883). King also drew for the Pall Mall Magazine and Punch. He exhibited paintings at the Royal Academy, the Royal Society of British Artists, and the Royal Institute of Painters in Oil-Colours, and worked in

East Mosley toward the end of his life. He was elected NEA in 1888.
[Houfe]

KING, H.W.
Draughtsman of animal subjects wood engraved in The Graphic, 1871.

KING, Henry John Yeend 1855-1924
Illustrator and landscape painter. He was born in London on 25 August 1855 and apprenticed to the glass painters, Messrs O'Connors, of Berners Street. After three years he left to study painting, under William Bromley, then in Paris under Bonnat and Cormon. He began to exhibit at the Royal Academy, 1876, and was elected RBA, 1879, RI, 1887 and VPRI, 1901. He is listed here for his drawings, usually of rural or domestic subjects, for wood engravings in The Graphic, 1888-92; and the Illustrated London News, 1887-94. He died on 10 June 1924.

KING, Walter
London draughtsman for wood engraving, who worked at 73 Farringdon Street, EC (Kelly's, 1900).

KINGDON, Charles
Wood engraver, one of the earliest engraving pupils of the Dalziel Brothers (q.v.). He and his colleague Harry Fenn (q.v.) worked on blocks, although Kingdon had by far the greater talent for engraving, despite his disadvantages -- a 'restless nature and had not the persistent industry of his companion', according to the Dalziels. Kingdon left after his apprenticeship for Canada, found work in America, and settled in New York City, marrying an American. The Dalziels recall, 'He died young'.
[White; Dalziels' Record]

KINNEAR, James fl.1872-92
Scottish wood engraver and landscape painter. He worked as wood engraver at 5 Crichton Street, Edinburgh (Kelly's, 1872-76), then began exhibiting landscape paintings in London at the Royal Academy and the New Watercolour Society, from 1880-92.
[Bénézit; TB; Graves]

KIRBY, Thomas and Sons Limited
Provincial draughtsmen firm, with an office at The Bridge, Walsall (Kelly's, 1900).

KIRCHNER, John fl.1840s
London wood engraver, who worked at 15 Bridge Street, Southwark (POD, 1840). Bohn in Chatto and Jackson reproduces his cut after John Gilbert's (q.v.) drawing 'Prince Arthur and Hubert de Bourg' to Percy Tales of the Kings of England, 1840. Kirchner used the fine black-line style, the figures modelled by dark hatching and a stark white highlight. He signed his work: 'KIRCHNER Sc'.

[Chatto]

KIRKPATRICK, David M. fl.1880s
Provincial draughtsman on wood, who worked at 101 Durham Street, Newcastle-upon-Tyne (Kelly's, 1889).

KIRKPATRICK, Miss Ethel fl.1891-c1941
Colour woodcut designer, landscape and marine oil and watercolour painter. She was the sister of Ida Kirkpatrick, a noted painter. She studied at the Royal Academy Schools, and the Central School, and exhibited work in London from 1891, notably at the Royal Academy, the Royal Institute of Painters in Watercolours, and the Royal Society of British Artists. Her colour woodcuts were praised by Gusman, who linked them to the work of the woodcut artists Mabel Royds and H.G.Webb (qq.v.). She was a member of the Society of Graver Printers, and Colour Woodcut Society. She lived in Harrow, Middlesex.
[Gusman; Waters]

KITTON, Frederick George 1856-1903
Occasional draughtsman, wood engraver, author and illustrator. He was born in Norwich on 5 May 1856 where he was educated before moving to London. There, he trained as a wood engraver and draughtsman on wood for W.L.Thomas (q.v.), who was then editor of The Graphic. He contributed drawings for engravings there, 1874-85, also for the Illustrated London News, 1889-90; then as a prolific but mundane pen and ink draughtsman for the English Illustrated Magazine, 1891-92; Black and White, 1892; and Sunday Magazine, 1894. His skill as a draughtsman engraver prepared him for his greatest contribution, his numerous books written on Dickens and his illustrators. He also exhibited work at the Royal Society of British Artists, 1880, and in Norwich, 1886-87. He died in St Albans on 10 September 1903.
[Houfe; Bénézit; TB; DNB; Sketchley]

KLEBOE and Franklin fl.1895-1901
London wood engraving firm, with an office at 75 Fleet Street, EC (POD, 1895-1901).

KLINKICHT, Moritz (Karl M.Johannes) 1845-?
German wood engraver, who was born in Neustadt on 18 April 1845. He studied in Dresden with August Gaber (q.v.) 1859-62, and worked in Stuttgart and Paris. From 1868-83 he worked in London where he served for four years as director of the wood engraving studio of the publisher Cassell, Petter and Galpin. Among his employees was the wood engraver John Greenaway (q.v.). During this English period Klinkicht also set up an office as wood engraver, as 'Maurice Klinkicht', at 15 Wine Office Court, EC (POD, 1875-78). Here, he engraved full-page cuts for the Illustrated London News, 1875-76, after

various minor painters and illustrators like
E.Buckman, Arthur Hopkins, H.S.Marks and
Charles Gregory. He adopted a clear outline style,
although detail was often sacrificed to his concern
to pick out the entire background. By the 1880s he
was a capable portrait engraver of large-format
engravings, especially for the Illustrated London
News,1886-93, working after photographs of his
subjects. They included Herbert Spenser, after a
Mayall photograph, 9 October 1886; Cardinal
Manning, after a photograph, 3 April 1886; Robert
Browning, after a photograph, December 1889;
G.F.Watts, after a Julia Margaret Cameron
photograph, 1889; Henry Irving and Thomas Huxley,
1891; Thomas Hardy, 1892; and John Tyndale, 1893.
He also engraved a portrait bust of Sir Joseph Noel
Paton, painter, for the Magazine of Art,1880. All
of these are in the British Museum. Much of this
work was done for English publications while he
lived out of the country, from 1883 in Freiburg. The
British Museum also owns two large engraved
portraits. He signed his work: 'M KLINKICHT'.
[Hake; TB]

KNESING, Theodor 1840-?
German wood engraver and draughtsman illustrator.
He was born in Leipzig on 24 July 1840, where he
learned wood engraving. He was a pupil of the
Leipzig Academy, 1856-58 and then the Munich
Academy, 1866-67. He then travelled to Rome, 1867,
Paris, 1867-68 and finally to Munich, 1869, where he
established a reputation for wood engravings after
Doré (q.v.), Grützner, Kaulbach and Keller. He is
listed here for his full-page engravings on wood to
the English Illustrated Magazine,1883-85. These
include a portrait of Martin Luther after Cranach,
1883-84; a stipple engraving after Rossetti's watercolour, 'Lady Lilith', 1883-84; 'Shy' after Lawrence
Alma-Tadema and 'Mrs Siddons' after Gainsborough,
both 1883-84; and 'The Baby's Lullaby', after
Lawrence Alma-Tadema, 1884-85.
[TB]

KNIGHT, Charles 1791-1873
Influential publisher of wood engravings, colour
printer. Knight is listed here for his promotion of
most of the talented wood engravers of the mid
nineteenth century, whom he employed for his
numerous publications: Penny Magazine,1832-45;
Penny Cyclopedia,1833-44; History of England; Knight's
London,1841; Lane's Arabian Nights' Entertainments,
1839; Pictorial Shakespeare,1842; and the 'Land We
Live In' series. Among his engravers were J.Jackson,
T.Williams, S.Sly, the Whympers, A.J.Mason,
Murdon, Wragg, M.Hampton, Landells, Holloway,
Sears, Leonard, Slader, G.P.Nicholls, F.J.Smyth,
J.Andrew, Quartley, Welch, Mead, Crowe, E.Evans,
and the Dalziel Brothers (qq.v.). Knight was also a
competent colour printer who patented in 1838 the

'Patent Illuminating Process' which allowed him to
offer for the first time colour-plate illustrations to
a wide popular audience. The Bodleian Library
owns a large collection of his books and magazines.
[C.Knight, Passages from a Working Life,1865;
DNB; C.T.Lewis; McLean; Chatto; Dalziels' Record]

KNIGHT, Isaac fl.1823-24
London wood engraver, who worked at Old Bethnal
Green Road (Pigot,1823-24).

KNIGHT, John fl.1849-80
London wood engraver, who worked at 22 Kirby
Street, Hatton Garden (POD,1849-51), then at
7 Clerkenwell Close (POD,1853-80). He may be the
engraver in early partnership with W.C.Walker
(q.v.) as Walker and Knight (q.v.), 1840-48. The
Constance Meade Collection, Bodleian Library, has
a penny dreadful, The Little Woodman and His Dog
Caesar,n.d. with wood engravings signed: 'J.Knight
sc'.

KNIGHT, John William Buxton 1843-1908
Occasional illustrator for wood engravings, watercolourist and landscape painter. He was born in
Sevenoaks in 1843, studied with J.Holland in Kent,
and then attended the Royal Academy Schools, 1860.
He also illustrated the article 'Hops and Hop-picking'
in the English Illustrated Magazine, 1886-87. His
drawings were wood engraved by H.S.Percy,
H.F.Davey, C.Streller, R.Paterson, and
J.A.Quartley (qq.v.). Knight also exhibited paintings
at the Grosvenor Gallery and the Royal Academy. He
was elected member of the Royal Society of British
Artists, 1875; and the Royal Society of Painter-
Etchers and Engravers, 1881. He died in Dover on
3 January 1908.
[Bénézit; TB; Graves; A.Lingfield, Work of
J.B.Knight; Magazine of Fine Arts,1906; Art
Journal,1908]

KNIGHT, P.
The British Museum attributes a series of fine black
outline engravings to P.Knight. These are of
classical statuary and signed: 'P Knight'. They
were acquired in 1866.

KNIGHT, Richard fl.1866-1881
London wood engraver, who worked at 11 Carey
Street, Lincoln's Inn, WC (POD,1866-67), 4 Symond's
Inn, WC (POD,1868-70), and then 34 later 15 Cursitor
Street, WC (POD,1872-81).

KNOTT, Lewis fl.1886-1910
London wood engraver, who worked at 89 Farringdon
Street, EC (POD,1886-1910). He shared this office
with several engravers, F.Appleton, W.J.Potter,
H.Prater, F.Thorp(e), J.Dixon, and W.Ginn (qq.v.).

KNOWLES, Davidson fl.1879-1902
Draughtsman illustrator, landscape and figure
painter. He worked in London drawing for wood
engravings in The Graphic,1880; the Illustrated
London News,1883-96; and the English Illustrated
Magazine,1893-94. He also illustrated the book,
W.D.Cummings' Songs and Lyrics for Little Lips,
n.d. He specialised in country subjects and
animals, the painted versions being exhibited
1879-96 at the Royal Academy, the New English Art
Club, and the Royal Society of British Artists, where
he became a member,1890.
[Houfe; Bénézit; TB]

KNOWLES, William Henry fl.1870s
Provincial wood engraver, who worked at Market
Place, Denton, Manchester (Kelly's,1872).

KOPPEL, Charles W. fl.1875-82
London wood engraver, who worked at 74 Fleet
Street, EC (POD,1875-82).

KRAKOW, S.
Wood engraver, who engraved cuts to the penny
dreadful, Lonely Lily, by M.L.C., published by
John F.Shaw, London, n.d. This is in the Constance
Meade Collection, Bodleian Library.

KRETSCHNER, Albert 1825-91
Occasional draughtsman on wood, and genre painter.
He was born in Burghof, Germany on 27 February
1825 and studied at the Berlin Academy. He exhibited
once in London at the Royal Academy, 1852. He is
listed here for his drawing for a wood engraving in
Henry Vizetelly's Illustrated Times,1859. He died
in Burghof on 11 July 1891.

KRONHEIM, Joseph Martin 1810-96
Prominent lithographer, colour printer, engraver,
listed here for his influence over the Baxter wood
engraving pupils Charles Gregory, Thomas Dowlen,
and Thomas Thompson (qq.v.), whom he employed.
Kronheim was born in Magdeburg on 26 October
1810, and appears in Paris during the 1830s, where
he learned lithography. He was in Britain by about
1835, worked in Edinburgh, 1839, as an engraver
and lithographer and by 1846, he was working in
London. The city directories list 'Joseph Kronheim
and Company' patent stereotype founders, 3 Earl
Street, Blackfriars (POD,1846), then by 1849 he was
an engraver, stamp and die cutter, printer and
embosser of fancy stationary at 32 Paternoster Row
(POD,1849). By that year he was employing the
Baxter pupils Gregory, Dowlen and Thompson and
together they established a colour printing business
of great influence: they printed over 1,000 subjects
before 1854 alone. By 1855 Kronheim had sold up to
his partner Frauenknecht and moved to America and
Germany, then returned to his old firm to retire in

1887. He produced two types of colour print: a
variation upon Baxter's process using zinc or copper
plates drawn on by anonymous artists; and a straight
letterpress from wood or metal blocks, which he used
in the famous Warne and Routledge 'Toy Books' series
(see Routledge's 'Reynard the Fox', designed by
Walter Crane). Kronheim had offices in Manchester,
Glasgow and London by 1867. He died in Germany on
25 March 1896.
[For colour work see Wakeman and Bridson;
E.Etheridge 'Kronheim Prints', Baxter...Print
Values for 1923; articles for F.Seeley in Quarterly
Journal of the Baxter Society,1923-25 (passim);
Baxter Times,1924-25; Lewis; Burch]

L and R, or L.R. fl.1872-76
Draughtsman and wood engraver. He was employed
by the Illustrated London News, as draughtsman,
1872, then as an engraver after Alfred Hunt's (q.v.)
drawings. By 1874 he had produced numerous double-
page supplements after noted Victorian artists: 'Low
Life' after the late Edwin Landseer, 14 February
1874; the full page fantasy, 'A Christmas Dream'
after Kate Greenaway (q.v.), 26 December 1874;
'The Barley Harvest' after John Linnell, 24 April
1875, and the foldout supplement 'The Arab at
Prayer' after Horace Vernet, 15 January 1876;
followed by 'The Gamekeeper's Daughter' after Frank
Dadd (q.v.), 25 March 1876. Most of these were
rather crude engravings which suffered for their
large size, the detail and figures being stretched and
picked out by large areas of parallel lines and a
dependency on dark shadow.

LABY, Alexander fl.1840-1879
Draughtsman and painter of historical subjects. He
worked in Paris where he exhibited,1840-44. He is
listed here for his drawings of Flemish industry
wood engraved in the Illustrated London News,1879.
He also exhibited in London at the Royal Society of
British Artists, 1864-66.

LACOUR, Octave L. fl.1880s
Wood engraver, watercolourist, lithographer and
etcher. He worked from Teddington and adopted the
grey flat-style of the process block to imitate painted
washes. He engraved after the most prominent paintings
of the day, or after drawings by such popular
illustrators as Hugh Thomson, Harry Furniss,
Du Maurier, and Randolph Caldecott (qq.v.), all
in the English Illustrated Magazine. He also engraved
a series, 'English Art', after Turner, Girton and
Cozens; and after various 'Old Master' paintings of
Reynolds, Frans Hals and Moroni. He was especially
good at engraving after Millais, Alma-Tadema and
G.F.Watts. He engraved Millais' portrait of Disraeli
for the Magazine of Art. He also etched reproductions
of paintings and exhibited these at the Royal Academy,

1887-91. The British Museum owns several of his engravings. He signed his work: 'LACOUR' or 'Octave L. Lacour' (script).
[Bénézit; TB; Hake; see Volume I for his etchings]

LADER, A.S.
Draughtsman, who contributed topographical drawings for wood engravings in the Illustrated London News, 1889.

LAING, Charles D. fl.1838-53
London wood engraver and draughtsman. He worked at 1 Long Lane, W. Smithfield (POD,1842), 5 Upper Smith Street, Northampton Square (POD,1848), then 13 (18) Guil Street, East Spitalfields (POD,1851-53). According to Gusman, Laing engraved for French magazines such as Magasin Pittoresque and Vues de Paris, and made cuts after Théophile Fragonard to Les Evangiles,1835. He also engraved for an early issue of the Illustrated London News, 13 August 1842 -- a small vignette, 'View of the City of Bath', which combined stipple-cut foliage with a distinctive parallel lined hillside.
[Gusman]

LAING, John Joseph 1830-62
Scottish wood engraver, born in Glasgow in 1830, where he set up as a wood engraver for some time. Later he moved to London, where he found work engraving architectural subjects for the magazine, The Builder. He died in Glasgow in 1862, aged thirty-two, cutting short a promising career.
[Bénézit; Bryan; Redgrave]

LAMBERT, George 1873-1930
Illustrator and portrait painter. He was born in Russia in 1873, came to England in 1878, and visited Australia in 1891 where he studied and won a scholarship to Paris. During his English period he drew for wood engravings in The Graphic,1887-88; the Strand Magazine,1891; and the English Illustrated Magazine, 1893-94. He taught at the London School of Art, 1910, but returned to Australia, 1928, although elected ARA,1922. He died on 29 May 1930.

LAMBERT, Mark 1781-1855
Newcastle draughtsman and engraver. He was apprenticed in the city, then served as assistant to Thomas Bewick (q.v.). Redgrave claimed that 'He was distinguished for the truth and carefulness of his drawings'. He established his own business in 1807, taking his son, Mark William Lambert (?-1893) in as a partner in 1838. During this period the father engraved chiefly ornamental work 'of a mechanical character'. Fincham lists several engraved bookplates dated 1810, 1830, 1840 and signed 'Lamberts', 'Lambert, Newcastle' or 'M & M W Lambert, Newcastle'. Mark Lambert died in Newcastle on 28 September 1855, aged

seventy-four.
[For more information see John Pinycomb, Lambert as an Engraver of Book Plates,1896, for colour work by Mark Lambert,Junior, see Wakeman and Bridson; also Redgrave; Bénézit; TB]

LAMONT or LA MONTE, Elish c1800-70
Draughtsman on wood, painter of miniatures. She was born in Belfast about 1800, where she worked as well as in Dublin. She painted portraits for The Court Album,1857, and according to Houfe 'did some illustrations for Joseph Swain (q.v.) in the 1860s'. She also exhibited at the Royal Academy, 1856-69, and the Royal Hibernian Academy, 1842-57.

LAMONT, Thomas Reynolds 1826-98
Draughtsman illustrator and landscape painter. He was born in Scotland in 1826 and studied art in Paris with George Du Maurier (q.v.) who used him as 'the Laird' in his own novel Trilby. Lamont drew on wood for London Society,1865, and contributed to the Shilling Magazine,1865-66. He was elected ARWS, 1866, for his landscape painting which appeared also at the Grosvenor Gallery and the Old Watercolour Society, but he did little work after 1880.

LANCASHIRE Wood Engraving Company fl.1880s
Provincial wood engraving firm, with an office at 54 Arcade Chambers, St Mary's Gate, Manchester (Kelly's,1889).

LANCELOT, Dieudonné Auguste 1822-94
Draughtsman on wood, lithographer. He was born in Sezanne in 1822, became a pupil of J.F.Arnaud de Troyes and exhibited at the Salon from 1853-76. He is listed here for his views of Paris which appeared in the Illustrated London News,1857.

LANCON, Auguste André 1836-87
Draughtsman illustrator, painter, engraver and sculptor. He was born in Saint-Claude in 1836 and studied art in Lyons and Paris. He contributed drawings for wood engravings in the Illustrated London News,1870, and after being implicated in the Paris Commune, 1871 and imprisoned, he was re-established as a reputable artist-illustrator under the new regime. He became a 'special artist' for L'Illustration and went to the Balkans for them in 1877.

LANDELLS, Alexander fl.1840s
Wood engraver, brother of the prominent wood engraver Ebenezer Landells (q.v.). He was employed by his brother when Ebenezer set up on his own, first at 76 Fleet Street, then c1840 at his private residence, Thornhill Road, Barnsbury. Alexander was a kind-hearted overseer of the apprentices, such as young Edmund Evans (q.v.), who recalled: 'he gave me ten shillings for cutting the margins of

proofs and sticking them into a scrap-book'.
(Evans Reminiscences, p.8).

LANDELLS, Ebenezer 1808-60
Prominent wood engraver, draughtsman illustrator and
originator of various illustrated papers, including
Punch. He was born in Newcastle-upon-Tyne on
13 April 1808, the son of a Scottish merchant and
was educated locally at Mr Bruce's Academy. At
fourteen he was apprenticed to Thomas Bewick (q.v.),
but remained there only a short time, his father being
unable to arrange terms with Bewick. The Dalziel
Brothers record the conversation between Mr Landells
and Bewick: 'Well, Mr Bewick, I hope you will make
my son a clever fellow'. Bewick's reply: 'Mr Landells,
I'll do my best to teach him what I know, but if God
Almighty hasn't put brains into your son's head, it's
impossible for me to put them there!' The DNE
claimed that 'He was a favourite pupil of Bewick' and
only after Bewick's death in 1828 did Landells go to
London. However the Dalziels record a different
story: '...Landells did not remain long with him
[Bewick], but served his apprenticeship with Isaac
Nicholson (an old pupil of Bewick, who had opened an
office on the opposite side of the way to his old
master, in St Nicholas' Churchyard, Newcastle) with
whom Charles Gray was also a pupil' (Dalziels'
Record, p.10). After a seven years apprenticeship,
young Landells moved to London, where he lived for
some time from November 1824 with the engraver
John Jackson (q.v.) at Clarendon Street, Clarendon
Square. There he joined forces with Charles Gray
(q.v.) and was commissioned to engrave William
Harvey's drawings to the 1833 edition of Northcote's
Fables, for which he engraved the initial letters. He
also engraved with Gray the drawings by Phiz and
Cattermole (qq.v.) to Dickens' Master Humphrey's
Clock. Other engravings of the 1830s included: Mary
Howitt's Sketches of Natural History, 1834, engraved
in a Bewick-style; Thomas Bingley's Tales of
Shipwrecks and Other Disasters at Sea, 1839, drawn
and engraved by Landells; and a few cuts for Charles
Knight's edition of Lane's Arabian Nights'
Entertainments, 1839, and Knight's Pictorial
Shakespeare series. During this period Landells'
worked from an office shared with the printer
Whitehead and Company, 76 Fleet Street. About 1840
the Whitehead firm collapsed and Landells moved
premises. He chose to establish his engraving
business in his home at Thornhill Road, Barnsbury,
near Islington. There he had a staff of apprentices,
including the young Edmund Evans (q.v.), supervised
by his brother Alexander Landells (q.v.). He was
made supervisor of fine art engraving to the firm of
Branston and Vizetelly (q.v.). This was followed by
a move to 22 Bidborough Street, New Road, St
Pancras, presumably made to accommodate Landells'
new venture, namely the short-lived illustrated journal
of fashion, Cosmorama. Landells was associated

with the birth of Punch, 17 July 1841 and became its
exclusive engraver on 24 December 1842. To
accommodate the workload which a weekly illustrated
paper demanded, he gathered together a considerable
and impressive staff of assistants: Birket Foster,
Edmund Evans, John Greenaway and William Galter
(qq.v.) were 'in house' wood draughtsmen engravers,
while Edward and George Dalziel, T. Armstrong and
Charles Gorway (qq.v.) were employed as 'outside
wood engravers. Together they worked for 'old
Tooch-it-oop', 'The Skipper' or 'Daddy Landells',
as they affectionately called their employer, and
built up an impressive workshop under his control.
Unfortunately the Punch proprietors, dissatisfied
with his engravings, were to turn to Joseph Swain
(q.v.) to replace him in 1843. The demands on the
business increased when Herbert Ingram consulted
Landells about engraving for his new paper, the
Illustrated London News, 1842: after several months,
the paper's proprietor needed a skilful and reliable
engraver. Landells' work appeared there as early as
14 May 1842, a small line engraving of 'Rufford Old
Hall'. Such work continued throughout the 1840s and
50s, when almost all the engravings done by his
assistants were signed only 'Landells'. Exceptions to
this were the half and full-page engravings which
demanded great detail such as a meeting of the 'British
Association, Cambridge', and the atmospheric
nocturnal scene, 'Fireworks Temple, Vauxhall',
both published in the 21 June 1845 issue. These were
signed 'LANDELLS, GORWAY & PROVART' or
'LANDELLS & GRAY', to signify the work done by
his outside engravers. Other engravings appeared
borrowed from work which Landells had originally
done for his own newest venture, the Illuminated
Magazine, 1843, for which he supplied all the wood
engravings. Landell's engravings in the Illustrated
London News appeared until within months of his
death, which terminated an association of almost
twenty years with the paper. The paper called upon
his skills as a draughtsman when it sent him with
the Queen on her first visit to Scotland, and on her
subsequent visits to the Rhine, in order to make
sketches for engravings. The Queen later bought his
sketches, the first of their kind to be made for a
paper on the spot. Landells was an ambitious,
inventive projector of numerous publishing ventures,
his energies being much admired by his staff. They
followed him to his various premises with an optimism
that was infectious. Unfortunately Landells lacked the
business acumen necessary to sustain his numerous
ideas. His most successful venture was The Lady's
Newspaper, 2 January 1847, 'the earliest paper
devoted to female interests' (DNB) which was
incorporated with The Queen. He was also connected
as artist or proprietor with The Great Gun, begun in
1844; Diogenes, 1853; and Illustrated Inventor. Seeing
the growth of the children's book market, he
illustrated his own: Boy's Own Toy Maker, 1858

(10th edition by 1881), followed by Girl's Own Toy Maker, 1859 (by Alice Landells, probably his daughter); and Illustrated Paper Model Maker, 1860, 'with 12 engraved subjects, descriptive text and diagrams for construction'. All of these projects were initiated from the variety of premises Landells chose. With the Illustrated London News work, he needed to be more centrally located and so moved to the printing district, 6 Bride Court, New Bridge Street (POD, 1844-46). He then moved to 12 Holford Square, Pentonville (POD, 1851) which he maintained as a second office with one at Water Street, Strand (POD, 1854-55), then 188 Strand (POD, 1857-59). His apprentices and assistants were devoted and grateful always for his help. Edmund Evans spoke affectionately of his apprenticeship with Landells, which ended at Holford Square; he could have continued as Landells' assistant if he hadn't wanted to set up on his own. The Dalziel Brothers, who worked for about ten years for Landells, from 1840-50, and lived nearby in Barnsbury recalled: 'In the early part of our career, that is to say during the Forties, we, George and Edward, worked very much in association with Ebenezer Landells... in fact we were largely indebted to him for much sincere help at a time when such help was invaluable ...' (Dalziels' Record, p.4). They were especially associated with the Punch engravings and cut the first Leech (q.v.) drawing, 'Foreign Affairs' for Landells. Landells' prolific if financially unsuccessful career came to an end on his death at Victoria Grove, West Brompton, on 1 October 1860. His son, Robert Landells (q.v.) was also an illustrator. Landells was important as a major contributor to the boom in illustrated journalism during the 1840s and 50s. He employed and trained some of the period's most competent and influential engravers and draughtsmen. His own drawings were rather weak, such as those to the Sporting Review, 1842-46; and the Illustrated London News, 1844-56. He exhibited engravings at the Royal Society of British Artists during his early days in London, 1833 and 1837. Redgrave concluded of his engraving style: 'He worked in a broad, clever manner, but wanted delicacy and refinement both in his line and his drawing'. The DNB notes: 'His later engravings lack any special excellence...' presumably owing to his having a finger in so many publishing pies. The British Museum owns several nature vignettes signed: 'LANDELLS & GRAY'.
[For his work on Punch see Spielmann; also Dalziels' Record; DNB; Redgrave; McLean; Houfe; TB]

LANDELLS, Robert Thomas 1833-77
Draughtsman, 'special artist' illustrator and painter. He was born in London on 1 August 1833, the eldest son of the wood engraver Ebenezer Landells (q.v.). He was educated in France but studied drawing and painting in London, specialising in military scenes. Under the influence of his father, he followed in his footsteps as a 'special artist' for the Illustrated

London News, 1855-71. He was sent to the Crimaea in 1856 to draw scenes of the campaign, and also covered the Schleswig-Holstein War, 1864; the Austro-Prussian War, 1866; and the Franco-Prussian War, 1870-71. For the latter, he was awarded the Prussian Iron Cross. He also drew on wood for the Illustrated London Magazine, 1853-55. He illustrated G.A.Henty's Young Franc-Tireurs, 1872. As a painter, he was employed by the Queen to paint various ceremonials which she attended, and he exhibited at the Royal Society of British Artists, 1863-76. He died at Winchester Terrace, Chelsea, on 6 January 1877. [Redgrave; DNB; Bénézit; Dalziels' Record]

LANDSEER, Thomas 1795-1880
Draughtsman on wood, metal engraver, etcher and illustrator. He was born in London in 1795, the eldest son of John Landseer, ARA, and brother of Charles and Edwin Landseer. He was a pupil and assistant to his father, and studied also with Benjamin Haydon. He drew sprightly, humorous compositions of animals in flight or fighting with men, which were mostly published by Moon, Boys and Graves in the 1820s and 30s: Monkeyana or Men in Miniatures, 1827-28; S.T.Coleridge's The Devil's Walk, 1831; Characteristic Sketches of Animals, 1832; or Emily Taylor's The Boy and the Birds, 1840. Most were etchings although he had begun to draw on wood, notably for his few contributions to magazines: a small third-page drawing on wood after his brother Edwin's sketch, 'Deer-stalking in the Highlands of Scotland', the Illustrated London News, 21 October 1843; followed by a contribution to The People's Journal, 1846. These suggested where Thomas' skills might have led, had he not been so seriously overshadowed and later dependent on his famous brother Edwin, whose animal paintings he devoted most of his life to engraving on metal. Landseer is listed here for work as a draughtsman on wood. Hee had early attracted considerable admiration from Henry Vizetelly (q.v.) who recalled in his Glances Back: 'Deaf old Thomas Landseer, who was a draughtsman on wood--chiefly known for his illustrations to the "Devil's Walk"...'. W.J.Linton (q.v.) described Thomas as 'a short, broad-shouldered deaf man... evincing more originality and vigour of drawing than is to be seen in the excellently painted pictures of the more famous Sir Edwin'. Thomas achieved some small success for his later metal engraved and painted work which he exhibited at the British Institution, the New Watercolour Society, the Royal Academy, where he was belatedly elected ARA, 1868, and the Royal Society of British Artists. But nevertheless he grew more dependent on Edwin's patronage. He died in St John's Wood in 1880.
[For bibliography and list of his metal engravings see Volume I; see also LeBlanc; TB; DNB]

LANGSTON, Arthur Joseph fl.1880s
Provincial draughtsman and wood engraver. He
worked at 8 Newhall Street, Birmingham (Kelly's,
1889). An advertisement in the directory listed
Langston as a 'Photographer, artistic and mechanical
draughtsman, engraver on wood'.

LANGTON, Robert Fulshaw fl.1851-89
Provincial wood engraver, draughtsman. He worked
as 'Robert Fulshaw Langton' in Wilmslow, Cheshire
(Kelly's,1872), then as Robert Langton at Albert
Chambers, Fennel Street, Manchester (Kelly's,
1876-89). According to Wakeman (p.76) Langton
was the first wood engraver to achieve much success
using photography as a means to fix a drawing onto a
wood block, a process which he experimented on for
over four years before he achieved satisfactory
results. Examples of his early engravings were
published in the Art Journal,1854. He also exhibited
an engraving from a photograph of the moon at the
Caxton Exhibition,1877, with the claim that it was an
example of 'the earliest invention of photography on
wood'. The British Museum owns a topographical
print by him.

LARSEN, Carl Christian 1853-1910
Danish draughtsman, painter. He was born in Viborg,
Denmark on 16 March 1853 and studied at the
Copenhagen School of Art. He is listed here for his
drawings for wood engravings of Siberia during his
term as 'special artist' for the Illustrated London
News,1882. He died in Vienna on 6 June 1910.

LASCELLES, E. and T.W. fl.1883-93
Wood engravers, who worked for the English
Illustrated Magazine. E.Lascelles engraved views of
Bath, drawings by Albert Morrow (q.v.), and C.Napier
Hemy's illustrations to 'An Unsentimental Journey
through Cornwall',1883-84. T.W.Lascelles engraved
from 1883-85 after drawings of Albert Morrow, A.Danse,
and W.J.Hennessy (qq.v.); and J.W.North's (q.v.)
drawings to Richard Jeffries' 'Summer in Somerset',
1887-88. The British Museum owns a portrait of Sir
Walter Raleigh engraved for the Illustrated London News,
1891. (See also Lascelles and Richardson)
[Hake]

LASCELLES and Richardson fl.1889-93
London wood engraving partnership, between the
Lascelles and J.T.Richardson (qq.v.). They worked
from 11 New Court, Carey Street, WC (POD,1891-93).
Among their commissions were cuts for the English
Illustrated Magazine,1889-90, notably landscape views
of Osterley Park; and after a series of photographs
depicting 'An August Ramble Down the Upper Thames'.

LAUCHARD, J.
Wood engraver, who engraved a half-length portrait
of the Victorian painter William Etty. It is in the
British Museum collection.
[Hake]

LAURENS, Jules Joseph Augustin 1825-1901
Draughtsman on wood and watercolourist. He was
born in Carpentras, France, on 26 July 1825 and
became a pupil of his brother J.J.B.Laurens. As a
draughtsman on wood he worked for Henry Vizetelly
and provided various views of Persia for his
Illustrated Times,1856. He also regularly exhibited
at the Salon, and died in St Didier on 5 May 1901.

LAURIE, Milton and Company fl.1876-90
London wood engraving firm, with an office at
38 Surry (sic) Street, Strand, WC (POD,1876-77),
then as Laurie and Company, 97 Fleet Street, EC
(POD,1878-86) which it shared with T.D.Collins
(q.v.). After a year at 41 Gracechurch Street, EC
(POD,1887), the firm moved to 36 King William
Street, EC (POD,1888-90).

LAWLESS, Matthew James 1837-64
Draughtsman illustrator and etcher, one of the most
talented of the 'Sixties School'. He was born in
Ireland, the son of a Dublin solicitor, Barry Lawless,
but was educated at Prior Park School, Bath, the
Langham, and Cary's and Leigh's art schools in
London. He studied with Henry O'Neill, RA and was
influenced by the Pre-Raphaelites and the 17th
century Dutch School, known for its mastery of
detail, which he developed in his own drawings on
wood for various 'Sixties School' magazines. This
work began with Once a Week,1859-64. For this he
drew most of his published work, engraved on wood
by Joseph Swain (q.v.). He soon developed a broader,
less solid style, more dependent on a freer use of
white and delicate line and less reliant on dark shaded
masses, and transferred this into the later pages of
Once a Week. He served a short stint for Punch,
1860-61 with six drawings (again engraved by Swain);
and did illustrations to Lyra Germanica,1861; and
the Life of St Patrick,1862. By this time, he had
become acquainted with the Dalziel Brothers (q.v.)
who engraved his drawings on wood for Good Words,
1862-64; also London Society,1862-70, although Reid
claimed that his first Dalziel cut for this ('Beauty's
Toilet',1862) was 'ruined by Dalziel'. Perhaps his
most successful wood engraver interpreter, apart
from Swain and the Dalziels, was Walter Barker
(q.v.), who engraved his touching drawings to the
Churchman's Family Magazine,1863, with a light,
sureness of touch reminiscent of a fine pencil line
or lithograph. Some of this sense of delicacy Lawless
learned while etching plates for the Junior Etching
Club's Passages from English Poets,1862. Lawless
also exhibited at the Royal Academy and the Royal

Society of British Artists, 1857-63. In 1860 Lawless became ill, and died in Bayswater on 6 August 1864, aged twenty-seven, cutting short a promising career. Despite his early death, pleas went out for his reputation not to be forgotten, although sadly they were mostly ignored. His draughtsmanship on wood was often linked to that of Millais and Sandys, though just below their standard. White claimed this was unfortunate: 'but, while a few of the men of the period have less deservedly dropped out of notice, one feels that to repeat such an estimate were to do an injustice to a very charming draughtsman... For fancy and feeling, no less than for his loyal adherence to the Dürer line, at a time it found little favour, Lawless deserves to be more studied by the younger artists of today' (White, pp. 27-28). Perhaps more to the point, Strickland called him 'One of the most brilliant and promising young artists to whom Ireland has given birth...'. The British Museum owns several proof engraved designs, done for the Dalziel Brothers, 1862-63.
[Houfe (book list); White; Reid; Strickland; Chatto; Redgrave; Bénézit; Bryan]

LAWRENCE, William fl. 1872-87
London wood engraver. He worked at 73 Fleet Street, EC (POD, 1872-74), premises which he shared with C.A. Ferrier (q.v.), then at 28 Ludgate Hill, EC (POD, 1875-78), 5 Castle Street, Holborn, EC (POD, 1879-80), 1 Norfolk Street, Strand, WC (POD, 1882), and 32 later 33 Fetter Lane, EC (POD, 1883-87), which was shared with R.H. Keene (q.v.).

LAWSON, Cecil Gordon 1851-82
Draughtsman on wood and landscape oil painter. He was born in Wellington, Shropshire, in 1851, the son of the Scottish portrait painter, William Lawson. He came to London with his father in 1861 and here, by 1870 had set up as a draughtsman on wood for various magazines. He contributed landscape drawings to The Quiver, Good Words, The Sunday Magazine, Dark Blue, 1871-72; as well as illustrations to Poems and Songs by Robert Burns, 1875. He also painted proto-impressionist oils of Kent and Yorkshire countryside which he exhibited at the Grosvenor Gallery, the Royal Academy and the Royal Society of British Artists. He suffered acute ill health and after a trip to France in 1881, died in London on 10 June 1882. His elder brother was the noted illustrator Francis Wilfrid Lawson (q.v.), who taught Cecil for a time.
[DNB; Reid; Bryan; Houfe; TB; Bénézit]

LAWSON, Edward fl. 1872-89
Provincial wood engraver. He worked at 20 (10) South John Street, Liverpool (Kelly's, 1872-89).

LAWSON, Francis Wilfrid 1842-1935
Draughtsman on wood and painter. He was born in 1842, the son of the Scottish painter, William Lawson, elder brother of Cecil Lawson (q.v.) who taught him drawing. He was a prolific figure and landscape draughtsman on wood during the 'Sixties School' period and drew for Foxe's Book of Martyrs, 1866; and Heber's Hymns, 1867. He contributed to such magazines as Once a Week; London Society; the Cornhill, 1867-69; Shilling Magazine; Sunday Magazine; Cassell's Magazine; Broadway; Dark Blue; Auny Judy's Magazine; the Dalziels' Fun; The Graphic, 1869-76; and Punch, 1876. He also collaborated with Luke Fildes on Wilkie Collins' The Law and the Lady, 1876. He exhibited work at the Grosvenor Gallery, the New English Art Club, the Royal Academy, the Royal Society of British Artists, the Royal Institute of Painters in Oil-Colours, the Royal Institute of Painters in Watercolours and the Royal Scottish Academy. The British Museum owns proof engravings by the Dalziel Brothers (q.v.) dated 1865-66.
[Spielmann; Houfe; TB; White]

LAWSON, John fl. 1865-1909
A competent though secondary draughtsman on wood and wood engraver of the 'Sixties School'; also a landscape painter. He worked in Scotland until about 1880, when it may be he who appears in the provincial directories as the wood engraver 'John Lawson, 26 Carver Lane, Sheffield' (Kelly's, 1880), since Houfe claims he worked in Sheffield as late as 1892-93. Lawson is unrelated to Cecil or Francis Lawson (qq.v.) although he contributed numerous drawings to periodicals and books at the same time as they were working. According to Reid, although Lawson was not a major artist, '...his work is often good, and at its best is distinguished by a purity of line and a pleasing use of rich solid blacks'. He began with drawings engraved by Joseph Swain (q.v.) in Once a Week, 1865-67; Sunday Magazine; Cassell's Magazine; The Quiver, 1865; Children's Hour, 1865; Shilling Magazine, 1866; Argosy, 1866; British Workman, 1866; and Pen and Pencil Pictures, 1866. He also exhibited at the Royal Scottish Academy and the Royal Institute of Painters in Watercolours. The British Museum owns proof engravings by the Dalziel Brothers (q.v.) to Goldsmith's Works, and Ballad Stories, 1863-67.
[Houfe (for full list); Reid; White; TB (bibliography)]

LAWTON, William Arthur and Company fl. 1888-91
London wood engraver, who worked at 174 Fleet Street, EC (POD, 1888-91), premises shared with the Commercial and Artistic Publishing and Engraving Company (q.v.). By 1892 this had changed to Lawton and Riley, wood engravers, 174 Fleet Street, EC (POD, 1892).

LAWTON and Riley
(see Lawton, William Arthur and Company)

LAZARUS, Eleazer fl.1830s
London wood engraver, who worked at 51 Mansell
Street, Minories (Pigot,1839).

LEAR, Edward 1812-88
Draughtsman illustrator of comic subjects,
topographical painter and lithographer. He was born
in Holloway on 12 May 1812, and by the age of fifteen
was earning his living by making bird drawings. In
1831 he became a draughtsman at the Zoological
Gardens, and published his first book, coloured
plates of parrots, in 1832. He worked as drawing
master for the Earl of Derby's family,1832-36, for
whom he composed his famous Book of Nonsense,1846,
1861, and the Knowsley Menagerie,1856. He taught
the Queen drawing in 1846. From 1831 onwards,
Lear travelled the Continent and drew, painted and
lithographed his observations, which he published
in various books. He studied briefly at the Royal
Academy Schools, where he met the Pre-Raphaelite
William Holman Hunt (q.v.), but preferred to live
abroad, in France, Corfu and Italy. He died in San
Remo in January 1888. Lear's drawings were mainly
done in pen and ink with wash, rather than water-
colour. He is listed here for his Nonsense book
(revised edition) designs wood engraved by the Dalziel
Brothers (q.v.),1861,1865. (The proofs are in the
British Museum.) He also exhibited work at the Royal
Academy and the Royal Society of British Artists.
[For a biographical account see V.Noakes, Edward
Lear,1968; for a list of illustrated work see Houfe]

LEBLOND, Abraham and Robert fl.1850-60s
Colour printers and lithographers, noted for their
colour prints engraved on boxwood using the Baxter
methods. It was a family firm of Robert LeBlond
(1816-63) and Abraham LeBlond (1819-94). They
appear in the London directories in 1840, as Abraham
LeBlond, 5 Old Road, Stepney, where he worked as
engraver; then in 1845 Robert LeBlond appears as
lithographer at 4 Walbrook, Stepney. They were
granted a Baxter licence in 1849 and produced a
large number of colour plates for books, magazines
and as special large prints. The British Museum
owns a full-length portrait of Prince Albert, with
the Great Exhibition in the background, engraved by
the Baxter process. By 1865 they were appearing as
LeBlond and Company, Hawks Road, Norbiton,
Kingston SW (LSDS,1865).
[For a discussion of their colour work see C.T.Lewis,
The Story of Picture Printing,1928,pp.209-25;
also Wakeman and Bridson; Hake]

LEBON and Company fl.1883-85
London wood engraving firm, with an office at
23 Southampton Buildings, WC (POD,1883-85).

LE BRETON, Miss Rosa fl.1857-65
Draughtsman on wood and domestic painter. She
contributed domestic scenes for wood engraving in
Cassell's Illustrated Family Paper,1857. She also
exhibited paintings in 1865.

LEE, Edward fl.1860s
London wood engraver, who worked at 219 Strand,
WC (POD,1863).

LEE, James fl.1800-75
Prolific London wood engraver, the son of the wood
engraver John Lee (q.v.) with whose work his is
often confused. He appears in the directories at
Anderson's Buildings, City Road (Pigot,1822-27);
and later 97 later 39 Princess Square, Kennington
(Pigot,1839; POD,1851-75). Lee was most
successful at engraving the designs of William
Craig (q.v.): an early work was A Wreath for the
Brow of Youth,1804 (Redgrave). He was also
employed by Charles Whittingham, Senior (q.v.) for
whom he engraved in clear black-line style the
natural history and scientific cuts for which he became
famous: Whittingham's Thornton's A New System of
Botany; Bohn praises his intricate engravings to
Dr Mantell's Medals of Creation, and Petrifactions
and Their Teachings. Lee also engraved portraits to
Hansard's Typographia,1805 (DNB); cuts to the early
numbers of the French Magasin Pittoresque; and for
children's books. His last cut, a tailpiece to Temple
of the Fairies, is in the Douce Collection, Bodleian
Library. Fincham lists seven bookplate engravings
after Craig designs, dated 1800-30. There is a large
collection of Lee's engravings in the Bodleian Library;
the British Museum owns a few animal engravings.
[Redgrave; Chatto; DNB; Gusman]

LEE, John fl.1794-1804
London wood engraver, father of the noted engraver
James Lee (q.v.) with whose work his is often
confused. John Lee is best known for his contributions
to what Chatto and Jackson call the 'London School' of
wood engraving -- post Bewick, and most recognisable in
the work of Robert Branston (q.v.). Lee's contribution
was the series of black-line cuts to The Cheap
Repository,1796, printed 1794-98 and sold
by Marshall, London and S.Hazard, Bath (Bryan).
'Those cuts, though coarsely executed, as might be
expected, considering the work for which they were
intended, frequently display considerable merit in
the design; and in this respect several of them are
scarcely inferior to the cuts drawn and engraved by
John Bewick in Dr Trusler's Progress of Man and
Society' (Chatto,pp.534-35). Towards the end of his
life, Lee took on Henry White (q.v.) as an apprentice,
but died in March 1804, before White's term was
completed. White subsequently trained under Thomas
Bewick (q.v.) in Newcastle. There are several small
vignettes and figure engravings in the Bodleian

Library signed 'J.Lee Engraver on wood, No 68
Hatton Garden', found in the Whittingham Papers, in
a folder dated 'Dec 5 1801' which may be John Lee's
work. Hake lists a portrait of John Baskerville
engraved by 'J Lee'.
[DNB; TB; Chatto; Nagler; Bryan]

LEE, John Ingle fl.1866-91
Houfe lists this draughtsman as the possible artist
for illustrations in Foxe's Book of Martyrs,1866, the
illustrations being signed 'J.Lee'. He was a figure
artist who exhibited at the Royal Academy and the
Royal Society of British Artists,1868-91.

LEE, Joseph fl.1869-72
London wood engraver, who worked at 16 Beaufort
Buildings, Strand (POD,1869-72). He shared the office
with E.S.Gascoine and A.Oswin (qq.v.).

LEE, R. fl.1832-34
London wood engraver, who worked at 7 Union Place,
City Road (Robson's,1832, Pigot,1834).

LEE, Sydney 1866-1949
Wood engraver, etcher, landscape and urban painter
in oil and watercolour. He was born on 27 August 1866
in Manchester and studied at the local art school, then
in Paris, eventually working extensively on the
Continent. He produced wood engravings in a Japanese
style which Gusman praised for their sense 'of bold
style'. These appeared in such influential revivalist
magazines as the Venture,1903: 'The Gabled House'.
He exhibited at the Royal Society of Painter-Etchers
and Engravers, where he was elected ARE in 1905,
and RE in 1915. He was elected ARA in 1922, RA in
1930, ARWS in 1942 and RWS in 1945. He died in
London on 31 October 1949. He signed his engravings:
'S L' (superimposed).
[Gusman; Waters]

LEE, Thomas Wales fl.1850s
The British Museum owns a wood engraved certificate
for the South East Middlesex Agricultural Society,
dated 1852, and attributed to Thomas Wales Lee. It
was cut in a competent black-line style, and was of
wheat sheafs with an ornamental border. He signed
his work: 'Lee'.

LEE, William 1810-65
Draughtsman on wood and watercolourist. He was born
in 1810, and began work as a draughtsman on wood for
Charles Knight's (q.v.) publications. He drew for Knight's
Penny Magazine, September 1841, engraved by Witby
(q.v.); and Knight's London,1841. He also served as
a member and secretary of the Langham Sketch Club,
was elected NWS,1848, and exhibited also at the
Royal Academy and the Royal Society of British
Artists. He died in London on 22 January 1865.
[Houfe; Bodleian Library]

LEECH, John 1817-64
Prominent and prolific draughtsman on wood, etcher
and painter. He was born in London in August 1817,
the son of a vintner, and showed a special talent for
drawing at an early age. He was educated at
Charterhouse and trained for medicine but abandoned
it for drawing, producing his first book, Etchings and
Sketchings,1835. This was a series of caricatures of
Londoners and was followed by another series of
satirical and political lithographs, which established his
style for dexterous comical yet accurately observed
draughtsmanship. He was then taught to draw on wood
by John Orrin Smith (q.v.) and his earliest efforts
were engraved in Bell's Life,1836, 'very rudely cut'
(Bryan); followed by illustrations to Percival Leigh's
Comic Latin Grammar and Comic English Grammar,
1840. He became established in 1840 when he joined
the staff of Bentley's Miscellany, contributing over
140 etchings there. In August 1841 his first drawing
for the newly established Punch appeared, engraved
over a two day period which delayed the paper's
publication while the engravers, the Dalziel Brothers
(q.v.) adjusted Leech's pencil drawing. They recalled
how this full page 'Foreign Affairs' drawing 'had to be
worked at from the moment it came into our hands till
it was given to the printer'. The delay involved the
block itself which was engraved whole rather than
split up among various engravers and later rejoined,
as was the subsequent practice. Nevertheless Leech
contributed about 3,000 drawings to Punch,1841-64.
He occupied the chief cartoonist role (for which he
drew 720 cartoons) until John Tenniel (q.v.) took over
in 1861. Most of this drawing, always in pencil on the
block, was engraved by Joseph Swain (q.v.). Though
an expert interpreter, Swain, in Leech's eyes, failed
to reproduce his original intentions: showing a block
drawing to a friend he commented with a sigh, 'But
wait till next week and see how the engraver will
spoil it!' Most of his objections centred around his
never being reconciled to the blackness of the
printer's ink, as opposed to the subtle silvery
greyness of his original pencil line; he shared this
view with his colleague Tenniel. Leech was a prolific
illustrator. Apart from his Punch work, he is known
to have drawn or etched for some fifty books, the
most widely known Dickens' Christmas Carol,
1843-44. And yet his engravers were often the
cause of his public reputation for rather slap-dash,
certainly quick sketchiness of style. Percy Muir
comments, 'Most of what we have of his was printed
from wood-blocks and it may be permitted to wonder
how far the fairly frequent crudities in Punch
illustrations were due to the clumsiness of the
engraver. The artist would have been quite safe in
the expert hands of such as Orrin Smith, W.J.Linton
and any of the Dalziels; but it may have been a quite
different matter when a block had to be divided
between several members of the Punch staff and
rushed through to meet the dead-line of the printing

shop. Leech may also have to shoulder some of the responsibility, not only because of dilatoriness, but because there is considerable evidence that, like Tenniel, he sometimes handed in the merest outline of his conception leaving the filling in of much of the detail to the engraver'. Much also depended on Leech's working method. He rarely used a pen and ink, but drew almost entirely in hard pencil cut to a fine point to create the 'exquisite delicacy' of his block drawings. Sadly these latter were destroyed by the engraver. Bryan gives an account of his working method for wood block drawings: 'As the idea of a subject came into his mind, he would set it down in pencil with extraordinary rapidity and with a complete sense of composition; these "first thoughts", as they have been named, bearing a close resemblance to the final issue. From these "first thoughts" he selected and traced the leading lines on vegetable tracing paper. These tracings are often extremely slight, but more often they are drawn with a sensitive delicacy and artistic expression which is quite remarkable considering the material on which they are drawn and the transitory purpose for which they were intended...The final drawing on the wood has, of course, disappeared in the process of cutting, and it is probably true that no finished independent drawing by John Leech in his best period can now be appealed to'. In later years Leech also painted oil sketch versions of his Punch drawings, which he exhibited at the Egyptian Hall Gallery, Piccadilly, in June 1862. He was a long suffering depressive and his poor health soon broke down. He died of angina pectoris on 14 October 1864, leaving a considerable reputation as a draughtsman. But when W.P.Linton praised his limited abilities in Masters of Wood Engraving he was rather unfair: 'I admire his facility in catching character and see improvement from long practice; but he was not an artist'. The British Museum owns proof engravings by the Dalziel Brothers, 1839-51, 1866.
[For biography see F.G.Kitton, John Leech, 1863; W.P.Frith, John Leech, 2 volumes, 1891; also Houfe (full bibliography and list of work); Muir; Chatto; Dalziels' Record; DNB; Spielmann; Bryan]

LEIGH, Hubert S. fl.1880
Provincial wood engraver, who worked at 14 Biggin Street, Dover (Kelly's, 1880).

LEIGHTON Brothers
(see Leighton, George Cargill)

LEIGHTON, Frederic, Lord Leighton of Stretton
1830-96
Occasional draughtsman illustrator on wood, prominent neoclassical painter. He was born in Scarborough in 1830, the son of a doctor who took him on extensive tours of the Continent. He learned drawing from F.Meli in Rome, attended the Florence Academy, and studied under the German Nazarene J.E.Steinle in Frankfurt. He worked for three years in Rome, having set up a studio in 1852, then settled in London from 1859, where he had caused a sensation with his first Royal Academy exhibit, 'Cimabue's 'Madonna''. He quickly rose to the heights of his profession and was elected ARA in 1864, RA in 1868 and PRA in 1878. He also exhibited at the Grosvenor Gallery, the Royal Hibernian Academy, the Royal Scottish Academy and the Fine Art Society, was created baronet in 1886, and a peer in 1896 (the only artist to be honoured in this way). He died on 25 January 1896. Leighton is listed here for his powerful drawings for the period's major wood engravers. Joseph Swain and Linton (qq.v.) engraved those which appeared in the Cornhill, 1860-63, 1867. These were a set of twenty-four full-page and initial drawings, made to illustrate George Eliot's Romola, and three additional drawings: 'Drifting', 'An Evening in a French Country House', and 'The Great God Pan'. Reid dismissed them for their poor engraving, especially the Romola drawings. That they are 'the work of a highly trained draughtsman is clear, that several have a kind of cold, formal dignity is also clear, but that they are sympathetic drawings will hardly be proposed. On the other hand, having seen photographs of the original design, I must add that Swain and Linton have let the artist down badly. The subjects, and Leighton's technique, I should have thought, present fewer difficulties than usual, nevertheless the cutting is below average, and in several cases the entire character of a drawing has been altered.' The Cornhill's publisher George Smith recalled Leighton's initial reluctance to take on the illustrations: 'Leighton had never drawn on wood before, and when the proofs of the first wood engraving were sent to him, he came to me in great agitation. The engraver, he declared, had entirely spoilt his drawing, leaving out certain essential lines, and putting other irrelevant ones of his own. If Leighton did not tear his own hair, or mine, it was only because his natural courtesy as a gentleman overcame his wrath as an artist. I sent for the wood engraver [Swain?] -- one of the best of his class -- who swore by all his gods, he had engraved every line conscientiously. I found myself between two exasperated artists, and looked forward with some dismay to what might happen during the next twelve months. Lying awake one night, it suddenly occurred to me that I might manufacture evidence. I sent the next drawing to a photographer, and instructed him to photograph it with the utmost care. When Leighton next made his appearance to complain of the injustice done to his drawing, I produced my photograph, sent for the engraver and the two fought it out together. Leighton became more accustomed to drawing on wood, and the other engravings gave him great satisfaction' (quoted in L.Huxley, The House of Smith and Elder, 1923, p.140). Nevertheless

the Romola illustrations rank among the most powerful of the 'Sixties School'. More successful as engravings were those nine drawings which Leighton did for the Dalziel Brothers (q.v.), who published them in their Bible Gallery, 1881. For these Leighton selected his own biblical passages, first wanting to do twelve scenes but eventually asking for a reprieve after long delays. He had obviously found drawing on wood increasingly trying: his blocks were sent in messy conditions ('the white touches are of course only corrections--not highlights'), and he asked for more time: 'I very much regret that I find that the minute work--without which I cannot satisfy myself--on these drawings has proved terribly trying to my eyes...', wanting to give them up temporarily. When they were published the Dalziels were as pleased as the critics, declaring 'Cain and Abel' 'will always rank as one of the grandest examples of biblical art of modern times'; a critic called them Leighton's 'greatest achievement'; and Forrest Reid declared the engravings 'wonders'. Two other Leighton contributions for the engravers appeared: in Punch, 1886, a portrait of his favourite model, Dorothy Dene ('one of the few tint blocks that have appeared in the paper...not a woodcut at all, but a wood engraving'); also in Black and White, 1891. [For biographical detail see R. and L. Ormond, Lord Leighton, 1975; also Dalziels' Record; Spielmann]

LEIGHTON, George Cargill 1826-95
Wood engraver and colour printer. He was born in 1826, the son of Stephen Leighton. He was apprenticed in 1836, aged ten, to the wood engraver George Baxter (q.v.) where he trained for seven years. Later, when involved in his own colour printing dispute with Baxter, he claimed that he had been taught colour printing not engraving as an apprentice. But he left Baxter and set up as a wood engraver about 1847. He is listed in the London directories at 19 Lamb's Conduit Street (POD, 1849-52). His real interest was in colour printing and when he had failed to get Baxter's licence, he joined with fellow Baxter pupils Gregory, W. Collins and W. Reynolds (qq.v.). When they split up about 1849, he established his own firm under the name Leighton Brothers, in partnership with his brother Charles Blair Leighton, who had trained with a silver engraver. Leighton Brothers were responsible for some of the most effective colour-printed illustrations from wood blocks of the 1850s and 60s. They printed colour-plates for the Art Journal, 1851, exhibited work at the Great Exhibition, and took new premises the following year at 4 Red Lion Square, once the office of the engraver Basire. When Charles Leighton died in 1855, George continued the business and became a regular printer of colour-plates to the Illustrated London News; two years later he became its publisher. His firm continued to produce influential colour-plates, notably after Harrison Weir's animal drawings and for Routledge.

That publisher's Gems of English Art, 1869, is one of Leighton's finest. George Leighton eventually moved to a Drury Lane factory, Stanhope House, and worked there until his retirement about 1884. The name Leighton Brothers last appears in the directories in 1885, after which time Leighton sold up to the lithographers Vincent Brooks, Day and Son. He turned over the colour wood blocks for Warne and Routledge's 'Toy Book' series to the prominent wood engraver Edmund Evans (q.v.). He died at Fairlight, Shepherd's Hill, Highgate, on 8 May 1895, aged sixty-eight. He left a substantial reputation as the advancer of colour printing from wood blocks, whose work improved and perfected advances made by Savage, Baxter, Gregory, Collins and Reynolds (qq.v.). [For a list of work see C.T.Courtney Lewis, Picture Printing, 1928; also McLean; Wakeman and Bridson; Printing Times, NS7, 1881, p.242]

LEIGHTON, Henry fl.1851-72
Wood engraver of the designs of his brother, John Leighton (q.v.). He may be the apprentice whom the Dalziel Brothers (q.v.) listed as Harry (sic) Leighton. He set up as a wood engraver in London and according to the directories shared the offices of a family relation's firm, J. and J. Leighton, 40 Brewer Street, Golden Square, 'high-class bookbinders and booksellers'. He worked there from 1851-57, then possibly at the office of 'Leighton and Leighton', 9 Buckingham Street, WC (POD, 1858-72). Henry Leighton was a competent engraver of his brother's ornate emblamatic designs for numerous books, magazines, and pieces of commercial work, once John had drawn them on the wood block. Many of these he engraved for colour printing in various tints. The best of Henry's work after his brother's drawings appeared in Quentin Durward, 1853; and some of the 247 total designs to Richard Pigot's Moral Emblems of all Ages and Nations, 1860-62. These he engraved with the Dalziels, Green, Harral, De Wilde and Joseph Swain (qq.v.). The British Museum owns his early vignette engraving of a courting couple, unattributed. He signed his engravings: 'H. LEIGHTON S^C', 'LEIGHTON'. [Chatto; Evans Reminiscences; Dalziels' Record]

LEIGHTON, John 'Luke Limner' 1822-1912
Draughtsman illustrator, book designer and writer. He was born in London on 22 September 1822, the brother of Henry Leighton (q.v.) and cousin of George Cargill Leighton (q.v.). He studied under Henry Howard, RA. He compiled sixty-four designs to The Comic Art Manufacturer, 1848; followed by twelve designs wood engraved by the Dalziels (q.v.) to Christmas Comes but Once a Year, 1850. By that year he had designed for lithography, Contrasts and Conceits, c1850; London Out of Town, c1850; and as a lecturer published Suggestions in Design...for the Use of Artists, 1853. This was the year he joined

with the photographer Roger Fenton to found the present day Royal Photographic Society. Leighton had joined forces with his brother Henry by the early 1860s, and together they established a reputation for distinctive book decorations, which Henry engraved from John's drawings on wood blocks. John drew for title pages, frontispieces, head and tailpieces, many of which were colour printed; he also designed bindings for nearly every London publisher from 1845 onwards. He was in fact one of the earliest commercial professional artists who designed for books, magazines, Christmas cards, bank-notes, seals and medallions and playing cards, and even took his own photographs. His design for the title page of the newly established Graphic, 1869, of which he was a founder proprietor, remained in use until 1930. His best work appeared during the 1860s in Lyra Germanica, 1861; Moral Emblems, 1860-62; Good Words, 1864; Once a Week, 1866; all the illustrations to Life of Man Symbolised, 1866; and the cover of London Society, 1868. He drew for the Dalziels' Bible Gallery, 1881. The Dalziels had in turn engraved some of his early drawings on wood, notably Moral Emblems. He had an interest in the Pictorial World, contributed to Chambers' Journal, and wrote extensively under his pseudonym, Luke Limner. He continued to contribute to various magazines and books well up to and past the turn of the century: Puck and Ariel, 1890; to the Dalziels' Fun, 1890-92; all the illustrations to Poems of William Leighton, 1894; and drawings to Punch, 1900-02. Leighton as a designer on wood held the position that the design should harmonise with, and illustrate the character and content of each book for which his drawings were intended. He would draw directly on wood, then turn the block over to Henry for engraving. If a design was to be colour printed in several tints from wood blocks, Henry would return proofs to his brother, who then coloured them. McLean concludes of Leighton's influence as a designer that 'Leighton was a good craftsman, who fully understood the limitations and possibilities of the media he employed; humour creeps pleasantly into some of his designs, but his lack of originality would make it difficult to identify most of them if they were not signed...' (Victorian Book Design, 1963, p.220). Leighton was also related to various influential figures in the London book world. His brother Alfred was largely responsible for introducing the rubber stamp to England. The firm J. and J. Leighton, 'high-class bookbinders and booksellers' at Brewer Street, Golden Square, London was owned by family relations who commissioned work from John and Henry Leighton. Their nephew, Archibald Leighton, was a founder of the bookbinding firm, Leighton, Son and Hodge, and inventor of cloth binding in 1822 (when the firm was Leighton and Eeles, Spitalfields). John Leighton died in Harrow on 15 September 1912. The British Museum owns two proof engravings by the Dalziel Brothers,

1863.
[For a complete account of Leighton and his family see S. Pantazzi in Connoisseur, Vol. CLII, 1963, pp.263-65; Chatto; White; Houfe; Fincham; McLean; TB; Who's Who, 1912; British and Colonial Printer, 19 May 1904, pp.2-3 (photograph portrait)]

LEIGHTON and Leighton
(see Leighton, Henry)

LEITCH, Richard Principal fl.1840-75
Draughtsman, illustrator and 'special artist', brother of the noted artist W.L. Leitch (q.v.). He began his draughtsman's career for the Illustrated London News, 1847-61, providing various landscape and topographical drawings for wood engraving. Especially proficient was his half-page drawing, 'Scene of the geological discoveries at Swanage, Dorset', Illustrated London News, 26 December 1857, drawn from a photograph and reproduced with a clear understanding of contrast. This was followed by the full-page 'The Harbour at Hong Kong', 27 December 1857, which set the pace for various nautical drawings in the early 1860s. He was also sent to cover the Franco-Italian War by the Illustrated London News in 1859. Leitch also drew for Poets of the Nineteenth Century, 1857; Good Words, 1864; the Sunday Magazine, 1865; Idyllic Pictures, 1867; and the Quiver. His painted landscapes were exhibited at the Royal Academy, 1844-60, and the Royal Society of British Artists until 1862. The British Museum owns a proof engraving of a biblical landscape and others engraved by the Dalziel Brothers (q.v.), 1857, 1860.
[Bénézit; Graves; Houfe; White]

LEITCH, William Leighton 1804-83
Draughtsman on wood and watercolourist. He was born in Glasgow on 22 November 1804, the son of a businessman and brother of R.P. Leitch (q.v.). He trained first as a lawyer, then learned art under D. Macnee and worked as a sign painter and a scenery painter at Glasgow's Theatre Royal, 1824. He moved to London where he befriended David Roberts and Clarkson Stanfield (qq.v.), then travelled extensively, teaching and sketching. He returned to London and set up first as a fashionable watercolourist (patronised by the Queen), and then draughtsman on wood for various topographical books. He worked for the wood engraver W.J. Linton (q.v.) who remembered him during the early days of the Illustrated London News, to which Leitch contributed a drawing in 1859. It seems he had a fastidious technique for drawing on the wood block, using Indian ink or sepia, 'with so much pencilling as might be sometimes needed for clearer definition'. The result was a wash drawing on the block 'as well studied and as carefully drawn as his exhibited pictures'. Among his illustrations for books were

those for R.Walsh's Constantinople and the Turkish Empire,1838; Reverend G.N.Wright's The Rhine, Italy and Greece,1840; Shores and Islands of the Mediterranean,1841; W.Brockedon's Italy,1843; and J.P.Lawson's Scotland Delineated,1847-54. He also exhibited paintings at the British Institution, the New Watercolour Society, the Royal Academy and the Royal Society of British Artists. He died on 25 April 1883. The British Museum owns proof engravings by the Dalziel Brothers (q.v.), 1856.
[For biographical detail see A.MacGregor, Memoir of William Leitch,1884; DNB; Bryan; TB; Linton, Masters of Wood Engraving]

LE JEUNE, Henry L. 1819-1904
Draughtsman on wood and genre painter. He was born in London on 12 December 1819 and studied at the Royal Academy Schools, later serving there as drawing master, 1845, and curator,1848. By the 1850s he was drawing illustrations on wood, most notably figure subjects for Ministering Children, 1856, engraved by Edmund Evans (q.v.); Lays of the Holy Land,1858; and The Poetry of Thomas Moore. These were cited by Bohn in Chatto and Jackson. He exhibited pictures at the British Institution and the Royal Academy, being elected ARA,1863.
He died in Hampstead on 5 September 1904.
[Chatto; Evans Reminiscences; Bénézit; Houfe]

LELOIR fl.1830-60
French wood engraver, best known for his associations with Andrew, and with Adolphe Best (qq.v.) as Best and Leloir, then Best, Leloir, Hotelin and Regnier. He worked with them on such engraved books as Kugler's History of Frederick the Great, 1842; Raczynski's History of the New German Art, 1836-41; and Goldsmith's Vicar of Wakefield. He also wood engraved cuts for such magazines as the Gazette des Beaux Arts, and the Illustrated London News,1845. He is best known for cuts after Adolphe Menzel,1842. He signed his work: 'Leloir' or 'B L' (superimposed) (Best and Leloir).
[LeBlanc; Gusman; TB; Bénézit; Nagler; Beraldi]

LEMON, Arthur 1850-1912
Draughtsman illustrator and painter. He was born on the Isle of Man in 1850, spent his youth in Rome, worked in California and spent two years under the painter Carolus Duran in Paris, then returned to England where he exhibited work at the Royal Academy from 1880. He also drew illustrations for wood engravings in the English Illustrated Magazine, 1884-85. These were to Mabel Collins' 'In the New Forest' and were wood engraved by O.Lacour, E.Gascoine, R.S.Lueders, J.A.Quartley, Waterlow and Company, and E.Ohme (qq.v.). Lemon died in April 1912.
[TB; Graves]

LENG, William Christopher and Company fl.1880
Provincial draughtsmen firm, with an office at 17 High Street and Aldine Court, Sheffield (Kelly's, 1880). They were also proprietors of the Sheffield Daily Telegraph ('the oldest newspaper in the provinces').

LEONARD fl.1840s
Wood engraver, who worked for Charles Knight's (q.v.) publications, often in partnership with M.U.Sears (q.v.) as Leonard and Sears. Leonard's wood engravings included cuts for Knight's Penny Magazine, after Fairholt, November, December 1841. As Leonard and Sears he engraved after Wells (q.v.) September 1841, and after Shepherd, November 1841.
[Bodleian Library]

LEONARD and Sears
(see Leonard, also Sears, M.U.)

LEPERE, Auguste Louis c1848-1918
Prominent French wood engraver, born in Paris on 30 November 1849 (TB), (1848,Gusman), the son of a sculptor. He was a pupil of Rude and the English expatriot wood engraver Burn Smeeton (q.v.), with whom he worked in Paris from 1862. He made his debut at the Salon,1870, and by 1875 he had begun to exhibit wood engravings. He established a reputation for architectural engraving as well as for reproductions of works by such famous painters and artists as Constable ('The Cottage', for Magasin Pittoresque), Watelin, Daumier and Doré. He had first learned to transfer drawings onto the block and worked after drawings of Haenen, Scott, Morin, and Vierge. His first wood engraving was of a drawing after Busson for Monde Illustré. He continued to engrave for this constantly from 1880 and soon became associated with various French engraving and publishing firms. In 1881 he won a third class medal, in 1887 a second class, and finally he won a gold one in 1889. He became one of the most influential wood engravers during the period of revival of the art. He taught Lucien Pissarro (q.v.), and with Pierre Gusman, helped to found the Societé des Graveurs sur Bois,1897. His influence in England was felt by many members of the Society of Wood Engravers, among them Gwen Raverat. His style was painterly, impressionistic rather than reproductive, noted for pure white, broad black effects and linear harmony; and for this reason his followers viewed him as the true painter-engraver. By 1900 he and Beltrand had designed a series of colour wood engravings to J.Richepin's Paysages et Coins de Rues, while his own engravings were exhibited at Colnaghi's in London at the same time as the first London exhibition of the Society of Wood Engravers. On the Continent the Monde Illustré, 1918, wrote his eulogy in glowing terms as 'the grand master of wood [engraving] ...He upgraded it

again to the level of art and gave to it nobility and independence. He liberated and glorified it.'
[For a full bibliography see TB; Gusman; also Benedite, Oeuvre Gravée de Lepère, 1905; and a survey article 'A French Wood-Engraver -- Auguste Lepère', Studio, December 1897, pp.143-55]

LESLIE, Alexander Duff fl.1873-89
London wood engraver, who worked at 303 Strand, WC (POD, 1873), 319 Strand (POD, 1874-75), 295 Strand (POD, 1876-83), 173 Strand (POD, 1884-85), and then 10 (11) Ludgate Hill, EC (POD, 1886-89).

LESLIE, Charles Robert 1794-1859
Occasional draughtsman illustrator, prominent painter of historical subjects and portraits. He was born of American parents in Clerkenwell in 1794 and left for America in 1799, but returned to England in 1811. He was a student at the Royal Academy Schools, 1813, the year he began to exhibit there. He was later elected ARA, 1821 and RA, 1826. He served as Professor of Painting there, 1847-52, and specialised in 17th and 18th century revivalist oil paintings. He is listed here for illustrations to the works of Washington Irving, and several designs wood engraved by the Dalziel Brothers and J.M.Williams (qq.v.), which are in the British Museum.
[For biographical detail see T.Taylor (ed.), Autobiographical Recollections, 1865; Fielding]

LESLIE, George Dunlop 1835-1921
Occasional draughtsman on wood, landscape and figure painter. He was born on 2 July 1835, the younger son and pupil of the painter C.R.Leslie, RA. After his education at Mercer's School and the Royal Academy Schools, 1856, he set up as a landscape painter, specialising in views of the Home Counties and Thames Valley. During this period he also drew some of the nineteen wood engraved illustrations to Walter Thornbury's Two Centuries of Song, 1867, engraved by W.J.Linton, Horace Harral and Gavin Smith (qq.v.). He shared the commission with the illustrators H.S.Marks, T.Morten, W.Small (qq.v.) and others. He also drew for a wood engraving in the Illustrated London News, 1878. Leslie was most successful as a painter and was elected ARA, 1868, then RA, 1876. He died in Lingfield, Sussex on 21 February 1921.
[White; Houfe]

LEVEILLE, Auguste-Hilaire 1840-1900
French wood engraver, born in Joue-du-Bois, Orne on 31 December 1840. He was the engraving pupil of the influential and prolific Adolphe Best (q.v.) and his partner Hotelin. His own engraving style began to appear from 1879 onward; by 1889 he had reached maturity and could be classed alongside such important French wood engravers as Lepère, S.Pannemaker and C.Bellenger (qq.v.). He exhibited

work at the Salon from 1873, and gradually became known for his wood engraved illustrations to such French magazines as Magasin Pittoresque, Revue Illustrée, and Gazette des Beaux Arts. Of these he was best known for engravings after Rodin's sculpture, as well as engravings after L.Dubois and Michelangelo. Some of these appeared in England: Rodin's portrait bust of the artist Alphonse Légros appeared in the English Magazine of Art, 1888. Leveille died in Paris on 13 April 1900, leaving a son Ernest Leveille, who also wood engraved until he abandoned it for music.
[Gusman; Bénézit; Beraldi; L'Art, 1888; Hake]

LEVERETT, Arthur fl.1893-1901
London wood engraver, who worked at 27 Chancery Lane, WC (POD, 1893-1901). He shared the address with the noted wood engraver C.Roberts (q.v.).

LEVESON, Major A.H. fl.1860s
Houfe lists this amateur draughtsman for wood engravings of the Abyssinian Expedition of 1868. These appeared in the Illustrated London News.

LEWIN, Walter fl.1880s
London draughtsman on wood, who worked at 10 Bolt Court, Fleet Street, EC (Kelly's, 1880). He shared the premises with the engravers T.Coman, E.Scrivens, R.G.F.Sweeting and A.J.Wilson (qq.v.).

LEWIS, John William fl.1883-1910
London wood engraver, who worked at 6 Balaclava Road, Bermondsey (POD, 1883-85) and 21 Trothy, Southwark Park Road, SE (POD, 1889-93). He then moves to 115 Peckham Park Road, SE (LSDS, 1894) until five years later, when he reappears in the printing centre of London, 68 Farringdon Street, EC (POD, 1899-1910). This premises he shared with the noted engraver A.Mullord (q.v.).

LIDDELL, J. fl.1875-76
Draughtsman on wood, who specialised in large, full-page drawings of crowds and architectural detail. These appeared in the Illustrated London News, 1875-76, often drawn in collaboration with 'C.R.'. The most notable of these was 'The Royal Visit to the City', Illustrated London News, 27 May 1876, a full-page crowd scene drawn with C.R.

LILLIE, Charles T. fl.1881-82
Comic draughtsman for Punch, and poster designer. He trained as an engineer and travelled throughout Africa and America before settling in London, at Haverstock Hill, Hampstead where he worked as an artist and author. He first made his name as a poster designer, then submitted a series of comic sketches for wood engraving in Punch, 1881. These were adaptations of advertisements for various wines, with personifications of the attributes of each: e.g. 'Port:

Old and Crusty' was a typical Colonel of the Raj, 'a fire-eating Anglo-Indian'; 'Claret: Very Light and Delicate' drawn as a dainty and graceful maiden. Lillie also exhibited flower paintings at the Royal Society of British Artists,1882.
[Spielmann; Houfe]

LIMMING, William fl.1886-89
London wood engraver, who worked at 9 Essex Street, Strand (POD,1886-89). He shared the premises with J.Desbois and G.Puttock (qq.v.).

LINDSELL, Alfred Henry and Company fl.1882-88
London wood engraving firm, with an office at 28 Ludgate Hill, EC (POD,1882) and 150 Fleet Street, EC (POD,1884-88). This latter office was shared with H.Shade, D.W.Williamson and E.C.Mitchell (qq.v.).

LINNEY, W.
Draughtsman on wood, who contributed a drawing to the early issue of Good Words,1861.

LINTON, Henry Duff 1816-99
Wood engraver, assistant to his elder brother W.J.Linton (q.v.). He was born in London, 1816, the son of a Stepney 'riverside businessman' and was employed by his brother's firm, Smith and Linton (q.v.) during the early 1840s, to engrave for the Illustrated London News. One of his earliest appearances here was a quarter-page, 'The Confirmation of St Andrew's, Holborn', after John Gilbert (q.v.), 13 May 1843 after which he became especially proficient as an engraver of Gilbert's drawings on wood. He moved to Paris in 1844-51 where he was employed as engraver for various French publications: Mary Lafon's La Dame de Bourbon,1860; Castagnary's Artists of the Nineteenth Century,1861; and Le Bois de Boulogne,1861. Gusman considered this work good enough to list and reproduced Linton's 'Les Femmes du Treizième au Seizième Siècle', done for Magasin Pittoresque, 1861. While in Paris Linton befriended Edmond Morin (q.v.) and brought him back to London for training as a draughtsman engraver, later engraving his drawings. Linton set up as wood engraver in London during the 1850s; he appears in the City's directories at 14 Chatham Place, Blackfriars (POD,1856-57), then 18 Bouverie Street, Fleet Street, EC (POD,1858-59), an address near to his brother's office at 33 Essex Street. He also worked from his home, 8 Jamaica Place, Kennington (Graves,1855-57). His work during this period included large and quite proficient engravings after Old Masters like Rembrandt and Moroni, and after prominent Victorian paintings; notably full and double-page to the Illustrated London News. He also engraved for his brother's new paper, Pen and Pencil, from 1855. He was especially good as an

interpreter of Alma-Tadema, whose work appeared in the Illustrated London News throughout the 1870s; he also engraved there the Pre-Raphaelite work, 'Autumn Leaves', after J.E.Millais, 30 August 1856. He had an ability to lend clarity to the slightest sketch, notably a series of 'American Sketches', 1875-76. His work was quickly recognised when five were hung at the Royal Academy, 1855-57: 'Portrait of Byron', after a drawing by E.Morris, 1855; 'Prisoners in the Vaults of the Hotel de Ville, Paris, June 1848', after Gavarni,1855; 'In the Forest of Fontainebleau',1856; 'Lullingsworth', after a drawing by S.Reid, 1857; and 'The Cradle', after the painting by N.Maes,1857. He also engraved cuts of various exhibits for the Art Treasures Examiner, at Manchester,1857; and numerous portrait engravings of Tennyson, the Duke of Wellington, David Wilkie, Richard Wilson, Dickens and Sir Charles Eastlake, after paintings, photographs of Mayall or more notably the drawings of E.Morin, his friend. (Many of these are in the British Museum.) Henry Linton was a 'shiftless, complaining man', largely at the mercy of his family. By the early 1860s he was existing primarily on allowances given by his brother and his nephew Willie. In March 1868, his brother, then engraving in New York, offered him a hundred dollars a week if he would join him there and Henry accepted and moved his four children and wife (at William's expense) to New York. He remained there 1868-73, but after four months he quarrelled with his brother-benefactor, and eventually returned to England. While in America he engraved large double-page illustrations for his brother's short-lived venture, American Enterprise, 1870-72. (A copy is in the British Museum.) During the 1870s he existed on occasional work for the Illustrated London News, notably after large popular paintings, and occasional book engravings. His most notable of these appeared in Trollope's The Way We Live Now,1874-75, after L.G.Fawks (q.v.). In this year Henry needed the money which he eventually obtained from his brother, to pay legal costs for yet another of the scrapes he unavoidably encountered. On his death on 18 June 1899, in Norbiton, Surrey, a year after his brother's death, the Athenaeum called him 'the last of the "old true wood engravers"'. His brother's biographer concluded in another way: 'He was competent, but less skilled than William; yet he shared his brother's feckless way with money and was fated always to live in his brother's shadow' (F.B.Smith, W.J.Linton,1973,p.166). The British Museum owns his engravings after J.Gilbert, J.Lauder, J.N.Paton, S.Read, G.Doré and Rembrandt. Linton signed his engravings 'HENRY LINTON'.
[For biographical information see DNB; TB; Gusman; also Times,23 June 1899; Hake; Graves; Bénézit]

LINTON, Sir James Drogmole 1840-1916
Occasional draughtsman illustrator for wood
engravings, lithographer and prominent historical
painter. He was born in London on 26 December
1840, educated at Clevedon House, Barnes and in
art at Leigh's Art School in Newman Street. He first
exhibited work at the early Dudley Gallery exhibitions
for young, unknown artists, then at the more
prestigious Royal Institute of Painters in Watercolours
from 1863, being later elected member in 1870, and
its first president, 1883-97. It was during the early
part of his career that he drew for wood engravings
and his sense of clarity, strong figure drawing and
understanding of spatial composition made his
drawings especially successful. These were noted
and admired by Van Gogh ('superb...very striking')
when they appeared as 'London Sketches', engraved
in The Graphic,1871-74. He also contributed drawings
to Good Words,1870; and Cassell's Magazine,1870;
and illustrated an edition of Pilgrim's Progress. His
paintings appeared at the Grosvenor Gallery, the New
Gallery, the Royal Academy, the Royal Hibernian
Academy, the Royal Institute of Painters in Watercolours and the Royal Institute of Painters in Oil-
Colours. He was knighted in 1885 and died in London
on 3 October 1916. The British Museum owns a
collection of his wood engraved designs.
[Houfe; TB (bibliography); Wood]

LINTON, William James 1812-98
Prominent wood engraver, poet and socialist. He was
born in Ireland's Row, Mile End Road, London on
7 December 1812, the son of a Stepney businessman
and brother of Henry Duff Linton (q.v.) with whom he
worked. William moved to Stratford in 1818, where
he was educated at Chigwell School and in his spare
time received drawing lessons and studied early
engraved illustrations in the Portfolio, Mirror,
Legends of Horror and Newgate Monthly, and collected
and engraved lottery bills of Robert Branston (q.v.).
His father helped him by paying for his drawing
lessons and apprenticed him to the draughtsman
engraver George Wilmot Bonner (q.v.), who was
himself once a pupil of Branston, for a period of six
years from 1828. William moved in with Bonner's
family at 12 Canterbury Row, Kennington, and
recalled of his training there: 'Bonner was a clever
artist, and a good master, making his pupils learn
and do everything connected with their work, even to
sawing up a box-wood log and planing and smoothing
the rounds of wood to fit them to receive the drawings.
For these we might also sometimes have to make the
sketches and draw them on the wood for our own
engraving. It was good artistic training (Memories,
p.8). He became adept at the black-line reproduction
technique of his master, but also admired Bewick's
white-line methods and attempted to imitate that
master as well. By the age of twenty-one he had
become quite outspoken about the merits of white-line

which was 'quicker and more flexible', and the role
of the engraver as collaborator/translator with an
artist, each 'members in the great Guild of Art' and
not 'mere mechanics'. His abilities as draughtsman
were tested by Bonner, who often sent him out to
draw from nature -- the Thames bridges, animals at
the zoo, or pictures in the Dulwich Art Gallery. He
also prepared blocks and used the trade method of
woodcutting drawings with a knife along the grain,
for Astley's Circus posters. Near the end of his
apprenticeship with Bonner, he was thought good
enough to engrave Thomas Hood's drawings for
Comic Cuts, which he dismissed as 'queer pen-and-
ink drawings to be cut in facsimile'. He also engraved
with Powis and Jackson (qq.v.) for Martin and Westall's
Pictorial Illustrations of the Bible,1833. In 1834 he
joined with his fellow pupil, William Henry Powis,
(q.v.) and worked on engravings until Powis died in
1836, aged twenty-eight. William then joined briefly
with John Thompson (q.v.) until he was employed by
the master engraver John Orrin Smith (q.v.). His
work for Orrin Smith began with seven of the eleven
total engravings after William Harvey for Solace of
Song,1836; also engravings for an edition of Cowper's
works, Kenny Meadows' Portraits of the English,
1840, and Meadows' Shakespeare,1839-42. During
this period he specialised in the intricate landscape
foregrounds which demanded a crisp cut from the
graver. It was a period when his engraving ambitions
were briefly overshadowed by painting and poetry,
when he used a calling card which described him not
as engraver but as 'artist'. A mark of his success
came when his first picture was hung at the Royal
Academy, 'Nereids',1837, which he completed from
his home at 67 Great Titchfield Street, London. He
became interested in social conditions and political
agitation and established the weekly paper, The
National,1839, which reprinted articles from other
papers for the working man, engraving his own
drawing, 'Tintern Abbey' as its frontispiece. The
1840s saw the establishment of Linton the engraver
and politician, as well as literary figure. In the
autumn 1842, he joined with his employer John Orrin
Smith to found Smith and Linton, principally to engrave
for the newly formed Illustrated London News,1842-.
He found Orrin Smith 'a most prolific draughtsman,
most amiable of men', and with him and their
friends, like William Harvey, William Bell Scott,
Thackeray, Leech and Kenny Meadows (qq.v.), they
established a thriving engraving business. They
moved from Judd Street to Brunswick Square and
managed to engrave not only the weekly cuts to the
Illustrated London News, but also those for Bell's
Life in London, and the commercial failure but
artistically influential S.C.Hall's Book of British
Ballads,1842. They achieved a great part of their
success by employing for the first time prominent
watercolourists and painters to draw on wood for
them, figures like Harvey, Meadows and Duncan,

who copied the works of 'Old Masters' or exhibited work at the Royal Academy or the Royal Watercolour Society. They had a staff of engraver assistants to translate these drawings into engraved line which included Alfred and Horace Harral, Henry Linton, C.Mins, C.S.Cheltnam, E.K.Johnson and G.Pearson (qq.v.). Linton was eventually more of a supervisor than engraver, although he claimed that he did engrave a few cuts exclusively: 'Choosing the Wedding Gown', after Mulready, was 'only cut entirely by my own hand'; later Archer's drawing of Lance's paintings 'Peacock at Home' and 'Dead Birds'; and Duncan and Dodgson's drawings of 'Old Mill' and 'Landscape', he also reserved for his graver alone. When Orrin Smith died in October 1843, the business which he and Linton had built up was threatened, but Linton was determined to carry on. He moved to new premises at 85 Hatton Garden (POD,1844-48), then in 1845 returned to his early home in Woodford, retaining the Hatton Garden business as well. He became the principal engraver to the Illuminated Magazine, and in 1845 succeeded Douglas Jerrold as its editor. He had also edited the Illustrated Family Journal, from 1844, which ceased in July 1845; and helped finance the equally ill-fated People's Journal, which he gave up in June 1848. He coupled these ventures with the Illustrated London News engravings, which were his most successful: 'the best specimens of wood-engraving of their kind that had ever been printed by means of a steam-press (Chatto in History of Wood Engraving,1848), 'unsurpassed in their vivacity and delicate accuracy', a 'staggering number of various subjects'. These ranged from political meetings to portraits; landscapes to reproductions of paintings. By 1847 Linton's interest in his engraving business had waned and he became less regular in supervising his business and more active in politics. The Illustrated London News also began to build up its own section of engravers, largely poached from Linton's staff. This 'broke up my business', Linton later recalled. By February 1848, when his commissions from the Illustrated London News had almost ceased, Linton was again in debt and faced a number of angry creditors. The firm of Smith and Linton finally collapsed in April 1848. The 1850s were a period of innovation and experiment for Linton. He had mastered anatomical illustration after only one visit to a dissection room, and drew and engraved what one critic called 'some of what are surely the finest anatomical illustrations of the nineteenth century'. They appeared in London Medical Gazette,1848, but paid poorly, so Linton abandoned further work in the field. He turned to nature illustrations and moved with his family to Brantwood, on Lake Coniston in the Lake District, which provided a stimulus for the illustrations he engraved in various natural history books. His most successful were to Harriet Martineau's The English Lakes,1858, 'Memorials to the tenderness of Linton's

life at Brantwood'. He entered a political row over the attribution of the picture 'Apollo and Marsyas', attributed to Raphael by the radicals, to a minor artist by the Tories, and in the end rejected by the National Gallery. Linton engraved a large copy of it and published it in his new political paper, Leader, 7 September 1850. This version had to be censored with a fig leaf; but ever-rebellious, Linton issued an uncensored version printed on better paper which he sold from the Leader's offices. His most famous commission while at Brantwood was the fourteen engravings after Rossetti, Stanfield and Millais to Moxon's edition of Tennyson's Poems, 1857, for which he charged about £5 a cut. When the publisher Moxon arrived at Brantwood to check the progress he was turned away, but it was a mark of Moxon's confidence in Linton that he returned to give him a cheque for £10 'advance payment'. Such work, and occasional free-lance engravings for the Illustrated London News supported him and his large family and assistants in a sort of 'day-commune' at Brantwood. His failures with illustrated papers did not dampen his ambitions and he tried to establish a number of new illustrated papers over the next few years. He founded The English Republic, which folded in 1855. Pen and Pencil, launched on 10 February 1855, with engravings by his brother Henry, had an eight week life, despite the financial backing of Henry's French friend Daniel (sic) Morin. The Farthing Times & Advertiser,1862, folded after one issue. Linton married a second time in 1858, to the homosexual writer Eliza Lynn (q.v.), which proved a disastrous step to further alienate him from his family and force him deeper into his work. He left his children at Brantwood, his wife at Hastings, and returned to London where he set up a new engraving business with Harvey Orrin Smith (q.v.), at 33 Essex Street, Strand (POD,1859-60), an old house which was replaced by the 'ramshackle premises' of the past, 85 Hatton Garden (POD,1861-72). There he employed about five apprentices, some deaf but capable as specialist block cutters for mechanical reproductions, or the tint, line and figure men who worked from pieces of broken up blocks. Linton's biographer claimed that 'Linton genuinely despised this kind of work, but his workshop, like its competitors, seems to have done a great deal of it'. Among his apprentices was the young Walter Crane (q.v.) who recalled his master 'as five feet, five & a half' tall, a slight man who moved at a nervous scamper and spoke rapidly in a high-pitched voice, leaving his sentences unfinished. Acquaintances thought him amiable and trustworthy, but not friendly' (quoted in Smith, W.J.Linton, 1973,p.44). The work during this period was indeed impressive: by the early 1860s it included cover designs to the new Cornhill and Macmillan's magazines; engravings to Pictorial Tour of the Thames; Burns' Poems and Songs; some of Leighton's drawings to George Eliot's Romola (with Joseph Swain) in Cornhill, 1862; and some 'particularly lucid and elegant' engravings to W.H.G.Kingston's Boys' Own Book of Boats, 1861. He engraved sixty-three cuts and his young apprentice Walter Crane's vignette drawings to J.R.Wise's The New Forest, 1863. His 'tour de force' was the album Thirty Pictures by Deceased British Artists, 1865, for the London Art Union, for which he did almost all the drawing and engraving after Constable, Gainsborough, Reynolds, Blake and others. These engravings were praised for their 'extraordinary faithfulness and bravura'. Linton's status as a wood engraver was well recognised by the 1860s. He was awarded one of two wood engraving medals at the Paris International Exhibition in 1862. This was the year in which he produced one of his most perfect pieces -- London International Exhibition Certificate, after Alfred Stevens. He had a series of eleven engravings selected for exhibition at the Royal Academy from 1855-64, which were: 'The Ivory Carver', after E.H.Wehnert, 1855; Wilkie's 'Rabbit on the Wall', drawn by J.Beech, 1857; Lawrence's 'Calmady Children', 1857; Fuseli's 'Witches', drawn by W.B.Scott, 1857; his engravings of Clarkson Stanfield's drawings to Moxon's edition of Tennyson's Poems, 1857; a T.Creswick drawing, 1857; Constable's 'Cornfield', drawn by Duncan, 1857; 'Burlington Old Pier', after Copley Fielding, 1858; 'The Castaway', after George Harvey, 1859; 'Sinai' and 'Jonah', both after Gustave Doré, 1863; and 'Dead Ripe', 1864. He also exhibited work at the Royal Society of British Artists and the London Fine Art Society. Bohn's appendix 'Artists and Engravers of the Present Day' to Chatto and Jackson in 1861 devoted two pages to Linton 'both as a draughtsman and an engraver on wood' and cited as illustrations Linton's engravings after John Martin's Bible Prints; after R.R.McIan's drawing in S.C.Hall's Book of British Ballads; and to Milton's L'Allegro. 'Many of the illustrated books of the last twenty years exhibit the talents of Mr Linton. We may name, besides the Book of Ballads, The Pictorial Tour of the Thames, The Merrie Days of England, 1859; Burns' Poems and Songs, Favourite English Poems, 1859, Shakespeare's Birthplace, and the illustrated edition of Milton's Poetical Works...'. The extraordinary output of Linton and his workshop during the 1850s and 1860s is best seen by the large number of proofs now in the Constance Meade Collection, Bodleian Library, dated 1859-64. Not only are there engravings for books but numerous trade cuts: a series of beds for Heal and Son, 1862; a 'Mucilage Bottle and Brush' for Winsor and Newton's catalogue, 1862; intricate scientific engravings for the British Medical Journal, 1862; a series of women's fashions to Ladies Treasury, 8 August 1862; and intricate geometric diagrams of 'Optics of the Eye' by J.L.Laurence, 1862. There are numerous popular works: a wrapper design to Agatha,

A Magazine of Social Reform, 1861; a series of thumbnail children's books for Mr C.Honeysuckle, 85 Hatton Garden; and some watercolours and proofs to Watt's Hymns. The British Museum owns his engraved Honourable Mention Certificate for the London International Exhibition, 1862. In November 1866 Linton intended just to visit America; but he was eventually to spend the remainder of his life there. He first taught women wood engraving for three years at the Cooper Institute. He soon built up a remarkable reputation as free-lance engraver and the critic responsible for 'the regeneration of American wood engraving' (DNB). In less than two years he had earned $5,000 in engraving commissions, enough to pay off his English creditors and subsidise his brother Henry Duff Linton (q.v.) who joined him in New York in 1868. During that period he became an out-spoken critic of the tonal-block engravers who caused the demise of clear, crisp wood engraving. Those European wood engravers exhibiting in Paris at l'Exposition Universale, 1867, he declared were merely following 'the fashion of the Dalziel mania in England' with their 'rotten' lines and 'muddy' prints: 'The art is dead in Europe'. He set out to show the American public what could be done on wood by engraving for various American magazines such as Aldine and Scribner's (to 1881), was engaged by Frank Leslie as Artistic Director, Frank Leslie's Illustrated Newspaper, and even started his own illustrated paper, American Enterprise, with Hennessy's drawings, engraved by his brother Henry and Alfred Harral (q.v.), whom he had also persuaded to join him in America. This large folio-sized paper lasted only two issues, 1870-72, despite critical raptures like 'the handsomest illustrated sheet ever printed in this country or abroad'. He also became a member of the exclusive Century Club of American Artists, a founder-member of the American Society of Painters in Watercolours, and in 1870 he was elected to the American Academy of Design. By 1881 Linton (aged seventy), was still engraving ten hours a day, seven days a week, despite his prodigious poetic output and printing work. At his Appledore Press, near New Haven, Connecticut, he lived and gathered disciples around him. Eventually he was elected the first wood engraver member to the American National Academy of Arts, 1881; and was also given an honorary MA at Yale, 1891. He died in New Haven on 1 January 1898, aged eighty-five. Apart from his own engravings, Linton is important for his writings on the history and practice of wood engraving. These included the articles, 'The Engraver: His Function and Status', Scribner's Magazine, June 1879, p.241 and 'Art in Engraving on Wood', Atlantic Monthly, Vol.43, 1879, pp.706-13. He also wrote books to aid the engraver and the collector: Practical Hints on Wood Engraving, 1879; A History of Wood Engraving in America, 1882; and Wood Engraving, a Manual of Instruction, 1884.

His magnum opus was Masters of Wood Engraving, 1889, prepared from 200 photographs and study at the British Museum while on a return visit to England in 1884,1887. Linton's reputation as an engraver, especially his outspoken championing of Bewick's white-line technique, earned him great respect amongst his fellow countrymen. Edmund Evans (q.v.) himself a pioneering wood engraver of the period, wrote as late as 1904 how Linton 'and his followers were sincere artists, were they not?--I have a great reverence for J.W.L. himself--he was a martyr--himself, I always thought it such a waste of a good man to take the political turn he took; I reckon any man good enough to be such a radical & if he had "stuck to his last" he would have lead (sic) a happier life, and done better work--I reckon that he was our best wood engraver...' (Evans MS, University of California Library). His crusade against the 'speckled' tonal engraving, which reproduced greyness and not clear form, was much admired by the more worried practitioners of an art form threatened by photo-engraving. He taught them to translate, never merely reproduce in mindless mechanical fashion; for to him, an engraver must never allow his art to become 'servile'. Above all it was this campaign to make the engraver an artist in the public's eyes which never lost strength. It appealed to the burgeoning Arts and Crafts movement of the nineties, on which Linton exerted indirect influence, notably over such figures as Arthur Mackmurdo, Emery Walker, and William Morris, and the whole birth of the private press movement. By the 1920s Linton the engraver was ready for the collectors' marketplace, and assessment. An article in the Bookman's Journal and Print Collector,1921, outlined his most collectable work from 1835-65, including his various large prints after famous paintings. Douglas Bliss, writing in his History of Wood Engraving,1928, offered a more critical view of Linton the engraver: 'One cannot help admiring the old man. He is so thorough, so sincere, so solemn, so monumental. But it is clear that this vast intelligence is exercising itself in the narrowest possible groove. Technique in general, and in particular a certain kind of white-line technique, seen at its highest in the pupils of Bewick, is Linton's cultus. Of the aesthetic of line, though he be eloquent for pages upon it, he seems to have had no clear grasp, and of the beauty of design per se he had no thought whatsoever. The elaborate reproduction of insipid and merely pretty pictures by inferior artists of Victoria's age, such was the vocation of this distinguished man--poet and historian, as well as engraver' (Bliss,p.201). A large collection of proofs (including 136 large prints mounted by Linton) is in the British Museum; also some work is in the Victoria and Albert Museum and the Bodleian Library. He signed his engravings: 'W.J.LINTON', 'W.J.L.', 'W.L.'.
[For the full account of his life with extensive

bibliography see F.B.Smith, Radical Artisan, W.J.Linton,1973; also Linton's autobiography Memories,1895; his Masters of Wood Engraving, 1889; articles in English Illustrated Magazine,1891; collector's viewpoint in Bookman's Journal and Print Collector,8 July, 12 August 1921; see also DNB; Hake; Chatto; Graves; Reid; British Library catalogue (books engraved and illustrated under pseudonym 'Abel Reid')]

LINTON, William Wade ('Willie') c1839-92
Willie Linton as he was known, was the son and assistant of the wood engraver W.J.Linton (q.v.). He was probably born in Woodford about 1839, his birth being later registered on 21 December 1841. He was devoted to his father, taking charge of Brantwood, their Lake District home, when Linton went to London to engrave, and managing the engraving business from November 1866, after his father left for America. Although it is unknown whether he actually engraved, he was a substantial influence on his father's work, 'his steady faith in his father's undertakings and his long researches in the British Museum towards them had warmed Linton's feelings towards him' (F.B.Smith, W.J.Linton,1973,p.208). He even lent money to his father and his engraver uncle Henry Duff Linton (q.v.) for their various projects. He was a scruffy withdrawn bachelor character who ended his life as a lowly railway clerk and died in 1892, following a mental and physical collapse two years earlier.

LINVECKER, J.B.
Draughtsman of animal subjects, who contributed a drawing for wood engraving in The Graphic,1872.

LISTER, Walter Llewellyn 1876-1951
Woodcut artist, and watercolourist. He was born on 28 November 1876 and studied at the Westminster School of Art and St Martin's School,1900-04. He exhibited colour woodcuts at the Society of Graver Printers, of which he was an associate member. He lived near Bodmin, Cornwall and died on 18 January 1951.
[Waters]

LITTLEBURY and Company fl.1889-1900
Provincial wood engraving firm, with an office at Ye Ancient Commandery, Worcester (Kelly's,1889), and as The Worcester Press from 1900.

LIX, Frédéric Théodore 1830-97
Occasional draughtsman on wood, genre painter. He was born in December 1830 and made his debut at the Paris Salon in 1859. He is listed here for his drawings of equestrian subjects wood engraved in the Illustrated London News,1862-63. He died in Paris, 1897.

LOCKWOOD, Joseph and Bridges fl.1872-76
Provincial wood engraving firm, with an office as
Lockwood and Bridges at 85 Queen Street, Sheffield
(Kelly's,1872). The partnership had broken up by
1876 when Joseph Lockwood worked alone as wood
engraver from the same address (Kelly's,1876).

LODGE, George Edward 1860-1953
Wood engraver, draughtsman on wood, figure and
landscape painter. He was apprenticed to a wood
engraver before he set up as wood engraver draughtsman in London, at 28 Holborn Viaduct, EC
(POD,1883-86), then at 99 Gower Street, WC
(POD,1887). During this time he produced and
engraved ornithological illustrations for the English
Illustrated Magazine,1886, such as 'Sketches of
Bird-Life in S. Sweden' engraved to emphasise
the detail of each bird, set against an even grey
background. He also drew the series 'Modern
Falconry' in the same year. Lodge also collaborated
with J.G.Millais (q.v.) the animal illustrator,
engraving and drawing for Lord Walsingham's
Shooting: Moor and Marsh,1909. This was perhaps
the most famous of hundreds of commissioned small
drawings and vignettes which he produced towards the
end of the century. Other work was drawn and
engraved on wood for Howard Saunders' An Illustrated
Manual of British Birds,1889; W.H.Hudson's British
Birds,1895; A.H.Evans' Birds,1899; and W.T.Greene's
Birds of the British Empire,1898. By this time he had
returned briefly to draw and engrave again in the
English Illustrated Magazine,1893-94, and also for the
Pall Mall Magazine. He also exhibited paintings at the
Royal Academy, the Royal Society of British Artists
and the Royal Institute of Painters in Oil-Colours,
working in later life from Camberley.
[Houfe; C.Jackson]

LODGE, Reginald B. fl.1886-1911
Wood engraver, who specialised in detailed landscape
and decorative borders and initials. He engraved
various full-page landscapes by William Biscombe
Gardner (q.v.) and James T.Watts for the English
Illustrated Magazine,1886-89. The most noted and
successful of these was the series of full-page
engravings after Gardner's drawings to Grant Allen's
'Surrey Mill Wheels', 1886-87, which were engraved
with a fine understanding of light and dark in the
foliage and tree trunks. Lodge also collaborated with
fellow engravers H.F.Davey and J.D.Cooper (qq.v.)
to complete the full-page engraving 'Glan Conwat'
after James T.Watts,1888-89. By the turn of the
century he had wood engraved with Clemence Housman
(q.v.) from various designs by and for James Guthrie
(q.v.) at his Pear Tree Press. Among these were an
edition of D.G.Rossetti's (q.v.) The Blessed Damozel,
1911, with end-papers, title-page, borders and
initials designed by Guthrie; and John Milton's Hymn
on the Morning of Christ's Nativity, again with end-

paper, title-page and initial designs by Guthrie.

LONDON Drawing and Tracing Company fl.1880s
London firm of draughtsmen on wood, with an office
at 79 New Oxford Street, WC (Kelly's,1889).

LONDON Drawing Association
(see Taylor, Arthur)

LONDON Ruling Company fl.1883-84
London firm of wood engravers, under the manage-
ment of Edward Hodge, with an office at 281 Strand,
WC (POD,1883-84)

LONDON Wood Engraving Company fl.1894-96
London firm of wood engravers, with an office at
21 Bride Street, EC (POD,1894-96).

LONG, Arthur Robert fl.1890s
London wood engraver, who worked at 84 Fleet
Street, EC (POD,1892), previously the office of
Frederick Edmund Long (q.v.). The following year
the office was taken over by A. & H.Quartley (q.v.).

LONG, Frederick Edmund fl.1879-88
London wood engraver, who worked as Frederick
Long at 84 Fleet Street, EC (POD,1879), premises
shared with F.Babbage and A.Myerson (qq.v.). He
reappears in the London directories as Frederick
Edmund Long at 75 Fleet Street (POD,1888), an
address he then shared with F.W.Davis (q.v.)

LONG, Henry fl.1880-89
London draughtsman on wood, who worked at
25 Bouverie Street, EC (Kelly's,1880), and then
92 and 93 Fleet Street (Kelly's,1889).

LONG, Robert Richard and Company fl.1867-90
London firm of draughtsmen and wood engravers,
who worked at 22 Chancery Lane, WC (POD,1867),
an address shared with A.R.Dorrington (q.v.). By
1880 the firm appears in the directories at Hare
Place, 47 Fleet Street, EC (POD, Kelly's,1880-81).
They move yet again, six years later appearing in
the directory working from 75 Fleet Street, EC
(POD,1887), which they shared with F.W.Davis
(q.v.). Finally as Robert Richard Long and Son they
worked from 8 Pleydell Street, EC (POD,1889-90).

LORETZ and Company fl.1880s
Provincial wood engraving firm, with an office at
66 King Street, Manchester (Kelly's,1889).

LORSA(Y), Louis Alexandre Eustache 1822-?
French draughtsman and portrait painter. He was
born in Paris on 23 June 1822, and studied there and
at Monvoisin. He made his début at the Salon in 1847,
and returned 1859. He is listed here for his drawings
for wood engravings of figure subjects secured by

Henry Vizetelly (q.v.) for his Illustrated Times,1855.

LOSS, Peter fl.1880s
Provincial draughtsman on wood, who worked at 8 Kent
Street, Jarrow, Durham (Kelly's,1889). He specialised
in marine subjects. Among his local competitors
were A.Bain and G.Johnstone (qq.v.).

LOUDAN, Robert fl.1855-95
Prominent London wood engraver, who worked at
28 Ludgate Hill (Hodgson's,1855), then 38 Hatton
Garden (POD,1856). He then joined forces with Henry
Vizetelly (q.v.) as Vizetelly and Loudan, 15 and 16
Gough Square (POD,1862-64) until the partnership
broke up. He returned on his own to wood engrave
from 37 Essex Street, Strand, WC (POD,1865-92),
later moving briefly to 40 Norfolk Street, Strand,
WC (POD,1893-95), before he disappears from the
London directories. Among his commissions for
various magazines is a portrait engraving of Rt. Hon.
Sir George Lewis, after a photograph, Illustrated
London News,1863. More impressive is the large
foldout wood engraving, 'New York from Bergen
Hill, Hoboken', drawn on wood by T.Sulman, which
appeared in the Illustrated London News as a special
supplement (the size of six pages), 19 August 1876.
He signed his work: 'R.Loudan sc'.

LOUDON, J. fl.1860s
Bohn in Chatto and Jackson lists this wood engraver
as 'current'. His engravings included cuts for Henry
Vizetelly's Illustrated Times.

LOVEJOY, Henry fl.1867-68
London wood engraver, who worked at 15 Essex
Street, Strand, WC (POD,1867-68). He shared the
premises with F.Gifford and R.S.Marriott (qq.v.).

LOWE
(see Whitehead, Morris and Lowe)

LOWE, Arthur W. fl.1880s
Provincial wood engraver, who worked at Clifton's
Yard, Corn Market, Derby (Kelly's,1880).

LUARD, John Dalbiac 1830-60
Occasional draughtsman on wood, and genre painter.
He was born at Blythborough Hall, Lincolnshire in
1830, became a soldier and served in the Crimean
War. He then joined the Langham Sketching Club and
studied under John Philip,RA, exhibiting his first
paintings at the Royal Academy,1855-58. As an
illustrator he was dismissed by White thus: 'J.Luard,
an artist, whose work floods the cheaper publications
of the time, shows, in an early drawing, 'Contrasts'
[Once a Week,iii,p.84] , a Pre-Raphaelite manner,
and a promise which later years did not fulfil, if
indeed this be by the Luard of the penny dreadfuls'.
By 1859 his health had failed; he travelled to America

and back, with only temporary effect, and retired to
a relative's house Winterslow, in Salisbury where he
died in August 1860, aged thirty, 'leaving much
promise of a reputation in art'.
[White; Redgrave; Houfe]

LUCAS, Alfred fl.1880-1900
Provincial wood engraver, draughtsman on wood,
who worked at 35 Great Charles Street, Birmingham
(Kelly's,1880-89), then 120 Edmund Street (Kelly's,
1900).

LUCAS, Henry fl.1872-80
Provincial wood engraver, who worked at 90 Suffolk
Street, Birmingham (Kelly's,1872-80).

LUCAS, Horatio Joseph 1839-73
Occasional draughtsman on wood, amateur etcher.
He was born on 27 May 1839 and began an illustrator's
career, drawing for magazines. White lists his one
drawing 'The Sangreal' for a wood engraving in Good
Words,1863, but claims Lucas was 'a name rarely
encountered'. He also exhibited at the Royal Academy,
1870-73. He died on 18 December 1873. The British
Museum owns a proof engraving of a design done for
the Dalziel Brothers (q.v.), 1863.

LUCAS, John Seymour 1849-1923
Occasional draughtsman on wood, prominent painter
of historical subjects and portraits. He was born in
London on 21 December 1849, the nephew of the
portrait painter John Lucas. He attended St Martin's
and the Royal Academy Schools, and specialised in
sculpture but later turned to painting. He did a large
number of illustrations of historical subjects, some
of which were wood engraved by the Dalziel Brothers
(q.v.). They quote a letter from Lucas (Dalziels'
Record,p.160) concerning his judgement of their
translation of his drawing into engraved line: 'I
consider the cutting of my drawing quite a masterpiece, and in every respect up to my expectation.
There is nothing I can suggest that would improve it'.
Lucas generally made historical drawings in grey
wash with heavy body colour, which must have given
the Dalziels considerable trouble when they attempted
to translate such work into line. Nevertheless Lucas
continued to illustrate with The Cruise of the River,
1883 and throughout the 1890s, for The Graphic,
1893,1901-06, as well as for S.R.Crockett's The
Grey Man,1896. He was elected member of the New
Watercolour Society and the Royal Institute of Painters
in Watercolours in 1877, ARA in 1886 (the year he
visited the Royal Academy), RA in 1898. His work
appeared at the Royal Academy, the Royal Institute of
Painters in Oil-Colours, the Royal Scottish Academy,
the Royal Society of British Artists, the Royal
Cambrian Academy and the Royal Hibernian Academy.
He died in Blythborough, Suffolk on 8 May 1923.
[Dalziels' Record; TB; Who's Who,1913]

LUCAS, John Templeton 1836-80
Occasional draughtsman on wood, portrait painter,
metal engraver and author. He was born in 1836, the
son of the portrait painter John Lucas and cousin of
John Seymour Lucas (q.v.). He is included here for
his drawings for wood engravings in the Illustrated
London News, 1865, 1876 and 1879. These were
generally of genre or seasonal subjects. He wrote a
farcical play and some fairy tales, 1871. He also
exhibited paintings at the British Institution, 1859-76;
the Royal Academy, 1861-75 and the Royal Society of
British Artists. He died in Whitby in 1880.
[DNB; Bénézit; TB; Redgrave; Bryan; for his metal
engravings see Volume I]

LUDLOW, Henry Stephen 'Hal' 1861-?
Wood engraver, draughtsman on wood, portrait and
domestic painter. He was born in 1861 and studied at
Heatherley's Art School and Highgate College then was
apprenticed to the Dalziel Brothers (q.v.) to learn
wood engraving. He made little progress here but
was soon recognised for his draughtsmanship which
he developed into designs in pen and ink for wood
engraved children's books and various magazines.
The Dalziels set him to work on their Pictorial World,
for which he drew numerous social events, river and
racing scenes, theatrical, operatic and music hall
performances. Such work attracted the attention of
Mason Jackson (q.v.), art editor of the Illustrated
London News, who asked the Dalziels if Ludlow might
make similar drawings on wood for his magazine,
although his expert pen drawings lost much of their
vitality when reproduced by process (photo-engraving)
techniques; the Dalziels claimed 'it was a pity that
such clever drawings should all be reproduced by
process'--but then they never accepted the merits of
process over wood engraving. Ludlow contributed to
the Illustrated London News for seven years, 1882-89.
He also drew for Dalziels' comic magazine Fun,
1879-87. His comic skills earned him the post of
chief cartoonist for Punch's rival comic magazine,
Judy, 1889-90. He continued to draw for various
1890s magazines, such as the Queen, 1892; Rambler,
1897; Sketch; the Dalziels' own Ally Sloper's Half
Holiday; for Illustrated Bits; Cassell's Family
Magazine; Chums; and Strand Magazine. As a painter
Ludlow made small watercolours in the intricate,
detailed style of Dutch masters and exhibited at the
Royal Academy and the Royal Institute of Painters in
Watercolours. By the turn of the century he was still
working, away from London in Hanwell, 1902-25.
[Dalziels' Record; Houfe]

LUDLOW, Joseph W. fl.1880s
Provincial wood engraver, who worked at 96 Vauxhall
Road, Birmingham (Kelly's, 1880).

LUDLOW, S.
Draughtsman who contributed bird illustrations for
wood engravings in The Graphic, 1870.

LUEDERS, R.S. fl.1884-87
Wood engraver, who worked for the English Illustrated
Magazine, 1884-87. His wood engravings here
included landscapes and nautical subjects after
A.Lemon, C.J.Staniland, P.Hardy (qq.v.), H.Fitton
and J.Fulleylove. He signed his work 'R.Lueders'.

LUMLEY, Arthur 1837-1912
Draughtsman illustrator, who was born in Dublin in
1837 but who emigrated to the United States where he
worked in New York as an illustrator and painter. He
is included here for his drawings wood engraved
in the Illustrated London News, 1875-76, 1881. These
included a series of 'American Sketches' depicting
aspects of American life: 'Sunday on the Union
Pacific Railway', 20 March 1875; 'Salon of a Steam-
boat', 8 May 1875, engraved on wood by Henry
Linton (q.v.); 'Christmas in Florida', 30 December
1876, engraved by Linton; and 'Christmas in Hudson's
Bay Territory', 30 December 1876, engraved by
Henry Hollidge (q.v.). Lumley exhibited one work at
the Royal Academy, 1876. He died in Mount Vernon,
New York on 27 September 1912.

LUNDIE
(see Martin and Lundie)

LUXMOORE, Douglas Henry fl.1880s
London wood engraver, who worked at 64 Fleet
Street, EC (POD, 1880). He may be related to the
London painter and sculptor Arthur C.H.Luxmoore,
fl.1854-88.
[TB]

LYDON, Alexander Francis 'Frank' 1836-1917
Prominent wood engraver, draughtsman on wood of
ornithological and natural history subjects, best
known for his association with Benjamin Fawcett
(q.v.). Lydon was born in 1836, of a family of
soldiers, and apprenticed with his brother Frederick
(q.v.) to learn wood engraving from Benjamin
Fawcett (q.v.). Thus began his famous association
with Fawcett, where, according to C.T.Courtney
Lewis, he 'was to add lustre to the Driffield workshop, and as author, poet, watercolour artist,
engraver, and general utility man was to spend
upwards of thirty years there'. In fact Lydon, with
his draughtsmanship skills, was to instigate picture
printing at Fawcett's works and was responsible for
a 'vast output' which he drew and engraved on wood
for Fawcett's workers to print. Indeed even before
Lydon's apprenticeship was over, Fawcett had set
him to work drawing and preparing various colour
plates for publication. His earliest work was probably
for Agnes Strickland's Floral Sketches, Fables and

Other Poems, 1861. The list of Lydon's prolific
achievements is staggering. His abilities ranged
from drawing on blocks, and watercolour painting
(he exhibited at the Royal Academy, 1861) to
supervising the various aspects of Fawcett's
printing works. His apprenticeship had proved
invaluable for this since Fawcett had insisted that
Lydon train in each department of his printing works,
not just the engraving workshop. His most remarkable
early achievement was drawing all seventy-nine colour
and 909 black and white illustrations to E.J.Lowe's
A Natural History of Ferns, British and Exotic,
1856-60. This involved over 1,000 wood blocks and
set the pace for subsequent natural history work,
most notably for Reverend Lowe's A Natural History
of British Grasses, 1857 (the seventy-four illustrations
for which Lydon drew on wood from nature) and Lowe's
Beautiful-Leaved Plants, 1859-?, with the sixty colour
illustrations all drawn by Lydon. His work for Lowe
totalled 630 colour plates, and 1,460 wood engravings.
He also persuaded Fawcett to branch out beyond
natural history printing: he watercoloured twenty-
nine illustrations to Gems for the Poets, 1860; followed
by Gems of Nature and Art. This led to Fawcett's
greatest printing project: the six volume The County
Seats of the Noblemen and Gentlemen of Great Britain
and Ireland, 1864-80. All 240 houses chosen were
drawn (though not engraved) on wood by Lydon and
printed in eight colours by Fawcett. When published
it was hailed as a 'a triumph of colour printing' which
had required 1,920 separate wood blocks. His last
work for Fawcett was twenty-five drawings each to
English Lake Scenery, 1880, and Scottish Loch
Scenery, 1882, which Fawcett printed at his Driffield
works. After this he left Fawcett, about 1883, for some
unknown reason, and went to London. There he continued
to provide black and white and watercolour illustrations
to magazines and books which were commissioned and
printed independent of his old employer. These included
colour plates to the Animal World and Band of Mercy.
He made thousands of bird drawings to various bird
magazines such as Fancier's Gazette, Feathered
World, Canary and Cage Bird Life and Poultry. Other
magazines he illustrated were the Boy's Own Paper,
Cassell's Popular Education, Harper's Monthly,
Harper's Young People, the Illustrated London News,
1890; the English Illustrated Magazine, 1891-92,
Leisure Hour, Pictorial World, Sporting and Dramatic
News, and Church Monthly, 1895. He even drew a series
of four colour prints: 'The Requiem', 'Frozen Out',
'Stoke Poges Church', and 'Burnham Beeches', two
of which some consider to be his finest work. Lydon
did some work with Fawcett after his departure from
his business, notably on the eighty-one colour plates
to Dr W.T.Greene's Parrots in Captivity, 1887. But
he largely remained in London, until his death on
20 March 1917, aged eighty. He left a wife, Catherine
Fitzgerald, five sons and two daughters. He signed
his engravings: 'F.L.' (early 1860s work)', 'A.F.L.'

(usual signature) or 'A.F.Lydon'.
[For a complete list of work drawn and engraved see
C.T.Lewis; also M.C.F.Morris, Benjamin Fawcett,
1925; Print Collector's Quarterly, Vol.12, 1925, p.342;
also Bénézit; McLean, Victorian Book Design; TB]

LYDON, C.
Wood engraver, who engraved 'The Morning Meal'
after a drawing by A.F.Lydon (q.v.) for the Church
Monthly, 1895. It is a strong engraving, noted for its
good understanding of contrasts.

LYDON, Frederick
Trainee wood engraver, apprenticed with his brother
Alexander Francis Lydon (q.v.) to the noted wood
engraver Benjamin Fawcett (q.v.). Unlike his
brother, Frederick did not complete his apprenticeship,
but was taken away by his parents to Dorchester.
[C.T.Lewis]

LYNCH, J.F.A.
Draughtsman on wood of topographical subjects,
which he drew for wood engravings in the Illustrated
London News, and Vizetelly's Illustrated Times in
1860.

LYNE, Gerard fl.1850s
London wood engraver, who worked at 48 Salisbury
Square, Fleet Street, EC (POD, 1858). These
premises, once the office of Greenaway and Wright
(q.v.), Lyne shared with S.V. and A.Slader (qq.v.).

LYNN, Eliza fl.1850s
Trainee wood engraver, poet, novelist and journalist
for various Victorian papers such as the Morning
Chronicle. She is listed here as the second wife of
the prominent wood engraver W.J.Linton (q.v.). She
had befriended his sister and in 1854 he gave her
wood engraving lessons. Linton was apparently
flattered by her interest in his profession although he
had little patience or sympathy with anyone less
dexterous than himself. Her engraved work is
unrecorded. Her tragic marriage to Linton (she was
homosexual) was one of the age's more bizarre
domestic arrangements and she maintained her own
professional career quite independent from her
husband.
[F.Smith, W.J.Linton, 1973; G.S.Layard, Mrs Lynn
Linton, 1901]

LYNN, Godfrey fl.1877-78
London wood engraver, who worked at 139 Fleet
Street, EC (POD, 1877), shared with F.Barnard
(q.v.); then at East Temple Chambers, Whitefriars
Street, EC (POD, 1878), which he shared with
R.Paterson (q.v.).

M., W.C.
A wood engraved portrait of Isaac Disraeli, by the
artist A.D'Orsay, engraved for a newspaper, was
signed 'W.C.M.'. It is now in the British Museum.
[Hake]

MACBETH, James 1847-91
Draughtsman illustrator, and landscape painter. He
was born in Glasgow in 1847, the son of the artist
Norman Macbeth, RSA, and brother of R.W.Macbeth
(q.v.). He drew for wood engravings in the Illustrated
London News, 1872-73; and The Graphic, 1872-74,
after his brother left the paper. At the same time he
exhibited paintings from 1872 at the Royal Academy,
the Grosvenor Gallery, the Royal Society of British
Artists, the Royal Institute of Painters in Watercolours,
the Royal Institute of Painters in Oil-Colours, and the
Royal Scottish Academy. He worked from London and
Churt, Surrey and died on 6 March 1891.
[TB; Bénézit; Houfe; Clement]

MACBETH, Robert Walker 1848-1910
Draughtsman, etcher and painter. He was born in
Glasgow on 30 September 1848, the son of Norman
Macbeth, RSA, and brother of James Macbeth (q.v.)
He was educated in Edinburgh and Friedrichsdorf,
Germany and studied art at the Royal Academy Schools.
By 1870 he was working in London for the newly
established The Graphic as draughtsman for wood
engravings. These engravings covered a large variety
of subjects, including sketches of the Paris Commune,
and appeared from 1870-71. He also drew for Once a
Week, 1870, and Sunday Magazine, 1871. During the
1880s he contributed illustrations for wood engravings
in the English Illustrated Magazine, 1883-85, most
notably a series of landscapes to 'In the Fens', 1883-84.
He was even better known for his intricate landscape
etchings and was elected RE at the foundation of that
group. He also exhibited paintings and his etchings
at the Grosvenor Gallery, the New Gallery, and the
Royal Academy, where he was elected ARA, 1883 and
RA, 1903, the Royal Institute of Painters in Watercolours, the Royal Institute of Painters in Oil-Colours,
the Royal Scottish Academy, and the Royal Watercolour Society. He died in London on 1 November
1910.
[Bénézit; Houfe; for etchings see Volume I]

McCOMB, George fl.1870s
Provincial wood engraver, who worked at 11 Church
Lane, Liverpool (Kelly's, 1872).

McCONNELL, William ?-1867
Trainee wood engraver, draughtsman on wood of
comic subjects. He was the son of an Irish tailor who
had set up business in London's Tottenham Court
Road. He showed an early talent for drawing and
showed his sketches to the Punch editor, Mark
Lemon, who was impressed enough to recommend

McConnell for training as draughtsman and wood
engraver by the Punch engraver Joseph Swain (q.v.).
Swain not only taught him to draw on blocks and cut
on the wood, he also took the young man in as a
lodger 'for a time; but not living long enough to prove
his individuality, he remained to the end an imitator
of Leech', according to Spielmann. He became an
official Punch cartoonist in 1852, his work having
appeared there from 1850, but even the fact that 'He
was a good and improving draughtsman, especially
of horses; and he revelled in beggars, 'swells', and
backgrounds' (Spielmann) could not compensate for
what he regarded as his unfair treatment by Lemon.
Luckily he had also begun drawing for wood engravings
in the Illustrated London News, 1851-58, 1860, and
was appointed cartoonist of the Illustrated Times from
1855-56, following his supposed mistreatment by Punch.
He was also a friend of G.A.Sala, who described
McConnell as 'a handsome little fellow, alert, and
full of originality', and secured his illustrations to
Sala's Twice Round the Clock, 1859. Henry Vizetelly
(q.v.) also published his drawings on wood in his
Illustrated Times, 1855-61, but dismissed McConnell
as 'a somewhat vulgarised imitator of John Leech'.
Edmund Evans (q.v.) used McConnell to draw on
wood for his new series of colour railway book
covers, and the Dalziel Brothers (q.v.) also engraved
his early work. By the 1860s McConnell had illustrated
The Adventures of Mr Wilderspin, 1860; and for the
magazines Welcome Guest, 1860; London Society,
1864; Churchman's Family Magazine, 1864; and
Sunday Magazine, 1865. He died in 1867. The British
Museum owns his political cartoons. He signed his work:
'Mc' 'W M^{C}onnell' (script).
[Dalziels' Record; Bénézit; Spielmann; Houfe;
Vizetelly, Glances Back; Evans Reminiscences]

McCORMACK, Arthur David 1860-1943
Draughtsman, etcher and travel artist. He was born
in Coleraine on 14 October 1860 and educated there
and in Belfast, before studying art at South Kensington.
He began as a draughtsman for wood engravings in the
English Illustrated Magazine, 1884-88, notably a series
of illustrations to John Lomas' 'Legends of Toledo',
1884-85, engraved on wood by H.F.Davey and
A. and W.Dawson (qq.v.); illustrations to 'A Month
in Sicily', 1885-86, engraved by J.C.Griffiths,
T.S.Bayley, O.Jahyer, H.F.Davey, Waterlow and
Sons and J.D.Cooper (qq.v.); and illustrations to
'A September Day in the Valley of the Arno', 1886,
engraved by O.Lacour (q.v.). He established himself
as a travel artist in these and in numerous later book
illustrations throughout the 1890s (see Houfe for a
list). He also contributed drawings for wood
engravings in the Illustrated London News, 1886-97;
Good Words, 1898; Arabian Nights' Entertainments,
1899; and Strand Magazine, 1906. He exhibited at
various galleries including the Royal Academy, the
Royal Society of British Artists, to which he was

elected member,1897; the Royal Hibernian Society, the Royal Society of Painters in Oil-Colours, to which he was elected member,1905; the Royal Institute of Painters in Watercolours, to which he was elected member,1906; and at the Royal Water-colour Society. He died in St John's Wood, London in 1943.
[For a list of etched work see Volume I; see also TB; Bénézit; Who's Who,1924; Houfe]

McCROMBIE, Francis Valentine fl.1889-93
London wood engraver, who worked as McCrombie and Todhunter, a partnership with E.M.Todhunter (q.v.), at 5 New Court, Carey Street, WC (POD,1889-90). He then appears on his own, working at the same address (POD,1891-93).

McCROMBIE and Todhunter
(see McCrombie, Francis)

MacDONALD
(see Maclure, MacDonald and MacGregor)

MacDONALD, Georgiana
(see Burne-Jones, Georgiana)

MacDOUGALL, William Brown ?-1936
Wood engraver, illustrator, painter and etcher. He was born in Glasgow, educated at the Glasgow Academy and studied art in Paris at Julian's and under Bougereau, J.M.Laurens, and R.Fleury. He exhibited regularly at the Paris Salon. His illustration and engraved work showed a distinct change of style after appearing in the Yellow Book,1894, and his contact with Beardsley: his engravings and drawings turn heavy with stark contrast. Such work appeared in the Evergreen,1894, Savoy, and in various 1890s books. He exhibited at the New English Art Club, where he was elected member in 1890. He also exhibited at the Royal Academy and the Royal Scottish Academy. He died in Loughton, Essex on 20 April 1936. The British Museum owns a series of marine engravings by him.
[Houfe (list of 90s books); Sketchley]

McDOUGLE and Dolling fl.1870s
London firm of draughtsmen on wood, who worked at 48 Paternoster Row, EC (Kelly's,1872).

MacFARLANE and Erskine fl.1872-1900
Scottish wood engraving and colour printing firm. It was founded in 1859 at 19 St James Square, Edinburgh, by F.Schenck, who sold the firm to W.H.Farlane (d.1875) who adopted the name 'MacFarlane'. Later William Erskine took over, adopting 'MacFarlane and Erskine', and continued the business which was still in operation in 1975. They appear in Kelly's Stationers' directory as a wood engraving firm, 13,14,19 St James Square (Kelly's,1872-80).
[Wakeman and Bridson]

McIAN, Robert Ronald 1803-56
Draughtsman on wood, genre painter. He was born in 1803 and combined acting with painting. He abandoned the theatre after 1840 and took up drawing on wood for various publications. The earliest work seems to have been small vignettes for the Book of British Ballads,1842, engraved on wood by W.J.Linton (q.v.). One is reproduced by Bohn in Chatto and Jackson (p.590) as a good example of Linton's early engraving; it depicts a cauldron surmounted by predatory birds and encircled by wolves. McIan went on to illustrate two volumes of James Logan's Clans of the Scottish Highlands, 1845-47, and cuts to the London Art Union Prize Annual,1845. He was a successful painter as well and exhibited at the Royal Academy from 1836, also the British Institution, the Royal Society of British Artists, and the Royal Scottish Academy, being elected ARSA. He died in Hampstead in 1856. The British Museum owns proofs of his designs engraved by John Orrin Smith and the Dalziel Brothers (qq.v.).
[Bryan; Bénézit; Chatto; Houfe]

MacKAY, Wallis 'W.V.' fl.1870-93
Comic draughtsman, caricaturist. He achieved notice as cartoonist for Punch,1870-74, where he had twenty-seven drawings wood engraved. He left abruptly in 1874 after drawing an offensive cartoon, which upset the editor Tom Taylor. 'Even the blocks already in hand and paid for were suppressed, with the exception of four, of which the last appeared in 1877', Spielmann recalled. Mackay subsequently drew comic cuts for Judy, the rival paper to Punch, and for the Illustrated London News,1880. He became cartoonist of Fun in 1893, the year in which the paper was sold by the Dalziel Brothers (q.v.).
[Spielmann; Dalziels' Record]

McKELVIE and Dobson fl.1889-1900
Provincial wood engraving firm, with offices at 24 Waterloo Buildings, 2 Wood Street, Liverpool (Kelly's,1889) and then, as 'Samuel McKelvie', at 12 Waterloo Buildings, Liverpool (Kelly's,1900).

MacKENZIE fl.1830s
London wood engraver, who worked at 23 Prospect Place, Cambridge Heath (POD,1832).

MacKENZIE, William fl.1847-1900
Scottish wood engraver and colour printer. He worked for the firm founded by Duncan MacKenzie at 154 Trongate, Glasgow in 1806, by 1841 known as MacKenzie, White and Company. In 1847 William MacKenzie appeared as a colour printer at 48 London Street, Glasgow, then had moved to 45-47 Howard Street, by 1854. He exhibited colour work at the Great Exhibition of 1851, and also printed Library Shakespeare,c1873, after J.Gilbert, Cruikshank and R.Dudley. He appeared as wood engraver in

Kelly's Stationers' directory at 43 Howard Street
(Kelly's,1880), where he remained until at least
1900.
[For colour work see Wakeman and Bridson]

MacKENZIE, William Henry fl.1865-70
London wood engraver, who worked at St Leonard
Street, Bromley (POD,1865-70).

MACLISE, Daniel 1806-70
Prominent draughtsman on wood, lithographer,
painter of historical subjects and portraits. He was
born in Cork in 1806 (Maclise always claimed 1811),
the son of a former Scottish soldier. He attended
the Cork School of Art during which time he received
attention for a lithographed sketch of Sir Walter Scott
which he drew from life, 1825. He eventually saved
enough from portrait sketches to go to London in
July 1827, where he attended the Royal Academy
Schools and won the silver and gold medals in 1828.
He exhibited there from 1829, then by 1830 had set
up as a book illustrator, adopting a firm, Germanic
outline style. He continued to alternate painting with
illustration until the 1860s. His most interesting
drawings were lithographic caricatures for Fraser's,
1830-36, and various drawings for his friend Charles
Dickens' books: The Chimes,1844 and The Cricket on
the Hearth,1845. He drew on wood for Thomas Moore's
Irish Melodies,1845; Gottfried Burger's poem Leonora,
1847, wood engraved by J.Thompson (q.v.). His most
noted drawings were to Moxon's edition of Tennyson's
Poems,1857; and Tennyson's Princess,1860, wood
engraved by W.L.Thomas (q.v.). Excerpts from the
Tennyson works are reproduced by Bohn in Chatto
and Jackson as examples of Maclise as a draughtsman
on wood, 'who in his own peculiar manner has
furnished drawings on wood for several finely
illustrated publications...'. The DNB remarks that
as a draughtsman Maclise 'was a master, scarcely
rivalled by any British artist. His line was somewhat
cold and strict, but full of spirit and expression, as
elastic and as firm as steel. It was rather that of a
sculptor or an engraver, than a painter, preserving
precision and completeness of outline at all costs.'
As a painter, Maclise exhibited at the British
Institution and the Royal Society of British Artists,
and was elected RA in 1840, refusing the presidency
there in 1866. He died at 4 Cheyne Walk, Chelsea on
25 April 1870. The British Museum owns proofs of
his designs engraved by the Dalziel Brothers (q.v.),
1853,1856-57.
[Chatto; Wood; Houfe; R.Ormond, Daniel Maclise,
1972; Bryan; DNB]

MacLURE, MacDonald and MacGregor
Firm of draughtsmen for wood engravings, lithographers and colour printers. The firm was started
by Archibald Gray MacDonald (1813-1900), a Glasgow
born apprentice to the engraver and lithographer

James Miller. He joined with fellow apprentice
Andrew MacLure (1812-85) in 1835 and set up an
engraving and lithographic printing business.
MacLure concentrated on the artistic side of the
firm and was a competent lithographer and oil and
watercolour painter, who exhibited at the Royal
Academy. The firm grew with colour printing work
and earned the distinction of being the first to use
steam power for lithographic printing in Britain.
They opened branches in Liverpool,1840, London,
1845, and Manchester,1850. They appear as
MacLure and MacDonald in Kelly's Stationers'
directory: as draughtsmen on wood at 97 Queen
Victoria Street, EC (Kelly's,1876-1900), then as
MacLure and Company from 1889, with printing
works at 27 Ray Street, Clerkenwell.
[For colour work see Wakeman and Bridson]

MacMICHAEL, J. fl.1869-70
London wood engraver, who worked at 207 King's
Road, Chelsea, SW (POD,1869-70).

MackMURDIE, Alfred George fl.1894-98
London wood engraver, who worked at 36 Furnival
Street, EC (POD,1894-98). The following year the
address was that of W.Haywood (q.v.).

MacNAB, Peter ?-1900
Draughtsman illustrator and genre painter who
worked in London and Woking, Surrey. He drew for
wood engravings in the Illustrated London News,
1882-83; the Cornhill,1884; and for the English
Illustrated Magazine,1884-87, where his illustrations
to James Sime's 'The Crofters', 1884-85, were wood
engraved by E.Ohme, W. and J.R.Cheshire,
R.Paterson, E.Schladitz (qq.v.). He also collaborated
with Dewey Bates on illustrations to Richard Jeffries'
essay, 'Walks in the Wheatfields', 1886-87, engraved
on wood by O.Lacour, H.F.Davey, and R.Paterson.
As a painter Macnab exhibited from 1864 at the
British Institution, the Fine Art Society, the Royal
Academy, the Royal Institute of Painters in Watercolours, and the Royal Institute of Painters in Oil-
Colours. He was elected RBA in 1879.
[Houfe; Bénézit; Graves]

MACNAMARA, Joseph John fl.1889-1910
London wood engraver, who worked at 3 Chandos
Street, Covent Garden, WC (POD,1889), then
10 and 11 Bedford Street, Strand (POD,1890-91).
When he moved to Dacre House, Arundel Street,
Strand (POD,1892-94), then 10 Norfolk Street,
Strand (POD,1895-97) he shared both offices with
the noted wood engraver H.W.Bennett (q.v.). By
1910 Macnamara was listing his office as 3 Arundel
Street, Strand, WC (POD,1910).

McPHERSON, A. and J. fl.1850-57
Scottish wood engraving and lithographic firm,
listed in the directories in 1855-57 at 12 Royal
Exchange, Edinburgh. They specialised in lithographic
printing including a series of tinted views of Scotland,
c1850 for R.W.Fraser.
[see Wakeman and Bridson for colour work]

MACQUOID, Percy T. 1852-1925
Draughtsman illustrator, painter, theatrical designer
and furniture historian. He was born in 1852, the son
of the artist Thomas Robert Macquoid (q.v.), and
educated at Marlborough. He studied at Heatherley's,
the Royal Academy Schools and in France. He began
his illustrations for wood engravings in 1871, drawing
for The Graphic,1871-90, generally animal scenes or
genre subjects like 'The Mackerel Fishery--Sketches
in a Devonshire Village', 9 May 1874. These were
much admired by Van Gogh: 'Macquoid is one of the
most distinguished of English illustrators'. Such
work also appeared wood engraved in the Illustrated
London News,1874-82. These too Van Gogh
collected and found inspiring, such as 'Reflections',
Christmas,1874, and an engraving of his own painting
'Girl of Pont-Aven', 30 December 1876 which he
declared 'splendid'. Macquoid was in fact an
accomplished draughtsman for wood engravings, his
favourite device being a series of sketches over-
lapping each other on one page, for instance, 'Sketches
at the Mule and Dog Show', the Illustrated London
News,16 May 1874. He also illustrated an edition of
Walter Scott's The Bridal of Triermain, for the
Art Union,1886. His genre pictures of young society
girls were quite popular and were exhibited at the
Royal Academy and the Royal Institute of Painters
in Watercolours, where he was elected member 1882.
He also exhibited at the Royal Institute of Painters in
Oil-Colours, and was elected member in 1883. He
also designed theatrical costumes and in later years
compiled four volumes of History of English Furniture,
1905. He died on 20 March 1925.
[Bénézit; English Influences on Van Gogh; Houfe;
Connoisseur,1925,p.47]

MACQUOID, Thomas Robert 1820-1912
Draughtsman on wood, ornamental designer and
painter. He was born in Chelsea on 24 January 1820,
was educated in Brompton and then studied art at the
Royal Academy Schools. He became well known for
his ornamental borders and letters for which he was
praised by Bohn in Chatto and Jackson. These he
contributed as special titles to supplements of early
volumes of the Illustrated London News,1851-61,
1863-69. Some of these were wood engraved by
J. and A. Williams (q.v.). He could be linked with
Noel Humphreys (q.v.) although he was not as
proficient in his ornamental work. His cover designs
to the Illustrated London Almanack,1866, printed in
colours by the Leighton Brothers (q.v.) were

described by McLean as 'among the best things of
that kind of their period'. His drawings on wood
included illustrations to Favourite English Poems,
1857; Welcome Guest,1860; Churchman's Family
Magazine,1863; The Graphic,1873; Rhymes and
Roundelayes; Burns' Poems; Thornbury's Legendary
Ballads,1876; Good Words,1880; and the Pall Mall
Gazette. His drawings to 'In Umbria', in the English
Illustrated Magazine,1885-86, were engraved on wood
by C.Kellenbach, J.D.Cooper, O.Jahyer, and W.R.Quick
(qq.v.). As a painter he exhibited at the Royal Academy,
the Royal Society of British Artists, the Royal Scottish
Watercolour Society and the Royal Institute of Painters
in Watercolours, where he was elected member 1882,
and the Royal Society of Painters in Oil-Colours, where
he was elected member in 1883. He died on 6 April 1912.
The British Museum owns proofs of his designs engraved
by the Dalziel Brothers (q.v.),1857, 1862-63.
[McLean, Victorian Book Design; Chatto; Houfe;
Bénézit; White]

McTAGGART, William 1835-1910
Occasional draughtsman, etcher, painter and
Scottish impressionist. He was born in Aros, near
Campbeltown, and began by doing portraits of the
local inhabitants in his spare time. He attended the
Trustees Academy, Edinburgh, from 1852, with
fellow students W.Q.Orchardson and J.Macwhirter
(qq.v.). He contributed a drawing on wood to Good
Words about this time,1860, for which he is listed
here. But he concentrated mostly on his painting,
was elected ARSA,1859, RSA,1870 and exhibited at
the New English Art Club, the Royal Academy, the
Royal Hibernian Academy, and the Royal Scottish
Watercolour Society, serving as its Vice-President,
1878. He died in Broomieknowe on 2 April 1910.
The British Museum owns proofs of designs engraved
by the Dalziel Brothers (q.v.),1861.
[For a list of his etched work see Volume I; see also
White; Houfe]

MacWHIRTER, John 1839-1911
Draughtsman illustrator, etcher and landscape
painter. He was born in Slateford near Edinburgh in
1839 and educated at Peebles School, the Edinburgh
School of Design and the Trustees Academy. He began
drawing on wood for various publications: Good
Words,1861; Golden Thread,1861; Wordsworth's
Poems for the Young,1863; Sunday Magazine,1869;
Pen and Pencil Pictures from the Poets,1866, and
Poems and Songs of Robert Burns,1875. He was a
strong advocate of drawing direct from nature and
published a book on illustration. As a successful
painter of landscapes of Highland scenery he was
elected ARA,1879 and RA,1893. He also exhibited
at the Grosvenor Gallery, the New Gallery, the
Royal Society of Painter-Etchers and Engravers,
the Royal Hibernian Academy, the Royal Institute of
Painters in Watercolours, the Royal Institute of

Painters in Oil-Colours, and the Royal Scottish
Watercolour Society. He died in St John's Wood,
29 January 1911. The British Museum owns proofs
of his designs engraved by the Dalziel Brothers
(q.v.),1861-62.
[For a list of his etched work see Volume I; see also
DNB; TB; W.M.Sinclair, 'Life of John MacWhirter',
in Art Journal, December 1903]

MADOT, Adolphus M. ?-1864
Draughtsman on wood of figure subjects. He was a
pupil at the Royal Academy Schools and at Julian's in
Paris and exhibited work at the Royal Academy, the
British Institution, and the Royal Society of British
Artists from 1852-64. During this time he drew on
wood for some of the one hundred illustrations to
Charles Mackay's The Home Affections, 1858,
engraved by the Dalziel Brothers (q.v.) (the proofs
are in the British Museum); also illustrations to the
Poetical Works of E.A.Poe, 1858. White dismissed
these as the work of A.W. (sic) Madot, and other
'draughtsmen whose names are certainly not household words to-day'. Part of the reason must lie in
the fact that Madot died young, in 1864.

MAHONEY, J. fl.1865-76
Draughtsman on wood and wood engraver. He is not
to be confused with James Mahoney (q.v.), although
the two were contemporaries and fellow 'Sixties
School' illustrators. J.Mahoney, according to Harold
Hartley, was practically uneducated and untrained
when he began work as an errand boy to the lithographic printers Vincent, Son and Brooks (see
Volume I). He was noticed by Edward Whymper (q.v.),
to whom he delivered proofs, and was eventually
engaged to train as a draughtsman on wood for a
pound a week. Reid takes up the story: 'Such a
beginning seems promising, but unfortunately this
is the brightest period in Mahoney's troubled career.
Though he was soon earning plenty of money, he
developed at the same time habits that faced the
Whympers with a second problem--namely, how to
get rid of him.' And yet Mahoney made quick progress
and was given substantial draughtsman commissions,
primarily for magazines, such as Leisure Hour,
1865-66; Sunday Magazine, 1866-70; Argosy, 1866;
Cassell's Magazine, 1867; Touches of Nature, 1867;
Cassell's Illustrated Readings, 1867; People's
Magazine, 1867; Quiver, 1868; Nobility of Life, 1869;
Good Words for the Young, 1869; National Nursery
Rhymes, 1870; Little Folks, 1870; the Dalziel Brothers'
magazine Fun; and the Day of Rest. He illustrated
numerous books, including Whymper's Scrambles on
the Alps, 1870; Trollope's Three Clerks (frontispiece
only); Jean Ingelow's Little Wonder-Horn, 1872; and
collaborated with George Du Maurier on Wilkie
Collins' Frozen Deep, 1875. Mahoney also worked
for the wood engravers, the Dalziel Brothers (q.v.),
although here too the relationship was plagued with

difficulties. The Dalziels had been given the engraving
commission of the Household Edition of Dickens, and,
on the strength of Mahoney's reputation as a draughtsman on wood, secured him for the first and subsequent
two stories: Oliver Twist, Little Dorrit, and Our
Mutual Friend, 1871. They praised his understanding
of drawing on wood for their engravers, noting in
their Record (p.332) he 'had a firm, clear style of
manipulation and no one knew better than he how to
make work look solid and firm by leaving large
masses of white in his arrangement of colour'. They
clearly liked his abilities, bought the few watercolours he did, and commissioned illustrations to
their own comic paper Judy, ('crude and clumsy',
according to Reid). But in the end they too found
Mahoney a trial: 'It was not only that he was usually
drunk, but that he was singularly unpleasant when
he was drunk--quarrelsome, aggressive, reckless.
One day, in the Dalziels' office, he assaulted an
inoffensive person who, in addressing him, had
stressed the second syllable of his name, a
peculiarity to which the English are prone, but
which Mahoney would only tolerate when accompanied
by a commission for drawings. And such incidents
were frequent. His life seems to have been a
passionate and disreputable one, haunted no doubt by
visions of an utterly different kind, but of which we
can know nothing. It ended sordidly in a public
latrine', Reid concluded, and added a critical note
that he had an unfortunate tendency to dwarf his
figures, and relied on a sense of ugliness to hide
poor draughtsmanship, especially in his Judy drawings.
[Houfe; Reid; White; Strickland]

MAHONEY, James 1816-79
Irish draughtsman, engraver on wood, watercolourist.
He is not to be confused with J.Mahoney (q.v.), a
contemporary and fellow illustrator. He was born in
Cork about 1816 (1810,TB), the son of a carpenter.
He studied in Rome and spent some years travelling
abroad, returning to Cork, where he set up in 1842
as an artist at 34 Nile Street. He exhibited watercolour views of his travels at the Royal Hibernian
Academy until 1846, then went abroad, primarily to
Spain. In 1859 he resigned his ARHA and left Ireland
for London, where he painted for the Royal Academy
from 1866-77, and the Royal Watercolour Society,
being elected ARWS in 1867. He found employment as
a draughtsman on wood for the Illustrated London
News, having contributed there in 1847. He died at
26 Charles Street, Marylebone, on 29 May 1879.
[Bénézit; Strickland; Hardie; Houfe; Hayden, Chats
on Old Prints, 1908]

MALDEN, Benjamin John fl.1860-72
London wood engraver, who specialised in
scientific and technical work. An advertisement in
the London directory, 1869, claimed that these were
'executed with exactitude, estimates given for

illustrating manufacturers' catalogues in an artistic
and effective manner'. He and his assistants worked
in London at 29 Hart Street, Bloomsbury, WC
(POD,1860-62), 5 Chichester Place, WC (POD,1863),
253 Gray's Inn Road, WC (POD,1864), then again at
29 Hart Street (POD,1865-70). The following year
they moved to 14 Great Coram Street, Russell Square,
WC (POD,1871-72).

MALINS, Clement fl.1880s
Provincial wood engraver, who worked at 58 Howard
Street, Birmingham (Kelly's,1880).

MALIPHANT, William 1862-?
Apprentice wood engraver, landscape and genre
painter in oils and watercolour. He was born in
Brynmawr, South Wales, but spent his early years
in Pennsylvania, encouraged by a travelling portrait
painter to become an artist. He moved to London and
was apprenticed about 1875, aged thirteen, to a wood
engraver. He studied art at the Westminster School
of Art under Frederick Brown and Loudan. He lived
in London and exhibited landscapes at the Royal
Academy, the Royal Institute of Painters in Watercolours and the Royal Society of British Artists from
1887.
[Waters]

MALLET(T), Richard W. fl.1859-75
London wood engraver and draughtsman, who worked
first as a commercial engraver at 84 Fleet Street, EC
(POD,1859-60), then at 200 Fleet Street (POD,1861-71).
Houfe lists R.W.Mallett (sic) as a draughtsman who
contributed industrial subjects for wood engravings in
the Illustrated London News,1875.

MANCHESTER Wood Engraving Company fl.1889-1900
Provincial firm of wood engravers, under the
proprietorship of Sword and Brown, 2 Brown Street
and 46A Market Street, Manchester (Kelly's,1889-1900).

MANSEL, Miss (afterwards Mrs Bull)
Amateur draughtsman for wood engraving. She was
about seventeen years old when she drew on wood
one work for Punch, which John Leech (q.v.) touched
up before publication in 1863.

MARCH, I(ssac)
Little is known of this early wood engraver, known to
have engraved cuts to Salter's Angler's Guide,1818.

MARCH or Marsh, James fl.1832-39
London wood engraver, who worked at 15 Cobourg
Place, Borough Road (Pigot,1832-34), then 2 (4)
Oxford Place, Waterloo Street (Robson,1834,
Pigot,1838-39).

MARCHANT, John Joseph fl.1880s
London wood engraver, who worked at 119 Salisbury
Square, EC (POD,1880). Fincham lists a bookplate
engraved for a Mr Buller by 'Marchant, Hampstead
Road', dated 1860, and of a seal design.

MARDARA, M. and Company fl.1880-89
London wood engraving firm, with offices at 53 Hyde
Road, N (POD,1880), 126 St John Street, EC
(POD,1881) and 158 Strand (POD,1882-83). As
Mardara and Company the firm established itself
at Temple Chambers, Falcon Court, Fleet Street,
EC (POD,1884-89), an address which they shared
with H.Harral and T.Hobbs (qq.v.).

MARIE, Adrien-Emmanuel 1848-91
French draughtsman, wood engraver and painter.
He was born in Neuilly-sur-Seine on 2 October 1848,
was the pupil of Bayard, Camino and Pils and
regularly exhibited at the Salon from 1866-81. He
became known as a draughtsman for wood engravings
of French genre and social subjects in The Graphic,
from 1873 and thereafter became a prolific
draughtsman. From 1885-89 his work appeared in
English magazines, 'supplementing a rather weak
period for English illustrators' (Houfe). As a wood
engraver Gusman claimed that he worked in
association with Navellier (q.v.) as Navellier and
Marie, and specialised in cuts after Garnier towards
the end of the century. He died in Cadiz in April 1891.
[Bénézit; TB; Bryan; Houfe; Gusman]

MARK, of Wellington fl.1830s
Provincial wood engraver, noted for his bird
engravings in a style similar to that of Bewick. He
worked in Wellington, Shropshire, most notably for
T.C.Eyton, author of a supplement to Bewick's
British Birds, after Eyton's own bird drawings. The
result was Mark's eighty engravings, including
thirty-eight vignettes, for A History of the Rarer
British Birds,1836. These were engraved in Bewick's
style, but the ovals of several were in thicker line
and not cut with the short strokes used by Bewick
(cf. Bewick's trees and stones). Eyton went on to a
more distinctive reputation as Edward Lear's patron,
employing Lear to illustrate his next book.
[C.Jackson]

MARKS, Henry Stacy 1829-98
Draughtsman on wood, etcher, painter of animals,
especially birds, and stained glass designer. He
was born in London on 13 September 1829 and
studied at Leigh's and the Royal Academy Schools,
1851, where he exhibited from 1853. By the mid
1850s he was beginning to supplement his painting
income by drawing on wood for various books and
magazines: Home Circle,1855; and Thornbury's
Legends of the Cavaliers and the Roundheads,1857.
He had established his position as a competent

draughtsman, especially in pen and ink, by the 1860s, and contributed to various publications, such as Punch, 1861, 1882; and Willmott's Sacred Poetry, 1862. He etched for Passages from Modern English Poets, 1862; and drew on wood for Once a Week, 1863; Churchman's Family Magazine, 1863; Two Centuries of Song, 1867; and Ridiculous Rhymes, 1869. He continued to draw for illustrations throughout the 1870s, for London Society, 1870; National Nursery Rhymes, 1871; Quiver, 1873; Child's History of England, 1873; the Illustrated London News, 1876, 1879; and The Graphic. His book illustrations also appeared in T.J.Ellis's Sketching from Nature, 1876 and E.Stuart's The Good Old Days, 1876. However, from the 1860s onwards he lost his sense of clarity, his style became lazy, and his skills turned toward the bird paintings for which he became famous, as well as the ludicrous medieval themes he loved. Nevertheless his skills at drawing for wood engraving were admired by Edmund Evans (q.v.) who commissioned him to design for his 'Toy Book' series, c1865, which he drew in the spirit and style of his greatest admirer, young Walter Crane (q.v.). Marks also drew for the wood engravers, the Dalziel Brothers (q.v.), who claimed that he 'gave us some of the best drawings he ever made for the wood engraver'. He was also adviser to the meteoric career of Kate Greenaway (q.v.) and was quite shrewd in his comments concerning her wood engraved drawings once they had been cut by Edmund Evans. Marks was also a stained glass designer and interior designer of decorative painted panels, notably of his favourite birds. He also etched illustrations (for a list of etched work see Volume I). He exhibited paintings at the British Institution, the Royal Institute of Painters in Oil-Colours, and the Fine Art Society. He was elected ARA, 1871, RA, 1878 and member of the Royal Society of Painters in Watercolours. He died in Primrose Hill on 9 January 1898. The British Museum owns proofs of his designs engraved by the Dalziel Brothers (q.v.), 1861.
[For biographical detail see his autobiography, Pen and Pencil Sketches, 1894; DNB; Wood; Houfe; Spielmann; Dalziels' Record; British Library catalogue; R.Engen, Kate Greenaway, 1981]

MARRIOTT, Richard Samuel fl.1863-75
London wood engraver, who worked during the boom years of reproductive wood engraving. He is first listed with an office at 6 Fetter Lane, EC (POD, 1864) which he shared with H.Crane and R.Pringle (qq.v.). Here he probably worked on the illustrations to Romantic Passages in English History, 1863. Reid explained that though commonly attributed to Robert Barnes (q.v.), the illustrations to this were probably done totally by Marriott. He next moved to 15 Essex Street, Strand, WC (POD, 1865-68), shared with F.J.Smith, F.Gifford and H.Lovejoy (qq.v.), then to 8 Palsgrave Place, Strand (POD, 1869-72), which

he shared with R.H.Wells (q.v.). The following year he appeared at 166 Strand (POD, 1875). His engravings during the mid 1870s included a full-page engraving, 'Sketches at Berlin', after Ludwig Töeffler, for the Illustrated London News, 8 March 1873. He signed his work: 'R.S.Marriott sc'.

'MARS' Maurice Bonvoisin 1849-1912
Comic draughtsman, engraver and cartoonist of the Belgian School. He was born in Verviers on 26 May 1849 and became a regular draughtsman illustrator for the French papers Journal amusant and Charivari. Houfe claims that 'He was the only continental artist to be used consistently for cartoon work by British periodicals', and lists his contributions for wood engraving in The Graphic, 1880-91; the Illustrated London News, 1882-92; Daily Graphic, 1890; the Sketch, 1894; and Illustrated Bits. For these and his illustrated books he often used British subjects, which made him popular in England.

MARSH, Henry fl.1870s
Prominent American wood engraver, listed here for his violent controversy with the English engraver W.J.Linton (q.v.). Marsh was linked with his fellow American, Timothy Cole (q.v.), as the most skilful of wood engravers. He was praised for his 'excellent work' by the editor of Scribner's Magazine, who declared his engravings to Harris's Insects Injurious to Vegetation 'the greatest single engraving enterprise in the world'. Linton attacked Marsh for sloppiness and was so outraged by his apparently undeserved success that he claimed, 'There is not a line left'.
[For the controversy see Atlantic Monthly, 1879]

MARSH, James
(see March, James)

MARSHALL, C.A. fl.1889-90
Amateur draughtsman, who contributed two drawings for wood engravings in Punch, 1889, noted for the competent horse drawing. He also drew once for the Dalziel Brothers' magazine, Judy, 1890.
[Spielmann; Houfe]

MARSHALL, J.R. fl.1820-40s
Wood engraver, noted by Bohn in Chatto and Jackson for his cuts after Robert and George Cruikshank's drawings to the Universal Songster, 1828. These showed 'rather a coarse hand' and were signed 'J.R.M.'. Gusman lists Marshall as an important English wood engraver after George Cruikshank and Harrison Weir (qq.v.).
[Chatto; Gusman]

MARSHMAN, J.
Draughtsman who worked in Bangor, North Wales and drew sporting subjects for wood engravings in The Graphic, 1876.

MARTIN, Alfred 1839-1903
French wood engraver, who worked in London at the
end of the century. He was born in Mauriac, Cantal,
on 15 July 1839, was a pupil of J.Fagnion in Paris
and made his Salon début in 1870. He became noted
for wood engravings after Vierge in Monde Illustré
which Gusman called 'aux actualités'. In 1885 he
became a wood engraving instructor at the Ecole des
Beaux Arts, Geneva, where he also exhibited
paintings. The London directories list Alfred Martin,
wood engraver, working at 160 Fleet Street, EC
(POD,1891-94), 32 Grafton Terrace, Haverstock
Hill, NW (LSDN,1894), then Falcon Court, 32 Fleet
Street, EC (POD,1897-1900), shared with W.Andrews
(q.v.). He died in Geneva on 22 April 1903.
[TB; Gusman]

MARTIN, Charles fl.1830-?
Draughtsman caricaturist and watercolourist. He
was the son of the Victorian painter John Martin,
and drew full length portraits of literary people for
wood engravings in Henry Vizetelly's Pictorial Times,
and three comic drawings for Punch,1853. He
preferred the life of the social climber and was a
dandy who preferred to make occasional watercolours
than to work hard at black and white illustrations. He
may be the draughtsman of illustrations signed
'Martin' in Knight's Penny Magazine,July 1842,
engraved on wood by S.Sly (q.v.).
[Vizetelly, Glances Back; Houfe; Bodleian]

MARTIN, D. fl.1883-84
Wood engraver, who engraved the drawing by
G.H.Thompson (q.v.) of the north transept of
Winchester Cathedral for the English Illustrated
Magazine,1883-84. The engraving was uninspired
but showed a clear understanding of solid form and
was well shaded. The British Museum owns a number
of sharp, clear proofs of his work. One, a jungle
scene after C.O.Murray, is inscribed 'sc. for
J.D.Cooper'.

MARTIN, David 1730-85
Wood engraver, draughtsman and painter, friend
and fellow apprentice of Thomas Bewick (q.v.).
Martin is listed here for his influence on the career
of Bewick, although strictly speaking he falls outside
the scope of this book. He was born in London in
1730, and exhibited work there as a painter. As a
wood engraver he reproduced the drawings of
J.Watson and tried to encourage Thomas Bewick to
remain working in London. Writing to Bewick on
29 January 1777, when Bewick wished to return to
Newcastle after a disappointing stay in London,
Martin explained, 'I can't say but I have been much
deceived with regard to the encouragement they give
to wood cutting in London for I tho't as there was not
any body there in that way who could do anything
worth looking at & yours being so much superior

thereto that you would get any price you asked...'
(Hack MS).
[For a list of Martin's engravings see Nagler;
see also Bewick Memoir,p.237]

MARTIN, Gilbert Nelson fl.1880-1900
London draughtsman, who worked at
267 Strand, WC (Kelly's,1880), which he shared
with the engraver C.T.Jago. Later he moved to
81 Chancery Lane, WC (Kelly's,1889-1900) and
shared the new premises with R.Boston (q.v.).

MARTIN, John
Little is known of this wood engraver, described by
Bohn in Chatto and Jackson,1861, as one of several
wood engravers 'best entitled to honourable mention'
(p.544).

MARTIN, John 1789-1854
Prominent painter of biblical scenes and metal
engraver, listed here for designs from his 'Biblical
Prints',1831-35 which were wood engraved by
W.J.Linton, F.W.Branston, Ebenezer Landells,
W.H.Powis, Thomas Williams, and W.T.Green
(qq.v.). Martin prepared his designs in wash and
brown and black ink before metal engraving.
[Chatto; see Volume I for metal engravings (with
full bibliography)]

MARTIN, Leopold fl.1848-56
London wood engraver, who engraved John Tenniel's
(q.v.) designs for Aesop's Fables,1848. Martin
engraved about a hundred of these in a clear, sharp
black-outline style which proved successful enough
to help Tenniel establish himself as a competent
illustrator, candidate for and eventual holder of
the post of Punch cartoonist. Martin may be half of
the engraving firm Martin and Corbould (q.v.) in
1848; later Martin and Lundie (q.v.) from 1855-56.
[British Library catalogue; F.Sarzano, J.Tenniel,1948]

MARTIN, Paul 1864-?
Wood engraver and prominent Victorian photographer.
He was born in France in 1864, and emigrated with
his family to England after the siege of Paris. In 1880
he was apprenticed to a wood engraver and excelled
in the art. Despite the threat of the new photo-engraving
process which eventually took away the wood engraver's
work, Martin learned to use photography and to
regard it as a useful tool for the wood engraver. He
is known to have taken various photographs for the
same purpose that his predecessors, the draughtsmen
on wood and illustrators, had made preliminary
sketches; and he used these in the preparation of
his engravings on the block. An example, done in
1892, shows a photograph of a group of boys fishing
at a river bank, which Martin altered in his
engraving, making the group smaller, dropping the
half-concealed figures for clearer outlines, and

altering the boy's fish net to a fishing pole.
[For full account and discussion see R.Flukinger,
L.Schaaf, S.Meacham, Paul Martin,1978]

MARTIN, Thomas and Company fl.1880s
Provincial wood engraving firm, with an office at
Albert Street, Dale End, Birmingham (Kelly's,1889).

MARTIN and Corbould fl.1849
London wood engraving firm, a partnership between
Leopold Martin and E.Corbould (qq.v.). They were
listed once in the London directory, working at
10 Buckingham Street (POD,1849). Their engraving
commissions included eight cuts to Dickens'
Christmas Books, which included Tenniel's drawings
to the Haunted Man,1848.
[British Library catalogue]

MARTIN and Lundie fl.1855-56
London wood engraving partnership, probably with
Leopold Martin (q.v.). They listed their address in
the London directory as 100 (101) Long Acre, Covent
Garden (Hodgson's, POD,1855-56).

MARX, George Walter fl.1871-84
London wood engraver and author on wood engraving
technique. He worked as a wood engraver at 6 Red
Lion Court, Fleet Street, EC (POD,1871-72),
5 Racquet Court, Fleet Street, EC (POD,1873-74)
and 146 Fleet Street, EC (POD,1875-79). Then he
appeared as the firm of George Walter Marx and
Company, 211 Strand and 1 and 2 Chancery Lane.
Under this name Marx published his Art of Drawing
and Engraving on Wood,1881. The book has a helpful
text and includes a note about the author to the effect
that Marx was willing to give private lessons in the
'Art of Engraving on Wood' either at his Chancery
Lane offices or at a pupil's home, 'on moderate and
inclusive terms'. Marx's firm also supplied the
skills of artists' colourmen and sold engraving tools.
They moved to 5 Hind Court, Fleet Street, EC
(POD,1883-84) where they remained for two years.
They still appear in the directories in 1910, at
184 Blackfriars, SE (POD,1910).

MASON, Abraham John 1794-?
Draughtsman and wood engraver, who was born in
London on 4 April 1794, and lost his parents early
on. He was educated in Devonshire, then moved to
London to be apprenticed to Robert Branston (q.v.)
in 1808, for seven years. He stayed on with Branston
for five years after his training had finished, but by
1821 had set up as a wood engraver on his own. He
appeared in the London directory working at
23 Spencer Street, Clerkenwell (Pigot,1826-27).
During this time his engravings included cuts for
George Cruikshank's Tales of Humour,1824 and four
cuts after William Harvey's designs for Northcote's
Fables,1828. He used a fine black-line style. He also

lectured on wood engraving at the London Mechanic's
Institution, the Royal Institution, and the London
Institution. He exhibited at the Royal Society of
British Artists in 1829, before emigrating to New
York in November of that year. There he became
an associate member of the National Academy of
Design, and a professor of wood engraving,
lecturing on the subject in Boston. He returned
to London in 1839. There he set up an engraving
office at 106 St John Street Road (POD,1839-40),
10 Bolt Court, Fleet Street, EC (POD,1842),
3 Acton Place, Gray's Inn Road (POD,1843),
28 Liverpool Street, Kings Cross (POD,1847-51)
and 46 Argyle Square, New Road (POD,1853-56).
His engravings appeared in Charles Knight's
Penny Magazine,July 1842, engraved after his
own drawings on wood. He also engraved the
five full-page illustrations to an elaborate
supplement 'The Queen's Visit to the City of
London', in the Illustrated London News,12 July
1851; followed by a full-page 'Allegorical Picture
by Absolon and Fenton for the Inauguration Dinner
of the Lord Mayor',11 November 1854. His
engraving abilities were best used on such works,
where masses of ornate detail were treated in a
fine, etched black-line style. He died in England.
The British Museum owns his engravings after
J.Gilbert and H.C.Selous, also a series of
churches and landscape vignettes. He signed his
engravings: 'MASON'.
[LeBlanc (as 'A.Mason'); Bruillot; Nagler;
Bodleian Library; Redgrave; Bénézit; Bryan;
Fielding]

MASON, Ernold E. fl.1883-1902
Draughtsman, figure painter. He worked in
London, where he contributed a series of comic
sketches for wood engravings in the Illustrated
London News,1889. He also exhibited at the
Royal Academy,1883. He was living in Tilford,
Surrey in 1902.

MASON, George Finch 1850-1915
Draughtsman, caricaturist, and painter of sporting
scenes. He was the son of an Eton master, and
attended the school, 1860-64, which inspired a set
of painted caricatures. He is listed here for his
comic drawings for wood engravings in Punch, three
in 1881, three in 1882, and one 1883. He also
exhibited in London from 1874-76.
[Houfe; Spielmann]

MASON, Henry Charles fl.1854-84
London wood engraver who worked from various
offices over a period of thirty years. He first
appears in the directories at 53 Exmouth Street,
Clerkenwell (POD,1854-55), 6 Sudeley Street,
Islington (POD,1856) and then 90 Aldersgate Street
(POD,1857-58). He merges with Frederick Watkins

(q.v.) as Mason and Watkins, 1859-62 (q.v.), but returns independently at 67 Snowhill, EC (POD, 1863-68). By 1871 he was sharing his office at 9 Essex Street, Strand (POD, 1871) with J.Bye, J.Desbois and T.Robinson (qq.v.). Finally Henry Mason worked at 11 St Bride Street (POD, 1883-84).

MASON, Walter George fl.1842-57
London wood engraver and draughtsman, who worked at 48A Paternoster Row (POD, 1843), 59 Fleet Street, EC (POD, 1844), 186 Fleet Street, EC (POD, 1845), 135 Fleet Street, EC (POD, 1846), and 9 Thanet Place, Temple Bar (POD, 1848-49). Mason was not a particularly skilful engraver although much of the overall greyness of his work was due to poor printing. He worked for numerous books and magazines, such as J.F.Murray's Environs of London, 1842, his one cut being engraved with J.Whymper (q.v.). He was predominently commissioned by the Illustrated London News, for which he engraved after John Gilbert during its first year, 1842; also after H.Warren, E.H.Corbould (qq.v.), and various theatrical sketches. He was probably the W.O. (sic) Mason, engraver of Richard Doyle's Merry Pictures, 1857. The British Museum owns his engraved portrait of Queen Victoria on horseback after T.N.Nicholson; also proofs after J.Absolon, and a crudely engraved reproduction of a Louis Haghe painting. He signed his work: 'W G Mason Sc' (script).
[Stauffer; Hake; Houfe; TB and LeBlanc (as 'William' Mason)]

MASON and Strong fl.1840s
London wood engraving firm, with an office at 22 Warwick Square (POD, 1842).

MASON and Watkins fl.1859-62
London wood engraving firm, a partnership between Henry Charles Mason (q.v.) and Frederick Watkins (q.v.). Their office was at 55 Fleet Street, EC (POD, 1859-60), then 67 Snowhill, EC (POD, 1861-62). After this time Mason continued on his own at the Snowhill address.

MASSEY, Benjamin fl.1872-80
Scottish wood engraver, who worked at 11 Miller Street, Glasgow (Kelly's, 1872-80).

MASTERS, ? fl.1840s
Draughtsman on wood, who contributed drawings for wood engravings in Charles Knight's London, 1841. He also drew on wood for Knight's Penny Magazine, December 1841, his drawings being engraved by Welch and Mead (qq.v.).
[Bodleian Library]

MASTERS, Tertius fl.1879-1901
London wood engraver, who worked for over twenty years at 54 Paternoster Row, EC (POD, 1879-1901).

He shared these premises at various times with J.Walmsley, G.P.Nicholls, A.Berry, and C.A.Ferrier (qq.v.).

MATHES, Louis
Ornamental draughtsman for wood engraved ornamental headpieces in the English Illustrated Magazine, 1883.

MATHEWS, William H. fl.1832-60
London wood engraver, who worked at 22 Lant Street, Southwark, SE (Robson's, 1832, POD, 1859-60).

MATTHEWSON, Arthur fl.1880s
London draughtsman on wood, who worked at 61 Fleet Street, EC (Kelly's, 1889). By 1891 he had joined with A.Palmer (q.v.) as Palmer and Matthewson (q.v.).

MAY, Philip William 'Phil' 1864-1903
Successful black and white draughtsman and caricaturist, primarily for 1890s magazines. He is listed here for his early drawings for wood engravings in the Yorkshire Gossip, 1878; Busy Bee, 1878; St Stephen's Review, 1883-85, 1890-91; journeyman's drawings in the Penny Illustrated Paper, 1883; Pictorial World, 1883; Society, 1885; Sydney Bulletin, 1886-94, and various other magazines, before being taken up by Punch, from 1895, and The Graphic, 1891-1903. (For a complete account and list see Houfe, also D.Cuppleditch, Phil May, 1981). He was elected RI in 1897, also exhibited at the Royal Academy, and the Fine Art Society. He died on 5 August 1903, aged thirty-nine.
[DNB; Bryan; Spielmann; Houfe (book list)]

MAY, Captain Walter William 1831-96
Draughtsman on wood, watercolourist of marine subjects. He served in the Royal Navy, 1850-70, during which time he began to draw for wood engraved books, doing illustrations to S.C.Hall's Book of South Wales, 1861; and various nautical drawings for wood engravings in The Graphic, 1869-75; and the Illustrated London News, 1875-76. He was elected ANWS, 1871 and NWS, 1874.
[Bénézit; Houfe]

MEAD, Joseph fl.1836-46
London wood engraver, who worked at 1 Corporation Row, Clerkenwell (Pigot, Robson's, 1836-37), then 9 Upper Smith, Northampton Square (POD, 1845-46). His engravings included cuts for Charles Knight's Penny Magazine, December 1841, after Masters (q.v.).
[Bodleian Library]

MEADOWS, Joseph Kenny 1790-1874
Prolific draughtsman on wood, caricaturist. He was born in Cardigan on 1 November 1790, the son of a

retired naval officer. He struggled at first, drawing for wood and metal engravings, but by the 1830s he had begun drawing on wood for various books. He collaborated with Isaac and Robert Cruikshank on The Devil in London, 1832, and by the end of the 1830s had begun his own magnum opus--the 1,000 drawings for wood engravings to an illustrated Shakespeare, 1839-43 (partly drawn on wood by W.B. Scott (q.v.)). These drawings and Portraits of the English, 1840 (both published by Robert Tyas) were wood engraved by W.J. Linton aided by Orrin Smith (qq.v.). This fortunate coincidence helped to establish Meadows as a competent draughtsman on wood and he was one of the first illustrators whose work recommended wood engraving to publishers (who had previously used metal engravings printed separately). His work on wood blocks increased and the list of Meadows' illustrations grew to encompass most of the mid century wood engraved publications: Knight's London, 1841; Punch, from 1841 onward; S.C. Hall's Book of British Ballads, 1842-43; the Illuminated Magazine, 1843-45; Henry Vizetelly's Pictorial Times, 1843-47; the Illustrated Musical Annual; Cassell's Illustrated Family Paper, 1853; the Illustrated London News, 1854-55, his best work here being full-page Christmas fantasies; Vizetelly's Illustrated Times, 1855-59; and Welcome Guest, 1860. Meadows had his 'British Ballads' drawings wood engraved by the Dalziel Brothers (q.v.) ('unsurpassed by anything he has since done', according to Bohn). Thus began his long association with the influential Dalziels, who remembered Meadows as 'a clever, erratic genius, and an artist of great ability...intimately connected with Orrin Smith, the distinguished wood engraver; their earliest work being character sketches and heads of the people done for Bell's Life in London'. So highly regarded were the Dalziels by Meadows that when he was asked to draw on wood for Punch, he stipulated that the Dalziels should have all his drawings to engrave. Typically, this was soon forgotten, but then, Meadows never recovered from his early unpleasant struggles, grovelling for money from his wood engraver employers. He once recalled how his early years were spent in 'great straights' (sic) with only a few commissions drawing on wood blocks and occasional watercolours for steel engravings in 'Byron's Beauties or Shakespeare's Heroines'. When Henry Vizetelly met Meadows on the stairway of a notoriously bad paying wood engraver, the young artist shrugged, 'I never go up this staircase unless I want money very badly, and then always with the certainty of not getting it' (Glances Back, pp.152-53). Even his early friend and fellow workman, W.J. Linton, recalled how handicapped Meadows had been by this early restrictive training, or lack of it. After often visiting Meadows at his house at Cottage Place, Camden Town, presumably to collect the Shakespeare drawings, he pronounced his drawings the products of 'a witty man, with some inventive talent, but a

poor draughtsman, having had little artistic education, brought up, one might say, on Finden's Book of Beauty, and the like wishy-washiness' (Memories, p.72). Moreover, Meadows could 'turn nasty', especially if he drank too much. The Dalziels recall how once, in his cups, he told John Leech to change his style, 'such as I do mine, sir'. Such were the capable but temperamental qualities of this influential yet largely unoriginal draughtsman. He found, by the 1840s and 1850s that his own brand of delicate fantasy had been superseded by the more aggressive and competent draughtsmanship of Leech and Doyle. He did provide illustrations to numerous books, however, including an edition of Moore's Lalla Rookh, 1842; Leigh Hunt's Palfrey, 1842; The Family Joe Miller, 1848; Blanchard's Sketches from Life, 1849; the Mayhew brothers' Magic of Kindness; and S.C. Hall's Midsummer Eve, 1849. His work was specially popular in Germany, praised by Nagler as 'gehört zu den fruchtbarsten englischen Künstlern neuer zeit'. Meadows also exhibited work at the Royal Society of British Artists from 1830-38, also the Royal Academy, 1830, 1845, 1853. He married the sister of the artist Archibald S. Henning and died in London in August 1874. The British Museum owns proofs of his designs engraved by the Dalziel Brothers 1839-51, 1860.
[Chatto; Spielmann; Evans Reminiscences; Everett; Dalziels' Record; Houfe; TB; Bryan; Vizetelly, Glances Back; W.J. Linton, Masters of Wood Engraving and Memories]

MEARNS, Miss Louisa
Little is known of this draughtsman for wood engravings, who contributed four drawings to Once a Week, Vol.xiii, which White described as being 'of genuine interest'. The British Museum owns two proof designs engraved by the Dalziel Brothers (q.v.), 1865.

MEARS, Arthur Herbert fl.1891-1910
London wood engraver, who worked at 84 Fetter Lane, EC (POD, 1891). In 1910 he appeared in the directories as Arthur Herbert Mears, 33 Milk Street, EC (POD, 1910).

MEASOM, Allen fl.1870-71
London wood engraver, who worked at 8 Palsgrave Place, Strand, WC (POD, 1870), which he shared with R.S. Marriott and R.H. Wells (qq.v.). The following year he appeared in the directories at 165 Strand, WC (POD, 1871).

MEASOM, George S. fl.1845-62
London wood engraver, brother of William Frederick Measom (q.v.) with whom he worked during the 1840s and early 1850s. One of their earliest collaborations was a musical border, 'My Writing Desk', after 'G.J.' for the Illustrated London News, 25 October

1845. This was signed 'W & G.M.'. George Measom
engraved from his London office, listed in the
directories at 46 Liverpool Street (POD, 1851-53),
then from 1855 at 74 Charrington Street, Somerstown
(Hodgson's, 1855, POD, 1856-62). His commissions
included the engraving of twenty designs on wood by
John Gilbert to B.Foster's Ye History of ye Priory
and Gate of St John, 1851, published by William
Pickering (a copy is in the Bodleian Library). He
also engraved the drawings of T.Sulman, Junior,
taken from Indian MSS in the British Museum and
published as Sakoontala, 1855. Bohn in Chatto and
Jackson reproduces an engraving after Henry Anelay
(q.v.) for Bohn's edition of Sandford and Merton,
'engraved by Mr.Measom, whose practice is
extensive and of long standing'. Edmund Evans (q.v.)
described his associations with George and William
Measom in a letter dated 1899 (now in UCLA library):
'I knew Measom. His brother "Sir George" is still
alive. I saw him 4 years ago, he is a swell--lives at
Twickenham. He never engraved [sic] though he was
"an Engraver" !! as sure and easy [sic] most of these
old fellows have joined the majority'. The British
Museum owns his engravings after R.Doyle,
G.F.Sargent, T.Sulman and W.Phillips, and a series
of fine black-line style vignettes of buildings, classical
sculpture and landscape with figures. He signed his
work: 'GEO MEASOM', 'M', 'G MEASOM SC'.
[Chatto; McLean; Bodleian Library]

MEASOM, William Frederick fl.1840s-76
London wood engraver and draughtsman, brother of
George Measom (q.v.) with whom he worked during
the 1840s and 1850s. William first appears in the
London directories at 46 Liverpool Street (POD, 1845)
(his brother's office) but by the 1860s he had set up on
his own, at 7 Percy Circus (POD, 1861-64), then
268 Strand, WC (POD, 1865-66) and finally 32 Fleet
Street, EC (POD, 1872). Measom first worked with
his brother on engravings for the Illustrated London
News, 1845, 1851, and continued work there engraving
various 'special' artists' sketches, for instance,
those of Regamey and V.Bromley (qq.v.) in the mid
1870s. He engraved in a firm, black-line style
suggestive of copper or steel engravings. He engraved
a drawing of dogs after Thomas Landseer in 1840,
which is now in the British Museum and worked on a
series of dog portraits, also in the British Museum,
which he engraved and signed 'A Measom del'. But
he was particularly good at landscape work, which he
often drew on wood himself and engraved using dense
blacks and a chisel-like effect to modulate shadows
and define form. The British Museum owns a superb
tree after E.Wagner done in this way, which is a
masterwork of intricate detail, yet fails on the whole
as a complete, well considered tonal composition.
Another attempt was a large reproduction drawn and
engraved after Constable's 'The Cornfield' (also in
the British Museum). He also engraved the pencil

sketches for David Wilkie's famous 'Village
Politicians'. Measom worked on a portrait engraving
of Jenny Lind for Howitt's Journal, 1847 and a large
fold-out plate for the 'Cartoons for the People' series
in the London Journal, 7 June 1848. By the 1860s he
was working sporadically for various 'Sixties School'
publications, such as Sunday at Home, 1869. He
exhibited his engravings of James MacLaren Smith's
(q.v.) illustrations to The Pearl Fountain at the
Royal Academy, 1876. The British Museum owns
proofs after W.J.Blacklock, Birket Foster,
F.Goodall, R.Huskisson, W.L.Leitch, J.N.Paton,
L.Price, H.Weir and T.Landseer. He signed his
work: 'W MEASOM', 'WILLIAM MEASOM SC',
'W MEASOM, DEL Sc' or 'W Measom del et sculpt'.
[Chatto; Graves; Hake]

MEASOR, W. fl.1837-70
Draughtsman and painter of scriptural and marine
subjects. He worked in Exeter, but exhibited in
London at the British Institution, the Royal Academy,
and the Royal Society of British Artists, 1837-64.
He is listed here for drawings for wood engravings in
the Illustrated London News, 1848, and The Graphic,
1870.

MEAULLE, Fortuné-Louis 1844-?
French wood engraver, painter and novelist, who
contributed various engravings to British magazines.
He was born in Angers on 11 April 1844, was a pupil
of Suiton and Isabey, and made his Salon début in
1861. He wood engraved for L'Art, and achieved
great success interpreting the drawings of Chifflart,
Giacomelli, E.Lambert, and Meissonier. He was a
frequent visitor to Victor Hugo's home and engraved
some of his drawings. He maintained an engraving
studio and produced engravings for a Paris Guide,
1867. He also contributed various full-page engravings
to the Illustrated London News, 1875-80, notably
'Going to Market in East Turkestan' after Régamey,
6 February 1875; and 'Wagtails', after H.Giacomelli,
29 May 1880. For this latter work, he used a stark
white cut-out technique or severe gouged effect to
define foliage; this left the overall impression of
crudity rather than of a delicate sylvan landscape.
[Gusman; Bénézit; Beraldi]

MEEK, George fl.1883-97
London wood engraver, who worked in 1883 with
Wright, Greatwood and Meek (q.v.), then set up on
his own at 1 Norfolk Street, Strand, WC (POD, 1884-97).
During his time there he shared the premises with
J.C.Saunders, A.E.Fisher, R.Cousins and
A.Shepherd (qq.v.).

MELLISH, Frederick fl.1858-66
London wood engraver, who worked at 3 Lansdowne
Cottage, South Lambeth (POD, 1858-59), then at
48 Salisbury Square, EC (POD, 1860), and 6 Fetter

Lane, Fleet Street, EC (POD,1865), which he
shared with H.Crane and R.Pringle (qq.v.). His
last appearance in the directories was at 5 Red Lion
Court, EC (POD,1866).

MELLOR, Sir John Paget, Bt. 'Quiz' 1862-1929
Amateur draughtsman illustrator and caricaturist.
He served as a barrister and solicitor to the
Treasury but did draw for three comic wood
engravings in Punch,1886-88. He also drew for
Vanity Fair,1890, 1893, 1898. He was created
CB,1905, and KCB,1911, and died on 4 February
1929.
[Spielmann; Houfe]

MELVILLE, Harden Sidney fl.1837-82
Draughtsman and painter of landscapes, animals
and sport subjects. He began as a draughtsman on
wood for Charles Knight's London,1841; then did
some drawings on wood for the Illustrated London
News,1848, 1865-66; Henry Vizetelly's Illustrated
Times,1865; and Welcome Guest,1860. He developed
a skill for drawing animals and exotic locations
which he turned into illustrations for various books,
namely W.Dalton's The War Tiger,1859;
J.Greenwood's Wild Sports of the World,1862; his
own Curiosities of Savage Life,1864; and finally The
Adventures of a Griffin,1867. Houfe believes that
although he worked in London he may have travelled
to Australia and other foreign parts to research his
drawings. He exhibited work from 1837-79 at the
British Institution, the Royal Academy, and the
Royal Society of British Artists.
[Bénézit; Houfe]

MERRITT, F.R.
Draughtsman illustrator, who contributed one work
for wood engraving in The Graphic,1884.

METCALF, William John fl.1892-99
London wood engraver, who worked at 11 (12) Bow
Lane, EC (POD,1892-99). Fincham lists a London
engraver named Metcalf, at 8 Pall Mall, who
engraved eight armorial bookplates between 1830-50.

METTAIS, Charles-Joseph fl.1846-57
French draughtsman illustrator and portrait painter.
He exhibited at the Salon from 1846-48. He is listed
here for a drawing on wood to Cassell's Illustrated
Family Paper,1857, which appeared during the early
years of the magazine, when its primary interest
was the prolific illustrations of John Gilbert (q.v.).

METZNER, Frederick John and Son fl.1889-1902
London wood engraver, who listed his premises at
19 Brookland Road, Lewisham, SE (LSDS,1880-88),
then as Frederick Metzner and Son at 118 Holborn,
EC (POD,1889-90). He reappeared in the directories
at 181 High Street, Lewisham, SE (LSDS,1902).

MEYERSTEIN, Emil fl.1880-85
London wood engraver, colour printer and litho-
grapher. He worked as a colour printer at 1 Hatton
Garden (POD,1880), then wood engraver at 280 High
Holborn (POD,1884-85). He was the author of a book
on 'Stenochromy' colour printing.
[See Wakeman and Bridson for colour print work]

MICHAEL, J.B.
Draughtsman on wood, particularly of architectural
subjects, which he contributed to the Illustrated
London News,1873.

MICHAEL, L.H. fl.1845-74
Architectural draughtsman on wood, who contributed
drawings to Wyatt's Industrial Arts of the Nineteenth
Century and to the magazines Welcome Guest,1860,
and the Illustrated London News,1865-66, where he
first appeared with a full page illustration of 'A
Visit to Greenwich Hospital', 1865, wood engraved
by Mason Jackson (q.v.). The British Museum owns
proof engravings of his designs, engraved by the
Dalziel Brothers (q.v.), 1854-55.

MIDLAND Educational Company Limited fl.1880s
Provincial wood engraving firm, with offices at
91 New Street and 40 High Street, Birmingham
(Kelly's,1880).

MIDLAND Printing Company Limited fl.1889-1900
Provincial wood engraving firm, with an office at
Simpson Street, Oldbury, Birmingham
(Kelly's,1889-1900).

MIDDLETON
(see Beesley, Arthur)

MILLAIS, Sir John Everett, Bt. 1829-96
Draughtsman on wood, occasional etcher, major
Victorian portrait and genre painter, founding
member of the Pre-Raphaelite Brotherhood. He was
born in Southampton in 1829, and studied in London
at Sass's Academy and the Royal Academy Schools,
1840. He joined with Holman Hunt and D.G.Rossetti
to found the Pre-Raphaelite Brotherhood in 1848,
and began his career drawing on wood for their
publication, The Germ,1850, followed by his most
powerful work on wood, done between 1851-55.
However, their strong moral subject matter led to
these drawings being left unpublished. He also drew
on wood for Wilkie Collins' Mr Wray's Cashbox,1852,
then most notably with Rossetti for the influential
Pre-Raphaelite work, William Allingham's The
Music Master,1855, engraved by the Dalziels. This
was followed by illustrations to an equally influential
work, Moxon's edition of Tennyson's Poems,1857,
in which he developed two styles of drawing on wood:
a highly finished romantic technique for the
sentimental subjects and a slightly more sketchy,

contemporary manner. Luckily he again had the master wood engravers, the Dalziel Brothers (q.v.) to interpret his designs. Millais contributed drawings on wood to most of the major books and magazines of the period. The Dalziels engraved his drawings to Willmott's Poets of the Nineteenth Century, 1857, ('quite as fine as the Tennyson', White claimed). He also contributed to Lays of the Holy Land, 1858; to Mackay's Home Affections, 1858 (all hundred illustrations engraved by the Dalziels); and to numerous 'Sixties School' magazines, mostly wood engraved by the Dalziels. First was Cornhill, 1860-63, with illustrations to Trollope's Framley Parsonage which secured Millais' reputation as the most skilful and talented draughts-man for wood engravers of his time. Then came drawings for Good Words, 1861-64, 1878, 1882; London Society, 1862-64; a brief appearance in the Illustrated London News, 1862; the Churchman's Family Magazine, 1863; and Punch, 1863, 1865. Also he made contributions to various other books, such as Pennell's Puck on Pegasus, 1862; the Dalziels' Parables of our Lord, 1863; Touches of Nature by Eminent Artists, 1866; Mackay's Gems of Poetry, 1867; Passages from Modern English Poets, 1876; Thackeray's Barry Lyndon (complete works edition), 1879; and a frontispiece for his son's book, Game Birds and Shooting Sketches, 1892. Millais is best known, and rightly so, for his masterful interpret-ations of the works of Trollope. He first drew on wood for their publication as serials, in various magazines and it appears he was able to work rapidly upon the block. The time he took varied from one evening to two days per drawing, while the final plate to Framley Parsonage had to be redrawn three times upon the block before he was pleased enough to pass it. Nevertheless even Trollope was ecstatic in his praises of Millais' talent for understanding his literary intentions; he called the Orley Farm drawings 'the best I have seen in any novel in any language'. N.John Hall, in Trollope and His Illustrators, 1980, went further and claimed 'it would not be rash to call them the best of an English novel of the "golden decade" of wood engraving'. The Millais-Trollope collaborations included, apart from Framley Parsonage, 1860-62: Orley Farm, 1861-62; Small House at Allington, 1862; Phineas Finn, 1869; and Kept in the Dark, 1882. All of these drawings were engraved by the Dalziel Brothers who had a fruit-ful association with Millais by the 1860s. They had been introduced to the young artist by Richard Doyle (q.v.), and immediately commissioned a drawing on wood for Moxon's edition of Tennyson's Poems, 1857, which led to further collaborations on books and such magazines as the Cornhill and Good Words. By 1860 in fact Millais' friend William Allingham could write to the Brownings that Millais was rapidly becoming self-sufficient by his drawing on wood blocks alone, earning £15-20 'any time by a slight sketch on wood'. However, Allingham noted, there was 'a tendency to hasty productions and [Millais] knows it'. Nevertheless, such work soon taught Millais to regard drawing on wood with enough seriousness for the Dalziels to admire his perfectionist tendencies. He would return proofs with elaborate corrections and notes on the minutest errors ('...the mother's face is too full of little fine lines...'). When the Dalziels commissioned him exclusively for their Parables of Our Lord, published in 1863, after agreement was reached in 1857, Millais asked for the blocks and a list of parables needing illustrations. His letter to the Dalziels concerning this commission provides the best insight we have into his working methods as a draughtsman on wood: 'There is so much labour in these drawings that I trust you will give me my own time, otherwise I could not undertake the commission. I should make it a labour of love like yourselves.' He continued, 'It is almost unnecessary for me to say that I cannot produce these quickly, even if supposing I give all my time to them. They are separate pictures, and so I exert myself to the utmost to make them as complete as possible. I can do ordinary illustrations as quickly as most men; but these designs can scarcely be regarded in the same light--each Parable I illustrate perhaps a dozen times before I fix, and the "Hidden Treasures" I have altered on the wood at least 6 times. The manipulation of the drawings takes less time than the arrangement, although you cannot see how carefully they are executed. Believe me, I will not again occasionally delay in the production. I know you will take every care in the cutting, so I will not say anything about that...' (Dalziels' Record, p.94). And yet Millais was often late with his drawings. After his marriage to Effie Ruskin in 1855, she undertook the business letters for 'wood drawings' and apologies for her husband's tardiness. To the Dalziels she wrote, 'But he often makes designs, and continues to improve them until he is quite satisfied that it is as good as he can make it, and this takes a long time'. By the late 1860s Millais concentrated more upon his paintings, especially portraits of the famous, which brought him wealth and position. He was elected RA, 1863 and created a baronet in 1885. He served as PRA for only six months in 1896, before his death of cancer of the throat on 13 August 1896. He left a son, the animal artist John Guille Millais (q.v.) and artist brother William Henry Millais (q.v.). The British Museum owns proofs of his designs engraved by the Dalziel Brothers, 1853, 1861-63. [For a discussion of Millais as illustrator see J.G.Millais, Life and Letters of J.E.Millais, 1899; N.John Hall, Trollope and His Illustrators, 1980; and Martin Hardie, Catalogue of Prints, Wood engravings of Millais in the Victoria and Albert Museum, 1908. For a discussion of Millais as etcher see Volume I. See also Houfe; Wood]

MILLAIS, John Guille 1865-1931
Draughtsman for wood engravings, who specialised
in animal subjects, also painter. He was born on
24 March 1865, the fourth and youngest son of the
noted illustrator John Everett Millais (q.v.). He
was educated at Marlborough, and Trinity College,
Cambridge and travelled as a big game hunter in
Africa, Canada, America, and the Arctic, which
provided material for the numerous books which he
published on the animals of these places. He is
listed here for his drawings on wood and text
figures, begun during the 1880s and continued after
1900 (although they were then reproduced photo-
graphically). This wood engraved work included
contributions to The Graphic,1886; Pearson's
Magazine, and book illustrations to A Fauna of
Sutherland,1887; and A Fauna of the Outer Hebrides,
1888. He drew for twenty-eight wood engravings of
feathers, wings and heads to Henry Seebohm's
Geographical Distribution of the Family Charadriidae,
1887-88; and for wood engravings in his own book,
Game Birds and Shooting Sketches,1892, the wood
engravings being signed 'J.G.M.'. His drawings to
Lord Walsingham's Shooting Moor and Marsh,1909,
were engraved on wood by George Lodge (q.v.).
Millais exhibited work at the Fine Art Society,1901,
1919, and 1923, and died on 24 March 1931.
[TB; Who's Who; Sketchley; Houfe; C.Jackson]

MILLAIS, William Henry 1828-99
Draughtsman for wood engravings, watercolourist.
He was the elder brother of John Everett Millais
(q.v.), and worked at Farnham, specialising in
landscape paintings. He exhibited at the Fine Art
Society, the Royal Academy, and the Royal Institute
of Painters in Watercolours. He is listed here for
his drawings on wood for Mrs Gatty's Parables from
Nature,1861, 1867, 'of average interest' (White); and
some of the nineteen illustrations, engraved on wood
by Horace Harral (q.v.) for A.A.Procter's Legends
and Lyrics,1865.
[White; TB; Bryan; Houfe]

MILLARD, George fl.1876-95
London wood engraver, who worked at 3 Bouverie
Street, EC (POD,1876-80), then at 49 Essex Street,
Strand, WC (POD,1887-95), shared with
W.Spreadbury (q.v.).

MILLER, ?
Wood engraver, assistant to Edmund Evans (q.v.),
with whom he worked for thirty years (Evans letter,
UCLA). Miller was the son of the metal engraver
William Miller, 1796-1882, best known for his steel
engravings after Turner.
[For metal engravings see Volume I]

MILLER, Felix Martin
Draughtsman on wood, who contributed a series of
four scenes, 'Passages in the Voyage of Life', for
the Art Journal,1853,pp.90-91.

MILLER, Hugh fl.1870s
London wood engraver, who worked at 45 Speke
Road, Battersea, SW (LSDS,1876).

MILLER, John Fenwick fl.1882-84
London wood engraver, who worked at 64 Fleet
Street, EC (POD,1882-84). He shared the premises
with E.A.D.Mins and G.F.Sheern (qq.v.).

MILLER, Stephen 1872-80
Scottish wood engraver, who worked at 52 Renfield
Street, Glasgow (Kelly's,1872-76), then at
100 N. Hanover Street, Glasgow (Kelly's,1880-89).

MILLS, Alfred ?-1833
Wood engraver of the early nineteenth century.
Redgrave claimed that, 'He was for about 40 years
engaged in designing and cutting works for the
illustration of children's books, in which he showed
much ability'. He engraved illustrations to Pictures
of Grecian History,1812. He died in Walworth on
7 December 1833, aged fifty-seven.
[Bénézit; TB; Redgrave]

MILLS, Frederick W. fl.1880s
Provincial wood engraver, who worked at 13 Market
Passage, Cambridge (Kelly's,1880).

MILLS, Nathaniel Pearl fl.1892-96
London wood engraver, who worked at Temple
Chambers, Falcon Court, 32 Fleet Street, EC
(POD,1892-96). He shared the address with
W.Hampshire, W.P.Mills and W.Spielmeyer (qq.v.).

MIN(N)S, C. fl.1835-41
Wood engraver, landscape painter. He exhibited
landscape paintings in London at the Royal Academy
and other galleries from 1835-39, then became a
wood engraving assistant to Smith and Linton (q.v.)
during their early days as chief engravers to the
Illustrated London News. He specialised in engravings
after watercolours of the prominent painters of the
1840s. He also engraved after Wells (q.v.) for
Charles Knight's Penny Magazine,June 1841.
[Linton, Masters of Wood Engraving; TB;
Bodleian Library]

MINNS, Edward Alfred fl.1882-83
London wood engraver, who worked at 64 Fleet
Street, EC (POD,1882-83). He shared the premises
with John F.Miller and G.F.Sheern (qq.v.).

MINTON and Stranders fl.1870s
London firm of wood engravers, who worked at
33 Castle Street, Holborn, EC (POD,1871).

MITCHELL, Edward (D.) fl.1880-87
London draughtsman on wood, 'herald painter,
writer and designer'. He worked at 44 and 46 Ludgate
Chambers, EC (Kelly's,1880). Fincham listed three
bookplates engraved by E.D.Mitchell, London,
dated 1880, 1887.

MITCHELL, Ernest Charles fl.1886-98
London wood engraver, who worked from 150 Fleet
Street, EC (POD,1886-88), premises shared with
A.H.Lindsell (q.v.). He then joined with Henry Pitt
(q.v.) as Mitchell, Pitt and Company (q.v.).

MITCHELL, Frederick William fl.1880-86
London wood engraver, who worked at 6 Wine Office
Court, EC (POD,1880-86). He shared the address
with J.Reindorp, G.F.Sheern and C.Murray (qq.v.).

MITCHELL, Pitt and Company fl.1890-98
London wood engraving firm, a partnership between
Ernest Charles Mitchell and Henry Pitt (qq.v.).
They worked from 30 Holborn, EC (POD,1890-98)
before Henry Pitt took over the office on his own.

MOFFAT, George fl.1872-80
London draughtsman on wood, who worked at 5 Wine
Office Court, Fleet Street, EC (Kelly's,1872), then
at 12 Copeland Terrace, Copeland Road, Peckham,
SE (LSDS,1880).

MOLLER, Frederick William fl.1862-65
London wood engraver, who worked at 8 Sergeants'
Inn, EC (POD,1862-65). He may be related to the
Danish portrait artist, Frederick Moller, 1797-1871.
[Bénézit]

MONNIER, G.
French draughtsman, who contributed a drawing for
wood engraving in the Illustrated London News,1870.

MONSELL, Elinor
Woodcut designer and artist. She contributed 'Daphne
and Apollo' to Laurence Housman's The Venture,1903.
She may be related to the illustrator J.R.Monsell,
who drew for Grimms Fairy Tales,1908 and Cassell's
edition of The Buccaneers,1908. She signed her work:
'WE' (superimposed).
[Houfe]

MONTAGU, H.Irving fl.1873-93
Draughtsman, war artist and figure painter. He
served as 'Special Artist' to the Illustrated London
News from 1874, his duties including providing
drawings for wood engravings of the Carlist uprising
in Spain, later scenes from Hungary, Turkey and

Russia. He contributed one drawing to the Sunday
Magazine,1881. He also exhibited work at the Royal
Academy and the Royal Society of British Artists.
[Houfe; H.I.Montagu, Wanderings,1889; Strand
Magazine,1891,pp.576-85]

MONTAGU, J.A. fl.1840s
Ornamental draughtsman for wood engravings. He
worked for the Chiswick Press, drew various designs
for them, including the press's initial colophon and
designs to The Book of Common Prayer,1844. These
were wood engraved by Mary Byfield (q.v.).
[McLean; Warren, C.Whittingham,1896,p.224]

MONTAGUE, Charles Joseph fl.1890s
London draughtsman on wood, who worked at Falcon
Court, 32 Fleet Street, EC (Kelly's,1900). He
shared the address with W.Hampshire, W.F.Jeffries
and W.A.Monypenny (qq.v.).

MONTALBA, Clara 1842-1929
Occasional illustrator, landscape and marine painter,
primarily of Venetian scenes. She was born in
Cheltenham, studied in Paris under E.Isabey,
travelled throughout France and lived in Venice for
many years. She is included here for her Venetian
illustrations to H.F.Brown's article, 'Venice', in
the English Illustrated Magazine,1886-87. These
were wood engraved by O.Lacour and Waterlow
and Sons (qq.v.). She primarily worked as a painter,
however, exhibiting from 1866 at the Royal Academy,
the British Institution, the Society of British Artists,
the Old Watercolour Society (eighty-six works), the
Grosvenor Gallery and the New Gallery, and helping
to advise Kate Greenaway and Helen Paterson (qq.v.),
later Allingham on their watercolour technique.
She died in Venice on 13 August 1929.
[TB; Wood; Bénézit; Who's Who; Clement]

MONTBARD, G. Charles Auguste Loyes 1841-1905
Draughtsman illustrator, caricaturist, etcher and
landscape painter. He was born in Montbard on
2 August 1841, and adopted the town's name as his
own, professionally. He began as a draughtsman for
wood engravings, first with O'Shea on Chronique
Illustrée, then was introduced to the English public
with his drawings of Compiègne, wood engraved in
the Illustrated London News,1868. He soon became
a regular contributor to this magazine from 1868-99,
and by the 1870s was proficient enough at drawing
for their wood engravers to be given various 'Special
Artist' sketches to polish and transfer onto wood
blocks, for instance, 'The War: Egyptian Troops in
Bulgaria', 9 June 1877. By the 1880s he had produced
drawings of various seasonal landscapes, poorly
engraved on wood, but competent as nature studies.
He also drew various country houses, usually without
figures, which he found difficult to draw well. He
also drew for wood engravings in The Graphic,1871-73;

for the comic paper Judy,1871; Vanity Fair,1872; Good Words,1880-99; English Illustrated Magazine, 1895; St James's Budget; Windsor Magazine; and the Pall Mall Gazette. He exhibited work in London from 1870, at the Royal Academy, the Royal Society of British Artists, the Royal Institute of Painters in Watercolours and the Royal Institute of Painters in Oil-Colours. He died there on 5 August 1905.
[TB; Houfe; Beraldi]

MONYPENNY, William Arthur fl.1880-1910
London wood engraver, who worked at Falcon Court, 32 Fleet Street, EC (POD,1896-1910). He shared the address with W.F.Jeffries and W.Andrews (qq.v.). Fincham lists a bookplate for Flora, Duchess of Norfolk, engraved by 'Monypenny' after a seal design by G.A.Lee, dated 1880.

MOORE, Albert Joseph 1841-93
Occasional draughtsman illustrator, neo-classical figure painter. He was born in York in 1841, the son of the portrait painter William Moore. He moved to London after the death of his father in 1855, and there was employed by architects as a mural painter. He made occasional drawings on wood for book illustrations, notably to Milton's Ode on the Morning of Christ's Nativity,1867, wood engraved by W.J.Palmer (q.v.) to capture Moore's firm, even outline reminiscent of the later Walter Crane (q.v.). He also illustrated W.Eden Nesfield's Specimens of Medieval Architecture,1862. As a painter, he was noted for classical figures, a precursor of Alma-Tadema, and exhibited these at the New English Art Club, the New Gallery, the Royal Academy, the Royal Institute of Painters in Watercolours and the Royal Watercolour Society, where he was elected member in 1884. He died in London in 1893. The British Museum owns a proof engraving by the Dalziel Brothers (q.v.), 1862.
[Wood; McLean, Victorian Book Design; White]

MOORE, Richard Hewitt fl.1863-90
Wood engraver, draughtsman of birds and animals, and sculptor. He set off as a wood engraver with J.D.Cooper (q.v.) at 188 Strand, WC (POD,1863-66), then on his own at 268 Strand (POD,1867-68). By 1875 he had begun drawing birds and animals for wood engravings in the Illustrated London News, 1875-90, many of his drawings being engraved by the master animal wood engraver John Greenaway (q.v.), for instance, the full-page 'The Prince of Wales' Animals from India', 27 May 1876. He also contributed to Lady's Pictorial and Sporting and Dramatic News,1890. He exhibited paintings at the New Watercolour Society and the Royal Society of British Artists.

MOORE, Thomas Sturge 1870-1944
Wood engraver, illustrator and poet. He was born on 4 March 1870 in Essex, and studied wood engraving under Charles Roberts (q.v.) at the Lambeth School of Art, after being persuaded by his new friends Charles Ricketts and Charles Shannon (qq.v.). He joined the Dial Group, 1897-99, while he developed wood engravings of a more balanced, less formalised nature than William Morris. In fact Hind claimed that his wood engravings recaptured some of the inspiration of William Blake. They first appeared in the Dial,1895, alongside wood engravings by Lucien Pissarro (q.v.). He established strong ties with the private press movement, especially the Essex House Press, and was a member of the Society of Twelve. He illustrated The Centaur; De Guerin's The Bacchante,1899; and William Penn's Some Fruits of Solitude,1901. He also produced decorations for rhyme sheets of Harold Monro's Poetry Bookshop. He exhibited work at the Royal Scottish Academy, and wrote poetry and a monograph on Dürer,1905. The British Museum owns a small wood engraving by him.
[For a discussion of his wood engravings see Studio, 1916; Winter,1923-24; and Print Collector's Quarterly,1921,p.276; also David Chambers, 'Checklist of books illustrated by T.S.Moore', The Private Library,1971,pp.38-46,190; Malcolm Easton, 'T.S.Moore Woodengraver', Private Library,1971,pp.24-37; also his essay to Hull Univeristy catalogue on W.B.Yates,1970]

MORGAN, Harry fl.1860-65
London wood engraver, who worked at 17 Tooks Court, Chancery Lane (POD,1865). He probably engraved the wood engraving, 'The Village Smithy', after a painting by Lewis, in the Illustrated London News,8 September 1860. It is a poor work, with too much emphasis on intricate detail and shows a deficiency in perspective. He signed his work: 'MORGAN Sc'.

MORGAN, Matt Somerville 1836-90
Prominent draughtsman on wood, primarily of figure and landscape subjects, caricaturist, lithographer and social realist painter. He was born in London in 1836, and by the late 1850s had established himself as a powerful draughtsman on wood. Bohn in Chatto and Jackson noted his work for Miles Standish; he also drew on wood for Henry Vizetelly's Illustrated Times,1859-66. During this period he served as 'Special Artist' in Italy, 1859-61, and sent sketches back for wood engraving in this paper and in the Illustrated London News,1859-86. Such work stirred his social conscience and he began to draw powerful records of reform demonstrations and poverty victims in London. His cartoonist talent was put to use in the Tomahawk, for which he became cartoonist in 1867; also for Broadway,1867-74; for the Dalziels'

comic paper Judy; for Britannia, 1869; Arrow; and
Will o' the Wisp, another short-lived comic paper.
Some of these sharply satiric drawings were wood
engraved and printed from tinted wood blocks,
heightening their impact. Morgan's later life was
spent in America, painting battle panoramas of the
American Civil War. He died in New York in 1890.
[Chatto; TB; Clement; Houfe; Fielding]

MORGAN, Walter Jenks 1847-1924
Draughtsman illustrator and genre painter. He
studied at the Birmingham School and at South
Kensington, then began drawing for wood engraved
illustrations in magazines such as The Graphic,
1875-76, and the Illustrated London News, 1877-81.
He also worked for the children's engravers and
publishers, Messrs Cassell (q.v.) drawing domestic
and juvenile subjects for their numerous wood
engraved books and magazines. He exhibited work
at the Royal Academy, the Royal Society of British
Artists and the Royal Institute of Painters in Watercolours. He died in Birmingham on 31 October 1924.

MORIN, Edward 1824-82
French born draughtsman on wood, lithographer,
watercolourist. He was born in Le Havre on 26 March
1824, was a pupil of Gleyre and exhibited landscapes
at the Salon from 1857. He came to London, probably
at the instigation of Henry Duff Linton (q.v.), who
was his friend in Paris, and trained as a draughtsman
on wood under John Gilbert (q.v.). His first work
appeared in Cassell's Illustrated Family Paper,
1853-55 (in which Gilbert was the primary contributor),
then he worked for Henry Vizetelly's (q.v.) Illustrated
Times, 1855-61. Vizetelly described his new artist on
wood as 'a spirited French artist'. Such work
inevitably led to commissions for the Illustrated London
News, 1856-57. Bénézit claimed that Morin lived for
several years in England, but returned to Paris in
1851, where he drew illustrations for L'Illustration
and other French papers. His work still appeared in
England during this time, until 1861. He died in
Sceaux on 18 August 1882. A 'Daniel Morin' is known
to have given W.J.Linton money to help finance his
magazine, Pen and Pencil, which was launched
10 February 1855. He was a friend of Henry Duff
Linton (q.v.) who brought him from Paris to London.
[F.Smith, W.J.Linton, 1973, p.119; Vizetelly,
Glances Back; Gusman; Bénézit; Houfe]

MORING, Thomas fl.1840-1900
Draughtsman and wood engraver, who specialised in
medieval designs for bookplates and heraldic
stationery. He worked for sixty years, first at
44 High Holborn, WC (Fincham, 1840, POD, 1876-82),
then at 323 High Holborn, WC (POD, 1883-89),
1st Avenue Buildings, High Holborn and 15 Warwick
Court, WC (POD, 1890-93), and finally at 52A High
Holborn, WC (POD, 1894-1900). Fincham lists

eighteen bookplates designed and engraved by
'T.Moring sc'.

MORISON, George A. fl.1870s
Scottish wood engraver, who worked at 3 Comely
Green Acres, Edinburgh (Kelly's, 1872).

MORRELL, John (Turner) fl.1865-82
London wood engraver, who worked as John Turner
at 37 Ludgate Hill, EC (POD, 1865), then 66 Ludgate
Hill (POD, 1866-70). A John Turner Morrell also
appears in the directories as wood engraver working
at 28 Essex Street, Strand, WC (POD, 1870-72). He
shared his address with C.C.Irons and F.Wentworth
(qq.v.).

MORRIS, E. fl.1850s
Graves lists a work by this draughtsman on wood, a
'Portrait of Byron' drawn for the Art Union of
London and engraved on wood by Henry Duff Linton
(q.v.). It was exhibited at the Royal Academy in 1855.
He may be Ebenezer Butter Morris, a portrait and
genre painter who worked in London from 1833-63.
[Graves; Bénézit]

MORRIS, Jane, née Burden
Wood engraver, embroiderer, wife of the artist
William Morris (q.v.). Jane Morris worked for her
husband's firm, Morris and Company with Georgiana
Burne-Jones (q.v.). They embroidered and wood
engraved together at the Red House during the early
1860s, as Georgiana recalled, 'Oh, how happy we
were, Janey and I, busy in the morning with needlework or wood-engraving...' (G.Burne-Jones,
Memorials, 1904, Vol.I, p.213).
[A.Callen, Angel in the Studio, p.223]

MORRIS, William 1834-96
Wood engraver, poet, designer, manufacturer and
socialist. He was born in Walthamstow on 24 March
1834, and attended Marlborough and Exeter College,
Oxford. He established Morris, Marshall, Faulkner
and Company in April 1861, a firm of manufacturers
and decorators which produced from its own
designers the influential textiles, tapestries,
embroideries, wallpapers, metal work and furniture
for which Morris is best known. During this period
at the Webb-designed Red House, in Upton, Kent he
tried to establish an artistic commune. Here, with
his wife Jane Morris, Edward Burne-Jones, and his
wife Georgiana (qq.v.) they worked on various
projects, including Burne-Jones' and Morris's
designs for wood engravings. It was during this
period that Georgiana engraved her husband's
designs, and Morris's firm engraved an illustration
by Dante Gabriel Rossetti to his sister Christina's
Goblin Market, 1862. Then followed the forty-four
known Burne-Jones designs on wood, thirty-five
engraved by William Morris, for a projected but

unpublished edition of The Tale of Cupid and Psyche, done about 1866 (published from recently discovered blocks by Clover Hill Editions,1974). Burne-Jones then designed the title page for Morris's The Earthly Paradise,1868, which Morris wood engraved himself (engraved in subsequent editions by G.Campfield (q.v.)). Other Morris wood engravings included a double-page map to E.Magnusson's, The Story of Grettir the Strong,1869. Morris had most of his early books printed by the Chiswick Press. In 1866 and again in 1877, he planned a fine edition of all his own writings with illustrations engraved by himself, but this was abandoned. It was not until he founded the Kelmscott Press in 1890, that he saw his dreams and aesthetic theories for book design materialise, and during the life of the press, he designed and supervised some fifty of the total fifty-three volumes published (see S.C.Cockerell, The Kelmscott Press, 1898; H.Sparkling, The Kelmscott Press and William Morris,1924). He also employed such draughtsman illustrators as Burne-Jones, Walter Crane, and C.M.Gere (qq.v.) and the wood engraver W.H.Hooper (q.v.). In addition N.Jones (q.v.) may have designed and engraved for Morris. His most famous volume, the Kelmscott Chaucer, appeared on 8 May 1896, a few months before Morris died, in Hammersmith on 3 October 1896.
[For a full account of Morris's work see A.Vallance, William Morris,1897; for biography see J.Lindsay, William Morris,1975; also McLean, Victorian Book Design; Hind; H.Sparling, The Kelmscott Press and William Morris,1924; DNB; TB (bibliography)]

MORRISON, George fl.1872-80
Scottish wood engraver, who worked at 62 Buchanan Street, Glasgow (Kelly's,1872), then 16 Hope Street, Glasgow (Kelly's,1876-80).

MORRISON, G. and M. fl.1889-1900
Firm of Scottish draughtsmen on wood, which specialised in 'illustrations for catalogues, books, magazines, labels and trade marks'. They worked from 166 Buchanan Street, Glasgow (Kelly's,1889), then 92 St Vincent Street (Kelly's,1900).

MORROW, Albert George 1863-1927
Draughtsman illustrator and poster artist. He was born in Comber, County Down, Ireland, in 1863 and studied in Belfast and in London at South Kensington. He began drawing for wood engraved illustrations in magazines in 1884, his first work appearing that year in the English Illustrated Magazine. This early work was drawn on the spot, generally of some industrial site, for instance a series of drawings of workshop and workers to H.J.Palmer's 'Cutlers and Cutlery at Sheffield', 1884, wood engraved by J.Cocking, J.D.Cooper, E.Lascelles, O.Jahyer and A.W.Dawson (qq.v.). This was followed by 'Nottingham Castle', engraved by A.C.Coats (q.v.);

'China-making at Stoke-on-Trent', engraved by J.D.Cooper and Waterlow and Sons (qq.v.); and scenes to B.H.Becker's 'Iron and Steel Making in South Wales', engraved on wood by O.Jahyer, T.W.Lascelles, E.Gascoine and J.D.Cooper (qq.v.). He also contributed to Illustrated Bits, 1890; Good Words,1890; Punch (not mentioned by Spielmann). He exhibited work at the Royal Academy and the Royal Society of British Artists and died in West Heathly, Sussex in October 1927.
[TB; Bénézit; Houfe; Who's Who]

MORTEN, Thomas 1836-66
Prolific draughtsman on wood and occasional painter, championed by Forrest Reid as an unfairly neglected artist of the 'Sixties School', competent in block work. 'It is true that it is uneven, but at its best it is brilliant and highly decorative, with frequently a fantastic element both original and attractive'. Morten was born in Uxbridge in 1836 and studied at Leigh's art school in Newman Street at an early age, where he specialised in drawing on wood blocks. He started work for Good Words,1861-63, under the tutelage of the Dalziel Brothers (q.v.) who engraved his best work; then for Once a Week,1861-66, aided by the other major wood engraver Joseph Swain (q.v.); then for Entertaining Things,1861-62; and Laird's Return,1861. His drawings to London Society,1862-69 were usually engraved by Horace Harral (q.v.) 'whose work is rarely so satisfactory as that of Dalziel or Swain' (Reid). He was soon contributing to most of the leading magazines of the 1860s period and continued to draw on wood until his tragic suicide in the autumn of 1866. Further work appeared in Every Boy's Magazine,1862-63; and he did four drawings to Churchman's Family Magazine, 1863-64, expertly engraved by the Dalziels, who had commissioned one drawing for their Dalziels' Arabian Nights' Entertainments,1863. Then came illustrations to A Round of Days,1865; Watts's Divine and Moral Songs,1865; Procter's Legends and Lyrics,1865; Jingles and Jokes for little Folks, 1865; Quiver,1865-66; Aunt Judy's Magazine,1866; Beeton's Annuals; and Cassell's Family Paper,1866. His finest illustrations were eighty designs 'by the late T.Morten', engraved by W.J.Linton to Gulliver's Travels,1866, 'in which the ill-fated artist is seen at his best level; they display a really convincing imagination, and if, technically speaking, he had some better work elsewhere, this is his most successful sustained effort', White claimed. Other posthumous appearances were in Foxe's Book of Martyrs,1867, engraved by W.L.Thomas (q.v.); Belgravia,1871; Thornbury's Legendary Ballads, 1876; and sections of Cassell's History of England. Morten's weakness was his tendency to borrow from his more powerful draughtsmen colleagues, like Doré, Sandys and J.D.Watson (qq.v.). This led Reid to conclude that 'Taking all these drawings into

consideration--drawings so uneven in conception
and execution--it becomes exceedingly difficult to
place Morten. When he is good he is very good; on
the other hand, just when he seems completely to
have found himself, he will produce a design that
looks like an imitation of so immature a draughtsman
as Paul Gray (q.v.). He had an excellent manner of
his own, which makes it all the harder to understand
why he should have troubled to show us that he can
"do" Sandys and other artists--some of whom require
a great deal of "doing"'. Morten occasionally exhibited
at the British Institution and the Royal Academy. He
died probably by suicide over money problems, on
23 September 1866, cutting short a promising career.
The British Museum owns a series of proof engravings
by the Dalziel Brothers, 1861-63.
[For a discussion of individual works see Reid;
White; see also Redgrave; DNB; Bryan; Bénézit;
Art Journal,1866,p.364]

MORTON, William fl.1870s
Provincial wood engraver, who worked at 2 Essex
Street, King Street, Manchester (Kelly's,1872). He
may be related to the William Morton, watercolour
painter of Manchester, who exhibited in London from
1869.

MOSSES, Thomas fl.1828-61
Wood engraver, noted by Chatto as one of the best
wood engravers entitled to 'honourable mention' next
to C.Nesbit and J.Thompson (qq.v.). Mosses engraved
eight of William Harvey's (q.v.) illustrations to
Northcote's Fables,1828. He engraved the illustrations
of Robert Cruikshank (q.v.) and numerous works for
Charles Whittingham (q.v.), who commissioned
engravings to a series of 'Painters and Paintings':
reproductions of 'Old Master' works such as Reynolds'
'Mrs Molesworth', Hogarth's 'Harlot's Progress', and
portrait works by Gainsborough, Gillray, Opie, and
Mengs. Mosses also engraved biblical drawings by
John Martin, R.Westall, C.Nesbit and W.H.Powis,
1835; also plates to Allan Cunningham's Lives of the
Most Eminent British Painters, Sculptors, and
Architects,1839. Mosses maintained his position as
a major wood engraver for book illustrations. The
British Museum owns a series of engravings after
W.Harvey, the Bodleian Library his Whittingham
engravings. He signed his work: 'T MOSSES SC'.
[see A.Warren, C.Whittingham,1896; Nagler;
LeBlanc; Brulliot; TB; Chatto]

MOSSES, W.I. fl.1880s
Wood engraver, who engraved numerous illustrations
to the Illustrated London News,1880. The most noted
of these were full and double-page illustrations of
R.C.Woodville, like 'The State of Ireland', 14 February,
6 March 1880. He also engraved after Frank Dadd,
W.H.Overend and C.J.Staniland (qq.v.).
His engraving style centred around an emphasis on

figure outlines, hard-edged to stand out against a
uniform background. His biggest challenge came
with R.C.Woodville's drawing, 'Polo Match by
Electric Light', Illustrated London News, 5 June
1880, with the polo players as black outlines set
against the glare of electric light. He signed his
engravings: 'W-I-Mosses Sc'.

MOTT, Edward (Edwin) fl.1869-74
London wood engraver, who worked at 2 Great New
Street, Fetter Lane, EC (POD,1869). He moved to
1 Upper Chadwell Street, EC (POD,1871-74).

MOULIN, M. fl.1859-60
French draughtsman of figure subjects, noted here
for his association with Henry Vizetelly (q.v.) who
described him as 'an amateur, but...of an unusual
kind'. When Vizetelly was in Paris, Moulin constantly
brought him sketches of court life in the Tuilleries,
having 'the run of the Tuilleries' because he said he
was related to Napoleon III's chef. In fact he was a
member of the palace secret police ordered to guard
the king. Nevertheless Vizetelly gratefully accepted
the sketches which, although 'utterly destitute of
artistic merit', could be easily sharpened up for his
wood engravers. These appeared in Vizetelly's
Illustrated Times,1859-60; then when Vizetelly
became the Paris correspondent to the Illustrated
London News he secured Moulin's sketches for this
paper as well. They appeared from 1860, including
the most intriguing sketch which Moulin made, on a
drum head in 1870, during a visit with Napoleon to
Mertz and Sedan. (The sketch survived and was
exhibited at the Crystal Palace.)
[Vizetelly, Glances Back; Houfe]

MOWATT, J.E.
Little is known of this wood engraver, who engraved
a portrait of the print and bookseller Edward Daniell
(1807-92), after an anonymous drawing. The wood
engraving is owned by the British Museum.
[Hake]

MULLORD, Alfred fl.1884-1910
London wood engraver, who worked at 7 Water Lane,
Ludgate Hill, EC (POD,1884-88), then as Mullord
and Company at 164 Queen Victoria Street, EC
(POD,1889-93), and 68 Farringdon Street, EC-
(POD,1894-1910). During this last period the firm
shared the address with the wood engraver J.W.Lewis
(q.v.).

MULREADY, William 1786-1863
Prominent genre painter, prolific illustrator of
small vignettes during the early nineteenth century,
and occasional draughtsman on wood of figure
subjects. He was born in Ennis, County Clare, on
1 April 1786, and came to London early in his life
where he developed his precocious talent for drawing.

He was soon accepted at the Royal Academy Schools, 1800, where he achieved distinction and exhibited his paintings, later being elected ARA,1815, and RA a few months later. His need for money drove him to try a variety of commissions and techniques; he taught drawing and produced a large number of children's book designs from 1807-09. Mulready is listed here for his later work as draughtsman on wood, his designs appearing with those of the Pre-Raphaelites in some instances. He drew illustrations wood engraved in facsimile by John Thompson (q.v.) to Goldsmith's Vicar of Wakefield,1843, a work which 'did much to shape the manner of book illustrations in the fifties' (White). It was a subject which he afterwards painted. He drew illustrations to The Mother's Primer,1844; Walter Scott's Peveril of the Peak,1846; and a frontispiece to Moore's Irish Melodies,1856. His four illustrations on wood to Moxon's edition of Tennyson's Poems,1857, were noted by Bohn in Chatto and Jackson. However, he is perhaps best known today for his design of the first Penny Postage envelope for Sir Rowland Hill,1840, engraved on brass by John Thompson (q.v.). As a draughtsman Mulready was never a strong artist, his delicate touch being more suited to etchings than wood engraving. Indeed, White makes the valid point, that 'The more one studies the matter, the more one fancies that certain drawings not intended for engraving by Mulready, and others by Maclise, must have had a large share in the movement [etching revival] which culminated about 1865 and died out about 1870'. Mulready continued his drawing throughout his later years, and died in Bayswater on 7 July 1863. The British Museum owns a proof engraving by the Dalziel Brothers (q.v.),1855; also a postage stamp envelope engraved proof. [Chatto; Houfe; DNB; Wood]

MUMBY, George fl.1876-89
London draughtsman on wood, who worked at 33 Fetter Lane, EC (Kelly's,1876-89).

MUNRO, George fl.1872-1900
Scottish wood engraver, who worked at 46 Earl Grey Street, Edinburgh (Kelly's,1872-1900).

MURCH, Arthur fl.1871-81
Draughtsman for wood engravings. He worked in Italy, 1871-73, and knew Walter Crane (q.v.) who described him as 'a meticulous man who produced little'. He did produce four of the total of sixty-nine drawings for the Dalziels' Bible Gallery (dated 1880, published 1880-81), and this alone secured his position as a competent draughtsman for wood engraving.

MURDEN, William fl.1860-83
London wood engraver, who worked for the Illustrated London News from 1860. That year he engraved a full-page series of vignettes after A.Hunt's sketches, 'Home for the Holidays', 22 December 1860. It was

followed by various portrait engravings such as 'Associates of the RA in 1861', 23 February 1861. He worked at 9 Essex Street, Strand, WC (POD,1868-83), premises shared with P.Roberts, J.Bye, H.C.Mason, and G.J.Baker (qq.v.). He signed his work: 'MURDEN SC'.

MURDON, ? fl.1840s
Wood engraver, who worked for Charles Knight (q.v.). He engraved various cuts to Knight's Penny Magazine,after Anelay, October 1841 and after Standfust and Wells (qq.v.), November 1841. [Bodleian Library]

MURRAY, Charles fl.1874-1900
London wood engraver, who worked at 6 Wine Office Court, EC (POD,1874-1900). He shared this address at various times during this twenty-six year period with J.Reindorp, H.Izod and G.F.Sheern (qq.v.), later with W.H.Franklin and W.H.Joyce (qq.v.).

MURRAY, Charles Oliver 1841-1924
Occasional illustrator, prominent etcher and painter. He was born in Denholm in 1842, educated at the Minto School, the Edinburgh School of Design and the Royal Scottish Academy. He started as an illustrator and engraver for magazines, and contributed wood engraved illustrations to Golden Hours, 1869 and Good Words,1880. He illustrated A.R.Hope's Spindle Stories,1880; and produced illustrations for wood engravings in the English Illustrated Magazine, 1883-84, 1891-92. The most noted of these were to Reverend Alfred Ainger's article, 'Shakespeare in the Middle Temple', 1883-84, wood engraved by E.Gascoine, W. and J.R.Cheshire, O.Jahyer, J.A.Quartley, and E.Stankowski (qq.v.). Murray was later a prolific etcher after paintings of famous artists.
[For etchings and bibliography see Volume I]

MURRAY, Sir David 1849-1933
Occasional illustrator, landscape painter. He was born in Glasgow in 1849, where he studied at the art school, then came to London and became a fashionable landscape painter. He was elected ARA,1891, and RA in 1905. He is included here for his drawings, 'Picturesque Picardy', wood engraved by H.F.Davey, O.Lacour and R.Paterson (qq.v.) in the English Illustrated Magazine,1887.
[Houfe; Clement; Who's Who; Bénézit; TB (full bibliography)]

MURRAY, William Bazett fl.1871-90
Talented draughtsman for wood engravings of social realist subjects. He remains an elusive figure who exhibited in London at the Dudley 'Black and White' exhibitions and the Royal Academy, 1871-75, then stopped submitting work to devote his time to drawing for The Graphic,1874-76 and the Illustrated London

News, 1874-90. His subjects included various industrial themes like 'Sugar-making at the Countership Refinery, Bristol', Illustrated London News, 29 November 1873, well engraved to show good contrasts by F.Wentworth (q.v.); various Scottish subjects like 'New Year's Eve in Edinburgh', Illustrated London News, 30 December 1876, well engraved with strong contrasting darks by W.B.Gardner (q.v.). He recorded London life in a more sympathetic manner than Doré, and his work for The Graphic was collected and much admired by Van Gogh: especially competent were 'London Life: Sack Making by Lamplight', The Graphic, 3 April 1875; and 'Market Gardening -- A Winter's Journey to Covent Garden', The Graphic, 12 February 1876.
[Houfe; English Influences on Van Gogh]

MYERSON, Alfred fl.1878-81
London wood engraver, who worked at 84 Fleet Street, EC (POD, 1878-81). He shared the address with F.Babbage (q.v.) and C.Ridgway.

MYERSON and Nicholas fl.1890s
London wood engraving firm, with an office at 1 Norfolk Street, Strand, WC (POD, 1896). The address was shared with J.C.Saunders and A.Shepherd (qq.v.).

NAIRN
Draughtsman for wood engravings of the New Zealand Gold Rush in the Illustrated London News, 1863. He may be the father of J.M.Nairn, a New Zealand artist (d.1904).

NALL, James fl.1880s
Provincial wood engraver, who worked at 6 Queen Street, Leicester (Kelly's, 1889).

NANTEUIL, Célestin François 1813-73
French reproductive wood engraver, etcher, lithographer, and genre painter. He was born on 11 July 1813 in Rome, and properly named Leboeuf. He was the brother of the sculptor Charles François, and pupil of Charles Langlois and Ingres. He began his wood engraving career with reproductions of various French artists' work, notably a half-page engraving 'The Passage over the Styx', from Dante's Inferno, after Ary Scheffer, in the Illustrated London News, 29 November 1856. Nanteuil's style showed in this a tight, almost steel-like line, the figures picked out by strong cross-hatches against a dark, evenly ruled sky. Nanteuil also reproduced Barbizon landscape paintings, and illustrations to various contemporary French novelists: Victor Hugo, Dumas, and Theophile Gautier. In 1867 he became the Director of the Academy of Dijon. He died on 4 September 1873 in Marlotte, Seine-et-Marne.

[TB; Bénézit; Beraldi; Glaser]

NASH, John Franklin fl.1867-80
London wood engraver and draughtsman, who worked at 144 Strand, WC (POD, 1867), 58 Nelson Square, SE (POD, 1878), and 75 Fleet Street, EC (POD, 1879-80), which he shared with the wood engraver William Gibbs (q.v.).

NASH, John Northcote 1893-1977
Wood engraver, painter and book illustrator. He was born in Kensington on 11 April 1893, the brother of Paul Nash (q.v.) with whom he worked. He received no formal training but was encouraged by Paul and exhibited with him at the Dorien Leigh Gallery, South Kensington, 1913. He was a founder member of the Society of Wood Engravers, 1920. Although he falls outside the general scope of this book, he is listed for his influence, together with that of his brother, on turn of the century wood engraving. He exhibited frequently in London at the Royal Academy and was elected member in 1951.
[For a book list see Houfe; see also Garrett]

NASH, Joseph 1808-78
Occasional draughtsman on wood, lithographer and watercolourist. He was born in Great Marlow, Buckinghamshire on 17 December 1808 (DNB, 1809), and studied architecture under Augustus Pugin, who took him to Paris to prepare his Paris and Its Environs, 1830. Nash also drew figure subjects within architectural settings illustrating poets and novelists; for this he was included by Bohn in Chatto and Jackson as a painter who occasionally drew on wood. His most noted wood engraved drawings were to E.A.MacDermott's Merrie Days of England, 1858-59, published with drawings by Birket Foster, G.Thomas and E.Corbould (qq.v.). He also exhibited at the Old Watercolour Society, where he was elected member in 1842, and at the British Institution, the New Watercolour Society and the Royal Academy. In later years his output declined due to illness and he died in Bayswater on 19 December 1878. His son was the painter of marine subjects Joseph Nash, Junior (q.v.). He signed his work: 'J.N.'.
[DNB; Chatto; Bryan; Houfe; TB (with bibliography); Nagler; for lithographs see Volume I]

NASH, Joseph, Junior ?-1922
Illustrator for wood engravings, painter of marine and landscape subjects. He was the son of the noted draughtsman Joseph Nash (q.v.) and worked in London from 1859, later at Bedford Park. He began work illustrating for wood engravings in The Graphic, 1872-1902, choosing primarily shipping subjects. He was elected RI in 1886 and also exhibited at the Royal Academy, the Royal Hibernian Academy and the Royal Institute of Painters in Oil-Colours. He died in 1922.

NASH, Paul 1889-1946
Wood engraver, illustrator, designer and landscape
painter. He was born in London on 11 May 1889, the
elder brother of John Nash (1893-1977), also a wood
engraver (q.v.). He was educated at St Pauls, then
part-time at the Chelsea Polytechnic, taking evening
classes at Bolt Court Street, then the Slade. He held
his first exhibition of drawings at the Carfax Gallery,
1911-12. He became a noted war artist, and after the
war shared a studio with his brother. In 1919 he
engraved his first work on wood, Disuse, and was
elected member of the Society of Wood Engravers in
1921. He exhibited frequently in London, notably
wood engravings at the Redfern Gallery,1928. His
last dated wood engraved print was in 1930. He died
in Boscombe, Hampshire on 11 July 1946.
[For a bibliography see Houfe; also Paul Nash, Poet
and Painter,1955; Garrett; A.Posten, Complete
Graphic Work of Paul Nash,1973]

NASH, Thomas fl.1864-74
Draughtsman illustrator, who contributed drawings
for wood engravings to the Broadway,1867-74.

NAST, Thomas 1840-1902
Draughtsman caricaturist, who was born in Landau
on 27 September 1840 of German parents. He was
taken to New York in 1846 where he began as a
magazine illustrator for various American press
publications, being self-taught. He worked there for
Frank Leslie's Illustrated Magazine from 1855, and
in 1860 came to England for the New York Illustrated
Newspaper to cover sporting events. His drawings
were also snapped up by Henry Vizetelly (q.v.) for his
Illustrated Times,1860; and also for the Illustrated
London News,1860-61. Later his caricatures
appeared in Vanity Fair,1872. He returned to
America in 1861, where he fought in the Civil War
and became a leading political cartoonist of his age,
'noted for the power of his images and his draughtsmanship' (Houfe). He died on 7 December 1902 in
Guayaquil, Ecuador.
[TB; Bénézit; Clement; Houfe]

NAUMANN, Paul Hermann 1851-?
German reproductive wood engraver, born in Leipzig
on 25 October 1851. He attended the Dresden Academy,
where he later taught. He appeared as a wood engraver
in the London directories at 69 later 65 and
71 Pentonville Road, N (POD,1896-97). During this
time he worked in collaboration with R.Taylor and
Company (q.v.). Naumann was best known for his
portrait engravings, often after photographs, which
appeared in the Illustrated London News,1888-95,
Queen,1892, Strand Magazine, and the Magazine of
Art,1889. His most notable portraits included 'Our
Literary Contributors - Past and Present', a series
of thirty-two heads, Illustrated London News ,1892;
'Tennyson Family', a series after photographs,

Illustrated London News,1892; Thomas Carlyle,
after G.F.Watts,Illustrated London News,1892;
Gladstone, aged eighty-three, after W.B.Richmond,
Magazine of Art,1889. These are in the British
Museum collections. Naumann signed his work:
'P.N.' or 'P.Naumann' or 'P.N. & R.T.' (R.Taylor).
[Hake; TB]

NAVELLIER, Narcisse fl.1870s
French wood engraver, born in Marly. He was the pupil
of Belhotte and made his Salon début in 1876. Gusman
explained that he often engraved in association with
Adrien Marie (q.v.) after drawings by Garnier.
Navellier is listed here for his double-page engraving,
'Salut aux Blessés' after Edouard Detaille, which was
published as a supplement to the Illustrated London
News,16 June 1877. The engraving style was skilful
enough to reproduce the various painterly surfaces of
the original Detaille work, and incorporated irregular
parallel lines or set figures against stark white backgrounds, for the purpose of clarity.
[Gusman; Bénézit; TB]

NEALE, Edward c1833-1904
Draughtsman on wood, illustrator of birds, born the
son of a grocer in Speenhamland, Berkshire, where
he was baptised in May 1833. He established himself
as a bird and animal artist, with paintings of birds
exhibited at the British Institution, the Royal Academy
and the Society of British Artists from 1858-80. He
is listed here for his eleven signed drawings of birds
to the new edition of Yarrell's History of British
Birds,1871-85, wood engraved by R.C.West,
Madame Pearson, and the Dalziel Brothers (qq.v.).
Houfe claims that he illustrated for the Illustrated
London News,1899. He worked in London where he
died, a life-long bachelor, on 11 November 1904.
The British Museum owns proof engravings after his
designs for the Dalziel Brothers,1861-62, including
cuts to Wood's Natural History,1862.
[C.Jackson; Houfe]

NESBIT, Charlton 1775-1838
Wood engraver and draughtsman on wood. He was
born in Swalwell, near Gateshead in Durham in 1775,
the son of a keelman. He was apprenticed to the
Newcastle wood engraver, Thomas Bewick (q.v.),
from 5 June 1790-97, where he worked on the first
volume of Bewick's British Birds, drawing and
engraving a bird's nest for the preface. He also
engraved the majority of vignettes and tailpieces to
Poems by Goldsmith and Parnell,1795; and to Le
Grand's Fabliaux,1796, 1800 (see I.Bain, Thomas
Bewick Vignettes,1978). At the end of his apprenticeship he engraved a memorial block to his fellow
pupil, Robert Johnson (q.v.), who had died in 1796,
and about a year later (1799, Chatto) he published for
Johnson's parents a large engraving of St Nicholas'
Church from one of Johnson's watercolours. It

measured 15" x 12", was engraved from twelve blocks and mounted on a cast-iron plate, and at the time was declared one of the largest wood engravings 'ever attempted in the present mode'. (A copy is in the British Museum.) Nesbit presented a copy to the Society of Arts, who presented him with a silver palette premium. W.J.Linton described it as 'a very astonishing performance in those ante-illustrated-news days'. Nesbit left for London about 1799, where he set up in Fetter Lane and established a reputation for skilful engraving after the most prominent draughtsmen of the day. Bewick seemed to take some pride in the fact that his old apprentice succeeded in London. He described him as 'The first of my pupils, who made a figure in London, after my Brother...' and noted the reason for Nesbit's success: 'he went at the nick of time, when wood cuts seemed to claim something like universal attention & fortunately for that Art it was under the guidance of the ingenious John Thurston who pencilled his designs stroke by stroke on the wood, with the utmost accuracy, & it would appear that Nesbit was the first, by his mechanical excellence, to do justice to these designs'. His work after Thurston (q.v.) included a frontispiece to Bloomfield's Farmer's Boy, 1800; and cuts to Grey's edition of Butler's Hudibras, 1801. A collection of these in the British Museum is marked, 'Engraved by Nesbit but "finished" by Bewick at 6/-'. Linton divided Nesbit's engraving career into early pre-1805 works, during which time he was awarded a second silver medal by the Society of Arts, 1802; then by 1806 he had reached maturity with engravings after William Marshall Craig (q.v.) to Scripture Illustrated, 1806; and Wallis and Scholey's edition of Hume's History of England. He engraved with Branston and Clennell (qq.v.) head and tailpieces to Cowper's Poems, 1808; and his most ambitious work, again after Thurston's drawings, to Ackermann's Religious Emblems, 1809, was engraved with fellow Bewick pupils Clennell and Hole (qq.v.). He engraved two cuts in Puckle's The Club, 1817, and a specimen block, 'Rinaldo and Armida', after Thurston's drawing, which was published by William Savage in his Practical Hints on Decorative Printing, 1818, and considered by Savage to be one of the two (alongside work of Robert Branston, Senior) finest specimens of wood engraving ever produced. (The block was later restored by G.W.Bonner (q.v.).) Most references note that Nesbit remained in London until 1815, although he appeared in London directories as late as 1817, then working in Chelsea (Johnstone, 1817). He returned to his native Swalwell, after coming into an inheritance, and there continued to engrave sporadically until 1830, mostly for London and Newcastle booksellers. His most notable engravings during this last period were a portrait of his master Bewick, after Nicholson, published in Charnley's Select Fables, 1820; and the excellent series of seven cuts after William Harvey's drawings to Northcote's

Fables, 1828, several of which are now in the British Museum. He returned briefly to London in 1830 to work upon the second Northcote series, 1833 (which Chatto called his best); also upon Harvey's designs to Blind Beggar of Bethnal Green, 1832; White's Selbourne, 1836; and Latrobe's Scripture Illustrations, 1838. It was during his return to London that he died, at Queen's Elm, Brompton on 11 November 1838, aged sixty-three. Nesbit's reputation as a skilful engraver, particularly after Thurston and Harvey, continued after his death. W.H.Linton in Masters of Wood Engraving, 1889, placed him alongside the influential Luke Clennell, praised his later work for its 'finish', and claimed the second series of Northcote's Fables and White's Selbourne engravings were the best of his later work: 'Nothing can be more daintily sweet in line than the cuts in these two books'. Redgrave claimed that 'He attained a broad, clever style, his textures were variously and truly rendered, and great brilliancy of effect preserved. His figures were well drawn and simply treated'. But the DNB offered the most succinct assessment: 'As a wood-engraver pure and simple, he was the best of Bewick's pupils'. The British Museum owns a large collection of his work after W.M.Craig, W.Harvey and J.Thurston. He signed his work: 'CN' (superimposed), 'C Nesbit' (script). [For a list of illustrations and engravings see DNB; Linton, Masters of Wood Engraving; for Bewick connections see I.Bain in Bewick Memoir, 1975, Thomas Bewick Vignettes, 1978; T.Bewick catalogue, Laing Art Gallery, 1979; see also Chatto; Nagler; Redgrave; Houfe; C.T.Lewis; Bryan; British Library catalogue]

NESFIELD, William Eden 1835-88
Draughtsman and architect, the son of the artist William Andrews Nesfield. He was much associated with the romantic Victorian country house ideal and Richard Norman Shaw. He illustrated his own Specimens of Medieval Architecture, 1862. The British Museum owns a proof of his design engraved on wood by the Dalziel Brothers (q.v.), 1862.

NEWITT
(see Barford and Newitt)

NEWMAN, Frederick E. fl.1880s
Provincial wood engraver, who worked at Ponder's End, Middlesex (Kelly's, 1880).

NEWMAN, William fl.1842-64
Draughtsman of comic cuts, best known for his work in Punch, 1846-50. He had been introduced to Punch by his friend, the wood engraver Ebenezer Landells (q.v.) and for some time he was the most prolific draughtsman on wood for the magazine: he made eighty-seven cuts in 1846, 127 in 1847, 164 in 1848 and 121 in 1849. His numerous silhouettes, called

'blackies', were pictorial puns in the style of
Thomas Hood, for which he was paid 18s a dozen.
Spielmann described Newman as an unfortunate
individual: 'He was a very poor man, who in point
of payment for his work suffered more than the rest;
and when he asked for a slight increase in terms, he
was met with a refusal on the ground that "Mr Leech
required such high prices"'. He was not popular
with the Punch staff, who did not care to associate
with him because of his poor breeding and common
manners. His other drawings appeared in the Squib,
1842; Puppet Show; Diogenes; and Comic News, 1864.
During this time the wood engraver Edmund Evans
(q.v.) admired his 'very free pencil, but rather
coarse', style. Dissatisfied with his career in England,
Newman emigrated to the United States, where he was
better paid for work for various magazines during the
1860s. Spielmann concluded that 'He had a greater
sense of beauty and a more refined touch than most
of his colleagues; and though he did not shine as a
satirist, he was always well in the spirit of Punch'.
[Spielmann; Evans Reminiscences; Houfe]

NICHOLAS
(see Myerson and Nicholas)

NICHOLL, Andrew 1804-86
Irish draughtsman illustrator and landscape painter.
He was born in Belfast in 1804, trained as a newspaper printer on the Northern Whig, and taught
himself to draw and paint. He was elected ARHA,
1837, and RHA, 1860; but worked in London from
1840, where he exhibited at the Royal Academy,
1832-54, and other galleries until 1864. He moved to
Ceylon in 1846, where he taught drawing at the
Columbo Academy, and sent back two half-page
drawings, 'Sketches in Ceylon', which appeared as
wood engravings in the Illustrated London News,
5 July 1851. His work as an illustrator began with
landscape views to the Dublin Penny Journal, about
109 drawings from July 1832 onwards; also plates to
Views of the Dublin and Kingston Railway, Dublin, 1835,
engraved by Robert Clayton; and drawings to S.C.Hall's
Ireland Its Scenery and Character, 1841. He died in
in London on 16 April 1886. The British Museum
owns proof engravings by the Dalziel Brothers (q.v.),
1839-47.
[TB; Bénézit; Strickland; Houfe]

NICHOLLS, D.F. fl.1860s
Wood engraver, who engraved cuts to the short-lived
magazine, Sunday at Home, 1869. These appeared
alongside drawings of Charles Green (q.v.).

NICHOLLS, George Pike and John fl.1841-87
London wood engravers, who worked for some of the
most important publications of the mid-century.
George Pike Nicholls first appeared in the London
directories, at 53 Paternoster Row (POD, 1845-49).

He was then joined by John Nicholls as J. and
G.P.Nicholls, at 54 Paternoster Row (POD, 1855-57),
then at Aldine Chambers, 13 Paternoster Row
(POD, 1858-78), then at 17 Holborn Viaduct, EC
(POD, 1879-86), premises shared with the wood
engraver T.Williams (q.v.). George Nicholls
engraved from the 1840s onwards, namely cuts to
Contes des Fossoyeurs, after a German artist;
cuts to Charles Knight's Penny Magazine, after
Wells in June 1841, and after Elmes in December
1841; cuts to S.C.Hall's Book of British Ballads,
1842, after J.Franklin and H.J.Townsend; vignettes
to an edition of Sterne's A Sentimental Journey; and
cuts for Curmur's The Beaux Arts. His half-page
engraving, 'The Covenant of Judas', after J.Franklin's
painting, Illustrated London News, 13 April 1850, was
wood engraved in a rather poor imitation of etched
or steel engraved line, heavy-handed and too varied
to be successful, despite an even-ruled background.
Nevertheless, George Nicholls was competent
enough to exhibit three engravings at the Royal Academy,
1870-73: 'English landscape', 1870; a landscape after
B.W.Leader, 1872; and 'Pont-y-Pant on the River
Lledr', after G.W.Gill, 1873. Among the collaboration
engravings of J. and G.P.Nicholls were full-page
reproductions like 'The Lake of Como', after a drawing
by T.A.Aylmer; and a series of sketches, 'An Artist's
Rambles from Antwerp to Rome', both for the Art
Journal, 1853. The British Museum owns George
Nicholls' work after J.Gilbert, P.Macquoid,
J.Thorne, and his proof of 'Chester' for Charles
Knight's 'Land we Live In' series. He signed his work:
'NICHOLLS', 'G P NICHOLLS', 'G P N' (script).
[Gusman; TB; Bénézit; LeBlanc; Bodleian Library]

NICHOLLS, John
(see Nicholls, George)

NICHOLLS, William Alfred 1816-?
English wood engraver, born in London in 1816. He
worked in Leipzig in 1840 and joined with John
Allanson (q.v.) there, as Allanson and Nicholls.
This firm was quite possessive about its development
of English wood engraving techniques in an alien and
inferior German engraving environment: Muir
records how one budding German engraver was
turned away by the firm 'with an abrupt refusal even
to let him see any stage of their work in progress'.
Nicholls was competent as an engraver of Ludwig
Richter's (q.v.) work.
[J.F.Hoff, Ludwig Richter, 1877; Bénézit; TB;
Nagler; P.Muir, Victorian Illustrated Books,
p.216]

NICHOLSON, Isaac 1789-1848
Newcastle wood engraver. He was born in Melmerby,
Cumberland in 1789, and apprenticed to the
Newcastle wood engraver Thomas Bewick (q.v.)
from 18 May 1804 - 6 July 1811. During that period

he and fellow apprentice Edward Willis (q.v.) engraved tailpieces to an edition of Burns' Poems, 1808. Bewick seemed pleased with Nicholson's copyist skills; later in his autobiography he described Nicholson as 'both a good apprentice & a good artist--his engravings on wood are clearly, or honestly cut, as well as being accurately done from his patterns'. However, he proved a rather mechanical, uninspired engraver who, after leaving his apprenticeship and setting up on his own in Newcastle, opposite Bewick's workshop, was scolded by Bewick for copying his work and passing it off as his own. His engravings appeared in Charnely's Select Fables, 1820; followed by his most successful cuts, vignettes to Charnely's Fisher's Garland, 1822-42 (work often incorrectly attributed to Bewick). He also engraved Flower's Heraldic Visitation of the County of Durham, 1820; cuts to Sharp's History of the Rebellion; a History of England; Robinson Crusoe; and Watts' Hymns. He is perhaps best known as the instructor of that influential mid-century wood engraver, Ebenezer Landells (q.v.), and he also apprenticed Charles Gray (q.v.). He died on 18 October 1848, aged fifty-nine.
[Redgrave; Bénézit; TB (as 'Isaak'); Bryan; Slater; I.Bain, Thomas Bewick, 1979; Bewick Memoir]

NICHOLSON, Thomas Henry ?-1870
Wood engraver, draughtsman illustrator, and sculptor. He worked in London, where he began drawing and wood engraving for various magazines and established a reputation for his skilful drawings of horses. These caught the attention of Henry Vizetelly (q.v.) who commissioned drawings for his Illustrated Times, 1855-59, and later recalled that 'He was a crack draughtsman of horses, delineating them with considerable spirit, but in a rather conventional style' (Glances Back, p.391). He had also contributed to the Illustrated London News, 1848, and became the principal artist for wood engravings in Cassell's Illustrated Family Paper, 1853-57. He also illustrated the books Faces in the Fire, 1850, and Works of Shakespeare, n.d. (wood engraved by C.W.Sheeres (q.v.)). He was patronised by Count Alfred d'Orsay, in whose Gore House studio he worked as an equestrian sculptor, but by 1848 he had turned to wood engraving again. Redgrave concluded, 'but of a shy and retired disposition, he did not enjoy the credit which his works deserved'. He died in Portland, Hampshire in 1870.
[TB; Bénézit; Bryan; Redgrave; Houfe; Graves; Vizetelly, Glances Back]

NICHOLSON, Sir William 1872-1949
Wood engraver, illustrator and painter. He was born in Newark-on-Trent in 1872, the son of W.N.Nicholson, MP and studied at Julian's in Paris and at the Herkomer School in Bushey in 1888. From about 1894 Nicholson joined with his brother-in-law James Pryde (q.v.) as

'The Beggarstaff Brothers' and together they experimented with a series of French-inspired posters and books illustrated with woodcuts hand coloured, then lithographed. The total object was designed as a unit after the manner of the early chapbooks they so admired. Nicholson made his early appearance as a woodcut artist (using the side rather than the end grain of the block) in the influential magazine, the Dome, 1897, in which he cut 'A Fisher', a bold, expressive portrait of a mackintoshed fisherman which was cut from four blocks. This exploited the technique of stark, almost total white background and the evocative, suggestive qualities of overall blackness, from which the figure seems to emerge. This became a hallmark of Nicholson's woodcut style, one he used in his justly famous colour woodcut portraits, of Queen Victoria, Kaiser Wilhelm II, Bismarck, and Cecil Rhodes. Most of his experimentation with woodcut illustrations came before 1900, although he contributed spasmodically until the 1920s, notably illustrations to Siegfried Sassoon's Memoirs of a Fox-Hunting Man, 1929. His work then included: Tony Drum, 1898; An Alphabet, 1898; Rudyard Kipling's An Almanac of Twelve Sports, 1898; W.E.Henley's London Types, 1898; Arthur Waugh's Square Book of Animals, 1899; Characters of Romance, 1900; W.H.Davies' Moss and Feather, 1928; Pirate Twins; and endpapers for Lady Horner's Time Remembered, 1930. Nicholson's later career was almost entirely spent painting portraits. He exhibited at the Fine Art Society, the Grosvenor Gallery, the New English Art Club, the Royal Hibernian Academy, the Royal Institute of Painters in Oil-Colours, the Royal Scottish Academy, and the Royal Scottish Watercolour Society, and was elected RP in 1909. He was knighted in 1936, lived in Rottingdean, Sussex from 1920, and died in 1949.
[For a complete bibliography see TB; also Idler, Vol.8, pp.519-28; Studio, 12, 1897, pp.177-83 (G.White on Nicholson's Colour Prints); 53, 1911, pp.3-11 (A.L.Baldry on Nicholson's paintings); see also M.Steen, William Nicholson; Houfe; Garrett]

NICOL, Erskine 1825-1904
Occasional draughtsman, illustrator, painter of Irish genre works. He was born in Leith on 3 July 1825, and at the age of twelve was trained at the Trustees Academy and studied under W.Allen and Thomas Duncan. He worked as a drawing master in Leith, then moved to Dublin in 1846, where he established his reputation for painted Irish scenes. He settled in London in 1862, although he made frequent return visits to Ireland for material. He contributed two genre drawings on wood to the influential magazine Good Words, 1860, the full-page 'Mary Macdonell and Her Friends' 'being most probably, a thoroughly good sketch, but here again

the translator [i.e. wood engraver] has produced
hard scratchy lines that fail to suggest the freer play
of pencil or pen, whichever it was that produced the
original', claimed White. Nicol then turned most of
his attention to painting for the galleries, exhibiting
from 1851 at the Royal Scottish Academy, where he
was elected member in 1859, and the Royal Academy,
where he was elected ARA in 1868. He also exhibited
in Edinburgh from 1851-62. He returned as an
illustrator in the early 1900s with A.M.Hall's
Tales of Irish Life and Character,1909, and
W.Harvey's Irish Life and Humour,1909, both
published posthumously. He died in Feltham on
8 March 1904. The British Museum owns proofs of
his designs engraved by the Dalziel Brothers (q.v.),
1854.
[Wood; DNB; Bénézit; TB; Houfe; White]

NIEUWENKAMP, Wynard Otto Jan 1874-?
Dutch born wood engraver, etcher, lithographer and
painter, praised by the wood engraver G.Mackley as
one of the leading figures in the late nineteenth
century revival of wood engraving. His work is often
linked in influence with that of Bernard Sleigh,
Robert Bryden and Louise Glazier (qq.v.). Nieuwenkamp
was born in Amsterdam on 27 July 1874 and largely
self-taught as an artist. He exhibited his first wood
engraving in 1899, and received an honourable
mention at the Paris Salon,1900. It was in this year
that he had engraved three Dutch and Belgian scenes
for reproduction in the influential Dome magazine. By
1927 his output included seventy-six wood engravings,
twenty-five lithographs and 200 etchings. After 1920
he turned to line engraving, which he practised in
Italy. He signed his wood engravings: 'W O J N'.
[For a discussion of his prints see Print Collector's
Quarterly,1930,pp.332-51; also Mackley,p.112;
Bénézit; TB]

NIGHTINGALE, Charles Thrupp
Woodcut artist. The British Museum owns a series
of competent woodcut borders and figure designs
done by this artist. They are inspired by the
medievalism of William Morris, using plant forms
and interlace, and probably done c1900. They are
signed: 'CTN'.

NISBET, Thomas fl.1880-1900
Glasgow wood engraver, who worked at 166 Buchanan
Street, Glasgow (Kelly's,1880), then 95 Hutcheson
Street (Kelly's,1889), and finally 62 St Vincent
Street (Kelly's,1900). His advertisement in Kelly's
directory claimed that he was an engraver on wood
and zincographer, who specialised in large
illustrations for walls. The British Museum owns
a small, dark wood engraving 'Judas Betrayeth Christ'
after John Martin, attributed to T.Nesbitt (sic), but
most probably engraved by Nisbet..

NORBURY, Edwin Arthur 1849-1918
Draughtsman illustrator for wood engravings,
illustrator and painter. He was born in Liverpool in
1849, where he was educated at Dr Wand's School.
When fifteen years old he began to contribute
drawings on wood to the Illustrated London News,
and Henry Vizetelly's Illustrated Times. Later he
joined The Graphic as an artist correspondent,
sending sketches of various events for wood
engraving. He acted as 'Special Artist' during the
Franco-Siamese War,1893. He lived in North Wales,
1875-90, taught art in Siam in 1892 and was a
founding member of the Royal Cambrian Academy.
He later illustrated Ernest Young's Kingdom of the
Yellow Robe,1898; Arabian Nights' Entertainments,
1899; and Animal Arts and Crafts. He exhibited
paintings at the Royal Academy, the Royal Cambrian
Academy, the Royal Hibernian Academy, the Royal
Institute of Painters in Watercolours, and the Royal
Institute of Painters in Oil-Colours. He ran his own
Norbury Sketching School and St James' Life School
in Chelsea. He also served as Principal of the Henry
Blackburn Studio and died in London on 16 October
1918.

NORMAN, William St Claire fl.1883-84
Wood engraver, who worked in London with
G.F.Frasher (q.v.) at 42 Essex Street, Strand,
WC (POD,1883-84).

NORMAN, William Thomas fl.1844-49
London wood engraver, who worked at
28 Aldermanbury (POD,1844-46), then 15 Low
Whiters Street (POD,1848-49). He may be related
to the landscape painter W.T.Norman, who exhibited
paintings in London from 1834-42.
[TB; Bénézit; Graves]

NORMAND, B.
Draughtsman on wood, who contributed drawings
of Italy which were wood engraved in the Illustrated
London News,1847.

NORTH, John William 1842-1924
Draughtsman on wood, watercolourist and landscape
painter. He was born near London in 1842 and
apprenticed to the wood engraver J.W.Whymper
(q.v.) where he met fellow students Charles Green,
Frederick Walker and G.J.Pinwell (qq.v.). While
there he suffered under Whymper's doctrinaire
manner, forced mainly to copy drawings onto wood
blocks, generally after Birket Foster's (q.v.)
nature drawings. He later claimed that 'all the art
teaching he ever got at the Whymper's was that
when a subject was given him, a print of one of
Foster's was placed before him, with instructions
to make his drawings in that manner'. Dissatisfied
with Whymper as an employer, he was introduced
by G.J.Pinwell to the Dalziel Brothers (q.v.) and

given a series of private commissions for books they
proposed to produce themselves. These included
A Round of Days, 1865; Poems of Jean Ingelow, 1867;
and the most successful Wayside Poesies, 1867, all
of which North illustrated with brush drawings of
extreme delicacy, which the Dalziels adequately
engraved on wood blocks. But as Forrest Reid points
out, North's delicate brushwork could never be wood
engraved totally successfully. Such work set North up
as a prolific draughtsman illustrator for numerous
'Sixties School' publications: English Sacred Poetry
of the Olden Time, 1864; Our Life Illustrated by Pen
and Pencil, 1864; Touches of Nature by Eminent Artists,
1866; Longfellow's Poems, 1866; Spirit of Praise, 1867;
Months Illustrated with Pen and Pencil; and the gift
book Illustrated Book of Sacred Poems, 1867. He also
illustrated the influential magazines Good Words,
1866; Sunday Magazine, 1865-67; and Once a Week,
1866-67. Later he illustrated Richard Jeffries'
'Summer in Somerset', for the English Illustrated
Magazine, 1887. These drawings were wood engraved
by J.D.Cooper, H.F.Davey, T.W.Lascelles,
W. and R.Cheshire, and J.A.Quartley (qq.v.). Much
of this illustration work was probably done to support
North's greater ambition, to exhibit successfully
paintings of country landscapes in the London galleries.
He moved to Somerset in 1868 to collect material
for works exhibited, but it was not until 1871 that
he was elected ACWS, later RWS in 1883, and
finally his greatest ambition, ARA, in 1893. He
also exhibited at the Fine Art Society, the Grosvenor
Gallery, the New Gallery, the Royal Hibernian
Academy and the Royal Scottish Watercolour Society.
He spent the later years of his life patenting and
marketing a special watercolour paper which
impoverished him. He died in Washford on 20 December
1924. The British Museum owns proofs of his designs
engraved by the Dalziel Brothers, 1863-64,
including cuts to Goldsmith's Work, and Ballad Stories,
1863-67.
[TB; Bénézit; Sketchley; White; Reid; Hardie; Dalziels'
Record]

NORTH, Samuel William fl.1870s
London wood engraver, who appeared in the London
directories once. He listed his office at 29 Maddox
Street, W (POD, 1873).

NORTHCOTE, James 1746-1831
Draughtsman illustrator, painter of portraits and
author. He was born in Plymouth in 1746 and
apprenticed to a watchmaker before coming to London
in 1771 to become Joshua Reynolds' assistant. He
studied at the Royal Academy Schools, and in Italy in
1777, and set up as a successful London portrait
painter in 1780, being elected ARA in 1786, and RA
in the following year. He also exhibited at the British
Institution and the Royal Society of British Artists.
Towards the end of his career he turned to painting

animals and to writing a standard life of Reynolds,
1813, and Conversations, published by William
Hazlitt in 1830. Northcote is listed here for his
280 wood engraved illustrations to an edition of
One Hundred Fables, 1828, published in London,
printed by J.Johnson. These animal and
landscape vignettes, head and tailpieces come
nearest to Bewick's own work, and were wood
engraved by the most prominent engravers of the
day, notably G.W.Bonner (thirteen cuts), F.W.Branston
(four cuts), R.Branston (ten cuts), D.Dodd (three
cuts), J.Dodd (two cuts), J.Jackson (148 cuts),
Jackson and Smith (one cut), A.J.Mason (four cuts),
T.Mosses (eight cuts), C.Nesbit (seven cuts),
M.U.Sears (three cuts), S.Slader (nineteen cuts),
J.Smith (twenty-nine cuts), Elizabeth Thompson
(two cuts), H.White (thirteen cuts), H.White, Junior
(two cuts), J.Wright (one cut) and T.Williams (two
cuts) (qq.v.). Northcote's illustration method was to
clip figures of animals from books and papers and
paste them down, filling in pencil backgrounds. These
were set at the head of each fable, and then drawings
were 'most excellently drawn on wood, and prepared
for the engravers by Mr William Harvey, one of the
most distinguished artists in his profession; and
many of them have been improved by his skill', according to Northcote in the book's introduction. Harvey
(q.v.) also designed and drew all tailpieces and initial
letters. The style of these engravings combined the
popular black-line technique with the newer white-
line effects. They are most striking for the engravers'
understanding of light, in objects such as glow worms,
mirrors, metal pieces and the sunlight in landscapes.
All were originally planned as oval headpieces.
After Northcote's death, a second edition, the Artist's
Book of Fables, 1833, appeared with wood engravings
again under the direction of William Harvey.
[Redgrave; Houfe; Bryan]

NUGENT, John fl.1871-74
London wood engraver, who worked at 310 Strand,
WC (POD, 1871-73). His engravings appeared in the
Illustrated London News, notably the full-page 'A
Water Seller at Cairo', after W.J.Webb, 12 September
1874. He signed his engravings: 'Nugent sc'.

OAKLEY, William Harold fl.1887-1925
Draughtsman, illustrator, and architect. He practised
as an architect in London 1881-88 and during this
time drew architectural subjects for wood engravings
in the English Illustrated Magazine, 1887-92; also
the Strand Magazine, 1891.

OAKMAN, John c1748-93
One of the late eighteenth century wood engravers,
whose work for children's books 'and cheap literature'
(DNB) influenced the rising generation of new wood
engravers. He was born about 1748 in Hendon,

Middlesex and apprenticed to the map engraver
Emanuel Bowen. He set up his own shop in the
Haymarket, selling prints, later engraving
illustrations on wood for various children's books,
engraved 'with some ability' (Redgrave). The failure
of his shop led him to write 'several worthless and
disreputable novels' (DNB) and various ballads. He
died 'in distress' in December 1793.
[DNB; Redgrave; Bénézit; TB; Bryan; Gentleman's
Magazine,1793,p.1080]

O'BRIEN, L.R. 1832-99
Draughtsman illustrator, born on 15 August 1832. He
contributed drawings to F.Pollock's 'Clovelly', for
the English Illustrated Magazine,1884, which were
wood engraved by J.D.Cooper, E.Ohme, J.A.Quartley,
E.Gascoine, R.Paterson, and A.C.Coats (qq.v.).
O'Brien died in Toronto, Canada on 13 December 1899.
[Bénézit]

O'CONNOR, J. fl.1880s
Draughtsman illustrator of topographical subjects. He
contributed illustrations to Austin Dobson's series of
London scenes in the English Illustrated Magazine,
1884, wood engraved by J.D.Cooper (q.v.). He may
be John O'Connor, ARHA,(1830-89), a popular landscape and theatrical scenery painter.
[Strickland]

OFFOR, Edward fl.1880
London draughtsman on wood, who worked at
24 Bucklersbury, EC (Kelly's,1880).

OFFORD, John James fl.1860-86
Occasional draughtsman on wood of figure subjects.
He contributed these to the Illustrated London News,
1860. He also exhibited at the Royal Academy, 1886.
Fincham lists the bookplate designer, engraver,
'Offord, of Ipswich, Essex', who engraved a crest
design for Reverend W.Nassau St Leger, signed
'Offord sc Ipswich' and dated 1860.

OHME, E.J. fl.1883-86
Wood engraver, who worked for the English Illustrated
Magazine,1883-86. His engravings here were primarily
after paintings: by J.Downman,1884; W.J.Hennessy,
1885; Gainsborough and P.Macnab, both 1885; and the
topographical work, 'Newcastle from the River', after
R.Jobling,1886. His work was not especially good
with proportions and he cut outlines in a bold if not
crude manner which could destroy the delicacy of a
face (for instance, P.Macnab's 'Peat Gathering',
1885). He signed his engravings: 'E.Ohme'.

OLIVER, Lieutenant Samuel P.
Amateur draughtsman and Royal Artillery officer. He
drew for wood engravings in the Illustrated London
News,1867.

ONWHYN, Thomas ?-1886
Comic draughtsman for wood engravings, and prolific
etcher. He was born in London about 1820, the
youngest son of Joseph Onwhyn, a bookseller and
publisher of the magazine Owl,1864. Onwhyn began
illustrating with illegitimate drawings to an edition
of Dickens' Pickwick Papers,1837, signed 'Sam
Weller', followed by Nicholas Nickleby,1838, both
drawn in the style of H.K.Browne and George
Cruikshank (qq.v.). He was taken on by Punch, where
he contributed several cuts from 1847-48. 'But
Onwhyn was better used to the etching-needle than
the pencil, and his drawing on wood was hard and
unsympathetic, and his figures were usually rather
strained than funny,' according to Spielmann. He
continued to etch illustrations for various books under
the pseudonym Peter Palette, and even etched other
artists' works, for instance, W.H.Holmes' drawings to
Oakleigh,1843. He also drew scenery for guidebooks
and letter paper, but abandoned his artistic work for
the last twenty to thirty years of his life. He died in
London on 5 January 1886. A small vignette wood
engraved, signed 'F. (sic) Onwhyn', of 'Mademoiselle
Caroline at Vauxhall' appeared in the Illustrated
London News,27 August 1842.
[DNB; Bénézit; TB; Houfe; Bodleian Library]

ORCHARDSON, Sir William Quiller 1836-1910
Occasional draughtsman on wood, painter of genre
pictures and portraits. He was born in Edinburgh in
1836, entered the Trustees Academy in 1850 and then
moved to London in 1863 where he first exhibited
Shakespearean subjects at the Royal Academy. Also
during this period he drew on wood for Good Words,
notably nine drawings poorly engraved by F.Borders
(q.v.),1860-61, and again in 1878. He also appeared
in the compilation volume Touches of Nature,1866.
Orchardson was best known for his High Life paintings
which he exhibited to great success at the Grosvenor
Gallery, the New Gallery and the Royal Academy.
He was elected ARA in 1868 and RA in 1877. He also
exhibited at the Royal Hibernian Academy and the
Royal Scottish Academy. He was knighted in 1907
and died on 13 April 1910. The British Museum owns
a proof engraving by the Dalziel Brothers (q.v.),
1864.
[Wood; TB; Bénézit; DNB; Houfe]

ORDOYNO, Allamby fl.1872-80
Provincial wood engraver, who worked at 10 Ann
Street, Birmingham (Kelly's,1872), later 9 Upper
Priory, Birmingham (Kelly's,1876-80).

O'REILLY, Rear-Admiral Montague Frederick
1822-88
Amateur draughtsman for wood engravings, who
contributed numerous sketches of the Crimean War
to the Illustrated London News,1854-56. He explained
these in the 21 October 1854 issue, and was given a

fitting obituary in the 7 June 1888 issue.

ORRINSMITH, Harvey
(see Smith, Harvey Orrin)

ORRINSMITH, John
(see Smith, John Orrin)

OSWIN, Arthur fl.1869-72
London wood engraver, who worked at 16 Beaufort
Buildings (POD,1869-72). He shared these premises
with E.S.Gascoine and J.Lee (qq.v.).

OUTHWAITE, Jean Jacques fl.1836-77
English wood engraver, born in London. He was the
pupil of E.Goodall (q.v.), and worked in Paris where
he became a naturalised French citizen in 1855. He
set up as a wood engraver in Paris and collaborated
on such French magazines as the Magasin Pittoresque;
Memorial de Sainte-Hélène,1842; Notre-Dame de
Paris,1844; and L'Inde Pittoresque,1861. He exhibited
wood engravings and book illustrations at the Paris
Salon from 1836-77. He contributed in England to the
Art Journal,1855, 1857.
[Gusman; TB; Bénézit; Beraldi]

OVEREND, William Heysman 1851-98
Draughtsman illustrator for wood engravings, painter
of marine subjects. He was born in Coatham in
Yorkshire in 1851, educated at Charterhouse, and
started as a book illustrator with F.F.Moore's Fate of
the Black Swan,1865. He soon became known for drawings
of marine subjects which he contributed to the Illustrated
London News,1872-96. Among these were striking full
and double-page drawings of Arctic life, 1875, wood
engraved by W.J.Palmer (q.v.). The following year
he provided several full-page drawings of the Prince
of Wales in India, followed by the double page
'Between Decks of a Turkish Ironclad', 1877, wood
engraved again by W.J.Palmer. But it was his skill
at depicting fishermen and their gruelling life for the
magazine which secured his reputation. He also
illustrated for the English Illustrated Magazine,
1891-94; Good Words,1894; Rambler,1897; Boy's Own
Paper; Chums; Pall Mall Magazine; as well as for such
books as J.C.Hutcheson's On Board the Esmerelda,
1885; G.A.Henty's One of the 28th,1889;
R.H.S.Bacon's Benin the City of Blood,1897; and
Bret Harte's Devils Ford,1897. He also exhibited
paintings at the Royal Academy from 1872; and was
elected ROI,1886. He died in America in April 1898.
[TB; Bénézit; Houfe; Bryan; for his etchings see
Volume I]

OXLEY, Henry Mercer fl.1880s
Provincial wood engraver, who worked at 97 Bridge
Street, Manchester (Kelly's,1889).

PADGETT, William 1851-1904
Occasional draughtsman, landscape painter. He
worked in Twickenham in 1881 and Campden Hill,
London from 1882. He is listed here for his satirical
drawing, wood engraved in Punch,1882, of a spoof on
the 'greenery-yallery' fashions of the Grosvenor
Gallery with Ariadne mourning Oscar Wilde's
departure for America. He also exhibited landscape
paintings at the Grosvenor Gallery (which gave
credence to his Punch drawing); also at the New
Gallery, the Royal Academy, the Royal Society of
British Artists and the Royal Institute of Painters in
Oil-Colours.
[TB (bibliography); Bénézit; Spielmann]

PAGE, John fl.1874-1900
London wood engraver and draughtsman, who worked
at 172 Strand, WC (POD,1874-81), an office which he
shared with the wood engravers P.Grenier and
T.P.Collings (qq.v.). He then moved to 110 Hatton
Garden, EC (POD,1882-91, Kelly's,1900).

PAGE, P.N.
Architectural draughtsman for wood engravings, who
contributed a drawing for a colour-plate, wood
engraved and printed in the Illustrated London News,
1858.

PAGET, Henry Marriott 1856-1936
Draughtsman illustrator and painter. He was born in
London on 31 December 1856, the brother of artists
Sidney and Walter Paget. He entered the Royal
Academy Schools in 1874 and began drawing for wood
engravings in The Graphic,1877-1906, for which he
is listed here; followed by Quiver,1890; Illustrated
London News,1890; and Windsor Magazine. Such
work led to foreign tours, to Italy, Greece in 1879,
and Western Canada in 1909. He illustrated numerous
adventure stories: G.A.Henty's Bravest of the Brave,
1887; Walter Scott's The Talisman and Kenilworth,
1893, and Quentin Durward,1894. He continued to
work well into the twentieth century, as 'Special
Artist' to the Sphere during the Balkan War,1912-13.
He exhibited at the Fine Art Society, the Grosvenor
Gallery, the Royal Academy, the Royal Institute of
Painters in Oil-Colours and the Royal Society of
British Artists, where he was elected a member in
1889. He died in London on 27 March 1936.
[Bénézit; TB; Houfe]

PAIN, William Bowyer fl.1881-95
London wood engraver, who worked at 45 later 52
Imperial Buildings, New Bridge Street, EC
(POD,1881-83), premises shared with F.Godart
(q.v.). He moved to 319 Strand, WC (POD,1884-91),
then 62 Strand (POD,1892-95).

PALLISTER, George fl.1880-1900
Provincial wood engraver, who worked at Belgrave
Terrace, Belgrave Street, Leeds (Kelly's,1880-89)
and later as George Pallister and Sons at Albion
Street, Leeds (Kelly's,1900). They specialised in
wood engravings, 'mechanical and ornamental by
skilful artists', according to their directory
advertisement.

PALMER, Alexander fl.1889-1910
London wood engraver, draughtsman on wood. He
worked as a draughtsman on his own from 61 Fleet
Street (Kelly's,1889), then about 1891 joined forces
with Arthur Matthewson as Palmer and Matthewson
(q.v.). They retained Palmer's Fleet Street
office where they remained until the turn of the
century (Kelly's,1900).

PALMER, John fl.1856-87
Draughtsman for wood engravings and genre painter.
He specialised in industrial and theatrical scenes,
and domestic genre subjects. These he contributed
for wood engravings in Henry Vizetelly's Illustrated
Times,1856-61; and the Illustrated London News,
1864-66. His industrial scenes for the Illustrated
London News were much admired by Van Gogh. These
included his drawings in the series, 'Trades of
Sheffield', 6, 20 January and 10 March 1866. Van Gogh
called his 'Sheffield Trades: Fork Grinding',
10 March 1866, 'a marvellous thing of the steel
workers in Sheffield; it is called "The Fork Grinders".
It is in the style of Edmond Morin, that is to say, his
most compact and concise style'. Palmer also
exhibited at the Royal Academy and the Royal Society
of British Artists.
[Houfe; English Influences on Van Gogh]

PALMER, Samuel 1805-81
Occasional illustrator, wood engraver, etcher,
prominent landscape painter of visionary themes.
He was born in Newington on 27 January 1805, the
son of a bookseller, and began painting at thirteen
years old, exhibiting at the Royal Academy in 1819,
aged fourteen. He was greatly influenced by Varley,
Stothard and Linnell, but most of all by William Blake
(q.v.), who inspired not only his painting but the only
known wood engraving he made, 'a highly romantic
pastoral scene' (Chamberlain,p.51). He formed a
mystical circle of 'Ancients' at Shoreham where he
produced watercolours and etchings noted for their
poetic beauty. He turned to drawing later, and
although his work lost some of its initial intensity,
he exhibited at the Old Watercolour Society, where he
was elected member in 1856. His work also appeared
at the Royal Academy, the British Institute and the
Royal Society of British Artists. As a draughtsman
and illustrator for wood engravings, he contributed
four tiny vignettes to Dickens' Pictures from Italy,
1846, again inspired by Blake's wood engravings.

Gleeson White, however, lists Palmer as the
contributor to various 'Sixties School' publications.
His landscape drawings, in Adams' Sacred
Allegories,1856, wood engraved expertly by
W.T.Green (q.v.), brought White's rapturous
praises: 'The amazing quality of the landscapes by
Samuel Palmer stood even the test of enormous
enlargement in lantern slides, when Mr. Pennell
showed them at his lectures on the men of the sixties;
had W.T.Green engraved no other blocks, he might
be ranked as a great craftsman on the evidence of
these alone' (White,p.103). Then came drawings to
Joseph Cundall's A Book of Favourite Modern
Ballads,1860, wood engraved by Edmund Evans
(q.v.), which appeared with drawings by C.W.Cope,
J.C.Horsley and A.Solomon, and ornamental headings by Albert Warren (qq.v.), all printed uniquely with
a double process, 'black upon a previous printing in
grey, not solid, but with the "lights" carefully taken
out, so that the whole looks like a drawing on grey
paper heightened by white chalk', according to White.
Palmer's work also appeared in Household Song,1861;
and A.A.Procter's Legends and Lyrics,1865. In this
latter his work formed part of the total nineteen full
page wood engravings by Horace Harral (q.v.).
Palmer also etched: his posthumously published
Virgil's Eclogues,1883, and Milton's Minor Poems,
1888, were filled with etched illustrations. He died in
Redhill in 1881.
[For a bibliography see TB; for a list of etchings
see Volume I; see also Bénézit; Bryan; White
Houfe; Evans Reminiscences]

PALMER, William James fl.1858-96
Wood engraver, who rose to prominence during the
1860s. He began as an apprentice to the Jackson
brothers, John and Mason (qq.v.), then transferred
to Edmund Evans (q.v.). Evans recalled him as 'a
swell--but left me a very good engraver' (UCLA MS,
12 April 1904), and in his Reminiscences explained
how he took Palmer on (probably about 1850) to
enlarge his own engraving business: 'At first he was
a poor, dry, uninteresting engraver, but became a
valuable assistant afterwards'. The British Museum
owns a proof engraving, 'Castle of Inolance' (sic) after
Thompson, inscribed 'WJP for EVANS' and signed
'E.EVANS SC'. He set up in London on his own at
15 Wine Office Court, Fleet Street, EC (POD,1858)
but the following year he joined with E.M.Wimperis
(q.v.) as Palmer and Wimperis (q.v.). This lasted
just a year; then Palmer returned in the directories
on his own, at 15 Wine Office Court (POD,1860-61).
He moved to W.J.Linton's (q.v.) old address,
33 Essex Street, WC (POD,1862-80) which he shared
with G.L.Butlin, R.H.Keene and W.E.Hastie (qq.v.).
Then he moved to 22 Wellington Street, WC
(POD,1881-83) then 143 Strand, WC (POD,1884-91),
sharing the address with John Greenaway and T.Symons
(qq.v.). Symons followed Palmer to his next office,

59 and 60 Chancery Lane (POD,1892-96). Palmer
also taught the engraver Ernest Dalton (q.v.).
Palmer's engraving commissions varied from books
to magazines. His most successful work appeared in
the late 1850s when he worked after Birket Foster (q.v.)
for Lays of the Holy Land,1858; and Merrie Days of
England,1858; for Thomson's Seasons,1859; Gray's
Poems,1859; and an edition of The Merchant of
Venice,1860. These works were noted by Bohn in
Chatto and Jackson. They were followed by engravings
to Milton's Ode on the Morning of Christ's Nativity,
1867, after drawings by Albert Moore and William
Small (qq.v.). Later Palmer engraved H.R.Robertson's
drawings to Life on the Upper Thames,1875. He is
perhaps most successful and prolific in his engravings
to the Illustrated London News, 1860-80. He specialised
in various full and double-page sketches sent from
'Special Artist' reporters such as Felix Régamey
(q.v.), for instance, 'American Sketches: Blackwells
Island, Penitentiary', Illustrated London News,
4 March 1876, or an anonymous artist's sketches of
The Prince of Wales in India for the special supplement,
22 January 1876. He also engraved the drawings of
F.Barnard, T.Sulman and W.B.Murray, arctic
scenes by W.J.Overend. His marine coastal scene by
S.Read was especially good as a large fold-out plate,
3 June 1876. The British Museum owns his engravings
after B.Foster, R.P.Leitch, H.LeJeune, W.Small,
H.Weir, E.M.Wimperis. He signed his engravings:
'WJ Palmer Sc' or 'WJP Sc' (script).
[Reid; McLean; Chatto; Evans Reminiscences;
English Influences on Van Gogh; Dalziels' Record]

PALMER and Matthewson fl.1891-1910
London firm of draughtsmen and wood engravers, who
worked at 61 Fleet Street, EC (POD,1891-1901). The
firm was a partnership of Alexander Palmer and
Arthur Matthewson (qq.v.). They continued to
appear in the London directories until 1910, when they
were at 42 Fetter Lane, EC (POD,1910).

PALMER and Wimperis fl.1850s
London wood engraving partnership, between
W.J.Palmer and E.M.Wimperis (qq.v.). It
was a shortlived partnership of one year, according
to the London directories, which used
W.J.Palmer's office at 15 Wine Office Court,
EC (POD,1859).

PANNEMAKER, Adolphe François 1822-?
Belgian born wood engraver, noted for his engravings
after Gustave Doré (q.v.). He was born in Brussels
in 1822, was a pupil of William Brown (q.v.) at the
Brussels Academy and engraved his first work, in
colours, from 1840-45 after Hendrick's drawings for
L'Histoire Populaire de la Belgique. He moved to
Paris where he engraved for various French
publications, exhibited at the Salon,1855, then metal
engraved French and Belgian banknotes. He returned

to wood engraving for Jules Janin's La Revolution
Français,1862. He became the principal engraver
of Gustave Doré's drawings, engraving Doré's Dante's
Inferno,1861, and Contes de Perrault,1862,
which Glaser praised for the skilful black-line
technique he used and the various textures cut in the
manner of Goltzius. Pannemaker taught the wood
engraver Albert Bellenger (q.v.) and his own son,
Stéphane Pannemaker (q.v.). He died in Paris
sometime after 1890 (Hind).
[Gusman; Hind; Glaser]

PANNEMAKER, Stéphane 1847-1930
French wood engraver, painter, son of the noted
wood engraver Adolphe Pannemaker (q.v.). He was
born in Brussels on 27 February 1847, but taken to
Paris, aged eleven, where he was naturalised. From
the age of fourteen he began work engraving for his
father, producing a total of more then 300 works. He
also worked after Old Master paintings for various
French magazines, for instance, the double-page
engravings for L'Illustration, 'que restent comme des
types parfaits en ce genre' (Gusman). He engraved
after Bouguereau, C.Duran, Gainsborough, Reynolds,
Delacroix and Rousseau, for the Magasin Pittoresque.
He is listed here for his various full and double-page
engravings to the Illustrated London News,1876-80,
including after Doré's 'The Rime of the Ancient
Mariner', 15 January 1876; after Adrien Moreau's
'A Wedding in the Middle Ages', fold-out supplement,
17 June 1876; and after various landscape works of
E.Michel and Miss Edwards, engraved like etchings
in a fine, delicate line. He signed his engravings:
'PANNEMAKER' or 'PANNEMAKER FILS'.
[TB; Bénézit; Gusman]

PARKER, Edwin George fl.1870s
London wood engraver, who worked at 180 Fleet
Street, EC (POD,1877).

PARKER, Frederick fl.1833-47
London wood engraver, landscape painter, the son
of John Parker, publisher. He began his career
painting landscapes of the German Rhineland and
Scottish castles which he exhibited in London from
1833-47, notably four at the Royal Academy, 1845-46.
He appeared in the London directory as a wood
engraver at 10 Southampton Row, Strand
(POD,1845-46), then 70 Great Queen Street,
Lincoln's Inn (POD,1848). Redgrave claimed that
he had talent and did engravings 'of much promise'.
However he died young, on 16 December 1847. He
may be the Parker who Gusman lists as an early wood
engraver for the French Magasin Pittoresque from 1833.
[Redgrave; Bénézit; TB; Graves; Gusman]

PARKER, Thomas fl.1850s
London wood engraver, who worked at 24 Fetter
Lane, Fleet Street (POD,1854).

PARKER and Percy fl.1890s
Shortlived wood engraving partnership, which
occupied the original office of H.S.Percy (q.v.) at
10 Sergeant's Inn, Fleet Street, EC (POD,1898).

PARLBY, Frederick fl.1870s
London draughtsman on wood, who worked at
12 Leverton Street, NW (Kelly's,1876).

PARSONS, Alfred 1847-1920
Draughtsman illustrator, landscape painter and
watercolourist. He was born in Beckingham,
Somerset on 2 December 1847 and studied at South
Kensington. He soon specialised in illustrating
garden and plant themes for the gardener William
Robinson, and contributed to numerous books and
magazines from 1880. These included W.Robinson's
God's Acre Beautiful,1880; Poetry of Robert Herrick,
1882; R.D.Blackmore's Springham,1888; Old Songs,
1889; Sonnets of Wordsworth,1891; A.Quiller Couch's
Warwickshire Avon,1892; F.D.Millet's Danube,1892;
William Robinson's Wild Garden,1895; Freeman-
Mitford's Bamboo Garden,1896; Notes in Japan,1896;
and Andrew Lang's Wordsworth,1897. Parsons also
contributed expert initial letter designs and illustrations to magazines. These included drawings for
wood engravings in the English Illustrated Magazine,
1883-86, 1891-92, notably illustrations to Grant
Allen's 'Corn Cockles, 1884, wood engraved by
J.D.Cooper (q.v.); to Richard Jeffries' 'St Guido',
1885, his long borders, plants and wild flowers again
wood engraved by Cooper; and illustrations to Rose
Kingsley's 'Shakespeare Country', 1885, engraved by
J.Cocking, J.D.Cooper, E.Ohme, E.Gascoine, and
R.Paterson (qq.v.). He also illustrated with E.A.Abbey
for The Quiet Life,1890; Harper's Monthly,1891-92;
and Daily Chronicle,1895. He perfected a delicate
and intricate pen drawing technique and mastered a
superb soft-tone pencil technique. He also exhibited
paintings at the Fine Art Society,1885,1891,
1893-94, the Grosvenor Gallery, the New English
Art Club, the New Gallery and the Royal Academy,
where he was elected ARA in 1897, RA in 1911; at
the Royal Hibernian Academy, the Royal
Institute of Painters in Watercolours, the Royal
Institute of Painters in Oil-Colours, the Royal
Scottish Watercolour Society and the Royal Watercolour Society. He died in Broadway, Worcestershire
on 16 January 1920.
[Bénézit; TB; Wood; Houfe]

PARTRIDGE, Sir J.Bernard 1861-1945
Draughtsman for wood engravings, later prolific
illustrator for process engraving, noted as the
principal cartoonist for Punch. He was born in
London on 11 October 1861, educated at Stonyhurst
College, then trained as a stained glass artist,
1880-84. His theatrical interests (he acted in Shaw's
Arms and The Man) led to theatrical drawings for

wood engravings in the Illustrated London News,
1885-89. This was followed by drawings to the comic
magazine Judy,1886 and to the Quiver,1890. The
following year he was introduced to Punch by George
Du Maurier (q.v.), who predicted that here was his own
successor as Punch's cartoonist. Partridge appeared
first as its second cartoonist, 1901, and from 1909
until his death in 1945 as the chief cartoonist. During
this time he also contributed drawings for process
engravings to numerous 1890s magazines and books
(see Houfe for a list). Partridge easily modified his
early skills drawing on wood blocks for the newer
process engraving technique by sharpening up his pen
and ink line. He also exhibited oil, watercolour and
pastel works as well as Punch drawings at the Fine
Art Society, the Royal Academy and the New English
Art Club, where he was elected member, 1893, and
the Royal Institute of Painters in Watercolours,
where he was elected member in 1896. He died in
1945.
[Spielmann; Houfe; Bénézit; Who's Who; Sketchley]

PASCO(E), James H. fl.1858-66
London wood engraver, who worked at 22 Fetter
Lane, Fleet Street, EC (POD,1858-60). By 1864
he had taken over the office of John Dalziel, Junior
(q.v.) at 9 Essex Street, Strand, WC (POD,1864-66),
which he shared with the wood engravers W.Kelly,
T.Reynolds and C.Robinson (qq.v.).

PASQUIER, J.Abbott fl.1851-72
Draughtsman illustrator and watercolourist, genre
painter. He began work drawing on wood for
engravings in various magazines, such as the
Illustrated London News,1856, 1866; Henry
Vizetelly's Illustrated Times,1860; London Society,
1865-68; Aunt Judy's Magazine,1866; Beeton's
Annuals,1866; Broadway,1867; Sunday Magazine,
1867; and the Quiver,1868. He became associated
with the Dalziel Brothers (q.v.) when he contributed
to the hundred illustrations which they wood engraved
for Charles Mackay's Home Affections,1858, and the
Dalziels remembered Pasquier in their Record, as
'a very clever artist in black and white, and a skilful
painter in watercolours'. As a book illustrator,
Pasquier drew for wood engravings in the influential
Foxe's Book of Martyrs,1865, and collaborated with
J.B.Zwecker (q.v.) on a Routledge edition of Old Mother
Hubbard. He also made a collection of anatomical
drawings, Picturesque Groups, for art students.
Perhaps his most famous illustrations accompanied
Thomas Hardy's first published story, 'A Pair of
Blue Eyes', Tinsley's Magazine,1872-73, wood
engraved by Edmund Evans (q.v.). It is believed
that Pasquier worked from at least two sketches
which Hardy supplied of his fiancée, Emma Gifford,
to depict the story's heroine. The British Museum
owns a large collection of Dalziel proofs after his
designs,1861-63; also for an early work, Ida Wilson's

Our Native Land, which the Dalziels engraved for G.Routledge in 1857.
[Dalziels' Record; White; Houfe]

PATERSON, Helen (later Allingham) 1848-1926
Draughtsman for wood engravings, watercolourist of gardens and cottage scenes. She was born in Staffordshire on 26 September 1848, and attended the Birmingham School of Design, then moved to London as a pupil at the Royal Academy Schools from 1867 and studied (with Kate Greenaway (q.v.)) at the Slade. She was greatly influenced by the rural painter Frederick Walker, and began drawing country scenes on wood blocks for Joseph Swain (q.v.), who had taken her under his wing. Swain engraved and got published her earliest block drawings in Once a Week,1868, and through his connections with the newly established The Graphic and its editor W.L.Thomas (q.v.) Helen became the magazine's first woman draughtsman. She contributed various drawings from 1870-74, for full-page engravings of women in landscapes, which were admired by Van Gogh. She also drew for London Society,1870, engraved by Horace Harral (q.v.), the second most successful interpreter of her drawings on wood. By 1871 she had broken into the prestigious yet trying weekly, the Illustrated London News, for which she drew full-page domestic genre subjects -- couples blackberrying or playing croquet on the beach --from 1871. These were wood engraved by W.Hollidge (q.v.). Helen married the minor poet William Allingham in 1874, during her work for Thomas Hardy's Far from the Madding Crowd. This was serialised in the Cornhill,1874, and her drawings were wood engraved by Swain. Hardy was so pleased with these drawings that he called Helen Allingham his best illustrator, fell briefly in love with her, and tried in vain to commission further work. By this time the influential art critic John Ruskin had seen her watercolours of children and praised her drawings for wood engravings in his Academy Notes,1875, calling her 'an accomplished designer of wood-cuts'. She continued to draw sporadically for the children's stories of Mrs Ewing, but by 1878 had abandoned drawing on wood for watercolour paintings of gardens and cottages, with which she supported her family and gained a popular following. Her last illustrations for wood engravings appeared in her husband's Rhymes for Young Folk,1887, engraved by Edmund Evans (q.v.). She exhibited paintings at the Royal Academy and the Royal Watercolour Society, where she was elected its first woman member in 1890; and the Fine Art Society. She died in Haslemere, her favourite painting retreat, in 1926.
[Houfe; Wood; M.B.Huish, Happy England,1903; English Influences on Van Gogh]

PATERSON, Robert fl.1860-99
Wood engraver and etcher, who worked first at 3 East Register Street, Edinburgh (Kelly's,1872-76), then moved to London where he set up as a wood engraver at East Temple Chambers, Whitefriars Street, EC (POD,1877-92), which he shared with G.Lynn, W.H.Say and W.J.Watson (qq.v.). He later moved to 2 Whitefriars Street, EC (POD,1893-99). During this time he exhibited various etchings at the Royal Academy, 1870-89. He wood engraved successful cuts after J.W.MacWhirter's flower designs in Good Words,1860, praised by White as unusual in that context, particularly one which 'deserves especial notice as a much more elaborate piece of engraving than any other in the volume'. He wood engraved the twenty-eight drawings of C.Green, C.J.Staniland, P.Skelton, F.Barnard and Harrison Weir to Episodes of Fiction,1870. He apparently spent years with John H.Dell (q.v.) in perfecting his drawings to Warne's Nature Pictures, 1878; according to the preface, dated October 1878, it was the result of 'years of patient painstaking labour on the part of artist and engraver'. By the 1880s Paterson's engravings were appearing in the English Illustrated Magazine,1883-87. These included Cornish illustrations of T.Napier Hemy, landscapes of L.R.O'Brien, an excellent reproduction of Dürer's 'German Horse', 1884 and a full-page landscape, 'May' after J.MacWhirter,1885. From these alone it is clear that Paterson was capable of a variety of styles, from delicate landscape work to firm, hard-edged outline to dark, atmospheric landscapes.
[White; see Volume I for etchings]

PATERSON, W.J. fl.1871-80
Wood engraver, who contributed various full-page landscape engravings to the Illustrated London News, 1871-80. These included 'The Moated Grange', after Samuel Read,16 December 1871; 'Fettes College, Edinburgh', after J.R.Wells,13 June 1874; and an atmospheric seasonal engraving, 'The Months -- July', after Montbard, 17 July 1880. He signed his work: 'J Paterson Sc' (script).

PAT(T)ERSON, S. fl.1850s
In an 1898 letter, the wood engraver Edmund Evans (q.v.) claimed that an S.Patterson 'was one of my assistants 40 years ago', then refers to a Paterson (sic) as his assistant before the Nelson 'Nature' books series (Evans MSS in UCLA Library).

PATON, Sir Joseph Noël 1821-1901
Draughtsman illustrator, painter of religious subjects and fairies. He was born in Dunfermline on 13 December 1821 then moved to London to attend the Royal Academy Schools in 1843, where he twice won the Westminster Hall fresco design competition,1845 and 1847. He began illustrating with others on wood for A Book of British Ballads,1842, engraved by T.Armstrong (q.v.). Then followed designs to Compositions from Shakespeare's Tempest,1845; Compositions from Shelley's Prometheus Unbound,

1845; and James Wilson's Silent Love,1845. He became associated with the Pre-Raphaelites, and was an especial friend of the illustrator and painter John Millais (q.v.). It was through Paton's admiration for their Pre-Raphaelite illustrations to Moxon's edition of Tennyson's Poems,1857, expertly engraved by the Dalziel Brothers (q.v.), that he too turned to the Dalziels for help on his recent commission, W.E.Aytoun's Lays of the Scottish Cavaliers, published 1863. This was done with his brother, Walter Paton (q.v.) and was taken in hand by the Dalziels. As early as 1858, Paton wrote to the engravers: 'I can with perfect security and confidence recommend the Messrs. Blackwood to entrust you with as many of my drawings as you would care to undertake'. But Paton could be extremely critical of wood engravers, and even the Dalziels were criticised, in 1862: although their engravings were 'satisfactory', they all 'required careful overhauling'. He credited this to his 'desire, which so many must feel, that high class things of that sort [one of his drawings] could be got by themselves and printed in a manner worthy of their excellence--they are generally so indifferently printed in the periodicals in which they appear and dis-appear' (Dalziels' Record,p.108). Paton next completed his most popular illustrations, to Charles Kingsley's Water Babies,1863. He was even approached by but declined Lewis Carroll's offer to illustrate a second volume of the 'Alice' books. Instead he continued to paint the large fairy pictures and religious scenes which earned him a popular following when exhibited at the Grosvenor Gallery and the Royal Scottish Academy, where he became a member in 1850. His later occasional illustrations included drawings to Pennell's Puck on Pegasus, 1861; the Cornhill,1864; and drawings to the English Illustrated Magazine,1885-86, engraved by O.Lacour and E.Gascoine (qq.v.). His later book work comprised: Gems of Literature,1866; Story of Wandering Willie,1870; E.Strivelyne's Princess of Silverland,1874; and John Brown's Rab and His Friends,1878. Paton's popularity helped to make him Her Majesty's Limner for Scotland, 1866 and earn him his knighthood the following year. He died in Edinburgh on 26 December 1901. The British Museum owns several proofs after his designs engraved by the Dalziel Brothers,1862-63.
[Houfe; TB; Bryan; Bénézit; Dalziels' Record]

PATON, Walter Hugh 1828-95
Occasional draughtsman illustrator, and landscape painter. He was born at Dunfermline on 27 July 1828, the brother of Noël Paton (q.v.). He began as an industrial designer in textiles until 1848, then turned to painting landscapes for the galleries. He occasionally drew for wood engravings, notably with his brother on Aytoun's Lays of the Scottish Cavaliers, 1863, engraved by the Dalziel Brothers (q.v.). He also

drew for an edition of Poems and Songs of Robert Burns,1875. Paton was elected ARSA in 1866 and RSA in 1868, and also exhibited at the New Gallery, the Royal Academy, the Royal Institute of Painters in Watercolours, the Royal Hibernian Academy and the Royal Scottish Watercolour Society. He died in Edinburgh on 8 March 1895. The British Museum owns proof engravings of his designs for the Dalziel Brothers, 1862.
[Houfe]

PATTON, William fl.1840s
London wood engraver, who listed his office in the London directory at 7 Coldbath Square, Clerkenwell (POD,1840).

PAUQUET(TE), Hippolyte Louis Emile 1797-?
Draughtsman on wood, metal engraver and litho-grapher. He was born in Paris on 28 February 1797, a pupil of his father Louis Pauquet, brother of Polydore Pauquet (b.1800) with whom he worked. His brother-in-law was the illustrator Gustave Janet (q.v.). He drew vignettes on wood, for which he was best known. He exhibited at the Salon, 1821-49, and Bénézit claims that 'his engraved work is important'. Pauquet drew on wood for Henry Vizetelly (q.v.), then serving as Paris correspondent of the Illustrated London News. Nagler listed Pauquet in the firm of Piaud, Pauquet, and Perville, who signed their engravings 'P P P Sc' (script).
[Houfe; Bénézit; Gusman; Glaser; Vizetelly, Glances Back]

PAWSON and Brailsford fl.1857-1900
Provincial firm of wood engravers, colour printers. It was founded in 1857 by Henry Pawson (1820-1907), a Wakefield-born printer, and Joseph Brailsford (d.1891), with the intention of combining printing and stationery under one roof at Castle Street, Sheffield. Both men retired in 1878 and the firm was taken over by Henry W.Pawson and John A.Brailsford. By 1866 their office was at 10 Mulberry Street, Sheffield, where they printed in colour and wood engraved. They were listed as wood engravers in Kelly's Stationers' Directory,1880-89.
[For colour work see Wakeman and Bridson]

PAYNE, A.H. fl.1850s
English wood engraver, who worked in Leipzig. He was a publisher of several 'gallery' style publications with steel engravings like Orbis Pictus, and Hey's Fables,1852, all with London imprints, but produced in Leipzig. He later wood engraved the illustrations of Ludwig Richter (q.v.) under the name A.H.Payne and in collaboration as Payne and Gray. Payne is not to be confused with Henry Albert Payne (1868-1940), painter and illustrator.
[Muir, Victorian Illustrated Books,pp.215,231]

PAYNE and Gray
(see Payne, A.H.)

PEACH
(see Hay and Peach)

PEARSE, Alfred c1854-1933
Draughtsman, illustrator and wood engraver. He was born in St Pancras, London about 1854, and studied engraving there from 1872-75. He was proficient enough to be taken on as 'Special Artist' to the Pictorial World, for which he provided drawings to be wood engraved from 1879-86. He also drew for the Illustrated London News, 1882; Boy's Own Paper, 1890; Girl's Own Paper, 1890-1900; Strand Magazine, 1891-94, 1906; Wide World Magazine, 1898; Cassell's Family Magazine, 1898; and was 'Special Artist' for The Sphere, 1901-03, and a contributor to Punch, 1906. His book illustrations appeared in G.A.Henty's By England's Aid, 1890; and Gordon Stables' Westward with Columbus, 1894. He exhibited work in London at the Royal Academy and the Royal Society of British Artists, and died on 29 April 1933.
[Houfe; Waters]

PEARSON, Madame G. fl.1860-1909
Wood engraver of bird subjects. She engraved two cuts to the new edition of Yarrell's History of British Birds, 1871-85, the edition which added to A.Fussell's original drawings works by J.G.Keulemans, Edward Neale and Charles Whymper (qq.v.). These new drawings were wood engraved by Pearson, R.C.West and the Dalziel Brothers (qq.v.).
[C.Jackson]

PEARSON, George fl.1850-1910
London wood engraver, who worked specifically on animal and natural history subjects. Bohn in Chatto and Jackson gave two reproductions of his animal engravings and called him 'a rising artist' of natural history subjects, 'a department which he is cultivating by preference'. He set up his London engraving office first at 32 Stanhope Street, Hampstead Road (POD, 1851-55), then at 15 Wine Office Court, and 17 Albert Street, Camden Road (POD, 1856-61) which he shared with E.M.Wimperis and W.J.Palmer (qq.v.). The following year he moved to 3 Bolt Court, Fleet Street, EC (POD, 1862-99), then added 17 Lyme Street, Camden Road, NW (POD, 1866) briefly as a second office. By 1900 Pearson had joined with Hughes, as Pearson and Hughes (q.v.). Pearson's engraved work began in the 1850s when he was an assistant to Smith and Linton (q.v.), the wood engravers commissioned to engrave for the Illustrated London News. Pearson chose watercolours of animals to engrave from 1850-60, notably 'The Hippopotamus in the Regent's Park Zoo', 1 June 1850, after Harrison Weir; 'The Hippo in the Gardens', after J.D.Wolf, 8 June 1850; and various other zoo

animals to a series in 1854 and 1860. He also engraved after Joseph Wolf (q.v.) for T.W.Atkinson's Travels in the Region of the Upper and Lower Amoor (East Asia); cuts to Freeman and Salvin's Work on Falconry, c1860-61; fish drawings to Hartwig's Sea and Its Living Wonders; and a vignette, 'Falls of Niagara' to Bohn's Pictorial Handbook of Geography, c1861. Later he engraved cuts to the magazine Sunday at Home, 1869. Pearson also exhibited the engraving, 'Animal Life' after Joseph Wolf, at the Royal Academy, 1869. He signed his engravings: 'PEARSON Sc'.
[Chatto; Linton, Masters of Wood Engraving]

PEARSON, George William fl.1877-1900
London wood engraver and draughtsman on wood, who worked in partnership with John W.Kefford (q.v.) as Kefford and Pearson, then set up on his own at 99 Shoe Lane, EC (POD, 1883-88), 17 St Bride Street, EC (POD, 1889) and 105 Shoe Lane, EC (POD, 1890). By 1900 he listed himself as a draughtsman with an office at 75 Fleet Street, EC (Kelly's, 1900).

PEARSON, R.O.
Wood engraver of portraits, who engraved an unattributed half-length portrait of John Bright. The work is owned by the British Museum.
[Hake]

PEARSON and Hughes fl.1900-10
London wood engraving partnership, originally the office of George Pearson (q.v.) at 3 Bolt Court, Fleet Street, EC (POD, 1900-10).

PEARSON, Simmons and Knott fl.1891-93
London wood engraving firm, with an office at 12 Ludgate Square, EC (POD, 1891-93). The following year the firm was listed as Walter Simmons (q.v.).

PEINLIGH, Charles fl.1890s
London wood engraver, who worked at 9 Furnival Street, EC (POD, 1891).

PELCOQ, Jules fl.1866-77
French draughtsman on wood, who was born in Belgium of an old family, but after studies at Antwerp School went to Paris. He set up as a caricaturist, worked for Le Charivari (the French version of Punch), and Journal Amusant, illustrated the novels of Dumas, and specialised in subjects of Parisian life. For this he was employed by Henry Vizetelly (q.v.), then the Paris correspondent to the Illustrated London News, for which he drew on wood some 1,000 sketches. He became their chief artist in Paris during the Siege of 1870, sending his drawings to London by 'balloon post', after Vizetelly had had each photographed by Nadar for safety.

Vizetelly recalled that Pelcoq was an 'expert with pen and ink, but as a draughtsman on wood he was less successful'. He was forced to draw in bed, unable to afford fuel, and used pen and ink until the ink froze from the cold. Later Vizetelly took Pelcoq with him to cover the International Exhibition at Vienna in 1873. He also illustrated some of Vizetelly's own books.
[Vizetelly, Glances Back; Houfe]

PENGUILLY L'HARIDON, Octave 1811-70
French draughtsman illustrator, watercolourist and engraver. He was born on 4 April 1811, served as a professional soldier, then trained under Charlet. He exhibited at the Salon, 1835-70. He is listed here for his drawing wood engraved in the Illustrated London News, 1853. He also illustrated the works of Scarron.

PENNINGTON, Mrs Rooke fl.1880s
Provincial wood engraver, who worked at 15 Fold Street, Bolton, Lancashire (Kelly's, 1889).

PENSON, R.Kyrke 1815-66
Architectural draughtsman and architect. He is listed here for his drawings to the Waverley edition of Walter Scott's work, which proved influential to the young Edmund Evans (q.v.). Evans described them as 'memorable to me' when he first saw them during his early days as assistant to the Dalziel Brothers (q.v.). Penson also exhibited nine works at the Royal Academy, 1836-59, notably of Welsh subjects.
[Bénézit; TB; Evans Reminiscences; Cundall]

PERCY, Henry Stevens fl.1886-98
London wood engraver, who worked at 10 Sergeant's Inn, Fleet Street, EC (POD, 1886-97). He then formed a partnership as Parker and Percy (q.v.) (POD, 1898). Among Percy's wood engravings were the plate, 'Staghounds', after the animal illustrator Louis Wain, 1886, and a vignette, 'Peace after Toil', after J.Buxton Knight, 1887, both for the English Illustrated Magazine.

PERKINS, Arthur William 1897-1910
London wood engraver, who worked at 58 Fleet Street, EC (POD, 1897), then 154 Fleet Street, EC (POD, 1898-1910). He shared this second office with G.C.Hallam (q.v.).

PERRY, Harcourt
London wood engraver, who worked at 5 Fetter Lane, EC (POD, 1901).

PETERS, Mrs J. fl.1840s
London wood engraver, who worked at 8 Thanet Place, Temple Bar (POD, 1848).

PETHERICK, Horace William 1839-1919
Draughtsman illustrator and painter. He began as a draughtsman for wood engravings in the Illustrated London News, 1870-71, 1887 and 1890, notably of domestic and children's subjects such as 'The First Snowball', 16 December 1871. He also illustrated for children's books in the Kronheim 'Toy Book' series, drew for Home for the Holidays, 1880; for S.Hodges' Among the Woblins, and Among the Gibjigs, 1883; and for G.A.Henty's Cornet of Horse, 1892. Petherick exhibited work at the Royal Academy and the Royal Society of British Artists. He was working by 1891 from Addiscombe and by 1919 from Croydon.
[Bénézit; TB; Houfe; Fincham; Graves]

PETTIE, John 1839-93
Draughtsman illustrator and painter. He was born at East Linton, Scotland on 17 March 1839 and quickly developed his early talent for figure draughtsmanship. He studied at the Trustees Academy in 1856, under R.S.Lauder, with fellow students Orchardson, MacWhirter and McTaggart (qq.v.). He moved to London in 1862, where he shared a studio with Orchardson and began drawing on wood for engravings in Good Words, 1861-63; Wordsworth's Poetry for the Young, 1863, illustrated with MacWhirter; Pen and Pencil Pictures from the Poets, 1866; Touches of Nature by Eminent Artists, 1866; Sunday Magazine, 1868-69; and Good Words for the Young, 1869. He also illustrated books on his own, notably J. de Lefde's The Postman's Bag, 1865, L.G.Seguin's Boys of Axelford, 1869, later illustrations to Rural England, 1881. Pettie was also a noted etcher and produced plates for the Etching Club. He exhibited work at the Royal Academy from 1860, where he was elected ARA in 1866 and RA in 1873. He also exhibited at the Grosvenor Gallery, the Royal Hibernian Academy, the Royal Institute of Painters in Oil-Colours and the Royal Scottish Academy. He died in Hastings on 23 February 1893. The British Museum owns proofs of his designs engraved by the Dalziel Brothers (q.v.), 1861-62.
[TB; Bénézit; Bryan; Houfe; for etchings see Volume I]

PEYTON
English wood engraver of landscapes. The British Museum owns a small cut of a shepherd in the hills, after William Harvey (q.v.). It was engraved in a rather grey tinted manner and signed: 'PEYTON SC'.

PHILLIPS, A.Watts 1825-74
Draughtsman illustrator, and dramatist. He was born in 1825, was the only pupil of George Cruikshank (q.v.) and began drawing comic cuts for wood engravings in Punch, 1844-46. He turned from Punch to illustrate for Puck, then for Diogenes as its cartoonist. He also founded the short-lived Journal for Laughter; and at an early stage produced M.P.Drawn and Etched by Watts Phillips, c1840. He

settled in London from 1853-54, having contributed to the Illustrated London News,1852. He also wrote plays put on at the Adelphi Theatre,1857-59, and published novels in the Family Herald.
[Spielmann; Houfe]

PHILLIPS, Paul
Fashion draughtsman illustrator, who contributed a drawing for wood engraving in The Graphic,1871.

'PHIZ'
(see Browne, Hablot K.)

PICKERING, Jonathon fl.1840s
London wood engraver, who worked at 18 Shoe Lane (POD,1846).

PICKERING, T. fl.1850s
London wood engraver, who worked at 107 Fetter Lane (POD,1853).

PICKERSGILL, Frederick Richard 1820-1900
Occasional draughtsman illustrator on wood, painter of historical subjects. He was born in London on 25 September 1820, and studied at the Royal Academy Schools, exhibiting there from 1839. He began drawing on wood for S.C.Hall's Book of British Ballads,1842, then became associated with the Dalziel Brothers (q.v.) who commissioned drawings on wood for J.Burns' Poems and Pictures,1846. The Dalziels were pleased enough with Pickersgill's drawings here to commission further work, until they became his principle interpreter: they engraved his drawings to Willmott's Poets of the Nineteenth Century,1857; to Mackay's Home Affections,1858; to Montgomery's Poems,1860; and to an edition of the Lord's Prayer,1870. Pickersgill also drew five illustrations to their famous Bible Gallery,1880, and the Dalziels commissioned drawings for a Life of Christ which they planned to produce themselves, but which proved too expensive, and was later abandoned. Pickersgill was one of the 'painters who occasionally drew on wood' noted by Bohn in Chatto and Jackson and praised for his early work to the Poetry of Thomas Mocre, as well as the Book of British Ballads and Lays of the Holy Land,1858. Pickersgill's drawings on wood had a Germanic hardness, borrowed from the Nazarene influence of the period. He also painted carefully coloured historical pictures which he exhibited at the Royal Academy, where he was elected ARA in 1847 and RA in 1857. He also exhibited at the British Institution. He died on the Isle of Wight on 20 December 1900. The British Museum owns proofs of his designs engraved by the Dalziel Brothers 1846-51,1853,1855-61.
[Chatto; Houfe; Bryan; DNB; Dalziels' Record]

PILKINGTON, Margaret 1891-1974
Wood engraver and watercolourist, born in Salford, Lancashire in 1891. She was educated in Croydon, studied at the Slade,1913, and then studied wood engraving at the Central School. She received her first lesson from Lucien Pissarro (q.v.), then studied under Noel Rooke (q.v.), and is listed here as a disciple of both. She was successful enough as a wood engraver for an engraving to be hung in the first exhibition of the newly formed Society of Wood Engravers. She was invited to become a member in 1922 and two years later served as Honorary Secretary on the retirement of Robert Gibbings (q.v.). In 1954 she was elected chairman.
[Garrett]

PINWELL, George John 1842-75
Prolific and successful draughtsman for wood engravings, who specialised in scenes of rural life, also a painter. He was born in Wycombe on 26 December 1842 the son of a builder, and first worked for embroiderers. He studied art at the St Martin's Lane Academy, and Heatherley's in 1862, and while there he earned money drawing for Matthew Browne's Lilliput Levee, and H.Lushington's The Happy Home and Hacco the Dwarf, both 1864. He also made drawings for the comic paper Fun, and the silver-smiths, Elkingtons, while training with the prominent wood engraver J.W.Whymper (q.v.), who at the time had lost his figure draughtsmen Fred Walker and Charles Green (qq.v.). 'Pinwell was not regularly apprenticed to Mr Whymper, but a running arrange-ment, something on the lines of apprenticeship, was made between them. Mr Whymper greatly appreciated the instinct for design and character that he could discern in Pinwell, but his want of knowledge of drawing could not be overlooked by the publisher, and no great amount of success attended Mr Whymper's efforts with him' (Bryan). Pinwell shared a room with the novice draughtsman Thomas White (q.v.), then at work on drawings on wood for Fun and Once a Week, and he introduced Pinwell to these magazines, which were illustrated at that time by fellow Heatherley pupils such as Fred Barnard, H.Linton and Charles Green (qq.v.). So it was in 1863 that Pinwell had drawings published wood engraved drawings in Punch; Once a Week,1863-69; Good Words,1863-75; Churchman's Family Magazine, 1863-64; Sunday at Home,1863-64; and London Society,1863-67. His Once a Week commissions alone totalled about fifty drawings and almost all of these early commissions were wood engraved by Joseph Swain (q.v.). It was through Alexander Strahan, publisher of Good Words, that Pinwell was first introduced to the wood engravers the Dalziel Brothers (q.v.) and their commissions eventually amounted to hundreds of drawings in one of the most successful draughtsman-engraver collaborations of the 1860s. 'We recognised at once his cleverness and that study

and practice only were required to develop his great abilities', the Dalziels recalled. They gave him work on their recent acquisition, the comic paper Fun, and regular work on Good Words (which amounted to over a hundred drawings alone). Pinwell did a few drawings for the Dalziels' Arabian Nights' Entertainments,1865, having just completed his most trying commission for them. This was the hundred drawings on wood to one of the Dalziels' illustrated edition series, The Illustrated Goldsmith,1864. It took Pinwell six months to complete, working week by week to produce illustrations on the block for serial publication. The pressure taught him to hate working against time; 'money was not enough for him', according to the Dalziels. Yet the completed book was his personal triumph: 'His work on the "Goldsmith" is so thoroughly good, so full of his earnest desire to represent the author, that it can be taken as a model of what an illustrated book should be' (Bryan). Pinwell met fellow draughtsmen J.W.North and Fred Walker (qq.v.) through the Dalziels and the trio produced what is considered the best rural illustration of the period. This included contributions by Pinwell to such influential works as Touches of Nature,1866; the Spirit of Praise,1867; Golden Thoughts,1867; the Dalziels' A Round of Days, 1866; Wayside Poesies,1867; and perhaps his best, twenty illustrations to Jean Ingelow's Poems,1867. By the early 1870s Pinwell was contributing drawings to The Graphic,1870-73, notably 'The Lost Child', 6 January 1870; 'The Sisters', 6 May 1871; and 'London Sketches: A Country Visitor', 22 February 1873. They were collected by Van Gogh who praised Pinwell's abilities to draw the commonplace: 'He was such a poet that he saw the sublime in the most ordinary, commonplace things'. Pinwell's reputation as a draughtsman on wood was substantial; his friends E.G.Dalziel and A.B.Houghton (qq.v.) praised his abilities and Millais claimed 'no man could produce work like his who was not a man of exquisite taste and refined poetic feeling'. His style, although linked with Frederick Walker's, was less bold in outline, more dependent on fine, thin parallel lines which were sometimes split in two by an unsympathetic engraver so that they appeared greyer, almost tonal in places, although they were actually fine black and white lines. Pinwell's greatest champion and collector was Harold Hartley, whose article in the Print Collector's Quarterly,1924, was based on his own collection (now in the Boston Museum) and interviews with Pinwell's associates. Of the artist's engravers' difficulty in interpreting the drawings on wood Hartley wrote: 'Both Mr Edward Whymper and Mr Joseph Swain explained to me the difficulties they experienced in engraving many of his blocks, his drawings being so ineffectively adopted for facsimile reproduction... Yet Swain admitted that Pinwell was indefatigable in trying to work out his ideas with greater technical accomplishment'. A selection of Pinwell's drawings

uncut on wood blocks are in the British Museum and the Victoria and Albert Museum. According to Martin Hardie they 'are the work of a natural composer and show great sensitiveness of line, coupled with both interpretative and inventive power'. His greatest strength lay in his search for authentic textures in clothing, foliage, and the play of light and shadow on rustic objects. Even Forrest Reid devoted ten pages to Pinwell's work: 'It is an art extremely personal in its manner and therefore in its appeal; it is an art hampered constantly by an imperfect technique, and yet its very failures are frequently more interesting than the successes of cleverer draughtsmen, while successes are lovely as April primroses'. In later years Pinwell devoted more time to his finely finished rural paintings which he first exhibited at the Dudley,1865. He exhibited at the Old Watercolour Society, where he was elected Associate in 1869, and member in 1870. Unfortunately his health failed in 1873 and after a recuperative trip to Tangiers in 1875, he died in London on 8 September 1875. The British Museum owns proofs of his designs engraved by the Dalziel Brothers,1863.
[For a complete list of illustrations see Houfe; also G.C.Williamson, George Pinwell and His Work, 1900; also Reid; Dalziels' Record; Bryan; Print Collector's Quarterly,1924,pp.163-84]

PIPPET, Gabriel 1880-1962
Wood engraver and woodcut artist, known to have cut a portrait of William Morris as a frontispiece to his Poems,1923. He also worked as Paul Woodroffe's (q.v.) assistant in his stained glass studio during World War I.

PISAN, Heliodore Joseph 1822-90
French wood engraver and painter. He was born in Marseilles in 1822, and made his debut at the Salon in 1849. He engraved for various French magazines such as Magasin Pittoresque, and Histoire des Peintres de Toutes les Ecoles,1849-75, but with Pannemaker (q.v.) is best known for his engravings after Gustave Doré (q.v.). These included Doré's edition of Dante's Inferno,1861; and Don Quixote,1863; although his most successful work was for Doré's Bible and Perrault's Tales. Gusman goes so far as to claim that Pisan helped to establish Doré's reputation with his engravings: 'He developed his method in perfect harmony with wash and gouache tones of the master illustrator's designs on wood. In particular he had the art of determining with ease the various special planes of the design'. Pisan also engraved a portrait of the English landscape painter, Richard Wilson,RA, after a painting by R.Mengs, the engraving of which is in the British Museum.
[Gusman; Hake; Glaser]

PISSARRO, Esther (née Bensusan) 1871-?
Wood engraver, designer, illuminator and printer.
Born in England in 1871, she trained at the Crystal
Palace School of Art and specialised in book
decoration. She married the artist Lucien Pissarro
(q.v.) in 1892 and with him ran the Eragny Press,
from 1894. She shared her husband's concern in
perfecting hand woodblock colour and gold printing
to illustrate their press books and and she was given
most of the borders and initial letters to engrave.
'It is not clear--because the books all talk of Lucien
and none of Esther--whether or not she was little
more than a skilled hack-worker to Lucien. Various
sources note that she was skilled and talented in
her own right as an artist, but it does appear that
her creativity was made subservient to the demands
of Lucien's ideas' according to the historian Anthea
Callen. Lucien does acknowledge Esther in his
history of the Eragny Press: 'I must acknowledge
the valuable assistance given by my wife, both in
engraving and in printing. Her energy and skill have
been invaluable in the Press Room'. By April 1902
Esther and Lucien had moved the press to The Brook,
Stamford Brook, and there she engraved her only
known major work, in collaboration with Diana White.
This was Diana White's The Descent of Ishtar, with
frontispiece design by White, engraved on wood by
Esther. The book was finished in December 1903
and on publication was considered one of the finest
of the press's books. The British Museum owns a
small cut of three figures beneath a sun, taken from
the book.
[A.Callen, Angel in the Studio,p.182]

PISSARRO, Lucien 1863-1944
Wood engraver, designer and printer of books,
landscape painter. He was born in Paris on
20 February 1863, the eldest son of the French
painter Camille Pissarro, with whom he studied.
He also studied wood engraving and colour printing
under Auguste Lepère (q.v.) before coming to
England in 1883, having first visited in 1870, aged
seven. He stayed one year, then returned to France
until 1890, when he again returned to England. By
1893 he had settled permanently in England and the
following year established his Eragny Press with his
wife, the English wood engraver and decorative
artist Esther Pissarro (q.v.). He contributed
designs to The Dial; wood engravings to the spring
issue of L'Image,1897 a paper started by Lepère;
and also illustrated The Queen of the Fishes,1896;
Laforgue's Moralitès Légendaires, 1897; Ronsard's
Choix de sonnets,1902; Perrault's Peau d'Ane,1902;
and Areopagetica,1904, while his Livre de Jade of
Gautier,1911 and La Charue d'Erable,1912 broke
new ground and established the Eragny Press as a
successful producer of woodblock colour printing.
The methods employed were very similar to those
used in Edmund Evans' (q.v.) earlier successes,
which involved four colour blocks and an outline
block printed in dark green or black. Pissarro's
press work for over twenty years totalled thirty-
two books in French and English. His series of
illustrated French classics beautifully ornamented
by Esther and designed with T.Sturge Moore (q.v.)
retained the craftsman tradition of William Morris
(q.v.). His own wood engravings added a new
naturalism lacking in Morris's work, while he did
not attempt to join the new 'White-Line' school. He
exhibited wood engravings in 1911 and was a founding
member of the Society of Wood Engravers,1920. He
was also a landscape painter and caricaturist, and
exhibited work as a member of the New English Art
Club from 1906. Pissarro's work, like his mentor
Lepère's, was greatly influential to the new wave of
wood engravers including his pupil Margaret
Pilkington (q.v.). Pissarro's blocks and
engravings are in the Ashmolean Museum, Oxford,
which recently published 'Le Tennis' from the
original block, and a catalogue of the collection,
1981.
[see TB and C.Franklin, Private Presses,1969, for
full bibliography; Hind; Gusman]

PITT, Henry fl.1890-1910
London wood engraver, who worked first in partnership with E.C.Mitchell (q.v.) as Mitchell, Pitt and
Company (q.v.), then from 1899 on his own at
30 Holborn, EC (POD,1899-1901). By 1910 the engraver
is listed as Pitt and Reyner, a partnership with
P.Reyner (q.v.) at 2 Dyer's Buildings, EC (POD,1910).

PIXIS, H. fl.1860s
Draughtsman on wood, who produced wood-engraved
illustrations with J.D.Watson, H.C.Selous,
E.M.Wimperis and M.E.Edwards (qq.v.) to The
Illustrated Book of Sacred Poems,1867.

PLATT, John Edgar 1886-?
Colour woodcut artist and painter. He was born on
19 March 1886 at Leek, Staffordshire, studied at
the Royal College of Art,1905-08, and exhibited at
the Royal Academy from 1913, also the New English
Art Club. He exhibited at the International Society
of Painters, Sculptors and Gravers, from 1917 and
was president of the Society of Graver Printers,
1939-53.
[Waters]

PLUMMER, F. and Company fl.1895-1900
London wood engraving firm, with offices at 23 Great
New Street, EC and 1 and 2 Goldsmith's Court, Great
New Street, EC (POD,1895-99). The following year
only the 23 Great New Street office remained.

POCOCK, E.
Architectural draughtsman, who contributed a
drawing wood engraved in the Illustrated London

News,1875.

POPE, Louis A.
London wood engraver, who worked at 20 Martin
Street, Stratford, E (LSDN,1900).

PORTCH, Julian ?-1865
Draughtsman illustrator, who began as a self-taught
draughtsman of comic sketches which attracted the
Punch editor, Mark Lemon, who used them from
1858-61. 'It is true that it lacked strength, but it
showed a delicate pencil and a certain power of comic
expression sufficient to place him among "Mr Punch's
clever young men" of the second rank (Spielmann).
He was a pupil of Henry Vizetelly (q.v.) who
commissioned his earliest drawings and sent him as
'Special Artist' for the Illustrated Times,1855-61,
notably to cover British camp life in the Crimea in
1855. He returned paralysed after a bout of rheumatic
fever. He still managed illustrations for wood
engravings in Welcome Guest,1860; C.Pennell's Puck
on Pegasus,1861; London Society,1862; Poetry of the
Elizabethan Age,1862; an edition of Uncle Tom's
Cabin, and Boswell's Life of Johnson. He spent
several years on Punch's Pocket Books and continued
to do theatrical illustrations until his death 'after
three years of lovingly tended illness' in September
1865. The British Museum owns several proof
engravings of his designs for the Dalziel Brothers
(q.v.),1861.
[Spielmann; Houfe; Vizetelly, Glances Back]

PORTER, J.L. fl.1860s
Occasional draughtsman, probably the historical and
landscape painter John Porter, who worked in London
and Folkstone and exhibited at the British Institution,
the Royal Academy, and the Royal Society of British
Artists from 1826-70. He is listed here for a drawing,
wood engraved in Good Words,1861.

POSTLETHWAITE, Miss Elinor 1866-?
Colour woodcut artist, born on 21 February 1866 at
Hall Thwaites, Cumberland. She studied at Frank
Calderon's School and at the Westminster School of
Art, and exhibited at the Royal Academy and in the
provinces. She lived in South Devon.
[Waters]

POTTER, William John fl.1862-1910
London wood engraver, who worked at 1 Norfolk
Street, Strand, WC (POD,1862-64) and 123 Chancery
Lane, WC (POD,1875-82), which he shared with
W.H.Coldwell, E.T.Hartshorn and W.D.Willis
(qq.v.). He then worked at 89 Farringdon Street, EC
(POD,1884-1910), shared with L.Knott, J.A.Rogers,
F.Thorpe, H.Prater, F.Appleton and J.Dixon (qq.v.).
William Potter is not to be confused with William J.
Potter, the American landscape painter and pupil
of Walter Sickert.

POTTS, G. fl.1887-93
London wood engraver, who worked at 13A Salisbury
Square, EC (POD,1887-93). He may be related to
the landscape painter George B.Potts, fl.1833-60.

POTTS and Rogers fl.1894-97
London wood engraving firm, with an office at
44 Fleet Street (POD,1894-97).

POWELL, J.H.
Little is known of this draughtsman illustrator,
mentioned by the Dalziels (q.v.) in their Record
as the illustrator to their commission for E.Nisbet's
Lays of the Holy Land,1858. His drawing, 'Ruth and
Naomi', appeared engraved by the Dalziels alongside
works of J.Tenniel, F.Pickersgill, J.Millais,
B.Foster and J.R.Clayton. The British Museum owns
proofs of his designs to Pictorial Bible Stories,
engraved by the Dalziels in 1855.

POWER, Joseph Blakesley fl.1880-84
London wood engraver, who worked at 53 Ebury
Street, SW (POD,1880-81), then at 17 Jewry Street,
EC (POD,1882), and finally at 146 Fenchurch Street,
EC (POD,1884).

POWIS, William Henry 1808-36
London wood engraver, who trained under G.W.Bonner
(q.v.) and rapidly gained a reputation as a competent
engraver. He first worked for J.Jackson (q.v.) with
whom he is most associated. He engraved copies of
Holbein's Dance of Death for the publisher William
Pickering, and four headings to Northcote's Fables,
1833 (although they were signed by Jackson); he
engraved for Penny Magazine for Jackson. His best
cuts were to John Martin and Westhall's Illustrations
of the Bible,1833 and to Scott's Bible,1834, in which
some of W.J.Linton's (q.v.) early work appeared as
Powis's. These Linton later claimed were 'perhaps the
best landscapes for their size up to that time engraved
on wood'. Powis also engraved to Zoological Gardens,
1835; to a 'Farmer's Series for the Useful Knowledge
Society', and Spring,1836, engraved with S. and T.
Williams (qq.v.). Powis appeared in the London
directories working from 94 St John Street Road
(Pigot,1832-34), then 59 St John Street Road
(Pigot,1836). He shared this work premises with
W.J.Linton who praised his engraving talent
in his Masters of Wood Engraving: 'Most noticeable
in Powis's work is that everything has been cut at
once. In this he differed notably from [J.Orrin]
Smith, who depended on after-toning'. Powis was
one of the black-line imitators of copper engraving
but saw 'the virtue of engraving firmly graduated
colour without depending upon after-refinement',
although he was not as talented as his master, George
Bonner. Unfortunately Powis devoted too much
energy to his work and sapped his strength by accepting
numerous commissions. Linton claimed that he was

consumptive and died after realising he would be a
slave to his poor health. His death in 1836, at the
age of twenty-eight, left 'a very promising career...
cut short' (DNB). The British Museum owns his work
after W.Harvey, T.Landseer and J.Martin, also
vignettes to Romance of History,1833. He signed
his work: 'W POWIS Sc'.
[Redgrave; W.J.Linton, Masters of Wood Engraving;
Gusman; Nagler; Chatto; DNB; TB (bibliography);
Evans Reminiscences]

POWNEY, Thomas fl.1861-70
London wood engraver, who worked at 123 Chancery
Lane, WC (POD,1861-70). He shared the address
with G.C.Freudemacher, E.T.Hartshorn, W.D.Willis
and Robert Collins (qq.v.).

POYNTER, Ambrose 1796-1886
Occasional draughtsman on wood, still-life and
landscape painter, architect. He was born in London
in 1796, was a pupil of T.S.Boys and John Nash (qq.v.),
travelled to Italy,1819-21, and then set up in London
as an architect of government schools and churches.
He was a founder member of the Royal Institute of
British Architects in 1834, but retired because of poor
eyesight in 1858. During this period he also drew on
wood for Charles Knight's (q.v.) publications, 'the
most beautiful architectural drawings, which imparted
a character of truthfulness to many scenes' according to
Knight, namely Knight's Pictorial Shakespeare. He also
drew for wood engravings in Knight's London,1841-42.
He exhibited at the Royal Academy, and died in Dover
on 20 November 1886, leaving a famous artist son,
Sir E.J.Poynter (q.v.).
[For an account of Poynter's drawings see H.M.Poynter,
The Drawings of Ambrose Poynter,1931; also Houfe]

POYNTER, Sir Edward John, Bt. 1836-1919
Occasional draughtsman illustrator, prominent
Victorian painter of neoclassical and biblical subjects.
He was born in Paris on 20 March 1836, the son of
Ambrose Poynter (q.v.), and studied art in Paris
under Gleyre,1856-59, with Alma-Tadema,
Du Maurier and Whistler (qq.v.). He also attended
the Royal Academy Schools, where he was elected
ARA,1868 and RA,1877. He contributed drawings for
wood engravings in Once a Week,1862-67; London
Society,1862, 1864; Churchman's Family Magazine,
1869; Poems of Ingelow,1867; The Nobility of Life,
1869; and the Illustrated London News,1870. The
Dalziels (q.v.) saw his work exhibited at Newman
Street, and proposed illustrations to their Bible Gallery.
Poynter provided seven on the Joseph, Moses, Miriam
and Daniel stories, 'all remarkable for purity of
treatment' according to the Dalziels. Poynter was a
serious draughtsman for the Dalziels to whom he
often wrote about the intricate details of his drawings
engraved by them. The Dalziels quote from a letter,
dated 1871, where he comments 'the light on the floor

especially seems to want shading more gradually
into the background...The engraving is most
beautiful,...indeed, whatever is wrong is my own
fault'. The Bible Gallery drawings were published
in 1880, the result of Poynter's 'delightful times'
with the Dalziels. 'There is no part of my life or of
the practice of my art to which I look back with
greater pleasure', he wrote to them in 1896.
Poynter was best known for the paintings he exhibited
at the Grosvenor Gallery, the New Gallery, the Royal
Academy, the Royal Society of Painter-Etchers and
Engravers, the Royal Hibernian Academy, the Royal
Scottish Academy and the Royal Scottish Watercolour
Society. He developed a reputation as an educator
as well, teaching at the Slade,1871-75, South
Kensington,1875-81, became Director of the National
Gallery,1894-1904, served as President of the Royal
Academy,1896-1918, was knighted in 1896, and was
created baronet in 1902. He died in London on
26 July 1919. The British Museum owns proofs of his
designs engraved by the Dalziel Brothers.
[Wood; DNB; TB; Dalziels' Record; A.Margaux,
Art of E.J.Poynter,1905; M.Bell, Drawings of
E.J.Poynter,1906]

PRATER, Harry fl.1880-1910
London wood engraver, who worked at 152 Fleet
Street, EC (POD,1880-88), which he shared with
A.Scott, F.H.Cathcart and D.W.Williamson (qq.v.).
He then moved to 89 Farringdon Street, EC
(POD,1889-92), shared with W.J.Potter, L.Knott
and F.Thorpe (qq.v.). He returned to 152 Fleet
Street, EC (POD,1893-99), and by 1910 was working
at Falcon Court, 32 Fleet Street, EC (POD,1910).

PRATER, William fl.1885-89
London wood engraver and draughtsman, who worked
at 1 Norfolk Street, Strand, WC (POD,1885-89). He
shared the address with G.Meek (q.v.).

PREHN, William fl.1862-90
Occasional draughtsman and sculptor. He worked in
London and contributed two drawings wood engraved
in Punch,1865. He also exhibited at the Grosvenor
Gallery and the Royal Academy.
[Bénézit; TB; Spielmann]

PRESTIDGE, Edward C. fl.1880s
Provincial wood engraver, who worked at 20 North
Street, Bristol (Kelly's,1880).

PRICE and Andrew fl.1870s
London firm of draughtsmen and wood engravers,
who worked at 18 Southampton Street, Strand, WC
(Kelly's,1876).

PRIMROSE, Priscilla
Amateur draughtsman of wood engraved drawings
of Rome to Henry Vizetelly's (q.v.) Illustrated

Times,1859.

PRINGLE, Robert fl.1864-67
London wood engraver, who worked at 6 Fetter Lane, Fleet Street, EC (POD,1864-67). He shared the office with R.S.Marriott, H.Crane and C.Branston (qq.v.).

PRINSEP, Val C. 1838-1904
Occasional draughtsman, painter and author. He was born in Calcutta on 14 February 1838 and educated at home, then at the Royal Academy Schools and with Gleyre in Paris. He is listed here for his drawing wood engraved in Once a Week,1869. He also illustrated his own Imperial India, An Artist's Journal,1879. As a painter he exhibited at the Grosvenor Gallery, the New Gallery and the Royal Academy, where he was elected ARA,1879, and RA in 1894. He died on 11 November 1904.
[DNB; Houfe; Maas; Wood; TB]

PRINTING Block Engraving Company fl.1895-1901
London wood engraving and draughtsman firm, with an office at 49 Moorgate Street, EC (POD,1895-97), then 21 Camomile Street, EC (POD,1898-1901).

PRIOLO, Paolo fl.1857-90
Occasional illustrator, historical and biblical painter. He worked in Stockwell, London from 1857-90, and exhibited at the Royal Academy and the Royal Society of British Artists. He is listed here for his drawing for wood engraving in the Churchman's Family Magazine,1863.

PRIOR, Melton 1845-1910
Draughtsman illustrator and 'Special Artist' reporter. He was born in London on 12 September 1845, the son of the draughtsman William Henry Prior (q.v.), with whom he studied. He began drawing for wood engravings in the Illustrated London News from 1868 and after five years of contributing in England, he was sent out as the paper's first war correspondent in 1873, to Ashanti. Thus began thirty years of almost uninterrupted work drawing from such places as the Balkan peninsula,1876, South Africa,1877-81, the Sudan,1885, then South America,1889-92. His last assignment was the Russo-Japanese War,1904. He also accompanied various members of the Royal Family on tour, notably the Prince of Wales on his visit to Athens,1875. The DNB claimed that his work took him twice round the world, and that he knew every part of America. He also drew for the Sketch, and the English Illustrated Magazine,1893-94. 'Prior's art, if not of the highest order, was eminently graphic, and he had a keen eye for a dramatic situation. He worked almost entirely in black and white, with the pen or the pencil, and with extraordinary rapidity' (DNB). He died in Chelsea on 2 November 1910.
[DNB; TB; Bénézit; Houfe]

PRIOR, William Henry 1812-82
Draughtsman illustrator and landscape painter. He was born in 1812 and worked in London where he drew on wood for Charles Knight's (q.v.) publications, notably Knight's London,1841. He then drew for wood engravings in the Illuminated Magazine, 1845; the Illustrated London News,1850,1875; Cassell's Illustrated Family Paper,1853; the Illustrated London Magazine,1854; and Henry Vizetelly's Illustrated Times,1866. His early work on wood, engraved by the Dalziels (q.v.), was done under the influence of William Harvey (q.v.) to whom he served as assistant until he found his own commissions. Even then he retained the Harvey style, once saying to Harvey, 'I know you don't mind'. By 1876 he had set up in London as a draughtsman at 210 Strand, WC (Kelly's,1876-80), the office shared with H.W.Cutts (q.v.). He also exhibited landscape paintings at the British Institution, the Royal Academy and the Royal Society of British Artists.
[TB; Houfe; Dalziels' Record]

PRITCHARD
(see Blackstaffe and Pritchard)

PRITCHETT, Robert Taylor 1828-1907
Draughtsman and gunmaker. He was born in Enfield on 24 February 1828, the son of a gunsmith, with whom he worked as partner and inventor of various rifles and the 'Pritchett bullet'. As a draughtsman he exhibited views of Brittany and Belgium at the Royal Academy, 1851-52, then through the Punch cartoonist John Tenniel (q.v.) was introduced to the Punch editor. He contributed twenty-six drawings to Punch, 1863-69, the first taken by Tenniel to be wood engraved by Joseph Swain (q.v.). Swain also introduced Pritchett to Once a Week, for which he again drew for Swain to engrave. He also drew on wood for Good Words,1864-80; Sunday Magazine, 1865; Cassell's Magazine, 1867 (the DNB claims he did 100 drawings for Cassell, Petter and Galpin); Leisure Hour,1867; and The Graphic,1887. Pritchett became an intimate friend of fellow draughtsmen Birket Foster, John Leech and Charles Keene (qq.v.). He later turned to painting watercolours of the sea and ships, travelled and wrote and illustrated his own books, or records of his patron's travels. These include Brush Notes in Holland,1871; Gamle Norge,1878; Smokiana,1890; and Pen and Pencil Sketches of Shipping,1899. He exhibited work at the Royal Academy and the Royal Society of British Artists, and was patronised by various members of the Royal Family, including the Queen. He died in Burghfield, Berkshire on 16 June 1907.
[DNB; Spielmann; Houfe; TB; Bénézit]

PROCTOR, John fl.1866-98
Cartoonist who became known for his strong outline
drawings of animals. He became the chief cartoonist
for the Dalziels' Judy,1867-68, then served a period
on Will o' the Wisp, and Moonshine,1868-85; then
became chief cartoonist for the Sketch,1893; and the
Dalziels' Fun,1894-98. He also drew as 'Special
Artist' for the Illustrated London News, being sent
to St Petersburg in 1874. He worked for Cassell's
Saturday Journal, and illustrated the book, Dame
Dingle's Fairy Tales,1866-67. He exhibited at the
Royal Society of British Artists. The British Museum
owns proofs of his designs wood engraved by the
Dalziel Brothers (q.v.), 1862.

PROUT, John Skinner 1806-76
Occasional draughtsman on wood and architectural
painter. He was born in Plymouth in 1806, the nephew
of Samuel Prout, who influenced his work. When
young he visited Australia, and stayed long enough to
forfeit his membership to the New Watercolour
Society, earned in 1838, although he was re-elected
on his return in 1849. Prout is listed here for his
inclusion in Bohn's list of draughtsmen in Chatto and
Jackson, namely for his drawings on wood to Rhymes
and Roundelayes. (Houfe lists this work under Samuel
Prout.) John Prout also exhibited at the Royal Institute
of Painters in Watercolours, and died in Camden
Town, London on 29 August 1876.
[Chatto; Houfe; Redgrave; TB; Bénézit]

PROVART
(see Landells, Gorway and Provart)

PROVOST, W.(A.)
French draughtsman on wood, who contributed views
of Paris to Cassell's Illustrated Family Paper,1857.
Gusman lists 'A.Provost' who made his illustration
debut with vignettes for L'Illustration and also drew
for various 'livres de piété'.

PRYDE, James Ferrier 1866-1941
Occasional woodcut artist, book designer and painter.
He was born in St Andrews on 30 March 1869,
educated at the Royal Scottish Academy Schools and in
Paris at Julian's under Bouguereau. His marriage to
William Nicholson's (q.v.) sister brought the two
men together as the Beggarstaff Brothers, a
partnership which experimented with woodcuts and
produced the periodical The Page,1898, based on the
early chap-books which they admired. Pryde also
contributed illustrations to The Page,1898-99; also
Tony Drum,1898; and illustrated Wilhelm Hauff's
The Little Glass Man,1893. In later years he designed
stage scenery and painted dark, atmospheric paintings.
He exhibited at the Grosvenor Gallery, the New
English Art Club, the Royal Hibernian Academy and
the Royal Scottish Academy, being elected honorary
ROI in 1934. He died in 1941.

[D.Hudson, John Pryde,1949; Houfe]

PULLAN, Shipton and Company fl.1897-98
London wood engraving firm, with an office at
12 Ludgate Square, EC (POD,1897-98).

PURCHESE, William fl.1874-89
London wood engraver, who worked at 268 Strand,
WC (POD,1874-77), then joined in partnership with
Arthur Charles Canham (q.v.) as Purchese and
Canham (q.v.).

PURCHESE and Canham fl.1879-89
London firm of wood engravers, a partnership
between William Purchese (q.v.) and Arthur Canham
(q.v.). They worked from 168 Fleet Street, EC
(POD,1879-89), and shared the address with
W.E.Rouse, C.Branscombe and A.L.Appleton
(qq.v.). By 1890 Arthur Canham had broken away
from his partner and set up on his own.

PUTTOCK, George fl.1876-94
London wood engraver, who worked at 9 Essex
Street, Strand, WC (POD,1876-94). He shared the
address with J.Bye, J.Desbois, W.Murden,
H.C.Mason, R.Roberts, W.Limming and C.Trent
(qq.v.).

PYNE, William Henry 1769-1843
Occasional draughtsman on wood, landscape and
genre painter, etcher, and author. He was born in
London in 1769, studied with H.Pars, then took up
book illustration. His greatest successes were for the
colour-plate books of Rudolph Ackermann from about
1803-19. He is listed here for his drawing on wood,
engraved in Charles Knight's London,1841. He also
was an art critic and writer, editor of The Somerset
House Gazette. He died a debtor, although he had
exhibited as a founder member of the Old Watercolour
Society in 1804-09, also at the Royal Academy, and
had achieved some success as a painter. He died
at Pickering Place, Paddington on 29 May 1843.
[Hardie, Watercolour Painting; Houfe]

QUARTLEY, Alfred fl.1890-93
London wood engraver, who worked with Harry Quartley
(q.v.) at 3 Bouverie Street, EC (POD,1890-92),
sharing the address with E.C.Dalton and A.C.Coats
(qq.v.). By 1893 Alfred had appeared on his own at a
new address, 84 Fleet Street, EC (POD,1893), sharing
the office with E.J.Humphries (q.v.).

QUARTLEY, Frederick William 1808-74
Wood engraver, landscape painter, who was born in
London, became a wood engraver in 1852, then left
for New York where he created 'Picturesque America'
and 'Picturesque Europe', and various landscape paintings.
[TB; Bénézit; Fielding]

QUARTLEY, Harry James fl.1890-1910
London wood engraver, who worked first with Alfred
William Quartley (q.v.) at 3 Bouverie Street, EC
(POD,1890-92), then disappears from the London
directories until 1899. His office then was located
at 28 Clerkenwell Road, EC (POD,1899-1910).

QUARTLEY, John fl.1835-67
English born wood engraver, who settled in France
and worked in Tours. He directed the presses of the
publishing house of Mame and began a career as wood
engraver of illustrations for the Magasin Pittoresque;
followed by L'Illustration; Laurent's Histoire de
L'Empereur Napoleon,1839, the 500 illustrations for
which he engraved with C.Thompson, T.Williams,
J.Orrin Smith, J.Gowland, Whitehead and C.Sheeres
(qq.v.); twelve plates and vignettes to Lamartine's
Jocelyn,1841, engraved with Timms (q.v.); cuts for
Mme de Stael's Corinne ou L'Italie,1841-42, engraved
with Gowland and Orrin Smith; for the new edition
of Jules Janin's L'Ane Morte,1842, engraved with
Thompson, Harrison, Gray, Gowland, T.Williams
and Orrin Smith (qq.v.); for Jules Janin's La
Normandie, the 150 vignettes for which he engraved
with Harrison (q.v.). Quartley is best known for his
later work after Doré (q.v.): notably Doré's illustrations
to Dante's Inferno,1861, which Quartley engraved with
Linton, Pisan, Pannemaker and Best-Hotelin (qq.v.).
Gusman claimed that his best work using a fine black-
line style, was a plate after Bloteling for the Magasin
Pittoresque,1847. 'His technique has changed but
little, he has always remained an engraver of the
steel engraving method of the English school'
(Gusman,I,p.162). Quartley probably collaborated
with M.U.Sears (q.v.) as Quartley and Sears. Their
work appeared in Charles Knight's Penny Magazine,
September 1841, after a drawing on wood by Jarvis.
The Bodleian owns his C.Knight engravings.
[Nagler; Gusman; Beraldi; TB; Bénézit; Gazette de
Beaux Arts,IX,124,XVIII,388,XX,274,279,XXIII,118]

QUARTLEY, John Arthur fl.1876-88
London wood engraver, who worked at 13 Bouverie
Street, EC (POD,1876-80), also at 8 Eton Grove,
Dacre Park, SE (LSDS,1880). He specialised in
landscape engravings. His wood engravings appeared
in the English Illustrated Magazine,1883-88. They
included a full-page 'A Normandy Milkmaid', after
W.J.Hennessy,1885, engraved in firm outline style
although printed with an overall greyness; 'London
Commons', after Clough Bromley,1886; and landscape
engravings after J.W.North to illustrate Richard
Jeffries' article, 'Summer in Somerset', 1888. The
British Museum owns engravings after Claude
Lorraine and T.Lawrence; a portrait of 'Mrs Geddes',
after Andrew Geddes; and various Near Eastern
landscapes after K.Girardet. One small Moorish
scene is inscribed 'John Quartley for W.J.Palmer'.
He signed his work: 'J Quartley', 'J.A.QUARTLEY'.

QUARTLEY and Sears
(see Quartley, John)

QUEEN, John fl.1872-76
Provincial draughtsman, wood engraver, who
worked at 11 John Dalton Street, Manchester
(Kelly's,1872), then Wellington Chambers, Victoria
Street, Manchester (POD,1876).

QUEEN, Stockwin and Snell fl.1890s
London wood engraving firm, with an office at
3 Tudor Street (POD,1893). By 1899 the firm had
changed to Queen and Stevens (q.v.).

QUEEN and Stevens fl.1899-1901
London wood engraving firm, earlier Queen,
Stockwin and Snell (q.v.). Their office was at
3 Tudor Street, Blackfriars, EC (POD,1899-1901).

QUEEN'S Wood Engraving Company fl.1880s
Provincial wood engraving firm, with an office at
46A Market Street, Manchester (Kelly's,1889).

QUICK, John fl.1832-53
London wood engraver, who worked at 42 Bowling-
Green Lane, Clerkenwell (Pigot,1832-34), then
5 Weston Place, King's Cross (Pigot,1852-53).

QUICK, William Kerwood fl.1862-80
London wood engraver, who worked at 23 Garnault
Place, Clerkenwell (POD,1862-64), 144 Barnsbury
Road, N (POD,1865-72), then 369 Liverpool Road,
N (POD,1873-80).

QUICK, William Michael Roberts 1838-1927
London wood engraver, who worked from a variety
of addresses listed in the London directories,
1856-1902. They include 42 St John Square,
Clerkenwell (POD,1856-59), 2 Great New Street,
Fetter Lane, EC (POD,1860-65), 10 Symond's Inn,
WC (POD,1866-73) and 49 Fleet Street, EC
(POD,1874-77). He then disappears from the main
London directory until 1884. During that period he
worked at 15 Ambler Road, Finsbury Park, N
(LSDN,1880). He then moved back to the engraving
district of London, at 5 Sergeant's Inn, EC
(POD,1887), 1 Tudor Street, EC (POD,1888-89) and
7 Water Lane, Blackfriars, EC (POD,1890-91). By
the turn of the century he was working from Finsbury
Park, 38 Ennis Road (LSDN,1894-1902). He died in
London on 28 January 1927. As a wood engraver
Quick specialised in topographical engravings and
architectural subjects engraved in a tinted facsimile
manner. These include eight illustrations to the
English Illustrated Magazine,1883-88, notably
'Brass Work in Birmingham', after A.Morrow,1883;
facsimile reproductions of old sketches to Austin
Dobson's 'Changes at Charing Cross', 1884; and
illustrations by T.Napier Hemy to the story 'An

Unsentimental Journey through Cornwall', 1884. He engraved Hugh Thomson's drawings to Austin Dobson's article, 'The Tour of Covent Garden', 1884; produced a competent half-page facsimile of Rossetti's study for his famous picture, 'Found', 1884; and engraved a drawing by the comic artist Harry Furniss, 1887. The British Museum owns work done after drawings of W.H.Ohrend, W.Rainey, F.Dadd, T.Sulman and R.Caton Woodville. There is also a large sepia harbour scene inscribed 'Flora Russell 1916'. He signed his work: 'WQ'.
[TB; Bénézit]

RAFFET, Denis Auguste Marie 1804-60
French draughtsman illustrator, engraver, lithographer and battle painter. He was born in Paris on 2 March 1804, was apprenticed to a wood turner and then studied porcelain painting under Cabanel. He worked under Charlet as a lithographer, and from 1829 became a pupil of Gros. From 1831 he concentrated his energies entirely on lithography and illustration. He is listed here for his drawing on wood for a wood engraving in Henry Vizetelly's (q.v.) Illustrated Times, 1855. He also visited England and Scotland with his patron Prince Demidoff. He died in Gênes on 11 February 1860.

RAILTON, Herbert 1857-1910
Prominent draughtsman of architectural subjects and book illustrations. He was born in Pleasington, Lancashire on 21 November 1857 (1858, DNB) and educated in Belgium and Ampleforth, Yorkshire. He studied architectural drawing with W.S.Varley and eventually set up as a book illustrator in London from 1885. He is listed here for his early and, critics claim, his best drawings, wood engraved in the English Illustrated Magazine, 1884-96. These include drawings to Mowbray Morris's 'Eton', 1884, engraved by A. and W.Dawson, J.Cocking, R.Paterson, O.Lacour, W.M.R.Quick and J.C.Griffiths (qq.v.); which were followed by drawings to 'The London Charterhouse', 1885; and 'Old Chester', 1886, engraved by Waterlow and Sons and J.D.Cooper. By 1888 his drawings to Coaching Days and Coaching Ways, done with Hugh Thomson (q.v.), were first appearing, also engraved by Waterlow and Sons. This work launched Railton as an illustrator, not only for magazines such as The Graphic, 1887; the Illustrated London News, 1889-99; Sporting and Dramatic News, 1890; and Good Words, 1890-94, but also for books including Windsor Castle, 1886; Dickens' Pickwick Papers, Jubilee edition, 1887; Westminster Abbey, 1889; and the Poems of Goldsmith, 1889. The DNB claimed that his pen and ink drawings were best suited to process engraving and his work 'exercised a wide influence on contemporary illustration'. He was particularly proficient drawing textures and careful detailing in buildings. He died

on 15 March 1911.
[For a list of illustrated work see Houfe; DNB; TB]

RAINEY, William 1852-1936
Draughtsman illustrator, genre and landscape painter. He was born in London on 21 June 1852, studied art at South Kensington and the Royal Academy Schools before setting up as a book illustrator. He adopted the delicate eighteenth century revival style of Hugh Thomson (q.v.) for magazine work in the Illustrated London News, 1884-94; The Graphic, 1884-1901; and in various other 1890s publications. Rainey is listed here for his designs to Edmund Evans' (q.v.) new series of colour wood engraved book covers (see Evans Reminiscences, p.28). Rainey also exhibited work from 1876 at the Royal Institute of Painters in Watercolours, where he was elected member in 1891. He was elected ROI in 1892 and exhibited at the Royal Academy and the Royal Society of British Artists. He lived in Eastbourne towards the end of his life. He died on 24 January 1936.
[For a list of illustrations see Houfe; TB; Bénézit; Who's Who, 1924]

RAKE, Walter Henry fl.1885-86
London wood engraver, who worked at 1 Basinghall Street, EC (POD, 1885), then 53 Barbican, EC (POD, 1886).

RALSTON, John Mc L. fl.1872-80
Draughtsman figure artist and watercolourist. He was a young Scot who came to London and was employed as draughtsman on wood for various magazines, such as the Illustrated London News, 1872-73, 1880-81. He also illustrated Dickens' A Child's History of England, Household edition, 1873; and was employed by the Dalziel Brothers (q.v.) to make three drawings on wood, with F.Barnard (q.v.), to Pilgrim's Progress, 1880. He exhibited work at the Dowdeswell Galleries.
[Dalziels' Record; Houfe]

RALSTON, William 1848-1911
Draughtsman of comic subjects for Punch and other magazines. He was born in Dumbarton in 1848 and probably studied under his younger brother, 'whose artistic boots I was not fit to black'. He came to London and with an introduction from Joseph Swain (q.v.), took his drawings to the Punch editor Shirley Brooks: 'I remember how in walking down to business that day I tried to look unconscious of my greatness, and mentally determined that it would make no difference in my bearing'. He was taken on as a Punch draughtsman, and eventually contributed 227 genre, military subjects, comic initials and 'socials', 1870-86. He also drew for wood engravings in the Illustrated London News, 1870-73; The Graphic,

1870-1911; the Cornhill,1883-84; Daily Graphic; and Sporting and Dramatic News,1895. He developed the strip cartoon and compensated for his poor draughtsmanship by using humorous subjects. He died in Glasgow in October 1911.
[TB; Spielmann; Houfe]

RANKIN, Arabella Louisa 1871-?
Colour woodcut and landscape engraver, painter. She was born in Muthill, Perthshire in 1871, and worked in Edinburgh,1903, in Crieff,1914, and in London,1922-35. She exhibited at the Royal Scottish Academy and in the provinces. Her work appeared in the Studio,1896,p.252.

RANSOM, Frank 1874-?
Wood engraver and sculptor, born in Westminster on 8 October 1874. He studied at Lambeth School of Art and the Royal Academy Schools, where he exhibited. He also exhibited at the Royal Scottish Academy and in the provinces.
[Waters]

RANSOM, Henry Johnson fl.1887-89
London wood engraver, who worked at 6 Wine Office Court, EC (POD,1887-89). He shared the office with the wood engravers C.Murray and G.F.Sheern (qq.v.).

RATCLIFFE
Draughtsman on wood, who contributed drawings to Charles Knight's Penny Magazine,October 1841. These were engraved by Margaret Hampton (q.v.).
[Bodleian Library]

RAVERAT, Gwendolen Mary 1885-1957
Wood engraver and illustrator. She was born in Cambridge on 26 August 1885, daughter of Sir George Darwin, Professor of Astronomy, and studied at the Slade,1908-11, under Tonks, Steer and Fred Brown. She married Jacques Raverat,1911. She engraved for numerous books, her style influenced by Eric Gill (q.v.). She exhibited at the New English Art Club, the Royal Society of Painter-Etchers and Engravers, where she was elected member in 1934, at the Royal Hibernian Academy and at the Royal Scottish Academy. She worked in Cambridge, and London, and died on 11 February 1957.
[Waters; Houfe; Garrett]

RAWLINGS, Walter John fl.1894-1900
London wood engraver, who worked at 282 High Holborn, WC (POD,1894-99), then at 26 Ludgate Hill, EC (POD,1900).

RAWLINS, Thomas J. fl.1837-60
Draughtsman illustrator and topographer, who specialised in sporting subjects. He illustrated work by Nimrod and Charles James Apperley, with

H.T.Alken, and also illustrated Elementary Drawing as Taught at St Mark's College, Chelsea,1848. He drew for wood engravings in the Illustrated London News,1858-60, a period during which he possibly visited India. He also exhibited at the Royal Academy.

READ, Arthur Rigden 1879-?
Wood engraver, who specialised in landscape and figure subjects. He was born in London on 14 September 1879, exhibited extensively in London, and lived and worked in Winchelsea, Sussex.
[Waters]

READ, Samuel 1815-83
Occasional draughtsman on wood of landscape and architectural subjects, and watercolourist. He was born in Needham Market, Suffolk in 1815, and worked as lawyer's assistant then for an architect. He moved to London where he learned drawing on wood from the major draughtsman engraver J.W.Whymper (q.v.). He also studied watercolour painting with W.C.Smith, and exhibited at the Old Watercolour Society where he was elected member in 1880, the Royal Academy and the Royal Society of British Artists. As an illustrator, he first made drawings for Zoological Studies, published for the SPCK in 1844, the year he also began drawing for the Illustrated London News. He became well known for his Illustrated London News drawings of atmospheric seaside ruins, buildings hidden in undergrowth, and various coastal landmarks such as 'John O'Groats', 8 August 1874, engraved by John Greenaway (q.v.). Others were engraved by Edmund Evans (q.v.). Other work included a series of factory interiors such as 'A Visit to the Salt Mines of Cheshire', 24 August 1850, and a gun barrel manufacturers in Birmingham, 1 February 1851, engraved by Mason Jackson (q.v.). During the 1870s he provided full and double-page drawings on wood, such as the special supplement, 'Exeter Cathedral', double-page, 10 November 1877. He also became the first Illustrated London News 'Special Artist', sent out just prior to the Crimean War to draw scenes of Constantinople. He continued with drawings of Germany, Northern Italy and Spain, then returned to England to record most of the major ecclesiastical or manorial buildings in Britain. His work appeared in the Illustrated London News from 1844 until his death, since he was unofficially retained in old age as its art editor. He died in Sidmouth, Devon on 6 May 1883. Read is listed by Bohn in Chatto and Jackson as a worthy painter 'who occasionally draws on wood', and noted especially for his illustrations to Rhymes and Roundelayes. He also drew for Charles Mackay's Home Affections,1858; and Willmott's Sacred Poetry of the 16th, 17th and 18th Centuries, 1862. The British Museum owns several engraved proofs by the Dalziel Brothers (q.v.), 1860.
[Chatto; Houfe; TB; Bryan]

READE and Dixie fl.1885-86
London wood engraving firm, with offices at
12 and 14 Catherine Street, Strand, WC (POD,1885),
shared with Bartlett and Norman (q.v.). The
following year the firm moved to 66 Ludgate Hill,
EC (POD,1886).

REDGRAVE, Richard 1804-88
Occasional draughtsman on wood, who specialised
in figure subjects, also a genre painter. He was
born in Pimlico on 30 April 1804 and worked with
his father, a wire fence manufacturer, before
studying at the Royal Academy Schools. He became
a drawing master in 1830, was associated with
the Government School of Design from 1847,
and was Director of the Art Division, South
Kensington until 1875. Among his students was
Kate Greenaway (q.v.). He later became Surveyor
of the Queen's Pictures,1857-80 and was made
a CB that year. He exhibited at the Royal Academy
where he was elected ARA 1840, RA 1851, at
the British Institution and the Royal Society of British
Artists. His illustrations for wood engraving were
noted by Bohn as appearing in the Book of British
Ballads,1842; Favourite English Poems,1859; and
Early English Poems, Chaucer to Pope,1863. He was
also employed by Charles Whittingham (q.v.) to
design various ornamental devices (some incorporating
the familiar putti and mermaid) for Whittingham's
Chiswick Press. These were probably wood engraved
by the press's engraver, Mary Byfield (q.v.).
Redgrave also etched illustrations for the Etching
Club's publications, The Deserted Village,1841,
Songs of Shakespeare,1843, and The Song of the
Shirt. Redgrave died in London on 14 December
1888.
[For biographical information see F.M.Redgrave,
Richard Redgrave, a Memoir,1891; DNB; Bryan;
Wood; also Chatto; A.Warren, C.Whittingham,1896]

REES and Corpe fl.1890s
London wood engraving firm, with an office at 6 Red
Lion Court, Fleet Street, EC (POD,1894). The
following year the office was given over to J.Dalton
(q.v.).

REEVE, A.
Draughtsman illustrator, who contributed comic
genre subjects to The Graphic,1886.

REEVES
(see Gould and Reeves)

REGAMEY, Félix Elie 1844-1907
French draughtsman, etcher, engraver, portrait
and history painter. He was born in Paris on
7 August 1844, the son and pupil of the artist
L.P.G.Régamey, and the brother of Guillaume
Régamey (q.v.). He was the pupil of Lecoq de

Boisbaudran and began as an illustrator for various
French magazines, drawing caricatures in Journal
Amusant; La Vie Parisienne; Monde Illustré;
L'Illustration; L'Eclipse; and others, before he
founded his own paper, Salut Public in 1870. During
the Paris Siege Régamey remained in the city as
'Special Reporter Artist' for the Illustrated London
News. He produced strong, rather powerful drawings
which were wood engraved by W.J.Palmer and Henry
Linton (qq.v.), and in 1872 continued to draw and
record scenes on his travels: Van Gogh was
particularly taken by the double-page drawing, 'The
Diamond Diggings, South Africa', 31 August 1872.
In 1873 Régamey left France for England, then Japan
and the United States, where he made a series of
'American Sketches', of prison scenes again for the
Illustrated London News, which Van Gogh collected
and studied. He also drew for The Graphic; for the
American Harper's Weekly; and while in Japan
collected material for Japanese Promenades,1878.
He exhibited work in London in 1872 and became an
inspector of drawing at the Paris Schools in 1881.
He died in Paris on 7 May 1907.
[Beraldi; Art Journal,1907,pp.252,360; TB; Print
Collector's Quarterly,4,1914,p.198,11,1924,pp.327,
332; English Influences on Van Gogh]

REGAMEY, Guillaume Urbain 1837-75
Draughtsman, wood engraver, military painter. He
was born in Paris on 22 September 1837, the son of
the artist L.P.G.Régamey and the brother of Félix
Régamey (q.v.). Like his brother he was the pupil of
Lecoq de Boisbaudran, also of F.Bonvin and Bayre
at the Paris Academy, where he was awarded two
medals. He is listed here for his drawings as a
'Special Reporter' in Paris for the Illustrated London
News,1870-71; also for his work for The Graphic.
But unlike his brother he abandoned such work,
suffering from poor health. He spent the remainder
of the war working in London, then returned to Paris
briefly in 1872. The last three years of his life were
spent weakened by illness and he died in
London on 3 January 1875.
[Nagler; TB; Bénézit; E.Chesneau in Librairie de
l'Art,1879]

REGNAULT, Henri Alexandre Georges 1843-71
Occasional draughtsman, painter of genre and
historical subjects. He was born in Paris on
30 October 1843, and studied at the Ecole des Beaux
Arts from 1860. He won the Prix de Rome in 1866,
studied in Italy until 1868, then travelled to Spain and
Morocco. He enlisted in the 19th Infantry Regiment
in 1870 and was killed fighting with them. A carnival
drawing, wood engraved in The Graphic, appeared in
the year of his death,1871. Gusman listed a 'Regnault'
as wood engraver after Bertall and Gavarni for Les
Gens de Paris.
[Gusman; Houfe]

REGNIER, Isidore
Wood engraver, listed by Gusman as an assistant
to the prominent French engravers Adolphe Best
and Leloir and Hotelin (qq.v.). He also engraved
cuts for the Nouvelles Genevoises,1845; and for
Contes Rémous,1858. He trained his son Eugene
Regnier from 1887.
[Gusman]

REID, Andrew
The British Museum owns several proof wood
engravings after designs by this artist, engraved by
the Dalziel Brothers (q.v.), 1866.

REID, F.W.
The British Museum owns two proof wood engravings
after designs by this artist, engraved by the Dalziel
Brothers (q.v.), 1866.

REID, S.
Draughtsman on wood, who exhibited the work,
'Lullingsworth', wood engraved by Henry Duff
Linton (q.v.), at the Royal Academy, 1857. Fincham
lists two bookplates signed 'S Reid fecit' and dated
1880, 1890. He is not to be confused with the Scottish
illustrator Stephen Reid (1873-1948).
[TB; Graves; Fincham]

REINDORP, Jacques fl.1877-81
London wood engraver, who worked at 6 Wine Office
Court, EC (POD,1877-81). He shared the office with
H.Izod, C.Murray and F.W.Mitchell (qq.v.).

RENAUD, G. fl.1880s
Draughtsman of humorous subjects, who contributed
drawings for wood engravings in the Dalziel Brothers'
(q.v.) magazine Judy,1886-89.

REYNER, Percy Grout fl.1901-10
London wood engraver, who worked at 21 St John's
Square, EC (POD,1901). By 1910 he had formed a
partnership with Henry Pitt (q.v.) as Pitt and Reyner,
and worked from offices at 2 Dyer's Buildings, EC
(POD,1910).

REYNOLDS, Alfred 1818-91
Wood engraver, who, joining with his brother
William Reynolds (q.v.), was apprenticed in 1832 to
George Baxter (q.v.) to learn wood engraving.
C.T.Courtney Lewis believed that Alfred Reynolds
was 'probably Baxter's first apprentice', but William
Reynolds was trained earlier. Alfred left Baxter
about 1843 to become a partner in the engraving firm
of Gregory, Collins and Reynolds (q.v.),1844-48.
According to an advertisement the firm were
'Engravers on wood & printers in colour, gold &
bronze'. Sometime during 1848 or early 1849
Reynolds left the firm (probably replaced by George
Cargill Leighton (q.v.)) to manage the tile

department of Minton's pottery works, Stoke-on-
Trent.
[For colour work see Wakeman and Bridson;
C.T.Lewis]

REYNOLDS, Christopher fl.1880-1900
London draughtsman on wood, who worked at 10 (3)
Bolt Court, Fleet Street, EC (Kelly's,1880-1900).
He shared the office with the wood engravers
E.Scrivens, T.Coman and J.Harris (qq.v.).

REYNOLDS, Ernest G. fl.1880s
Draughtsman illustrator of humorous subjects who
contributed drawings to the Dalziel Brothers' (q.v.)
magazines Judy,1886, and Fun,1887.

REYNOLDS, Mary Henrietta 1856-1949
Wood engraver, daughter of William Reynolds
(q.v.). She was instructed in wood engraving as a
girl, but did not continue. She may be the engraver
of a work, signed 'M.H.R.', in the Jewitt box,
Constance Meade Collection, Bodleian Library.

REYNOLDS, Thomas fl.1864-69
London wood engraver, who worked at the office of
Charles and Thomas Robinson (qq.v.), 9 Essex
Street, Strand (POD,1864-69). Others who worked
with them included J.Bye and P.Roberts (qq.v.).

REYNOLDS, W.J.
Provincial wood engraver, who worked at
188 Warstone Lane, Birmingham (Kelly's,1900).
An advertisement in the directory for that year
claimed that Reynolds was a 'High class wood
engraver, draughtsman, and electrotyper,
specialising in jewellers' and silversmith
catalogues'.

REYNOLDS, Warwick fl.1871-79
Comic draughtsman, who contributed headpiece
drawings wood engraved in Judy,1871-79. He was
also a member of the New Watercolour Society
from 1864-65.

REYNOLDS, William 1815-88
Wood engraver, brother of Alfred Reynolds (q.v.),
before whom he was apprenticed to learn wood
engraving under George Baxter (q.v.). Reynolds
engraved with Orlando Jewitt (q.v.) during 1838-69,
then on Jewitt's death formed a partnership with his
brother Henry Jewitt and Charles Keates (qq.v.),
which lasted until Henry's death in 1875. William
then retired in 1885. According to William's
grandson, he engraved the name label for the Lea
and Perrins' sauce bottle, but most of his competent
engraving on wood was signed 'Jewitt & Co.' or
'J. & Co.'. This makes identification of William's
own technical skills extremely difficult. His grandson however, has a proof of an achievement of arms

(Earls of Pembroke) signed 'W.Reynolds sc.', as well as other proofs attributed specifically to him.

RHODES, James fl.1873-92
London wood engraver, who worked at 28 Essex Street, Strand, WC (POD,1873), which he shared with Irons and J.T.Morrell (qq.v.). By 1892 he was appearing in the London directory at 12 Furnival Street, EC (POD,1892).

RHYMER, Chadwick fl.1870s
London draughtsman on wood, who worked at 7 Tooks Court, Chancery Lane, EC (Kelly's,1876).

RICE
Draughtsman on wood, who contributed an illustration wood engraved in London Society,1868.

RICH, Anthony fl.1854-1914
Draughtsman and landscape painter, who worked in Croydon and Hassocks. He is listed here for his drawing in the influential 'Sixties School' publication, Thornbury's Legendary Ballads,1876, 'regarded as a most important volume in a collection of the sixties', according to Gleeson White. Most of the engravings were reissued from Once a Week.

RICHARDSON, Joseph Teale fl.1886-93
London wood engraver, who worked at 64 Fleet Street, EC (POD,1886), then at 55 and 56 Chancery Lane, WC (POD,1887-88). He probably formed a partnership with T.W.Lascelles (q.v.) as Lascelles and Richardson (q.v.) from 1891-93.

RICHES Brothers fl.1884-1901
London wood engravers Charles and William James Riches, who first appeared in the London directories as Riches Brothers, 74 Fleet Street, EC (POD,1884-88). Charles then set up on his own as a draughtsman wood engraver at 89 Farringdon Street, EC (POD,1889), and then 98 Fleet Street, EC (POD,1890), and William appeared as wood engraver at 108 Fleet Street, EC (POD,1890), then joined with Charles Branscombe (q.v.) for a year as Branscombe and Riches (q.v.). They returned in the directories as Riches Brothers in 1893, working at 108 (122) Fleet Street, EC (POD,1893, 1897-1901).

RICHTER, Adrian Ludwig 1803-84
German draughtsman illustrator, the son of a professor at the Dresden School of Art and graphic designer. Ludwig designed calendars with his father at the age of thirteen, and at sixteen drew his first book illustrations,1818-19, for J.C.Grote's Neuer Nord-Deutsche Robinson. He was popular in England for his sixty-three drawings to a German edition of The Vicar of Wakefield,1841, which were later offered in an English edition in 1857. This was followed by Müsaus, Volksmarchen der

Deutschen,1842, with 151 drawings on wood, engraved by John Allanson (q.v.); The Black Aunt, c1849; the Lord's Prayer,1856, wood engraved by A.Gaber (q.v.); and then two drawings to The Book of German Songs,1856, engraved by the Dalziel Brothers (q.v.). Richter's later work was sold by no fewer than six publishers who issued catalogues of clichés from his drawings for sale, for reproduction elsewhere. These were in circulation well into the 1890s and many were used in England. Some of Richter's drawings were also wood engraved by A.H.Payne (q.v.) the Leipzig engraver.
[See his autobiography, Lebenserinnerungen eines deutschen Malers,1885; J.F.Hoff's iconography,1877; A.L.Richter,Verzeichniss Seines Gesamten Graphischen Werkes,1922; also Muir, Victorian Illustrated Books]

RICHTER, Willibald fl.1840-56
Draughtsman illustrator and watercolourist. He was a pupil of the Vienna Academy in 1824, and worked in Vienna then travelled to England as well as Italy and Poland, painting views of these countries for the Vienna Academy,1840-50. He is listed here for his drawings of Turkey wood engraved in the Illustrated London News,1855-56.
[TB (bibliography); Houfe]

RICKETTS, Charles de Sousy 1866-1931
Wood engraver, illustrator, book designer, printer, painter, writer, stage designer and collector. He was born in Geneva on 2 October 1866, the son of a naval officer and illustrator, C.R.Ricketts (q.v.). He was brought up in France and Italy, was orphaned at sixteen years old while living in London, and apprenticed in 1882 to the wood engraver Charles Roberts (q.v.) at the City and Guilds Technical Art School, Kennington Park Road, Lambeth. There he learned to wood engrave and draw on wood; later he perfected his linear style under W.H.Hooper (q.v.). While at Lambeth he met his lifelong friend and collaborator, Charles Shannon (q.v.), also the young Laurence and Clemence Housman (qq.v.). Ricketts and Shannon completed their training by 1887, visited Puvis de Chavannes in Paris for advice on their future, and returned to London where Ricketts was to set up as illustrator while Shannon perfected his painting. They worked from The Vale, Chelsea, a house owned by Whistler, and there produced their first venture, The Dial,1889, a shortlived periodical which lasted for five numbers, until 1897, edited and illustrated by Ricketts, a lithograph by Shannon, and wood engravings by T.Sturge Moore and Lucien Pissarro (qq.v.). As part of the Dial's policy of experimental pictorial and literary publishing, the first volume claimed: 'all the woodcuts have been printed from the wood to ensure the greater sweetness of printing'. Ricketts financed their experimental work by drawing uninspired process engraved illustrations in Black and White,1891; and

the Magazine of Art,1892, 1895. He also designed most of Oscar Wilde's books (except Salome,1893), of which the most influential was Wilde's The House of Pomegranates,1891 (though four illustrations were by Shannon). Together Ricketts and Shannon drew and wood engraved Daphnis and Chlöe,1893, now recognised as the first book of the new 'woodcut revival'. Its thirty-seven illustrations and over 100 initials were divided between them: twenty-two illustrations drawn by Ricketts, who engraved most of the initials; and fifteen remaining illustrations by Shannon who wood engraved most of the intricate illustrations. Ricketts claim that 'the engraving alone of the pictures and initials occupied us for eleven months'. William Rothenstein recalled seeing the two engraving on wood at this time, 'bending over their blocks...[they] looked like figures from a missal'. This was followed by Hero and Leander,1894, with seven wood engraved illustrations. By 1894 they had established their own press, The Vale Press, and there they published some eighty-three books, many with the type, bindings and illustrations designed by them. (For a complete list see C.Franklin, Private Presses,1969; also Ricketts' A Bibliography of Books Published by Hacon and Ricketts,1904.) Ricketts perfected the ornate private press book, taking the work of William Morris further into the realms of inventive and experimental design. But his Vale Press ended after the last volume was published in 1904. By then the mass of blocks, drawings and initials, which took as long as three to four weeks each to design and engrave, had been destroyed by a fire at the storehouse, the Ballantyne Press, in 1899. From the turn of the century, then, Ricketts turned to oil painting, stage and costume design, jewellery-making and sculpture, as well as writing. As a wood engraver Ricketts was continually experimenting with the expressive quality of the technique. Not content with mere reproduction, he regarded the drawing on the wood block, intricately finished and watercoloured or inked, as a step in the inventive process which originated upon the block itself. T.Sturge Moore recalled how Ricketts would endlessly redraw his design on both sides of a sheet of thin paper until the basic arrangement was satisfactory. Then it would be pasted down on a firm card backing and squared for transfer to the block. However, once the drawing was set on the block, before he began cutting, he would move tiny pieces of white paper over the surface of the wood with a pin, trying out the infinite variations in altering and strengthening the design. Moore concluded, 'Actual sensuous proportions were in question, however slight'. Ricketts exhibited his work at numerous London galleries: The Fine Art Society, the Grosvenor Gallery, the Royal Society of British Artists, the Royal Institute of Painters in Watercolours, the Royal Institute of Painters in Oil-Colours, the Royal Scottish Academy and the Royal Academy, where he

was elected ARA in 1922 and RA in 1928. He died in London on 7 October 1931. The British Museum owns some of his engraved blocks.
[For biographical details see S.Calloway, Charles Ricketts,1979; J.Darracott, The World of Charles Ricketts,1980. For a discussion of his wood engravings see Cecil French, 'The Wood Engravings of Charles Ricketts', Print Collector's Quarterly,14, 1927,pp.195-217; also Ricketts on 'A Note on Original Wood Engraving', The Pageant,1897. For a full bibliography see TB]

RICKETTS, Charles Robert fl.1868-79
Occasional draughtsman illustrator for wood engravings, marine painter and naval officer. He was the father of Charles de Sousy Ricketts (q.v.) and worked in London where he exhibited marine pictures at the Royal Academy and the Royal Society of British Artists. He is listed here for his contribution to The Graphic,1871.
[Houfe]

RIDLEY, B.
Draughtsman illustrator, who contributed a drawing, wood engraved in London Society,1869.

RIDLEY, Charles fl.1880-83
London wood engraver, who worked at 84 Fleet Street, EC (POD,1880-83). He shared this office with the engravers A.Myerson and F.Babbage (qq.v.).

RIDLEY, Mathew White 1837-88
Occasional draughtsman illustrator of social realist subjects much admired by Van Gogh, also landscape painter and engraver. He was born in Newcastle-upon-Tyne in 1837, studied at the Royal Academy Schools under Smirke and Dobson and then became the earliest pupil of James Abbot McNeil Whistler (q.v.). He began drawing illustrations for wood engravings in Cassell's Family Magazine,1867; the Quiver,1867; and Every Boy's Magazine,1867; but he achieved his greatest notice with drawings for twenty pages in The Graphic,1869-77; also the Illustrated London News,1872-81. Van Gogh collected these for their technique. They included the grim series 'Pits and Pitmen' in The Graphic,28 January 1871, 4 February 1871, 11 February 1871, and 18 February 1871 which he claimed, 'remind one of etchings of Whistler or Seymour Haden'. His larger works for the Illustrated London News were engraved on wood by Joseph Swain (q.v.), who showed that 'that old style of engraving, that elaborate, honest, unembellished drawing is by far the best'. Ridley also exhibited work from 1857-88 at the Grosvenor Gallery, the Royal Academy and the Royal Institute of Painters in Watercolours, and died on 2 June 1888.
[TB; Bryan; Houfe; English Influences on Van Gogh; Country Life, 7 March 1974]

RIDLEY, W.D. fl.1860-c1925
Wood engraver, one of Benjamin Fawcett's (q.v.)
first competent engravers. He knew the early
copybooks which Fawcett drew and engraved, worked
with John Stabler (q.v.) and according to Reverend
M.C.F.Morris he photographed onto wood six
Sporting Prints,1890, engraved and coloured by
Fawcett but using a photographic process 'of his
own invention'.
[Reverend M.C.F.Morris, B.Fawcett,1925]

RIEBEN, Samuel fl.1880s
London wood engraver, who worked at 2 Ellington
Street, N (POD,1881).

RIMBAULT, Harry Augustus fl.1894-1910
London wood engraver, who worked at 33 Leicester
Square, WC (POD,1894-95), then 18 Green Street,
Leicester Square, WC (POD,1896-1910).

RIMBAULT, John Henry fl.1859-93
London wood engraver, who worked at 8 Dane's Inn,
Strand, WC (POD,1859-66), sharing the address
with P.Simon, C.M.Gorway and J.Watkins (qq.v.).
He moved to 13 Beaufort Buildings, WC (POD,1867-80),
then 30 Maiden Lane, Covent Garden, WC
(POD,1881-93).

RIMMER, Alfred 1829-93
Woodcut artist, illustrator and antiquary. He was
born in Liverpool on 9 August 1829, worked first as
an architect, then moved to Canada before settling in
Chester as an artist and writer. He illustrated
Ancient Streets and Homesteads of England; Pleasant
Spots about Oxford; Rambles about Eton and Harrow;
and About England with Dickens; also architectural
works such as On the Ancient Domestic Architecture
of Lancashire and Cheshire,1848-63; and Ancient
Halls of Lancashire,1852. He also drew for wood
engravings, notably 'Cheese Farming at Chester',
in the English Illustrated Magazine,1885, engraved
by O.Lacour (q.v.).
[TB; Bénézit; Art Journal,1873 (several illustrations);
Houfe]

RIOU, Edouard 1833-1900
Occasional draughtsman illustrator, landscape
painter. He was born in Saint-Servan on 2 December
1883 and exhibited work at the Salon from 1859. That
year he drew on wood for Henry Vizetelly's (q.v.)
Illustrated Times,1859. Later his work appeared
in the Illustrated London News,1894. He specialised
in illustrating Jules Verne and A.Riou's poetry. He
died in Paris on 27 January 1900.
[Houfe; Vizetelly, Glances Back]

RIPPON, John George fl.1884-85
London wood engraver, who worked at 40 Wellington
Street, Strand, WC (POD,1884-85).

RISCHGITZ, Edward 1828-1909
Occasional draughtsman, landscape painter. He was
born in Geneva on 28 July 1828, was a pupil of Diday
and worked in Paris but settled in London sometime
before 1878. He contributed a drawing wood engraved
in Good Words,1880. He also exhibited at the Grosvenor
Gallery and the Royal Society of Painter-Etchers and
Engravers, where he was elected a member in 1881.
He died at the home of his artist daughter, Mary
Rischgitz, on 3 November 1909.
[Houfe]

RIVIERE, Briton 1840-1920
Occasional draughtsman on wood, landscape and
animal painter. He was born in London on 14 August
1840, the son of William Riviere, drawing master
of Cheltenham College. He began making comic pen
sketches while at St Mary Hall, Oxford, and his work
was shown to the Punch editor, Mark Lemon, who
took him on for occasional work. He eventually
contributed twenty-three cuts, mainly of animals, to
Punch, from 1868-69; also while struggling for
recognition as a painter, he drew for Good Words,
1868; Good Words for the Young,1869; and the
Illustrated London News,1870. But such work turned
Riviere against drawing for wood engravings, mainly
because the pressure and close work permanently
injured his eyesight. By 1870 he had dropped it for
animal paintings which he exhibited at the Royal
Academy, where he was elected ARA in 1878 and RA
in 1881, the Royal Cambrian Academy, the Royal
Hibernian Academy and the Royal Scottish Academy.
He died in London on 20 April 1920.
[DNB; TB (full bibliography); Wood; Spielmann;
Houfe]

ROBERT, Charles-Jules 1843-98
French-born wood engraver, born in Chartres in
1843. He was a pupil of Chapon, made his debut in
1864, and worked for various French publications,
such as Magasin Pittoresque, L'Histoire des
Peintres, L'Illustration, and Monde Illustré, to
which he contributed portrait engravings on wood. He
engraved after Doré (q.v.); illustrations to Victor
Hugo's work; and various large wood engravings
after Neuville, J.P.Laurens and Henner, some of
which were known to a British public. He also
engraved French bank-notes. He died in 1898.
[Gusman]

ROBERTS, Charles fl.1870-97
Prominent London wood engraver, primarily of
portraits. He probably set up in partnership with
W.Biscombe Gardner (q.v.) as Roberts and Gardner,
47 Fleet Street, EC (POD,1872) where they engraved
for the Illustrated London News. They engraved a
full page cover to the fine art supplement, 18 May
1872, after a photograph of Jourdan's 'Le Favori'.
Charles Roberts then appeared on his own at the

same address, where he worked until 1878, then moved to J.D.Cooper's (q.v.) office at 188 Strand (POD,1879-80). He then worked from 27 Chancery Lane, WC (POD,1881-97), intermittently sharing the premises with G.M.Dodshon, H.Werdmüller and A.Leverett (qq.v.). Roberts' work included engravings after Luke Fildes to Dickens' The Mystery of Edwin Drood,1870, where he used a competent, atmospheric style which retained some of Fildes' intentions while glossing over his poor figure drawing. Roberts also engraved in 1873 after Helen Paterson (q.v.); and in 1875 after Hubert Herkomer (q.v.) for The Graphic. This was followed by his famous, extremely competent, large portrait engravings for the paper, notably that of Queen Victoria aged fifteen, after George Hayter, published as a special Jubilee supplement,1887. He also engraved for the English Illustrated Magazine,1885, notably 'Cley-next-the-Sea' after J.R.Wells. Roberts was a respected wood engraver who taught engraving at South Kensington from 1876-79, then at the Lambeth School of Art, where his pupils were the young T.S.Moore, Charles Ricketts, Charles Shannon and Clemence Housman (qq.v.), who worked as his freelance throughout the 1880s. By this time Roberts was considered 'one of the last those wood engravers upon whom then depended the existence of illustrated books and periodicals' (DNB). Gusman linked him with J.M.Johnstone and M.Klinkicht (qq.v.) and praised his portrait engravings: 'The work in wood is ingenious and varied in workmanship and solid in tone. The technique employed in the flesh tints, in the portraits, includes highlighting in white. The portrait of Cardinal Manning engraved by Roberts is a masterpiece in this genre' (Gusman,p.216).
[Gusman; Hake (as 'C.R.'); DNB]

ROBERTS, Charles J.Cramer 1834-95
Occasional draughtsman of portraits, military and social drawings, wood engraved in The Graphic, 1872-77. He was a professional soldier who joined the Army in 1853 and served in India and the Crimea, but retired in 1887. He also watercoloured landscape pictures.

ROBERTS and Gardner
(see Roberts, Charles)

ROBERTS, David 1796-1864
Occasional draughtsman on wood, prominent landscape and architectural painter. He was born in Stockbridge, near Edinburgh on 2 October 1796, and apprenticed to a house painter before working as a theatrical scenery painter in Carlisle, Edinburgh and Glasgow. He went to London in 1822, where he painted scenery for the Drury Lane Theatre and befriended the painter Clarkson Stanfield (q.v.). He travelled on the Continent in the 1820s and later visited Spain, Egypt and Palestine. His travels provided subjects for his

famous drawings and paintings of the Near East, some lithographed and published for private subscribers. He is listed here for his drawings on wood to Lockhart's Spanish Ballads, noted by Bohn in Chatto and Jackson. As a draughtsman Roberts excelled in accuracy and detail: 'It is as a draughtsman and as an organiser of masses that he shows most facility. He had a considerable sense of architectural effect; and he understood how to subordinate detail without losing richness' (DNB). Roberts was also a proficient painter, serving as Vice-President of the Society of British Artists in 1824, and President in 1830; he also exhibited at the Royal Academy where he was elected ARA in 1838 and RA in 1841. He died in London on 25 November 1864.
[For biographical information see J.Ballantine, The Life of David Roberts,1866; also Hardie; Redgrave; DNB; Chatto; Wood]

ROBERTS, Edwin fl.1862-90
Occasional draughtsman illustrator, genre and rustic painter. He drew comic figure illustrations for the Dalziel Brothers' (q.v.) Judy,1889. He also exhibited at the Royal Academy and the Royal Society of British Artists, working from Chelsea.

ROBERTS, Henry Benjamin 1832-1915
Occasional draughtsman, genre painter and water-colourist. He was born in Liverpool in 1831, the son and pupil of a landscape painter. He worked with W.H.Hunt and exhibited work at the Liverpool Academy, where he was elected member,1855, the New Watercolour Society, where he was elected member in 1867, and he was elected member of the Royal Society of British Artists in 1878. He is listed here for his drawings for wood engravings in the Illustrated London News,1871-75. He lived in Leyton, Essex from 1883, also briefly in North Wales.
[TB; Houfe]

ROBERTS, I.
Little is known of this draughtsman, who contributed a drawing of a social scene in The Graphic,1870, where it appeared as a wood engraving.

ROBERTS, Percy fl.1866-83
London wood engraver, who worked at 2 Surry (sic) Street, Strand (POD,1866-67), then at the C. and T. Robinson workshop (qq.v.) of 9 Essex Street, Strand (POD,1868-85). This was shared with J.Bye, W.Murden, G.Puttock and later J.Desbois and H.C.Mason (qq.v.). He specialised in dense landscapes which proved too dark or grey to be successful. The British Museum owns work after W.Small, and two waterfalls after H.Fenn inscribed 'for W.J.Palmer' and signed 'PALMER'.

ROBERTS, William fl.1889-92
London wood engraver, who worked at 61 Fleet Street,
EC (POD,1889-92). He shared the office with
E.Duvergier (q.v.).

ROBERTSON
(see Stubbs and Robertson)

ROBERTSON fl.1870s
Scottish wood engraver, who worked at 12 North Saint
David Street, Edinburgh (Kelly's,1876).

ROBERTSON, Henry Robert 1839-1921
Occasional draughtsman for wood engravings, landscape, genre and figure painter, and engraver. He
was born in Windsor in 1839, studied at the Royal
Academy Schools and began work drawing for wood
engravings in the Illustrated London News,1874,1881.
He also drew on wood for S.C.Hall's The Trial of Sir
Jasper,1870. He later drew 'Through the Cotes du
Nord' for the English Illustrated Magazine,1885,
wood engraved by O.Lacour, E.Ohme and R.Paterson
(qq.v.). Roberts also painted for the galleries, and
exhibited from 1861 at the New Gallery, the Royal
Academy, the Royal Society of British Artists, the
Royal Society of Painter-Etchers and Engravers,
where he was elected member in 1881, the Royal
Institute of Painters in Watercolours and the Royal
Institute of Painters of Oil-Colours. He died on
6 June 1921.
[TB; Bénézit; Hind; Houfe]

ROBERTSON, James (of Constantinople) fl.1855-56
Amateur draughtsman and photographer. He drew an
illustration of the Crimea, wood engraved in the
Illustrated London News,1855, and also photographed
subjects which Henry Vizetelly (q.v.) had wood engraved
for his Illustrated Times,1856. He later worked with
Felice Beato as an official British photographer.
[TB; Houfe; Vizetelly, Glances Back]

ROBERTSON, Thomas fl.1872-89
Glasgow wood engraver, who worked at 22 Dundas
Street, Glasgow (Kelly's,1872), then 89 Ingram
Street, Glasgow (Kelly's,1889). He may be related to
the Glasgow-born painter of marine subjects, Tom
Robertson (1850-?), who came to London by 1899.
[TB]

ROBERTSON, Thomas Bald fl.1886-99
London wood engraver, who worked at 11 Bride Street,
EC (POD,1886-92), sharing the office with B.D.Rudd
(q.v.). He moved to 15 Newcastle Street (POD,1895-96),
then Falcon Court, 32 Fleet Street, EC (POD,1898-99),
which he shared with W.Andrews (q.v.).

ROBINS, William Palmer 1882-1959
Woodcut artist, etcher and landscape painter. He was
born on 21 July 1882 in Southwark, London, and
studied architecture at King's College and art at St
Martin's, Goldsmiths' and the Royal College. His
woodcuts of landscape scenes are large but well
handled, showing a good use of linear contrast from
fine to bold line. He exhibited at the Royal Academy
from 1912, the New English Art Club and the Royal
Society of Painter-Etchers and Engravers, where he
was elected ARE in 1913 and RE,1917. He was also
elected ARWS in 1948 and RWS in 1955. He taught at
St Martin's 1904-21, and later at the Central School.
He lived in Sutton, Surrey and London and died on
14 July 1959. The British Museum owns several of
his best landscape woodcuts.
[Waters]

ROBINSON, C. ?-1881
London wood engraver, draughtsman illustrator on
wood. He was born in London, the son of a wood
engraver and book binder. He was apprenticed to the
lithographic firm Maclure, Macdonald and Macgregor,
attended the Finsbury School of Art,1857, then joined
the Illustrated London News about 1862, where he
contributed drawings and engraved until his death.
He also drew and engraved for Henry Vizetelly's
Illustrated Times,1865. He worked from his engraving
office, 9 Essex Street, Strand (POD,1864-69), which
he shared with W.Kelly, T.Reynolds, J.H.Pascoe
and W.Murden (qq.v.).
[Vizetelly, Glances Back; Houfe]

ROBINSON, Gerard fl.1870s
Provincial wood engraver, who worked at 97 and 101
Newgate Street, Newcastle-upon-Tyne (Kelly's,1872).

ROBINSON, H.R.
Comic draughtsman, who contributed two wood
engraved drawings to Punch,1864.
[Spielmann]

ROBINSON, Joseph James fl.1898-1902
London wood engraver, who worked at 107 Peckham
Road, SE (LSDS,1898-1902). He also appeared briefly
at 22A Southwark Street, SE (POD,1899-1900). He
may be related to the landscape painter Joseph
Robinson (fl.1882-85) who drew for the Illustrated
London News,1885.

ROBINSON, Thomas fl.1864-1900
London wood engraver and draughtsman on wood,
probably the father and teacher of the illustrators
Charles, T.H. and W.Heath Robinson. Thomas
Robinson worked as a London wood engraver from
9 Essex Street, Strand (POD,1864-69), sharing the
office with T.Reynolds (q.v.). He later moved to
8 Dane's Inn, Strand (POD,1871-84). He worked
chiefly on the Penny Illustrated Paper, and made
occasional drawings for Dark Blue,1871-73. The
London directory lists a Thomas Robinson,
draughtsman on wood, working as late as 1900 at

1 (sic) Dane's Inn, Strand (Kelly's, 1889-1900).
(See following entry)
[Houfe]

ROBINSON, Thomas fl.1865-69
London wood engraver, who worked at 34 Westbourne
Road (POD, 1865-69). He is probably the same as the
above, the new address being perhaps a second or
home address.

ROBINSON, Thomas Philip
(see De Grey, 1st Earl)

ROBLEY, Major-General Horatio Gordon 1840-1930
Amateur draughtsman illustrator for wood engravings
in Punch. He was born in Funchal, Madeira on
28 June 1840 and served as a soldier in the tropics.
He is listed here for his twenty-seven drawings for
Punch which he sent to Charles Keene (q.v.) during
his tour as member of the 91st (Argyle and Sutherland)
Highlanders. Keene considered him 'a very obliging
correspondent...I don't follow his drawings very
much, but they are very useful in military subjects'.
These appeared in Punch from 1873-78, touched up
by Keene before they were wood engraved. He also
drew for The Graphic and the Illustrated London
News. He died on 29 October 1930.
[Houfe; Spielmann; G.S.Layard, C.Keene, 1892, p.179]

RODGERS, Albert Ellison fl.1880s
Provincial draughtsman on wood, who worked from
Granville Terrace, High Street, Bracebridge,
Lincoln (Kelly's, 1889).

ROE
Wood engraver, who engraved after Wells (q.v.)
for Charles Knight's Penny Magazine, June 1841.
[Bodleian Library]

ROE, Richard Randall fl.1880s
Provincial wood engraver, who worked at East
Street, Blandford, Dorset (Kelly's, 1889).

ROGERS, James Edward 1838-96
Draughtsman illustrator, painter of architectural
and marine subjects. He was born in Dublin in 1838
and worked as an architect before turning to water-
colour. He illustrated More's Ridicula; Ridicula
Rediviva; and Mrs Mulock's Fairy Book, c1870. Later
he contributed illustrations to the English Illustrated
Magazine, 1893-94. He was elected ARHA, 1871,
RHA, 1872, and exhibited at the Royal Academy, the
Royal Society of Painter-Etchers and Engravers, the
Royal Institute of Painters in Watercolours and the
Royal Institute of Painters in Oil-Colours. He worked
in London from 1876, and died on 18 February 1896.
The British Museum owns three proof designs
wood engraved by the Dalziel Brothers (q.v.),
1866.

[Houfe; TB]

ROGERS, John Albert fl.1880s
London wood engraver, who worked at 89 Farringdon
Street, EC (POD, 1886). He shared the office with
L.Knott and W.J.Potter (qq.v.). He may be related
to John Rogers (1808-88) the English-born portrait
engraver, who died in New York.
[Stauffer; TB; Fielding]

ROGERS, John Frederick fl.1880s
London draughtsman on wood, who worked at
169 Fleet Street, EC (Kelly's, 1880).

ROGERS, Richard fl.1876-80
Provincial wood engraver, who worked at 61 (120)
High Street, Ashton Newtown, Birmingham
(Kelly's, 1876-80).

ROGERS, William Harry 1825-73
Occasional draughtsman on wood, designer of
ornamental letters and vignettes. He was the son of
the wood carver William Gibbs Roberts, and began
as a designer of intricate ornaments and emblems
based on 16th century German prototypes. These he
provided for the Art Journal, 1851, using plant
motifs with a gothic script. He designed wood
engravings in Poe's Poetical Works, 1858. By 1860
he had designed for Joseph Cundall a monogram and
decorative illuminations for an edition of Shakespeare's
The Merchant of Venice, 1860. He drew on wood for
Quarle's Emblems Divine and Moral, 1861, with
Charles Bennett (q.v.). Next he designed Spiritual
Conceits, or Emblems of Christian Life, 1862,
engraved on wood by Joseph Swain (q.v.). He worked
in Wimbledon and died there in 1873. The British Museum
owns his early designs wood engraved by the Dalziel
Brothers (q.v.); also a set of proofs engraved 1866.
[Nagler; DNB; Chatto; McLean, Victorian Book Design;
TB; Houfe]

ROGERS, William Thomas fl.1898-1900
London wood engraver, who worked at 2 Great New
Street, EC (POD, 1898), then at 3 Wine Office Court,
EC (POD, 1899-1900). He may have begun in
collaboration with G.Potts as Potts and Rogers (q.v.).

ROLLS and Company fl.1893-94
London wood engraving firm, with an office at
7 Featherstone Buildings, WC (POD, 1893-94).

ROMER, Mrs Frank (afterwards Mrs Jopling-Rowe)
Comic draughtsman for Punch, also portrait painter.
She was the niece of Mark Lemon, editor of Punch,
and for him made four drawings for wood engravings
in Punch, 1869.
[Spielmann]

RONKETTI, Anthony Joseph fl.1897-99
London wood engraver, who worked at 25 later 21
Northampton Road, EC (POD,1897-99). This was
also the address of the Engravers' Boxwood Block
Makers.

ROOKE, Noel 1881-1953
Wood engraver, book illustrator and decorator,
painter and teacher. He was born in London on
30 December 1881, the son of a watercolourist and
studied at the Slade,1899-1903 under Fred Brown,
Tonks, Steer and Russell, then at the Central School
under W.R.Lethaby and Edward Johnston. By 1904 he
had begun wood engraving, and the following year he
was appointed teacher of book illustration at the
Central School. He was given permission to teach
engraving there in 1912 and his pupils included
Margaret Pilkington (q.v.). He experimented with
colour in wood engraving and became head of the
School of Book Production, Central School in 1914,
teaching M.Anneslay and Robert Gibbings (qq.v.).
In 1920 he was a founding member of the Society of
Wood Engravers, also associate member of the Royal
Society of Painter-Etchers and Engravers. He also
exhibited at the New English Art Club and the Royal
Academy and showed wood engravings at the British
Empire Exhibition in Wembley,1924-25. He lived in
London and died on 7 October 1953.
[Garrett]

ROOKER, Edward fl.1876-77
London wood engraver, who worked at 227 Strand,
WC (POD,1876-77). He shared the office with
T.Hobbs and F.Watkins (qq.v.).

ROSS, Charles H. fl.1867-83
Comic draughtsman, dramatist and novelist. He
worked as a civil servant at Somerset House and drew
in his spare time. The publisher William Tinsley gave
him two Christmas annuals to edit and his drawings
and editorial skills came to the notice of the wood
engravers, the Dalziel Brothers (q.v.) who made
Ross editor of their magazine Judy,1867-78. He drew
on wood for this, signing his work 'Marie Duval', his
wife's maiden name. His drawings were slight,
although satiric. He later became proprietor of
C.H.Ross's Variety Paper. Other illustrations
appeared in Queens and Kings and Other Things; in
The Boy Crusoe, and Merry Conceits and Whimsical
Rhymes Written and Drawn by C.H.Ross,1883. The
British Museum owns several proof engravings after
his designs engraved by the Dalziel Brothers
1865.
[Dalziels' Record; Houfe; W.Tinsley, Random
Recollections,1900,pp.267-68]

ROSS, Thomas fl.1830s
London wood engraver, who worked at 8 Gilspur
Street (Pigot,1839).

ROSSETTI, Dante Gabriel 1828-82
Occasional draughtsman illustrator on wood, Pre-
Raphaelite painter and poet. He was born in London
on 12 May 1828, the son of an Italian refugee and
professor of King's College and the brother of William
Michael Rossetti and Christina Rossetti. He was
educated at King's College and studied drawing under
J.S.Cotman. He entered the Royal Academy Schools
in 1845 but dissatisfied, he turned for instruction to
Ford Madox Brown (q.v.). Brown together with
Millais and Holman Hunt later joined with Rossetti
to form the Pre-Raphaelite Brotherhood,1848-53, of
which Rossetti was the centre. Their paintings and
illustrations, however few, were to have a lasting
influence on Victorian art. As Gleeson White
commented of Rossetti, 'He, more than any modern
painter, would seem to be responsible for the present
decorative school of illustrators, whose work has
attracted unusual interest from many continental
critics of late, and is recognised by them as
peculiarly "English"'. Rossetti as a draughtsman on
wood executed a mere ten drawings (according to
White), yet he was paid handsomely, £30 each for
the small drawings on wood to Tennyson's Poems
which placed him alongside the more established
professional draughtsmen on wood at an early stage
in his career. The ten drawings on wood are: 'Elfen-
mere' in William Allingham's The Music Master,
1855, engraved on wood by the Dalziel Brothers
(q.v.); five drawings to Moxon's edition of Tennyson's
Poems,1857, again engraved by the Dalziels; two
illustrations to his sister Christina Rossetti's The
Goblin Market,1862; and two to her The Prince's
Progress,1866, engraved by W.J.Linton (q.v.).
Later appeared some drawings reissued from early
days e.g. Flower Pieces,1888, which contained the
'Elfen-mere' drawing, and the unpublished 'The
Queen's Page', drawn in 1854. Rossetti laboured long
over the blocks for all of these illustrations: over a
dozen studies survive for one block of the Tennyson
commission alone. He seems to have drawn in pencil,
ink, and red chalk directly on the whitened block,
with an intricacy of line and shading that the Dalziels
found impossible to reproduce in engraved line. One
of the Dalziels lamented his task, as White explained:
'When, however, the white coating had been rubbed
away in parts, and all sorts of strokes in pen, pencil,
and pigment added, it is not surprising that the
paraphrase failed to please the designer. Although
the drawings naturally perished in the cutting, and
cannot be brought forward as decisive evidence, we
may believe that the engraver spoilt them, and yet
also believe that no craftsman who ever lived would
have been absolutely successful' (White,p.160).
Rossetti's side of the story was given by his brother,
William Michael Rossetti (in Dante Gabriel Rossetti,
Letters and Memories,I,p.189): 'At the time they
gave him endless trouble and small satisfaction. Not
indeed that the invention or the mere designing of

these works was troublesome to him. He took great pains with them, but, as what he wrought at was always something which informed and glowed in his mind, he was not more tribulated by these than by other drawings. It must be said, also, that himself only, and not Tennyson, was his guide. He drew just what he chose, taking from his author's text nothing more than a hint and an opportunity. The trouble came in with the engraver and the publisher. With some of the doings of the engraver, Dalziel (not Linton, whom he found much more conformable to his notion), he was grievously disappointed. He probably exasperated Dalziel, and Dalziel certainly exasperated him. Blocks were re-worked upon and proofs sent back with vigour'. Rossetti himself wrote to W.Bell Scott in February 1857: 'I have designed five blocks for Tennyson, save seven which are still cutting and maiming. It is a thankless task. After a fortnight's work my block goes to the engraver, like Agag delicately, and is hewn in pieces before the Lord Harry. I took more pains with one block lately than I had done with anything for a long while. It came back to me on paper, the other day, with Dalziel performing his cannibal jig in the corner, and I have really felt like an invalid ever since. As yet I fare best with W.J.Linton. He keeps stomach aches for you, but Dalziel deals in fevers and agues. Address to Dalziel Brothers: "O woodman spare that block, O gash not anyhow! It took ten days by clock, I'd fain protect it now". Chorus--Wild laughter from Dalziels' Workshop'. Nevertheless Rossetti as a draughtsman illustrator broke the path for future 'Sixties School' illustrators to follow; he was 'the golden milestone where from all later work must needs be measured' (White). His impatience with wood engravers, and his singular insistence that his blocks should appear as accurately copied as possible were object lessons to future illustrators. For himself, as he once wrote William Allingham, 'As to the engraving, I suppose it is hardly possible that I can be satisfied'. Gilbert Dalziel's engraved blocks after Rossetti designs are in the Hartley Collection, Boston Museum; the British Museum also owns some Dalziel proofs.
[For Rossetti as draughtsman on wood see White; Dalziels' Record; also bibliographies in TB; DNB; Wood]

ROTHWELL, Thomas H. fl.1880s
Provincial wood engraver, who worked at 15 Fold Street, Bolton, Lancashire (Kelly's,1889).

ROUSE, Arthur Edmonds fl.1883-86
London wood engraver, who worked at 181 later 180 Fleet Street (POD,1883-86). He shared the office with H.Werdmüller (q.v.).

ROUSE, Walter Edmunds fl.1883-84
London wood engraver, who worked at 168 Fleet Street, EC (POD,1883-84). The address was shared with

Purchese and Canham (q.v.).

ROWBOTHAM, Thomas Charles Leeson 1823-75
Draughtsman, engraver, lithographer and landscape painter. He was the son and pupil of his artist father, Thomas Leeson Rowbotham (1783-1853) and exhibited from 1840-75 at the Royal Academy, the Society of British Artists, the New Watercolour Society and other galleries. He was elected RI in 1851. He illustrated his father's The Art of Sketching from Nature, and collaborated on The Art of Painting in Watercolours. In 1875 he produced small volumes of English Lake Scenery, and Picturesque Scottish Scenery. He also produced various chromolithographic plates of landscape scenery. The British Museum owns a collection of his designs wood engraved by the Dalziel Brothers (q.v.), 1848-51, and a small landscape mountain scene engraved in 1857.

ROWLAND
(see Carter and Rowland)

ROWLAND, Edward Jones fl.1880-89
Provincial wood engraver, who worked at 5 Snow Hill and 49A Dudley Street, Wolverhampton (Kelly's,1880), then 35A Dudley Street, Wolverhampton, (Kelly's,1889).

ROWLEY, The Hon. Hugh 1833-1908
Occasional illustrator on wood, painter of flowers. He was born in 1833, educated at Eton and Sandhurst, entered the army and retired in 1854. He then took up drawing and floral painting, drew on wood for London Society,1867, and illustrated Gamosagamnon, or Hints on Hymen,1870. He also wrote numerous humorous articles and edited the short-lived magazine, Puniana. He also exhibited at the Royal Academy, 1866, and died on 12 May 1908.

ROY, A. fl.1883-84
Wood engraver, who engraved illustrations in the English Illustrated Magazine,1883-84. These included engraved drawings to H.D.Traill's 'Two Centuries of Bath', 1883, and to the drawings of Hollar to Austin Dobson's 'Changes at Charing Cross', 1884.

ROYDS, Miss Mabel fl.1890s
Colour woodcut artist, praised by Gusman. He linked her work with that of the engravers E.Kirkpatrick and H.G.Webb (qq.v.).

ROYLE, C.
Amateur draughtsman illustrator. He drew on wood for an engraving in the Illustrated London News,1859.

ROYLE, Henry William fl.1888-1901
London wood engraver, who worked at 39 Regent Square, WC (POD,1888-91), then 21 Regent Square,

WC (POD,1897-98), and later 48 Burton Crescent, WC (POD,1899-1901).

ROZZELL, William O.P. fl.1871-79
London wood engraver, who worked at 52 Edward Street, Limehouse Fields, E (POD,1871-72), then 2 Blount Street, Limehouse Fields, E (POD,1873-79).

RUDD, Benjamin Dale fl.1864-1901
London wood engraver, who worked at 27 Fetter Lane, Fleet Street (POD,1864-66), shared with E.Heaviside and C.Bruwier (qq.v.). Rudd disappears from the London directories until 1888, when he worked at 11 St Bride Street, EC (POD,1888-1901), an office he shared with T.B.Robertson (q.v.).

RUDD Brothers
Provincial firm of draughtsmen on wood, with an office at 1 Opie Street, Norwich (Kelly's,1900).

RUDDOCK, John Candlish
London wood engraver, who worked at 97 Cheapside, EC (POD,1896).

RUFFLE, George William
London wood engraver, who worked at 380 New Cross Road, SE (POD,1869).

RUSDEN, Athelstan
Manchester draughtsman cartoonist on wood. He contributed a drawing on wood of a 'Disraeli Elephant', which appeared in Punch,1879, but soon 'drifted away' from Punch in favour of work on Moonshine.
[Spielmann]

RUSSELL, Frederick Howard
London wood engraver, who worked at 188 Strand, WC (POD,1901).

RYLAND, Henry 1856-1924
Draughtsman illustrator and painter. He was born in Biggleswade, Bedfordshire in 1856 and became a pupil of B.Constant, Boulanger, Lefebvre, and Cormon in Paris. Influenced by the Pre-Raphaelites, he turned to designing stained glass as well as book illustration. He illustrated Elizabeth Barrett Browning's Sonnets from the Portuguese, and drew for wood engraved illustrations in the English Illustrated Magazine,1883-85. These included drawings to Alfred Ainger's article 'The Women of Chaucer', 1883, wood engraved by J.D.Cooper and J.Cocking (qq.v.); and illustrations to Grant Allen's 'Primroses and Cowslips', 1885, wood engraved by H.F.Davey, W.M.R.Quick, W. and R.Cheshire and J.D.Cooper (qq.v.). Ryland also painted legends and various subject pictures which he exhibited at the Grosvenor Gallery, the New Gallery, the Royal Academy, the Royal Society of British Artists, the

Royal Hibernian Academy, the Royal Institute of Painters in Watercolours, where he was elected member in 1898, the Royal Institute of Painters in Oil-Colours and the Royal Scottish Watercolour Society. He died in Bedford Park, London on 23 November 1924.
[TB; Houfe; Who's Who; The Artist, September 1898, pp.1-9; Cassell's Magazine, Volume 194]

RYLAND, Howard and Company fl.1876-1900
Provincial wood engraver, who worked at 105-107 Newhall Street, Birmingham (Kelly's,1876), then 40 St Paul's Square, Birmingham (Kelly's,1880), and 217 Bradford Street, Birmingham (Kelly's,1900).

S., M.U.
Unidentified wood engraver, who engraved five sketches by Robert Cruikshank (q.v.) of Edward Irving (1792-1834), founder of the Catholic Apostolic Church. They are in the British Museum.
[Hake]

S., W.H.
Unidentified wood engraver, who engraved the drawings of Luke Fildes (q.v.) for Cassell's Magazine,1870.

SACHS, John fl.1858-99
London wood engraver and draughtsman on wood. He worked at 3 Red Lion Square, Holborn, WC (POD,1858-61), and 203 Strand, WC (POD,1862-63), then moved to the workshop of the prominent wood engraver W.J.Palmer (q.v.) at 33 Essex Street, Strand (POD,1864-71), working there with G.L.Butlin and R.H.Keene (qq.v.). He then moved to 223 Strand, WC (POD,1872-81) and then 57 and 58 Chancery Lane, WC (POD,1882-97), adding a second premises at 22 Camden Street, Oakley Square, NW (POD,1890-99). Fincham lists a bookplate for Johannis Sachs,1881, designed and engraved by J.Forbes Nixon and John Sachs.

SACHS, William J.
Topographical draughtsman on wood, who contributed a drawing on wood to Henry Vizetelly's (q.v.) Illustrated Times,1866.

SALA, George Augustus Henry 1828-96
Draughtsman illustrator, prolific journalist and author. He was born in London on 24 November 1828, the son of a hard-working actress and singer, who sent him to Paris and then to study with the miniature painter Carl Schiller in London. When just fifteen years old in 1843, he was a 'capable draughtsman' (DNB) and was employed by various London theatres to work on scenery design. He then became a book illustrator and edited Chat. He illustrated Alfred Bunn's Word with Punch,1847, followed by

illustrations to Albert Smith's The Man in the Moon, 1848, commissioned by the author. He taught himself to etch and afterwards learned engraving, nurturing an ambition to follow in his friends, George Cruikshank and Hablot K.Browne's ('Phiz') (qq.v.) footsteps. He illustrated a comic guidebook for Ackermann, Practical Exposition of J.M.W.Turner's Picture, 'Hail, Rain, Steam and Speed', 1850, and produced four large lithographs for the Great Exhibition. Later he prepared aquatint views of the Duke of Wellington's funeral, with Henry Alken,1852. Soon his journalism took precedence over his drawing. He was sent by Dickens to cover the Crimean War on the Russian side,1856; wrote articles for All the Year Round, 1858; founded and edited Temple Bar,1860-66; served as correspondent to the Illustrated London News,1860-86; and covered the American Civil War for the Daily Telegraph,1863. His novels were serialised first by Henry Vizetelly (q.v.) in his Illustrated Times from 1855, and more to the point here he wrote 'William Hogarth, Painter, Engraver and Philosopher', serialised in Thackeray's Cornhill, March-November, 1860 (issued in volume form 1866) which he illustrated on wood, engraved by the Dalziel Brothers (q.v.). Sala's letter to the Dalziels concerning their engraving of his drawings showed how carefully he worked so that his drawings should be clearly engraved: 'You will permit me to thank you for the exquisitely artistic manner in which my rude scratchings on Wood have been rendered by your graver...My chief defect appears to be heaviness and blackness of touch, caused by painfully defective sight. I will, however, endeavour to remedy this by using a harder point, and trusting more to your tasteful interpretation, without overloading my shadows with cross-hatching' (Dalziels' Record,p.136). The British Museum owns proof engravings of his designs by the Dalziel Brothers, 1863.
[For a complete account of Sala's career see DNB; Sala's own Life and Adventures of G.A.Sala,1895; Ralph Straus, G.A.Sala,1942; see also TB; Bryan; Houfe]

SALMON, Henry Rider fl.1855-69
London wood engraver, who worked at 2 Racquet Court, Fleet Street (Hodgson's,1855). He disappeared from the London directories until 1868, when he was working from 1 Racquet Court, Fleet Street, EC (POD,1868-69).

SALOP Stationery Stores fl.1880s
Provincial wood engraving firm, with an office at Cambrian Buildings, Oswald Street, Oswestry (Kelly's,1889).

SAMBOURNE, Edward Linley 1844-1910
Prolific draughtsman cartoonist for wood engravings, primarily in Punch. He was born in Pentonville, London on 4 January 1844 and educated at the City of

London School and Chester College, before being apprenticed to the marine engineers Messrs John Penn and Son, Greenwich. During that period he began to draw for Punch; his comic work was wood engraved and published there from 27 April 1867. He was made a regular staff member in 1871, later succeeding John Tenniel (q.v.) as chief cartoonist in 1901. Sambourne was largely self-taught, although he attended South Kensington for a fortnight, and it was the unexpected workload thrust upon him at an early stage that allowed him to develop a distinctive style for wood engravers such as Joseph Swain (q.v.) to transfer into engravings. As Spielmann explained: 'He began to form a style of his own, and that style did not lend itself to the representation of modern life. It was suited better for decoration than for movement; while the beauty of line and of silhouette which he sought and obtained, in spite of his intense, almost aggressive individuality, placed him absolutely apart from all the black-and-white artists of the day'. Sambourne was best when interpreting real life and drawing under pressure of deadlines. His eye for detail and sharp, clear line left some critics to wonder at his rather mechanical results, but these were mostly due to his working methods: he photographed and kept a record of over 10,000 photographs of various personalities, in a variety of dress, as well as animals, insects, and everyday objects; as he claimed, everything 'from a weasel to a Welshman'. He was an expert draughtsman in pencil and pen and ink: 'Like Giotto and his legendary feat, he can draw you a perfect circle with his pen--and perhaps he is the only man in the country who can do it' (Spielmann). Over a nearly forty year period on Punch he became the master cartoonist, whose distinctive style of linear clarity spilled over into occasional book illustrations as well. Such work included: The New Sandford and Merton,1872; Our Autumn Holidays on French Rivers, 1874; and The Royal Umbrella,1880. But his most famous commission was to Charles Kingsley's The Water Babies,1885, called by one critic 'the only distinguished woodcut book of the eighties'. Then came illustrations to Maurice Noel's Buz, or the Life and Adventures of the Honey Bee,1889; to Thackeray's The Four Georges,1894; and to The Real Adventures of Robinson Crusoe,1893. It is perhaps not surprising that Sambourne's work in periodicals other than Punch was rare, although he appeared early on in London Society,1868; and he contributed 'A Dream of Plum Pudding', an elaborate fantasy with numerous figures drawn full page and engraved by Joseph Swain (q.v.) in the Illustrated London News,Christmas supplement,1876. During the 1890s he contributed to Good Words,1890; Black and White,1891; Sketch,1893; Pall Mall Magazine, 1893; Daily Chronicle,1895; and the Minister,1895. He also exhibited Punch drawings at the Royal Academy, 1885-1904 and held an exhibition at the

London Fine Art Society,1893. He died in Kensington on 3 August 1910.
[Spielmann; TB; Houfe; Graves; Who's Who,1910]

SAMUEL, Samuel fl.1880s
London wood engraver, who worked at 3 Marlborough Road, Chelsea, SW (POD,1889).

SANDBY, T.
Draughtsman illustrator, who contributed illustrations to Austin Dobson's 'A Tour of Covent Garden', in the English Illustrated Magazine,1883, wood engraved by R.Davey (q.v.).

SANDERSON, H. fl.1862-65
Draughtsman of figure subjects on wood, who contributed to London Society,1862-63; Churchman's Family Magazine,1863; and Fun,1865. He also illustrated Holmeden's Legends from Fairyland, 1862. The British Museum owns proof engravings of his designs, engraved by the Dalziel Brothers (q.v.), 1861-64.

SANDERSON, James
Provincial draughtsman on wood, who worked at 31 Park Road, Jarrow, Durham (Kelly's,1889). His draughtsmen colleagues here were A.Bain, S.Kelly and George Johnstone (qq.v.).

SANDS, J. fl.1862-88
Amateur draughtsman on wood, primarily for Punch. He was trained to draw on wood by Charles Keene (q.v.), 'who made him practise drawing until he became dyspeptic and melancholy at the sight of his own feeble work' (Spielmann), and after their first meeting in 1862, Sands contributed drawings to various London magazines under Keene's supervision. He began to draw for Punch in 1870, and eventually contributed 'three-score' drawings from 1870-80, but gave up work here when dissatisfied by his treatment, being overshadowed by Keene's nephew A.Corbould (q.v.). He held a number of other jobs, and was an explorer in South America, where he drew for a Buenos Aires newspaper, and also explored the Hebrides, where he retired and became a recluse in Walls, Shetland. He published his record of life, Out of This World, or Life in St Kilda,1876.
[Spielmann; G.S.Layard, Life of C.Keene,1892, pp.123-28]

SANDYS, Frederick Augustus 1832-1904
Proficient draughtsman for wood engraving, portrait painter and chalk artist. He was born in Norwich on 1 May 1832, the son of a journeyman dyer and portrait painter who exposed his son to the work of early Flemish painters, and seeing that his son had talent, sent him to local art schools, the Norwich Grammar School and a newly opened branch of the Government School of Design. He drew his first illustrations to

The Birds of Norfolk, and The Antiquities of Norwich. He came to London in 1851, where he worked copying pictures in the National Gallery and exhibited that year at the Royal Academy a portrait crayon drawing. He continued to exhibit there, while earning his living as a draughtsman on wood for various magazines, coming under the influence of Rossetti (q.v.) and his circle, and their superbly finished designs for illustrations. He also studied and adopted the firm outline of Dürer (he copied his monogram from Dürer) and the work of the popular German draughtsman, Albert Rethel (1816-59). Drawing on wood became Sandys' most important contribution throughout the 1860s: Rossetti alone declared him 'the greatest of living draughtsmen'. He remembered his first commissioned drawing on wood, for Thackeray's Cornhill,1860, an illustration to George MacDonald's 'Legend of the Portent', for which he received the staggering amount of 40 guineas. 'He knew nothing of the correct way of preparing it; it was impossible to work on its smooth surface with either pencil or pen, and he finally drew "The Portent" line by line with a brush and Indian ink, and found the process so simple and the result so satisfactory that he always thereafter employed the same method' (White,p.56). Another observer remarked on Sandys' fine sable brush of nearly one hair, and his use of a quill pen cut by himself from the tip of the point upwards. 'He drew everything from life, seldom even making use of the lay figure for his draperies, and in fact did nothing without a model before him. It was his method to prepare most careful studies in pen and ink or pencil, before drawing direct on the wood block. He never used Chinese white to lighten or correct, but worked from a large slab of Indian ink' (White,p.56). For the most part he was satisfied with his engravers and perhaps was one of the most competent draughtsmen of the period because he knew the engraver's limitations and gave him only what he had learned would be possible to print: he never depended upon overlays of fine tints or washes to give atmosphere to his designs. Of his 'Danaë' block he wrote characteristically (in October 1880): 'My drawing was most perfectly cut by Swain, from my point of view, the best piece of wood-cutting of our time -- mind I am not speaking of my work, but of Swain's'. Gleeson White claimed that Sandys' designs totalled a mere thirty, thirteen of which appeared in Once a Week,1861-67, engraved by Joseph Swain (q.v.), as well as several in Cornhill, 1860, 1866; Good Words,1862-63; Willmott's Sacred Poetry,1862, engraved by the Dalziels (q.v.); and Churchman's Family Magazine,1863. Sandys' favourite drawing was 'Amor Mundi' to Christina Rossetti's poem in Shilling Magazine,1865. Then followed a steel-engraved frontispiece to Meredith's Shaving of Shagpat,1865 and to Mrs Craik's Christian's Mistake,1866. Further wood engraved drawings appeared in magazines such as Quiver,1866;

Argosy,1866; and the books Touches of Nature by
Eminent Artists,1866; Idyllic Pictures,1867;
Thornbury's Legendary Ballads,1876; and one
drawing for the Dalziels' Bible Gallery,1881. Sandys'
drawings on wood were admired by a new generation
of revivalist wood engravers. They were reprinted in
such influential new publications as The Quarto,1896,
where Joseph Pennell included an unfinished wood
block drawing in his eulogy article on Sandys. The
equally influential Century Guild Hobby-Horse,1888,
published his engravings, while such nineties critics
as Edmund Gosse and J.M.Grey admired and
praised his engraved contributions. On his death in
London on 25 June 1904 his wife had a selection of
twenty-five wood engravings published as Reproductions
of Woodcuts by F.Sandys,1860-66, although the
printing was poorly done. Proofs of most of his
illustrations are in the Hartley Collection, Boston
Museum; also the British Museum owns proof
engravings by the Dalziel Brothers.
[For a discussion of Sandys' illustrations see Reid;
White; The Artist,December 1897; F.Sandys
Brighton Museum catalogue,1974; also Volume I;
Wood; Dalziels' Record; DNB; Bryan]

SARGENT, G.F. fl.1840-60
Draughtsman on wood, who lived in London and special-
ised in topographical and antiquarian subjects. He began
drawing for wood engravings in Charles Knight's (q.v.)
London,1841-42, and Knight's Shakespeare Illustrated,
1842. He drew for the Pilgrim's Progress and the Holy
War Illuminated,c1850; Cassell's Illustrated Family
Paper,1853; the Illustrated London Magazine,1853-55;
the Seasons and The Castle of Indolence,1857; Welcome
Guest,1860; and the Illustrated London News,1860. He
also illustrated on his own T.L.Peacock's Polite
Repository and sixteen drawings to The Heather World,
1851. Sargent also painted watercolour landscapes but
was not proficient enough to be seconded for the New
Watercolour Society in 1854. The British Museum owns
proof engravings by the Dalziel Brothers (q.v.),
1839-47,1853, and J.Wakefield (q.v.).
[TB; Bénézit; Houfe; Nagler]

SARGENT, Henry fl.1875-76
London wood engraver, who worked at East Temple
Chambers, Whitefriars (POD,1875-76). He shared
the office with W.R.Buckman (q.v.). Gusman listed
a 'Sargent, --' wood engraver with W.J.Linton (q.v.) for
the French publication La Semaine des Enfants,1851.

SARGENT, Waldo
Draughtsman, who drew on wood for an engraving in
London Society,1863.

SAUNDERS, John Charles fl.1888-99
London wood engraver, who worked at 26 Oakfield
Road, Highgate Road, NW (LSDN,1888), then 1 Norfolk
Street, Strand, WC (POD,1892-99). He shared this

last office with R.Cousins, G.Cheshire, G.Meek
and A.Shepherd (qq.v.).

SAUNDERS, William Tyrie fl.1855-85
London wood engraver, who worked at 24 Little
Queen Street, Holborn (POD,1855-63). He disappears
from the directories until 1882, when he was working
at 13 Great Turnstile, WC (POD,1882-85).

SAUNDERSON
(see Burkitt and Saunderson)

SAUVE, Auguste fl.1887-91
London wood engraver, who worked at 136 Southampton
Row, WC (POD,1887-91).

SAVAGE, Reginald fl.1886-1905
Designer and illustrator for wood engravings,
portrait and figure painter. He was closely associated
with the Essex House Press and usually illustrated
history or poetry. He worked with Laurence Housman
(q.v.) for wood engravings engraved by Clemence
Housman (q.v.), for instance, the frontispiece to
Tennyson's Maude,1905. Walter Crane (q.v.)
admired his designs, which he called 'weird'. His other
drawings appeared in Black and White,1891; the Dial,
1892; Butterfly,1893; St Pauls,1894; Madame,1895;
Ludgate Monthly; Pageant,1896-97; and Fun,1901.
He signed his work: 'S' (reversed) 'R' (superimposed).
[For his Essex House Press work see Houfe; also
Sketchley; Studio,1914]

SAVAGE, William 1770-1843
Wood engraver, draughtsman and pioneering colour
printer. He was born in Howden, Yorkshire in 1770,
the son of a clockmaker, educated at the local church
school and in 1790 began a business as printer and
bookseller. He worked in partnership with his brother
James Savage (1767-1845) in Howden, but in 1797 he
moved to London where he was appointed printer to
the Royal Institution. About 1803 he began as a London
printer on his own and printed Foster's British
Gallery of Engravings, which established his
reputation. He experimented with printers' inks,
published Preparations in Printing Ink in Various
Colours,1832, and was awarded a medal 'for his
imitations of drawings, printed from engravings on
wood, with inks of his own preparing'. His most
influential work for wood engravers was Practical
Thoughts on Decorative Printing, issued in two parts,
1818 and 1823, which included his wood engravings
after Callcott, Varley, Thurston, Willement and
Brooke. He limited the edition and aroused considerable
indignation by claiming that he had destroyed his
wood blocks after the first printing. The colour
printing of specimens was done from as many as
twenty-nine wood blocks, although Chatto claimed
some were 'too soft and woolly'. Proofs are in the
British Museum, and the MS is in the John Rylands

University Library. Savage employed the young
G.W.Bonner (q.v.) and became the first true colour
printer to recognise the adaptability of wood blocks.
He was followed by George Baxter (q.v.) and his own
improvements to colour printing. He also was an
occasional draughtsman who made four drawings to
Britton's Beauties of England and Wales. The result
of a lifetime's collection of fine printing was his
Dictionary of the Art of Printing, 1840–41, which is
still consulted today. Oddly he does not mention his
colour printing experiments in the book. He died at
Dodington Grove, Kensington on 25 July 1843.
[For colour printing see C.T.Lewis; Wakeman and
Bridson; McLean, Victorian Book Design; see also
Chatto; DNB; Redgrave; TB; Bénézit; Gentleman's
Magazine, 1844, pp.98-100 (obituary by his brother)]

SAWERS, William Anderson fl.1878-86
London wood engraver, who worked at 49 Essex
Street, Strand, WC (POD, 1878-86). He shared the
premises with W.H.Trilby (q.v.).

SAY, William Henry fl.1879-1910
London draughtsman and wood engraver, who worked
at East Temple Chambers, Whitefriars, EC
(POD, 1879-1910). He shared the premises with
W.J.Watson (q.v.).

SCANDRETT, Thomas 1797-1870
Draughtsman on wood of architectural subjects, and
portrait painter. He was born in Worcester in 1797
and began as a portrait painter, exhibiting at the Royal
Academy, the British Institution and the Royal Society
of British Artists from 1824-70. During the early 1840s
he was commissioned by Charles Knight (q.v.), publisher
of popular engraved publications such as the excellent Old
England, 1844-45. This was issued in ninety-six parts
with twenty-four colour plates and 2,488 wood engravings
of which Scandrett probably drew most, engraved on wood
by S.Sly (q.v.). This was followed by Old England's
Worthies, 1847, with twelve colour plates and 'numerous
wood engravings'. Both works show that Scandrett had a
style similar to the architectural drawings of George
Cattermole (q.v.) in Dickens' Old Curiosity Shop.
[TB; Bénézit; Graves; Redgrave; McLean, Victorian
Book Design]

SCHARF, Sir George 1820-95
Draughtsman on wood, designer and art historian. He
was born in London on 16 December 1820, the son of
the noted lithographer and drawing master George
Scharf (see Volume I) with whom he trained. He also
attended the Royal Academy Schools in 1838, and the
following year published a set of theatrical etchings,
Recollections of Scenic Effects, after drawings of
Macready's Shakespearean revivals at Covent Garden.
He accompanied Sir Charles Fellows as draughtsman
illustrator to Asia Minor in 1840; three years later he
returned to draw the area for the government's

expedition. He painted oils for the London galleries,
the Royal Academy and the British Institution, but
was chiefly engaged in drawing on wood for book
illustrations for the publisher John Murray. Murray
had by the mid 1840s achieved remarkable success
with his publication of Owen Jones' (q.v.) designs
to Spanish Ballads, and commissioned Scharf to
follow and indeed collaborate with Jones on future
books. Scharf first drew numerous 'Old Master'
paintings on wood for Murray's Book of Common
Prayer, 1845, done under the supervision of Lewis
Gruner; he also drew 'from the antique' in
collaboration with Jones, who provided further
'monochrome designs' to Murray's edition of
Milman's Works of Horace, 1849. Further Scharf
illustrations appeared in Smith's Classical
Dictionaries; Keat's Poems, 1854; Schmitz's History
of Greece, 1856; and Mrs Speir's Indian Life, 1856.
He also assisted Charles Kean with costumes and
scenery for his revivals of Shakespearean plays, 1851,
1857 and he helped arrange and write the descriptions of
the Greek, Roman and Pompeiian courts at the Crystal
Palace, Sydenham. He wrote catalogues of numerous art
collections and was appointed Secretary then Director
of the National Portrait Gallery, 1857, 1882. He was
knighted in 1895, the year he died in London on
19 April. The British Museum owns proofs of his
designs engraved by the Dalziel Brothers (q.v.), 1848-53.
[TB; Bryan; Slater; McLean, Victorian Book Design;
Nagler; DNB]

SCHEU, Heinrich (Henry) 1845-?
Wood engraver, born on 19 October 1845 in Vienna.
He was the pupil of R.Von Waldheim, and served as
professor of decorative art in Florence, 1885. He
appeared as 'Henry Scheu' in the London directory
from 1889, working as a wood engraver for various
periodicals from his office at 3 and 4 Lincoln's Inn
Fields, WC (POD, 1889-90), then at 263 Strand, WC
(POD, 1891-92). Among his British commissions
were engravings in The Graphic, including a portrait
engraving of the Victorian painter Richard Ansdell,
after J.E.Hodgson which is now in the British
Museum. He also produced illustrations engraved
for the English Illustrated Magazine, 1889-90.
Bénézit claimed that he worked in Zurich in 1893.
[TB; Bénézit; Hake]

SCHLADITZ, Ernest 1862-?
German-born wood engraver and painter, born in
Leipzig in 1862. He contributed engravings to the
English Illustrated Magazine, 1883-84, notably after
rural drawings by C.Napier Hemy, Alfred Parsons,
G.Leslie and W.J.Hennessy (qq.v.). Bénézit claimed
that he worked in New York at one point.
[TB; Bénézit]

SCHNEIDER, Carl fl.1890s
Suburban London wood engraver, who worked at
34 Nightingale Road, Harlesden, NW (LSDN,1894).

SCHONBERG, Johann Nepomuk 1844-?
Draughtsman and figure artist. He was born in
Austria in 1844, the son of the lithographer Adolf
Schonberg (1813-68). He studied at the Vienna
Academy, then moved to France and worked as a
draughtsman on wood for Monde Illustré and Journal
Illustré. He was appointed 'Special Artist' by the
Illustrated London News while in Roumania in 1877
and remained employed by the paper until 1895. He
became adept at improving drawings for wood
engraving sent in by less proficient 'Special Artists'.
His style depended upon a rather heavy-handed use of
bodycolour and grey wash, which certainly challenged
his engravers. His own illustrated works were
Patuzzi's History of the Popes; Alvensleben's
Universal History; G.A.Henty's Young Buglers,1880;
and Henty's Dash for Khartoum,1892. Schonberg
also exhibited at the Royal Academy in 1895.
[Bénézit; Houfe]

SCOTT, A.
Amateur woodcut artist of the early nineteenth century.
The British Museum owns two large rather crude
woodcut portraits, dated 1802, 1803.These are signed:
'A Scott' (script).

SCOTT, Andrew fl.1880-86
London wood engraver, who worked at 152 Fleet
Street, EC (POD,1880-86). He shared the office with
H.Prater (q.v.).

SCOTT, David 1806-49
Draughtsman illustrator, engraver and painter. He
was born in Edinburgh in October 1806, the son of
the engraver Robert Scott, the elder brother of and
collaborator with William Bell Scott (q.v.). David
Scott worked as an engraver and draughtsman for
book illustrations before he turned, somewhat
unsuccessfully, to painting large historical canvases.
He studied at the Trustees Academy and worked
shortly in Italy,1832-34. He etched twenty-five plates
to Coleridge's Ancient Mariner,1837 'which...contain
a great many weird ideas, more or less adequately
portrayed, which should endear themselves to the
symbolist to-day' (White). He also engraved after
Stothard's designs to Thomson's Scottish Melodies.
His illustrations to an edition of Bunyan's Pilgrim's
Progress were wood engraved by his brother William,
and posthumously published in 1860. These show
Scott's borrowing from William Blake (q.v.).
According to White, Blake's influence limited Scott's
popularity: 'Founded on Blake, David Scott developed
a distinctly personal manner, that has provoked
praise and censure, in each case beyond its merit'.
Scott lived in Edinburgh from 1834, where he

exhibited paintings at the Royal Scottish Academy, to
which he was elected member in 1835. He died in
that city on 5 March 1849.
[For biographical information see W.B.Scott,
Memoir of David Scott,1850 and Autobiographical
Notes,1892; see also TB; Bryan; White; Houfe]

SCOTT, J.
Draughtsman figure artist. He contributed comic
illustrations for wood engravings in Thomas Hood's
Comic Annual,1837-38.

SCOTT, Robson John fl.1860s
London wood engraver, who worked at 8 Whitefriars
Street, EC (POD,1860).

SCOTT, Thomas D. fl.1850-93
Occasional draughtsman on wood of figures and
landscapes, also portrait engraver, painter and
miniaturist. He worked in Peckham and first drew on
wood for S.C.Hall's Book of British Ballads,1842;
and the Illustrated London News,1850. He drew
intricate compositions of figures in Examples of
Ornament,1855; drew for some of the 100 total
engravings in Heber's Hymns,1867; and drew for
Once a Week,1867. According to White he was 'a
well-known portrait engraver' by 1867. He engraved
a bust portrait of John Bright,MP, which is now in
the British Museum. Bohn in Chatto and Jackson
praised Scott's abilities as an 'able reducer and
copyist of pictures on wood'. He also exhibited
miniatures at the Royal Academy from 1889. The
British Museum owns a series of nine expertly
engraved butterflies to A.J.Stainton's A Manual of
British Butterflies and Moths,1857, attributed to
Thomas Dewell Scott; also Dalziel Brothers (q.v.)
proof engravings, 1862, 1865-66.
[Chatto; White; Bénézit; Hake; Graves]

SCOTT, William Bell 1811-90
Wood engraver, draughtsman, etcher, painter of
historical subjects, critic and poet. He was born in
Edinburgh on 12 September 1811, the son of the
engraver Robert Scott and younger brother of David
Scott (q.v.) whose works William wood engraved. He
studied art with his father, then at the Trustees
Academy in Edinburgh in 1831; then helped his father
to engrave before leaving for London in 1837. There
he 'supported himself precariously by etching,
engraving and painting' (DNB). He began as a draughtsman on wood with Kenny Meadows (q.v.), putting parts
of Meadows' designs on wood for his Illustrated
Shakespeare,1839-42. He also worked on the landscape
backgrounds. Henry Vizetelly remembered how the
young Scott at this time had 'a very moderate estimate
of his own abilities, and by no means disdained
journeyman's work...he remained to the last an
indifferent draughtsman' (Glances Back,p.153). His
illustrations appeared in The Ornamentist or Artisan's

Manual,1845; The Year of the World,1846; and
Landon's Poetical Works. He was a friend of the
prominent wood engraver W.J.Linton (q.v.) who
exhibited a wood engraving of Scott's drawing,
'Fuseli's Witches', at the Royal Academy, 1857.
Later Linton engraved Scott's Half-hour Lectures...
of the Fine and Ornamental Arts,1861. Scott also
contributed to The Family Bible,1867. He was a
proficient etcher, served as master of the Design
School, Newcastle, until 1863, worked on mural
paintings in numerous private patrons' homes, and
exhibited at the British Institution, the Royal Academy,
the Royal Society of British Artists and the Royal
Scottish Academy. As a wood engraver, Scott
engraved a portrait of John Blackett, MP for
Newcastle which is now in the British Museum, and
the illustrations by his brother David to Bunyan's
Pilgrim's Progress,1860. Scott also wrote and
published on the history of wood engraving, notably
A Descriptive Catalogue of Engravings, brought
together with a view to illustrate the Art of Engraving
on Copper and Wood...1880.
[For a discussion of Scott's etchings, see Volume I;
for biographical information see DNB; W.B.Scott's,
Autobiographical Notes...1892; Vizetelly, Glances
Back; Hake; Wood]

SCRIBBEN, William fl.1843-46
London wood engraver, who worked at 9 Westmorland
Place, City Road (POD,1843-46).

SCRIVENS, Edward fl.1877-79
London wood engraver, who worked at 10 Bolt Court,
Fleet Street, EC (POD,1877-79), shared with
T.Coman (q.v.).

SCRIVENS, Edwin fl.1885-96
London wood engraver, who worked at 65 Farringdon
Street, EC (POD,1885-90), then as Edwin Scrivens
and Company at 41 Imperial Buildings, EC and
149 Fleet Street, EC (POD,1891-94) and finally at
93 Fleet Street, EC (POD,1895-96). Both Edwin and
Edward Scrivens (q.v.) may be related to the
prominent metal engraver Edward Scrivens
(1775-1841) who had five children.

SEABROOK, Thomas fl.1854-80
London wood engraver, who worked at 9 Wine Office
Court, Fleet Street, EC (POD,1854), then 31 Bouverie
Street, Fleet Street, EC (POD,1855), then 23 Bouverie
Street and 2 Middle Brunswick Terrace, Barnsbury
Road (POD,1856-58) which he shared with F.P.Davis
and W.H.Webb (qq.v.). He moved to 7 Durham Place,
Dalston, NE (POD,1859-60), then Leah Cottage,
Lower Clapton, E (Kelly's Suburban,1868). He
returned to the city at 5A Wine Office Court, Fleet
Street, EC (POD,1872-75). By 1880 he was working
from 135 Pendlesham Road, Lower Clapton, E
(LSDE,1880).

SEABY, Professor Allen William 1867-1953
Colour woodcut artist. He was born in London on
26 May 1867 and trained as a woodcut artist under
F.Morley Fletcher (q.v.). He exhibited work at the
Society of Animal Painters, Graver Printers in
Colour, and also at the Colour Woodcut Society.
He became Professor of Fine Art, Reading University,
1920-33. He published several books, lived in Reading,
and died on 28 July 1953. Gusman praised his
Japanese-styled woodcuts and placed them in the
company of those by Sydney Lee, J.D.Batten and
W.Giles (qq.v.).
[Waters; Gusman]

SEARS, Henry fl.1830s
London wood engraver, who worked at 6 Graham
Street, Walworth Road (Pigot,1836). The British
Museum owns several small vignettes of landscapes
and figures competently engraved in a black-line
style. There is also a series of small ducks
attributed to 'SEARS'. He signed his work: 'SEARS',
'HY SEARS Sc'.

SEARS, Matthew Urlwin fl.1826-59
London wood engraver, who was born in the city
about 1800, and worked at 8 Angel Terrace,
Islington (Pigot,1826-27), 29 Charterhouse Square
(Pigot,1832-34), then 44 Paternoster Row
(Pigot,1836). He disappears from the London
directories until 1854, when he worked at 5 Bride
Court, Fleet Street, EC (POD,1854-58), then
36 Burton Crescent, WC (POD,1859). Sears' wood
engravings first appeared after William Harvey's
(q.v.) designs in the influential Northcote's Fables,
1828, amongst the work of some of the most
prominent wood engravers of the period. His three
cuts, engraved in a black-line style, are now in the
British Museum. He engraved eighty-five reproductions
to his Specimens of Historical Engraving on Wood,
1833, published in London, and continued to engrave
for various popular publications. The most unusual
is his Houses of Parliament, printed on a large
'Statistical Pocket Handkerchief', which is now in the
British Museum. By the 1840s he was engraving for
Charles Knight's Penny Magazine, after Wells,
Shepherd, Fairholt,October-December 1841; and
again in collaboration as Leonard and Sears and
Quartley and Sears (qq.v.), September,November
1841. However, about 1835 Sears had moved to
Leipzig and Paris and become one of the influential
expatriot English wood engravers to find work
engraving for various prominent French publications.
These included cuts to the Magasin Pittoresque;
Moliere's Oeuvres,1835-36; Les Evangiles,1838;
to Ct. de Laborde's Versailles,1839; and after
T.Johannot and Fragonard to La Fontaine Contes et
Nouvelles,1839. He engraved some of the 500 total
illustrations to Laurent's Histoire de L'Empereur
Napoleon,1839; and some of the ninety illustrations

to Abbé Prevost's Histoire de Manon Lescaut,1839. The British Museum owns a late work, a large comic cartoon, 'Quackery', 10 March 1869, possibly after Leech, Glaser praised Sears for his technical expertise in engraving 'smooth lines' which greatly influenced a new generation of French wood engravers. The Bodleian Library owns several of his Charles Knight commissions; the British Museum owns several engraved proofs of literary figures' houses and topographical views printed on yellow paper. He signed his engravings: 'SEARS', 'M U S', 'M U SEARS', 'M U', 'Sears' (script), 'Sears Sc' (script). [For his French work see Glaser; Gusman; Beraldi; Nagler; see also TB; Bénézit]

SEARY, Thomas fl.1872-73
London wood engraver, who worked at 15 Southampton Buildings, WC (POD,1872-73).

SECCOMBE, Colonel Thomas S. fl.1865-85
Military draughtsman, illustrator and painter. He was taken up by Punch while a subaltern, having joined the Royal Artillery in 1856, and he drew eight comic cuts on military themes which appeared 1864, 1866 and 1882. During that period he also drew for wood engravings in London Society,1865; and contributed to the Dalziel Brothers' Fun; also Henry Vizetelly's Illustrated Times. His book illustrations for children's books and period novels were done for Edward Moxon who published his drawings to the 'Popular Poets' series, namely the works of Thomas Moore, William Cowper and James Thomson, all c1870. He then drew for Thomas Hood's Miss Kilmansegg,1870; devised Army and Navy Drolleries, c1875; and illustrated The Rape of the Lock,1873; and finally The Story of Prince Hildebrand and the Princess Ida,1880. Seccombe also exhibited work at the Royal Society of British Artists. The British Museum owns proof engravings by the Dalziel Brothers (q.v.), 1865-66.
[Spielmann; Houfe]

SEDDON, Thomas B. 1821-56
Occasional draughtsman, minor Pre-Raphaelite painter. He was the son of a cabinet maker and brother of the architect, John Pollard Seddon. He travelled in France, accompanied William Holman Hunt to the Holy Land, 1853-54, and exhibited his small output of paintings at the Royal Academy, 1852-56. He is listed here for his wood engraved illustration, 'Landscape of Promise', engraved by the Dalziel Brothers (q.v.) posthumously on 19 September 1857. A proof of this is in the British Museum.

SELOUS, Henry Courtney 1803-90
Occasional draughtsman on wood, portrait and land-scape painter. He was born in Deptford in 1803, the son of a painter of miniatures, George Selous. He studied with John Martin (q.v.) and was a student at

the Royal Academy Schools 1818. By the 1840s he had begun drawing on wood for various influential publications: S.C.Hall's Book of British Ballads, 1842; Fouque's Sintram and His Companions,c1844; Poems and Pictures,1846; and the Art Union's Pilgrim's Progress in 1844. By the 1860s he was illustrating such books as Kingsley's Hereward the Wake,1869-70, to which he contributed twenty plates; followed by The Life of Robert The Bruce, for which he was awarded a prize. Other 'Sixties School' publications to which he contributed included: Cassell's Pilgrim's Progress,1863; Churchman's Family Magazine,1863; Cassell's History of England, 1865; Cassell's Shakespeare,1865; Heber's Hymns, 1867; and the Illustrated Book of Sacred Poems,1867. Selous was noted as a 'painter who occasionally draws on wood' by Bohn in Chatto and Jackson. He also exhibited at the British Institution and the Royal Academy to 1874, first under the name 'Slous' but changing his name to Selous by 1831. He also wrote children's books under the names 'Aunt Cae' and 'Kay Spen'. He died in Beaworthy in North Devon on 24 September 1890. The British Museum owns proof engravings by the Dalziel Brothers (q.v.), 1865. [Chatto; Bénézit; Bryan; TB; Nagler]

SENIOR, E. fl.1894-1902
London wood engraver, who worked at 219 Camberwell New Road, SE (LSDS,1894-1902).

SEYMOUR, George L. fl.1876-1916
Draughtsman illustrator, genre and animal painter. He drew architectural and topographical subjects for wood engravings in various magazines from 1876. These appeared in Good Words,1880, 1890-95; The Graphic,1886; the Illustrated London News,1887-92; English Illustrated Magazine,1888, 1897, wood engraved by R.Taylor (q.v.); and Pall Mall Gazette. He also illustrated W.D.Cummings' Songs and Lyrics for Little Lips.
[Bénézit; Houfe]

SEYMOUR, Robert 1798-1836
Draughtsman on wood, etcher, lithographer of illustrations and caricatures. He was born in Somerset in 1798, was apprenticed to a London pattern designer and during his leisure-time practised miniature painting. He set up as an artist and in 1822 had a painting accepted at the Royal Academy, his first and last appearance there. Seymour never wholly abandoned oil painting but most of his early energies were spent drawing on wood blocks for various magazines and books. Many were wood engraved by George Dorrington (q.v.). 'Nothing seemed to come amiss to him. He was as much at home with "Don Juan" as the "Book of Martyrs", and passed with the confidence of youth from illustrating Demosthenes and Ovid, to Shakespeare, Wordsworth, Gay, and Southey. He

thus spent six busy years, during which all his work was drawn on the wood, or at any rate with a view to the graver. He worked with extraordinary rapidity, and at a very low price. Most of his illustrations were remunerated at half a guinea apiece' (DNB). However, he turned to etching in 1827, when his employer for drawings on wood, Knight and Lacey, went bankrupt. 'This, although pecuniarily a disaster, gave Seymour the opportunity he had long desired of dispensing to a great extent with the middleman, the wood-engraver, by whom his work had been terribly mutilated.' He also turned to lithography and drew numerous 'Humorous Sketches', 1833-36. His occasional work for wood engravings during the early 1830s was drawings for The Odd Volume, 1830; cuts to Comic Magazine, 1832-34; and most important to the weekly Figaro in London, 1831-36, then under the editorship of Gilbert à Beckett. By 1834 Seymour was objecting to the careless engraving and printing of his blocks here and he resigned on 16 August, but resumed work there in 1835 until his death, working more successfully for the paper's new editor Henry Mayhew. Nevertheless Seymour continued to etch illustrations to numerous books and periodicals, his greatest contribution being that of the prototype for Dickens' Pickwick Papers -- that is, comic drawings of inept sportsmen from London out in the countryside. Dickens was commissioned to write the text round Seymour's sketches, to be issued in serial form but only two issues appeared before Seymour committed suicide, in London on 20 April 1836. The British Museum owns a series of Seymour drawings wood engraved by John Byfield (q.v.).
[For bibliographical information see Houfe; also DNB; TB; Redgrave; Bryan; Hake]

SHADE, Henry fl.1883-85
London wood engraver, who worked at 64 Fleet Street, EC (POD,1883). He then worked at 150 Fleet Street, EC (POD,1884-85), which was shared with A.H.Lindsell (q.v.).

SHANNON, Charles Hazelwood 1863-1937
Occasional wood engraver, painter, prominent lithographer. He was born in Quarrington, Lincoln-shire on 26 April 1863, educated at St John's School, Leatherhead, and then apprenticed to the wood engraver Charles Roberts (q.v.). There he met Charles Ricketts (q.v.) with whom he attended the City and Guilds Technical Art School, Kennington Park Road, Lambeth. They shared lodgings and began a life-long collaboration as illustrators, wood engravers and painters, first at The Vale, Chelsea. Their first joint work was the short-lived serial, The Dial, 1889-97, the five numbers of which were edited by Ricketts, the illustrations lithographed by Shannon, and wood engraved by Ricketts, T.Sturge Moore and Lucien Pissarro (qq.v.). Shannon also drew four illustrations with Ricketts

to Oscar Wilde's House of Pomegranates, 1891. Their most successful book was Daphnis and Chlöe, 1893, for which the thirty-seven illustrations and one hundred initials were divided between them: Shannon drew fifteen illustrations and wood engraved most of the hundred initials. This was followed by Hero and Leander, 1894, with seven illustrations. By 1894 they had formed their own press, The Vale Press, and with T.Sturge Moore and Lucien Pissarro, they published eighty-three books, a large number of which they designed and for which they engraved borders, initials and illustrations. Shannon was principally a lithographer and painter, having been left to perfect his art while Ricketts supported them both. During those early days he did contribute illustrations to the Dalziels' Judy, 1887; Black and White, 1891; and The Savoy, 1896. But his lithographs, early ones done almost wholly on the stone, later from a transfer, established his reputation. He also exhibited paintings and lithographs extensively at the Fine Art Society, the Grosvenor Gallery, the New English Art Club, the New Gallery, the Royal Society of British Artists, the Royal Society of Painter-Etchers and Engravers, the Royal Hibernian Academy, the Royal Institute of Painters in Watercolours, the Royal Institute of Painters in Oil-Colours, and the Royal Scottish Academy, and was elected ARA in 1911 and RA in 1921. He died in London on 18 March 1937. [For full bibliography see TB; DNB; Houfe; for list of prints see C.Ricketts, Catalogue of Mr Shannon's Lithographs, 1902; also entry in Volume I (with bibliography)]

SHARPE, W.
Draughtsman illustrator. The British Museum owns seven proof wood engravings after his designs engraved by the Dalziel Brothers (q.v.), 1861. He may be related to the metal engraver Charles William Sharpe (see Volume I).

SHARPLEY, Reginald 1879-?
Wood engraver and watercolourist. He began as a civil engineer and later studied at Heatherley's. He exhibited at the Royal Academy and in the provinces, working from Campden, Gloucestershire.
[Waters]

SHAW, Henry 1800-73
Occasional draughtsman on wood of architectural ornaments, letters and furniture decoration, book illuminator and antiquary. He was born in London on 4 July 1800, developed his architectural drawing skills while drawing for Britton's Cathedral Antiquities of England, 1832-36 and also drew and engraved A Series of Details of Gothic Architecture, 1829. He devoted himself to publishing a series of books illustrated with aspects of medieval and Elizabethan art and architecture, especially taken from illuminated manuscripts. Most of these were

published by William Pickering and printed at his Chiswick Press, 'among the finest achievements of Victorian book design and instruction' (McLean). Most of his early drawings were etched or lithographed, then hand coloured, but a selection were wood engraved, probably by Mary Byfield (q.v.). These included Shaw's Encyclopedia of Ornament, 1836-42, for which the colour plates were printed from wood blocks, 'probably the finest examples of colour printing by the Chiswick Press'; and his most ambitious project, a monthly serial, Dresses and Decorations of the Middle Ages, 2 volumes,1843, a total of ninety-four plates copper engraved, except for a few wood engraved by Mary Byfield. This earned the claim that it was 'the most handsome book produced in the whole of the nineteenth century'. Among Shaw's wood engraved publications are A Booke of Sundry Draughtes,1848, with a wood engraved title page; The Decorative Arts, Ecclesiastical and Civil of the Middle Ages,1851, both richly illustrated by wood engravings, hand coloured etchings and chromolithographs; A Handbook of the Art of Illumination,1866; and drawings to W.S.Gibson's The History of the Monastery Founded at Tynemouth,1846. Perhaps his most pertinent work was the designs on wood which he drew as decorative letters to the Longman edition of the New Testament,1864. As McLean concluded of such work, 'Shaw was not really an original designer: but he carried painstaking and faithful draughtsmanship almost to the point of genius. Much of Shaw's work, being reproductive, became unnecessary when photography was able to replace it...'. He was elected FSA in 1833, and died in Broxbourne, Hertfordshire on 12 June 1873. The Bodleian Library owns some of his Pickering commissions. [DNB; McLean, Victorian Book Design; Houfe; Chatto; Bénézit; TB; Fincham; Art Journal,1873,p.231; G.Keynes, W.Pickering,1969,p.89 (list of works)]

SHEERES, Charles William fl.1851-68
London wood engraver, draughtsman on wood. He worked at 14 Upper Barnsbury Street (POD,1851-61), then at 23 Bouverie Street, EC (POD,1862-64), which he shared with C.A.Ferrier (q.v.). The following year he appeared at 44 Paternoster Row, EC (POD,1865-66), then 23 Upper Barnsbury Street, N (POD,1867), and then 15 Paternoster Row, EC (POD,1868). During this period engraving in London, he also drew for wood engravings in the Illustrated London News,1855-59, notably industrial scenes such as 'Old and New Buildings in Threadneedle Street' 10 February 1855, engraved by John Brown (q.v.). In addition Gusman lists the wood engraver Scheeres (sic) who engraved cuts after Doré (q.v.) to the Journal pour Tous, 1855-62. Sheeres probably later joined in partnership with Thomas Symmons (q.v.) as Sheeres and Symmons (q.v.). The British Museum owns his engravings after John Gilbert (q.v.), and an engraved announcement of 'The Complete Works of Shakespeare'

illustrated by T.H.Nicholson (q.v.).
[Houfe; Gusman; Hake]

SHEERES and Symmons fl.1878-84
London wood engraving firm, probably a partnership between Charles Sheeres and Thomas Symmons (qq.v.). They worked at an office in St Bride Street, Ludgate Circus, EC (POD,1878-84); then Symmons broke up the business and set up on his own.

SHEERN, George Frederick fl.1870-93
London wood engraver, who worked first with A.J.Appleton (q.v.) as Appleton and Sheern (q.v.),, then appeared under his own name at 32 Fetter Lane, EC (POD,1872-73). He moved offices frequently, to 4 Red Lion Court, EC (POD,1875); 18 Bouverie Street, EC (POD,1876-80), shared with I.Holloway (q.v.); 64 Fleet Street (POD,1881-82); and finally 6 Wine Office Court, EC (POD,1883-93), which he shared with F.W.Mitchell and C.Murray (qq.v.).

SHEIL, Edward 1834-69
Irish occasional illustrator, figure painter. He was born in Coleraine in 1834, and attended the Cork School of Art where he taught. He worked in Cork, and contributed a drawing for wood engraving in Once a Week,1867. He also exhibited at the Royal Academy, the Royal Hibernian Academy and the Royal Society of British Artists. He died in Cork on 11 March 1869.
[Bénézit; TB; Houfe]

SHELDRICK, B. fl.1850s
London wood engraver, who worked at 11 Strahan Place, Ball's Pond (Hodgson's,1855).

SHEPHERD, Alfred fl.1884-98
London wood engraver, who worked at 7 New Inn, Strand, WC (POD,1884-95). He then moved to the workshop 1 Norfolk Street, Strand, WC (POD,1896-98), which he shared with H.W.Bennett, J.J.Macnamara and J.C.Saunders (qq.v.).

SHEPHERD, Thomas Hosmer c1817-c42
Topographical draughtsman on wood, wood engraver. He was the son of the architectural draughtsman George Shepherd, and, like his father, was noted for his drawings of London. He was commissioned by Frederick Crace to make these in watercolour and pencil, and hundreds of them are now in the British Museum. They were published in Elmes' Metropolitan Improvements,1827; and London and Its Environs in the Nineteenth Century,1829. He also drew for Modern Athens Displayed, or Edinburgh in the Nineteenth Century,1829, engraved on wood by Mary Byfield (q.v.). During the 1840s he continued to draw for wood engravings, notably for Charles Knight's Penny Magazine,1841, engraved by Sears and W.T.Green (qq.v.). He also served as wood engraver to

Ebenezer Landells (q.v.). According to the noted engraver Edmund Evans (q.v.) he worked at Landells' Holford Square cffice (see Evans Reminiscences, p.38). Shepherd also exhibited at the Royal Society of British Artists, 1831-32. The Bodleian Library owns his Charles Knight commissions, and the Mary Byfield Modern Athens engravings.
[Bryan; Bénézit; TB; Redgrave; Nagler]

SHEPHERD, Valentine Claud fl.1866-88
London wood engraver, who worked at 10 Wine Office Court, EC (POD,1866-67). By 1871 he was working at 2 Garrick Street, WC (POD,1871-84), then 20 Cranbourn Street, WC (POD,1885-88).

SHEPHERD, William H. fl.1861-62
London wood engraver, who worked at 7 Dane's Inn, Strand, WC (POD,1861-62). This was also the office of the noted engraver T.Bolton (q.v.).

SHERMAN, Welby
Occasional wood engraver, mezzotint and line engraver. He was a fellow student of Samuel Palmer (q.v.) at George Richmond's, but his master noted in his diary, that he 'did not turn out as he began-- alas!'. He line engraved 'Samson and the Lion' on metal in 1827, then engraved in mezzotint after Palmer's 'Evening', 1834. According to the Print Collector's Quarterly, Sherman also wood engraved 'The Bacchante', designed by Edward Calvert (q.v.). This was signed 'W.S.f'. The block and impression are in the British Museum.
[Print Collector's Quarterly,1930,pp.361-62; 1931, p.198ff]

SHERSBY, Hazard fl.1870-71
London wood engraver, who worked at 66 Ludgate Hill (POD,1870), and shared the office with G.Hewitt (q.v.). The following year he worked at 32 Whitefriars Street, Fleet Street, EC (POD,1871).

SHERWILL, Captain George fl.1848-56
Amateur draughtsman illustrator, officer in the Royal Marines from 1848. He drew views of India for wood engravings in the Illustrated London News, 1856.

SHERWIN, Alfred Henry fl.1860s
London wood engraver, who worked with Robert W. Sherwin (q.v.) at 230 Strand (POD,1868).

SHERWIN, Robert W. fl.1865-68
London wood engraver, who worked at East Temple Chambers, Whitefriars Street, EC (POD,1865-67), then took over an office at 230 Strand (POD,1868), which he shared with Alfred Henry Sherwin (q.v.).

SHIELDS, Frederic(k) James 1833-1911
Draughtsman illustrator for wood engravings, landscape and mural painter. He was born in Hartlepool on 14 March 1833, the son of a bookbinder and printer. He was sent to London after attending charity school, and studied from the antiques in the British Museum before being apprenticed to the lithographers Maclure, Macdonald and Macgregor (q.v.) for three years. He worked as lithographer in Halifax, preparing fourteen illustrations to A Rachde Felley's Visit to the Grayt Eggshibishun,1851 and on the strength of this success he set up as a watercolour landscape painter and occasional draughtsman for wood engravings in magazines and various 'Sixties School' publications. These included Touches of Nature by Eminent Artists,1866; Sunday Magazine,1866; Once a Week, 1867; and Punch,1867-75. He also illustrated on his own Defoe's History of the Plague of London,1862: and Pilgrim's Progress,1864, plates of which he sent to John Ruskin in 1861, who praised them highly. He later dropped illustrating for mural and oil painting for the galleries, exhibiting at the New Gallery and the Royal Watercolour Society, where he was elected ARWS in 1865. He died in Merton, Surrey on 26 March 1911.
[For biographical information see E.Mills, Life and Letters of Frederic James Shields,1912; also DNB; Hardie; Maas; Wood; Spielmann; White; Reid]

SHIPPERLEE and Quartly fl.1880s
London wood engraving firm, with an office at 90 London Wall, EC (POD,1887). It may be connected with A.W. or J.A.Quartley (sic) (qq.v.).

SHORTLAND and Company fl.1870s
Provincial wood engraver, who worked at 1 Lord Street, Liverpool (Kelly's,1872).

SILK, Oliver fl.1880-89
Provincial wood engraver, who worked at Leith Offices, 34 Moorfields, Liverpool (Kelly's,1880), then Trafford Chambers, 58 St John Street, Liverpool (Kelly's,1889).

SILVESTER, Henry Seymour fl.1880-89
London draughtsman on wood, who worked at 9 Adam Street, Adelphi, WC (Kelly's,1880), then at 92 and 93 Fleet Street, EC (Kelly's,1889).

SIMMONS, Walter and Company fl.1892-99
London wood engraver, who first worked as Pearson, Simmons and Knott (q.v.), then set up as Walter Simmons and Company, 12 Ludgate Square, EC (POD,1894-95), then 19 Ludgate Hill, EC (POD,1898-99).

SIMMS, C.
The British Museum owns a proof wood engraving after his design, engraved by the Dalziel Brothers (q.v.) for Goldsmith's Works,1863-67.

SIMON, Paul fl.1857-75
London wood engraver, who worked at 210 Strand (POD,1857) and 8 (1) Dane's Inn, St Clement's, WC (POD,1858-64). He shared this latter office with C.M.Gorway (q.v.). According to Gusman, Simon engraved cuts for French magazines, such as Histoire des Peintres de Toutes les Ecoles,1849-75, working with C.J.Roberts, S.Pannemaker, H.Linton, J.Quartley, Timms, Pisan, and the Etheringtons (qq.v.).

SIMONSEN, Niels 1807-85
Draughtsman illustrator, painter, lithographer and sculptor. He was born in Copenhagen on 10 December 1807 and became a pupil of J.L.Lund. He visited Italy and Algeria and was commissioned to draw for wood engravings the scenes which he found. These were published under the title, 'Our Danish Artist' in the Illustrated London News,1864.

SIMPSON, Clement fl.1870s
London wood engraver, who worked at 8 Palsgrave Place, Strand (POD,1874). He shared the office with A.J.Appleton and G.Humphreys (qq.v.).

SIMPSON, William 1823-99
Draughtsman, 'Special Artist' and early lithographer. He was born in Glasgow on 28 October 1823 and educated in Perth and Glasgow where he was apprenticed to a lithographer. He moved to Day and Sons, London lithographers in 1851, and drew for lithography a set of Crimean War drawings published by Colnaghi. He was the first 'Special Artist' sent into action (by Colnaghi), and contributed a series of drawings wood engraved in the Illustrated London News, being a permanent staff member from 1866 and reported on the Abyssinian campaign, accompanied the Prince of Wales to India,1875-76, and illustrated Dr Schliemann's excavations in 1877. 'For forty years [he] was an eye-witness of every great war and political event in the history of our country' (Bryan). He also exhibited fifty pictures at the Royal Institute of Painters in Watercolours, and he was elected a member in 1879. He died in London on 17 April 1899.
[For biographical information see William Simpson, RI, Autobiography,1903; also Houfe; TB; Bénézit; Bryan; for his lithographs see Volume I (with bibliography)]

SIMPSON, William fl.1880s
Provincial wood engraver, who worked at 22 Caroline Street, Birmingham (Kelly's,1880).

SKELTON, Percival fl.1849-87
Draughtsman on wood, landscape painter. He was related to Joseph Skelton, the eighteenth century engraver and illustrator. He drew on wood for the more competent engravers like W.J.Whymper and Edmund Evans (qq.v.) to interpret. He illustrated on his own for T.Jeans' Tommiebeg Shootings,1860; and S.E.Gay's Harry's Big Boots, 1873. He contributed to Samuel Lover's Metrical Tales,1849; the Poetical Works of Edgar Allan Poe, 1858; Childe Harold,1858-59, engraved by W.J.Whymper; the Illustrated London News,1860; the Book of Favourite Modern Ballads,1860, engraved by Evans; the Illustrated Times,1860; Welcome Guest,1860; Churchman's Family Magazine,1863; Kingsley's Water Babies,1863, drawn with Noel Paton (q.v.); Life and Lessons of Our Lord,1864; Once a Week,1866; Heber's Hymns, 1867; Episodes of Fiction,1870; The Graphic, 1870-71; and Thornbury's Legendary Ballads,1876. He exhibited work at the Royal Academy and the Royal Society of British Artists, but was an unsuccessful candidate for the New Watercolour Society from 1852-61. He specialised in Scottish and coastal scenes.
[Chatto; Houfe; Bénézit (as 'Perceval' Skelton); Evans Reminiscences]

SKIDMORE and Harris fl.1870s
Provincial wood engraving firm, with an office at South Parade Mills, Back South Parade, Manchester (Kelly's,1876).

SKILL, Edward 1831-73
Wood engraver, born near London on 23 June 1831. He set up as a London engraver at 156 Strand, WC (POD,1863-64), then moved to Sweden. He was the head of a studio there, engraving portraits from 1864-65, and working for the Swedish paper Ny Illustrerod Tidning. By 1870-72 he had moved to America but returned to Stockholm where he died on 5 May 1873. He also engraved for the Illustrated London News, notably 'On the Track', after H.B.Roberts, 23 December 1871.
[Gusman; Bénézit; TB (full bibliography)]

SKILL, Frederick John 1824-81
Draughtsman illustrator, landscape and portrait painter. He was born in 1824, and trained as a steel engraver then a portrait painter for the London Journal. He acted as 'Special Artist' for the Illustrated London News, his drawings wood engraved by W.Thomas (q.v.),1854-67. He also worked for Henry Vizetelly's Illustrated Times,1860-65; Cassell's Family Paper,1860-61; Welcome Guest, 1860; London Society,1862; Foxe's Book of Martyrs, 1866; Beeton's Annual,1866; and The Graphic, 1870-71. Many of these drawings on wood were engraved by Edmund Evans (q.v.). He also exhibited

at the New Watercolour Society, to which he was elected member in 1876. He also exhibited at the Royal Academy and the Royal Society of British Artists. He died in London on 8 March 1881, 'of a broken heart, having failed to attract public attention' (Bryan). The British Museum owns his drawings of a Spanish scene by John Phillips, wood engraved by H.Orrin Smith (q.v.).
[Bryan; Evans Reminiscences; TB; Bénézit; Houfe; Art Journal,1881]

SKIPPE, John 1771-1811
Chiaroscuro wood engraver, draughtsman on wood, the pupil of J.B.Malchair and probably of John Baptist Jackson (q.v.). Bryan claimed that he was a native of Ledbury, who studied landscape painting under Claude Vernet. He is best known for his chiaroscuro engravings on wood after 'Old Master' paintings for instance those by Parmigianino, Correggio, and Raphael, published 1770-1812. Chatto and Jackson claimed that he was the only chiaroscuro engraver in England and lists three works after Parmigianino. He is known to have engraved a plate after Salvator Rosa, dated 1809 and he possibly died on 8 April 1811 (Nagler). The British Museum owns a large collection of his colour engravings after Michelangelo, Rubens, and Parmigianino, mostly dated 1780,1783. He signed his work: 'JO' (superimposed) 'n scul', 'JS', 'JN' (script).
[For a list of work see Nagler; LeBlanc; see also Bryan; Chatto]

SLADER, Alfred G. fl.1854-58
London wood engraver, who worked with Samuel Vincent Slader (q.v.) at 126 Chancery Lane (POD,1854-55), and 48 Salisbury Square (POD,1856-58). Alfred Slader was also a draughtsman on wood, who contributed drawings for wood engravings in Henry Vizetelly's Illustrated Times, 1856-66, especially to Christmas issues. He also painted landscapes.

SLADER, Samuel Machin fl.1828-41
London wood engraver, who worked at 17 White Conduit Terrace (Pigot,1832-34), then 10 Nelson Terrace, City Road (Pigot,1836-38). His engravings appeared in the influential Northcote's Fables,1828, for which he engraved nineteen tailpieces and initial letters after William Harvey (q.v.). Twenty-five proofs of these are in the British Museum. He probably also engraved for Charles Knight's (q.v.) Penny Magazine, after Fairholt's drawings e.g. 'A Day in a Tobacco Factory', November 1841. According to Gusman he also contributed some of the 300 cuts to Dr C.Wordsworth's La Grèce Pittoresque et Historique,1841, engraved with Edmund Evans, J.Orrin Smith, W.T.Green, J.Jackson, M.A.Williams, R.Hart, R.Branston, Bonner, E.Gray, E.W.Whymper, Sly, and T.M.Williams (qq.v.). Slader died after 1861. The British Museum owns his work after J.R.Cruikshank,

T.Landseer, R.Seymour, and J.Martin; the Bodleian Library owns his Knight work.
He signed his work: 'SLADER', 'S SLADER Sc', 'SS'.

SLADER, Samuel Vincent fl.1854-65
London wood engraver, who worked with Alfred Slader (q.v.) at 126 Chancery Lane (POD,1854-55), and 48 Salisbury Square (POD,1856). By 1859 he was working independently of Alfred at 156 Strand (POD,1859-65), sharing the premises with W.A.Cranston and E.Skill (qq.v.).

SLEIGH, Bernard 1872-?
Wood engraver, illustrator, watercolourist and book decorator. He was born in Birmingham in 1872, and apprenticed to a Birmingham firm of wood engravers. He recalled the training: 'I learnt to leave lines standing as hairs, to graduate washes with scrupulous fidelity, to reproduce with accuracy flat masses from black to palest grey, to clear out open spaces without bruising the surrounding lines and edges'. He found especially challenging the task of engraving bicycles with their numerous spokes. Sleigh then took up a teaching post at the Birmingham Guild of Handicraft and wood engraved numerous commissions for the publisher George Allen. He engraved Arthur Gaskin's illustrations to Hans Andersen,1895, which the publishers claimed 'was the last book of that period illustrated throughout by wood blocks' and also Henry A Payne's A Book of Pictured Cards, 1893, for the Birmingham School, which was later described as influential: 'it showed an instinctive feeling for the right uses of the wood blocks, in that it was made with Chinese white upon black paper, every stroke of the brush corresponding to a graver cut...'. Sleigh also contributed to Aubrey Beardsley's Yellow Book,1896; and eight illustrations to The Dome, 1899-1900, drawn in the solid black-line medievalism pioneered by William Morris (q.v.). Sleigh was also associated with the Campden Guild of Handicraft and the Essex House Press, for which he illustrated and cut numerous wood blocks. Sleigh's position in the revival of interest in wood engraving was firmly linked to the Birmingham School of illustration: he was 'at the very heart of that particular school of Post Pre-Raphaelitism', according to Campbell Dodgson. He wrote on the revival in various art magazines, publishing his Wood Engraving Since 1890,1932, which gave a selection of colleagues' works against a background of his own experience with the medium. He also wrote the prophetic 'The Future of Wood Engraving', in the Studio,1898, pp.10-16, which he illustrated with his own medievalist inspired engravings. The article began: 'It can hardly be denied that there is in the present condition of the art of wood-engraving very serious cause for lamentation', then ends with a plea for purity and respect for the medium itself. Sleigh's reputation continued to influence a new generation of wood

engravers, for example George Mackley, who
included praises for Sleigh in his classic manual
Wood Engraving,1948. His work was included in such
anthologies as Sketchley's English Book Illustration of
Today,1903; the 'Special' Studio numbers The Artist
Engraver,1904, and The Graphic Arts of Great Britain,
1917. Sleigh exhibited work at the Fine Art Society,
the New Gallery and the Royal Academy, was elected
RBSA in 1928. The British Museum owns a small
roundel and a Christmas card dated 1928. He signed
his work: 'B S' (superimposed), '.S.'.

SLEIGH, John fl.1842-72
Draughtsman illustrator for wood engravings and
etchings, book decorator and landscape painter. He
worked in London where he was the friend of fellow
illustrator Charles Keene (q.v.). He drew on wood
for Charles Mackay's Home Affections,1858; and
drew for decorations surrounding the landscape
drawings by Birket Foster (q.v.) to Odes and Sonnets,
1859, engraved and colour printed by the Dalziel
Brothers (q.v.). These looked like chromolithographs:
'It is not a happy experiment; despite the exquisite
landscapes, the decoration accords so badly that you
cannot linger over its pages with pleasure', according
to Gleeson White. Sleigh also drew for the
compilation volume Sacred Poetry of the 16th, 17th
and 18th Centuries,c1862. He contributed to the
etchings in Passages from Modern English Poets,
1862, for the Etching Club, and also exhibited work
at the Royal Academy and the Royal Society of British
Artists. The British Museum owns a series of landscape designs engraved by the Dalziel Brothers,
1857, 1860.
[McLean, Victorian Book Design; Houfe; G.S.Layard,
C.Keene,1892,p.59; for his etchings see Volume I]

SLINGER, F.J. fl.1858-71
Draughtsman illustrator, genre painter. He worked
in London where he contributed drawings for wood
engravings in Once a Week and The Graphic,1871.
He served as assistant at the Slade School to
Alphonse Legros. He also exhibited at the British
Institution and the Royal Academy.
[White; Houfe]

SLOCOMBE, Alfred fl.1850-1900
Floral draughtsman, painter, watercolourist and
etcher, member of a family of painter-etchers. He
drew floral decorations wood engraved in the
Illustrated London News,1866; designed a 'yellow
back' cover to Routledge's Crab, Shrimp and,
Lobster Lore,1867, wood engraved by Edmund Evans
(q.v.); and drew illustrations to Shirley Hibberd's
The Ivy,1872, wood engraved and colour printed by
Benjamin Fawcett (q.v.). Slocombe was also a
member of the Royal Cambrian Academy, and
exhibited floral pictures at the British Institution,
the Old Watercolour Society, the Royal Academy,

and the Royal Society of British Artists. He was the
brother of Edward Slocombe (q.v.).
[McLean, Victorian Book Design; Houfe; TB; Bénézit;
for his etchings see Volume I]

SLOCOMBE, Edward C. 1850-1915
Draughtsman, etcher and painter, born in 1850,
into a noted family of artist-etchers, brother of
Alfred Slocombe (q.v.). He worked in Watford,
Hertfordshire from 1883. He drew for wood
engraving in The Graphic,1873, mainly social and
military subjects. He also exhibited from 1873-1904
at the Fine Art Society, the New Gallery, the Royal
Academy, the Royal Society of Painter-Etchers and
Engravers, and the Royal Hibernian Society.
[For full bibliography and etchings list see Volume I]

SLY, B.
Draughtsman on wood, who contributed drawings to
Charles Knight's (q.v.) publications. These included
Knight's London,1841, and Knight's Penny Magazine,
October 1841 and July 1842, engraved by J.Andrew
and Stephen Sly (qq.v.).
[Bodleian Library]

SLY, Stephen fl.1836-47
Prominent early wood engraver, best known for his
prolific cuts to Charles Knight's (q.v.) publications.
He set up in London first in partnership with Wilson
as Sly and Wilson, wood engravers, at 11 Bouverie
Street, Fleet Street, EC (Pigot,1836), then on his
own from 1838-40 at the same address. His work
included cuts to Charles Knight's Penny Magazine,
October 1841, after Freeman's drawings of the
Cartoons of Raphael; and July 1842, after drawings
of Martin, Webber, Anelay, Yarrell, and B.Sly (qq.v.).
He engraved after T.Scandrett's (q.v.) drawings to
Charles Knight's Old England,1844-45, a work which
totalled 2,488 wood engravings and twenty-four colour
plates; and to Knight's Old England's Worthies,1847,
with its 'numerous black and white engravings and
12 colour plates'. These were engraved in a style
reminiscent of George Cattermole's architectural
drawings in the Old Curiosity Shop. Sly's skills as
engraver for popular illustrated periodicals, which
demanded strict deadlines and a vast number of
small engravings, were learned under Henry
Vizetelly (q.v.). He was assisted by his protégé
Henry Anelay (q.v.), an equally prolific draughtsman
on wood. Both men worked for the early issues of
the Illustrated London News. Sly, in fact, engraved
the paper's first title heading in 1841, a view of London
along the Thames (the lettering done by Vizetelly's
firm). Sly followed this with quarter and half-page
engravings, then a double-page Scottish scene,
drawn by W.Dickes (q.v.), 4 June 1842. His style here
and in subsequent issues showed a mastery of landscape and topographical background at the expense
of the figures which often appeared in heavy drapery

or as black shapes against a stark white oval surround or vignette. He was also competent at engraving animals, notably a full-page series of Smithfield Show cattle, 3 December 1842; and a quarter page engraving after 'The Otter Speared' by Edwin Landseer, 13 July 1844. The British Museum owns his engravings after W.Kidd; an intricate border design after John, Earl of Westmoreland: and cuts to Scott's Waverley Novels. The Bodleian Library owns several of his C.Knight commissions. He signed his engravings: 'S SLY SC'.
[McLean; Houfe; Vizetelly, Glances Back]

SLY and Wilson
(see Sly, Stephen)

SMALL, William 1843-1929
Draughtsman illustrator, one of the most prolific of the 'Sixties School'. He was born in Edinburgh on 27 May 1843, studied at the Royal Scottish Academy Schools and worked illustrating story books for the publisher Thomas Nelson in the city. He came to London in 1865, where he developed a reputation for drawing on wood for numerous magazines and books. His quick, powerful drawings with skilful details were among the best of the period. His early drawings were done in line, upon the block, but gradually he was one of the first to break with this tradition by adopting heavy washes, especially seen in his pages for The Graphic for which he drew from 1869 until about 1900. 'His later drawings in wash, actually painted in body colour on the wood, and leaving the whole creation of the texture to the engraver, brilliant though they may be, coincide with the beginning of the decadence, for it was on these later drawings that the new school was founded, bringing our period of illustration to an end (Reid). Small was at his best during the sixties, but from the 1870s onwards he experimented and lost his way in a maze of wash drawing. Ruskin called this style 'Blottesque'. Yet he became the highest paid illustrator of his time, earning sixty guineas for each drawing for The Graphic. Small's drawings on wood were best engraved by the Dalziels and W.J.Palmer (qq.v.). They spanned the entire second half of the Victorian period. He contributed to Shilling Magazine, 1865-66; Once a Week, 1866; Good Words, 1866-68; Sunday Magazine, 1866-68, 1871; Cassell's Family Paper, 1866, 1870; Sunday at Home, 1866; Pen and Pencil Pictures from the Poets, 1866; Touches of Nature by Eminent Artists, 1866; Ballad Stories of the Affections, 1866; London Society, 1867-69; Argosy, 1867; Quiver, 1867; Poems by Jean Ingelow, 1867; Idyllic Pictures, 1867; Two Centuries of Song, 1867; Foxe's Book of Martyrs, 1867; Heber's Hymns, 1867; Spirit of Praise, 1867; the Illustrated Book of Sacred Poems, 1867; Golden Thoughts from Golden Fountains, 1867; Milton's Ode on the Morning of Christ's Nativity, 1867, engraved by W.J.Palmer; North Coast and Other Poems, 1868;

Pictures from English Literature, 1870; Good Words for the Young, 1871; Novello's National Nursery Rhymes, 1871; Judy's Almanac, 1872; Thornbury's Legendary Ballads, 1876; Dalziels' Bible Gallery, 1880; Chums, 1892; Fun; and Gypsy, 1915. The books he illustrated singlehanded were Words for the Wise, 1864; Miracles of Heavenly Love, 1864; Marion's Sundays, 1864; Washerwoman's Foundling, 1867; and Bret Harte's A Protégé of Jack Hamilton, 1894. Small was elected RI in 1883, and exhibited at the Royal Academy, 1869-1900, at the Royal Hibernian Academy, the Royal Institute of Painters in Oil-Colours, and the Royal Scottish Academy, being elected HRSA in 1917. He died on 23 December 1929. The British Museum owns proofs of his designs to Goldsmith's Works, 1865, engraved by the Dalziel Brothers.
[For a discussion of illustrations see Reid; also White; S.Haden, Chats on Old Prints, 1909; TB; Clement; McLean, Victorian Book Design; Dalziels' Record]

SMALLFIELD, Frederick 1829-1915
Occasional draughtsman illustrator for wood engravings, genre and portrait painter. He was born in Homerton in 1829, studied at the Royal Academy Schools and was elected ARWS in 1860. He is listed here for his wood engraved drawings in Willmott's Sacred Poetry, 1862. He also contributed etchings to Passages from Modern English Poets, 1862, for the Etching Club. He was also a prolific watercolourist, exhibiting from 1849-86 at the British Institution, the Grosvenor Gallery, the Royal Academy, the Royal Institute of Painters in Watercolours, and the Royal Institute of Painters in Oil-Colours, and worked in London. He died there on 10 September 1915. The British Museum owns proof engravings by the Dalziel Brothers (q.v.) dated 1861, and to Goldsmith's Works, 1865.
[Bénézit; TB; for his etchings see Volume I (with full bibliography)]

SMALLMAN, George fl.1880s
London wood engraver, who worked at 16 Clarence Street, Clapham, SW (LSDS, 1888).

SMALLWOOD, William Frome 1806-34
Draughtsman of architectural subjects, architect. He was born in London on 24 June 1806, was a pupil of the architect D.N.Cottingham, and travelled to the Continent to draw churches for publication in Charles Knight's Penny Magazine. He also drew for wood engravings in Knight's London, 1842. He exhibited landscapes at the Royal Academy and the Royal Society of British Artists, and died in London on 22 April 1834.

SMART and Company fl.1880s
Provincial wood engraver, who worked at 54 Ward's Buildings, Deansgate, Manchester (Kelly's, 1880).

There was a London lithographic and colour printing firm called Walter Smart at 10 Leather Lane (POD,1844-51). [see Wakeman and Bridson]

SMEETON, Burn fl.1840-70s
English wood engraver, who worked in Paris from 1840-60. He engraved cuts to the Magasin Pittoresque, with his partner Cossin, from 1870; and to Aubert's Le Littoral de la France,1883. He taught the noted engraver August Lepère (q.v.) and was a member of the group of engravers in Paris: Nanteuil, Best, Leloir and Pisan (qq.v.). Beraldi and Gusman listed and praised Smeeton's contributions to reproductive wood engraving in France. By the 1870s Smeeton had joined with Auguste Tilly (q.v.) as Smeeton and Tilly (q.v.). His work is in the British Museum.
[TB; Beraldi; Gusman; Bénézit]

SMEETON and Tilly fl.1870s
Wood engraving partnership in Paris, between the English engraver Burn Smeeton (q.v.) and the French engraver Auguste Tilly (q.v.). They engraved portraits for the French magazine L'art, notably English politicians and artists such as Sir John Gilbert, after Albert Gilbert's sculpted bust,1875. They also engraved after a painting by Lobrichon, which appeared full-page in the Illustrated London News,11 July 1874; and a portrait of 'The late M.Corot', after Alfred Gilbert, 27 February 1875, which was engraved in a fine, delicate black-line style with stipple-shaded facial features. The British Museum owns a number of their engravings. They signed their engravings: 'SMEETON TILLY SC'.
[Hake]

SMITH, E. fl.1862
The British Museum owns a collection of his designs engraved by the Dalziel Brothers (q.v.) for Wood's Natural History,1862.

SMITH, Edward and Company
Provincial wood engraving firm, with an office at Northwood Street, Birmingham (Kelly's,1880).

SMITH, Gavin fl.1860s
London wood engraver, who engraved in collaboration with W.J.Linton and H.Harral (qq.v.) after drawings on wood of H.S.Marks, T.Morten, W.Small (qq.v.), and others to the compilation volume, Two Centuries of Song,1867. The London directory lists a 'G.Smith', wood engraver at 2 Maritime Cottages, Gurney Road, Newtown, Stratford, E (Kelly's,1868).
[White]

SMITH, G.F. fl.1872-84
Wood engraver, who as 'F.Smith' worked for the Illustrated London News, where the full-page engraving 'The Derby Day: On the Road to Epsom', appeared 1 June 1872. As G.F.Smith he engraved

L.R.O'Brien's illustrations to 'Dartmoor and the Walkham' in the English Illustrated Magazine,1883. These were skilful atmospheric studies, the landscapes dark and brooding. They were engraved in collaboration with R.Paterson (q.v.). He signed his engravings: 'F S[superimposed]mith'.

SMITH, Harvey Orrin (later Orrinsmith) fl.1849-70
London wood engraver, who worked first in partnership with Harral (q.v.) as Smith and Harral, 85 Hatton Garden (POD,1849), then with C.S.Cheltnam (q.v.) as Smith and Cheltnam (POD,1850). They engraved various cuts for the Illustrated London News, and after drawings by Richard Doyle (q.v.); and various royal portraits, 1850-51. In 1852 Smith appeared in the London directories working on his own at 85 Hatton Garden (POD,1852-72). He was joined there by W.J.Linton (q.v.) about 1859. The two men also shared Linton's 'fine old house' at 33 Essex Street, but by 1861 Linton had also moved to the 'ramshackle' premises 85 Hatton Garden; premises which he had once had under the firm name of Smith and Linton (q.v.) (a partnership between Linton and John Orrin Smith (q.v.)). Harvey Orrin Smith worked with Linton until about 1866, when Linton emigrated to America, leaving his son William Wade Linton (q.v.) to act as his agent in the firm until at least 1872. Harvey Orrin Smith had changed his name to Orrinsmith by the late 1860s. By then his engraved work included numerous cuts for the Illustrated London News,1850-60, generally after royal portraits or full-page copies of exhibited paintings. One of his most successful engravings here was 'The Last Day of Old Smithfield', 16 June 1855, a full-page crowd scene (presumably drawn by Smith as well as engraved), and engraved with clarity despite the detail necessary to pick out members of the crowd. His most prestigious commission was to engrave Richard Doyle's illustrations to John Ruskin's fairy tale, The King of the Golden River,1851, a considerable achievement considering the outspoken attacks Ruskin had made on incompetent wood engravers at the time (see the introductory essay). He also engraved numerous cuts with Mason Jackson, the Dalziels and Bastin (qq.v.) to Charles Knight's 'Land We Live In' series. The British Museum owns several C.Knight commissions; also cuts after C.W.Cope, J.Gilbert, G.K.Johnson, J.Leech and E.Duncan; and a Spanish scene after John Phillips 'copied on wood by F.J.Skill'; the Bodleian Library owns further Knight engravings. He signed his engravings: 'H.O.SMITH' or 'H.Orrin Smith & Co.'.
[McLean, Victorian Book Design; Hake; F.Smith, W.J.Linton,1973; British Library catalogue]

SMITH, Henry Norris fl.1854-56
London wood engraver, who worked at 69 Coleman Street, W (POD, Hodgson's,1854-56).

SMITH, J. fl.1870s
Draughtsman on wood, who contributed genre
subjects wood engraved in the Illustrated London
News,1873. He may be related to the draughtsman
J.Clifford C.Smith, who contributed two landscape
drawings to the Royal Academy, 1868, 1872.
[Graves]

SMITH, J.Moyr fl.1870-1920
Draughtsman illustrator and decorative designer.
He trained as an architect 'but a natural love of
figure-drawing, intensified by the study of Sir John
Tenniel's comic illustrations of the historical
costume, faithfully and even learnedly delineated and
perfectly drawn, settled his career...' (Spielmann).
He began drawing comic illustrations for Fun, and
contributed 'mock-Etruscan' drawings to Punch,
1872-78. He alternated this work with drawing for
industry, but it was his ability to combine mythology
and historical detail with mild comedy that endeared
him to the Punch staff. He also drew decorative
details for Doré's Thomas Hood,1870, and later
illustrated Shakespeare for Children; and Lamb's
Tales,c1897. He also exhibited at the Royal Academy,
the Royal Society of British Artists, the Royal
Scottish Academy and the Royal Watercolour Society.
[Spielmann; Houfe]

SMITH, James Burrell 1822-97
Occasional draughtsman, landscape painter. He was
born in 1822, studied with T.M.Richardson and lived
in Alnwick, 1843-54. He set up as a London drawing
master in 1854, emulating his master, and exhibited
at the Royal Society of British Artists. He is listed
here for his landscape drawings for wood engravings
in the Illustrated London News,1883-87. He died in
London in 1897.

SMITH, James MacLaren fl.1873-76
Draughtsman illustrator and decorative designer. He
worked in Fulham and Putney, and exhibited decorative
interior designs and local sketches at the Royal
Academy, 1873-76. He also illustrated The Pearl
Fountain, his drawings being wood engraved by
W.Measom (q.v.).
[Graves]

SMITH, John Orrin (later Orrinsmith) 1799-1843
Prominent early Victorian wood engraver, noted for
his animal and landscape engravings in the black-line
style. He was born in Colchester in 1799, and first
learned wood engraving from Samuel Williams
(q.v.). He then briefly worked with an architect,
before resuming his wood engraving in 1824. He was
employed by William Harvey (q.v.) in London and
successfully engraved twenty-nine initial letters and
tailpieces after Harvey's designs to Northcote's
Fables,1828; he also collaborated here with John
Jackson as Jackson and Smith (q.v.). These engravings

marked Smith out as a competent engraver of
animals and were followed by cuts to Zoological
Gardens,1835. The British Museum also owns his
proof 'Brahmin Bull' engraved after Thomas
Landseer, dated 1832. However, it was his landscape
engravings for which he achieved the greatest
reputation. His colleague W.J.Linton (q.v.), who
had worked for Smith on Harvey's designs to Solace
of Song,1836, the proofs of which are in the British
Museum, declared: 'They mark the extreme of the
imitation of copper or steel, to which wood engraving
had long been tending. Allowing tone to be more
important than expressiveness of line or the distinct
assertion of form, these cuts may be considered
perfect' (Linton, Masters of Wood Engraving).
Other early engravings in this mould included cuts
to Seeley's Bible; Heads of the People; cuts after
his friend Kenny Meadows' (q.v.) designs to
Illustrated Shakespeare; numerous cuts to Charles
Knight's edition of Lane's Arabian Nights'
Entertainments; all seventy-five John Gilbert (q.v.)
drawings to Cowper's Poems; cuts to J.F.Murray's
Environs of London,1842; cuts to S.C.Hall's Book of
British Ballads,1842; and a large proportion of the
Harvey designs to J.Montgomery's Milton's Poetical
Works,1843. He was also commissioned for numerous
early issues of the Art Union (later Art Journal)
from 1839. Smith's work was known and praised in
France as well. He engraved for French publications
from about 1835, initially for Curmer on the French
edition of Paul et Virginie, 'his engraving for which
was so much esteemed that his portrait was given
in the book' (Linton). Among the other French
commissions, usually done in collaboration with
other noted English wood engravers (see separate
entries on each of those listed below) were the
following listed by Gusman: some of the 800 vignettes
after T.Johannot to Moliere's Oeuvres,1835-36,
engraved with M.Sears and Charles Thompson;
Les Evangiles,1838, engraved with G.H.Thomas,
T.Williams, Charles Gray, F.W.Branston, W.Powis,
Robert Hart, M.Sears, Charles Laing, John Wright,
and Folkard; cuts to J.B.Bossuet's Discours sur
L'Histoire Universelle,1839, engraved with
T.Williams; Ct. de Laborde's Versailles,1839,
engraved with Godard, Gowland, Charles Thompson,
W.T.Green, J.A.Wheeler, M.Sears, Jackson and
Best; Laurent's Histoire de L'Empereur Napoleon,
1839, the 500 illustrations engraved with Sears,
Thompson, Williams, Quartley, Gowland, Whitehead
and Sheeres; Abbé Prevost's Histoire de Manon
Lescaut,1839, the ninety illustrations engraved with
Sears, Thompson, Williams, Mary Ann Williams,
Gray, Gowland, and Timms; De Stael's Corinne ou
L'Italie,1841-42, engraved with Quartley and
Gowland; cuts to Wordsworth's La Grèce Pittoresque,
1841, engraved after Huet and Meissonier; Jules
Janin's L'Ane Mort,1842 edition, engraved with
Thompson, Harrison, Gray, Quartley, Gowland,

and T.Williams. He also engraved for a German edition of Herder's Cid,1839, after E.Neureuther. Nagler in fact claimed that Smith was one of the most prolific engravers of his country. John Orrin-Smith changed his name to Orrinsmith sometime after 1836. By that time he had as his apprentice the young Henry Vizetelly (q.v.), who came to him after a training with G.W.Bonner (q.v.). Vizetelly recalled that his new master was devoted to engraving and 'not only a great enthusiast in his profession, but had the knack of inspiring those associated with him with much of his own zeal'. The workshop was always filled with a stream of visiting artists, writers, and theatre people who were captivated by Smith's hospitable manner. One of the budding artists was the young John Leech (q.v.) whom Smith took under his roof and promoted by publishing his early sketches. Vizetelly also recalled his master's working methods during that important early French commission, the Paul et Virginie for Curmer. Smith insisted that he draw the Meissonier drawing of 'Paul and Virginia and the Indian Cottage' on the wood block himself, but he was so carried away by the landscape that he decided that the intricate pencil drawing he produced was too delicate to engrave, and he left the block out when he sent the remainder to Paris for printing. Indeed Linton remarked that Smith's true place in the history of English wood engraving was at the top of those men concerned with tone alone; his line remained weak in contrast to his background modulations. Towards the end of his life, Smith joined forces with his assistant (from 1836), W.J.Linton, as Smith and Linton, a company established in the autumn of 1842 to engrave all the illustrations to the new publication, the Illustrated London News. The firm quickly gained a reputation for quick, accurate press work, and developed the method of commissioning illustrations from the prominent watercolourists of the day. These were engraved by their assistants: Alfred and Horace Harral, Henry Linton, C.Mins, C.S.Cheltnam, E.K.Johnson, and G.Pearson (see separate entries on each engraver). Since much was engraved by their assistants, it is difficult to know which was Smith's own work at this period. The pressure of work for the Illustrated London News alone, with a weekly circulation of 66,000 copies, proved a trial. The variety of engravings from news illustrations, portraits, artistic inserts by William Harvey, Kenny Meadows and E.Duncan, as well as engraved copies of recently exhibited paintings at the Royal Academy and other galleries, all contributed to the success of the Illustrated London News. However, Smith died in London on 15 October 1843 leaving his partner to continue the engraving business single-handed. Smith and Linton in fact survived for another five years, during which time Linton continued engraving for the Illustrated London News. However, despite their appearance in the London directories,

at 85 Hatton Garden (POD,1844-48), in about April, 1848, the firm collapsed. This was no doubt as a result of Linton's inability to meet crucial deadlines. It was in April 1848 that the father of one of his apprentices tried to withdraw his boy from Linton's office, an office he noted that was 'not very busy' at that time; the father demanded payment 'in money or bill at 2 months'. The British Museum owns Smith's engravings after J.Gilbert, T.Landseer, R.McIan, K.Meadows, W.Harvey. He signed his engravings: 'J Smith', 'ORRIN SMITH', 'Smith & Linton', 'Smith sculp' (script), 'OSS'.
[For a list of French work engraved see Andresen; Gusman; LeBlanc; Nagler; see also F.B.Smith, W.J.Linton,1973; C.T.Lewis; Vizetelly, Glances Back; Linton, Masters of Wood Engraving; TB; Bryan; Spielmann; Hake]

SMITH, John Richard fl.1892-95
London wood engraver, who worked at 8 New Court, Carey Street, WC (POD,1892-95).

SMITH, T.J. Son and Downes
London firm of draughtsmen on wood, and stationers, who worked at 76 Newgate Street, with printing works at 26 Upper Thames Street, EC, and 26 Charterhouse Square (Kelly's,1900).

SMITH, W.Thomas 1862-?
Occasional woodcut artist, painter of portraits, figures and historical subjects. He worked in London in 1890 and contributed illustrations to various books and magazines including Oxley's The Wilds of the West Coast,1894; the Quiver,1890; Good Cheer, 1894; and the Boy's Own Paper. The British Museum owns a folio-size woodcut, 'Virgilantia' (limited to seventy-five copies) of a soldier in armour leaning on his lance. Smith exhibited at the Royal Academy, the Royal Society of British Artists and the Royal Institute of Painters in Watercolours.

SMITH, Worthington G. fl.1866-80
London wood engraver, botanical and archaeological draughtsman. He contributed drawings to R.Hogg and G.W.Johnson's Wild Flowers of Great Britain, 1866-80; and to the Gardener's Chronicle,1875-1910. These latter commissions were dismissed by the garden writer M.Hadfield as 'a regular flow of drawings...of monotonous accuracy combined with a peculiar feeling of staleness that no doubt increased by the now debased mechanics of wood engraving' (Gardening in Britain,1960,p.370). Smith also designed the later (post 1860) covers to the Illustrated London Almanack; and an initial letter wood engraved in Punch,1878. The British Museum owns his trade card, dated 1878: 'Worthington G.Smith, Wood engraver and artist Draughtsman to the British Archaeological Association, Artist & Engraver to the Cambrian

Archaeological Association, 38 Kyverdale Road, Upper Clapton, London, N'. This was skilfully engraved with a border of animals, plants and classical busts.

SMITH and Cheltnam
(see Smith, Harvey Orrin)

SMITH and Harral
(see Smith, Harvey Orrin)

SMITH and Jackson
(see Jackson, John; also Jackson and Smith)

SMYTH, Frederick James fl.1841-67
London wood engraver, who worked at 196 Strand (POD,1849), 15 Essex Street (POD,1851-64), then 2 Surrey Street, WC (POD,1866-67). He engraved cuts to Charles Knight's Penny Magazine, June 1841, after Wells. He was best known for his numerous engravings to the Illustrated London News, 1843-60, for which he quickly became a major engraver. He worked on the cover and most illustrations for the Anniversary edition, 27 May 1843, but a full-page 'The Lord Mayor's Procession', 11 November 1843, was engraved poorly, with block seams showing. Chatto claimed that his supplement pull out, eight feet long, 'Panorama of the River Thames in 1845', 11 January 1845, was the largest block engraving in England. This was followed by a fold-out double-page engraving 'The Royal Children', 25 December 1852. Smyth was a skilful portrait engraver. His numerous engraved portraits were taken after photographs or sculpted busts as well as paintings. Perhaps his most effective was the small, third page portrait, 'Captain M'Clure in his Arctic Dress', Illustrated London News, 7 October 1854, which utilised a silhouette technique against a stark white arctic landscape. He also engraved for the Illustrated London Almanack, 1851. The British Museum owns several portrait engravings, also work after J.Gilbert and H.C.Selous (a series of large individual prints); The Bodleian Library owns his Knight cuts. He signed his work: 'SMYTH SC' or 'Smyth Sc' (script).
[Hake; Chatto]

SMYTH, John Talfourd
Wood engraver, listed by the British Museum for a large sepia printed engraving of Christ (?) carving his crucifixion into a prison wall, after E.H.Wehnert. This was also printed in black ink, a copy of which is in the British Museum washed with grey to pick out the figure alone. He signed his work in a similar manner to Frederick J.Smyth: 'Smyth Sc' (script).

SMYTHE, Lionel Percy 1839-1918
Occasional draughtsman, illustrator, figure and landscape watercolourist. He was born in London on

4 September 1839, educated at King's College School and educated in art at Heatherley's. He contributed drawings which were wood engraved in the Illustrated London News, 1874, 1879, 1880. He was elected ARA in 1898 and RA in 1911, and exhibited at the Fine Art Society, the Royal Society of British Artists, the Royal Institute of Painters in Watercolours, the Royal Institute of Painters in Oil-Colours and the Royal Watercolour Society. He died on 10 July 1918.
[Hardie; Bénézit; TB; Houfe]

SNELL, Arthur Bartram fl.1891-95
London wood engraver, who worked at 2 (3) Tudor Street, EC (POD,1891-94), then as Snell and Company at 30 Essex Street, Strand, WC (POD,1895).

SNELL, Frank R. fl.1882-83
London wood engraver, who worked at 129 Tottenham Court Road, W (POD,1882-83).

SNOW, J.W. fl.1832-48
Occasional draughtsman, painter of horses. He illustrated Tattersalls British Race Horses, 1838, and drew for a wood engraving in the Illustrated London News, 1848. He also exhibited at the Royal Society of British Artists, 1832.

SOANE, Harry fl.1840-95
London wood engraver, heraldic draughtsman, stationer. He worked at 1 later 8 Green Street, Leicester Square, WC (POD,1876-87). Fincham lists numerous heraldic bookplates designed by Soane, c1840-95.

SOLOMON, Abraham 1824-62
Occasional draughtsman on wood of figure subjects, popular genre painter. He was born in London in May 1824, the brother of Simeon and Rebecca Solomon (qq.v.). He studied at Sass's in Bloomsbury, 1838, then at the Royal Academy Schools, 1839. He established a reputation for his paintings of railway carriage dramas from 1854 and became a regular Royal Academy exhibitor. His work also appeared at the British Institution. He was listed by Bohn in Chatto and Jackson for his drawings on wood to Book of Favourite Modern Ballads; he also drew on wood for Household Song, 1861. He contributed to the Illustrated London News, 1857. He died in Biarritz on 19 December 1862.
[Chatto; TB; Bryan; Maas; Redgrave]

SOLOMON, Rebecca fl.1852-69
Occasional draughtsman for wood engravings, painter of portraits and historical subjects. She was the sister of Abraham and Simeon Solomon (qq.v.) and drew for wood engravings in the Churchman's Family Magazine, 1864, and London Society. She also exhibited from 1852-69, notably at the Royal Academy. She collaborated and modelled

with J.E.Millais on his painting, 'Christ in the House of his Parents', 1850. She 'subsequently developed an errant nature and came to disaster' (DNB).
[TB; Bénézit; DNB]

SOLOMON, Simeon   1840-1905
Draughtsman illustrator, painter. He was born in Bishopsgate Without, on 9 October 1840, the brother of fellow artists Abraham and Rebecca Solomon (qq.v.). He was a pupil of Cary's Academy, Bloomsbury, then the Royal Academy Schools, where he exhibited from 1858. He also entered his brother's Gower Street studio and learned of a painter's life and ambitions there. His drawing came under the influence of Swinburne and Rossetti. He drew briefly for wood engravings in Once a Week, 1862, and Good Words, 1866, and this trained his abilities to draw for the engraver. He then produced his most notable work for wood engraving: 'Illustrations of Jewish Customs', ten drawings for Leisure Hour, 1866. It is these which Reid calls 'extraordinary', with an influence from Rembrandt's use of light that make them 'so completely unlike anything else that was being done at this time...They must have proved something of a puzzle to the orthodox engraver, though Butterworth and Heath [q.v.] have accomplished their task well...Each one of these drawings is brimmed up with atmosphere--an atmosphere strange, sad, exotic, alien...Its emotion is a kind of nostalgia, a homesickness, a sickness of the soul, but completely unlike the sensuous idealism of Rossetti, and still more unlike the weak, cloying idealism of Simeon Solomon's own later drawings'. Solomon also drew two heads for Dark Blue, 1871-73. He was commissioned by the Dalziels (q.v.) for their Bible Gallery, 1880 and made twenty designs, some in pen and ink (more than other contributors), though only six were used. He also drew for Mrs Jameson's Lives of the Minor Saints, c1860, and etched a plate for a Portfolio of Illustrations of Thomas Hood, 1858. Later his drawing of a Medusa head was wood engraved in Hobby Horse, 1893. But from 1872 on his career collapsed. He refused commissions, for a time worked as a pavement artist, and eventually was found lying insensible in Great Turnstile Street and died shortly afterwards. The DNB summarised this last period: 'His main source of income in the long years of ruin were the occasional few shillings earned by hasty drawings of a futile but, in reproductions, popular sentimentality'. The British Museum owns proof engravings of his designs for the Dalziel Brothers, 1862.
[Reid; DNB; Houfe; Wood; B.Falk, Five Years Dead, 1937; J.E.Ford, Simeon Solomon, 1964; The Bibelot, xiv, 1908; Apollo, 85, 1967, pp.59-61; for his etchings see Volume I]

SOPER, George   1870-1942
Wood engraver, etcher and watercolourist of figure subjects and town scenes. He was born in London in 1870, educated in Ramsgate and studied etching with Frank Short. He illustrated Kingsley's Water Babies, 1908; contributed drawings to the Illustrated London News, 1897; Cassell's Magazine, 1898; the Boy's Own Paper; Chums; and The Graphic, 1901-04. His wood engravings appeared in the Studio, Special Number, 1919. He worked in Harmer Green, Welwyn, Hertfordshire. He was elected ARE in 1918 and RE in 1920. He died on 13 August 1942. The British Museum owns a series of proofs of landscapes and agricultural workers.
[TB; Bénézit; Slater; Who's Who in Art, 1934]

SOUTHPORT Independent and General Printing Company   fl.1870s
Provincial wood engraving firm, with an office at 13 and 16 Newill Street, Southport, Lancashire (Kelly's, 1872).

SOUTHWOOD, Smith and Company   fl.1880s
London draughtsmen on wood, with an office at 4 King Street, Cheapside, EC and Ironmonger Lane, EC, with a printing works at Plough Court, Fetter Lane (Kelly's, 1889).

SOWERBY, G.B.
Draughtsman for wood engravings, who illustrated Reverend J.G.Wood's Common Objects of the Sea Shore, 1857, wood engraved by Edmund Evans (q.v.).
[Evans Reminiscences]

SOWERBY, J. DeCarle   fl.1840s
London wood engraver, who worked at 82 Pratt Street, Camden Town (POD, 1847).

SOWERBY, John G.   fl.1876-1925
Draughtsman illustrator of landscape and floral subjects, also painter. He worked in Newcastle, Gateshead, and Ross-on-Wye. He drew Greenaway-inspired children's illustrations, for instance, Afternoon Tea, c1880; and At Home, 1881. These were first sent to Edmund Evans (q.v.) for wood engraving, but had to be broken up among twelve separate engravers when Evans refused, incensed by this copyist of his new protégé, Kate Greenaway (q.v.). Sowerby also exhibited from 1876-1914 at the Royal Academy, the Royal Institute of Painters in Watercolours, and the Royal Scottish Academy.
[Bénézit; Houfe]

SPAWTON, Harry   fl.1890s
London wood engraver, who worked at 3 Rood Lane, EC (POD, 1899).

SPECKTER, Otto 1807-?
Draughtsman for wood engravings, born in Hamburg in 1804, who contributed to Mrs Gatty's Parables from Nature,1867. He was also a painter, lithographer and etcher.
[Nagler; Muir (with book list)]

SPIELMEYER, Wilhelm fl.1888-94
Prominent wood engraver after photographs, who worked at Falcon Court, 32 Fleet Street, EC (POD,1893-94). His engravings of photographs appeared in many places, notably the English Illustrated Magazine,1888-89; with the portrait 'Bill Beresford and His Victoria Cross', and illustrations to H.H.Cameron's 'The History of Billiards'. He also wood engraved the illustrations by G.H.Boughton (q.v.) to Rip Van Winkle,1893, for Macmillan's series of illustrated classics. These 'show a complete change from the sixties and seventies: mechanical methods are creeping in, the engraver is copying wash tones in the same style he has learned to use for photographs' (McLean). The British Museum owns a few landscape and nature engravings and signed proofs after G.H.Boughton. He signed his work: 'W SPIELMEYER Sc'.

SPON, F. fl.1853-55
London wood engraver, who worked at Clarehall Row, Stepney Green (POD, Hodgson's,1853-55).

SPREADBURY, William fl.1887-90
London wood engraver, who worked at 49 Essex Street, Strand, WC (POD,1887-90). He shared the premises with G.Millard (q.v.).

STABLER, John fl.1840s-90s
Long-standing assistant to the wood engraver Benjamin Fawcett (q.v.). When Fawcett established his stereotype foundry he took Stabler in, and trained him in the mechanics of wood engraving. He worked as block-planer, lead moulder, papier-mâché, plaster-of-paris and general wood preparer, for over fifty years. The engraver W.D.Ridley (q.v.) recalled how Stabler 'prepared the blocks, being at first an expert cabinet maker; he also managed the stereotype foundry long years before 1850; and was responsible for every piece of boxwood used until the early 70s, when it was impossible to do without outside help in that department...'.
[Reverend M.C.F.Morris, Benjamin Fawcett, 1925,p.13]

STANDFUST, G.B. fl.1841-44
Draughtsman on wood, who drew for Charles Knight's Penny Magazine,November 1841, engraved by Murdon (q.v.). He illustrated Shelley's Poetical Works,1844, and concentrated on humorous subjects. He also exhibited at the Royal Academy in 1844.
[Bodleian Library; Houfe]

STANESBY
Draughtsman on wood, who contributed drawings for wood engravings in Charles Knight's Penny Magazine, December 1841, engraved by J.Cunningham (q.v.).
[Bodleian Library]

STANFIELD, William Clarkson 1793-1867
Occasional draughtsman on wood, landscape and marine painter. He was born in Sunderland on 3 December 1793 and apprenticed to an Edinburgh heraldic painter before going off to sea, 1808, then into the Navy in 1812. He left service in 1818 to devote all his time to theatrical scene painting, then with his friend David Roberts went to London in 1820. There he worked for the Drury Lane Theatre, joined the 'Dickens set' and illustrated various books by his friends, Captain Marryat as well as Dickens. This work started with drawings for steel engravings in Heath's Album,1832-34, Heath's Gallery,1836-38, and for the Findens. Other works were etched after his designs. His work drawing on wood was infrequent and engraved by Henry Vizetelly (q.v.). This included twenty engravings to Marryat's Poor Jack,1840, and a commission from Vizetelly to illustrate a life of Nelson. Stanfield 'commenced the designs for the project work, but, like many other painters, found the difficulty of drawing on the boxwood block with the necessary neatness and precision almost insurmountable' (Vizetelly, Glances Back,p.160). Stanfield also drew on wood with T.Creswick (q.v.) for Moxon's edition of Tennyson's Poems,1857, engraved by W.J.Linton (q.v.), who exhibited his work at the Royal Academy, 1857. Stanfield also exhibited his landscape and marine pictures at the British Institution, the Royal Society of British Artists, and the Royal Academy, and was elected ARA,1832, then RA in 1835. He died in Hampstead on 18 May 1867. The British Museum owns his designs engraved by the Dalziel Brothers (q.v.), 1855.
[For a list of works see TB; Houfe; see also DNB; Bryan; Chatto; Wood; J.Dafforne, Clarkson Stanfield,1873; Vizetelly, Glances Back]

STANILAND, Charles Joseph 1838-1916
Draughtsman illustrator, marine painter and etcher. He was born in Kingston-upon-Hull on 19 June 1838, studied at the Birmingham School of Art, Heatherley's, South Kensington and the Royal Academy Schools, 1861. He began work drawing for wood engravings in Leisure Hour,1866; Cassell's Family Magazine,1867; Idyllic Pictures,1867; the Quiver,1868; and Episodes of Fiction,1870. His numerous drawings wood engraved in the Illustrated London News,1870-87, and The Graphic,1880-90 were social realism of a type that appealed to Van Gogh. These included mining scenes like 'The Rush to the Pit's Mouth', The Graphic, 31 January 1880; also a double-page drawing of the South Kensington

Museum, Illustrated London News, 3 June 1871; and
oriental subjects drawn with C.W.Cole (q.v.) in
The Graphic, 1887. His drawings to the English
Illustrated Magazine, 1886-92, were wood engraved
by R.Paterson, R.Lueders, J.D.Cooper and
O.Lacour (qq.v.). He also drew single-handed for
A.W.Drayson's Gentleman Cadet, 1875; G.A.Henty's
Dragon and the River, 1886; M.C.Rowsell's Traitor
or Patriot; and C.N.Robinson's Britannia's Bulwarks,
1901. Staniland was also a successful marine painter
and portrait, still-life and bird watercolourist. He
exhibited at the Fine Art Society, the Royal Academy,
the Royal Institute of Painters in Watercolours, where
he was elected ARI, 1875, and RI in 1879, and the
Royal Institute of Painters in Oil-Colours in 1883.
He died in London in 1916.
[For bibliography and list of his etchings see
Volume I; see also TB; Bénézit; Who's Who, 1911]

STANKOWSKI, E. fl.1884
Wood engraver, who engraved after C.O.Murray's
vignette drawing 'The Porch of the Temple Church',
in the English Illustrated Magazine, 1884.

STANLEY, L. fl.1860
Draughtsman of topographical subjects. He
contributed drawings of Palermo wood engraved in
Henry Vizetelly's Illustrated Times, 1860.

STANNUS, Anthony Carey fl.1862-1909
Occasional draughtsman illustrator, genre, landscape
and marine painter. He contributed a drawing wood
engraved in the Illustrated London News, 1867. He
specialised in views of Cornwall, also Ireland,
Belgium. He exhibited work at the British Institution,
the Royal Academy, the Royal Society of British
Artists, and the Royal Hibernian Academy.

STANTON, George Clark 1832-94
Occasional draughtsman for wood engravings,
sculptor, painter of genre subjects on eighteenth
century themes. He was born in Birmingham in 1832,
was a pupil at the Birmingham School of Art, worked
for Elkington and Company, visited Italy and then
returned to settle in Edinburgh in 1855. He drew for
wood engravings in Good Words, 1860, and contributed
to Poems and Songs of Robert Burns, 1875. He also
sculpted, designed stained glass, and exhibited work
at the Royal Scottish Academy, where he was elected
ARSA, 1862, and RSA, 1883. He died in Edinburgh on
8 January 1894. The British Museum owns a proof
engraved design for the Dalziel Brothers (q.v.), 1861.
[TB; White; Houfe]

STANTON, Horace Hughes 1843-1914
Occasional draughtsman illustrator, landscape painter.
He was born in 1843, and worked in Chelsea and
Kensington until 1913. He drew for wood engraving in
London Society, 1869. He later went to America where

he died in New York on 13 September 1914. While
in London he exhibited at the Grosvenor Gallery, the
Royal Academy, and the Royal Hibernian Academy.

STAPLES, Frederick fl.1857-58
London wood engraver, who worked at 41 St George's
Road, Southwark, S (POD, 1857-58).

STARLING, Henrietta P. fl.1842-55
London wood engraver, who worked at 8 Adelaide
Terrace, Islington (POD, 1845-48), then 36 Halliford
Street, Islington (POD, 1853-55). She engraved a
small drawing 'Nooks and Corners of Old England',
for the Illustrated London News, 27 August 1842.

STEEDMAN, William fl.1860-66
London wood engraver, who worked at 8 Wine Office
Court, Fleet Street, EC (POD, 1860). He moved later
to 13 Gough Square, Fleet Street, EC (POD, 1864-66).

STEELE, Gourlay 1819-94
Occasional draughtsman illustrator, painter of
animal subjects. He was born in 1819, and studied
at the Trustees Academy in Edinburgh under
R.S.Lauder. He drew for wood engravings in Good
Words, 1860, and contributed to Poems and Songs of
Robert Burns, 1875. He also exhibited at the Royal
Academy and the Royal Scottish Academy, where he
was elected ARSA in 1846, and RSA in 1859. He died
in Edinburgh in 1894. The British Museum owns a
proof engraving by the Dalziel Brothers (q.v.) after
'S.Steele', an execution scene dated 1854.
[White; Houfe]

STEMBRIDGE, Henry James fl.1872-80
Provincial wood engraver, who worked at 29A South
John Street, Liverpool (Kelly's, 1872-76). Later he
moved to 3 Cable Street, Liverpool (Kelly's, 1880).

STENSON, George Austin fl.1880s
Provincial draughtsman on wood, who worked in
Long Eaton, Nottingham (Kelly's, 1889).

STEPHENS, George fl.1870s
London wood engraver, who worked at 37 Thornton
Street, Brixton (Kelly's, LSDS, 1872).

STEPHENSON, James 1828-86
Occasional draughtsman on wood, prominent metal
engraver and lithographer. He was born in
Manchester on 26 November 1828, was a metal
engraving pupil of Finden in London in 1847, and
exhibited engravings at the Royal Academy, 1856-58.
He drew for wood engravings in Clever Boys, and
Bohn's edition of Wide Wide World. He was more
noted as a skilful engraver on steel, in line or
mezzotint, as well as an occasional etcher. He died
in London on 28 May 1886.
[For a complete account of his metal engravings

see Volume I; see also DNB; Bryan; TB; Chatto;
Houfe]

STEVENS, Charles fl.1858-65
London wood engraver, who worked at 7 Dane's Inn,
Strand, WC (POD,1858), the office of the prominent
engraver Thomas Bolton (q.v.). He moved later to
48 Essex Street, Strand, WC (POD,1863-65).

STEVENSON, Robert Louis 1850-94
Amateur wood engraver, best known as author of
numerous classic adventure stories. Stevenson
attempted to draw and engrave illustrations but none
of these were published during his lifetime.
[J.Pennell's,'Robert Louis Stevenson, Illustrator',
in Studio,1897,pp.17-24]

STEYERT, Auguste 1830-1904
French draughtsman on wood and designer of bookplates. He was born in Lyons in 1830, and did
drawings for Henry Vizetelly's Illustrated Times,1856,
which were wood engraved. He died in Lyons in 1904.

STIFF, C. fl.1840s
Wood engraver, who engraved for the early numbers
of the Illustrated London News,1842. His engravings
here included small fillers, 'Lord Mayor's Day' after
John Gilbert (q.v.), 12 November 1842; and a double-
page, 'The Christmas Pantomime' after Alfred
Crowquill (q.v.), 24 December 1842.

STOCKDALE, W.Colebrooke fl.1852-67
Draughtsman illustrator, who specialised in drawing
buildings and sporting subjects. He drew for a wood
engraving in the Illustrated London News,1852. He
also exhibited at the Royal Academy, 1860-67.

STOCKS, Lumb 1812-92
Occasional draughtsman on wood, generally of
figures and portraits, metal engraver. He was born
in Lightcliffe, Yorkshire on 30 November 1812, was
a pupil of Charles Cope (q.v.), then settled in
London in 1827. He learned engraving for six years
with Charles Rolls, and eventually became one of the
most prominent engravers of Fine Art prints. He
occasionally drew on wood, for Ministering Children,
engraved by Edmund Evans (q.v.); for Ministry of
Life; and English Yeoman. Stocks was one of the few
metal engravers elected to the Royal Academy, first
ARA in 1853, then as RA in 1872. He also exhibited
at the Royal Society of British Artists. He died in
London on 28 April 1892.
[For a description of his metal engravings see
Volume I (with full bibliography); also Nagler; Chatto;
LeBlanc; Art Journal,1892; Illustrated London News,
1892; Evans Reminiscences]

STOCKWIN, A. fl.1880s
Provincial wood engraver, who worked at Swan
Buildings, Edmund Street, Birmingham (Kelly's,1889).

STOKER, Matilda fl.1880-88
Draughtsman of ornamental book decoration. She
worked in London and Dublin, and drew for wood
engravings of Celtic ornaments to the English
Illustrated Magazine,1886-88. She also exhibited
at the Royal Hibernian Academy, 1880-84.

STOKES, A.E. and Company fl.1889-1900
Provincial wood engraving firm, with an office at
Queen Street, Wolverhampton (Kelly's,1889). This
became Stokes and Bradley, Midland Chambers and
162 Edmund Street, Birmingham (Kelly's,1900).

STONE, Marcus 1840-1921
Draughtsman illustrator, and genre painter. He was
born in London on 4 July 1840 and studied art with
his illustrator father Frank Stone. He exhibited at
the Royal Academy from 1858 and specialised in figures
in interiors. He drew for wood engravings in London
Society,1863-64; Sunday Magazine,1865; Touches of
Nature by Eminent Artists,1866; The Graphic,1872;
Cornhill,1873; and the Illustrated London News,1873.
He also illustrated Dickens' Great Expectations,
1860-61; and Our Mutual Friend,1865, for which he
is best known, although Stone thought such work 'very
immature'. Stone was perhaps more successful with
his illustrations to Trollope's serial novel, He Knew
He Was Right,1868-69, which were highly praised by
Reid as well as Henry James. Stone's drawings were
wood engraved for this by Joseph Swain (q.v.) after
being photographed onto wood--the first Trollope
work for which this new technique was used. The
original full-page pen and ink drawings and vignettes
(now in New York Public Library) were, therefore,
larger then necessary, drawn in ink rather than the
pencil earlier necessary for transfer by the
illustrator onto the wood block. 'One would be
tempted to think the plates had been made by a
photographic line engraving, were it not for the
most subtle variations and signature of the engraver
(here Swain)' (N.John Hall, Trollope and His
Illustrators,1980,p.156). As a result, all cross-
hatching and close parallel lines for texture are
Stone's original lines, not re-interpreted by the
engraver; this shows how expert Stone had become
in drawing for the wood engraver. Stone was also
a popular genre painter, who was successfully
elected ARA in 1877, and RA in 1887. He died in
London on 24 March 1921. The British Museum
owns several engravings after his designs, engraved
by the Dalziel Brothers (q.v.), 1861-62.
[see TB and Wood (complete bibliographies); Clement;
Houfe; White]

STOPFORD, Robert Lowe 1813-98
Draughtsman 'Special Artist' for wood engravings in
the Illustrated London News; also marine and scenery
painter, lithographer. He was born in Dublin in 1813,
became a drawing master in Cork, but was sent away
as 'Special Artist' for the Illustrated London News.
He also drew on wood for Henry Vizetelly's Illustrated
Times,1859, and for 'many other papers' (Strickland).
He died in Cork on 2 February 1898.
[Bénézit; Houfe; Strickland]

STOREY, George Adolphus 1834-1919
Occasional illustrator, genre and portrait painter.
He was born in London on 7 January 1834, was
educated in Paris under M.Morand, and then
returned to London to study with an architect. He
enrolled in Leigh's Art School, and the Royal Academy
Schools, 1854, and worked as a painter under the
influence of the Pre-Raphaelites. As a draughtsman
illustrator, some of his drawings appeared wood
engraved; namely a drawing of 'Little Snowdrop', in
Punch,1882, which Spielmann dismisses as, 'pretty
as it was, displayed but a very mild sort of humour'.
Storey drew for Homely Ballads and Old-Fashioned
Poems,1880. He also contributed later to Ludgate
Monthly,1892, and the Illustrated London News,1893.
As a painter, he was a founder member of the
St John's Wood Clique, was elected ARA in 1876 and
RA in 1914, and also exhibited at the Royal Institute
of Painters in Watercolours, the Royal Institute of
Painters in Oil-Colours, and the Royal Scottish
Academy. He died on 29 July 1919.
[Spielmann; Houfe; TB; Bénézit; Wood]

STOTHARD, Thomas 1755-1834
Draughtsman illustrator, occasionally on wood,
miniature painter, decorator. He was born in London
on 17 August 1755, educated at Tadcaster, and then
apprenticed to a draughtsman of silk patterns in
Spitalfields. He entered the Royal Academy Schools
in 1777, drawing his first book illustrations for
Harrison's The Novelists and The Poetical magazines.
By 1779 he had done work for Town and Country
Magazine; and Bell's British Poets series; then shop
card designs and fashion plates, as well as head and
tailpieces for books. Most of these were engraved on
metal, some notably by William Blake, others by
C.Heath, later by Finden. Stothard is listed here for
his occasional drawings for wood engravers. His
most successful were to Rogers' Pleasures of
Memory,1810, engraved on wood by Luke Clennell
(q.v.) in 'a very pure example of the facsimile style'
(Hind); or according to the DNB they are 'justly
prized for their close imitation of Stothard's beautiful
touch with the pen'. Stothard was also a favourite
with the publisher William Pickering, who often
commissioned drawings for steel or wood engravings
after his paintings, reduced in size to use as decorative
borders. These were wood engraved by John Thompson

(q.v.), notably an Alphabet,1830; thirty-one engravings
printed at the Chiswick Press. Other Stothard
drawings were wood engraved by Mary Byfield
(q.v.). In fact more than 3,000 Stothard drawings
were engraved on metal or wood. 'Few draughtsmen,
however, knew better than Stothard how far the
engraver might be trusted to interpret his drawings
or how little details it was necessary to give'
(Dudley Heath in Connoisseur,1910). Nearly all of
the engravings may be found in the British Museum;
also a selection is in the Bodleian Library's Constance
Meade Collection. Stothard was largely known
during his lifetime as an illustrator, although he
also designed interior decoration and exhibited
paintings at the Royal Academy being elected
ARA in 1785, and RA in 1794. He also exhibited at
the British Institution and the Royal Society of
British Artists. He generally worked in monochrome
wash, occasionally in full watercolour. He died at
his house at 28 Newman Street on 27 April 1834.
[For a list of illustrated work see DNB; Houfe;
see also A.E.Bray's Life of Thomas Stothard,1851;
Hind; Linton, Masters of Wood Engraving]

STOTT, Joseph and John fl.1822-1889
Halifax wood engravers, lithographers and colour
printers. Joseph Saville Stott (d.1879) set up a
colour printing and lithographic business in 1822 at
Hall End, Halifax. John Stott set up as engraver and
printer at Upper Brunswick Street in 1850. The two
combined in partnership in 1861 at Swine Street and
Mount Street. They appear as Stott Brothers, Mount
Street (POD,1887-1900). Kelly's Stationers'
directory lists them as wood engravers in 1889.
Fincham lists five bookplates of armorial designs
signed 'Stott Brothers, Halifax' or 'J.S.Stott',
dated 1840-60.
[For colour printing work see Wakeman and Bridson]

STOWERS, T.Gordon fl.1880-94
Occasional draughtsman illustrator, portrait painter.
He worked in London where he drew a clever wood
engraved parody of Millais' famous painting, which
he called 'Cherry Unripe', Punch, December 1880.
Spielmann claimed that after this Stowers 'rested on
his laurels'. He also exhibited work at the Royal
Academy and the Royal Society of British Artists.

STRANDERS
(see Minton and Stranders)

STRANG, William 1859-1921
Occasional woodcut artist of chiaroscuro work,
prominent etcher and painter. He was born in
Dumbarton on 13 February 1859, and studied at the
local Academy, then in London at the Slade, under
Alphonse Legros, who from 1875 taught him etching.
He achieved considerable success with etched book
illustrations, portraits, and social realist plates;

his etched oeuvres totalled 747 plates. (For a complete account see Volume I.) His work on wood included woodcut illustrations to his masterful A Book of Giants,1898, for the Unicorn Press; and The Doings of Death,1902, for the Essex House Press. For this latter work, done in collaboration with Bernard Sleigh (q.v.), Strang drew directly upon blocks of pear wood with a very fine pen, making his lines so thin as to suggest only the direction intended for the tool cuts, not the required tones to bring the subject to life. Sleigh recalled how traumatic this method could be, 'it became a difficult test of skill and knowledge quite invaluable to me'. When highlights were required, a second tone was used, and a total of twenty-six blocks made up the final printed work. The finished work became a primary example of chiaroscuro wood cut technique during the early turn of the century revival of wood engraving. A similar process was adopted for Strang's masterpiece, 'The Plough', published in The Dome,1900 as a fold-out plate, and signed 'W.STRANG 1899', which was sold by the Art for Schools Association, Bloomsbury. This cut measured originally 4' x 3'6", was produced from a number of joined planks, and was said to be 'one of the largest woodcuts ever made' (DNB). Strang's woodcut 'The Prodigal Son' was also a successful venture, published in Hans Singer's book of Strang's etchings and engravings, 1913. Strang was also a contributor of illustrations to the English Illustrated Magazine, 1890-91, the Yellow Book,1895, and The Dome, 1898-1900. He exhibited at the Fine Art Society, the Grosvenor Gallery, the New English Art Club, the Royal Academy, the Royal Society of Painter-Etchers and Engravers,1881, the Royal Hibernian Society and the Royal Scottish Academy. He was elected ARA in 1906 and RA (engraver) in 1921. He died on 12 April 1921. The British Museum owns a small woodcut of Icarus (?) signed 'WS'.
[For a list of illustrated work see Houfe; see also TB; DNB; Hind; Sketchley; Volume I for etchings]

STRASYNSKI, Leonard Ludwik 1828-89
Occasional draughtsman on wood, lithographer. He was born on 11 January 1828 in Tokarowka, Poland and studied at the St Petersburg Academy,1847-55. He travelled throughout the Continent, then came to London in 1867-68. There he drew for nine cuts for Punch,1867-68, 'very foreign in feeling and firm in touch' (Spielmann). He also contributed initial letters to London Society, and a drawing wood engraved in Once a Week,1867. He died in Shitomir on 4 February 1889.
[Spielmann; Bénézit; Houfe]

STRATHERN, J. and A.F. fl.1872-76
Glasgow firm of wood engravers, with an office at 33 Renfield Street, Glasgow (Kelly's,1872), then 153 W.Nile Street (Kelly's,1876). An advertisement

in Kelly's claimed that the firm were specialists as engravers on wood and metal as well as showcard manufacturers, lithographers, draughtsmen, embossers, letterpress printers and stationers.

STRECKER, Edward fl.1879-80
London wood engraver, who worked at 33 Catherine Street, Strand, WC (POD,1879-80).

STREET, Frederick fl.1890s
London wood engraver, who worked at 6 Red Lion Court, Fleet Street, EC (POD,1893).

STRELLER, C. fl.1884-88
Wood engraver, who contributed engravings to the English Illustrated Magazine,1884-88. These included 'The Birthday' after Alma-Tadema, 1884, and 'A Riverside Idyll' after Lucien Davis, 1885, both engraved in a flat, featureless style. Streller may be related to the Leipzig family of artists which included Heinrich (d.1865) and Carl (born in London,1889).

STRETCH, Matt fl.1880-96
Occasional draughtsman illustrator on wood, figure and humorous artist. He worked first for the wood engraver Edmund Evans (q.v.) drawing designs on wood for his early books, then contributed to The Gentlewoman; to the Dalziel Brothers' magazine, Fun,1886-96; and to Moonshine,1891. He also exhibited at the Royal Hibernian Academy in 1880.
[Evans Reminiscences; Houfe]

STRONG
(see Mason and Strong)

STUBBS and Robertson fl.1870s
Provincial firm of wood engravers, who worked at 63 Sackville Street, Manchester (Kelly's,1872).

STURGESS, John fl.1875-1903
Occasional draughtsman illustrator on wood, sporting painter. He worked in London, first drawing on wood for the Illustrated London News, 1874-97, as their principal hunting and racing artist for about ten years. His drawings, which were wood engraved by Edmund Evans (q.v.), were drawn in an accurate yet wooden style. One of his more successful non-sporting drawings wood engraved here was the full-page, 'Christmas Time Forty Years Ago', Illustrated London News,1874, which depicts a coach at the entry to a large country house. Later Sturgess contributed to the English Illustrated Magazine,1884; Sporting and Dramatic News,1890; and illustrated Nat Gould's Magic Jacket,1896. He also exhibited at the Royal Society of British Artists and the Royal Hibernian Academy.
[Evans Reminiscences; Houfe]

SULMAN, T. fl.1855-1900
Prominent draughtsman for architectural subjects, ornamental borders and vignettes, also wood engraver. He began drawing illustrations for Monier Williams' Kalidasa-Sakoontala,1855, taken from a British Museum manuscript, wood engraved by G.Measom (q.v.), then became topographical and architectural draughtsman for the Illustrated London News,1859-88. For this he drew ornate floral borders and decorative trellis patterns surrounding sketches of various topographical views. His skills were greatly tested by the drawing for a six-page fold-out wood engraving, 'New York from Bergen Hill, Hoboken', Illustrated London News,1876, engraved by R.Loudan (q.v.). During the 1860s Sulman contributed wood engraved drawings to Churchman's Family Magazine,1863; Illustrated Times,1860-65; Once a Week,1867; Good Words for the Young,1869; and Boy's Own Paper,1882. Chatto and Jackson cite his role as a painter who occasionally drew on wood, notably ornamental borders and vignettes which are best seen in Tenniel's edition of Lalla Rookh. Edmund Evans (q.v.) engraved and colour printed his drawings for the Christmas cover of Kind Words,1874. Sulman worked in London, and listed himself in the directories as T.Sulman,Junior, 15 King Edward Street, Liverpool Road, N (POD,1858-71), then 16 Essex Street, Strand, WC (Kelly's,1876-80), and New Court, Carey Street, WC (Kelly's,1889-1900). The British Museum owns a proof engraving by the Dalziel Brothers (q.v.) after 'S. [sic] Sulman', dated 1852.
[Chatto; Evans Reminiscences; McLean, Victorian Book Design]

SUMNER, George Heywood Maunoir 1853-1940
Draughtsman illustrator, one of the leading figures of the revival of wood engraving in the 1880s and 1890s; also an etcher and archaeologist. He was born in 1853 and began exhibiting work at the Royal Academy and the Royal Society of Painter-Etchers and Engravers from 1878. His style borrowed from the medievalism of William Morris, and the firm outline of Walter Crane, as well as the lyrical nature of Blake and Palmer. His drawings for wood engravings appeared in the English Illustrated Magazine,1883-86, where his Undine drawings, 1888, first appeared wood engraved by O.Jahyer, J.Cocking and Waterlow and Sons (qq.v.). He also illustrated Itchen Valley,1881; Avon from Naxby to Tewkesbury,1882; Epping Forest,1884; Sintram and His Companions,1883; Besom Maker,1888; and Jacob and the Raven,1896.
[Bénézit; Studio Winter No.1900-01; Sketchley; Country Life, 28 September 1978]

SWAIN, Joseph 1820-1909
Major London wood engraver, whose career proved, with that of the Dalziel Brothers (q.v.), to be one of the most influential for the 'Sixties School' of reproductive Victorian wood engraving. He was born in Oxford on 29 February 1820, the son of a printer, Ebenezer Swain, grandson of one-time apprentice engraver and hymn writer Joseph Swain (1761-96), his namesake. He was educated at private schools in Oxford, then moved with his father to London in 1829. There his father worked as printer to Wertheimer and Company, and apprenticed young Joseph to the wood engraver Nathaniel Whittock (q.v.) in 1834, 'to learn the art and craft of wood-cutting. But though Mr Whittock was something of an artist, he was less an engraver; and finding after a few years that he was making little progress, young Swain applied for instruction to Thomas Williams [q.v.] . That distinguished engraver was one of the few excellent "facsimile men" of the day; and he agreed to accept the applicant as "improver" ' (Spielmann, History of Punch,1895,p.248). Swain probably helped his master with preparing illustrations to the French edition of Paul et Virginie, 1838, published in Paris, with engravings after Meissonier, Johannot, and Horace Vernet. Swain set up in business as John (sic) Swain, a wood engraver at 18 Elder Street, Norton Folgate (POD,1842-45), then joined with Thomas Armstrong (q.v.) as Swain and Armstrong, 58 Fleet Street (POD,1855). He took over the premises 6 Bouverie Street, Fleet Street, EC (POD,1858-1900) which he retained for the next forty years, sharing the business with his son, Joseph Blomeley Swain (q.v.) from the 1880s. He worked for William Dickes (q.v.) during the first year of his business, when the Punch proprietors, dissatisfied with Ebenezer Landells' engravings, turned first to Thomas Orlando Jewitt (q.v.) as a replacement engraver. But Jewitt found the test block, a drawing by John Leech, too much of a strain and turned it over to his young acquaintance Swain, who had probably been engraving for Jewitt at the time (c1843). 'So pleased was Leech with the result that he strongly recommended that the man who had cut such a block should, in place of the middleman, be installed as manager of the engraving department', according to Spielmann. Swain was soon made the head of the engraving department of Punch. He took on six to eight assistants tor Punch engraving alone, and bid for exclusive engraving rights to the paper. This meant that he could expand his business, and give cheaper rates (he kept Punch engraving expenses down to under £30 a week) while he had more time for extra book and periodical commissions. Swain engraved for Punch until 1900; his most notable work was after John Tenniel (q.v.), who insisted that his cartoons were still to be wood engraved by Swain long after Punch had turned to process engraving. The business of engraving under pressure for a 'weekly' was a considerable strain for a less dedicated engraver, as Spielmann explained: 'The

cartoon, for reasons of economy of time, has always, up to 1893, been drawn upon the wood -- not upon paper, as has been possible to the rest of the Staff for a good many years past--and is delivered into Mr Swain's hands by Friday night. Twenty-four hours later the engraving of the block is completed, and it is handed over to the printers, who are already clamouring for it...'. Swain recalled: 'To myself, it has always been a pleasing reflection that during the whole time of my connection with Punch, extending over fifty years, I have never once failed to get my work done in time and without accident. Of course, now and again it has been a very near thing, but it has always been done somehow'. The pressure was tempered by Mark Lemon, Punch's editor, who 'would come down two or three times a week to edit and make up the paper, and would talk leisurely with Mr Swain of such matters as concerned the engraver. No block was hurried. If it could not be ready for one week, it was held over the next--a saving grace which the engraver has now and again acknowledged by drawing an initial or other simple design on the wood half an hour before going to press, when the Editor hurriedly required such a decoration--possibly to supply an artist's omission'. Swain became one of the most prolific wood engravers of the Victorian period. He was responsible for nearly all the engravings in the Cornhill; engraved for Once a Week (for which he employed the young draughtsman Frederick Walker (q.v.) for the first time); Good Words; Argosy; for the Illustrated London News; and for the numerous publications of the Religious Tract Society and Baptist Missionary Society. He engraved the paintings and drawings of Frederick Walker, J.E.Millais, Frederick Sandys, Richard Doyle, R.Ansdell, Frederick Barnard, 'and practically all famous illustrators from 1860 onwards' (DNB). Most of this work was signed 'Swain sc' which indicated the work of his assistants as well as the master. By the 1850s the firm had become large enough to employ a manager, and Swain obtained the wood engraver W.H.Hooper (q.v.). By the 1880s his son, Joseph Blomeley Swain (q.v.), who had trained as wood engraver, had joined his father as Joseph Swain and Son Limited. Swain occasionally contributed sketches 'at times of sudden need' for Punch fillers in the 1850s, but generally he was a wood engraver. It was Swain's practice, like that of most important engravers of the day, to search out new draughtsman talent and to commission drawings on wood, which his assistants would engrave for publishers to purchase. He was responsible for introducing various prominent figures into print: he started T.Harrington Wilson on Punch and he was the only engraver willing to help the struggling art student Helen Paterson (q.v.) who worked on Cornhill and Once a Week for Swain, though he was not always successful with his artists. Young Randolph Caldecott, while a struggling bank clerk in Manchester in 1871, wrote to Thomas

Armstrong of the trials to get Swain to accept his work: 'I sent one block to Swain, who returned it as too sketchy and asked me to try again. I did so; and he then sent me blocks for the other scenes. After these had been in his hands a few days I received a note from him to say that they were accepted, and if I liked to send any more drawings to him he would shew them for approval. So I look forward to seeing myself in 'Punch' shortly' (M.Hutchins, Yours Pictorially,1976,p.16). On the other hand, John Leech (q.v.) often complained of Swain's interpretations in Punch: 'But wait till next week and see how the engraver will spoil it!', which was an unfair criticism due to rapid printing rather than poor engraving. Charles Keene's (q.v.) work also suffered from interpretative engraving, largely owing to Swain's attempts to master the subtleties of Keene's grey washes in hard black engraved line. Swain's talent lay in his ability to strengthen a drawing for publication, which Thackeray recognised. He pleaded with Swain: 'Why don't you engrave my drawings to come out like John Gilbert's--his work always looks.to strong and mine so weak and scratchy?' (quoted in Dalziels' Record,p.44). Another illustrator for Punch, George Du Maurier (q.v.), wrote in disgust to Swain, 'I am very sorry the animal you mentioned should have turned into a dog when it got to Bouverie Street--I can assure you it was a Persian Cat when it left New Grove House and you must try and engrave it back again'. (Undated letter in Hartley Collection, Boston Museum). Swain was one of the few wood engravers, apart from the Dalziels and W.J.Linton (q.v.), to have work accepted for exhibition at the Royal Academy. There, from 1863-69, he hung ten engravings: 'Coming Home', after F.Leighton,1863; 'Endymion', after J.E.Millais,1863; 'Thanksgiving', after F.Walker, 1863; 'Harold Harfager', after T. (sic) Sandys,1863; 'Hogarth in his Studio', after F.Walker,1867; 'Animals', after a drawing by Basil Bradley,1867; 'Danaë', after F.Sandys,1867; 'Afternoon in the Highlands', after B.Bradley,1869; 'Scene from an Old Legend of Romeo and Juliet', after G. Du Maurier,1869; and 'Elijah and the Widow's Son', after B.Bradley,1869. He also wrote articles on the illustrators whom he admired: F.Walker, C.H.Bennett, G.J.Pinwell, and F.Eltze (qq.v.) which appeared in Good Words,1888-89, reprinted in H.C.Ewart, Toilers in Art,1891. Towards the end of his life Swain realised the threat of photo-engraving to the wood engraver's profession. In fact he learned to appreciate its merits, and took over the photo-engraving firm Leitch and Company, which was the first photo-engraving firm in England. The new process involved a photograph of the design pasted face down on the wood block, the wet paper being rubbed away to leave only the image on the wood, ready for engraving. It was this process which was 'afterwards adopted by the late John

Swain' (according to Hentschel in Journal of Society of Arts, 1900). Swain retired in 1890, however, and died in Ealing on 25 February 1909. The British Museum owns a large collection of his engravings after R.Ansdell, R.Doyle, F.Eltze, H.Furniss, H.B.Houghton, J.Lawson, J.Leech, Lord Leighton, Thackeray, J.E.Millais, J.N.Paton, F.Walker, A.F.Sandys, J.Tenniel, and G.Cruikshank. The largest collection of Swain's letters and engravings (from the estate sale) is in the Hartley Collection, Boston Museum. He signed his engravings: 'SWAIN', 'SWAIN SC' (although many were done by assistants). [For biographical and technical facts see Spielmann; Print Collector's Quarterly, 1924, pp.172f; DNB; TB (with bibliography); Bénézit; Muir; White: British Library catalogue; Hake; Dalziels' Record; Chatto: McLean, Victorian Book Design; Wakeman; F.G.Kitton in British Printer, 1894, pp.217-31; and Wakeman and Bridson]

SWAIN, Joseph Blomeley 1844-?
Wood engraver, process engraver and draughtsman on wood. He was born in 1844, the son of the famous engraver Joseph Swain (q.v.) with whom he probably trained. He first appeared in the London directories as a draughtsman wood engraver as John (sic) Swain, 266 Strand (POD, 1860-85), an office which he shared with fellow engravers F.Wentworth and J.Hustler (qq.v.). There he engraved for magazines and later helped to photograph designs on wood blocks as well. In 1886 he added a second office at 58 Farringdon Street, EC (POD, 1886-1900) and added departments for lithographic, copper-plate and chromo printing. It was not until 1894 that he appears with his father in the directories as Joseph Swain and Son, when two offices were listed, one at Farringdon Street (for engraving) and one High Barnet (for half-tone and colour printing) (POD, 1894-1900). When his father retired in 1890, however, Joseph Blomeley took over the firm, then specialising in process blocks and colour printing. Here he process engraved weekly Punch cartoons; colour printed the Illustrated London News, Christmas number, 1895; and printed and published Swain's Quarterly, from 1907. As a wood engraver he engraved C.M.Gere's (q.v.) illustrations to the Ashenden Press edition of Morte d'Arthur, the proofs of which are in the British Museum.
[Spielmann; British Library catalogue; Wakeman; for colour work see Wakeman and Bridson]

SWAIN and Armstrong
(see Swain, Joseph; also Armstrong, Thomas)

SWAINE, John Barak c1815-38
Occasional wood engraver, talented facsimile etcher and engraver on metal. He was born about 1815, the only son of the draughtsman engraver John Swaine (1775-1860). He studied at the Royal Academy Schools, having done some antiquarian drawings while a child.

He drew for Archaeologia, 1832, 1834. He was awarded the Isis Gold Medal of the Society of Arts, 1833, for an etching; and the following year he visited The Hague and Paris. While in Paris he painted 'and also tried his hand successfully at wood engraving' (DNB). 'Swaine was a versatile artist of great promise' (DNB), but his career was cut short when he died at Queen Street, Golden Square, London on 28 March 1838, aged twenty-three.

SWAINSON, William 1789-1855
Draughtsman on wood of zoological subjects. He travelled throughout Europe, lived in Brazil, 1816-18, returned to England in 1819, then emigrated to New Zealand, 1837, where he died in 1855. He wrote and illustrated many of his works. He is listed here for forty-one drawings wood engraved in Fauna Boreali-Americana; also 300 engravings in two volumes of On the Natural History and Classification of Birds, 1836-37. He also illustrated Ornithological Drawings, Birds of Brazil, 1834-35; and Sir L.Richardson's Birds of Western Africa, 1837.
[Houfe; C.Jackson]

SWEETING, R.G.Frederick fl.1880s
London wood engraver, who worked at 10 Bolt Court, EC (POD, 1880). He may be related to R.G.Sweeting, painter of genre and landscapes, who exhibited in London, 1845-65.
[Bénézit]

SYKES, Godfrey 1824-66
Occasional draughtsman, prominent decorative designer, landscape and interior painter. He was born in Malton in 1824 and studied at the Government School of Art, Sheffield while serving an apprenticeship to an engraver. On coming to London he was befriended by Alfred Stevens, and worked on various decorative interior commissions. He also drew copies of paintings by Correggio, Raphael and Titian. He is listed here for his cover design for the Cornhill, 1860, commissioned by Thackeray (probably wood engraved, after his pen and ink design, by Swain (q.v.), the magazine's chief engraver). His work was much admired by the wood engraver W.J.Linton (q.v.) who recalled how Sykes 'was starved on a low salary' and consequently died of consumption in London on 28 February 1866. The British Museum owns a proof engraving after his design, engraved by the Dalziel Brothers (q.v.), 1863.
[Redgrave; TB; Bénézit; DNB; Linton, Memories, p.182]

SYMMONS, Thomas fl.1872-96
London wood engraver, who worked at 10 Tooks Court, Chancery Lane, EC (POD, 1872). He disappears from the directories until 1885, when he worked at St Bride Street, Ludgate Crescent, EC (POD, 1885-88). He worked with the prominent wood

engraver W.J.Palmer (q.v.) at 143 Strand (POD,1889-91) and accompanied Palmer to new premises at 59 and 60 Chancery Lane, WC (POD,1892-95). The following year Symmons joined with a partner as Symmons and Thiele, 65-66 Chancery Lane, WC (POD,1896).

SYMONS, William Christian 1845-1911
Occasional illustrator, portrait, genre, landscape and still-life painter. He was born in London in 1845, studied at the Lambeth School of Art and the Royal Academy Schools. He drew for wood engravings in The Graphic,1885; Strand Magazine,1891; Good Words,1898; and Wide World Magazine,1898. He also designed stained glass and was elected RBA but resigned with Whistler in 1888. He exhibited at the New English Art Club, the Royal Academy, the Royal Society of British Artists, the Royal Hibernian Academy, the Royal Institute of Painters in Water-colours and the Royal Institute of Painters in Oil-Colours. He died in London in 1911.

TABART, George
Wood engraver of the Bewick School. The British Museum has a collection of his small cuts of eight-eenth century rural life, cuts to Aesop's Fables, and various ornamental pieces with cherubs. They also attribute a scene in the Italian lakes after Birket Foster (q.v.) to Tabart, although it is signed 'E.Evans'; also an engraved horse signed 'J.Jackson'.

TARLTON, J. fl.1872-75
Wood engraver and draughtsman on wood. He worked in London and contributed drawings to the Illustrated London News,1874-75. These included 'Christmas on the Ice Floe,1869', 26 December 1874, a full page engraving by 'LR'; a series of underwater sketches of Captain Boyton's voyage, 13 March 1875; and a full-page cover illustration, 'Giant Tortoises', 3 July 1875.

TARRANT, Percy fl.1881-1930
Occasional illustrator for wood engravings, land-scape, coastal and figure painter. He worked in South London, Leatherhead and Gomshall, Surrey. He drew for wood engravings in the Illustrated London News,1884-89; also for process blocks for the Quiver, 1890; Black and White,1891; Cassell's Family Magazine; Girl's Own Paper; and The Graphic,1911. He also illustrated Chambers' Tom's Boy,1901.

TAVERNER, J.
Draughtsman illustrator, who contributed railway scenes wood engraved in The Graphic,1870.

TAYLER, John Frederick 1801-89
Landscape and figure draughtsman, painter, litho-grapher and etcher. He was born in Boreham Wood,

Hertfordshire in 1802, educated at Eton and Harrow and then studied art at the Royal Academy Schools and in Paris under Horace Vernet. There he shared rooms with R.P.Bonington and worked with Samuel Prout. He worked in Rome before moving to London where he established a reputation for watercolour hunting scenes, some of which he etched and litho-graphed. He is listed here for his drawings (now in the British Museum) wood engraved by John Thompson, Charles T.Thompson, Joseph L.Williams, Thomas Williams, and Samuel Williams (qq.v.). He etched as a member of the Etching Club for their Goldsmith's The Deserted Village,1841; and also illustrated The Traveller,1851, for the Art Union. He was elected AOWS in 1831, OWS in 1834, and served as its president, 1858-71. He also exhibited at the Royal Academy and the Royal Cambrian Academy.
[For a discussion of his etchings and lithographs see Volume I (with bibliography)]

TAYLER, Miss Maria fl.1854-56
London wood engraver, who worked in Denmark Hill, Camberwell (POD,1854-56).

TAYLER, William Lewis fl.1870s
Provincial wood engraver, who worked at 2 Baldwin Street, Bristol (Kelly's,1872).

TAYLOR, Arthur fl.1864-74
London wood engraver, who worked at 13 Red Lion Court, Fleet Street, EC (POD,1864-66), then 172 Fleet Street, EC (POD,1867-72), then 48 Essex Street, Strand, WC (POD,1873-74). The British Museum owns a proof engraved by the Dalziel Brothers (q.v.) after 'A.W.Taylor',1855.

TAYLOR, Miss E. fl.1860s
Amateur draughtsman illustrator on wood. She was commissioned by Trollope to illustrate the last parts of Can You Forgive Her, published serially from January 1864. Trollope had apparently upset the original illustrator, Hablot K.Browne (q.v.) and convinced his publisher Chapman and Hall to accept Miss Taylor's twenty drawings. 'I am having the last ten numbers of Can You Forgive Her illustrated by a lady. She has as yet done two drawings on wood. They are both excellent, and the cutter [Dalziel] says that they will come out very well. She has £5.5s--a drawing for them...She is a Miss Taylor of St Leonards', Trollope wrote to Chapman (quoted in N.John Hall, Trollope and His Illustrators,1980, p.98). She may have been a personal friend of the novelist, who gave her unusually free reign in the drawings. 'Whatever Miss Taylor's limitations, she attempted to illustrate in the Millais fashion...Her work is stiff, excessively pretty, too serious, but it is not satiric in Browne's fashion. She is a Sixties-style illustrator' (Hall). One suspects that the

Dalziel Brothers (q.v.) did much to improve the
original drawings when they engraved them on wood.
By the third edition of the book,1866, Miss Taylor
was not credited on the title-page with her illustrations.
The British Museum owns several proof engraved
designs by the Dalziel Brothers (q.v.), 1864-65.

TAYLOR, Edward
(see Taylor, Richard)

TAYLOR, F.Bertram fl.1889-1900
Provincial wood engraver, who worked first as
Taylor and Dufton, 82 Albion Street, Leeds
(Kelly's,1889), then on his own at 97 Albion Street,
Leeds (Kelly's,1900).

TAYLOR, John,Junior
The British Museum owns a large number of proof
engravings after his designs, engraved by the Dalziel
Brothers (q.v.), 1865.

TAYLOR, Richard (and Edward) fl.1872-1901
London firm of draughtsmen and wood engravers.
They established a firm as R. and E.Taylor at
17 New Bridge Street, EC (POD,1872-99), then as
R.Taylor and Company, 32 and 34 Old Street
(Kelly's,1900). Richard and Edward Taylor began by
engraving numerous portraits for the Illustrated
London News,from 1872-92, some engraved with
P.Naumann (q.v.). These were engraved after
paintings, photographs or sculptures. They also
engraved George Seymour's illustrations for the
English Illustrated Magazine,1884-87, as well as
after a Velasquez portrait of Philip IV, 1887; a pastel
portrait of David Garrick,1889; and a drawing of
Andrea del Sarto,1890. A collection of engraved
portraits by the Taylors is in the British Museum
(see Hake). They signed their engravings:
'R & E Taylor', 'R.T.', 'R.Taylor & Co.', and
R.Taylor & Son'.

TAYLOR and Dufton
(see Taylor, Richard)

TEGGIN, William fl.1880s
Provincial wood engraver, who worked at 32 Booth
Street, Manchester (Kelly's,1889).

TELFER, John Robert fl.1840s
London wood engraver, who worked at 46 High
Holborn (POD,1847).

TEMPLE, William W. fl.1798-1830
Wood engraver, apprenticed to Thomas Bewick (q.v.)
in Newcastle, from ?August 1812-14 August 1819. He
shared the workshop with William Harvey (q.v.) and
together the two worked on Bewick's Aesop's Fables,
1818 (in production since 1811). Bewick recalled in
his Memoir (pp.131-32) 'In impatiently pushing

forward to get to press with the publication, I
availed myself of the help of my pupils, (my son,
Wm Harvey & Wm Temple) who were also eager to
do their utmost to forward me in the engraving
business & in my struggles to get the Book ushered
into the world...'. He also engraved for Bewick's
British Birds (Redgrave lists four plates: rough-legged
falcon, pigmy sandpiper, red sand-piper, and eared
grebe). Bewick described Temple as 'a faithful
copyest, & his pieces were honestly or clearly
cut...'. Unfortunately after his apprenticeship he
abandoned wood engraving to become a draper and
silk-mercer, in Newcastle.
[Bryan; Bénézit; TB; Redgrave]

TENNANT, Dorothy (Lady Stanley) ?-1926
Occasional illustrator, genre painter and writer.
She studied at the Slade and with Henner in Paris,
and began illustrations of domestic and child
subjects. She drew the series, 'The London
Ragamuffin', portraits of various children in
silhouette, which were wood engraved by E.Schladitz,
E.Gascoine, R.Paterson, O.Jahyer, and J.Cocking
(qq.v.). These appeared in the English Illustrated
Magazine,1885. She also illustrated the book, London
Street Arabs,1890. She exhibited at the New Gallery,
the Royal Academy, the Royal Hibernian Academy
and the Royal Institute of Painters in Oil-Colours.
She was elected RE in 1881, and married the African
explorer Sir H.M.Stanley in 1890. She died on
5 October 1926.
[TB; Who's Who,1924; Houfe]

TENNIEL, Sir John 1820-1914
Prolific draughtsman illustrator on wood, known for
his Punch drawings and 'Alice' illustrations. He was
born in London on 27 February 1820, and was largely
self-taught, although he briefly attended the Royal
Academy Schools and Clipstone Academy. He
preferred private study at the British Museum, where
he learned to draw costume and animals which he
incorporated into his early book illustration success,
Aesop's Fables,1848. This earned him the praise of
the Punch editor Mark Lemon, who invited him to
take over the second cartoonist position, vacated in
1850 by Richard Doyle (q.v.). By 1864 on the death
of John Leech (q.v.) he had become chief cartoonist,
and remained on the Punch staff until 1901, drawing
over 2,000 fine pencil cartoons largely engraved on
wood by Joseph Swain. His skill at drawing on wood
had been developed before Punch sent him to Swain
for instruction. 'The accomplished young draughtsman soon took keen delight in the smooth face of a
block, and at once began--and ever continued-- to
demand a degree of smoothness that was the despair
of Swain to engrave' (Spielmann). Indeed Tenniel's
methods for drawing on wood resulted in the highly
polished drawings of a perfectionist. He always
used a specially manufactured 6H pencil with which

he achieved a silvery, fine-edged line, 'so delicate
was the drawing that, firm and solid as were the
lines, it looked as if you could blow if off the wood'.
Swain then had to interpret and inevitably thicken
these fine lines, much to the chagrin of Tenniel, who
could not muster up enough courage to be the first in
his household to examine the final published drawing
each week. He described his working method in
preparing his weekly cartoon in an interview in
April 1889 (quoted in Spielmann): 'I never use models
or Nature for the figure, drapery, or anything else.
But I have a wonderful memory of observation--not for
dates, but anything else I see I remember. Well, I
get my subject on Wednesday night; I think it out
carefully on Thursday, and make a rough sketch; on
Friday morning I begin, and stick to it all day, with
my nose well down on the block. By means of tracing-
paper--on which I make all alterations of composition
and action I may consider necessary--I transfer my
design to the wood, and draw on that. The first
sketch I may, and often do, complete later on as a
commission...Well, the block being finished, it is
handed over to Swain's boy at about 6.30 or 7 o'clock,
who has been waiting for it for an hour or so, and at
7.30 it is put in hand for engraving. That is completed
on the following night, and on Monday night I receive
by post the copy of next Wednesday's paper. Although
case-hardened in a sense, I have never the courage to
open the packet...My work would be difficult to
photograph on to the wood, as it is all done in pencil;
the only pen-and-ink work I have done, so far, being
for the Almanac and Pocket-book'. The process was
grudgingly altered by 1892, when the age of
photo-engraving had circumvented the more time-
consuming and expensive wood engraving, and Tenniel
submitted to drawing cartoons on a Chinese-whitened
cardboard surface, which allowed them to be photographed onto the block. Occasionally photography was
also used for portraiture; 'As I never have a model,
I never draw from life, always when I want a portrait,
a uniform, and so on, from a photograph, though not
in quite the same spirit as [Linley] Sambourne does,
I get a photograph only of the man whom I want to
draw, and seek to get his character. Then, if the
photograph is in profile, I have to 'judge' the full
face, and vice versa; but if I only succeed in getting
the character, I seldom go far wrong--a due
appreciation is an almost infallible guide'. Tenniel
managed to draw on wood for a variety of book and
periodical illustrations while serving on the Punch
staff. The most notable, and prolonged, of these
commissions came from Lewis Carroll (Charles
Lutwidge Dodgson (q.v.)) for his 'Alice' books:
Alice's Adventures in Wonderland, 1865, and Through
the Looking Glass, 1872, which Tenniel refused to let
dominate his more important Punch work. His
drawings were wood engraved not only by Swain but
also in the early 1850s and 60s by the Dalziel Brothers
(q.v.); notably his superbly inventive moorish designs

to Lalla Rookh, 1861 ('fine examples of his varied
powers of design and delicate manipulation',
according to the Dalziels' Record); and Ingoldsby
Legends, 1864. The Dalziels were proud of their
association with so esteemed an illustrator, noting
in their Record: 'Outside his Punch work we believe
nearly all Tenniel's work for wood engraving was
executed by us'. Despite this, Tenniel was never
satisfied with his engraver-interpreters: 'I'm not a
first-rate artist, I know; but I'm not half as bad as
those fellows, the woodcutters make me...'. Tenniel
was also an aspiring painter, first in oil and frescoe,
later watercolour. He exhibited at the Royal Academy
from 1837-42, then sporadically until 1880; also at
the Royal Society of British Artists and the New
Watercolour Society, where he was elected
associate member and full member in 1874. He was
knighted for his contributions to Punch, in 1893, and
retired from the staff in 1901. He always lived in
London, gradually going totally blind (he was blinded
in his right eye in 1840), and died on 25 February
1914, aged ninety-three. He left over thirty-eight
illustrated books, sixty-nine cuts to Once a Week,
1859-67; four to Good Words, 1862-64; and two in the
Illustrated London News, 1857, 1868. The British
Museum owns several proof engravings by the
Dalziel Brothers. The Boston Museum owns
drawings and Punch proofs.
[For a complete list of illustrations see R.Engen,
John Tenniel, 1985; F.Sarzano, Sir John Tenniel, 1948;
see also Spielmann; Dalziels' Record; Chatto; R.Engen
in Country Life, 28 October 1982]

TERRAS, Robert fl.1889-1900
Scottish wood engraver, who worked at 84 Oswald
Street, Glasgow (Kelly's, 1889), then moved to
57 W.Nile Street, Glasgow (Kelly's, 1900).

TERRY, George W. fl.1854-58
Ornamental draughtsman on wood. He drew for wood
engravings in the Illustrated London News, 1854 and
contributed 'a dozen initials of no particular
importance' (Spielmann) to Punch, 1856-58.

THACKERAY, William Makepeace 1811-63
Occasional draughtsman illustrator on wood,
caricaturist and novelist. He was born in Calcutta
in 1811 and turned to drawing after his family's
fortune was lost, developing a style of pen and light
wash drawing borrowed from eighteenth century
models, especially Hogarth. He began with lithographs published in Flore et Zephyr, 1836, during
the time he was studying art in Paris. His more
substantial illustrations appeared in The Book of
Snobs and Paris Sketchbook, 1840; Comic Tales and
Sketches, 1841; Irish Sketchbook, 1843; Christmas
Books, 1846-50; Vanity Fair, 1847-48; and History of
Pendennis, 1849-50. His drawings are important if
only because he was the only major writer to illustrate

his own works during the mid Victorian period.
Thackeray's drawings gave him a keen understanding
of the caricaturist's role, and he became a critic and
lecturer on the subject, both in England and abroad.
He is listed here for his attempts to draw on wood
for the engraver. He contributed to Figaro in London,
1836; more importantly, drawings and humorous
articles to Punch, 1842-54, and as editor and
contributor to the Cornhill, 1860-61. It seems he
was not proficient enough to satisfy his engravers.
Henry Vizetelly (q.v.) recalls that the work which he
engraved on the Christmas Books, came from wood
blocks 'wrapped up in notes from his feminine
correspondents, who at times allowed their
admiration to wander somewhat indiscreetly beyond
the range of his books' (Glances Back, I, p.290).
His draughtsman's association with Punch (he wrote
for Punch from 1842) was through the engraver Joseph
Swain (q.v.): 'As Mr Swain lived for some time close
to Thackeray's house, it was an occasional custom of
his to call on his way to the office to see if the great
'Thack' had any blocks ready that he might carry
away with him. The novelist was usually at breakfast
when he called, and would request that his visitor
might be shown into the library. There he would
presently join him and, if he were behindhand with
his work, would request Mr Swain to have a seat, a
cigar, and a chat, while he produced a Punch drawing
"while you wait". "Ah, Swain!" he said one day,
looking up from his block, when he was more than
usually confidential, "if it had not been for Punch, I
wonder where I should be!"'. He contributed 380
Punch drawings, primarily on demand, without
preliminary studies, drawing on the block what
Spielmann described as: 'Burlesques of history and
parodies of literature, ballads and songs, stories and
jokes, papers and paragraphs, pleasantry and pathos,
criticism and conundrums, travels in the East and
raillery in the West, political skits and social
satire--from a column to a single line--'. But as a
draughtsman he was severely criticised for 'wooden'
drawings and after 1836 (the year in which Dickens
rejected his application to illustrate Pickwick Papers)
he seems to have softened his attitude about his
serious limitations as a draughtsman on wood.
Trollope declared that Thackeray 'never learned to
draw--perhaps never could have learned'. Yet as
Spielmann pointed out, 'He moved his pencil slowly,
with a deliberate broad touch, without haste, and
with no more attempt at refinement than was natural
to him. Yet his hand was capable of astonishing
delicacy of touch...'. By the 1860s Thackeray found
drawing on wood an increasing strain. His attempts
to illustrate his novel Adventures of Phillip for the
Cornhill, 1861, ended in failure, and eventually he
turned over the job of re-drawing his sketches on
paper onto wood blocks to the young Fred Walker
(q.v.). Walker soon insisted that he hated this soul-
destroying copying and convinced Thackeray to allow

his own drawings to be published; the first appeared
in May 1861.
[For a discussion of Thackeray's drawings see
G.Everitt, English Caricaturists, 1893; see also
Connoisseur, March 1904; White; Spielmann;
Redgrave; Nagler; Houfe]

THIELE
(see Symmonds, Thomas)

THIRIAT, Henri fl.1874-82
French wood engraver, who worked in Paris. He
was the pupil of Burn Smeeton (q.v.) and exhibited
at the Salon from 1874-82. He is listed here for his
numerous wood engravings to various magazines,
including portrait engravings of the English figures
Darwin and Sir John Gilbert for L'Illustration.
[Gusman; TB; Bénézit; Beraldi]

THOMAS, Geoffrey and Company fl.1894-96
London wood engraving firm, with an office at
9 Tottenham Street, W (POD, 1894-95). The following
year Thomas and Company appear at 11 Queen Street,
EC (POD, 1896).

THOMAS, George Housman 1824-68
Wood engraver and draughtsman illustrator, 'one of
our best draughtsmen of figure subjects' (Bohn in
Chatto and Jackson). He was born in London on
17 December 1824, the brother of the engraver
W.L.Thomas (q.v.). He served as apprentice to
George Bonner (q.v.) from the age of fourteen, in
London, then set up in Paris as engraver, and later
as draughtsman on wood. He had in fact been awarded
a silver palette prize by the Society of Arts for a
drawing, 'Please to remember the Grotto',
submitted when he was fifteen. In Paris he worked
in conjunction with Henry Harrison (q.v.). Their
firm was so successful that they employed six or
seven assistants. He went to New York in 1846 to
illustrate a paper set up by his brother, and
remained there for two years. After the paper
folded he turned to designing and engraving American
bank-notes for the Government 'estimated among the
most beautiful of their kind' (White). He returned to
Europe for health reasons and travelled to Italy for
two years. There he drew a series of illustrations of
Garibaldi's defence of Rome which established his
reputation as draughtsman reporter when they appeared
in the Illustrated London News, from 1848 and he
continued drawing for wood engravings for this
magazine, many of his drawings being engraved by
his brother, from 1848-67. Perhaps his most
ambitious drawing was a three foot long fold-out
supplement, 'Sketches in London in 1851', 23 August
1851, wood engraved by J.Williamson (q.v.). His
sketches of sailors of the Baltic Fleet, engraved for
the Illustrated London News in 1854, caught the
attention of the Queen, who commissioned paintings

from him of major events in her reign. But it was his skill at drawing from life which earned him many of the drawing commissions that followed. The Dalziels claimed that he 'was one of the first, if not indeed the very first, to draw on wood direct from life', and recalled how his early Crimean War sketches caused an immediate sensation. Thomas' illustrations on wood included 'a remarkable set of woodcuts' (DNB) to Uncle Tom's Cabin,1852; Longfellow's Hiawatha,1855-56, engraved by W.L.Thomas (q.v.), but later re-engraved by Horace Harral (q.v.) for Longfellow's Poems; Burns' Poems, engraved by E.Evans (q.v.); Vicar of Wakefield,1857; Pilgrim's Progress,1857; Robinson Crusoe,1865; Wilkie Collins' Armadale,1866; and thirty-two plates and thirty-two vignettes to Trollope's Last Chronicle of Barset,1867, engraved by W.L.Thomas. These latter earned a mixed reception from Trollope, who was disappointed in not securing Millais; they 'helped to kill Trollope's interest in his illustrators' (see N.John Hall, Trollope and His Illustrators,1980,pp.114-24). Thomas also contributed to numerous compilation volumes following a brief appearance in Punch,1851-52; Merrie Days of England,1858-59; Mackay's Home Affections,1858; Thomson's Seasons, 1859; Favourite Modern Ballads,1860, engraved by Edmund Evans (q.v.); Household Songs,1861; Early English Poems,1862; London Society,1863; Churchman's Family Magazine,1863; the Cornhill, 1864-65; Legends and Lyrics,1865; Aunt Sally's Life, 1866-67; Foxe's Book of Martyrs,1866; Cassell's Magazine,1867; Quiver,1867; Broadway,1867; and Idyllic Pictures,1867. Thomas' paintings in oils were 'bright and animated and gained him considerable popularity, but had none of the higher qualities of art' (DNB). They were exhibited at the British Institution and the Royal Academy from 1854. He lived in Kingston and Surbiton, then moved to Boulogne for his health after falling from a horse. He died there on 21 July 1868. The British Museum owns a proof engraving by the Dalziel Brothers (q.v.),1857.
[For a selection of about 100 engravings see In Memoriam, G.H.Thomas,1869; see also discussions of his illustrations in Reid; White; Redgrave; DNB; TB; Print Collector's Quarterly,23,1936,p.181]

THOMAS, John 1813-62
Draughtsman of medieval-style designs for Charles Whittingham (q.v.) and the Chiswick Press. These were initial letters and emblems, some done in collaboration with Charlotte Whittingham (q.v.) and wood engraved by Mary Byfield (q.v.). Bryan called Thomas 'a very clever architectural draughtsman'.
[see McLean, Victorian Book Design; Nagler; Bryan; A.Warren, C.Whittingham,1896]

THOMAS, W.Carmichael ('Car') 1856-?
Wood engraver, later administrator of The Graphic. He was the son of The Graphic's founder, W.L.Thomas (q.v.), and son-in-law of the painter of marine subjects J.W.Carmichael. He worked first as an engraver on The Graphic, presumably trained by his father. On his father's death he worked as the paper's managing director,1900-17.

THOMAS, William Luson 1830-1900
Prominent wood engraver, who 'deserves to rank among the foremost of our wood engravers' (Bohn in Chatto and Jackson); also a metal engraver, watercolourist and newspaper proprietor. He was born on 4 December 1830, the brother and collaborator of George H.Thomas (q.v.). The two brothers worked together first in Paris, then went to New York in 1846 where William established the short-lived papers The Republic and The Picture Gallery, employing George to draw on wood for them. They returned to Europe and lived in Paris and Rome before William set up on his own as a wood engraver working from 17 Essex Street, Strand (POD,1852-55). This was also the office of the prolific wood engraver Horace Harral (q.v.). By 1856 he had moved (with Harral) to 11 Serjeant's Inn, Fleet Street, EC (POD,1856-60), then 4 Palgrave Place, Strand (POD,1860-71), again shared with Harral. During this period he worked with W.J.Linton (q.v.) engraving cuts for the Illustrated London News, generally after his brother George's drawings on wood--notably two full-page drawings 'Troops for the War', 4 March 1854, followed by the double-page 'Man of Wars', 18 March 1854. These were engraved in a dark, heavy-handed style, the figures set against a pale ruled or completely white sky. He specialised in war subjects or large crowd scenes involving royalty, but could display virtuoso technical ability when engraving such apparently difficult effects as 'The Fireworks at Versailles', a double-page, 1 September 1855. He was also competent enough to reproduce paintings from some of the more successful exhibitions--'The Scotch Gamekeeper', after Richard Ansdell, full-page,9 June 1855; a Masaccio from the National Gallery; or numerous British Institution exhibition works. Such work gave Thomas the idea for his own illustrated periodical and he founded the influential Graphic in December 1869; the paper flourished throughout the 1870s, attracting a socially-conscious breed of artist-illustrator and the very best wood engravers to interpret their drawings. He turned the tables on the established publishing procedures involving wood engravings by commissioning drawings directly from the illustrators, rather than securing them from the engravers, who in turn found the draughtsmen illustrators. The immediacy and realism of The Graphic's illustrations on subjects relating to the Franco-German War ensured its early success. According to Thomas it was founded

as 'a weekly illustrated journal open to all artists whatever their method', and he refused to limit his artists to drawings on wood alone. His 'brilliant staff' included Pinwell, Fred Walker, Hubert Herkomer, R.W.Macbeth, E.J.Gregory, his first woman Helen Paterson, and the young novice Luke Fildes (qq.v.). Fresh from art school young Fildes was employed by Thomas first to re-draw other artists' work on wood to make it suitable for engraving. He commissioned Fildes to make two drawings for Foxe's Book of Martyrs,1866, then gave him an unrestricted commission to draw his own subject on wood for his then secret new venture, The Graphic. The result was Fildes' famous 'Houseless and Hungry'. Thomas also engraved for numerous books during the 1850s and 1860s. Bohn lists the drawings to Hiawatha by his brother George published in Bohn's Illustrated Longfellow's Work; drawings after Maclise (q.v.) for Tennyson's Princess; and all the John Gilbert subjects in Boy's Book of Ballads. Others done in collaboration with George or engraved separately appeared in Book of Favourite Modern Ballads; Poetry and Pictures from Thomas Moore; Burns' Poems; The Merrie Days of England; and Favourite English Poems. He also engraved for magazines of the period, namely J.Mahoney's 'Springtime' for London Society,1870; also F.Sandys' 'The Waiting Time', for Churchman's Family Magazine,1864. In 1890 he established the Daily Graphic, London's first illustrated daily paper. Thomas was also an accomplished landscape water-colourist who was elected ANWS in 1864, and NWS (or RI) in 1875; he also exhibited at the Royal Institute of Painters in Oil-Colours. He exhibited a total of 173 pictures. He died on 16 October 1900, leaving his son, W.Carmichael Thomas (q.v.) who engraved and took up the administration of The Graphic. The British Museum owns his engravings after J.Gilbert, G.Thomas, and various portrait engravings. He signed his work: 'W Thomas Sc' (script), 'W J Sc' (script).
[Houfe; TB; White; Bryan; Hake; Chatto; for his metal engravings and bibliography see Volume I]

THOMASON, G.T. fl.1850s
London wood engraver and printer, who worked at 8 Old Swan Lane, Upper Thames Street (POD,1853).

THOMPSON, Alfred ?-1895
Amateur draughtsman on wood, painter and caricaturist. He was a cavalry officer when he had work published in Diogenes,1854; then his few drawings, mostly comic initials, were accepted and published in Punch,1856-58, and he was persuaded by its editor, Mark Lemon to give up military life for drawing. He studied in Paris, where he contributed drawings to the French Journal Amusant. He returned to England and wrote for Punch while awaiting a promised staff position, for which he gave up hope when he was offered management of the Theatre Royal, Manchester. Later he designed costumes and scenery, wrote pantomimes and edited the magazine, Mask, as well as drawing for Comic News, 1865; The Arrow,1865; Vanity Fair,1862-76; Broadway, 1867-74; the Illustrated London News,1867; and for Dalziels' Fun,1870. His last Punch drawings appeared 1876,1877. 'The most that can be said of Mr Thompson's sketches is that they are bright and not without fancy; but since these were made, his power and charm of grace greatly increased' (Spielmann). He died in New Jersey in September 1895. The British Museum owns several proof engravings after his designs, engraved by the Dalziel Brothers (q.v.), 1865.
[Spielmann; Houfe; TB; Graves]

THOMPSON, Charles 1791-1843
Wood engraver, born in London in 1791, the brother of John and Eliza Thompson (qq.v.) and uncle of Charles Thurston Thompson (q.v.). He was a pupil of Robert Branston (q.v.) before setting up on his own. He moved to Paris in 1816 where he worked for the publisher Didot and was responsible for introducing the English method of black-line engraving from the end grain of the block to France. He developed a large practice in Paris. He engraved cuts to Fairfax's Tasso,1817; and Singer's Shakespeare,1826. He also introduced the superior talent of his brother John to the French. He was awarded a gold medal for his wood engravings exhibited at the Salon in 1824, and was much employed by the publisher Curmer. His French engravings included those listed by Gusman of which the most important were to L'Histoire de L'Ancien et du Nouveau Testament,1835; Fables de la Fontaine, 1836, engraved with his brother John; Jules Janin's L'Ane Mort (1842 edition of 1829 original); Moliere's Oeuvres,1835-36; Ct. de Laborde's Versailles,1839; Laurent's Histoire de L'Empereur Napoleon,1839; Abbé Prevost's Histoire de Manon Lescaut,1839; and Baron Holstein's Corinne,1841. There is an indication that Thompson worked in London during the early 1820s: according to the Post Office directories he had an office at Barden Place, Peckham (Pigot,1822-23), shared with John Thompson. However he chose to live mostly in France, where he died, in Bourg-la-Reine, near Paris on 19 May 1843. He had by then established a considerable French reputation for his engravings and the government awarded his widow a pension in consequence of his contributions to French literature. The British Museum owns a set of India proofs to Fairfax's Tasso; a set of sixty-five cuts to Singer's Shakespeare; and a large engraving, 'Vue du Pont de Montereau'.
[Muir; Redgrave; LeBlanc; Nagler; Andresen; Gusman (for large list of French work); Bryan]

THOMPSON, Charles Thurston 1816-68
Wood engraver and photographer. He was born in
Peckham on 28 July 1816, the son of the wood
engraver John Thompson (q.v.), brother of Richard
Anthony (q.v.) and nephew of Charles and Eliza
Thompson (qq.v.). He trained as a wood engraver and
achieved great success for the publications of Van
Voorst and Messrs Longman. One of his most success-
ful individual engravings was the frontispiece after
Richard Doyle (q.v.) to Ruskin's King of the Golden
River, second edition, c1851. That year he helped in
the arrangement of the Great Exhibition in Hyde Park.
Having developed a keen interest in photography he
was appointed by the exhibition commissioners to
superintend photographic printing at Versailles,
then commissioned to photograph works in Spain,
Paris and Portugal for the Science and Art Department at South Kensington, being made official
photographer. But while travelling his health
suffered and he died in Paris, after a short illness,
on 22 January 1868, aged fifty-two. The British
Museum owns his engravings after E.Armitage,
R.Doyle, R.Huskisson, J.Millais, F.Tayler, and
a group of intricate copies of fresco designs and
Duccio paintings. He signed his engravings:
'C T Thompson' (script), 'C T THOMPSON SC'.
[Bryan; DNB; Redgrave]

THOMPSON, Eliza
Wood engraver, sister of the prominent wood engravers
John and Charles Thompson (qq.v.) and aunt of Richard
Anthony and Charles Thurston Thompson (qq.v.).
She worked in London, often with her brothers. Her
early engravings included a tailpiece after William
Harvey's design for 'Falstaff at Gadshill'; and two
tailpieces after Forester, all published in Northcote's
Fables, 1828. Nagler called her engravings the work
of 'an excellent artist'. The British Museum owns
two Northcote's Fables cuts.
[Nagler]

THOMPSON, G.H. fl.1883-84
Draughtsman for wood engravings in the English
Illustrated Magazine, 1883-84. He specialised in
topographical and social scenes here, such as 'North
Transept, Winchester Cathedral', 1884, engraved by
D.Martin (q.v.) and the series, 'The Industries of
the Lake District', 1883-84, engraved by E.Schladitz,
B.Istvan, E.Lascelles, C.Barbant, and O.Lacour
(qq.v.).

THOMPSON, Isabel A.
Wood engraver, who engraved the initial letter 'S' and
cottage scene vignettes of Richard Doyle's illustrations
to Ruskin's King of the Golden River, 1850-51. She
signed her engravings: 'I A T' (script).

THOMPSON, John 1785-1866
Prominent wood and metal engraver, born in
Manchester on 25 May 1785, the brother of the
engravers Charles and Eliza Thompson (qq.v.) with
whom he worked. He was apprenticed at fourteen
years old to Robert Branston, Senior (q.v.). The
British Museum owns the tiny, crude squirrel
engraving which he claimed was 'My first engraving'.
During the latter half of his training he learned wood
engraving, eventually forming a distinctive style
under the influence of John Thurston (q.v.). He in
fact engraved about 900 of Thurston's designs on
wood, including cuts for Dibdin's London Theatre,
1814-18; Fairfax's Tasso, 1817 (engraved with Charles);
Puckle's The Club, 1817; and Butler's Hudibras,
1818. In this last year he produced his largest
engraving, the diploma of the Highland Society after
Benjamin West's design. A proof of this is in
the British Museum. His most notable engraved
illustration commissions appeared in Singer's
edition of Shakespeare, 1826, (printed by Chiswick
Press, proofs are in the British Museum), after
William Harvey, Stothard, and Corbould (qq.v.);
Mornings at Bow Street, and Beauties of Washington
Irving, both after George Cruikshank (q.v.); Rogers'
Italy, 1828, after Stothard and Landseer;
Goldsmith's Vicar of Wakefield, 1843, after Mulready
(q.v.); Bürger's Leonora, 1847, after Maclise (q.v.);
Sir Roger de Coverley, 1850, after Frederick Tayler;
Moxon's edition of Tennyson's Poems, 1857; Aytoun's
Lays of the Cavaliers, 1863, after Noel Paton (q.v.); and
Longman's New Testament, 1864. Thompson's skill
at engraving black-line to imitate metal engraving
was introduced into France by his brother Charles,
and much of John's work for the French market
returned to England in translations illustrated by
Grandville, Scheffer, Johannot, and others. He was
wholly or partly responsible for the engraved
illustrations of at least fourteen such volumes, and
occasionally joined with Charles on such works as
Fables de la Fontaine, 1836. He was awarded a grand
medal of honour for wood engraving at the Paris
exhibition of 1855, and even received but declined
an invitation to settle in Prussia. Instead he served
as superintendent of the Female School of Wood
Engraving at South Kensington, 1852-59, where he
delivered a course of useful lectures on wood engraving
to his students. As a wood engraver he worked in
a London office as early as 1817: 129 Houndsditch
(Johnstone, 1817), then Barden Place, Peckham
(Pigot, 1822-23), which he shared with his brother
Charles. He then moved to 3 (later 5) Bedford Place,
Kensington Gravel Pits (Pigot, 1832-38), to be near
his major employer, Charles Whittingham (q.v.) at
the Chiswick Press. From these offices he developed
a substantial reputation as a wood engraver. 'Thompson
was perhaps the ablest exponent that has ever lived
of the style of wood engraving which aimed at
rivalling the effect of copper, and his cuts in

Fairfax's Tasso and Puckle's Club may be instanced
as supreme triumphs of the art. For about fifty
years he stood at the head of his profession, and,
vast as was the amount of work he produced during
that period, he never allowed it to become mechanical
or degenerate into a manufacture' (DNB). Among his
assistants in his busy and expert workshop was the
influential engraver and historian of the art,
W.J.Linton (q.v.), who worked with Thompson from
about 1836 to the end of 1838. Linton described his
master in his own Masters of Wood Engraving, as an
expert with the graver, 'beyond question entitled to
rank above all the men who have engraved in wood'.
Bewick's engraving technique 'is weak as a child's
untaught attempts beside...'. Thompson was in fact
commissioned by William Yarrell to copy Bewick's
bird engravings, and engrave numerous bird cuts for
Yarrell's A History of British Birds, 1837-43, which
he engraved with his brother Charles and son Richard
(q.v.), with Charles Whymper and the Dalziel
Brothers (qq.v.). He was also a prolific metal
engraver of stipple and mezzotint plates. He cut on
brass Mulready's penny postage envelope, and cut on
steel the figure of Britannia on English banknotes.
He had two sons with whom he engraved: Charles
Thurston and Richard Anthony Thompson (qq.v.).
He died on 20 February 1866, in South Kensington,
London, aged eighty-one. The Victoria and Albert
Museum owns a collection of his proofs; the British
Museum has a large number of engravings, notably
after H.K.Browne, C.W.Cope, W.E.Frost,
J.Gilbert, W.Harvey, J.C.Horsley, W.H.Hunt,
E.Landseer, D.Maclise, J.Millais, W.Mulready,
F.Tayler and J.Thurston; various trade engravings
printed by C.Whittingham; a separate print of a
schoolboy after W.Collins engraved for Van Voorst,
June 1840; proof of his brass engraved design after
Mulready for the first postage stamp envelope, 1840;
and a series of engravings after Egyptian antiquities.
Thompson signed his work in various ways:
'JNᵒ THOMPSON', 'THOMPSON SC', 'JOHN
THOMPSON SC', 'JT' (superimposed), a cross
shape.
[For a list of engraved French work see L.Carteret,
Le Tresor du Bibliophile, 1924-28; LeBlanc; TB; for
a bibliography and discussion of his metal engravings
see Volume I; see also Chatto; Hake; Redgrave;
Gusman; A.Warren, C.Whittingham, 1896;
W.J.Linton, Masters of Wood Engraving; C.Jackson]

THOMPSON, Joseph fl.1871-77
London wood engraver, who worked at 102 Fleet
Street, EC (POD, 1871-73), then 97 Fleet Street, EC
(POD, 1875-77). He probably engraved the full-page
animal engraving, 'The Maccarte Lion', for the
Illustrated London News, 28 November 1874, signed
'Thompson sc'. It was engraved in a bold, confident
black-line style reminiscent of a lithograph.

THOMPSON, Richard Anthony c1820-1908
Wood engraver, museum administrator. He was
born about 1820, the son of the wood engraver John
Thompson (q.v.) and nephew of the engravers
Charles Thurston Thompson and Eliza Thompson
(qq.v.). He possibly engraved part of his father's
commission, Yarrell's British Birds, at the age of
seventeen, although his contribution was probably
only small. Thompson abandoned engraving when he
was appointed an administrator of the South
Kensington Museum, serving as assistant director
until 1892.
[C.Jackson]

THOMPSON, Thomas
Wood engraver, little known apprentice of the wood
engraver George Baxter (q.v.). He probably worked
for Kronheim about 1849, with the engraver Charles
Gregory (q.v.)
[C.T.Lewis]

THOMSON, (John) Gordon fl.1864-93
Comic draughtsman and figure artist. He began his
drawing career while training as a civil servant,
then abandoned drawing until he retired in 1870. He
had successfully drawn on wood thirty-three 'socials'
for Punch by 1864; also for London Society and The
Graphic, 1869-86. He established himself drawing
double-pages of the Franco-Prussian War for The
Graphic. He was engaged by the Dalziel Brothers
(q.v.) as chief cartoonist to their comic paper
Fun, from 1870, and 'remained for twenty years
without one week's break' (Spielmann). He was
especially noted for his parodies of major exhibition
pictures and the Dalziels noted his 'large pictures
for Christmas and other Holiday Numbers...
remarkable for the varied topical events he crowded
into them, and those who remember his "Academy
Skits" will know what quaint burlesques they were'.
He also drew illustrations to Dickens' Pictures From
Italy, 1870. He exhibited once, at the Royal Academy
in 1878. The British Museum owns proof engravings
of his designs by the Dalziel Brothers,
1865-66.
[Spielmann; Dalziels' Record; Houfe]

THOMSON, Hugh 1860-1920
Draughtsman, watercolourist and illustrator. He was
born in Coleraine, Co Londonderry on 1 June 1860
and left his home for Belfast in 1877, to work for the
colour printer of Christmas cards, Marcus Ward.
There he also attended a few art classes at the
Belfast School of Art. He made his name drawing
for wood engravings in Carr's English Illustrated
Magazine, 1883-92, notably his series 'Days with
Sir Roger de Coverley', 1885-86, wood engraved by
O.Lacour, O.Jahyer, and Waterlow and Sons (qq.v.),
published in volume form, 1886. Other drawings for
wood engravings here included illustrations to

H.D.Traill's 'Two Centuries of Bath', 1883, engraved by E.Gascoine (q.v.); Austin Dobson's 'Tour of Covent Garden', 1884, engraved by R.Davey (q.v.); and drawings to H.A.Jones' 'The Dramatic Outlook', 1884, engraved by O.Lacour, J.D.Cooper, W.M.R.Quick, J.A.Quartley, R.Paterson and A. and W.Dawson (qq.v.). Thomson's style was adopted from eighteenth century subjects and drawn with a light, sure touch borrowed from Randolph Caldecott (q.v.). From the 1880s he was constantly employed illustrating numerous classic novels, which were mostly process engraved. He was elected RI in 1897 and retired in 1907. He died in Wandsworth on 7 May 1920.
[For a complete list of illustrated work see Spielmann and Jerrold, Hugh Thomson, 1931; also DNB; TB; Houfe; Sketchley]

THORIGNY, Felix 1824-70
Draughtsman for wood engraving, landscape painter. He was born in Caen on 14 March 1824, where he studied with Julian. He worked in Paris for wood engraved illustrations in the Monde Illustré; Magasin Pittoresque; Musée des Familles; and Calvados Pittoresque. He drew for Henry Vizetelly's Illustrated Times, 1859, and for the Illustrated London News, 1859-68. He died in Paris on 27 March 1870.
[TB (with bibliography); Houfe]

THORNE, J.
The British Museum owns a series of proof wood engravings by the Dalziel Brothers (q.v.), engraved 1848-51 after designs by J.Thorne.

THORNELY, H.
Draughtsman of equestrian subjects. He drew these for wood engravings in the Penny Illustrated Paper.

THORNTON, Henry fl.1880-95
Draughtsman on wood and wood engraver, listed in Kelly's provincial directory at 12 Preeson's Row, Liverpool (Kelly's, 1880). Three years later Henry Thornton and Company appeared in the London directories at 89 Farringdon Street, WC (POD, 1883-87), where the firm employed W.J.Potter, J.A.Rogers and L.Knott (qq.v.). Later the firm moved to 328 High Holborn, WC (POD, 1890-92), 10 Thavies Inn, Holborn, EC (POD, 1893-94), then 3 Dyer's Buildings, EC (POD, 1895).

THORPE, Frederick fl.1877-1910
London wood engraver, who worked at 53 Tavistock Road, W (POD, 1877-82), then 30 Fleet Street, EC (POD, 1886-88). When he moved to 89 Farringdon Street, WC (POD, 1889-1901), he shared the office with the wood engravers G.F.Horne, F.Appleton, W.J.Potter, L.Knott, H.Prater, and J.Dixon (qq.v.). By 1910 Thorpe was working at 47 Red Lion Street, EC (POD, 1910). Among Thorpe's engraving

commissions was an illustration drawn by A.D.M'Cormick, 'Chateau de Cluiss', for the English Illustrated Magazine, 1886. This was poorly engraved, the graver marks gouged unevenly, the sky an uneven series of lines.

THORPE, John Hall 1874-?
Wood engraver and painter of landscapes and flowers. He was born in Victoria, Australia on 29 April 1874, studied at the Sydney Art Society and then moved to London to study at Heatherley's and St Martin's. He exhibited at the Royal Academy and the Royal Society of British Artists, was a member of the Langham Club and Art Workers' Guild, and worked in London.
[Waters]

THURSTON, John 1774-1822
Prominent early draughtsman on wood, wood engraver, and watercolourist. He was born in Scarborough in 1774, educated at the Hornsey Academy there and learned drawing under Mr Hornsey. He was engaged to the copperplate engraver James Heath, whom he helped engrave the two major plates, 'The Death of Major Peirson', after Copley, and 'The Dead Soldier', after J.Wright of Derby. He soon turned to drawing on wood and devoted himself to designing book illustrations for wood engravers and 'most of the editions of the poets and novelists published during the first twenty years of the present century, especially those issued by the Chiswick Press, were embellished by his pencil' (DNB). Although many of his drawings were engraved on copper (e.g. to Sharpe's and Cooke's classics) the majority were drawn on wood blocks and cut by Luke Clennell, Branston, Charlton Nesbit and Thompson (qq.v.). He drew for Thomson's Seasons, 1805 and Burns' Poems, 1808, engraved by Henry White, Isaac Nicholson and E.Willis (qq.v.), both books engraved in the Bewick workshop; also to Beattie's Minstrel, 1807; Ackermann's Religious Emblems, 1808; Shakespeare's Works, 1814; Somerville's Rural Sports, 1814; Puckle's The Club, 1817; and Falconer's Shipwreck, 1817; and his engraved work appeared in Savage's Hints on Decorative Printing, 1822. He also contributed to Hood's Comic Annual, which appeared posthumously in 1830. Thurston was described by Chatto and Jackson as 'one of the best designers on wood of his time. He drew very beautifully, but his designs are too frequently deficient in natural character and feeling'. One of his greatest contemporary admirers was Thomas Bewick (q.v.) who wrote of Thurston as a draughtsman on wood: 'Fortunately, for the Art [Wood engraving] it was under the guidance of the ingenious John Thurston-- who pencilled his designs stroke by stroke on the Wood, with the utmost accuracy--' (Bewick, Memoir). Thurston was a major influence on Victorian wood engravers. W.J.Linton (q.v.) in his Masters of Wood Engraving in fact blames Thurston, the draughtsman, for splitting the role of the engraver from the draughts-

man, which caused a decline in masterful cooperative wood engravings: 'His reign is undisputed. Such work as Craig could do bore no comparison with his; and though Stothard, most prolific of designers, and Corbould and others, made a few occasional drawings on wood, they could not be considered as rivals. Nearly all of better book illustrations on wood during all that period seems to have been entrusted to the able pencil of Thurston'. Thurston was also a water-colourist and was elected AOWS in 1805 (1806,DNB), sending in five Shakespearean groups that year; he also occasionally exhibited at the Royal Academy, 1794-1812. He died in Holloway, London in 1822, 'his life being shortened by excessive devotion to his art' (DNB). The Bodleian Library owns his drawings engraved by S.Williams (q.v.) for C.Whittingham.
[Redgrave; DNB; W.J.Linton, Masters of Wood Engraving; Chatto; Nagler; Slater]

TIDMARSH, H.E. fl.1880-1925
Occasional draughtsman for wood engravings of architectural subjects, figure and landscape painter. He worked in North London and Barnet, and drew for wood engravings in The Graphic,1886-87; also the Illustrated London News,1889-91. He also exhibited at the Royal Academy, the Royal Society of British Artists and the Royal Institute of Painters in Water-colours.

TIFFIN, Henry fl.1841-74 Walter Francis fl.1844-67
Draughtsman on wood and landscape painter, Henry Tiffin worked in London. He drew for Charles Knight's (q.v.) publications, such as Knight's London,1841, He also exhibited at the British Institution, the Royal Academy and the Royal Society of British Artists, from 1845-74. In addition Bénézit lists a Walter Francis Tiffin, draughtsman on wood, miniaturist and portrait painter, from Salisbury. He worked from 1844-67 and exhibited two landscapes at the Royal Academy,1844, also at the British Institution and the Society of British Artists. He drew for wood engravings in Charles Knight's Penny Magazine, 1841-42, engraved by C.Gray, M.Hampton and J.W.Whymper (qq.v.). The Bodleian Library owns his Knight commissions. He signed his work 'WTIFFIN'.

TILBY, Charles and William Henry fl.1868-90
London wood engravers, who worked at 3 Bouverie Street, EC (POD,1868-73), an office shared briefly with J.S.Dalziel (q.v.). They moved to 46 Fleet Street, EC (POD,1874), 4 Wine Office Court (POD,1875-76), shared with John Greenaway (q.v.); 49 Essex Street, Strand, WC (POD,1878-80), shared with W.A.Sawers (q.v.); 61 Fleet Street, EC (POD,1884) and finally as William Henry and Charles Tilby, at 272 Strand, WC (POD,1889-90).

TILLING, Alfred Thomas fl.1880
London draughtsman on wood, who worked at the workshop 9 Essex Street, Strand, WC (Kelly's,1880). He worked there with J.Bye, J.Desbois and H.C.Mason (qq.v.).

TILLY, Auguste ?-1898
French wood engraver, born in Toul. He studied with Coissier and most importantly with Burn Smeeton (q.v.) with whom he set up an engraving business, Smeeton and Tilly (q.v.). He made his debut at the Salon in 1874, and engraved after various English works for the Magasin Pittoresque. He collaborated with his son, the wood engraver Pierre Emile Tilly.
[TB; Bénézit; Gusman]

TIMBRELL, James Christopher c1807-50
Occasional draughtsman illustrator, marine and landscape painter. He was born in Dublin about 1807 (1810,DNB), the brother of the sculptor Henry Timbrell. He specialised in nautical subjects, having trained at the Dublin Society's Schools. He worked in London, drew on wood for Charles Knight's London,1841; also illustrations to Hall's Ireland, its Scenery and Character. He exhibited paintings from 1830-48 at the Royal Academy, the British Institution and the Royal Society of British Artists. He died in Portsmouth on 5 January 1850.
[DNB; Redgrave; TB; Nagler; Strickland; Art Journal,1850,p.100]

TIMMS fl.1839-65
English wood engraver who worked in Paris. He was one of a group of expatriot engravers who influenced the illustration of French magazines. He engraved numerous vignettes and was especially proficient at reproducing paintings for such publications as L'Illustration and Magasin Pittoresque, as well as the books Abbé Prévost's Histoire de Manon Lescaut,1839; Lamartine's Jocelyn, for which he engraved twelve plates and vignettes with Quartley (q.v.); Jules Janin's L'Ane Mort,1842, with 100 vignettes and twelve plates engraved after J.Johannot; numerous vignettes to L'Eté à Paris,1843, after Jules Janin; and cuts to Histoire des Peintres,1865. His work also appeared in the Gazette des Beaux Arts,1861,p.124; 1865, p.388. The British Museum owns his engravings of landscapes by G.F.Sargent and Claude Lorrain. He signed his work: 'TIMMS Sc'.
[Gusman; Bénézit; TB; Beraldi]

TIREBUCK, Joseph and Isaac fl.1876-80
London draughtsmen on wood, who worked at 3 Windsor Court and 40A Monkwell Street, EC (Kelly's,1876-80).

TODD, H.W.
The British Museum owns a proof wood engraving by the Dalziel Brothers (q.v.) after a drawing by this artist. It is a large print of a tower with figures, engraved in 1853.

TODHUNTER, Evans Murray fl.1889-93
London wood engraver, who worked in partnership as McCrombie and Todhunter (q.v.) then on his own at 5 New Court, Carey Street, WC (POD,1890-93).

TOMKINS, Charles F. 1799-1844
Occasional draughtsman, caricaturist, and landscape painter. He worked with David Roberts and Clarkson Stanfield (qq.v.) and is listed here for early drawings wood engraved in Punch during its first years (according to Houfe, although Spielmann fails to list his Punch work). He also exhibited at the British Institution and the Royal Society of British Artists, being elected a member of the Society of British Artists in 1838.

TOOMER, James fl.1880s
London wood engraver, who worked at 325 Strand, WC (POD,1884). He shared the premises with H.R.Edwards (q.v.).

TOPHAM, Francis William 1808-77
Occasional draughtsman on wood, watercolour painter of genre subjects, line engraver. He was born in Leeds on 15 April 1808 and apprenticed to his uncle, a 'writer engraver'. In 1830 he came to London and worked first as a coat-of-arms engraver, then for the engravers Fenner and Sears, where he met the engraver Henry Beckwith, later marrying his sister. He engraved for the publisher James Sprent Virtue some landscapes after W.H.Bartlett and Thomas Allom; he also drew and engraved illustrations to Fisher's edition of Scott's Waverley Novels. He studied figure drawing at the Clipstone Street Academy and proved good enough to draw on wood for numerous books, including the Poems of Burns; Thomas Moore's Melodies and Poems; and S.C.Hall's Book of British Ballads,1842. He contributed to the Sporting Review,1842-46; Pictures and Poems,1846; Mrs S.C.Hall's Midsummer Eve,1848; Dickens' Child's History of England, 1852-54; and Charles Mackay's Home Affections,1858. Some of these were singled out by Bohn in Chatto and Jackson as the work of a proficient draughtsman on wood, who specialised in 'Irish characters'. He later gave up engraving for watercolour paintings of his travels to the Continent, especially in Spain, and Ireland, and exhibited at the British Institution and the New Watercolour Society to which he was elected member in 1843; the Old Watercolour Society to which he was elected member in 1848; the Royal Academy and the Royal Society of British Artists. He died in Cordova on 31 March 1877. The British Museum

owns proof wood engravings by the Dalziel Brothers (q.v.), 1857.
[Chatto; Houfe; DNB; Kitton]

TORRY, John T. fl.1880s
Occasional draughtsman illustrator, landscape painter. He is listed here for his social scenes for wood engravings in the Illustrated London News, 1886. He also exhibited at the Royal Society of British Artists and the Royal Institute of Painters in Watercolours.

TOWNSEND, G.
Ornamental draughtsman on wood, who contributed a page decoration wood engraved in the Illustrated London News,1860. He worked at the time in Exeter.

TOWNSEND, Henry James 1810-90
Occasional draughtsman on wood, etcher, painter and surgeon. He was born on 6 June 1810 and taught at the Government School of Design, Somerset House from 1839-66. During that time he also etched numerous plates for the Etching Club's publications (see Volume I for a discussion and list). He also drew on wood for engravings in Mrs S.C.Hall's Book of British Ballads,1842 edition, engraved by G.P.Nicholls (q.v.); for Thomson's Seasons,1852; and for Henry Vizetelly's (q.v.) Illustrated Times, 1855. He also exhibited at the British Institution, the Royal Academy and the Royal Society of British Artists, from 1839-66, generally genre and history paintings.
[Houfe; Bryan; Volume I]

TOZER, Henry E. fl.1873-1907
Occasional draughtsman illustrator for wood engravings of marine subjects, also marine painter. He worked at Penzance. He drew for wood engravings in the Illustrated London News,1873-80, namely half or third-page nautical scenes such as 'HMS Raleigh', 13 June 1874, or 'Demolition of Old Fortifications at Portsmouth', 6 February 1875. These were anonymously engraved in a style which depended upon parallel lines for sky and water. He also exhibited paintings at the Royal Academy from 1892.

TREACHER, Harry and Charles fl.1889-1900
Provincial wood engravers, who worked at 170 North Street, 44 East Street, and 4 Brighton Place, Brighton (Kelly's,1889-1900).

TRENT, Charles fl.1882-95
London wood engraver, who worked at 310 Strand, WC (POD,1882) and 110 Shoe Lane, EC (POD,1884-86). By 1892 he had appeared at 9 Essex Street, Strand, WC (POD,1892-94), premises shared with the engraver G.Puttock (q.v.). He was last listed in the directories at 33 Fetter Lane, EC (POD,1895).

TRICHON, François Auguste 1814-?
French wood engraver, who was born on 1 November
1814 in Paris. He studied from 1835 at the Royal
School of Drawing, the studio of Montvoissin, and
learned wood engraving from Henry Brown (q.v.).
He engraved for the prominent French engraving
firm, Andrew, Best and Leloir (q.v.) from 1836-40.
He exhibited first at the Salon in 1848. His work
included numerous cuts to French art periodicals
such as L'Illustration, Le Journal pour Tous, Le
Magasin des Enfants, Journal du Dimanche and
C.Blanc's L'Histoire des Peintres. Towards the end
of his career he engraved for L'Univers Illustré,
and Musée de Familles. He taught the Doré engraver
Paul Jonnard (q.v.), having engraved Doré
drawings in the Gazette des Beaux Arts,1866,
p.278. His daughters Adèle and Adrienne were also
wood engravers.
[TB; Nagler; Beraldi]

TUCK, Harry fl.1870-1907
Comic draughtsman on wood, landscape and genre
painter. He drew on wood for Gilbert Dalziel's Fun,
serving on the staff from 1878-1900. He also drew
for Strand Magazine,1891. He worked at Haverstock
Hill, London, and exhibited at the Royal Academy,
the Royal Society of British Artists, the Royal
Institute of Painters in Watercolours, and the Royal
Institute of Painters in Oil-Colours.

TUCKLEY and Vince fl.1880s
Provincial wood engraving firm, with an office at
10 Parade, Birmingham (Kelly's,1889).

TURNBULL, F.J. fl.1850s
London wood engraver, who worked at 32 Red Lion
Street, Clerkenwell (POD,1853).

TURNER, Lewis fl.1830s
London wood engraver, who worked at 25 Upper
Rosamon Street, Clerkenwell (Pigot,1838).

UBSDELL, Richard Henry Clements fl.1828-56
Occasional draughtsman on wood, painter of
historical subjects, miniaturist, and photographer.
He worked in Portsmouth, and drew for wood
engravings of marine subjects in Henry Vizetelly's
Illustrated Times,1856. He also watercoloured
church views, and exhibited at the Royal Academy
and the Royal Society of British Artists.

UHLRICH, Heinrich Sigismund 1846-?
German wood engraver, noted for his portrait
engravings in The Graphic. He was born in Oschatz,
Germany in 1846 and worked in Chelsfield, Kent. He
became one of the major wood engravers for The
Graphic, noted especially for engravings after
Hubert Herkomer (q.v.), as well as after 'Old

Master' paintings by Hals, Van Dyck, Rembrandt,
Raphael, Velasquez, Murillo, and Dürer. Uhlrich
exhibited his wood engravings at the Royal Academy,
some twenty-one from 1889-1904, including the
following subjects: 'Viscount Wolseley', after
Frank Holl,1889; 'J.M.Swan', after Theodore B.
Wirgman,1894; 'Ha!Ha!Ha!', after George Hare,
1894; 'Duke of York', after George Greenhill,1897;
'Baptism of the First Prince of Wales', after Fred
Roe,1899; 'HRH the Duke of Connaught', after
Hubert Herkomer,1899; 'An Aristocrat Answering
in Summons to Execution in Paris, 1798', after
Frank L.Cooper,1902; 'Clouds That Gather Round
the Setting Sun', after J.Seymour Lucas,1902; and
'Lively Measure', after J.Seymour Lucas,1903. In
addition the British Museum owns a portrait of
'Leopold, Duke of Albany', after a photograph,
issued as an engraved supplement to The Graphic,
1884; and 'Albert, Duke of Clarence', after Hubert
Herkomer, supplement to The Graphic,1892.
[TB (with bibliography); Bénézit; Hayden, Chats on
Old Prints, 1908; Graves; Hake]

UNIVERSAL Printing Company fl.1884-85
London wood engraving and printing firm, with an
office at 280 High Holborn (POD,1884-85) and
printing works at Tichborne Court, WC.

UNWIN, Francis Sydney 1885-1925
Wood engraver, lithographer, etcher of architect-
ural subjects, and writer. He was born in Stalbridge,
Dorset in 1885 and was a pupil at the Winchester
School of Art and the Slade School from 1902-05.
He worked in London and travelled extensively on
the Continent. The British Museum owns two land-
scape wood engravings by Unwin. He signed his
engravings: 'UNWIN'.
[For a discussion, bibliography and list of his metal
engravings and etchings see Volume I; also C.Dodgson,
Francis Unwin,1928; TB; Bénézit]

UNZELMANN, Frederick Ludwig 1797-1854
German wood engraver, born in Berlin in 1797,
and pupil of Gubitz at the Berlin Academy, where he
became a member in 1843, then served as engraving
professor in 1845. He quickly established a
reputation for his wood engravings of architecture,
landscapes, portraits and genre subjects, many of
which appeared in Britain. His most famous and
successful were after drawings by Adolf Menzel to
History of Frederick the Great,1840, for which
Unzelmann used a knife rather than a graver to
engrave. Later he engraved Menzel's drawings to
the Works of Frederick the Great,1844. Apparently
Menzel's work was demanding to engrave, 'every
scribble had to be translated with complete self-
effacement by the executant'. Unzelmann died in
Vienna on 29 August 1854. He signed his work:
'U', 'UM', 'Uzl' (script).

[For a bibliography and list of work see Nagler; TB; and Glaser; see also Bénézit; Hind; Hake; Bliss]

UPTON, James fl.1872-89
Provincial wood engraver, who worked at 162-164 Great Charles Street, Cambridge (Kelly's,1872) then 16A Moor Street, Birmingham (Kelly's,1876-89). There was also a James Upton (1821-74), colour printer (see Wakeman and Bridson).

UTTING, Robert Brooke fl.1854-79
London wood engraver and draughtsman of intricate black-line engraved designs of antiquities. He worked at 13 Camden Terrace, Camden Town (POD,1854) and 34 College Street, Camden Town (POD,1855-59). He then moved to 9 Cornwall Crescent, Camden Town (POD,1860-65) and 47 later 33 Camden Road, NW (POD,1866-79). His engravings included a stained glass window design for the Great Exhibition, Illustrated London News, 26 July 1851. He also engraved five bookplates listed by Fincham. after seal designs dated 1850, 1860. The British Museum owns a number of his intricate black-line engravings of jewellery, Norman antiquities drawn by Mossman, vases, crest designs, antique gems, and an early Christian box lid. He signed his engravings: 'Utting sc', 'Utting del et sc'.

VALENTIN, Henry 1820-55
Draughtsman, illustrator for wood engravings, also a painter. He was born in Allarmoint in the Vosges in 1820. He drew for lithographs in French albums and drew on wood for L'Illustration and Journal Amusant, his figures being in the style of Gavarni (q.v.). He was French correspondent to various British papers, notably the Illustrated London News, 1848-56, and Henry Vizetelly's Illustrated Times. He also drew for a wood engraving in Cassell's Illustrated Family Paper,1855. He died in Paris in 1855.
[TB; Nagler; Beraldi; Houfe]

VALERIO, Theodore 1819-79
Occasional draughtsman for wood engravings, engraver, etcher, lithographer and painter. He was born in Herserange on 18 February 1819, was a pupil of Charlet, and exhibited at the Salon from 1838. He travelled throughout the Continent and made drawings of the Crimea as a member of the Turkish Omer Pacha's army. He travelled to England and contributed drawings of Arabia and Austria wood engraved in Henry Vizetelly's Illustrated Times,1856. He died in Vichy on 14 September 1879.
[TB (full bibliography); Beraldi; Clement; Bénézit; LeBlanc; Andresen]

VALLANCE, William Fleming 1827-1904
Occasional draughtsman for wood engravings, marine and landscape painter. He was born in Paisley on 13 February 1827, apprenticed to a gilder in 1841, studied at the local design school and Edinburgh Trustees Academy. From 1857 he set up as a full-time artist, and drew for wood engraved illustrations in Pen and Pencil Pictures from the Poets,1866, contributing to the forty illustrations by Keeley Halswelle, Pettie, MacWhirter, W.Small, and J.Lawson (qq.v.). Vallance was a noted painter, being elected ARSA in 1875 and RSA in 1881. He died in Edinburgh on 31 August 1904.
[DNB; Houfe]

VARDY, John fl.1880s
Provincial wood engraver, who worked at 56 Wyle Cop, Shrewsbury (Kelly's,1889).

VASEY
Wood engraver, who engraved cuts to Charles Knight's publication, William Lane's Arabian Night's Entertainments,1839, which is now in the Bodleian Library. The British Museum owns his advertisements for the series of four, A History of British Quadrupeds...Reptiles...Birds...Fishes, each with an engraved animal by Vasey. He signed his engravings: 'VASEY'.

VERPEILLEUX, Emile Antoine 1888-1964
Wood engraver of coloured views of London, portrait and landscape painter, engraver and illustrator. He was born of Belgian parents in London on 3 March 1888 and studied in London and at the Antwerp Academy. He is listed here for the series of coloured wood engravings which he exhibited as a member of the Society for Graver-Printers in Colour. These include the most successful 'St Paul's Cathedral'; 'Trafalgar Square'; 'Searchlights'; 'St Pancras Station'; 'Tower Bridge'; and 'Interior of King's College Chapel, Cambridge'. Gusman called them 'remarkable'. These were reproduced in various volumes of the Studio,1913, 1917, Special Numbers, 1919, 1922, and 1927. He also contributed to The Graphic,1915. He exhibited at the Royal Academy, the New English Art Club, the Royal Society of British Artists to which he was elected member in 1914, and the Royal Scottish Academy.
[For a complete bibliography see TB; also Houfe; Waters; Gusman]

VICKERS, Alfred fl.1876-77
London wood engraver, who worked at East Temple Chambers, Whitefriars Street, EC (POD,1876-77). He shared the premises with W.R.Buckman (q.v.). He may be related to the London landscape painter Alfred Vickers (1786-1868).

VIERGE, Daniel ('Vierge Urrabieta Ortiz') 1851-1904
Draughtsman on wood, genre painter. He was born in Madrid on 5 March 1851 the son of Vicente

Urrabieta Ortiz, a noted Spanish illustrator. He studied at the Madrid Academy and in 1867 drew for Madrid la Nuit. In 1869 he left for Paris hoping to establish himself as an artist illustrator. There he drew for Henry Vizetelly (q.v.), then Paris foreign correspondent to the Illustrated London News, but his plans were cut short by the Franco-Prussian War. He returned to Madrid, was taken up at the age of twenty by Yriarte (q.v.), editor of Monde Illustré, and worked for the paper from then onward. He soon became known for his illustrations especially to Victor Hugo's works, 1874-82, wood engraved by C.Bellenger, E.Froment and Frederick Florian (qq.v.). Demands on his time grew with his reputation: he claimed that he had three to four months work to complete in one month or at best six weeks. Indeed constant spells of overwork while completing his finest work, illustrations to Quevedo's Don Pablo de Segovia, 1881-82, led to paralysis on his right side by the age of thirty. Nevertheless he continued to draw with his left hand and completed illustrations to Cervantes, 1893. Vierge was championed by Joseph Pennell, who claimed that he had a considerable influence on French, Spanish and American illustration of the period; the Century Magazine, June (1893) claimed he was the 'father of modern illustration'. Towards the end of his life he won many honours, including the Legion of Honour, and wanted to exhibit in England. He drew again for the Illustrated London News in 1897. He died in Boulogne-sur-Seine on 4 May 1904.
[For a bibliography see TB; also Gusman; Bénézit; Vizetelly, Glances Back; Jules de Marthold, Daniel Vierge, 1906; Louis Morin, Quelques Artistes de ce Temps, 1898, pp.13-90]

VIGNE, Godfrey Thomas 1801-63
Amateur draughtsman illustrator, professional traveller. He was born in 1801, attended Harrow School in 1817, was called to the bar in 1824 and then in 1831 travelled to America, publishing his account as Six Months in America, 1832. That year he left for India, and spent 1833-39 in excursions on the way. He published his observations as A Personal Narrative of a Visit to Ghuzni, Kabul, and Afghanistan, 1840. He is listed here for his drawings wood engraved for the Illustrated London News, 1849. He also exhibited at the Royal Academy, and died in Woodford, Essex on 12 July 1863.
[DNB; Gentleman's Magazine, 1863, p.250; Houfe]

VILLIERS, Fred 1851-1922
'Special Artist', draughtsman for wood engravings, notably of military subjects. He was born in London on 23 April 1851 and studied art at the British Museum and South Kensington, 1869-70, then the Royal Academy Schools, 1871. He was employed by The Graphic in 1876 to make drawings for wood engravings on the spot and was first sent to Servia,

then Turkey, 1877. He toured the world for the paper and recorded numerous Eastern events. By the turn of the century he was the earliest correspondent to use a camera, working during the Great War, 1914-18. He is listed here for his drawings to The Graphic, and various wood engraved illustrations to the English Illustrated Magazine, 1883-84, engraved on wood by F.Babbage, O.Jahyer, H.F.Davey, W.M.R.Quick, A.Bucknell, T.W.Lascelles and R.Paterson (qq.v.). These were engraved as pencil drawings, brief sketches filled out by dots and shaded backgrounds. He also exhibited at the Royal Academy and the Royal Institute of Painters in Oil-Colours and died on 3 April 1922.

VINCE
(see Tuckley and Vince)

VINING, H.M.
The British Museum owns a series of proof wood engravings by the Dalziel Brothers (q.v.) after this artist's drawings. They were engraved in 1863.

VIZETELLY, Frank 1830-83
Prominent 'Special Artist' and draughtsman on wood. He was born in Fleet Street, London on 26 September 1830, the younger brother of Henry and James Vizetelly (qq.v.). He probably trained with his father, James Henry Vizetelly (q.v.), a wood engraver and printer member of Vizetelly and Branston (q.v.). He became an expert draughtsman on wood, trained with Gustave Doré (q.v.) and Blanchard Jerrold in Boulogne, and put his skills to work as travelling correspondent and draughtsman for the Pictorial Times. He worked there for his brother Henry who started the paper in 1843. Later he helped to found the Paris paper, Monde Illustré, serving as its editor, 1857-59. He then became a war correspondent for the Illustrated London News, covering the Italian campaign in 1859 and being with Garibaldi in Sicily, 1860. He was sent to America in 1861 and made sketches of Civil War battles published to outraged opinion in New York's Harper's Weekly, and republished in the Illustrated London News. By 1866 he was in Austria, covering the Prusso-Austrian War. He also founded the society periodical, Echoes of the Clubs, and made pencil sketches in the royal nursery for the Queen. In 1883 he was sent by The Graphic to accompany Hicks Pasha's army to the Sudan and is believed to have been killed at El Obeid during the massacre on 5 November 1883.
[For biographical detail see H.Vizetelly, Glances Back; also W.S.Hoole, Vizetelly Covers the Confederacy, 1957; DNB]

VIZETELLY, Henry R. 1820-94
Wood engraver, journalist pioneer of the illustrated press, colour printer. He was born in St Botolph, Bishopsgate, London on 30 July 1820, the son of the

printer-engraver James Henry Vizetelly (q.v.) and brother of James and Frank Vizetelly (qq.v.) with whom he worked. He was educated at Clapham and Chislehurst under Wyburn before he was apprenticed to his father's former trainee, G.W.Bonner (q.v.) to learn wood engraving. Henry remained with Bonner about a year, c1835-36, accepting the rigours of a 72 hour week, and found his master 'a second-rate wood engraver, who itensified in his woodcuts the conventional mannerisms of the bold watercolours which he was somewhat adept at producing'. Bonner died in 1836 and Henry transferred to John Orrin Smith (q.v.) whom he admired for his enthusiasm and energy. There he helped engrave for Charles Knight's edition of Lane's The Arabian Nights' Entertainments, 1839, and to Wordsworth's La Grèce Pittoresque no doubt learning the technical skills Smith once gained from William Harvey (q.v.). Among his other early works were cuts to Marryat's Poor Jack, 1840, after Clarkson Stanfield, engraved with Robert Branston, Junior (q.v.); etched illustrations for the Etching Club's Thomson's Seasons; and also a portrait of 'Old Parr' for the proprietors of 'Parr's Life Pills', notably Henry Ingram, who later initiated the Illustrated London News on the profits of these pills and employed Henry Vizetelly to engrave its illustrations. When Henry's father's firm, Vizetelly and Branston failed, about 1841, Henry joined with his elder brother James (q.v.) to form Vizetelly Brothers, Peterborough Court, Fleet Street. Among their earliest commissions was an edition of Lockhart's Ancient Spanish Ballads, 1842, for the publisher John Murray, who had originally commissioned Vizetelly and Branston. The pressure to succeed was great, as Henry recalled; 'I sacrificed everything that I possess' for the firm to thrive. Fortunately this book, engraved with S. Williams and John Orrin Smith (qq.v.), with colour lithographs by Owen Jones (q.v.) was a 'conspicuous success'. Thus began a fruitful collaboration with Murray and Owen Jones. The brothers continued throughout the 1840s until a quarrel and split-up about 1849, when James remained at Peterborough Court and Henry went to Gough Square. Their accomplishments included wood engraving, printing letterpress, and the colour plates from wood blocks that earned Henry the accolade of being one of the most successful colour printers of the early period, alongside George Baxter and Charles Knight (qq.v.). Much of this work was after the rural drawings of his protégé, Birket Foster (q.v.), whom he first commissioned to draw water-colours for T. Miller's Country Year Book, 1847, which he printed in colours from wood blocks probably for the first time; then Illustrated Book of Songs for Children, 1850; followed by Christmas with the Poets, 1851. One of his more famous clients was the critic John Ruskin, who had his children's story, The King of the Golden River, 1851, with Richard

Doyle (q.v.) illustrations engraved by Henry; also he engraved Ruskin's small sketches for the Stones of Venice, 'but I regret to say not to the great art critic's entire satisfaction,' he later recalled. He was intimately associated with illustrated journalism from the early days of the Illustrated London News, 1842, and formed his own rival paper, Pictorial Times, 1843. He recalled in his autobiography the role of the engraver in these early ventures; how he and Henry Ingram believed illustrations of current events such as the Afghan and Chinese wars, would make 'telling' engravings and sell the papers. Henry Vizetelly's job each morning was to scan the early editions of newspapers and cut out paragraphs on subjects which he felt would make good engravings. He sent these with a necessary collection of boxwood blocks to his various draughtsmen who returned the blocks with the scene drawn on wood. John Gilbert (q.v.) was one of these unfortunate draughtsmen who became so proficient that he merely sent the messenger away for an hour during which time he had the required drawing completed and ready for collection. The problem was the small number of draughtsmen capable of such work: 'So few were the designers employed on the new paper during the first few months of its existence that they might almost have been told off on the fingers of one hand' (Glances Back, pp.232, 238). Henry recalled the difficulties of engraving the blocks, once the drawing was made, especially when a portrait of a prominent figure was attempted. John Bright, MP, refused to approve of his thumb-sized portrait for the Pictorial Times until he had stood over Vizetelly and watched him alter it: '...I had to make repeated attempts before I succeeded in satisfying the new MP whose childish vanity amused me immensely'. The 1850s brought much book engraving, and colour printing work. He engraved landscape vignettes after Birket Foster (q.v.) to Longfellow's Evangeline, 1850, which the DNB claimed was his best work. He also engraved the influential Tupper's Proverbial Philosophy, 1854, after Tenniel, Gilbert (qq.v.), and B. Foster. His colour printing of Birket Foster's designs to Christmas with the Poets, 1851, was exhibited at the Great Exhibition of 1851, as an example of modern British printing. After this, Vizetelly turned away from colour printing from wood blocks, to the more popular chromolithographic techniques. He even attempted an English edition of Uncle Tom's Cabin, 1853, which had to be reduced in price to attract substantial sales. But the high point of the fifties was Vizetelly's establishing the Illustrated Times, 1855, for which he secured numerous draughtsmen: Edward Morin, Phiz, B. Foster, Kenny Meadows, Doré, C.H.Bennett, Charles Doyle, G.H.Andrews, G.Janet, G.Cruikshank, Harrison Weir, Matt Morgan and Charles Keene (qq.v.). The paper was eventually a success, despite the problems of quick printing from wood for a large circulation and

constant rivalry to print the first news engravings. He
continued on the paper until 1865, when it was suppressed
by its rival the Illustrated London News, for which
he then worked as its Paris correspondent for the
next seven years. He had long planned, following the
break-up with his brother James, to 'engage in
business as a printer & Engraver whether in
connection with a new partner or else on my own
account', and during the 1860s he lived up to his
promise. The London directories list him in
partnership with the wood engraver Robert Loudan
(q.v.) as Vizetelly and Loudan, 15 and 16 Gough
Square, Fleet Street, EC (POD,1862-64), after
which he continued as Henry Vizetelly, 15 and 16
Gough Square, EC (POD,1865). The following year,
while in Paris, he secured numerous drawings on
wood from a variety of French draughtsmen for
publication in the Illustrated London News. Henry
Vizetelly lived in Paris until 1872, then moved to
Berlin before returning to London. There he worked
on translations of Russian and French novels and
wrote classic books on wine, published from
Henrietta Street, Covent Garden. He was imprisoned
(for publishing Zola's novels) in 1889, but survived
the ordeal despite his sixty-nine years and poor
health. He published his autobiography, Glances
Back, 1893, a year before his death at Heatherlands,
Farnham, on 1 January 1894, aged seventy-three.
Vizetelly's reputation as a wood engraver was overshadowed by his publishing and journalistic ventures.
Bohn in Chatto and Jackson claimed (1860) that he
'has been so indefatigable for the last twenty years
in producing illustrated works in every department,
that examples of his wood engraving are extensively
distributed. He is besides a printer, well skilled in
bringing up wood-cuts, which is a most delicate and
artistic process.' His colleague, the engraver Edmund
Evans (q.v.) eulogised him in the 1890s, as 'a very
clever fellow...poor fellow, he died very poor
indeed, in a village near here...his was a most
eventful life (Evans MSS, UCLA). The British
Museum owns engravings after B.Foster, J.Gilbert,
J.D.Harding, R.Redgrave, J.Millais, and a trade
card for 'Puck'--132 Fleet Street. He signed his
engravings: 'H VIZETELLY SC'.
[For a discussion of Vizetelly's colour printing see
Wakeman and Bridson; McLean; C.T.Lewis; for
biographical detail see Vizetelly's, Glances Back;
DNB; British Library catalogue]

VIZETELLY, James 1817-97
Wood engraver and printer, the son of the printer-
engraver James Henry Vizetelly (q.v.). He set up as
printer-engraver 'while not yet of age' with his brother
Henry (q.v.) as the Vizetelly Brothers, c1841-49, and
helped to engrave and print numerous book illustrations
for John Murray and other major publishers. He was
a friend of the engraver W.J.Linton (q.v.).
[Vizetelly, Glances Back; McLean]

VIZETELLY, James Henry 1790-1838
Printer-engraver, member of the Stationers' Hall. He
formed a partnership with Robert Edward Branston
(q.v.) as Vizetelly and Branston, 135 (later 76)
Fleet Street. He trained G.W.Bonner and W.H.Wills
(qq.v.). His sons, Henry and James Vizetelly
(qq.v.) took over the firm about 1841, changing its
name to Vizetelly Brothers, and engraved some of
the work for John Murray originally commissioned
for Vizetelly and Branston.
[see also Vizetelly, Glances Back]

VIZETELLY and Branston
(see Vizetelly, James Henry; also Branston, Robert
Edward)

VIZETELLY and Loudan
(see Vizetelly, Henry)

VOYEZ, C.
Draughtsman on wood, who contributed designs to
Shirley Hibberd's Rustic Adornments for Homes of
Taste and Recreations for Town-folk in the Study
and Imitation of Nature,1856. These were wood
engraved by Benjamin Fawcett (q.v.). C.T.Courtney
Lewis claimed Voyez was 'no doubt a Frenchman'.
[see also Reverend M.Morris, B.Fawcett,1925,
p.37; C.T.Lewis]

W., H.
Wood engraver, who engraved a portrait of George
Cruikshank (q.v.) after an anonymous artist for the
London Journal,1847. The work is in the British
Museum.
[Hake]

W., W.
Wood engraver, who engraved a three-quarter length
portrait of the actor, W.G.Ross as 'Mr Johnson',
after an unattributed artist. The work is in the
British Museum.
[Hake]

WADDY, Frederick fl.1878-97
Ornamental draughtsman and illustrator for wood
engravings. He drew initial letters which were wood
engraved in the Illustrated London News,1883-84,
and also exhibited pencil drawings in London from
1878. He later illustrated with A.Forrestier (q.v.)
for Walter Besant's For Faith and Freedom,1897.

WADE, Henry fl.1885-88
London wood engraver, who worked at 5 Arundel
Street, Strand, WC (POD,1885-88).

WADSWORTH, Edward Alexander 1889-1949
Wood and copper engraver, tempera painter of
nautical, landscape and still life subjects. He was

born in Cleckheaton, Yorkshire on 29 October 1889, studied art in Munich at the Knirr School,1906, and returned to England to study at the Bradford School of Art,1907, and at the Slade,1908-12. He exhibited at Roger Fry's Second Post-Impressionist Exhibition, 1912, and joined Wyndham Lewis and the Vorticists. His woodcuts were first exhibited at the Society of Wood Engravers,1920. He died in London on 21 June 1949.
[Garrett; Waters]

WAGNER
(see Andrew and Wagner)

WAIBLER, F.
German draughtsman illustrator. He contributed a drawing wood engraved in the Illustrated London News,1872, according to Houfe.

WAIN, Louis William 1860-1939
Animal caricaturist and illustrator, whose early works were wood engraved. He was born in London on 5 August 1860, and educated at the West London School of Art,1877-80, later serving as assistant master there. He began his career as an illustrator by drawing for wood engravings in the Illustrated Sporting and Dramatic News in 1882 and the following year for the Illustrated London News,1883-99. He began at this period to specialise in drawings of cats and was known to have spent eleven days drawing one picture of 150 cats. In 1884 he drew for wood engravings in the English Illustrated Magazine, 1884-1900, notably to Mowbray Morris's 'Eton', 1884, wood engraved by R.Paterson, A. and W.Dawson, W.M.R.Quick and H.F.Davey (qq.v.); 'Dogs of the Chase', 1885, wood engraved by O.Jahyer, O.Lacour, H.S.Percy and E.Schladitz (qq.v.); and 'Cats and Kittens', 1889, engraved by O.Jahyer, H.F.Davey and Waterlow and Sons (qq.v.). Wain continued to illustrate throughout the nineties and into the 1900s, worked in America on the staff of the New York American, and illustrated short stories, gift books, postcards. He also exhibited work at the Royal Society of British Artists. He died in poverty, on 4 July 1939, after having slowly turned insane.
[For a list of work see Houfe; also R.Dale, Louis Wain,1968; Idler,8,pp.550-55]

WAKE, Richard 1865-88
Amateur 'Special Artist', born on 24 September, 1865. He was appointed 'Special Artist' to The Graphic at Suakim in 1888, and made a few drawings wood engraved in the paper before his death there on 6 December 1888.

WAKEFIELD, T. or J. fl.1840s-60s
Wood engraver, who engraved with J.Bastin (q.v.) the drawings on wood of Edward Corbould (q.v.). These appeared in S.C.Hall's Book of British Ballads,

1842. The British Museum attributes to J.Wakefield two small cuts after G.F.Sargent, engraved in a fine, black-line style; one is a student with a wheelbarrow, the other a crowd scene. They are signed: 'J WAKEFIELD SC' and dated 1860.

WAKEMAN, William Frederick 1822-1900
Draughtsman illustrator of landscapes and topographical subjects. He was born in Dublin in 1822, and worked for the Ordnance Survey, and later as drawing master in Dublin, at St Columba's College, Stackallan, and the Royal School, Portora. He illustrated the works of his friend G.Petrie, such as Ecclesiastical Antiquities; and various Irish subjects in S.C.Hall's Ireland, Its Scenery and Character; Wilde's Catalogue of Antiquities in the Royal Irish Academy; and O'Hanlon's Lives of the Irish Saints. He also drew for the Irish Penny Journal; Dublin Saturday Magazine; and Hibernian Magazine. He exhibited work at the Royal Hibernian Academy, and died in Coleraine in 1900. The British Museum owns a series of proof wood engravings after his designs, engraved by the Dalziel Brothers (q.v.) in 1863.

WALKER, D. fl.1862
The British Museum owns a series of wood engraved proofs after designs by this artist. They were engraved by the Dalziel Brothers (q.v.) in 1862.

WALKER, E.J. fl.1878-86
Occasional illustrator, painter of domestic subjects. He worked in Liverpool,1878-79, then moved to Regents Park, London. He is listed here for his wood engraved Christmas illustration to the Illustrated London News,1886.
[Houfe]

WALKER, Francis S. 1848-1916
Draughtsman on wood, mezzotint engraver, etcher, genre and landscape painter. He was born in County Meath, Ireland in 1848, and studied art at the Royal Dublin Society and the Royal Hibernian Academy Schools where he received a scholarship to study in London. He arrived there in 1868, during the height of the 'Sixties School' illustration boom, and was taken up by the engravers, the Dalziel Brothers (q.v.), who employed him to draw on wood. They engraved his drawings to Cassell's Family Magazine,1868; Good Words,1869; Sunday Magazine,1869; Good Words for the Young,1869-72; Nobility of Life,1869; London Society,1870; and later for their own Bible Gallery,1880; and secured drawings for their comic publication Fun. Walker was successful enough as a draughtsman on wood to be taken up by The Graphic,1870, during its early stage of development and drew scenes of the Franco-Prussian War for them. He also drew for the Illustrated London News,1875. Some of these

drawings were wood engraved and colour printed. He took up etching and mezzotint engraving and exhibited this work at the Royal Academy. He also painted for the galleries and exhibited at the Royal Institute of Painters in Oil-Colours and the Royal Hibernian Academy. He was elected ARHA in 1878 and RHA in 1879, also member of the Royal Society of Painter-Etchers and Engravers in 1897. He worked primarily in North London where he died in Mill Hill on 17 April 1916.
[see Volume I for bibliography and list of his metal engravings: also Houfe; Wood]

WALKER, Frederick 1840-75
Draughtsman illustrator on wood, painter of land-scapes and rural subjects. He was born in Marylebone on 24 May 1840, studied at the British Museum, and then was apprenticed to an architect, whom he left to return to the museum. There he concentrated on drawings of Greek sculpture and took life classes at Leigh's to improve his figure drawing. He was eventually admitted to the Royal Academy Schools on the strength of his museum drawings but wished to train as an illustrator for wood engravings and sought the advice of the Dalziel Brothers (q.v.) who then commissioned drawings on wood. The Dalziels advised him to copy engravings from the Illustrated London News in pen and ink, especially the drawings of J.Gilbert (q.v.) and their protégé Birket Foster (q.v.). He also showed specimen drawings to the illustrator Daniel Maclise (q.v.). By 1858 he was apprenticed to the wood engraver J.W.Whymper (q.v.) who took in assistants to draw on wood. He shared his apprenticeship with J.W.North and Charles Green (qq.v.). Here Walker worked three days a week for two years. During this time the Dalziels gave him drawing commissions for various boys' books published by Routledge, also for Dickens' Hard Times, and Reprinted Pieces,1861. Walker was firmly established as a draughtsman on wood when he took drawings to the editor of Once a Week, where his second published drawing appeared, 18 February 1860 and he continued to contribute until 1866. This followed his earliest published drawing, in Everybody's Journal, 14 January 1860. His drawings for wood engraving appeared throughout the 1860s: in Leisure Hour,1860; Tom Cringle's Log,1861; Twins and Their Stepmother,1861; Good Words, 1861-64, engraved by the Dalziels; the Cornhill, 1861-69; London Society,1862; Willmott's Sacred Poetry,1862; Cornhill Gallery,1864; English Sacred Poetry,1864; Punch,1865, 1869; A Round of Days, 1866, engraved by the Dalziels; Barham's Ingoldsby Legends,1866; Touches of Nature by Eminent Artists, 1866; Wayside Poesies,1867, engraved by the Dalziels; Story of Elizabeth,1867; Village on the Cliff,1867; The Graphic,1869; Daughter of Heth,1872; and Thornbury's Legendary Ballads,1876. Walker's connection with the Cornhill gives some indication

of his early struggles to establish himself. He called twice at the office, the first time being dismissed as too young to be serious in the eyes of a clerk. But the second time he was eventually given the chance to re-draw Thackeray's (q.v.) illustrations on wood to Adventures of Phillip. Walker passed his test with the novelist and was given the commission, but gradually he grew dissatisfied with re-drawing rather than inventing his own designs. He drew for Thackeray's daughter's stories in the magazine as well. (For a full discussion, see Reid,pp.138-45). Walker's draughtsman methods involved, according to the Dalziels, 'the mixture of pencil, paint work, in some instances ink and wash; the delicate colour of the wood, and the skilful use of body colour'. Although the Dalziels engraved a considerable number of Walker's wood blocks, Joseph Swain (q.v.) engraved the greater part of his work. Their relationship, through correspondence and exchange of blocks was instrumental in moulding Walker's innovative technical ability on the block. According to Swain, Walker was one of the first draughtsmen to introduce brushwork into his drawings, 'using the spreading of the brush to give texture, and also producing the same effect by the peculiarity of his lines. He was exceedingly particular as to the way in which his blocks were cut.' Indeed Walker's letters to Swain were full of minute corrections to the engraved proofs. For instance, of a girl's face engraved in 1869 he re-drew a detail and noted '...I think rather too definite as to her frown, so I think that the little line between the eyebrows might be almost taken away or dotted as I have served it here'. Swain concluded that Walker was never satisfied with what he called 'the beastliness of wood drawing. The cutting of the blocks was a source of constant anxiety, notwithstanding the care that was always given to his work; and it was with a certain flutter of excitement in the home circle that the proofs were generally received.' Although Walker was often linked with George Pinwell (q.v.) as a draughtsman of rural subjects, his own technique varied considerably. Mostly he used heavy black out-lines to create effective contrast with wide areas of white, unlike Pinwell's overall grey effects upon the block. He built up his drawings slowly and carefully upon the block. Walker's paintings were exhibited at the Old Watercolour Society, where he was elected AOWS in 1864 and OWS in 1866; also at the Royal Academy, being elected ARA in 1871. He travelled extensively on the Continent but failing health sent him to Algiers in 1873-74 and he returned and died in St Fillan's, Perthshire on 5 June 1875. A collection of Walker's wood block drawings and proofs are in the Hartley Collection, Boston Museum; and the British Museum owns a number of Dalziel proof engravings after his designs.
[For an account of Walker's career see DNB; J.Comyns Carr, Frederick Walker,1855; C.Phillips,

The Portfolio, June 1894; J.G.Marks, Life and Letters of Frederick Walker, 1896; also Reid; White; Redgrave; Hind; Dalziels' Record; Houfe]

WALKER, J. and J. fl.1832-40
London wood engravers, who worked at 3 Finsbury Market, East Side (Robson, 1832), then 65 High Street, Hoxton Old Town (POD, 1840).

WALKER, Marcella M. fl.1872-1917
Occasional illustrator for wood engravings, painter of flowers. She worked at Haverstock Hill and is listed here for wood engraved drawings to the Illustrated London News, 1885-94, 1903; also the Girl's Own Paper. She also exhibited at the Royal Academy and the Royal Hibernian Academy.

WALKER, Vernon Henry fl.1880s
London draughtsman on wood, who worked at the prominent engraving workshop, 4 Bouverie Street, EC (Kelly's, 1889). He shared the premises with the engravers A.J.Appleton, F.Wentworth and W.L.Webb (qq.v.).

WALKER, William Chester fl.1826-48
London wood engraver, who worked at 15 (later 10) Guildford Place, Spitalfields (Pigot, 1826-38). The following year he joined in partnership as Walker and Knight, working from their 10 Guildford Place premises (Pigot, POD, 1839-48).

WALKER and Boutall fl.1888-97
Wood engravers and block makers. They engraved with H.F.Davey (q.v.) the illustrations by Harper Pennington to Oscar Wilde's story, 'London Models'. This was published in the English Illustrated Magazine, 1888. They also prepared the wood blocks for a map drawn by H.Cribb for William Morris's The Sundering Flood, 1897, published by the Kelmscott Press and overseen by May Morris.

WALKER and Brown fl.1880-1900
Provincial wood engraving firm, with offices at 99 and 100 High Street, Hull (Kelly's, 1880-1900).

WALKER and Knight
(see Walker, William Chester)

WALL, G.H.
The British Museum owns a wood engraving of a marine battle, attributed to G.H.Wall. It is a rather crude, heavy-handed work engraved in the black-line style reminiscent of a mid nineteenth century trade engraver. He signed his work: 'G H WALL'.

WALL, James Charles fl.1884-1901
London wood engraver, who worked in partnership as Collins and Wall (q.v.) until 1885, then as Ford and Wall. He set up on his own from 1891, working

at 31 Paternoster Square, EC (POD, 1891-95), then 4 Paternoster Buildings (POD, 1896-1901).

WALL, John Peter fl.1854-68
London wood engraver, who worked at 154 Strand (POD, 1854-56). He then moved into the workshop of the noted wood engraver J.D.Cooper (q.v.) at 188 Strand (POD, 1861-68).

WALLACE, Robert Bruce ?-1893
Draughtsman illustrator and figure artist in watercolour, who lived and worked in Manchester. He began drawing for wood engraved initials and comic inserts in the style of C.H.Bennett and Linley Sambourne. These appeared in Punch from 1875-78, then occasionally until his death in 1893, with one posthumously in 1894. He had been introduced to the paper by the wood engraver Joseph Swain (q.v.) who engraved these early drawings on wood and presumably was encouraged enough to become what Spielmann called 'a very prolific contributor'. He hoped to succeed the hunting artist Georgina Bowers (q.v.) on the Punch staff, but when this failed to occur, after he had prepared himself by a move to Worcestershire for landscape and horse and hound sketching, Wallace was annoyed and refused to continue his steady stream of initial letters on wood. He concentrated on illustrations elsewhere: to an edition of Thackeray's Adventures of Phillip; to Thackeray's Catherine, 1894 (cheap edition); and a drawing to the Illustrated London News, 1898. He served as Secretary to the Manchester Academy of Fine Arts and was a friend of fellow artists Frederic Shields and Ford Madox Brown (qq.v.) whom he helped to paint a series of Manchester frescoes. He also exhibited work at the Royal Society of British Artists and in his native Manchester, where he died in 1893. [Houfe; Spielmann]

WALLER, Samuel Edmund 1850-1903
Occasional draughtsman illustrator for wood engravings, genre and animal painter of English country life. He was born in Gloucester in June 1850, the son of an architect with whom he trained. He also attended the local Gloucester School of Art, studied with John Kemp there, and then went to London where he was admitted to the Royal Academy Schools in 1869, exhibiting his first picture there in 1871. He began drawing for wood engravings about this time and was admitted to the staff of The Graphic in 1873, contributing numerous illustrations for the paper's highly proficient wood engravers from 1874-81. He also contributed later to the Illustrated London News, 1895; and Sporting and Dramatic News, 1899. His brief venture into book illustration resulted in drawings to William Black's Strange Adventures of a Phaeton, 1874; and his own written and illustrated account of a visit to Ireland in 1872, Six Weeks in the Saddle; also the book Sebastian's Secret.

Especially proficient at horse drawings, he exhibited his country scenes at the Fine Art Society, the Royal Academy and the Royal Institute of Painters in Oil-Colours where he was elected member in 1883. He died in Haverstock Hill on 9 June 1903.
[DNB; Art Journal,1903; Houfe]

WALLIS, E.J.
Wood engraving apprentice to the Dalziel Brothers (q.v.). He may be related to the Wallis family of metal engravers, Robert, William and Charles (see Volume I). The Dalziels noted that by 1901 E.J.Wallis had become a proficient landscape photographer.
[Dalziels' Record]

WALLIS, Henry 1830-1916
Occasional draughtsman illustrator, painter of landscapes and historical subjects and writer. He was born in London on 21 February 1830 and studied at Cary's Academy, in Paris, and at the Royal Academy Schools. He is most famous for his painting 'The Death of Chatterton', 1856, but he did draw for a few wood engravings. The British Museum owns a proof engraving by the Dalziel Brothers (q.v.), engraved in 1863 from his design. He later illustrated his own books on ceramics. He was elected RWS,1880, and died in Sutton, Surrey in December 1916.

WALMSLEY, John fl.1839-78
London wood engraver, according to Nagler also a draughtsman, painter in oils. He appeared in the London directories as wood engraver at Aldine Chambers, Paternoster Row (Pigot,1839, POD,1841), then moved to 3 North Place, Gray's Inn Road (POD,1847), 2 Walbrook Buildings, EC (POD,1858-61), apparently also working at 6 Melbourne Square, North Brixton (LSDS,1860). By 1862 he had moved to the premises, 17 Devonshire Square, NE (POD,1862-74) which he shared briefly with the wood engraver A.Berry (q.v.). He finally moved, as Walmsley and Son, to 54 Paternoster Row and 8 Frith Street, Soho (POD,1875-78). Walmsley's wood engraving commissions included S.H.Hall's Book of British Ballads,1842, after drawings by J.Franklin, H.J.Townsend, E.M.Ward (qq.v.) in collaboration with fellow engravers J.Bastin and T.Wakefield (qq.v.). He also engraved for the Illustrated London News,1842-60, mostly small vignettes after H.G.Hine (q.v.), 16 and 23 July 1842; also a half-page cover engraving, 'Choir of Litchfield Cathedral', after Drayton Wyatt, 12 May 1860. He signed his work: 'W J[superimposed]ALMSLEY Sc'.
[Nagler; British Library catalogue]

WALTERS, Thomas fl.1856-75
Draughtsman illustrator, painter of domestic subjects. He drew on wood for Punch,1867-75, and worked in London, where he also exhibited at the British Institution, the Royal Academy and the Royal Society of British Artists.
[Spielmann; Houfe]

WALTGES, F.S.
Draughtsman illustrator, who drew one illustration which was wood engraved by the Dalziel Brothers (q.v.) for their Bible Gallery, but was apparently not used. It was eventually published in a subsequent compilation, Art Pictures from the Old Testament, 1897, published by SPCK. White lists this artist as 'Waltges' (sic).

WALTON, T.
Draughtsman illustrator, who contributed a drawing wood engraved in the Illustrated London News,1860.

WARBURTON, Joseph fl.1850s
London wood engraver, who worked at 119 High Holborn (POD,1852).

WARD, Arthur Thomas fl.1880s
Provincial wood engraver, who worked at 122 High Street, Hull (Kelly's,1889).

WARD, Sir Leslie Matthew ('Spy') 1851-1922
Caricaturist for wood engraving and lithography, portrait painter. He was born in London on 21 November 1851, the son of a painter of historical subjects, E.M.Ward, and grandson of the engravers George Raphael Ward and James Ward. He was educated at Eton, studied architecture with Sydney Smirke, and studied at the Royal Academy Schools from 1871. He was taken up by J.Millais (q.v.), who admired his caricatures, and eventually introduced him to the editor of Vanity Fair, then in need of a new cartoonist. It is for Ward's thirty-six year stint drawing for colour lithographic plates in Vanity Fair that he is most remembered, first as understudy then as successor to Carlo Pellegrini, 1873-1909. But he also at this early period drew caricatures for wood engravings in The Graphic from 1874, and contributed drawings on wood to Cassell's Family Magazine. He was elected member of the Royal Society of Portrait Painters,1891, knighted in 1918 and died in London on 15 May 1922.
[DNB; Houfe; R.T.Matthews, In Vanity Fair,1982]

WARREN, Albert H. fl.1860-65
Ornamental draughtsman on wood, whose drawings were generally wood engraved by Edmund Evans (q.v.). These included ornamental headings to A Book of Favourite Modern Ballads,1860, described by McLean as 'the third of Evans's early colour printing masterpieces' and especially noteworthy for Warren's double title-page surrounding two pictures by Birket Foster (q.v.). They make 'one of the most charming openings in mid-Victorian book production'. The book was reissued c1865. Warren also designed

a cloth binding to Thomas Miller's Common Wayside Flowers, 1860.
[McLean, Victorian Book Design; Evans Reminiscences]

WARREN, George C. fl.1891-1901
London wood engraver, who worked at 11 Milford Lane, Strand, WC (POD, 1891-1901).

WARREN, Henry 1794-1879
Occasional draughtsman on wood, landscape and genre painter. He was born in London on 24 September 1794 and studied under Joseph Nollekens, the sculptor, and at the Royal Academy Schools in 1818. He abandoned his early oil paintings for watercolour and was elected member of the New Watercolour Society in 1835, and President from 1839-73. He published several manuals on watercolour, drawing and anatomy. He is listed here as a 'painter who occasionally drew on wood', noted by Bohn in Chatto and Jackson for his figure and architectural subjects. These appeared wood engraved as a title-page to Lockhart's Ancient Spanish Ballads, 1842; illustrations in S.C.Hall's Book of British Ballads, 1842; Book of Common Prayer, 1845, ('charming woodcut illustrations with J.C.Horsley', McLean); an illustration to the Illustrated London News, 1848; a cover design wood engraved by W.Dickes (q.v.) to Simms and McIntyre's Parlour Library, 1847-62; in Lays of the Holy Land, 1858; Welcome Guest, 1860; A Winter's Tale; Wordsworth's Pastoral Poems; Moore's Paradise and the Peri; and Children's Picture Book of Scripture Parables, 1861. Warren was also a lithographer and musician. He exhibited work at the British Institution, the New Watercolour Society, the Royal Academy and the Royal Society of British Artists. He died in London in 1879. The British Museum owns several proof engravings by the Dalziel Brothers (q.v.) engraved 1847, 1852, 1857.
[Chatto; Nagler; McLean, Victorian Book Design; Houfe]

WARRY, Daniel Robert fl.1855-1913
Occasional draughtsman illustrator and architect. He worked in Lewisham and Eltham. He specialised in architectural and antiquarian drawings which were wood engraved in The Graphic, 1881-82, 1884. He also exhibited at the Royal Academy.

WASGOTT, E.
Wood engraver, who engraved 'The Confession of Love', after F.A.Delobbe, in the English Illustrated Magazine, 1885. It was a flat, rather grey engraving of a woman, her suitor and a dog.

WATERHOUSE, Annie fl.1850s
Wood engraving instructor at South Kensington from 1853-59. She worked there with the noted engraver J.Thompson (q.v.) until it was discovered by the authorities that their students could not secure work after training, and the engraving course was closed

down (see HMSO Report of the Departmental Committee on the Royal College of Art, 1911).

WATERLOW and Sons fl.1883-99
Prominent wood engraving firm, process block supplier, collotype printer. The firm was started by George S.Waterlow, manager, Paul Waterlow and J.G.Geddes about 1883 and exhibited work at the International Exhibition in 1885. Their first engravings appeared in the English Illustrated Magazine, 1884-90, using process and facsimile techniques to reproduce with great clarity the ink drawings of Walter Crane, Hugh Thomson, Heywood Sumner (qq.v.) and Reginald Blomfield. They later appeared in the directories as the 'wood engravers', Waterlow and Sons Ltd, 73 Temple Row, Birmingham (Kelly's, 1889-1900).
[For colour work see Wakeman and Bridson]

WATKINS, Frank fl.1859-94
Architectural draughtsman illustrator on wood, who began drawing for wood engravings in the Illustrated London News, 1859, 1875, then contributed continuously, 1884-94. He worked in Feltham, 1875-76 and Maida Hill, London in 1890. He also exhibited at the Royal Hibernian Academy.

WATKINS, Frederick fl.1858-81
London draughtsman on wood and wood engraver. He worked at 7 Frederick Place, Old Kent Road, SE (POD, 1858) then joined in partnership with H.C.Mason (q.v.) as Mason and Watkins (q.v.) until 1863. He then set up on his own at 9 Essex Street, Strand (POD, 1863-74), a popular office shared by engravers like J.Bye, T.Reynolds, J.Desbois, H.C.Mason and briefly for John Dalziel, Junior, and W.Kelly (qq.v.). He moved to 227 Strand (POD, 1875-81), shared with T.Hobbs and E.Rooker (qq.v.).

WATKINS, John fl.1857-75
London wood engraver, who worked at 14 Albert Street, Pentonville (POD, 1857), then at the workshop of C.M.Gorway (q.v.) at 8 Dane's Inn, St Clement's, WC (POD, 1858-62). He worked here with the engravers P.Simon, J.M.Rimbault and E.T.Hartshorn (qq.v.). He then worked in the suburbs, at Lothian Road, Camberwell New Road, S (LSDS, 1865). By 1873 he was working at 5 Arundel Street, Strand, WC (POD, 1873). His engravings were commissioned for the Illustrated London News, for which he specialised in large intricate detailed architectural views such as three views of 'The Freemasons Benevolent Institutions', 24 April 1875. He was a fairly competent engraver of clear tradesman-like work.

WATKINSON, Henry and Company fl.1876-1900
Provincial wood engraving and draughtsman firm, with an office at 2 Essex Street, King Street, Manchester (Kelly's, 1876-80), then 34 John Dalton

Street (Kelly's,1889-1900). 'Henry Watkinson, AMA', engraved Randolph Caldecott's Pictures,1888, for the Brasenose Club, Manchester. Caldecott's posthumous loan exhibited catalogue. He signed his work: 'H WATKINSON Sc', 'H.W.Sc'.

WATMOUGH, William C.
Wood engraver, nephew of Orlando Jewitt (q.v.) with whom he was apprenticed to learn wood engraving. He was the son (or stepson) of Jewitt's sister, Marianne. In 1851 he lived in Headington, near Oxford, with his grandfather Arthur Jewitt, and described himself as an 'engraver's apprentice'. (see The Library,1964,p.326).

WATSON, John Dawson 1832-92
Occasional draughtsman on wood, prominent illustrator and painter of figure subjects. He was born in Sedbergh, Yorkshire on 20 May 1832, left for the Manchester School of Art in 1847, aged fifteen and then went to London. There he was admitted to the Royal Academy Schools in 1851 and studied under A.D.Cooper, but returned to Manchester the following year where he exhibited at the Manchester Royal Institution from 1851. He returned to London in 1860, where he successfully established a reputation as a draughtsman for wood engravings, in numerous 'Sixties School' magazines and books. The Dalziel Brothers (q.v.) apparently commissioned Watson to make drawings for a series of nursery tales, and when their collaborator, the publisher George Routledge asked the Dalziels for a 'new man' to illustrate a new edition of Pilgrim's Progress, the commission of a hundred designs was given to Watson, and published in 1861. Then followed 110 drawings on wood to Eliza Cook's Poems,1861. Both books were praised by Bohn in Chatto and Jackson. Other books completely illustrated by Watson included Dr Norman Macleod's Golden Thread,1861; Bennetts Poems,1862; Golden Harp,1864; Robinson Crusoe,1864, again commissioned (as a companion volume to Pilgrim's Progress) and engraved by the Dalziels; Old Friends and New,1867; Wild Cat Tower,1877; and Princess Althea,1883. Watson contributed drawings to numerous magazines and books as well; many drawn on wood for the Dalziels to engrave. They include Once a Week, 1861; Good Words,1861-63; Illustrated London News, 1861,1872; London Society,1862-67; Willmott's Sacred Poetry,1862; Churchman's Family Magazine, 1863; British Workman,1863; The Arabian Nights' Entertainments,1863; English Sacred Poetry of the Olden Time,1864; Our Life Illustrated by Pen and Pencil,1865; Shilling Magazine,1865; A Round of Days, 1866; Legends and Lyrics,1866; Ellen Montgomery's Bookshelf,1866; Ballad Stories of the Affections, 1866; Foxe's Book of Martyrs,1866; Sunday Magazine, 1867; Touches of Nature,1867; Savage Club Papers, 1867; Illustrated Book of Sacred Poems,1867; Cassell's Illustrated Readings,1867; Cassell's

Magazine,1868-69; Tinsley's Magazine,1868-69; Nobility of Life,1869; Pictures from English Literature,1870; The Graphic,1870-77; Leslie's Musical Annual,1870; Quiver,1873; People's Magazine,1873; and Thornbury's Legendary Ballads, 1876. Watson's best illustration work was done before 1865, after which he experimented with oil painting and watercolours and occasionally etchings. He exhibited 372 works at the London galleries between 1859-92, following his election as associate to the Old Watercolour Society in 1864, and full member in 1869, and as member of the Royal Society of British Artists in 1882. Other venues he exhibited at were the British Institution, the Grosvenor Gallery, the Royal Academy and the Royal Cambrian Academy. The Dalziel Brothers were among his patrons, as Watson once remarked: 'I believe if I were to spit upon a piece of paper and smear it over with my hand they would declare it beautiful, and have a scramble who was to buy it'. He died in Conway, North Wales on 3 January 1892. The British Museum owns a large collection of Dalziel proofs,1860-63; also a small cut of two trees expertly engraved and inscribed: 'J Greenaway Watson sc 1840 to 1850'; and a small house engraving inscribed: 'Watson sc after Sheeres ? 1850-60'. [For a discussion of his illustrations see Reid; White; see also Houfe; Chatto; Dalziels' Record; for a discussion and list of Watson's etchings see Volume I]

WATSON, William fl.1880-1900
Scottish wood engraver, who worked at 3 East Register Street, Edinburgh (Kelly's,1880), 30 (21) St James 'Square, Edinburgh (Kelly's,1889-1900).

WATSON, William James fl.1872-83
London draughtsman on wood and wood engraver, who worked at East Temple Chambers, Whitefriars Street, EC (Kelly's, POD,1872-83). He shared his workshop with the engravers W.H.Say, A.Vickers, H.Sargent, R.Paterson, and W.R.Buckman (qq.v.). An advertisement in Kelly's directory claimed that Watson specialised in illustrations for books, periodicals, catalogues, original designs from manuscripts, ornamental headings and borders. Such work received praise from the Printing Journal, March 1875: 'Mr Watson's charges are reasonable and his work good'. The British Museum owns a good black-line vignette, 'The Holy Bible', after Cruik-shank (?) attributed to W.J.Watson.

WATSON and Scott fl.1884-87
London wood engraving firm, with offices at 40 and 41 Imperial Buildings, New Bridge Street, EC (POD,1884-87). This may be a partnership between William J.Watson and Andrew Scott (qq.v.).

WATT, T. fl.1850s
Draughtsman and ornamental illustrator, who
provided head and initial pieces to a Lumsden
edition of Pilgrim's Progress and the Holy War,
Illuminated, c1850.

WATTS, George fl.1820s
Wood engraver, who worked in London. He was
apprenticed to the prominent and influential wood
engraver Robert Branston (q.v.), but left for
Germany when Branston's workshop became too
crowded. He worked in Leipzig for a year, wood
engraved Cruikshank's drawings to Irish Tales;
seven cuts to Goethe's Hermann und Dorothea; and
many vignettes for numerous books, especially after
the drawings of Schwind.
[See Nagler for a list of German work]

WATTS, George Frederick 1817-1904
Prominent Victorian painter of historical subjects
and portraits, who occasionally drew on wood. He
was born in London in 1817, entered the Royal
Academy Schools, 1835, studied in Italy, and then
returned to London where he exhibited at the Royal
Academy, 1837-1904, the British Institution, the
Society of British Artists, the Grosvenor Gallery
and the New Gallery. He is listed here for his three
drawings on wood for the Dalziels' Bible Gallery,
1881. These were commissioned about 1863, when on
19 July 1863 Watts wrote apologies to the Dalziels
(q.v.) for the delay: 'The fact is I have not the habit
of making designs for wood cutting, and the subject
is not a good one...'. About two weeks later he
proposed, 'perhaps I had better send you back the
wood block'. By December he had completed the
work and defended himself against the Dalziels'
criticism of it: a drawing of Noah's head to show 'the
might and style of the inspired Patriarch' (Dalziels'
Record, p.244).
[For complete bibliography see Wood; also Volume I]

WATTS, Simon fl.1736-80
London wood engraver, who established a reputation
in the mid eighteenth century. He continued to
influence the early Bewick school of engravers for
which he is listed here. He also engraved on copper
and steel. He specialised in portrait engravings.
Two or three large wood cuts dated 1736, and some
small circular portraits of painters were known to
be his work; also a portrait of Queen Elizabeth, 1773
and one of Dudley, Earl of Leicester, 1775. His work
was being praised by 1839 in Chatto and Jackson.
He signed his work: 'SW'.
[Redgrave; Nagler; LeBlanc; Andresen; Chatto]

WEBB, Clifford Cyril 1895-1972
Wood engraver, lithographer and painter of landscapes and animals. He was born in London on
14 February 1895, was apprenticed to a London

lithographer, and spent his spare time during the
First World War painting. He studied art at the
Westminster School of Art under Walter Bayes in
1915-22. The same year he began wood engraving,
becoming proficient enough to exhibit engravings at
the Society of Wood Engravers, 1928, to which he
was elected member in 1935. He illustrated a
number of books and taught at Westminster School,
and St Martin's School of Art, 1945-65. He lived in
Surrey until his death on 29 July 1972.
[Garrett; Waters]

WEBB, Harry George 1882-1914
Wood engraver, etcher, landscape painter. He
specialised in architectural drawings and is listed
here for his wood engraving, 'The Palace of the
Popes', after a drawing by Frank Brangwyn
(reproduced in Art Chronicle, 1913). Gusman linked
his engraving skills with E.Kirkpatrick and M.Royds
(qq.v.) and praised his engraving style for its
originality and sense of 'daring freedom'.
[Gusman; Houfe]

WEBB, William H. fl.1850s
London wood engraver, who worked at 23 Bouverie
Street, Fleet Street, EC (POD, 1858).

WEBB, William J. fl.1853-82
Draughtsman illustrator, animal and genre painter.
He studied in Düsseldorf, then worked in Niton, Isle
of Wight, 1855-60, London 1861-64, and Manchester,
1882. He drew on wood for engravings of topography
and travel scenes for the Illustrated London News,
1872-76. These included a full-page, 'A Water-
Seller at Cairo', 12 September 1874, engraved by
J.Nugent (q.v.); a cover drawing, 'The War (Servia):
Scene in a London Drawing Room', 7 October 1876,
engraved by 'F.S.W.'. He later illustrated a cheap
edition of the Great Hoggarty Diamond, 1894. He
also exhibited at the Royal Academy, the Royal
Society of British Artists and British Institution.

WEBBE, William Chitty fl.1880s
London wood engraver, who worked at 2 Gough
Square, EC (POD, 1884).

WEBBE, William Linton fl.1875-91
London wood engraver, who worked at 10 Red Lion
Court (POD, 1875), then 8 Red Lion Court, Fleet
Street, EC (POD, 1880), shared with H.Evans (q.v.).
He later shared the workshop of the prominent wood
engravers F.Wentworth and A.J.Appleton (qq.v.)
at 4 Bouverie Street, EC (POD, 1888-91).

WEBBER fl.1840s
Draughtsman on wood, who contributed illustrations
for wood engravings in Charles Knight's Penny
Magazine, July 1842. These were wood engraved by
S.Sly (q.v.). Houfe lists a 'H.Webber', who

exhibited scriptural subjects at the British Institution in 1830.
[Bodleian Library; Houfe]

WEBSTER, Thomas 1800-86
Occasional draughtsman on wood, genre painter. He was born in London on 20 March 1800, entered the Royal Academy Schools in 1821, and established a reputation for paintings of children. He exhibited at the Royal Academy, the British Institution and the Royal Society of British Artists. He occasionally drew for wood engravings of children, notably in S.C.Hall's Book of British Ballads,1842; and Favourite English Poems,1859. Both were cited by Bohn in Chatto and Jackson. He also etched illustrations for the Etching Club. He was elected ARA in 1840, and RA in 1846. He died in Cranbrook on 23 September 1886. The British Museum owns a Dalziel (q.v.) proof of his design, engraved in 1855.
[Chatto; Houfe]

WEEDON, E. fl.1848-72
Draughtsman illustrator for wood engravings of marine subjects, also painter. He was the chief marine illustrator for the Illustrated London News, 1848-72, where he drew for wood engravings, mainly elaborately detailed ship portraits. His work was wood engraved by W.J.Linton (q.v.), notably seascapes, ship's rigging and construction illustrations in W.H.G.Kingston's Boy's Own Book of Boats,1861. He exhibited once, at the Royal Academy in 1850. Fincham lists an armorial book-plate engraved by 'E.Weedon sc. Pimlico', dated 1820, which may be an early work.

WEEDON, J.F. fl.1888-95
Draughtsman on wood, who worked in London at 86-87 Fleet Street, EC (Kelly's,1889). His drawings appeared wood engraved in The Graphic,1888, and Church Monthly,1895. He specialised in sporting subjects.

WEEKES, William fl.1856-1909
Occasional illustrator, animal and genre painter. He was the son of the sculptor, Henry Weekes (1807-77) and lived at Primrose Hill, London. He had a drawing wood engraved in the Illustrated London News,1883. He also exhibited work from 1865-1904 at the Fine Art Society, the Grosvenor Gallery, the Royal Academy, the Royal Society of British Artists and the Royal Institute of Painters in Oil-Colours.

WEGUELIN, John Reinhard 1849-1927
Prolific draughtsman illustrator and painter. He was born in South Stoke, Sussex on 23 June 1849, became a Lloyd's underwriter,1870-73, then entered the London Slade School, under Poynter and Legros. He illustrated for wood engravings in The Graphic,

1888-1906, for which he is listed here, and also drew for books: Macaulay's Lays of Ancient Rome, 1881; G.A.Henty's Cat of Bubastes,1889; and various others. He exhibited at the Fine Art Society, the Grosvenor Gallery, the New Gallery, the Royal Academy, the Royal Society of British Artists, the Royal Hibernian Academy, the Royal Institute of Painters in Oil-Colours where he was elected member in 1888 and the Royal Watercolour Society where he was elected member in 1897. He worked in Sussex and died in Hastings on 28 April 1927.

WEHNERT, Edward Henry 1813-68
Prominent draughtsman on wood, painter of historical subjects. He was born in London in 1813, the son of a German tailor, educated at Göttingen, and worked in Paris and Jersey before coming back to London in 1837. There he established a reputation as a painter of historical subjects and prolific draughtsman illustrator on wood for books and magazines. His abilities led Bohn in Chatto and Jackson to describe him as 'essentially German' in his strong use of firm outline. His drawings on wood first appeared in books: Hutchinson's History of the British Nation, c1835; Grimm's Household Stories,1853; Poetical Works of E.A.Poe,1853; Bohn's edition of Longfellow's Poems,1854; Keats' Eve of St Agnes,1856; Coleridge's Ancient Mariner,1856-57, engraved on wood by H.Harral or Edmund Evans (qq.v.); Bunyan's Pilgrim's Progress,1858; thirty-four drawings in collaboration with Birket Foster, Cope and Creswick (qq.v.) to Favourite English Poems,1858; Grimm's Tales,1861; Hans Andersen's Fairy Tales,1861, for which electrotypes were produced by W.J.Linton (q.v.) from a new process; and Defoe's Robinson Crusoe,1862. Wehnert's drawings on wood for magazines appeared in Art Union Annual;1845; the Illustrated London News,1848-49; for the Art Union's The Traveller,1851; in Churchman's Family Magazine,1863; and Aunt Judy's Magazine. Wehnert exhibited work at the British Institution, the New Watercolour Society where he was elected member in 1837, at the Royal Society of British Artists and the Royal Academy. It was at the Royal Academy that he exhibited 'The Ivory Carver', a wood engraving after his drawing, by W.J.Linton,RA,1855. He died in Kentish Town on 15 September 1868. The British Museum owns a Dalziel proof collection,1839-52.
[McLean, Victorian Book Design; Chatto; Nagler; Graves]

WEIGALL, Charles Harvey (Henry) 1794-1877
Occasional draughtsman on wood, landscape and genre painter. He was born in 1794 and became a proficient draughtsman of animals and birds. He first drew for wood engravings in the Illustrated London News,1844-50; the Illustrated London Magazine,1853; and The Graphic,1873. He drew for the Juvenile Verse and Picture Book,1848. He also wrote various technical manuals on drawing. He

exhibited at the New Watercolour Society, to which he was elected member in 1834, and treasurer from 1839-41; also at the Royal Academy and the Royal Society of British Artists. He may have some connection with Griffiths and Weigall, a London heraldic stationers, which produced numerous bookplates for the famous, 3 St James' Street. The British Museum owns his designs engraved by the Dalziel Brothers (q.v.).

WEIR, Harrison William 1824-1906
Prolific draughtsman on wood and painter of animal subjects. He was born in Lewes, Sussex on 5 May 1824. and educated at Camberwell; then he withdrew to pursue his talent for drawing. He was apprenticed to the wood engraver and colour printer George Baxter (q.v.) for seven years. 'Baxter employed Weir in every branch of his business, his chief work being that of printing off the plates. Weir soon found his duties uncongenial, and he remained unwillingly to complete his engagement in 1844. While with Baxter he learnt to engrave and draw on wood' (DNB). He was employed while with Baxter to draw and engrave for the first number of the Illustrated London News, and remained a consistent contributor there, 1842-1900, being the longest serving artist on the paper. He was a prolific and dedicated draughtsman for wood engravings, most of which were engraved by John Greenaway, some by his partner W.Wright (qq.v.) as Greenaway and Wright. Following a turbulent argument, Weir left Baxter and first worked for the colour printers, Gregory, Collins and Reynolds, who opposed Baxter's bid to renew his colour printing licence. Later he collaborated with his fellow Baxter apprentice, George Cargill Leighton (q.v.) who had also left Baxter with a grievance. One of Weir's earliest published drawings on wood was the frontispiece and title-page to Peter Parley's Annual for 1846, engraved by Gregory, Collins and Reynolds. Weir's total output of drawings for wood engravings was considerable. He drew on wood for Mrs Loudon's Domestic Pets,1851; to Reverend J.G.Wood's Illustrated Natural History,1853; (some of his best animal drawings); Cat and Dog Memories of Puss and Captain,1854; Bloomfield's Farmer's Boy,1857-58, engraved by J.Greenaway; Poetry of Nature,1860, engraved by J.Greenaway; 300 drawings for Aesop's Fables,1867; J.Greenwood's Wild Sports of the World,1862; Mrs Trimmer's History of the Robins,1868; Animals and Birds,1868; and Tiny Natural Histories,1880. Weir also wrote and illustrated his own work: Every Day in the Country, 1883; Our Cats and All about Them,1889; and his classic exhaustive volume, Our Poultry and All about Them,1903. He also compiled and illustrated Animal Stories Old and New,1885; and Bird Stories Old and New. He drew for Edmund Evans (q.v.), notably cover designs to the Routledge and Warne 'Toy Books'. Weir contributed animal drawings on wood to

numerous magazines and books: Poetical Works of E.A.Poe,1853; Scott's Gertrude of Wyoming,1857; Cornwall's Dramatic Scenes,1857; Mackay's Home Affections,1858; Comus,1858; Favourite English Ballads,1859, engraved by J.Greenaway (q.v.); Montgomery's Poems,1860; Welcome Guest,1860; the Illustrated Times,1860; Sacred Poetry,1862; Parables from Nature,1867; Episodes of Fiction, 1870; British Workman; Band of Hope Review; Chatterbox,1880; Black and White; Field; Poultry and Stock Keeper; and 'Fowls' in the English Illustrated Magazine,1887, wood engraved by Waterlow and Sons and O.Lacour (qq.v.). Weir also exhibited numerous animal paintings at the British Institution and the New Watercolour Society, where he was elected associate in 1849 and member in 1851; also at the Royal Academy and the Royal Society of British Artists. He died at Poplar Hall, Appledore, Kent on 3 January 1906. The British Museum owns a series of proof engravings by the Dalziel Brothers (q.v.),1861-62.
[Chatto; Evans Reminiscences; Houfe (book list); C.T.Lewis; DNB]

WELCH, Alfred fl.1841-54
London wood engraver, who worked at 17 Brunswick Place, Barnsbury (POD,1848-51), then 19 Brunswick Street, Barnsbury Road (POD,1852-54). His engravings appeared in Charles Knight's publication, Penny Magazine,December 1841, after a drawing on wood by Masters (q.v.).
[Bodleian Library]

WELCH, Joseph
London wood engraver, who worked at 6 Francis Street, White Conduit Fields (Pigot,1836). Fincham lists a J.Welch, engraver and printer of Exeter, who produced two bookplates,1840, 1860. In addition Bénézit lists a T. (sic) Welch, London engraver of bookplates who worked from 1794-1820, who may be a relation.

WELCH, William James fl.1864-1900
London draughtsman on wood and wood engraver, who worked at 140 Strand, WC (POD,1864-65), then at his major office, 24 Wellington Street, Strand (POD,1866-95). By the following year he had appeared as 'direct photo engraver' in the directories at 2 Tavistock Street, Covent Garden, WC (POD,1896-1900). An early advertisement in the directories claimed that Welch was an 'artist and colour block engraver of every description', who specialised in pictorial, architectural and mechanical drawings on wood for books, catalogues and periodicals, 'illustrated either plain or in colours'. He won two medals in London and an honourable mention in Paris,1878, for such work.

WELLS (Charles)
Draughtsman on wood of topographical subjects,
which he made for Charles Knight's (q.v.) illustrated
publications. His work appeared in Knight's London,
1841; and in Knight's Penny Magazine, June, September,
October and November 1841, wood engraved by
G.P.Nicholls, F.J.Smyth, Roe, Minns, Leonard
and Sears, and Murdon (qq.v.). Wells may be related
to Charles Wells, a London cabinet maker, boxwood
importer and block manufacturer. From about 1860
(according to Spielmann) he was 'sole inventor and
manufacturer of the bolted and amalgamated block
for woodcuts of any dimensions'. He worked at
24 Bouverie Street (Hodgson's, 1855) and supplied
blocks to the Illustrated London News from its start,
also to Punch, the Art Journal, and 'all principal
illustrated periodicals'.
[Bodleian Library]

WELLS, Henry Gustavus fl.1860-68
London wood engraver, who worked at 162 Strand,
WC (POD,1860), then 3 Dane's Inn, WC (POD,1868).

WELLS, Joseph Robert fl.1872-95
Draughtsman for wood engravings of marine subjects
to the Illustrated London News, 1873-83. These were
generally full-page portraits of ships, engraved by
R.Paterson (q.v.) in a clear black-line style with
parallel-line skies. His most ambitious drawing for
this was a fold-out supplement, 'Russian Circular
Iron Ship', 1 January 1876. Wells later drew for
wood engraved illustrations to the English Illustrated
Magazine, 1885-86, notably to B.H.Becker's series
'Decayed Seaports', wood engraved by T.W.Lascelles, ,
J.D.Cooper, O.Jahyer, and C.Roberts (qq.v.); and
'Our Fishermen', engraved by J.D.Cooper,
R.Paterson, O.Lacour, and W.M.R.Quick (qq.v.).
His figures in these marine drawings were usually
drawn by C.J.Staniland (q.v.). Wells also exhibited
at the Royal Academy, the Royal Society of British
Artists, the Royal Institute of Painters in Water-
colours, and the Royal Institute of Painters in Oil-
Colours.

WELLS, L. fl.1855
The British Museum owns a proof wood engraving of
a hunting scene by this artist, engraved by the
Dalziel Brothers (q.v.) in 1855.

WELLS, Robert H. fl.1869-73
London wood engraver, who worked at 8 Palsgrave
Place, Strand, WC (POD,1869), an office which he
shared with R.S.Marriott (q.v.). He moved to
3 Union Street, Kingsland Road, E (POD,1873).

WELLS, William Henry 1842-80
London wood engraver, who according to Bénézit was
born in 1842, and worked at 32 Whitefriars Street,
EC (POD,1877). He died in 1880.

WENTWORTH, Frederick fl.1865-94
London wood engraver, who worked at 266 Strand,
WC (POD,1865-66), which he shared with
E.Whymper and W.A.Cranston (qq.v.). He worked
at 28 Essex Street, Strand, WC (POD,1874),
166 Strand, WC (POD,1875), then moved to the
noted workshop, 4 Bouverie Street, EC (POD,1883-92),
which he shared with A.J.Appleton (q.v.). He moved
finally to 3 Tudor Street, EC (POD,1893-94).
Wentworth's engravings were appearing by the early
1870s in The Graphic, after Arthur Boyd Houghton
(q.v.); after William Small (q.v.) to Wilkie Collins'
Man and Wife, Cassell's Magazine, 1870; and the
Illustrated London News. Here he specialised in
wood engraving the paintings of E.N.Downard and
Edward Hughes; a double-page supplement, 'Nero
amongst the Ruins of Rome', after K.Piloty;
followed by a double-page supplement, 'The Execution
of Sir Thomas More', after W.F.Yeames,
13 February 1875. The British Museum owns a large
historical scene engraved by Wentworth. He signed
his engravings: 'F.Wentworth sc'.

WERDMULLER, Hermann (Heinrich) 1843-?
fl.1884-92
Swiss-born wood engraver, born in Zurich on
28 October 1843. He was the pupil of Jacob Büchi,
worked first in Dresden under H.Bürkner, and
established a reputation for engravings after
A.L.Richter. He worked in London from 1884, at
180 Fleet Street, EC (POD,1884-85), then with
C.Roberts (q.v.) at 27 Chancery Lane, WC
(POD,1886-92).
[TB (with bibliography); Bénézit]

WEST, R.C. fl.1870s
Wood engraver of birds and animals. He was
commissioned with Madame G.Pearson and the
Dalziel Brothers (qq.v.) to engrave a bird illustration
to the new edition of Yarrell's History of British
Birds, 1871-85. He also engraved small animal
drawings for the Illustrated London News, 1875-77.
The British Museum owns two competent topographical views after J.Thorne and Johnson
engraved by West. He signed his engravings:
'R.C.West sc'.

WHEELER, Edward J. fl.1872-1902
Draughtsman illustrator and painter. He began
drawing on wood for Punch about 1880 when the
wood engraver Joseph Swain (q.v.) introduced him
to the paper's editor Tom Taylor. He continued to
draw theatrical sketches, initials and illustrations
to stories until 1902. He also drew on wood for the
Cornhill, 1883; and later illustrated Smollett's
Tristram Shandy, 1894; and W.Besant's Captains
Room, 1897. He exhibited once in London in 1872.
[Spielmann; Houfe]

WHEELER, John Alexander fl.1838-48
London wood engraver, who worked at 14 Calthorpe
Street (Pigot,1838), and 7A Little James Street,
Bedford Row (POD,1841-45). He engraved cuts to
Ct de Laborde's Versailles,1839, engraved with
Gowland, Charles Thompson, J.Orrin Smith,
W.T.Green, M.Sears, J.Jackson, and Best (qq.v.);
also some of the 300 cuts to Dr C.Wordsworth's
La Grèce Pittoresque et Historique,1841.
[Gusman]

WHELLOCK, Robert Phillips fl.1870s
London draughtsman on wood, who worked at
1 Vicarage Road, Camberwell (Kelly's,1876). He
drew for the Illustrated London News, notably a half
page drawing on wood, 'West Area of St Paul's
Churchyard', 24 January 1874.

WHIMPER
(see Whymper)

WHISTLER, James Abbot McNeil 1834-1903
Occasional draughtsman on wood, painter, etcher,
lithographer and caricaturist. He was born in Lowell,
Massachusetts on 11 July 1834, brought up in Russia
and England, later became a Navy cartographer,
learned etching, and then studied under Gleyre in
Paris in 1855. There he met the struggling artist
draughtsman George Du Maurier (q.v.) and the
painter E.J.Poynter. He settled in London in 1859,
and became a prominent artistic figure and painter,
etcher. He is listed here for the six known drawings
which he made on wood in 1862, engraved by the
Dalziel Brothers (q.v.). 'Had we nothing of
Whistler's but his six wood engravings I think we
might still claim that he was a great artist. They do
not display all his qualities, of course, but they
display his poetic imagination, his feeling for
decoration, his beauty of line, his sense of
composition, and that impeccable taste which in him,
as Arthur Symons has said, was carried to the point
of genius (Reid). These six drawings were: two
drawings to illustrate the story, 'The Trial Sermon'
in Good Words,1862; and four drawings to Once a
Week,1862: 'The Mayor's Daughter', 'The Relief
Fund in Lancashire', 'The Morning before the
Massacre of St Bartholomew', and 'Count Burckhardt'.
'That they show the exquisite sense of the value of a
line, and have much in common with the artist's
etchings of the same period, is evident enough'
(White); the Good Words drawings were republished
in Thornbury's Legendary Ballads,1876, 'absurdly
renamed'. Whistler also contributed etchings to the
Etching Club's Passages of Modern English Poets,
1862. All of these illustrations showed Whistler as
a powerful draughtsman, who used a freedom of line
unusual among the 1860s draughtsmen on wood. This
over-zealous style certainly proved a trial to his
engravers, the maze of spidery and entangled lines

on wood demanding the infinite patience of a Dalziel
or at best a Swain (q.v.). The British Museum owns
Dalziel proof engravings after Whistler,1862.
[For an account of Whistler's etched work see
Volume I; also bibliographies in Houfe and Wood]

WHITAKER, Walter Ethell fl.1854-58
London wood engraver, who worked at 262 Strand
(POD,1854-58). Bénézit lists a W.Whitaker, who
exhibited at the Royal Academy in 1828.

WHITE, Edmund Richard fl.1864-1908
Occasional draughtsman illustrator, landscape and
genre painter in watercolour. He drew comic genre
subjects which were wood engraved in the Illustrated
London News,1871, for which he is listed here. He also
exhibited at the Royal Academy, the Royal Society
of British Artists, the Royal Institute of Painters in
in Watercolours and the Royal Watercolour Society,
working in London, and Walham from 1880.

WHITE, Ethelbert 1891-1972
Wood engraver, book illustrator, poster designer,
landscape painter. He was born in Isleworth on
26 February 1891 and studied at the St John's Wood
School of Art under Leonard Walker,1911-12. He
was proficient enough as a wood engraver to have
two engravings shown at the first exhibition of the
Society of Wood Engravers,1920, where he was
elected member in 1921. He resigned in 1925 and
joined the newly formed English Wood Engraving
Society, but produced his last wood engraving in
1930. He was, however, re-elected member of the
Society of Wood Engravers in 1935.
[Garrett; Waters]

WHITE, Henry ?-1861
Wood engraver, apprenticed first to John Lee (q.v.)
until his death in 1804; then White served the
remainder of his apprenticeship under Thomas
Bewick (q.v.). He stayed with Bewick in Newcastle
from 29 November 1804-9 January 1808, where he
also worked with Robert Bewick (q.v.). Thomas
Bewick recalled his apprenticeship: 'When the term
of his engagement with me was ended--he returned
to London, & chiefly turned his attention, to the
imitation of sketchy cross hatching on Wood, from
the inimitable pencil of Mr Cruikshanks, & perhaps
some other artists in this same way--Henry White
appears to have taken the lead of others, who
followed that manner of cutting, which shortly
became quite the Ton ['black line' engraving which
faithfully reproduces the drawn line]' (Bewick
Memoir,pp.199-200). He set up in London at
Wynyatt Street, Northampton Square (Pigot,1822-23)
and St John's Lane, Clerkenwell (Pigot,1823-24).
White's engravings appeared as early as 1808, with
cuts to Burns' Poems,1808, published by Catnack
Davison of Alnwick; cuts to Puckle's The Club,1817;

thirteen cuts made with his son Henry William White
(q.v.) to Northcote's Fables, 1828; cuts to Major's
edition of Walton's Angler, 1824; and cuts to William
Yarrell's History of British Fishes, 1836. Redgrave
claimed that he made 'clever illustrations' to Hone's
House that Jack Built; and Matrimonial Ladder. He
also engraved a portrait of the actress, Mary Anne
Keeley for the London Journal, 12 August 1848, which
is now owned by the British Museum. He died in
1861, leaving a son, Henry William White.
The British Museum owns his engravings after
J.R.Cruikshank, and cuts to Northcote's
Fables. He signed his work: 'H WHITE',
'White' (script), 'H W' (superimposed).
[Redgrave; Nagler (as Henry Whyte); Bénézit]

WHITE, Henry William, Junior fl.1828-87
London wood engraver, the son of Henry White (q.v.),
with whom he engraved for Northcote's Fables, 1828.
Henry Junior engraved just two cuts: 'Loadstone and
Mirror' and 'Rats and Cheese'. He signed these
'H.White Jun'. By 1861, the year his father died,
he had set up as a wood engraver at 16 Arlington
Street, New North Road, N (POD, 1861) adding a
second premises at 14 Little New Street, Shoe Lane,
EC (POD, 1862-75). The following year he appeared
in the directories as draughtsman on wood at
14 Carthusian Street, EC (POD, 1876-84), then
28 Clerkenwell Road, EC (POD, 1885-87). The
British Museum owns his several competent engravings
after George Cruikshank, done in a black-line style;
also his Northcote's Fables cuts.

WHITE, James Norman fl.1880s
London wood engraver, who worked at 152 Fleet
Street, EC (POD, 1880). This was the workshop of
the prominent wood engravers H.Prater and A.Scott
(qq.v.).

WHITE, Mansfield fl.1876-80
London draughtsman on wood, who worked at
15 Southampton Street, Strand, WC (Kelly's, 1876-80).

WHITE, T.
London wood engraver, who worked at 22 Wynyatt
Street, St John's Street Road (Johnstone's, 1817). His
neighbours here were the engraving colleagues
J.Armstrong and H.Hughes (qq.v.).

WHITE, Thomas or D.T. fl.1860s
Draughtsman on wood, who shared a room in the early
1860s with the young G.Pinwell (q.v.) in London. At
the time White was drawing for wood engravings in
Once a Week and Fun. Gleeson White notes his
drawing for Dark Blue, 1871, to the serial by
J.C.Freund, 'Lost'.

WHITE, Thomas Edward
London wood engraver, who worked at 391 Strand
(Robson, 1834).

WHIT(E)HEAD
English wood engraver, listed by Gusman for his
engravings to the French magazine, Magasin
Pittoresque. These were engraved in a style both
'delicate and brilliant'. He may have collaborated
with C.Sheeres (q.v.) as Withead (sic) and Sheeres,
engravers for Laurent's Histoire de L'Empereur
Napoleon, 1839. For other work see Robert Branston
(q.v.). The British Museum owns several French
prints after Girardet, and animal engravings after
W.Freeman signed 'WHITEHEAD SC'. They are
notable for the sense of strong contrasts, from deep
black foliage to stark white highlights on the figures.
[Gusman]

WHITEHEAD, Morris and Lowe fl.1876-80
London firm of draughtsmen on wood, with offices at
167-168 Fenchurch Street, EC, and 1-2 Love Lane,
Eastcheap, EC (Kelly's, 1876-80). They also
specialised in supplying 'copying paper', according
to a directory advertisement.

WHITHAM, Mrs Sylvia Frances 1878-?
Wood engraver, etcher and painter. She was born
in London on 13 October 1878, studied at the Royal
Academy Schools, and exhibited work at the Royal
Academy and the New English Art Club. She worked
from Combe Martin, Devon.
[Waters]

WHITING, Charles
(see Branston, Robert Edward)

WHITING, Thomas (Tom) fl.1884-85
London wood engraver, who worked at 28 Cursitor
Street, EC (POD, 1884-85).

WHITLEY, George fl.1856-57
London wood engraver, who worked at 9 Clephane
Road, Lower Road, Islington (POD, 1856-57). He may
be related to Whitley of the engraving firm Wilton
and Whitley (q.v.).

WHITLOW, William Henry
Provincial wood engraver, who worked at
9 Corporation Street, Manchester (Kelly's, 1889).

WHITTINGHAM, Albert
Provincial wood engraver, who worked at 1 Cherry
Street, Birmingham (Kelly's, 1889).

WHITTINGHAM, Charles, Senior 1767-1840
Prominent pioneer printer of wood engravings,
founder of the Chiswick Press. He is listed here for
his contributions to wood engraved illustration and

because he employed and printed the work of such prominent engravers as John Thompson, John Jackson, Robert Branston and Thomas Williams (qq.v.). He was born in Caludon, Warwickshire on 16 June 1767, apprenticed to the printer, bookseller, Richard Bird, and set up in Dean Street, London as a printer from 1789. His first printed book of woodcut illustrations was Pity's Gift, 1798, followed by companion volumes, The Village Orphan, and The Basket Maker. As work increased he moved to Islington, then Chiswick, where in 1811 he founded the famous Chiswick Press. The period 1810-15 earned him a reputation as one of the first printers to develop fully the overlaying of wood engravings for book illustrations, and 'the first to print wood engravings perfectly' (DNB). He joined with William Hughes (q.v.), a wood engraver to form Whittingham and Hughes, 1819-21, at 12 Staining Lane, London, and there produced the famous Chiswick edition of 100 volumes, British Poets, 1822. His nephew Charles (q.v.) joined him in 1824 as a Chiswick Press partner, but after four years went his separate way. Charles Whittingham's finest printing achievements with wood engraved illustrations were after William Harvey's 280 drawings on wood for Northcote's Fables, 1829 and 1833 editions; also Tower Menagerie, 1829; and animals and birds of the Zoological Gardens, 1830-31. The most influential of his engravers was John Thompson (q.v.), who engraved thirty cuts to the Vicar of Wakefield, 1813; cuts to Shakespeare, 1813; and several hundred to Dibdin's London Theatre, all of which Whittingham printed. In fact he commissioned over a hundred wood engravers and many draughtsmen during his working life of about forty years. They included such well known names as Armitage, John Byfield, George Cattermole, Derby, Drummond, Finden, Goodall, Hughes, Humphreys, Landells, the three Landseer brothers, W.J.Linton, Nesbit, Seymour, Smirke, Scheffer, Stanfield, Westall, and Willement (qq.v.). Mason Jackson (q.v.) recalled the process Whittingham used to obtain drawings on wood: 'I have heard William Harvey relate that when Whittingham, the well-known printer, wanted a new cut for his Chiswick Press Series, he would write to Harvey and John Thompson, the engraver, appointing a meeting in Chiswick, when printer, designer, and engraver talked over the matter with as much deliberation as if about to produce a national monument. After they settled all points over a snug supper, the result of their labours was the production a month afterwards of a woodcut measuring perhaps two inches by three' (quoted in Mason Jackson, Pictorial Press). Whittingham's achievements with clear distinct wood engraved printing were developed after much experimentation. According to Arthur Warren, in The Charles Whittinghams, 1896, the exact date of his successful development of printing from wood engravings is unknown: 'But we know that he was always experimenting in one way or another, and it is not improbable that he made many attempts

before he hit upon the best method...Perhaps the engravers were the first to suggest the practice, and in that case I am inclined to think that John Thompson was the helper.' The first success was probably for Croxall's version of Aesop's Fables, 1813, with 'a promise of Thompson in the blocks'. Whittingham also experimented with inks to achieve a clarity rarely known at the time, when wood engravings still appeared flat and grey. By the end of his career, he had established over forty presses to print his numerous commissions and was one of the first in England to use a steam engine to make paper-pulp and to warm his workshops with steam pipes. He never had an engine for printing, however, believing the hand press was far superior. Following an illness early in 1838, he turned over the control at Chiswick to Charles, his nephew, and died in Chiswick on 5 January 1840. He died having established, in the Chiswick Press, the foremost name in Victorian book design, which continued to exert influence on good typography and printing continuously until its closure in 1962. Throughout his days at the press Whittingham retained his belief in proper wood engraved printing, not for profit but for the love of fine work. He was 'the first printer to print woodcuts perfectly' (Warren). The large collection of proof engravings annotated for (by?) Whittingham is in the Bodleian Library.
[For a biography and list of works produced see A.Warren, The Charles Whittinghams, 1896; also DNB; British Bookmaker, September 1890; Linton, Masters of Wood Engraving; McLean, Victorian Book Design; White]

WHITTINGHAM, Charles, Junior 1795-1876
Printer of wood engravings and colour plates from wood blocks, influential typographer, the nephew of Charles Whittingham (q.v.) with whom he worked and whom he eventually succeeded at the Chiswick Press. He is listed here for his influence as a printer upon wood engraved illustration, and for his support of such draughtsmen as his daughters, Charlotte and Elizabeth Whittingham (qq.v.), and the engraver Mary Byfield (q.v.). He was born in Mitcham, Surrey on 30 October 1795, was apprenticed at fifteen to his uncle and made a freeman of the Company of Stationers in 1817. The following year his uncle sent him to Paris, which resulted in the Chiswick Press series, French Classics. He became partner with his uncle in 1824-28, after which time he set up a printing office at 21 Took's Court, Chancery Lane. He became associated with William Pickering, the bookseller, for whom he printed numerous influential books, noted for their expert ornamental initials and wood engraved borders. These were mostly drawn on wood by his daughters Elizabeth and Charlotte and engraved by Mary Byfield. Whittingham sought a reputation for producing the finest ornamental editions and it was his practice when he saw a good design to

buy it immediately before his competitors could do so. He was 'a most particular critic, and every scrap of work that came from the little circle was minutely examined by him before the graving-tool made its first incision', according to his biographer, A.Warren. His family of five children were pressed into the family firm, the sons William and Charles John became apprentice printers, the daughters Charlotte, Elizabeth Eleanor and Jane 'almost invariably drew upon wood'. From the 1830s he produced books after drawings by Robert and George Cruikshank (qq.v.) including W.T.Moncrieff's March of Intellect, with 'eight splendid engravings on wood', after Robert, the whole series collected in Cruikshank's Comic Album,1831. In June 1838 his uncle turned over the Chiswick Press to him, and he maintained Took's Court and the Chiswick business until 1848. He also began colour printing from wood blocks in 1840, for Shaw's Elizabethan Architecture,1842 and some of his finest work can be found in his Shaw commissions. Between 1843-44 he joined with Henry Cole in the revival of 'old-fashioned' expert book production and produced over the next few years some remarkable volumes. He lost his wife, however, in 1854, and by 1860 had turned over his firm's affairs to his former apprentice and new partner, John Wilkins who died in 1869. Then B.F.Stevens and Wilkins' son took over and tried to use Whittingham's wood engravings on their own account (see Whittingham vs Wilkins,1876). The business then passed to George Bell, the London publisher. Whittingham died on 21 April 1876, having continued the high standards of the Chiswick Press, which 'largely contributed to raise the standard of English printing in the nineteenth century and its productions are as distinctive in character as those of Baskerville' (DNB). The Constance Meade Collection in the Bodleian Library has a selection of proofs annotated by Whittingham, also the court documents to Whittingham vs Wilkins,1876.
[For a biography see A.Warren, The Charles Whittinghams,1896, with list of works; also DNB; Sir G.Keynes, W.Pickering,1924, rev.ed.1969; David Butcher, The Whittingham Press,1982]

WHITTINGHAM, Charlotte 1829-1903
Skilful draughtsman of ornamental designs for the Chiswick Press. She was born on 30 January 1829 in London, the daughter of Charles Whittingham, Junior (q.v.), for whom she worked, also sister-collaborator of Elizabeth Eleanor Whittingham (q.v.). Her father pressed her into drawing the numerous ornamental headpieces, tailpieces, and borders for his Chiswick Press. From early childhood she and her sister were trained for such work, which was wood engraved by Mary Byfield (q.v.). They included border designs to Queen Elizabeth's Prayer Book; and to Keble's Christian Year; and borders surrounding sixteenth century designs of Geoffrey Tory in the Book of Common Prayer,1844 (re-used in Singer's

Shakespeare). She designed various letters with her sister Elizabeth for Grotesque Alphabet. Her working method involved an initial highly finished pencil or ink drawing, which she then re-drew onto the wood block for Mary Byfield to engrave. Many of these were specifically drawn as individual blocks so that they could be arranged around a design, as a border, and later re-used in a different way -- as a headpiece or tailpiece, perhaps. Charlotte was particularly adept at floral vignettes and borders using a fine stipple pen and ink technique. A collection of these highly finished drawings are in the Constance Meade Collection, Bodleian Library. One incorporated her initials in the centre of a border; some were ruled over with a red ink grid, presumably so that they could be transferred onto the wood block. These she signed 'C W'. Charlotte was also an oil painter; her portraits of her father and grandfather appear in Warren (op.p.184). She was a plain, rather dumpy woman who in 1865 married the American antiquarian B.F.Stevens, who became a partner in the Chiswick Press from January 1872 - August 1876. Charlotte died at Sheaves, Surbiton Hall, on 22 July 1903, aged seventy-four. The DNB concluded, 'Charlotte and Elizabeth were educated as artists, and from their designs came the greater part of the extensive collection of borders, monograms, head and tailpieces, and other embellishments still preserved and used'.
[A.Warren, The Charles Whittinghams,1896; McLean, Victorian Book Design; DNB; Sir G.Keynes, W.Pickering,1969]

WHITTINGHAM, Elizabeth Eleanor ?-1869
Talented ornamental designer for wood engraved decorations of the Chiswick Press. She was the daughter of Charles Whittingham, Junior (q.v.) who pressed her at an early age into training to draw ornamental vignettes, borders and especially initials, monograms for his Chiswick Press. She designed many of these with her sister, Charlotte Whittingham (q.v.) which were wood engraved by Mary Byfield (q.v.) the press's major engraver. This work included the title initial 'B' to Breviarium Aberdonense; re-drawing Thomas Stothard's alphabet designs for Mary Byfield to engrave; drawing alphabet designs of her own with Charlotte for Grotesque Alphabet; and adopting various initial letters from the Gulden Bible. She was in fact most proficient at initial letters which she drew in finished form on paper, then re-drew onto the wood block for the engraver to follow. The Constance Meade Collection in the Bodleian Library has a selection of these highly finished drawings, some in violet ink, which she signed 'E E W', presumably to distinguish her work from her sister's 'C W'. Elizabeth died in 1869, but her sister continued to work for the Chiswick Press with her husband, B.F.Stevens.
[see also A.Warren, The Charles Whittinghams,1896; DNB]

WHITTINGHAM and Hughes fl.1819-22
Wood engraving and printing firm, owned by the
printer Charles Whittingham, Senior (q.v.) and
the wood engraver William Hughes (q.v.). They
established an office at 12 Staining Lane, and
produced the famous Chiswick Press series, British
Poets, 1822, in 100 volumes.

WHITTOCK, Nathaniel fl.1828-51
Influential draughtsman and lithographer. He was
the drawing instructor of the prominent wood
engraver Joseph Swain (q.v.) about 1834, and
described by Spielmann as a 'draughtsman of Islington...
though Mr Whittock was something of an artist, he
was less of an engraver'. He was principally known
as a draughtsman and lithographer of topographical
and drawing books. He worked in London and at
11 London Place, St Clements, Oxford (Fincham),
where he was a professor of drawing and perspective
at Oxford University.
[For a list of work see TB; Houfe; see also
Spielmann; Bryan]

WHYMPER, Charles H. 1853-1941
Occasional wood engraver, landscape and animal
draughtsman and painter. He was born in London on
31 August 1853, the son of the wood engraver Josiah
Whymper (q.v.) with whom he briefly worked, and
brother of Edward and Frederick (qq.v.). He also
studied at the Royal Academy Schools, travelled to
Egypt, and then spent three years with the animal
illustrator and painter Joseph Wolf (q.v.). He
travelled during most of his working life, collecting
illustrations for his numerous books of travel,
natural history and sport. He is listed here for
his wood engravings of birds to Yarrell's History
of British Birds, 1871-85; also for other wood
engravings which appeared in Henry Seebohm's
Siberia in Europe, 1880; and Siberia in Asia, 1882,
for which he engraved ten of the 112 total cuts. The
British Museum lists wood engraved illustrations
drawn by Charles to F.H.H.Guillemard's Cruise of
the Marchesa, 1886. He also drew for wood engravings
in the Illustrated London News, 1887-89; Good Words,
1891; and natural history drawings to the English
Illustrated Magazine, 1883, engraved by W. and
J.R.Cheshire (q.v.). Whymper was also a watercolour painter and used this work to illustrate his
books. He exhibited at the Fine Art Society, the New
Gallery, the Royal Academy, the Royal Society of
British Artists and the Royal Institute of Painters in
Watercolours, where he was elected member in 1909.
He worked in London, then Houghton, Huntingdonshire
from 1915. He died on 25 April 1941. The British
Museum attributes to him proofs engraved by the Dalziels
(q.v.), 1861, but these were probably by Edward.
[For a list of later illustrated works see Houfe;
British Library catalogue; Who's Who, 1906;
Sketchley; Hake; Bénézit]

WHYMPER, Ebenezzar fl.1833-42
Wood engraver, brother of Josiah Wood Whymper
(q.v.) and uncle of Edward and Charles Whymper
(qq.v.). He was the son of an Ipswich brewer,
became dissatisfied with life there as a youth, and
joined with his brother Josiah to set up a London
wood engraving firm. They established an office at
35 Little Bartholomew Close (Robson, 1833) and the
following year moved to Paradise Street, Lambeth
(Robson, 1834). Ebenezzar last appeared in the
London directory at 20 Paradise Terrace
(Pigot, 1838). When his brother turned to watercolour painting, he hoped to give most of the
engraving business responsibilities to Ebenezzar,
but Josiah soon discovered that his brother was
'more incapable than ever'. Eventually he was
replaced by Josiah's son, his nephew, Edward
Whymper (q.v.).

WHYMPER, Edward J. 1840-1911
Occasional draughtsman and engraver on wood,
illustrator, landscape watercolourist and alpinist.
He was born on 27 April 1840, the second son of the
wood engraver Josiah Whymper (q.v.), and brother
of Charles and Frederick Whymper (qq.v.). He
trained from the age of fifteen, in 1855, as a
draughtsman engraver in his father's engraving
business in Lambeth. His father had just returned
from Paris with a wood engraved architectural guide
and challenged his son to produce drawings of equal
merit since 'no one in England could draw architecture
like they were'. This architectural work became the
basis of his career drawing various monuments for
his father's numerous commissions: 'Castle of St
Angelo' and 'Baths of Caracalla' for Brown's
History of Rome in 1857; 'Peterboro Cathedral' in
1858, which John Gilbert praised 'as good as that
kind of drawing could possibly be'. In that year
young Edward declared his ambition to become 'a
correct architectural draughtsman'. But the training
was largely drudgery, as his diary recorded:
'Dec.1855--Cut up wood and cut out the overlay of a
most ridiculous mythological outline drawn by Chas.
Kingsley'. Two years later he was still disheartened:
'22 Sept. [1857] --Cut up wood. Drew diagrams, etc.
Diagrams! Oh, sickening job. I have lines frequently
one-sixth of an inch thick and that for many weeks
together. Oh, how I should rejoice to escape from
this thraldom with scarcely any prospect of better
times...'. Indeed Edward seems to have battled
valiantly with his conscience during these trying
times: 'I, when I first came to business, did not like
it at all, and wished myself to go to sea'. By 1859 a
slump in the engraving business did not bring even a
brief respite for Edward's drudgery: '19 Jan.1859--
Finished list of birds, marked out 30 pcs of wood'.
A projected book on birds with 150-200 cuts meant
'This will keep us going briskly for some months';
but by February even that drawing of mackerel on

wood lost its fascination: 'stinking job' (quoted in
F.S.Smythe, Edward Whymper,1940). During the
1860s he first set up in London on his own, at
266 Strand, WC (POD,1865) and contributed drawings
for wood engravings in Sunday Magazine,1865;
Leisure Hour,1867; and the Illustrated London News,
1868-69. He alternated such work with explorations
and mountaineering expeditions. He wrote Peaks,
Passes and Glaciers,1862, which helped his
illustrations for such works as A.Bethell's Helen in
Switzerland,1867; and T.G.Bonney's Alpine Regions
of Switzerland,1868. These culminated in his own
classic account, Scrambles amongst the Alps in the
Years 1860-69, published 1871, and praised by
Sir Leslie Stephen (Alpine Journal, V,pp.230-44):
'Mr Whymper's woodcuts seem to bring the genuine
Alps before us...'. The British Museum owns a set
of fifty unused proofs to the book, engraved with his
father after drawings by W.H.J.Boot, C.Johnson,
J.Mahoney, J.W.North, P.Skelton and Edward
himself. In the 1870s Edward returned to drawing
and engraving on wood, occasionally with his father.
Together they did twenty engravings to Life and
Habits of Wild Animals,1873-74, after drawings of
Joseph Wolf (q.v.). By 1876 Edward was listing two
offices in the directories: Edward Whymper and
Company, 30 Essex Street, Strand and 19 Canterbury
Place, Lambeth Road (POD,1876-81), keeping the
Lambeth address to be near his father's premises.
By 1882 the two appear in the directories, as
J.W. and Edward Whymper, 43 and 45 Lambeth
Road (POD,1882-86). Eventually Edward took over
his father's engraving affairs and continued to run the
firm at 29 Ludgate Hill (POD,1893-1900). Among the
'outside' engravers he employed was G.L.Butlin
(q.v.). Edward Whymper specialised in alpine land-
scapes but he also drew and engraved various portraits,
many of which appeared in British Heroes and
Worthies,1871. A collection of portraits, foreign
stamp designs, and wood blocks is in the British
Museum. He exhibited watercolours at the Royal
Society of British Artists, 1857, and the Royal
Academy,1857-61. He continued to write throughout
the 1890s, and published Travels among the Great
Andes, 1892; Chamonix and Mont Blanc,1896; and
Zermatt and the Matterhorn,1897, among others.
The British Library catalogue lists some
sixteen books written, illustrated and/or engraved
by Whymper. He died in Chamonix on 16 September
1911. The British Museum (print room) owns his
engravings after W.H.J.Boot, F.Barnard,
M.E.Edwards, G.D.Giles, W.Hennessy, J.Mahoney,
J.N.Paton, J.Wolf, C.Whymper, Caton Woodville,
and J.B.Zwecker (qq.v.); also a large collection of
early proofs, annotated by Whymper. He signed his
work: 'E WHIMPER', 'WHIMPER', 'E Whimper' (script).
[For biographical detail see F.S.Smythe, Edward
Whymper,1940; B.E.Young, Edward Whymper,
Alpinist,1914; W.Unsworth, Matterhorn Man,1965;

also TB (bibliography); DNB; Wakeman and
Bridson (for colour work); British Library catalogue]

WHYMPER or Whimper, Elijah fl.1848-73
London wood engraver, who worked at 66 later 20
Paternoster Row (POD,1848-60), then 144 Fleet
Street, EC (POD,1868-73). He may be related to
the Whymper family of engravers (q.v.).

WHYMPER, Emily Hepburn (Mrs Josiah Wood
Whymper) ?-1886
Draughtsman illustrator and watercolourist. She was
the second wife of the wood engraver Josiah Wood
Whymper (q.v.), and lived and worked in London.
She illustrated Beauty in Common Things, c1874.
She exhibited watercolour landscapes in London from
1877-85, at the Royal Academy and the New Water-
colour Society.
[Bénézit; British Library catalogue]

WHYMPER, Frederick fl.1857-84
Occasional wood engraver, landscape draughtsman
and painter and traveller. He was the eldest son of
the wood engraver Josiah Wood Whymper (q.v.) who
planned to train him to continue his engraving
business, alongside his brother Edward Whymper
(q.v.). He turned instead to landscape painting and
drawing, first working in London from 1857-61, then
in America. There he explored Alaska, publishing his
observations as Travel and Adventure in...Alaska,
1868. He also drew for wood engravings of Russian
America in the Illustrated London News,1868-69.
His second love was the sea, about which he wrote
various books: The Sea,1877-80, in four volumes;
and The Romance of the Sea. He also exhibited
paintings at the Royal Academy and the Royal Society
of British Artists.
[British Library catalogue; Houfe]

WHYMPER, Josiah Wood 1813-1903
Prominent wood engraver and watercolourist. He
was born in Ipswich on 14 March 1813, the son of a
local brewer, and brother of Ebenezzar Whymper
(q.v.) with whom he set up a wood engraving
business in London, after an unsuccessful apprenticeship with a stone mason. He taught himself to draw,
then in London from 1829 studied watercolour
painting with W.Collinwood Smith. He established
himself as an illustrator with an etching of 'London
Bridge', 1831. In the early 1830s he and Ebenezzar
wood engraved from a premises in 31 Paradise Road,
Lambeth (POD,1836). In 1840 he changed the spelling
of his name to Whimper, which he believed was the
correct spelling and began to paint for the London
exhibitions, but later signed his work as Whymper,
as did his relations. His brother gradually proved too
irresponsible to run the business, which moved to
20 Canterbury Place, Lambeth (POD,1842-76), and
Josiah took on a series of impressive apprentices:

Frederick Walker, Charles Keene (for five years), J.W.North (from 1860), Charles Green and G.J.Pinwell (qq.v.) -- in other words some of the most prominent 'Sixties School' draughtsmen. He also employed his sons Edward and (probably) Frederick (qq.v.). Whymper's wood engraving business began with work for Charles Knight (q.v.) on Arabian Nights' Entertainments,1839; Pictorial Shakespeare; and Penny Magazine, but thrived on most of the engraving work for Murray's, the publishers, for the Religious Tract Society and S.P.C.K. He purposely had a large family of eleven children so that the business would continue to thrive: 'But shall we finally keep to this--I think, in fact I know we shall not', he confessed in his diary. The most successful members to adhere to his plan were Alfred, who was sent to train with the Edinburgh printer R.Clark about 1857, Charles, Frederick and Edward (qq.v.), whom Josiah trained as draughtsmen on wood, and who eventually took over the business. Indeed, they worked together on various natural history commissions including Life and Habits of Wild Animals,1873-74, after Joseph Wolf's drawings. This followed the book which some consider to be Josiah's most successful: C.A.John's British Birds in Their Haunts,1862, with 190 engravings after Wolf, engraved under the influence of Thomas Bewick (q.v.) and from drawings of birds done at a third of their actual size. Whymper contributed engravings to periodicals such as the Illustrated London News,1855 and Sunday at Home, 1869. His best book engravings appeared in Scott's Poetical Works,1857; Murray's edition of Byron's Childe Harold; and Schliemann's Works. He was especially good at engravings after his friend John Gilbert's drawings: Lady of the Lake,1853; and Lay of the Last Minstrel,1854. By the early 1880s his engraving business at 43 and 45 Lambeth Road, was under joint control with his son Edward and appeared in the directories as J.W. and Edward Whymper, draughtsmen and engravers on wood. Josiah retired and turned over the firm to Edward, who ran it throughout the 1890s. Over a period of some sixty years the name of Whymper had become prominent and a successful mark of quality wood engravings for numerous books and magazines. Whymper was also a competent draughtsman illustrator, often engraving his own natural history illustrations. These appeared in C.R.Conder's Child's History of Jerusalem,1874; L.J.Jennings' Field Paths and Green Lanes,1877; and C.R.Conder's Tent Work in Palestine,1878. He aspired to become a more successful watercolourist for the galleries than his engraving work allowed, but he did frequently exhibit at the New Watercolour Society from 1844, where he was elected associate in 1854 and member in 1857; also at the Royal Institute of Painters in Watercolours and the Royal Institute of Painters in Oil-Colours. He worked in London, later Haslemere,

Surrey where he died on 7 April 1903. The British Museum owns his engravings after G.Balmer, J.Gilbert, E.Landseer, T.Landseer, W.Parrot and S.Read; the Bodleian Library owns a series of engravings of animals colour printed, and engravings for C.Knight. He signed his work: 'WHIMPER SC' or 'JW WHIMPER' (early work), 'JW WHYMPER' (later).
[For a discussion of Whymper as colour printer see Wakeman and Bridson; as engraver see Chatto; Nagler; DNB; Bénézit; TB (bibliography)]

WIEGAND, W.J. fl.1869-82
Decorative draughtsman on wood, who worked in London for various magazines. He drew for wood engravings in Good Words for the Young,1869-73; and contributed decorative headpieces to the Sunday Magazine,1870. His drawings were reissued by Novello in Elliott's Nursery Rhymes,1870.

WILD, Ebenezer fl.1842-55
London wood engraver, who contributed small cuts to early numbers of the Illustrated London News. He engraved 'The Chub', to head the 'Angling' column, 2 July 1842; and a small view of 'Dale Abbey, Derbyshire', to the series, 'Nooks and Corners of England', 18 February 1843. He worked in London at 3 Long Lane, Smithfield (POD,1844-45), 11 Wellington Street, N (POD,1848), 313 Strand (POD,1851-52), and 7 St Paul's Terrace, Camden Town, N (POD,1855).

WILDE, D. or De
Wood engraver, who collaborated with the Dalziel Brothers, Leighton, Green, Harral and Joseph Swain (qq.v.) to engrave the 247 blocks after John Leighton's (q.v.) designs to Richard Pigot's Moral Emblems, 1860-62.
[White]

WILKINSON, James F. fl.1870s
Provincial draughtsman on wood, who worked at 32 and 34 Oxford Street, and Gutenburg Works, Pendleton, Lancashire (Kelly's,1876).

WILKINSON, John fl.1832-36
London wood engraver, who worked at 6 Ann Street, Spitalfields (Pigot,1832-34), then 38 Margaret Street, E (Pigot,1836).

WILLCOCK, Joseph fl.1863-65
London wood engraver, who worked at 89 Chancery Lane, WC (POD,1863). He probably formed a partnership with W.H.Brewer (q.v.) the following year as Willcock and Brewer, wood engravers at the same address (POD,1864-65).

WILLCOCK and Brewer
(see Willcock, Joseph)

WILLES, William ?-1851
Occasional draughtsman for wood engravings, born
in Cork, who was a pupil of the Royal Academy
Schools, then Master of the Cork School of Design,
1849. He is listed here for his drawing wood
engraved by M.A.Williams (q.v.) to S.C.Hall's
Ireland,1841. He exhibited at the British Institution
and the Royal Academy and died in Cork in 1851.
[TB; Redgrave; Strickland; Art Journal,1851,p.44]

WILLETT, H.B. and Company fl.1889-1900
Provincial wood engraving firm, with an office at
24 (26) Bath Street, Bristol (Kelly's,1889-1900).

WILLIAMS, Alfred 1832-1905
Occasional draughtsman on wood, painter of alpine
scenes. He was born in Newark-on-Trent on 4 May
1832, educated at University College School, London
and taught drawing privately under the watercolourist
William Bennett (1811-71). 'As a young man he
supported himself by drawing on wood for book
illustrations' (DNB). His drawings included work
for the Religious Tract Society and Cassells, as well
as his brother Frederick Smeeton Williams' Our
Iron Roads,1852. He also served as assistant to
the prominent draughtsman on wood, John Gilbert
(q.v.). From 1861-86 he worked as a maltster in
Salisbury, during the summer travelling to alpine
regions to draw and paint. He exhibited at the Royal
Academy, the Royal Society of British Artists,
the New Gallery and the Alpine Club. He died in
St Maxime-sur-Mer, France on 19 March 1905.
[DNB; Graves]

WILLIAMS, Alfred Mayhew fl.1855-75
London wood engraver, who worked at 5 Gloucester
Place, Regent's Park (POD,1855). He disappears
from the directories until 1872, then working at
50 Carey Street, WC (POD,1872-75). His wood
engraved work included architectural cuts to the
Illustrated London News, notably 'The Minton
Testimonial Museum', after J.Murray, 11 February
1860. He had the unusual engraving technique of
cutting clouds as white patches without firm outlines.
He also engraved a portrait of Sir William Frederick
Williams, Bart, in uniform, which is in the British
Museum. Alfred Williams may be related to the
noted engraving partnership John and Alfred Williams
(q.v.).
[Hake]

WILLIAMS, Alfred Sheldon fl.1871-75
Draughtsman illustrator of equestrian subjects and
farmer. He lived and worked in Winchfield, the son
of the artist Inglis Sheldon-Williams. He began
drawing for wood engravings in The Graphic,1871,

then the Illustrated London News,1874-75. Here he
drew the double-page 'Prize Animals at Smithfield
Club Show', 19 December 1874, engraved by John
Greenaway (q.v.). He also drew illustrations to
Cassell's Book of the Horse,1875. He exhibited
paintings at the Royal Academy and the Royal Society
of British Artists.

WILLIAMS, Captain
Amateur draughtsman illustrator on wood and army
officer. He is listed here for drawings of Canada
wood engraved in the Illustrated London News,1860.

WILLIAMS, Miss E. fl.1842-60
Wood engraver, daughter of the noted engraver
Samuel Williams (q.v.) and sister of Joseph Lionel
Williams (q.v.). She collaborated with her brother
and father on engraving illustrations to S.C.Hall's
Book of British Ballads,1842, after drawings on wood
by J.Franklin and T.M.Joy (qq.v.). Bohn in Chatto
and Jackson cites her engravings in collaboration
with W.Thomas, W.T.Green, and the Dalziel
Brothers (qq.v.) to an illustrated edition of
Tennyson's Princess,1860, after D.Maclise (q.v.).
[Chatto]

WILLIAMS, Edward Morrett fl.1842-75
Wood engraver and portrait painter. He worked in
London at 144 Fleet Street (POD,1842-56), then
1 Gloucester Cottages, Loughborough Park, Brixton
(POD, LSDS,1857-60). He exhibited in London as a
portrait painter from 1843-75.
[TB]

WILLIAMS, Frederick Thomas fl.1858-87
London wood engraver, who worked at 6 Great
Russell Street, Covent Garden, WC (POD,1858).
He entered the workshop of the prominent engraver
J.D.Cooper (q.v.) at 188 Strand, WC (POD,1861-62).
He taught the noted engraver Thomas Johnson (q.v.).
He disappears from the London directories until
1878, when he was working at Aldine Chambers,
13 Paternoster Row, EC (POD,1878), then joined
the workshop of J. and G.P.Nicholls (q.v.) at
17 Holborn Viaduct, EC (POD,1879-85). The
following year he appears as Frederick Thomas
Williams and Son, 22 Holborn Viaduct, EC
(POD,1886-86).

WILLIAMS, J.M.
The British Museum owns wood engravings after
A.H.Forrestier, W.Harvey and C.R.Leslie (qq.v.)
attributed to J.M.Williams.

WILLIAMS, John and Alfred fl.1853-58
London wood engravers, who worked at 6 Palsgrave
Place, Strand (POD,1855-56). They engraved
primarily intricate detailed drawings and architectural subjects for the Illustrated London News,

1853-58. These appeared as the floral virtuoso full-page, 'Prize Plate and Flowers --Cheltenham', after T.Marquoid,16 July 1853; 'The Sultan's New Palace of Dolmabaghdsche',22 October 1853; and the intriguing challenge for engraving tonal contrast, the double-page surface of the moon, after a photograph, 30 September 1854. A portrait engraving, Victoria Adelaide Mary Louise, after the marble bust by Hamo Thornycroft, published in the Illustrated London News,1858, is in the British Museum. Alfred Williams may be related to the noted engraver Alfred Mayhew Williams (q.v.). They signed their engravings: 'J. & A.W.' or 'J. & A.Williams'.
[Hake]

WILLIAMS, Joseph Lionel c1815-77
Wood engraver, draughtsman on wood, and water-colourist. He was the son of the wood engraver Samuel Williams (q.v.) with whom he worked; also the brother of Miss E.Williams (q.v.). He first worked with his father on Scott's Bible,1833-34; also Solace of Song,1836. The three worked together on cuts to S.C.Hall's Book of British Ballads,1842, Joseph engraving after F.R.Pickersgill and T.Creswick (q.v.). Glaser linked his wood engravings with the early English school of Hart, Smith and Slader (qq.v.), best seen in cuts to Paul et Virginie and Gil Blas. His major contributions were drawings and engravings on wood to the Illustrated London News,1846-52. Here, unusually, he was given a full-page commission at an early stage, the Christmas drawing, 'Bring in the Boar's Head, Queen's College, Oxford', 26 December 1846, which he drew on wood and engraved. This was followed by a series of architectural engravings, some of which he drew and engraved, and culminated in the fold-out double page, 'Funeral of the Late Duke of Wellington', 11 December 1852, a vertical composition which exaggerated the dome of St Paul's Cathedral. He also drew for the Art Journal, and engraved various portraits: Albert in Roman Dress, after Wolfe; Viscount Palmerston, after a photograph, and Thomas Denham, all of which are now in the British Museum. He was an engraver for Charles Whittingham (q.v.) for whom he engraved the full-page plate, 'The Virgin and Child attended by Angels' in Henry Shaw's Handbook of the Art of Illumination as Practised during the Middle Ages,1866. This had a border engraved by J.D.Cooper (q.v.). Williams was a competent wood engraver, adept at cutting clear details in the numerous buildings he engraved; also foliage which appeared with a sense of spatial depth unusual for most engravers on wood at the time. W.J.Linton (q.v.) praised Williams' skill as a wood engraver in his Masters of Wood Engraving,1889. He noted Williams' engravings to 'Scripture Illustrations, A High Priest on the Day of Atonement' but lamented that Williams had 'long since abandoned the art'. By then Williams had also exhibited his watercolours and paintings at the British Institution, the Royal Academy and the Royal Society of British Artists. He died in London in 1877. The British Museum owns his engravings after J.Absolon, J.Bell, W.Carpenter, J.Burnet, C.W.Cope,, E.H.Corbould, T.Creswick, G.H.Dodgson, F.W.Fairholt, J.Gilbert, B.Foster, W.Harvey, F.W.Hulme, R.S.Lauder, J.N.Paton, W.L.Leitch, A.Powis, J.R.Pickersgill, S.Read, R.Redgrave, H.C.Selous, F.Tayler, and W.J.Linton. He signed his work: 'Joseph L.Williams', 'JOSEPH WILLIAMS', 'J L W' (script).
[Hake; Glaser; Bénézit; A.Warren, C.Whittingham, 1896,p.285]

WILLIAMS, Mary Ann 1788-?
Wood engraver, genre painter and illustrator, sister of the influential Samuel and Thomas Williams (qq.v.) and aunt of Joseph Lionel Williams and Miss E.Williams (qq.v.). As one of the 'Williams School' of wood engraving she worked with her brothers on various commissions, and Spielmann claimed that for this she should be better remembered: 'a brilliant engraver she, who never gained her due of reputation'. Her engraved work appeared in Percy's Beggar's Daughter of Bendall Green,1832; as cuts after French artists to the influential French edition Curmer's Paul et Virginie, 1838 (not engraved in the familiar Williams style); and as cuts to Poetical Works of Goldsmith,1840. The following year she worked for Charles Knight's numerous wood engraved publications: cuts to Knight's 'Land We Live In' series, after drawings on wood by William Harvey (q.v.) and some of the 600 cuts after Harvey to Knight's edition of Lane's Arabian Nights' Entertainments,1839. She engraved after J.Franklin to Leigh Hunt's The Palfrey,1842; and S.C.Hall's Ireland,1841. She was especially known to French readers and engraved for various illustrated French editions: Abbé Prevost's Histoire de Manon Lescaut,1839; and Wordsworth's La Grèce Pittoresque,1841. The British Museum owns her engravings after W.Harvey, G.F.Sargent and J.Thorne; the Bodleian Library owns her engravings for C.Knight. She signed her engravings: 'M.A.WILLIAMS sc', 'MARY ANN WILLIAMS Sc'.
[Spielmann; Bénézit; Gusman; Nagler; Houfe]

WILLIAMS, Richard James 1876-1964
Occasional wood engraver, painter and illustrator of children's books. He was born in Hereford on 16 March 1876 and studied in Hereford, Cardiff, where he won a gold medal,1893, at Birmingham and London. He worked as a wood engraver and also became Headmaster of Worcester School of Arts and Crafts. He exhibited at the Royal Institute of Painters in Watercolours and the Royal Cambrian Academy, to which he was elected member in 1936.
[TB; Bénézit; Houfe; Waters]

WILLIAMS, Samuel 1788-1853
Prominent wood engraver, draughtsman and natural
history illustrator. He was born in Colchester on
23 February 1788 'of poor but respectable parents',
and was the elder brother of Thomas Williams and
Mary Ann Williams (qq.v.), with whom he often
engraved. He was apprenticed to a house painter and
taught himself to etch and wood engrave, frequently
engraving after his own drawings on the block. He
was given his first commission in 1810, to wood
engrave illustrations to a natural history, which
Linton dismissed as 'of no great merit', but which
earned him future commissions. He engraved several
'clever cuts' to Mrs Trimmer's Natural History,
1822-23; and was commissioned by Charles
Whittingham, Senior (q.v.) to engrave cuts to the
Chiswick Press's Noble and Renowned History of Guy,
Earl of Warwick,1821. Williams tried to engrave
these to imitate a delicate etched line but they were
unfortunately too roughly cut. He continued to engrave
for Whittingham, notably after Thurston's (q.v.)
drawings (a group of proofs are in the Bodleian Library,
Oxford). He designed and engraved illustrations to
Britten's Picturesque Antiquities of English Cities,
1820; and Defoe's Robinson Crusoe,1822; there are
good cuts after Corbould to Wiffen's Jerusalem
Delivered,1823; some good early engravings in
Hone's Every-day Book,1825; numerous cuts to the
weekly magazine, Olio, 1828-33; and cuts after
Cruikshank to History of Napoleon,1829. He worked
with his son Joseph Lionel Williams (q.v.) on
engraving Scott's Bible,1833-34; also Solace of Song,
1836; after William Harvey's drawings, which included
what Linton called his best cut, 'Architecture of Titus'.
He faltered in cuts to Lady C.Guest's Mabinogion,
1838; and later engraved forty-eight cuts to Thomson's
Seasons,1841 which W.J.Linton (q.v.) dismissed:
'the engraver's manner is most conspicuous and
unpleasant, though the cuts are effective and
delicately finished'. On the other hand Bohn claimed
that they earned Williams 'a conspicuous niche in the
Walhalla of Artists'. He worked for Charles Knight's
edition of Lane's Arabian Nights' Entertainments,
1839, which he engraved with his brother Thomas
and sister Mary Ann; also for Knight's Penny
Cyclopedia. By the late 1830s and early 1840s
Williams was established as a competent wood
engraver in England as well as on the Continent.
Nagler and Gusman list several praiseworthy works
and point out that he engraved for various Paris
published editions from 1836-41, notably for the
publisher Curmer: Livre de Marriage,1838; and
Paul et Virginie,1838. (For a list see Gusman,p.156;
also Nagler.) Samuel Williams as a wood engraver
was admired and an influential figure among his
contemporaries. Thomas Bewick (q.v.) as a child
admired the animal engravings in A.D.McQuin's
A Description of Three Hundred Animals, which
Williams engraved in a later edition,1812. And when

Bewick died and left a group of drawings of rural
scenes on blocks, they were bought by William
Howitt in 1841, from the Bewick family, and
engraved by Samuel Williams ('quite in his own
manner', Bain) to a second edition of Howitt's Rural
Life in England,1842. Williams also trained some of
the period's most important engravers, notably
George Baxter, about 1829, and John Orrin-Smith
(qq.v.). He most probably also trained his son
Joseph Lionel and daughter Mary Ann (qq.v.) with
whom he worked on various late commissions. He
continued to produce wood engravings which were
often re-printed in reviews in the Illustrated London
News, as examples of exemplary architectural or
topographical works: his cuts to E.Jesse's A Summer's
Day at Hampton Court,1842, engraved with Orlando
Jewitt (q.v.); and some of his 120 engravings after
William Harvey's designs to J.Montgomery's edition
of Milton's Poetical Works,1843, engraved with
W.Green and Orrin Smith. Chatto linked Williams'
style as a wood engraver with that of his contemporaries, Charlton Nesbit and John Thompson (qq.v.).
In his Masters of Wood Engraving,1889, the engraver
W.J.Linton devoted a large section to Williams and
his related engravers, and concluded of his style:
'His manner is peculiarly his own, unborrowed,
and distinct from all others. In his cuts he prefers a
brilliant effect, the sharp accentuation of blocks with
fine grey tints to enhance their brightness; but his
line is always thin and meagre, without beauty or
distinctive character, and he depends for effect too
entirely on contrast...'. Nevertheless the engraver
Edmund Evans (q.v.) wrote in praise of Williams'
engravings to Ancient Rome, engraved with Joseph
Lionel Williams, 'They are wonderful bits of good
engraving, most elaborate...' (Evans MSS, UCLA
Library). He was also 'skilful in rural scenery'
(Redgrave) and exhibited a few painted miniatures
and oil paintings at the Royal Academy and the
British Institution. He died on 19 September 1853
in London, aged sixty-five. The British Museum
owns a large folder of proofs, including small cuts
of toys and domestic utensils in a firm black outline;
also his engravings after J.Absolon, W.Allen,
C.E.Aubrey, R.W.Billings, H.K.Browne, J.Burnet,
J.W.Carmichael, C.W.Cope, E.H.Corbould,
T.Creswick, J.R.Cruikshank, T.Duncan, R.Farrier,
A.Fraser, C.Landseer, C.R.Leslie, J.Meissonier,
D.Roberts, G.Scharf, W.Simson, M.Stanley,
J.G.Strutt, F.Tayler and H.Warren. The Bodleian
Library owns his engravings after J.Thurston for
C.Whittingham and those for C.Knight. He signed
his engravings: 'S.WILLIAMS', 'S.W.'.
[Chatto; Spielmann; Evans Reminiscences; Nagler;
Gusman, Hake; Linton, Masters of Wood Engraving;
McLean, Victorian Book Design; I.Bain, Watercolours
of T.Bewick,1981,p.221]

WILLIAMS, Thomas 1800-?
London wood engraver, brother of Samuel and Mary
Ann Williams (qq.v.) with whom he often engraved.
He trained under his elder brother Samuel, although
according to Linton he lacked his brother's 'faculty
of design'. His work appeared during the late 1820s,
notably a fable and tailpiece after William Harvey
(q.v.) to Northcote's Fables, 1828 (eight fables and five
tailpieces in the 1833 edition); cuts to Martin and
Westall's Pictorial Illustrations to the Bible, 1833;
after G.Cruikshank's designs to Sunday at Home, 1833;
and after William Harvey's drawings to Solace of Song,
1836, engraved with his brother. He was associated
with Charles Whittingham, Senior (q.v.), whose portrait
he painted, and whose Chiswick Press emblem he
designed (engraved on wood by Mary Byfield (q.v.)).
He engraved after Charlotte Whittingham (q.v.) designs
in a fine, etched-line style; engraved numerous
vignettes after William Harvey to Whittingham's
'Pocket Novels' series (thirty-nine volumes); and to
Whittingham's Peter Parley's Tales of the Sun (a copy
of which is in the Bodleian Library, Oxford). He
accepted for training young Joseph Swain (q.v.) in
1837, taking over from N.Whittock (q.v.). Williams
was employed by various French publishers to engrave
for such influential works as Paul et Virginie, 1838;
Wordsworth's La Grèce Pittoresque, 1841; and Jules
Janin's L'Ane Mort, 1842 edition. It was while working
on the Paul et Virginie engravings that the young
Joseph Swain (q.v.) approached him for engraving
instruction, having become disillusioned with his
limited drawing lessons on wood with N.Whittock
(q.v.). Williams, 'one of the few excellent "facsimile
men" of the day...agreed to accept the applicant as
"improver"' (Spielmann, p.248). During the 1840s
Williams engraved for the popular wood engraved
publications of Charles Knight (q.v.): Knight's 'Land
We Live In' series; Knight's Penny Magazine, July,
1842, after a William Harvey design; and also with
Samuel for cuts to Knight's edition of Lane's
Arabian Nights' Entertainments, 1839. He engraved
for S.C.Hall's Book of British Ballads, 1842, after
J.Franklin's designs, engraved with his brother,
his nephew, Joseph Lionel Williams, and his niece,
Miss E.Williams (qq.v.). By the 1850s he had
appeared in the London directories, working at
15 Wine Office Court, Fleet Street, EC (POD, 1855),
later 37 Ludgate Hill, EC (POD, 1862). His work
during this period included small cuts to the Illustrated
London News, notably 'A Street in Constantinople'
after Thomas Allom, 29 November 1851, engraved
with an emphasis on dark details which emerge from
stark white areas. He seems to have been well enough
regarded to be commissioned to engrave cuts to the
Moxon edition of Tennyson's Poems, 1857. However,
with a consistently large work load 'he attracted the
habit of debt, and never forsook it', according to
Charles Whittingham (A.Warren, Charles
Whittingham, 1896, p.73). The British Museum owns

a large collection of his engravings, including those
after W.Allen, E.Armitage, C.W.Cope, T.Creswick,
W.Dickes, W.A.Fraser, A.D.Fripp, J.Gilbert,
W.Harvey, F.W.Hulme, W.H.Hunt, E. and T.
Landseer, J.Leech, D.Maclise, J.Millais,
R.Redgrave, C.Stanfield, M.Stanley, F.Tayler,
J.Thorne, D.Wilkie and J.Meissonier (qq.v.).
There are also engravings for a 'Deaf and Dumb'
alphabet, antiquities and sculpture, engraved in a
fine, even black-line style; a cut to Richard Doyle's
'Brown, Jones and Robinson' series; and numerous
small engraved conjuring tricks, animal traps and
domestic objects, to indicate the scope of Williams'
trade engravings. The Bodleian Library owns his
C.Knight engravings. He signed his engravings:
'THOS WILLIAMS sc', 'T WILLIAMS', 'T W', 'TW'
(superimposed and script).
[Nagler; Spielmann; Hake; Evans Reminiscences;
Gusman; W.J.Linton, Masters of Wood Engraving,
1889]

WILLIAMS, Walter fl.1887-1901
Wood engraver, who worked in London. He was a
pupil of the Dalziel Brothers (q.v.) and appears in
the London directories at 9 East Harding Street,
Gough Square, EC (POD, 1887-1900).
[Dalziels' Record]

WILLIAMS, William fl.1840s
London wood engraver, who worked at 101 Park
Street, Camden Town (POD, 1845).

WILLIAMSON, David Wallace fl.1872-98
Wood engraver, who worked first in Edinburgh, at
11 Melbourne Place (Kelly's, 1872-80), then moved
to London. There he worked from 150 Fleet Street,
EC (POD, 1884-85), sharing the premises with
A.H.Lindsell and H.Shade (qq.v.). He joined forces
with A.Bradstock, first at 154 Fleet Street, EC
(POD, 1886), then at 7 New Court, Carey Street, WC
(POD, 1890-98).

WILLIAMSON, J. fl.1839-67
Wood engraver, who worked in London first for
Charles Knight's popular publication, Arabian
Nights' Entertainments, 1839. He was most
successful engraving for the Illustrated London News,
1851-60. His engraving of G.Thomas's drawing,
'Sketches in London in 1851', was a three foot long
pull-out engraving, 23 August 1851; followed by
'Wellington's Funeral', after John Gilbert (q.v.), a
three foot supplement, 27 November 1852. He engraved
after paintings, photographic portraits, and sketches by
various 'Special Artists': 'The Prince of Wales Landing
at Quebec', double-page, 29 September 1860, after
'Special Artist', G.H.Andrews (q.v.). He also
engraved William Small's (q.v.) drawing on wood,
'Between the Cliffs' in the Quiver, 1867. The
British Museum owns his engravings after G.Dodgson,

J.Gilbert, G.F.Sargent. He signed his engravings:
'Williamson Sc' (script), 'WILLIAMSON'.

WILLIAMSON, James
Scottish wood engraver, who worked at 34 St Andrews
Square, Edinburgh (Kelly's,1900), an office he shared
with C. and A. Young (q.v.).

WILLIAMSON, Joseph fl.1891-95
London wood engraver, who worked at 10 Red Lion
Court, Fleet Street, EC (POD,1891-95), the office
of the prominent wood engraver F.Appleton (q.v.).

WILLIS, Edward fl.1800-39
Wood engraver, apprenticed to Thomas Bewick (q.v.)
in Newcastle, from ? July 1798 -17 August 1805,
during the period of the second volume of Bewick's
British Birds. Bewick wrote of Willis: 'The next of
my pupils, who chiefly turned his attention to Wood
engraving was Edward Willis, who while he remained
with me was much upon a par with [Charlton] Nesbit,
but did not equal him in the mechanical excellence
Nesbit had attained to in London--I had a great regard
for Edward Willis on account of his regular good
behaviour while he was under my tuition--' (Bewick
Memoir,p.199). By the end of his apprenticeship
Bewick recalled how there was 'never a cross word
passed between us'. Willis used his knowledge of the
period with Bewick to help Chatto and Jackson with
their Treatise on Wood Engraving, giving details to
the Bewick section of the book. Willis engraved many
tailpieces to Burns' Poems,1808, with fellow Bewick
apprentice Isaac Nicholson and colleague Henry White
(qq.v.). By the early 1820s he had moved from
Newcastle to London where he set up as a wood
engraver at 62 Compton Street, Clerkenwell
(Johnstone,1817; Pigot,1822-23), then 14 Market
Street, Clerkenwell (Pigot,1823-24), and 11 Leather-
seller's Buildings, London Wall (Pigot, Robson,
1832-34). While there he worked for Charles
Whittingham,Senior (q.v.), notably for his Family
Robinson Crusoe, engraved in a fine copper-plate
style; also for Whittingham's Sandford and Merton,
engraved with John Jackson and Jackson and Smith
(qq.v.) (which are now in the Bodleian Library). The
British Museum owns a small cut of a man working
with an assistant, signed 'Willis'.
[Nagler; Bewick Memoir; I.Bain, Watercolours of
T.Bewick,1981]

WILLIS, G.W.
Wood engraver, who engraved a portrait of William
Dargan, the Irish railway projector,1799-1867, after
an anonymous drawing. The work is in the British
Museum.
[Hake]

WILLIS, M. fl.1830s
London wood engraver, who worked at 31 Charles
Street, City Road (Robson,1837).

WILLIS, William Dalrymple fl.1860-95
London wood engraver, who worked at 123 Chancery
Lane, WC (POD,1864-82) which he shared with the
engraver E.T.Hartshorn (q.v.), then W.J.Potter
(q.v.) with whom he moved to 89 Farringdon Street,
EC (POD,1884-95). They were joined there by
F.Appleton, L.Knott, H.Prater, F.Thorpe, and
G.F.Horne (qq.v.). He was a rather crude engraver
responsible for cutting the young Walter Crane's
(q.v.) early drawings on wood. These included five
landscape vignettes after Crane's sketches to
Reverend Henry Stern's Wandering among the
Falashas in Abyssinia,1860; Crane's drawings to
Reverend P.B.Power's The Eye Doctor,1862; and
after six drawings of Crane to Agnes de Haviland's
Stories of Memel for the Young,1863. He signed his
engravings: 'W.D.WILLIS'.
[For reproduction see I.Spencer, W.Crane,1975,p.23]

WILLS, William Henry 1810-80
Wood engraver, journalist and writer, one of the
original Punch staff, and editor for Dickens'
Household Words. He was born in Plymouth on
13 January 1810, and brought up as a wood engraver
in Henry Vizetelly's father's firm Vizetelly and
Branston (q.v.). Later he turned to journalism,
edited Chamber's Journal, and published numerous
illustrated books, some published by Henry Vizetelly
(q.v.). He died in Welwyn, Hertfordshire on
1 September 1880.
[DNB; Spielmann; Vizetelly, Glances Back]

WILLSON, John J. 1836-1903
Occasional illustrator for wood engravings, painter
of landscapes and sporting subjects. He was born in
Leeds in 1836, worked at Headingley, Leeds and
was a pupil of Edwin Moore and Richard Waller.
He is listed here for a work wood engraved in The
Graphic,1875. He exhibited at the Royal Academy
and died in Leeds in 1903.

WILMER
(see Dawson and Wilmer)

WILSON, Arthur James fl.1880s
London wood engraver, who worked at 10 Bolt
Court, EC (POD,1880). He shared the premises
with T.Coman, E.Scrivens and R.G.F.Sweeting
(qq.v.).

WILSON, C.E.
Draughtsman illustrator, who drew for wood engravings
in the English Illustrated Magazine,1884. These were
illustrations to J.E.Panton's 'Highways and Byways',
wood engraved by A. and W.Dawson, J.A.Quartley,

O.Jahyer, R.Paterson and O.Lacour (qq.v.).

WILSON, Charles Walter fl.1894-97
London wood engraver, who worked at 5 Furnival
Street, EC (POD,1894-95), then 84 Fetter Lane,
EC (POD,1896-97), which he shared with B.Earl
(q.v.).

WILSON, Dower fl.1875-97
Draughtsman illustrator of domestic subjects. He
drew for wood engravings in the Illustrated London
News, notably a small sketch, 'St Valentine's Day',
13 February 1875; Judy,1878-79; Punch's Almanac,
1879; later Punch,1897; and Moonshine,1891.

WILSON, Miss M.O.
Wood engraver, who contributed engravings with
H.F.Davey (q.v.) to 'A Suburban Garden', after
J.E.Hodgson, in the English Illustrated Magazine,
1888.

WILSON, Thomas Harrington fl.1842-86
Draughtsman illustrator, occasional engraver on
wood, landscape, portrait and genre painter. He
studied art at the National Gallery with John Tenniel
and Charles Martin (qq.v.) and was introduced to
Mark Lemon, editor of Punch, by the wood engraver
Joseph Swain (q.v.). Wilson drew on wood for Punch
from 1853, also for Punch's Pocket Books,1854-57.
Spielmann described his drawings for these as 'a
dozen clever, but hardly striking, drawings. These
were "socials" dealing with society or fashions, stage,
situations from behind the scenes, and grotesque
ideas, such as the "effect of wearing respirators
on burglars" (October,1853). He in fact specialised
in theatrical portraiture which he drew on wood as
special correspondent for the Illustrated London
News,1854-61,1876; also for the Illustrated London
Magazine,1855; and a brief appearance in an early
issue of The Graphic,1871. He was particularly
proficient with the portraiture which he may also have
engraved on wood: Sir Charles Eastlake, RA, for the
Illustrated London News,1860, owned by the British
Museum; also 'The late Sir William Charles Ross,RA',
Illustrated London News,6 February 1860. He also
exhibited work at the British Institution, the Royal
Academy, the Royal Institute of Painters in Water-
colours and the Royal Institute of Painters in Oil-
Colours. His son was the artist Thomas Walter Wilson
(q.v.). He signed his engravings: 'T H WILSON Sc'.
[Spielmann; Hake; Houfe]

WILSON, Thomas Walter 1851-1912
Draughtsman illustrator and landscape painter. He
was born in London on 7 November 1851, the son of
the draughtsman T.H.Wilson (q.v.), and educated
in Chelsea then at South Kensington,1868, where he
won a scholarship the following year. He was sent
by the Department of Science and Art to Bayeux, and

worked in Holland and Belgium. He is listed here
for his drawings wood engraved in the Illustrated
London News,1876-99, notably the full-page series,
'Objects from the Prince of Wales' Presents' [of his
Indian tour], July 1876. Wilson was adept enough at
drawing for the wood engraver to be employed by The
Graphic to finish the rapid sketches of the 'Special
Artist' Fred Villiers (q.v.), and his own work
appeared in the paper 1880-85. He continued his
magazine work throughout the 1890s for the English
Illustrated Magazine,1895; Good Words,1898-99;
Sketch; Minister; and Idler. He also exhibited work
at the Royal Institute of Painters in Watercolours and
the Royal Society of Painters in Oil-Colours, being
elected ARI in 1877, RI in 1879 and ROI in 1883.

WILTON and Whitley fl.1852-54
London wood engraving firm, with an office at
48A Paternoster Row (POD,1852-54). (See also
Whitley, George)

WIMPERIS, Edmund Morrison 1835-1900
Wood engraver, draughtsman on wood and landscape
painter. He was born in Chester on 6 February 1835,
and worked there in business until the age of fourteen,
when he came to London as an apprentice wood
engraver to Mason Jackson (q.v.). He also learned
to draw on wood from Birket Foster (q.v.) and as a
result drew and engraved on wood for the Illustrated
London News. He set up as wood engraver first on
his own at 15 Wine Office Court, EC (POD,1857-58),
then joined with W.J.Palmer (q.v.) as Palmer and
Wimperis (q.v.). He reappears on his own at
2 Whitefriars Street, EC (POD,1860). His wood
engraved work during this period included cuts to
Merrie Days of England,1858, after Birket Foster
and various cuts to the Illustrated London News.
His drawings on wood appeared in various 'Sixties
School' magazines and books: Poetry of the
Elizabethan Age,1861; S.C.Hall's Book of South
Wales,1861; and Once a Week,1866-67; and his
drawings to Gray's Elegy,1869 were colour printed.
By the 1870s he had turned from illustration to
watercolour landscape painting, in the style of
Birket Foster. He was elected ARI in 1873, and
RI in 1875, serving as its Vice-President in
1895. He also exhibited at the Royal Society of
British Artists, Grosvenor Gallery, New Gallery,
Fine Art Society. He died in Christchurch, Hamp-
shire on 25 December 1900. His son, Edmund
Wimperis,Junior, was a landscape watercolourist.
[Chatto; White; DNB; Houfe; Wood (full
bibliography)]

WINGFIELD, James Digman 1800-72
Occasional draughtsman for wood engravings. He
worked in London, specialising in costume subjects,
often with Hampton Court as a background. Houfe
points out that he made drawings of the Great

Exhibition of 1851, and the 'two poetic works of his being engraved by Dalziel', for which he is included here.

WINSTON, Charles Edward fl.1850s
London wood engraver, who worked at 87 St Martin's Lane (POD, 1857).

WINTER, Cornelius J.W. ?-1890
Draughtsman on wood, engraver, lithographer and watercolourist. He worked in Norwich, at 5 Castle Hill (Kelly's, 1880-89). His work included lithographed illustrations to Reverend J.Gunn's Roodscreen at Barton Turf, 1869; and a watercolour copy of an Edwin Landseer painting which is now in the British Museum. He also drew four bookplates, which he engraved 1880-89, signed 'Winter sc' (Fincham).
[TB (bibliography)]

WIRGMANN, Charles 1832-91
Occasional draughtsman for wood engravings, figure artist and caricaturist. He was born in 1832, the brother of the London artist Theodore Wirgmann (q.v.) and worked in London before settling in Yokohama, Japan, 1860, to paint Japanese life. He contributed drawings of Manila, 1857 and China, 1860 for wood engravings in the Illustrated London News, for which he is listed here.
[TB (bibliography); Houfe]

WIRGMANN, Theodore Blake 1848-1925
Draughtsman illustrator and portrait painter. He was born in Louvain, Belgium on 29 April 1848, of a Swedish family, brother of Charles Wirgmann (q.v.). He entered the Royal Academy Schools and won a silver medal there in 1865; also studied with E.Hebert in Paris. When he returned he worked as draughtsman for wood engravings in The Graphic from 1875, having once drawn for a wood engraving in Cassell's Family Magazine, 1868. He also worked as assistant to the prominent painter John Everett Millais (q.v.). He is best known, however, for his chalk drawing of politicians, writers and royalty for later editions of The Graphic, 1884-89; he also contributed to the Daily Chronicle, 1895. He was elected RP in 1891, and exhibited extensively at the Grosvenor Gallery, the New Gallery, the Royal Academy, the Royal Hibernian Academy, the Royal Institute of Painters in Watercolours and the Royal Institute of Painters in Oil-Colours. He died in London on 16 January 1925.
[Houfe; TB (bibliography); Who's Who, 1916-28; Bénézit]

WITBY or Withy, Thomas fl.1841-59
London wood engraver, who worked at 12 Gough Square, Fleet Street, EC, and 35 New Street, Kennington Common (POD, 1844-45), 1 James Place, Harleyford Road (POD, 1846-49), 8 Thanet Place,

Strand (POD, 1854-57), and 5 Cook's Court, Lincoln's Inn Fields and a second office at Three Mile Cottage, Upper Holloway, N (POD, 1858-59). His engravings appeared in Charles Knight's (q.v.) popular publications, namely Knight's Penny Magazine. The Bodleian Library owns his cut for September 1841, after a drawing on wood by W.Lee (q.v.).

WITTON, Joseph fl.1880s
London suburban wood engraver, who worked at 16 Tonsley Hill, Wandsworth, SW (LSDS, 1880).

WOLF, Joseph 1820-99
Prominent draughtsman on wood of animal and bird subjects. He was born in Mors, near Coblenz in 1820, studied lithography at Darmstadt, then entered the Antwerp Academy. He came to England in 1848, where he was patronised by the Duke of Westminster and befriended by D.G.Rossetti and the Dalziel Brothers (qq.v.). They remembered him for his love of nature: 'Bred amid field, woodland and hedgerow, he gathered his love of all things beautiful, animate and inanimate, direct from Nature'. His boyhood had been spent studying and dissecting birds, the basis for his later drawings and paintings, and his early commission, Gray's Genera of Birds. He illustrated as 'Special Artist', for the Zoological Society, working at Regent's Park and the Science Museum and visited Norway in 1848 and 1856, with John Gould, the ornithologist and illustrator. Wolf is listed here for his numerous wood engraved drawings of animals and birds, engraved by such prominent figures as the Dalziel Brothers, the Whympers and G.Pearson (qq.v.). His early work was praised by Bohn in Chatto and Jackson who concluded that he 'like Mr Harrison Weir, has a preference for animal drawing, and excels in it'. Bohn cites Wolf's drawings wood engraved by G.Pearson in T.W.Atkinson's Travels in the Region of the Upper and Lower Amoor; and Freeman and Salvin's work on falconry, c1861. The Dalziel Brothers cite one drawing which Wolf did for their Pilgrim's Progress and the 'large number' (twenty) of drawings he did with J.B.Zwecker (q.v.) to Reverend J.G.Wood's Illustrated Natural History, 1862. Wolf began his career drawing on wood for various publications: he was commissioned to improve the early illustrations of John Tenniel (q.v.) for the second edition of his Aesop's Fables, 1851; contributed drawings on wood to the Illustrated London News, 1853-57, 1872; to Eliza Cook's Poems, 1856; Wordsworth's Selected Poems, 1859; Montgomery's Poems, 1860; Band of Hope Review, 1861; Good Words, 1861-64; Willmott's Sacred Poetry, 1862; Sunday Magazine, 1866-68; Once a Week, 1866; Poems of Jean Ingelow, 1867; Buchanan's North Coast and Other Poems, 1868; sixty-five drawings to L.Lloyd's Game Birds of Sweden and Norway; and J.E.Hastings' Sketches of Bird Life, 1883. Wolf also exhibited work at the Royal Academy, the British Institution and the

Royal Institute of Painters in Watercolours where he was elected member in 1874. He died in London on 20 April 1899. The British Museum owns a series of proof wood engravings by the Dalziel Brothers, after Wolf's designs.
[For biographical detail see A.H.Palmer, Life of Joseph Wolf, 1895; also The Artist, May 1899, pp.1-15; also Chatto; Houfe; Dalziels' Record]

WOLFE, Major W.S.M. fl.1855-62
Amateur draughtsman illustrator, Royal Artillery officer. He contributed drawings for wood engravings of the Crimean War to the Illustrated London News, 1855.

WOOD fl.1840s
Wood engraver, proficient draughtsman on wood. Spielmann claimed the young artist H.G.Hine (q.v.) was commissioned to make drawings on wood of London's dockland, c1840-41: 'The work was not new to him, as Wood, a master-engraver of the time, taking pity on the sense of foolish powerlessness with which every beginner is afflicted, had explained to him the secret of the craft. Landscape was thus his acknowledged line when he found himself at the Docks with his round of boxwood in his hand' (Spielmann, pp.414-15).

WOOD, Fane
Draughtsman on wood, who contributed figure subjects for wood engravings in London Society, 1868. The British Museum owns several designs engraved by the Dalziel Brothers (q.v.), 1865-66.

WOOD, James Edmund fl.1876-1900
Provincial wood engraver and draughtsman, who worked at 5 Queen Street, Plymouth (Kelly's, 1876-1900).

WOOD, John Henry fl.1880s
Provincial wood engraver, who worked at 22 Mill Street, Macclesfield, Cheshire (Kelly's, 1880).

WOOD, Thomas fl.1870s
Provincial wood engraver, who worked at 16 Brazenose Street, Manchester (Kelly's, 1872).

WOOD, Thomas W. fl.1855-75
Draughtsman on wood, who specialised in animal and bird subjects. He contributed these to the Illustrated London News, 1855-58, then 1865-75, notably small vignettes of animals from the Regent's Park Zoo. These were generally wood engraved by J.Greenaway or the Dalziel Brothers (qq.v.). He also drew for Gems of Nature and Art, c1860, with A.F.Lydon (q.v.); and bird and butterfly drawings on wood for the Dalziels to engrave in Reverend J.G.Wood's Illustrated Natural History, 1862. The Dalziels concluded of Wood's draughtsmanship, 'Though always technically correct, he was deficient in artistic treatment--in fact, a

playful artist friend once dubbed him the "Wooden Wood". His son was the illustrator T.W.Wood, Junior (q.v.). The British Museum owns the Dalziel proofs to Wood's Illustrated Natural History; also proofs engraved 1861, 1865, after Wood's designs.
[Spielmann; Dalziels' Record; Reverend M.Morris, B.Fawcett, 1925, p.53]

WOOD, T.W., Junior fl.1865-80
Draughtsman illustrator, son of the animal illustrator Thomas W.Wood (q.v.). He contributed four drawings for wood engravings in Punch, 1865 and illustrated Reverend J.G.Wood's Common Moths of England, c1880. He also exhibited at the Royal Academy.
[Spielmann (as Woods); Houfe]

WOODHEAD, Alfred T.
London wood engraver, who worked at Love Lane, Tottenham (LSDN, 1900-02).

WOODROFFE, Paul Vincent 1875-1954
Occasional illustrator for wood engraving, painter and stained glass artist. He was born in Madras, India in 1875, educated at Stonyhurst and studied art at the Slade. He specialised in book decoration, covers and end-papers in the style of his friend Laurence Housman (q.v.). He drew illustrations for Housman's sister Clemence (q.v.) to wood engrave, notably The Confessions of St Augustine, 1900, and the four published (ten drawn originally) illustrations to Laurence Housman's translation, Aucassin and Nicolette, 1902. He also contributed to various process engraved publications. His drawing appeared in the influential periodicals, The Quarto, 1896 and The Parade, 1897. From 1904 he lived in Campden, Gloucestershire where he was associated with the local Arts and Crafts Movement and designed stained glass. He was a founder member of the Art Workers Guild, exhibited at the Fine Art Society, the New English Art Club, the Royal Academy, and the Royal Hibernian Academy, and died in Eastbourne, 7 May 1954.
[For a list of illustrated work see Houfe; also Sketchley; J.R.Taylor, Art Nouveau Book, 1966; also exhibition catalogue William Morris Gallery, Walthamstow, 1982]

WOODS, F. fl.1874
Spielmann lists this draughtsman for Punch, who contributed a drawing on wood in 1874, which appeared 'having been practically redrawn although his initials were allowed to stand'.

WOODS, Henry 1846-1921
Draughtsman illustrator, painter of genre, Venetian and landscape subjects. He was born in Warrington on 22 April 1846, studied at the local art school, where he won a travelling scholarship, and then moved to London to attend the South Kensington Schools. He joined The Graphic in 1870, and

worked with his friend and brother-in-law Luke
Fildes (q.v.) and in collaboration with the 'Special
Artist' on The Graphic, S.P.Hall (q.v.). Woods
also drew illustrations to Trollope's The Vicar of
Bullhampton,1870, and with Fildes the illustrations
to Wilkie Collins' Miss or Mrs?,1885. He settled
in Venice from 1876, but exhibited at the Royal
Institute of Painters in Oil-Colours and the
Royal Academy, being elected ARA in 1882,
and RA in 1893. He died in Venice on
27 October 1921.
[Houfe; N.John Hall, Trollope and his
Illustrators,1980]

WOODS, Henry N. fl.1855-69
Wood engraver of ornamental borders and vignettes.
He worked in London at 8 John Street, Adelphi, WC
(POD,1855-69). His engravings included decorative
initials by Noel Humphreys (q.v.) to W.Falconer's The
Shipwreck,1858; and to Wordsworth's The White Doe
of Rylstone,1859. Bohn in Chatto and Jackson points
out his engravings to Moore's Lalla Rookh: these
were probably the Persian designs of T.Sulman,
Junior, to Tenniel's Lalla Rookh,1861 (mostly
engraved by the Dalziels (q.v.)).
[McLean, Victorian Book Design; Chatto]

WOODS, Walter R. fl.1870-74
London wood engraver, who worked at 10 Symmond's
Inn, WC (POD,1870-72), then 41 Richmond Road,
Caledonian Road, N (POD,1873-74).

WOODS, William fl.1860
Draughtsman illustrator of military subjects. He
contributed these to the Illustrated London News,
1860.

WOODVILLE, Richard Caton, Senior 1825-55
Occasional draughtsman illustrator, painter of battle
scenes. He was born in Baltimore in 1825 but worked
in London in the 1850s. He contributed a drawing for
a wood engraving in the Illustrated London News,
1852. He also exhibited at the British Institution and
the Royal Academy, and died in London in 1855.

WOODVILLE, Richard Caton, Junior 1856-1927
Draughtsman illustrator, 'Special Artist' and painter
of battle scenes. He was born in London on 7 January
1856, the son of R.C.Woodville,Senior (q.v.). He
studied art in Düsseldorf under Kamphussen, and
lived in Paris until he settled in London in 1875. There
he immediately worked drawing for wood engravings
in the Illustrated London News,1876-1911, serving as
their 'Special Artist' during various wars in Turkey,
Egypt and Albania. His drawings there often merited the
cover or double-page supplements and were successful
for their figure drawing alone. He also illustrated for
the Cornhill,1883; the Sketch; the Boy's Own Paper;
Windsor Magazine; the English Illustrated Magazine,

1895-97; and Pearson's Magazine,1896. He had
turned to oil painting by the 1880s, and exhibited at
the Fine Art Society, the New Gallery, the Royal
Academy, the Royal Hibernian Academy, the Royal
Institute of Painters in Watercolours and the Royal
Institute of Painters in Oil-Colours, being elected
RI in 1882, and ROI in 1883. He died in North London
on 17 August 1927.
[For biography see R.C.Woodville, Random
Recollections,1913; The Idler,1897,10,pp.758-75;
Houfe; Wood (bibliography)]

WOOLLEY, John James fl.1872-1910
London wood engraver, who worked at 9 Essex
Street, Strand, WC (POD,1872-73), which he shared
with J.Desbois, H.C.Mason, W.Murden, P.Roberts
and F.Watkins (qq.v.). He moved to Howard Chambers,
Howard Street, WC (POD,1874-83), then 34 Fetter
Lane (POD,1885-88), and 15 Cursitor Street, EC
(POD,1889-1910).

WORMS, Jaspar von 1832-1924
Illustrator, etcher and painter. He was born in
Paris on 16 December 1832 and studied at the Ecole
des Beaux Arts from 1849. He exhibited at the Salon
from 1859, specialising in Spanish genre subjects.
He is listed here for his drawings of the Crimea,
wood engraved in Cassell's Illustrated Family Paper,
1853-57.

WRAGG, G. and Thomas Dodd fl.1841-60
London wood engravers. G.Wragg worked at 38
Ludgate Hill (POD,1855), and became proficient
as a portrait engraver. He engraved a life-
size oval portrait of Queen Victoria, after
T.D.Scott, for the Illustrated Times,7 June 1856.
The work is in the British Museum. Thomas Dodd
Wragg worked in London at 16 Ebury Street, Pimlico
(POD,1852), 17 Glasgow Terrace, Thames Bank
(POD, Hodgson's,1854-57), and later 2 Park Villas,
Park Place, S.Lambeth (POD,1858-60). He probably
engraved for Charles Knight's Penny Magazine,
November and December 1841, after Fairholt's
drawings, the engravings being signed 'Wragg'.
[Hake; Bodleian Library]

WRIGHT, Edward fl.1883-1910
London wood engraver, who worked first as Wright,
Greatwood and Meek (q.v.), then alone at 9 Red Lion
Court (POD,1884), 64 Fleet Street, EC (POD,1885-87),
and 6 Red Lion Court (POD,1888-89), which he shared
with E.Campbell (q.v.). He then worked as 'Edward
Wright and Company' at 180 Fleet Street, EC
(POD,1891-1900). By 1910 he was working at 13 Wine
Office Court (POD,1910).

WRIGHT, John fl.1828-41
London wood engraver, who worked on his own, then
with Robert Branston (q.v.) as Branston and Wright

(q.v.), then with William Folkard (q.v.) as Wright and Folkard, 4 New London Street (Pigot, POD, 1836-40). Wright began with an engraved tailpiece after William Harvey (q.v.) to Northcote's Fables, 1828; followed by engravings after Harvey to Children in the Wood, 1831; Dr Percy's Beggar's Daughter of Brendell Green, 1832; and some fifty-four cuts after Harvey's drawings of London Zoo animals, (as Branston and Wright) and for a German publication, A.Grafen's History of New German Art, 1836. He engraved well enough for Nagler to list his contributions to the French editions of Paul et Virginie, 1838; and Les Evangiles, 1838. When Wright joined with Folkard about 1836 some of their major commissions came from the publisher Charles Knight (q.v.), who secured engravings to his Lane's edition of the Arabian Nights' Entertainments, 1839; also Knight's Penny Magazine, October 1845, notably after W.Harvey's drawings. The British Museum owns a cut to Northcote's Fables, and engravings after H.Weir. The Bodleian Library owns his C.Knight engravings. He signed his engravings: 'J WRIGHT', 'B & W sc' (Branston and Wright), 'W & F', 'W et F' (Wright and Folkard).
[Nagler; Gusman]

WRIGHT, W. fl.1846-57
London wood engraver, who worked originally with Henry Vizetelly (q.v.). He formed a partnership with John Greenaway as Greenaway and Wright (qq.v.) and helped to engrave Appleton's illustrated series of Dickens' stories. When Appleton went bankrupt Wright abandoned his partner to face the debts alone. He was especially proficient at animal engravings after Harrison Weir (q.v.), notably cuts to Bloomfield's Farmer's Boy, 1857. The British Museum owns a small cut of children at a well, after G.Cruikshank. He signed his engravings: 'W WRIGHT Sc'.
[Chatto]

WRIGHT, Walter fl.1880s
Provincial wood engraver, who worked at Great Western Buildings, 6 Livery Street, Birmingham (Kelly's, 1889).

WRIGHT, Greatwood and Meek
Short-lived London wood engraving firm, probably comprising Edward Wright and George Meek (qq.v.). Their office was at 1 Norfolk Street, WC (POD, 1883), which the following year became the office of George Meek alone.

WYBURD, Francis John 1826-?
Occasional draughtsman on wood, genre painter. He was born in London in 1826, studied in Lille and with the lithographer T.Fairland (see Volume I). He was admitted to the Royal Academy Schools in 1848, and travelled to Italy in the 1850s. He is listed by Bohn in Chatto and Jackson for his figure subjects, wood engraved in Poetry and Pictures of Thomas Moore,

c1845. He exhibited at the British Institution, the Royal Academy, the Royal Institute of Painters in Oil-Colours and the Royal Society of British Artists, where he was elected member in 1879. He died some time after 1893.
[Chatto; Houfe]

WYLLIE, Charles William or Charlie 1859-1923
Draughtsman illustrator and marine painter. He was born in London on 18 February 1859, the brother of W.L.Wyllie (q.v.). He studied at Leigh's and the Royal Academy Schools, and began in 1881 to draw for wood engravings of coastal and genre subjects in The Graphic, 1881-90; later for the Illustrated London News, 1893-96; and Sunday Magazine, 1894. He exhibited work at the Grosvenor Gallery, the New Gallery, the Royal Academy and the Royal Society of British Artists, to which he was elected member in 1886; also member of the ROI in 1888. He died in St John's Wood on 28 July 1923.

WYLLIE, William Lionel 1851-1931
Draughtsman illustrator, etcher and marine painter. He was born in London in July 1851, the brother of C.W.Wyllie (q.v.) and half-brother of Lionel Percy Smythe (q.v.). He studied at Heatherley's and the Royal Academy Schools, and joined the staff of The Graphic where he drew for wood engravings of marine subjects, 1880-1904. The paper sent him to the United States in 1893. He also exhibited work at the Fine Art Society, the Grosvenor Gallery and the New English Art Club, to which he was elected member, 1887 and the Royal Academy, where he was elected ARA in 1889, and RA in 1907. He also exhibited at the Royal Society of British Artists, the Royal Society of Painter-Etchers and Engravers, the Royal Hibernian Academy, the Royal Institute of Painters in Watercolours and the Royal Institute of Painters in Oil-Colours. He died on 6 April 1931.
[For a list of etchings see Volume I (with bibliography)]

Y, W.
Wood engraver, talented draughtsman trainee of the Dalziel Brothers (q.v.). He was apprenticed to the Dalziel workshop at the age of nineteen, the younger son of a 'good county family', his elder brother also accompanying him for training as a wood engraver. 'His development in our art was simply wonderful, his manipulative power was quite extraordinary; it was the one case in our experience where it seemed as if the pupil had come to teach the masters. He was steady, punctual to his long day's work, and in every way exemplary, a gentleman in manner, and a great favourite with all the assistants and other pupils...', the Dalziels recalled. He left the Dalziels and set up on his own for two to three months, but he inherited the family fortune and gave up engraving. The Dalziels lamented,

'he suddenly disappeared, and the last we heard was that he was spreading his time, and his money chiefly in the immediate vicinity of the Surrey Theatre, ...seen in the pub lighting his pipe with a £5 note. Poor fellow! it was the old, old story--the drink-- the drink that did it' (Dalziels' Record,p.347). The anecdote is interesting for shedding light on the Dalziel workshop methods, rather than the engravings of W.Y., whom the Dalziels kept anonymous ('for obvious reasons').

YARRELL
Draughtsman on wood, who drew illustrations to Charles Knight's Penny Magazine,July,1842. These were wood engraved by S.Sly (q.v.) and are now in the Bodleian Library.

YOUNG, Alexander and Charles fl.1864-1901
London wood engravers. Charles worked at 21 Paternoster Row, EC (POD,1864-66), then was joined by Alexander at 51 and 52 Imperial Buildings, New Bridge Street, EC (POD,1883-1901). They shared the premises with James Williamson (q.v.).

YOUNG, C. and A. fl.1872-89
Scottish wood engravers, who worked at 63 North Bridge, Edinburgh (Kelly's,1872-80) then 34 St Andrews Square (Kelly's,1889). An advertisement in Kelly's directory claimed that they were 'Artists and Engravers on wood of landscape, figure and ornamental subjects in the "first style of the Art"'.

YOUNG, Frederick C.E. fl.1860s
London wood engraver, manager of the London Drawing Association, 7 Duke Street, Adelphi, WC (POD,1865). (See Taylor, Arthur)

YOUNG, Henry fl.1895-99
London wood engraver, who worked at 82 Great Bland Street, SE (POD,1895), 44 Upper Bland Street, SE (POD,1896), and 178 New Kent Road, SE (POD,1897-99).

YOUNG, Robert fl.1850s
London wood engraver, who worked at 3 Furnival's Inn, Holborn, during the 1850s. He engraved the frontispiece design by Richard Doyle (q.v.) to Thackeray's The Newcomers,1854-55.

YRIARTE, Charles 1832-98
Occasional draughtsman on wood, architectural painter, writer and editor. He was born in Paris on 5 December 1832, was a pupil of Constant-Dufeux, and became editor of the illustrated paper, Monde Illustré. He employed the young Daniel Vierge (q.v.) and many other prominent draughtsmen as well as expatriot English wood engravers. He also contributed a Spanish subject wood engraved in Henry Vizetelly's Illustrated Times,1860, followed by a Turkish subject wood engraved in the Illustrated London News,1876.
[Houfe]

ZWECKER, Johann Baptist 1814-76
Occasional draughtsman of animal subjects on wood, etcher, and painter of historical subjects. He was born in Frankfurt on 18 September 1814, trained at the Institute Stadel and worked in Düsseldorf, 'a highly educated artist of the Düsseldorf school' (Dalziels' Record,p.270). He settled in London about 1850 where he drew on wood for numerous books and magazines, his work being mostly wood engraved by the Dalziel Brothers (q.v.). He specialised in natural history subjects: his animal drawings first appeared in the Illustrated London News,1860-66,1872, followed by brief appearances in Good Words,1861, 1868; Churchman's Family Magazine,1863; London Society,1864; Good Words for the Young,1869-70; and The Graphic,1875. His book illustrations began when the Dalziel Brothers commissioned Zwecker to help Joseph Wolf (q.v.) with animal drawings on wood for Reverend J.G.Wood's Natural History of Man,1862. The Dalziels remembered how Zwecker, 'an accomplished athlete, a genial companion, a kind-hearted man, and an enthusiastic son of the "Fatherland"', was a most cooperative draughtsman who 'always received his lists and instructions from the author; our portion being the engraving of the wood blocks and a general supervision of the printing ...'. This book commission was followed by others, namely contributions to Krilof and His Fables,1867; and Buchanan's North Coast and Other Poems,1868. He illustrated the following completely: J.Greenwood's Wild Sports of the World,1862; and G.A.Henty's Out on the Pampas,1871. His Child's Zoological Garden,1880; and S.W.Baker's Rifle and the Hound in Ceylon,1891 appeared posthumously. Zwecker's abilities as an occasional draughtsman on wood were recognised by Bohn in Chatto and Jackson. He also painted in oils and watercolour, and exhibited at the British Institution, the Royal Academy and the Royal Society of British Artists. He died in London on 10 January 1876. The British Museum owns several proof engravings of his designs engraved on wood by the Dalziel Brothers,1860-66.
[Chatto; Nagler; Houfe; Dalziels' Record]